W9-CSK-022

architectural heritage – the medieval Old Town, dominated by the famous castle, and Georgian New Town – its prestigious museums and its international arts festival.

MELROSE
A small Border town dominated by the pink sandstone ruins of Scotland's first Cistercian abbey. Associations with Walter Scott have made it a place of Romantic pilgrimage.

GLASGOW
Today Scotland's largest city is renowned for its dynamism and the rich cultural heritage of its eclectic architecture and many museums.

STIRLING
The former 'Gateway to the Highlands' is like Edinburgh on a much smaller scale, with impressive mansions nestling at the foot of its much-disputed castle.

ST ANDREWS
The home of Scotland's first university, an impressive ruined cathedral and prestigious golf courses.

GLEN COE
All the tragic beauty of the Highlands is encapsulated in this desolate valley, dominated by volcanic peaks.

IONA
A sacred island: the birthplace of Scottish Christianity and the burial place of the first Scottish kings.

ISLE OF SKYE
The largest island in the Inner Hebrides is renowned for its mountain landscapes whose summits are reflected in its lochs.

CALLANISH
A circle of standing stones shrouded in mystery, in the wild setting of the Outer Hebrides.

ORKNEY
These northern islands have a low relief and mild climate, and an exceptional architectural heritage.

SHETLAND
The most northerly of the Scottish islands lie at the crossroads between Scandinavia and Great Britain. They provide sanctuary for seabirds and are a favorite destination for bird-watchers.

IONA ▲ 204

ISLE OF SKYE ▲ 248

CALLANISH ▲ 252

ORKNEY ▲ 256

SHETLAND ▲ 262

SCOTLAND

KNOPF GUIDES

● Encyclopedia section

NATURE The natural heritage: species and habitats characteristic to Scotland, annotated and illustrated by naturalist authors and artists.

HISTORY AND LANGUAGE The history of Scotland, from the arrival of the first inhabitants to the present day, with key dates appearing in a timeline above the text.
The history of regional languages (Gaelic and Scots).

ARTS AND TRADITIONS Customs, traditions, festivals and cuisine and their continuing role in contemporary life in Scotland.

ARCHITECTURE The architectural heritage, focusing on style and topology, a look at rural and urban buildings, major civil, religious and military monuments.

AS SEEN BY PAINTERS A selection of paintings relating to Scotland by different artists and schools, arranged chronologically or thematically.

AS SEEN BY WRITERS An anthology of texts focusing on Scotland, arranged thematically.

▲ Itineraries

Each itinerary begins with a map of the area to be explored.
○ SPECIAL INTEREST These sites are not to be missed. They are highlighted in gray boxes in the margins.
★ EDITOR'S CHOICE Sites singled out by the editor for special attention.
INSETS On richly illustrated double pages, these insets focus on subjects deserving more in-depth treatment.

◆ Practical information

All the travel information you will need before you go and when you get there, plus a bibliography.
PLACES TO VISIT A handy table of addresses and opening hours.
USEFUL ADDRESSES A selection of hotels and restaurants compiled by an expert.
APPENDICES List of illustrations and general index.
MAP SECTION Maps of Scotland, with plans of the main cities, Edinburgh and Glasgow.

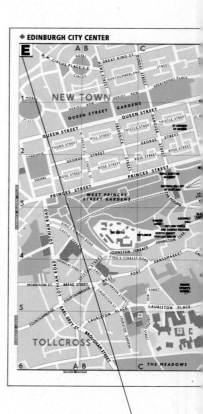

◆ EDINBURGH CITY CENTER

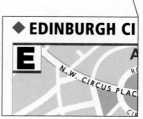

Each map in the map section is designated by a letter. In the itineraries, all the sites of interest are given a map reference

The mini-map pinpoints the itinerary within the wider area covered by the guide.

The itinerary map shows the main sites, the editor's choices and the places of special interest.

● ▲ ◆ The above symbols within the text provide cross-references to a place or a theme discussed elsewhere in the guide.

★ The star symbol signifies sites singled out by the editor for special attention.

◆ D B3 This reference pinpoints the location of a site on one of the maps at the end of the guide.

✪ This symbol indicates places of special interest.

▲ EAST CENTRAL

STIRLING AND SURROUNDINGS ▲

1. Stirling and surroundings ▲169
2. Fife ▲174
3. Perthshire ▲179
4. Angus ▲185

THE TROSSACHS ★
The 'bously country' so dear to Walter Scott has retained all its wild beauty. In summer its unforgettable landscapes are best enjoyed before the tourists flock onto the hills and along the wooded shores of the lochs.

STIRLING
OLD BRIDGE ◆ D B3
(north of Stirling)
The stone bridge built across the Forth in the early 15th century was of great strategic importance. It was the river's most southerly crossing until a second bridge, Main Road Bridge, was built below it in 1831. All the Scottish sovereigns, from Robert III to Charles II, are said to have passed over Stirling Old Bridge. The wooden bridge that gave its name to the famous battle in which William Wallace defeated the English, in September 1297 ● 38, stood nearby.

168

The central regions of Stirlingshire and Perthshire, and the eastern regions of Fife and Angus, are bounded by the Highlands to the north and the Southern Uplands to the south. Most of Stirlingshire lies to the north of the Highland Boundary Fault ● 76, the large geological fault that runs northeast/southwest and passes through Perthshire and the Trossachs. To the south of the fault lie the rich agricultural lands of Strathmore and the Carse of Gowrie, whose fruit production formed the basis of the Dundee jam and marmalade industry. Major coal and slate deposits played an even more important role in the region's economy in the 19th century. Angus, one of the main centers of Pictish settlement, has a remarkable legacy of symbolic carved stones ▲ 184. One of these is thought to commemorate the decisive victory of the Picts over the Angles in 685, which prevented the expansion of the kingdom of Northumbria. In the 11th century the center of power was displaced to the southwest when Scone ▲ 180 became the capital of the kingdom of the united Scots (Picts and Scots) of Dalriada. During the wars of Scottish independence ● 38 it was Stirling's turn to become the 'key to the kingdom' and the focus of crucial battles, with Scottish independence finally proclaimed at Arbroath ▲ 185 in 1320. Fife also played a major role in the history of the kingdom. In the 11th century Malcolm III married Margaret at Dunfermline ▲ 174, where they founded the first Benedictine abbey. They also encouraged the worship of the relics of St Andrew, the patron saint of Scotland, at St Andrews ▲ 176. In the 15th century St Andrews, the ecclesiastical capital and first university town in Scotland, lived through some of its darkest hours during the Reformation. Perth ▲ 179, a former royal residence, also experienced some troubled times, while Perthshire was the theater of great battles during the Jacobite ● risings: Killiecrankie in 1690, and Sheriffmuir in 1715. Finally, the Trossachs ▲ 172 owe their success as a tourist venue to the poet and novelist Walter Scott who immortalized their lochs and wild valleys in one of his poems and made Rob Roy, a famous local outlaw, the hero of one of his novels (Rob Roy, 1817).

The plain of central Scotland lies on either side of the River Forth, forming a natural corridor between the Southern Uplands and the North. It is dominated by Stirling Castle, which played a major role in the history of the kingdom. To the west the magnificent landscapes of the Campsie Fells, Trossachs and Loch Lomond, with their wooded hills, sparkling lochs and delightful villages, are only an hour by road from Edinburgh and Glasgow.

STIRLING ◆ D B3

This small town, with its former royal residence and historic center, is one of Scotland's leading tourist destinations. It is not unlike Edinburgh, only on a smaller scale, with its castle perched on a steep rock and an urban development that combines the old (cobbled streets and houses with stepped gables) and the new (shopping malls and streams of traffic), and University, nearby, at Airthrey.

GATEWAY TO THE HIGHLANDS.
The history of Stirling is closely linked to that of its castle, which stands on a 250-foot volcanic outcrop above the best crossing on the River Forth, a strategic position which explains its turbulent past. The rock was fortified during the Iron Age and may have been occupied by the Romans. The castle was first mentioned in history in connection with the death of Alexander I in 1124. The town was elevated to the status of a royal burgh by David I and soon became one of the 'courts of the four burghs', along with Berwick, Edinburgh and Roxburgh. It occupied a strategic position on the road to the Highlands and whoever controlled it also held the 'key to the kingdom'. As a result the castle became the focus of bitter struggles. It fell into the hands of the English in 1296 but was recaptured a year later by William Wallace. In 1304 it was captured by Edward I after a long siege, but his son Edward II had to abandon it to Robert Bruce in 1314, following his defeat at the Battle of Bannockburn ● 39. Dismantled on the order of Robert Bruce, the castle was rebuilt by the English in the 14th century and subsequently became the permanent royal residence of the Stewarts. It was the birthplace of James III in 1452, James V spent the first years of his reign there, his nine-month-old daughter Mary was crowned queen there in 1543, and his grandson James VI was baptized there in, 1566. Although Stirling lost its status as a royal residence when the court moved to London in 1603, it continued to prosper. Today Stirling is an active agricultural and commercial center and has been a university town since 1967.

STIRLING ✪
This old town and former royal residence has always been an obligatory crossing point to the North. It is dominated by its castle which synthesizes the long struggle for Scottish independence.

WALLACE MONUMENT ◆ D B3
1½ mile northwest of Stirling, on the A9 and B998)
This 220-foot tower was erected on Abbey Craig hill in 1869 in memory of William Wallace (c. 1270-1305) ● 38. It houses an exhibition which includes Wallace's two-handed sword, while beneath his battle tent is an audiovisual display tracing the exploits of the Scottish hero and patriot, and a series of marble busts of famous Scotsmen. The top of the tower (246 steps) offers sweeping views of the Ochil hills to the east, Stirling to the south and the Trossachs to the west.

Stirling in the time of the Stuarts, by Johannes Vorsterman (late 17th century).

FRONT MAP Sites of special interest
END MAP Scotland
02 How to use this guide
06 Introduction to the itineraries
07 The authors

● Encyclopedia section

15 NATURE
16 Biogeography
18 Marine mammals
20 Cliffs
24 Moorland
26 Peat bogs
28 Lochs
30 Rivers

31 HISTORY AND LANGUAGE
32 Chronology
38 The wars of Scottish independence, 1296–1357
40 Mary Stuart and the Reformation
42 The Jacobite Risings
44 The Scottish Enlightment
46 Language

49 ARTS AND TRADITIONS
50 Tartan
52 Music and dance
54 Highland Games
56 The 'Little People'
58 Golf
60 Scotch whisky
62 Food: cranachan and shortbreads
64 Specialties

65 ARCHITECTURE
66 Early Scottish architecture
68 Popular architecture

70 Churches and monasteries
72 Feudal castles and tower-houses
74 Scottish Renaissance palaces
76 Country residences
78 Urban and rural planning
80 The industrial age: housing
82 The industrial age: public and commercial buildings
83 Mackintosh and the Glasgow Style

85 SCOTLAND AS SEEN BY PAINTERS
86 From royal portraits to personal portraits
88 Wild and romantic landscapes
90 Modern Scotland: myth and reality
92 The sea, a boundless source of inspiration

93 SCOTLAND AS SEEN BY WRITERS

▲ Itineraries in Scotland

111 EDINBURGH, GLASGOW AND THE SOUTH
114 Edinbugh
128 Lothian
134 The Borders
140 Dumfries and Galloway
142 *Robert Burns*
148 Ayrshire
150 Glasgow
162 *Charles Rennie Mackintosh in Glasgow*
164 The outskirts of Glagow and the Clyde Valley

167 EAST CENTRAL
170 Stirling and surroundings
174 Fife
179 Perthshire
184 *Pictish stones*
185 Angus

187 THE WEST
189 The right bank of the Firth of Clyde
190 Argyll
196 *Scotland's gardens*
200 The inner Hebrides

207 THE NORTHEAST
210 Aberdeen
214 Aberdeenshire
220 *The Whisky Trail*
224 Moray

225 THE NORTH
228 *The Caledonian forest*
230 The Highlands
234 *The Cairngorms*
240 *Nessie, the Loch Ness Monster*
248 The Isle of Skye
252 The Outer Hebrides
256 Orkney
262 Shetland

◆ Practical information

270 Getting there
272 Getting around
274 Staying in Scotland
276 Festivals and events
277 Places to visit
300 Bibliography
301 Hotels and restaurants
315 List of illustrations
318 Index

325 Map section
   A The north
   B The northeast
   C The west
   D The center and the south
   E Edinburgh city center
   F Glasgow city center
   G Southwest Glasgow
   H Glasgow Underground

EDINBURGH, GLASGOW AND THE SOUTH ▲ 105

Discover Edinburgh, the 'Athens of the North', and the ancient royal burghs, luxurious mansions, ruined castles and attractive coastal resorts of Lothian. Travel to the gently rolling hills of the South and through the Borders beloved by Walter Scott, with their magnificent mansions and ruined abbeys. Walk on the deserted beaches of the Southwest, the 'Land of Robert Burns', and visit early Christian sites, abbeys and the impressive Culzean Castle. Finally discover the dynamic city of Glasgow and linger in its museums before journeying up the Clyde Valley.

EAST CENTRAL ▲ 167

From the former royal burgh of Stirling, head west to the wooded slopes of the Trossachs – the 'Bristly Country' made famous by Walter Scott – and Loch Lomond, Britain's largest freshwater lake. Head east to Fife with its fishing villages and historic towns: Dunfermline, Culross, Falkland and St Andrews, a golfers' paradise. Travel through the wild, open landscapes of Perthshire and visit the busy towns of Perth, Dunkeld and Pitlochry, and such legendary castles as Scone Palace and Blair Castle. Explore Angus, from the busy port of Dundee to the fairytale castle of Glamis, taking time out to admire the famous Pictish Stones.

THE WEST ▲ 187

The right bank of the Firth of Clyde will take you to Helensburgh, with the magnificent Hill House designed by Mackintosh, and on to Argyll, the mountainous and extremely rugged 'coast of the Gaels' that forms the southwest Highlands. As you pass from one peninsula to another, visit the archeological sites around Kilmartin and the distilleries of Campbeltown and Oban, or follow quiet minor roads leading to grandiose lochs guarded by ancient castles. Make a detour to the 'white town' of Inveraray on the way to the legendary valley of Glen Coe. Take a boat to the islands of the Firth of Clyde and the Inner Hebrides.

THE NORTHEAST ▲ 207

From Aberdeen, 'the Granite City', you can visit the Grampians, the land of whisky, hunting, fishing... and seventy castles. Travel up the Dee Valley to Balmoral Castle, the home of the British Royal Family, and Braemar, famous for its Highland Games. The less touristic Don Valley has an important archeological heritage and some prestigious castles, including Drum, Craigievar and Fraser. Follow the 'Whisky Trail' along the Spey Valley and the northeast coast to Forres, stopping en route to visit major fishing ports (Peterhead, Fraserburgh), nature reserves, little fishing villages and Elgin Cathedral.

THE NORTH ▲ 225

Northeast of Inverness, the capital of the Highlands, Fort George dominates the entrance to the Moray Firth. The Spey Valley runs to the foot of the Cairngorms, a favorite destination for mountain sports enthusiasts. From Fort William, at the foot of Ben Nevis, the 'road to the isles' runs west to Mallaig, while the geographical fault of Glen More ('Great Glen') runs northeast to the world-famous Loch Ness. Follow the northwest coast, whose impressive relief attracts walkers and climbers, and visit the exotic gardens of Inverewe. Shiver on the high cliffs and desolate moors of the North before returning to Inverness along the east coast with its attractive coastal resorts and prehistoric sites. Take a ferry to the Isle of Skye, the Outer Hebrides, Orkney and Shetland.

→ **ALL INFORMATION CONTAINED IN THIS GUIDE HAS BEEN APPROVED BY THE MANY SPECIALISTS WHO HAVE CONTRIBUTED TO ITS PRODUCTION.**

LIZ ARTHUR
Former conservator for the Glasgow Museums and the Burrell Collection, specializing in ancient costumes and textiles. Author of the spread on 'Tartan'.

DICK BALHARRY
Naturalist and one of the pioneers of Scottish Natural Heritage (SNH), which promotes nature and landscape conservation. Author of the pages on 'The Caledonian Forest'.

SYD BANGHAM
Guide and lecturer. Author of 'The North Coast' and 'The Northeast Coast'.

CALLUM BRINES
Author and editor of travel guides and documentaries. Author of 'Dumfries and Galloway', 'Ayrshire', 'Glasgow', 'The outskirts of Glasgow and the Clyde Valley' and 'Stirling and surroundings'.

YVES COHAT
PhD and specialist in marine life and fishing. Author of the section on 'Marine mammals'.

MARTIN COLLINSON
Biologist at Edinburgh University. Contributes to the journal British Birds and coordinates local action groups for the preservation of biodiversity in Scotland. Author of Biogeography', 'Cliffs', 'Moorland', 'Peat bogs', 'Lochs' and 'Rivers' in the 'Nature' section.

GREG CORBETT
Contributes to various ornithological journals. Lectures for the Royal Society for the Protection of Birds and other 'nature conservation' organizations in Scotland. Author of 'The Cairngorms'.

JOAN DOBBIE
Guide and lecturer. Author of 'Inverness', 'Inverness to Nairn', 'Fort William', 'The Road to the Isles', 'The "Great Glen"', 'Invergarry to Kyle of Lochalsh' and 'The Northwest Coast'.

PIERRE DUBOIS
An accredited 'elfologist' who spends a great deal of time in the company of gnomes, ghosts and fairies. He has written extensively on the subjects, including *La Grande Encyclopédie des Lutins* (sprites and goblins) and *La Grande Encyclopédie des Fées* (fairies). Author of 'The "Little People"'.

MARC DUQUET
Ornithologist and chief editor for the French journal *Ornithos*. Consultant for the 'Nature' section.

CLAUDINE GLOT
Has contributed to the journal Artus and helped to create the Centre de l'Imaginaire Arthurien in the forest of Broceliande (Brittany). Involved in the production of *Écosse, Blanches Terres* and *Scotland, Highlands and Islands* (Artus) and has published a number of articles on Scotland. Author of 'Orkney'.

CATHERINE IANCO
Author and translator who has traveled widely in Scotland. Author of the 'Perthshire' itineraries.

JOHN AND JULIA KEAY
Chief editors of the Encyclopaedia of Scotland (Collins). Julia Keay is a biographer who is currently writing a children's history of Scotland. John Keay has published historical works on India and the Far East. Co-authors of 'Chronology', 'The wars of Scottish independence', 'Mary Stuart and the Reformation', 'The Jacobite Risings', 'The Scottish Enlightenment' and the introductions to 'The West' and 'The North'.

JOHN KENNY
A well-known trombonist and composer for stage and screen who teaches music in London and Glasgow. Author of the spread on 'Music and dance'.

WENDY LEE
Author and editor who was involved in the publication of the first Rough Guides. Author of the 'Edinburgh' and 'Lothian' itineraries.

HILARY MACARTNEY
Art historian, former assistant-conservator of fine art for the Glasgow Museums and Art Galleries, and researcher in art history at Glasgow University. Has contributed to a number of travel guides on Scotland and Spain. Author of 'Popular architecture', 'Churches and monasteries', 'Feudal castles and tower-houses', 'Scottish Renaissance palaces', 'Country residences', 'Urban and rural planning', 'The industrial age' sections, 'Mackintosh and the Glasgow Style', 'Scotland as seen by painters', 'Charles Rennie Mackintosh in Glasgow', 'Pictish Stones', 'The Northeast', and the introductions to 'Edinburgh, Glasgow and the South' and 'East Central'.

ANN MACSWEEN
Archeologist attached to Historic Scotland who has published articles and a number of books on the archeology and history of Scotland. Author of 'Early Scottish architecture (from the Stone Age to the Viking invasions)', 'The Isle of Sky' and 'The Outer Hebrides'.

MARIE MCGRIGOR
Writer and journalist who has published two history books and a guide book on her home region of Argyll. Author of 'The West'.

GEORGE MCMURDO
Lecturer in computing at Queen Margaret University College, Edinburgh. He has been a keen golfer since childhood, and contributed to the *Encyclopaedia of Scotland* (Collins) and the *Edinburgh Encyclopaedia*. Author of the spread on 'Golf'.

RUTH NOBLE
Writer and editor. Author of 'The Borders' and 'Fife' itineraries.

MARTINE NOUET
Writer and journalist, and a connoisseur of brandies. Author of 'Scotch whisky', 'Food: cranachan and shortbreads' and 'The Whisky Trail'.

OLWYN OWEN
Archeologist and chief inspector of ancient monuments for Historic Scotland. She has published a number of books and articles on the Vikings, the early Middle Ages and the growth and development of Scottish towns. Author of 'Shetland'.

A.J. PATERSON
Teacher and translator. Author of 'Robert Burns'.

NICOLA TAYLOR
Writer and teacher. Author of 'Angus', the section on 'Nairn', 'Strathspey and the Cairngorms' and 'Nessie, the Loch Ness Monster'.

PATRICK TAYLOR
Writer and photographer who loves gardens. He has published several books on the subject and contributes to a number of specialist journals. Author of 'Scotland's gardens'.

JUDY URQUHART
Writer and journalist who has published a history of the island of Eigg. Author of the 'Specialties' section.

KEITH WILLIAMSON
Linguist specializing in the Scots language. Researcher at the Institute for Historical Dialectology, School of Scottish Studies, Edinburgh University. Author of the pages on 'Language'.

→ **ADVISORS: JULIA AND JOHN KEAY**
Historians.

This is a Borzoi Book
published by
Alfred A. Knopf

Copyright © 2001
Alfred A. Knopf, New York

All rights reserved under International
and Pan-American Copyright
Conventions. Published in the United
States by Alfred A. Knopf, a division of
Random House, Inc., New York, and
simultaneously in Canada by Random
House of Canada Limited, Toronto.
Distributed by Random House, Inc.,
New York.

www.aaknopf.com

Knopf, Borzoi Books, and the colophon
are registered trademarks of Random
House, Inc.

Scotland: ISBN 0-375-70659-3

First American Edition

Originally published in France by
Nouveaux-Loisirs, a subsidiary of Editions
Gallimard, Paris, 2000. Copyright © 2000
by Editions Nouveaux-Loisirs

SCOTLAND
■ **EDITOR**
Anne-Valérie Cadoret,
assisted by Solène Bouton, Jim Charmetant
■ **GRAPHICS**
Yann Le Duc
assisted by Isabelle Dubois-Dumée
■ **NATURE**
Frédéric Bony, Marc Duquet
■ **ARCHITECTURE**
Bruno Lenormand
assisted by Isabelle Bembo
■ **PICTURE RESEARCH**
Isabelle Latour, Suzanne Bosman,
Anaïk Bourhis
■ **LAYOUT**
Olivier Brunot
■ **PHOTOGRAPHY**
Patrick Léger
■ **MAPS**
Édigraphie, Patrick Mérienne (nature)
■ **RESEARCH**
Virginie Maubourguet

ILLUSTRATIONS
■ **NATURE**
Jean Chevallier, François Desbordes, Claire
Felloni, Catherine Lachaud, Alban
Larousse, Dominique Mansion, Pascal
Robin
■ **ARCHITECTURE**
Bruno Lenormand, Claude Quiec, Jean-
François Penneau, Maurice Pommier,
Amato Soro

TRANSLATED BY
Wendy Allatson

EDITED AND TYPESET BY
Book Creation Services Ltd, London

**We would like to thank the following for
their valuable help:**
Jane Anderson (Blair Castle), Lynda Clark
(Hunterian Art Gallery, Glasgow),
Douglas Corrance, Éric Duboüays,
Marianne Binet, Hervé Glot (Artus),
Fraser Hunter (Museum of Scotland),
John Hutchinson (Still Moving Picture
Company), Bertrand Lematinel (Edinburgh
University), Isla Robertson (National Trust
for Scotland), Magda Salvasen, Sylvie
Séchet (British Tourist Office, Paris),
Jean-Marc Terrasse (French Institute of
Scotland, Edinburgh), Winnie Tyrrell
(Glasgow Museums)

Special thanks to
Duncan McAra

Printed in Italy by Editoriale Lloyd

Encyclopedia section

15 Nature

31 History and language

49 Arts and traditions

65 Architecture

85 Scotland as seen by painters

93 Scotland as seen by writers

Rural scene, c. 1920.

Nature

Martin Collinson, Yves Cohat

16   Biogeography
18   Marine mammals
20   Cliffs
24   Moorland
26   Peat bogs
28   Lochs
30   Rivers

● Biogeography

Some of the western mountains are the remains of volcanoes. The region is dominated by extremely resistant basalt rocks which remained intact as the more fragile surrounding rocks were worn away.

The landscape of Scotland was formed from volcanic and sedimentary rocks which, over the past 550 million years, have been pushed together by the movement of the earth's crust. This is why the fertile, undulating landscape of the Lowlands suddenly gives way to the mountainous terrain of the Highlands along the Highland Boundary Fault. Glacial action during the Ice Age significantly altered these landscapes. When the ice retreated, about 15,000 years ago, flora and fauna recolonized the region, adapting to a climate that combined continental and oceanic influences.

THE GREAT GLEN FAULT (GLEN MORE)
This depression, occupied by a series of lochs stretching from Fort William in the southwest to Inverness in the northeast, lies along a major fault line which attests to a turbulent geological history.

GLACIAL ACTION
During the Ice Age glaciers hollowed out circles (semicircular depressions) at the heads of mountain valleys. They also created U-shaped valleys, which can be particularly spectacular.

GEOLOGICAL HISTORY
Some 500 million years ago Scotland was part of the paleocontinent of Laurentia, which was separated from the continent of Avalonia (which included present-day England and Wales) by the Iapetus Ocean. These land masses collided about 410 million years ago. Over the ages Avalonia drifted across to become isolated in the North Atlantic.

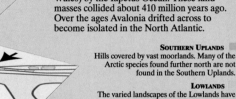

SOUTHERN UPLANDS
Hills covered by vast moorlands. Many of the Arctic species found further north are not found in the Southern Uplands.

LOWLANDS
The varied landscapes of the Lowlands have much in common with the English countryside.

THE SOUTH COAST
This coast, which enjoys mild winters and warm summers, has many of the species and habitats found in England.

THE INNER HEBRIDES
A surprisingly temperate, wet climate with rare animal and plant species, some of which are thought to have links with American plant communitites.

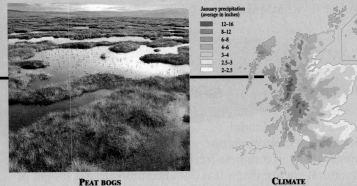

PEAT BOGS
The wet region of northern Scotland has the most extensive peat bogs in Europe. Plants have had to adapt to be able to grow in this acid peat environment, which is 95 percent water.

CLIMATE
In spite of its latitude (55–60° N) Scotland has mild winters and warm summers due to the influence of the Gulf Stream and westerly winds. However, the weather is extremely changeable and wet throughout the year.

January precipitation
(average in inches)
- 12–16
- 8–12
- 6–8
- 4–6
- 3–4
- 2.5–3
- 2–2.5

ORKNEY AND SHETLAND
These more or less treeless islands have a unique coastal vegetation, with a few rare plants such as the Scottish primrose growing on certain sites.

OUTER HEBRIDES
Rough pastureland with Arctic and alpine plants at low altitude.

THE WET WESTERN SHORES
The heavy rainfall on these predominately rocky, undulating shores favors the growth of broad-leaved forests rich in mosses, ferns and lichens.

FLOW COUNTRY
Peat bogs contain a rich variety of plant, insect and bird life.

PLAIN OF BUCHAN
Rich arable land climbing to the Grampians, with a few large forests and hunting reserves.

THE LOWER SLOPES OF THE HIGHLANDS
Forests, grassy hills and moorland.

HIGHLAND SUMMITS
Cold winters; Arctic and alpine flora and fauna.

Shetland

ATLANTIC OCEAN

Orkney

NORTH SEA

Outer Hebrides

MOINE THRUST

Northern Highlands

Moray Firth

GREAT GLEN FAULT

● Inverness

● Aberdeen

Grampian Mountains

Mull

● Dundee

Jura

Edinburgh

Firth of Forth

Islay

Glasgow ● ● Edinburgh

SOUTHERN UPLAND FAULT

Southern Uplands

SOLWAY FAULT

● MARINE MAMMALS

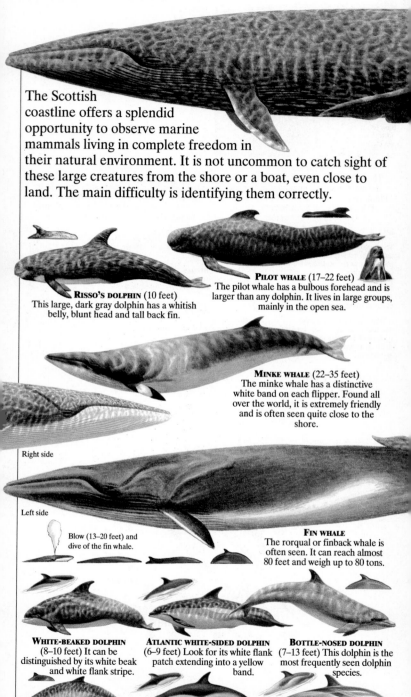

The Scottish coastline offers a splendid opportunity to observe marine mammals living in complete freedom in their natural environment. It is not uncommon to catch sight of these large creatures from the shore or a boat, even close to land. The main difficulty is identifying them correctly.

RISSO'S DOLPHIN (10 feet)
This large, dark gray dolphin has a whitish belly, blunt head and tall back fin.

PILOT WHALE (17–22 feet)
The pilot whale has a bulbous forehead and is larger than any dolphin. It lives in large groups, mainly in the open sea.

MINKE WHALE (22–35 feet)
The minke whale has a distinctive white band on each flipper. Found all over the world, it is extremely friendly and is often seen quite close to the shore.

Right side

Left side

Blow (13–20 feet) and dive of the fin whale.

FIN WHALE
The rorqual or finback whale is often seen. It can reach almost 80 feet and weigh up to 80 tons.

WHITE-BEAKED DOLPHIN (8–10 feet) It can be distinguished by its white beak and white flank stripe.

ATLANTIC WHITE-SIDED DOLPHIN (6–9 feet) Look for its white flank patch extending into a yellow band.

BOTTLE-NOSED DOLPHIN (7–13 feet) This dolphin is the most frequently seen dolphin species.

COMMON PORPOISE (6 feet) In summer, they can be seen in groups of 2–5 offshore.

COMMON DOLPHIN (5–7 feet) They live in groups, sometimes in considerable numbers.

STRIPED DOLPHIN (6–8½ feet) Though rarely seen, this dolphin often plays near boats.

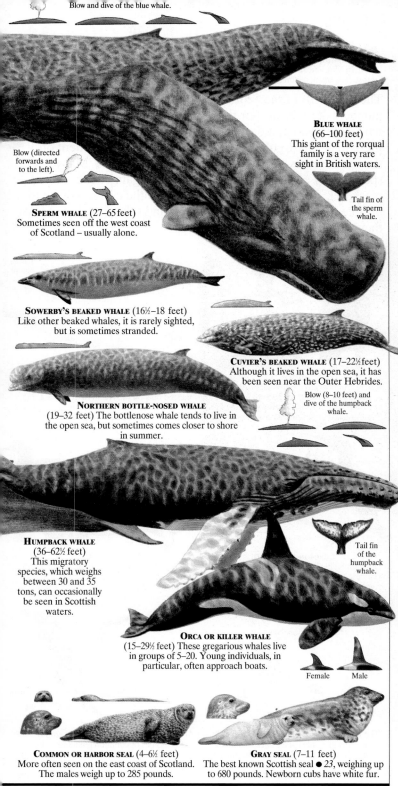

Blow and dive of the blue whale.

BLUE WHALE
(66–100 feet)
This giant of the rorqual family is a very rare sight in British waters.

Tail fin of the sperm whale.

Blow (directed forwards and to the left).

SPERM WHALE (27–65 feet)
Sometimes seen off the west coast of Scotland – usually alone.

SOWERBY'S BEAKED WHALE (16½–18 feet)
Like other beaked whales, it is rarely sighted, but is sometimes stranded.

CUVIER'S BEAKED WHALE (17–22½ feet)
Although it lives in the open sea, it has been seen near the Outer Hebrides.

Blow (8–10 feet) and dive of the humpback whale.

NORTHERN BOTTLE-NOSED WHALE
(19–32 feet) The bottlenose whale tends to live in the open sea, but sometimes comes closer to shore in summer.

HUMPBACK WHALE
(36–62½ feet)
This migratory species, which weighs between 30 and 35 tons, can occasionally be seen in Scottish waters.

Tail fin of the humpback whale.

ORCA OR KILLER WHALE
(15–29½ feet) These gregarious whales live in groups of 5–20. Young individuals, in particular, often approach boats.

Female   Male

COMMON OR HARBOR SEAL (4–6½ feet)
More often seen on the east coast of Scotland. The males weigh up to 285 pounds.

GRAY SEAL (7–11 feet)
The best known Scottish seal ● 23, weighing up to 680 pounds. Newborn cubs have white fur.

19

● CLIFFS

CLIFF FLORA
Between April and August the cliff tops are carpeted with the pink tufts of thrift or sea pink. In May and June the delicate Scottish primrose flowers on northern coastal pastures.

SEA PINK OR THRIFT   **SCOTTISH PRIMROSE**

The high cliffs of the Scottish coastline are the habitat of large numbers of seabirds. For those species that can adapt to the narrow windswept ledges, they offer a nesting place safe from predators. These colonies of nesting birds are dependent on the fish reserves of the Atlantic and the North Sea. Many species prey on sand-eels, while the larger gannet eats a lot of mackerel. The plant species that grow on the cliff face have to be able to withstand the drying winds and salt spray, but at least they are safe from grazing animals.

Adults, summer

Tubular nostrils

Adult

Taking off with feet trailing

PUFFIN
This comical large-billed seabird digs a burrow on the cliff tops where it breeds between May and July. During the rest of the year it lives far out in the open seas of the North Atlantic.

NORTHERN FULMAR
About 120 years ago, the northern fulmar nested only on the island of St Kilda ▲ *255*, off the Outer Hebrides. Today, it is widely found on Scotland's coastal cliffs and even nests in the center of Edinburgh.

Summer

Winter

Winter

Winter

Summer

COMMON GUILLEMOT
Common guillemots live in huge colonies on narrow ledges high above the sea. They do not build a nest as such, but lay their eggs directly onto the ledge.

BLACK GUILLEMOT
This guillemot is widely found in the north and west, but is scarce in eastern Scotland south of Caithness. Unlike other seabirds it lives close to the coast all year round.

Young bird

Winter

Summer

Adult

KITTIWAKE
The most sea-based of all the Scottish gulls, the kittiwake only comes back to land to nest. It tends to build its nest on small outcrops of rock on the cliff face, even on sheer cliffs.

RAZORBILL
Although sometimes found among colonies of common guillemots, the razorbill prefers to nest in pairs or small groups in cavities in the cliffs or among boulders.

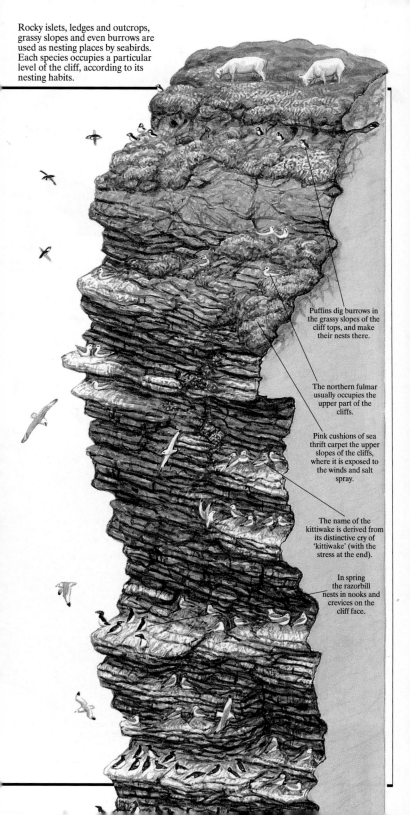

Rocky islets, ledges and outcrops, grassy slopes and even burrows are used as nesting places by seabirds. Each species occupies a particular level of the cliff, according to its nesting habits.

Puffins dig burrows in the grassy slopes of the cliff tops, and make their nests there.

The northern fulmar usually occupies the upper part of the cliffs.

Pink cushions of sea thrift carpet the upper slopes of the cliffs, where it is exposed to the winds and salt spray.

The name of the kittiwake is derived from its distinctive cry of 'kittiwake' (with the stress at the end).

In spring the razorbill nests in nooks and crevices on the cliff face.

CLIFFS

GANNET

When fishing, gannets perform some spectacular dives into the sea. More than half the world's gannet population nests in huge colonies on the Scottish islands.

1-year-old

3-year-old

Young bird

Adult

ARCTIC SKUA

This aerial acrobat can be seen in summer near the coast where it attacks other seabirds, such as seagulls and terns, and steals their fish.

Young bird

Adult

GREAT SKUA

This migratory bird is a summer visitor to the extreme north and west of Scotland. It attacks, and can even kill, seabirds as large as the gannet.

Adult

Young bird

Adult, breeding plumage January–April.

SHAG

The crest of the shag, visible during the breeding season, distinguishes it from the cormorant. The bird is often seen swimming and diving for fish along the coast.

Gannet

Shag

Gray seal

The lower, tidal parts of the cliffs are covered in seaweed and harbor a great many mollusks and shellfish.

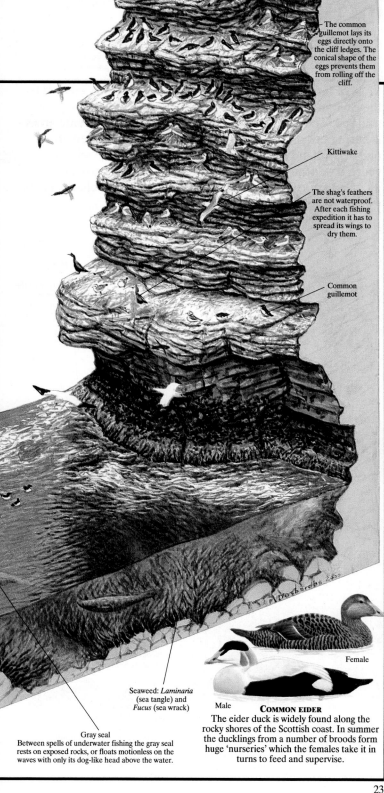

The common guillemot lays its eggs directly onto the cliff ledges. The conical shape of the eggs prevents them from rolling off the cliff.

Kittiwake

The shag's feathers are not waterproof. After each fishing expedition it has to spread its wings to dry them.

Common guillemot

Seaweed: *Laminaria* (sea tangle) and *Fucus* (sea wrack)

Gray seal
Between spells of underwater fishing the gray seal rests on exposed rocks, or floats motionless on the waves with only its dog-like head above the water.

Female

Male

COMMON EIDER
The eider duck is widely found along the rocky shores of the Scottish coast. In summer the ducklings from a number of broods form huge 'nurseries' which the females take it in turns to feed and supervise.

23

● MOORLAND

BANK VOLE
The woodland-dwelling bank vole has a redder
coat than the short-tailed field vole, which lives
on the moors and other open habitats.

Most of the Scottish moors are an artificial habitat, created by
the clearance of forests or the draining of peat bogs on poor,
acid soil. They are dominated by heather, which in some areas
is burnt periodically to maintain the habitat of the red grouse,
one of Scotland's most widely hunted birds. These moors,
which cover the hills and mountain-sides with a carpet of
green and purple, form one of the country's most characteristic
wild landscapes.

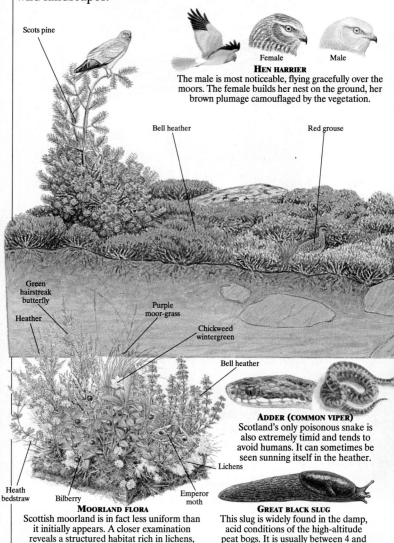

Scots pine

HEN HARRIER

Female   Male

The male is most noticeable, flying gracefully over the
moors. The female builds her nest on the ground, her
brown plumage camouflaged by the vegetation.

Bell heather

Red grouse

Green
hairstreak
butterfly

Heather

Purple
moor-grass

Chickweed
wintergreen

Bell heather

ADDER (COMMON VIPER)
Scotland's only poisonous snake is
also extremely timid and tends to
avoid humans. It can sometimes be
seen sunning itself in the heather.

Lichens

Heath
bedstraw

Bilberry

Emperor
moth

MOORLAND FLORA
Scottish moorland is in fact less uniform than
it initially appears. A closer examination
reveals a structured habitat rich in lichens,
flowers and insects, dominated by heather
(ling) and often with a variety of grasses.

GREAT BLACK SLUG
This slug is widely found in the damp,
acid conditions of the high-altitude
peat bogs. It is usually between 4 and
6 inches long but can occasionally
grow to almost 8 inches.

STOAT (ERMINE)
This formidable predator crosses the moors to hunt voles. In winter its fur turns white (apart from the tail tip) to provide better camouflage in the snow.

Winter

Summer

Winter

Summer

Female

Male

GOLDEN PLOVER
This wader nests on the moors in summer and winters in the lowland fields and estuaries. The subtle gold of its plumage is only visible at close range. It has a plaintive whistling cry.

MERLIN
This small, fast-flying falcon nests among the heather. It feeds on small birds caught on the wing after twisting pursuits, often skimming just above ground level.

RED GROUSE
The grouse is a well-known inhabitant of the moors where its plumage provides excellent camouflage. Numbers vary in 4–8 year cycles.

Golden plover

Red grouse

Heather (ling)

Merlin (male)

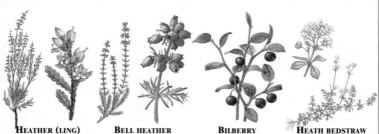

HEATHER (LING)
One of the emblems of Scotland. In late summer and fall its tiny flowers bring color to the moors.

BELL HEATHER
This plant grows in the driest areas of the moors. It flowers earlier than the more dominant heather.

BILBERRY
Its presence attests to the deforestation of what is now moorland. It has edible purple berries.

HEATH BEDSTRAW
The clusters of tiny white flowers are visible from a long way off across the moors.

● PEAT BOGS

SHORT-EARED OWL
This spectacular bird can be seen in broad daylight hunting for field voles over the moors and peat bogs. It often glides with its long wings held up in a shallow 'V'.

In areas that are badly drained or with a heavy rainfall, moorland gives way to sphagnum moss and other characteristic peat-bog vegetation. Peat is an accumulation of vegetable matter that has rotted very slowly due to the damp conditions and lack of oxygen. Over the centuries it forms layers several feet deep. The region known as the Flow Country, in the north of Scotland, is the largest area of peat bogs in Europe and one of the largest in the world.

Female

Male

SNIPE
This wader feeds on worms and insect larvae by probing mud and boggy ground with its very long beak.

MEADOW PIPIT
Widely found in the peat bogs and moors, this little brown bird is a favorite prey of the merlin.

DUNLIN
Large numbers of these little waders breed in the peat bogs of the Flow Country.

WHEATEAR
One of the first migratory birds to return in spring. Its white rump is clearly visible in flight.

Merlin

Short-eared owl

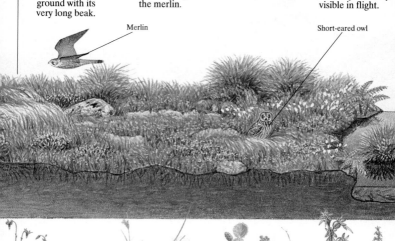

CRANBERRY
A relative of the bilberry, it flourishes in the damp soil of the peat bogs. It has small, red, edible berries.

COMMON COTTON-GRASS
The presence of this grass is a sign of very wet ground that could be treacherous underfoot.

DWARF BIRCH
This rampant bush grows on the edge of peat bogs and on the moors. It provides food for grouse ● 25 and insects.

LESSER TWAYBLADE
This small orchid is quite common but hard to see beneath the heather. It is recognized by its two heart-shaped leaves.

FROM PEAT BOGS TO MOORLAND
When the layer of peat becomes extremely deep, it begins to dry out. Sphagnum moss becomes increasingly sparse and is replaced by lichens and shrubby growth. The peat bog becomes heather-covered moorland.

Common cotton-grass

Bog asphodel

Bog pimpernel

SPHAGNUM MOSS
The different species of sphagnum moss form the basis of the peat-bog ecosystem. They also form the raw material for peat.

CROSS-LEAVED HEATH
This heather has pale pink flowers and characteristic cross-shaped whorls of leaves.

COMMON SUNDEW
This carnivorous 'flytrap' catches insects with its sticky red filaments.

Sphagnum moss

Cross-leaved heath

Peat is formed from an accumulation of dead sphagnum moss.

THE SYNERGY OF PEAT-BOG PLANTS
Sphagnum moss acts like a sponge, soaking up the water of the peat bogs and creating an almost dry environment, which explains the presence of heathers.

Meadow pipit

Cotton-grass

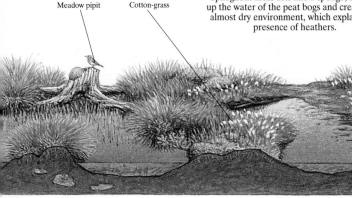

NORTHERN EMERALD
This large, dark-colored dragonfly is seen in summer over the peat bogs of the west, but not in the extreme north.

MIDGE
The bites of this tiny insect, one of the hazards of the Scottish summer, can be unbearable. Only the female bites.

EMPEROR MOTH
The caterpillar of this large nocturnal moth weaves a pear-shaped cocoon on sprigs of heather and willow branches.

GREEN HAIRSTREAK BUTTERFLY
The only British butterfly with green underwings. It is very bold and will even land on your hand.

27

There are more than 30,000 freshwater lochs in Scotland. They range from the Highland lochs, poor in nutrients and plant life, which are dominated by the black-throated diver and char, to the more shallow lochs of the Lowlands, which support a much richer flora and fauna. The west coast is famous for its sea lochs, deep indentations in the coastline which provide refuge for thousands of ducks, swans, geese, grebes and divers during the winter.

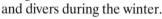

Young swan

Adult

PINK-FOOTED GOOSE
On winter evenings huge flocks of pink-footed geese gather on a number of Scottish lochs.

WHOOPER SWAN
Although only a few pairs of whooper swans nest in Scotland, thousands of these birds arrive from Iceland in winter.

GREY HERON
The heron can be seen fishing along the shores of shallow lochs, both saltwater and fresh. It nests in the trees.

Young bird

Mating plumage

Female

Male

RED-NECKED PHALAROPE
This dainty Arctic bird breeds in small numbers in Shetland. It swims in circles to bring food to the surface.

COMMON SANDPIPER
This little wader, a common sight on the gravelly, rocky shores of lochs, has a distinctive three-note whistling cry.

GOLDENEYE
Although a frequent sight in winter, only 200 or so pairs nest in Scotland, almost all in artificial nest-boxes.

Sea lochs are tidal. Cormorants can often be seen perching on the seaweed-covered rocks at low tide.

SEA LOCHS

Like the Scandinavian fjords, saltwater lochs provide a habitat for a number of coastal, marine and inland species. Dolphins and porpoises often venture into their deep waters.

Winter   Young bird   Summer

BLACK-THROATED DIVER
Much rarer than its red-throated cousin, this bird nests on the large northern and western lochs. Do not disturb it near the nest.

Winter   Young bird   Summer

RED-THROATED DIVER
Although it feeds at sea, this bird nests on the shores or islands of vegetation of small freshwater lochs. On spring nights its melancholy wails echoes across the moors.

FRESHWATER LOCHS
Some are huge lakes, others small, shallow pools. They are scattered across the Scottish moors, offering a unique habitat to many species of birds.

Female

GOOSANDER
Large flocks of these divers over-winter on some of the Scottish lochs. They feed on small fish caught beneath the surface.

Male

OTTER
An early morning walk along the shores of a quiet loch gives an ideal opportunity to catch a glimpse of this fish-eating mammal. Although fairly common, it is extremely timid.

CHAR
This survivor of the Ice Age is found in a few deep lochs. The lack of contact between the different populations means that each loch has its own genetic type.

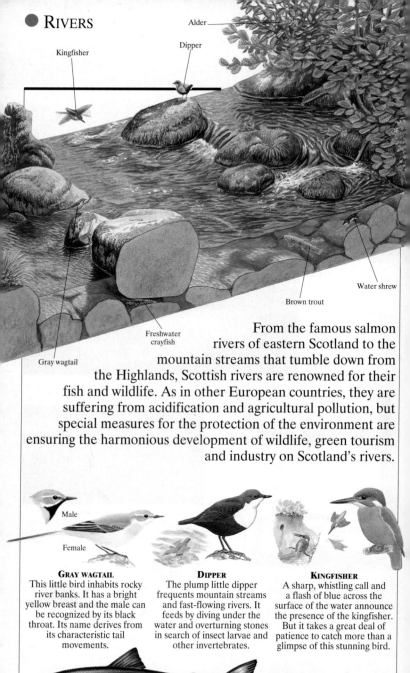

RIVERS

Alder

Dipper

Kingfisher

Water shrew

Brown trout

Freshwater
crayfish

Gray wagtail

From the famous salmon
rivers of eastern Scotland to the
mountain streams that tumble down from
the Highlands, Scottish rivers are renowned for their
fish and wildlife. As in other European countries, they are
suffering from acidification and agricultural pollution, but
special measures for the protection of the environment are
ensuring the harmonious development of wildlife, green tourism
and industry on Scotland's rivers.

Male

Female

GRAY WAGTAIL
This little bird inhabits rocky
river banks. It has a bright
yellow breast and the male can
be recognized by its black
throat. Its name derives from
its characteristic tail
movements.

DIPPER
The plump little dipper
frequents mountain streams
and fast-flowing rivers. It
feeds by diving under the
water and overturning stones
in search of insect larvae and
other invertebrates.

KINGFISHER
A sharp, whistling call and
a flash of blue across the
surface of the water announce
the presence of the kingfisher.
But it takes a great deal of
patience to catch more than a
glimpse of this stunning bird.

ATLANTIC SALMON
The Atlantic salmon swims
up the Scottish rivers to its
spawning grounds. Anglers
come from all over the world
to fish for salmon.

BROWN/SEA TROUT
Two forms – the freshwater
brown trout and the sea trout,
which returns to the rivers to
spawn – are found in shallow
rivers and streams.

RIVER LAMPREY
This strange parasitic fish uses
its mouth as a sucker to attach
itself to other fish and feed on
their blood. It migrates to
coasts when 6 years old.

History and language

Julia and John Keay
Keith Williamson

32 Chronology
38 The wars of Scottish
   independence, 1296–1357
40 Mary Stuart and the
   Reformation
42 The Jacobite Risings
44 The Scottish Enlightenment
46 Language

−10000 BC

4th century BC
The Celts occupy the
British Isles

AD 43–50
Britannia
annexed by the
Roman Empire

c. 400 The Romans
leave Caledonia

0   100   500

8000–7000 BC
The settlement of
Scotland

4000 BC
Stone Age

2000–1000 BC
Bronze Age

700 BC–AD 400
Iron Age

AD 78 Romans
occupy southern
Scotland

398 Saint Ninian
founds one of the firs
Christian centers in
Britain, at Whithorn

PRE-CHRISTIAN SCOTLAND

THE PREHISTORIC PERIOD

Man-made deposits dating back 8500 years have been found on the Fife peninsula. These provide evidence that the early peoples of Scotland, who may have arrived from Germany or Scandinavia in leather or wooden boats, were nomadic groups of hunter-fisher-gatherers.
Around 4000 BC, probably due to the gradual warming of the climate, the Stone Age people began to plant crops and keep livestock. They also developed the art of pottery and weaving, and built mud and stone houses. Between 2500 and 1000 BC the art of metalwork was imported from the east via Germania and Gaul.

The Bronze Age people erected tumuli (barrows), and large circles and alignments of standing stones, such as those still to be seen at Callanish. The Iron Age people built circular or underground houses. They also built defensive dry-stone towers, high and round, which are known as *brochs*. Some still exist.

CELTIC SETTLEMENT

From c. 1000 BC the peoples of Scotland spoke Celtic dialects, and place names throughout Scotland incorporate such Celtic elements as *dun* (fortress). However, linguistic variations suggest that the Celtic immigration occurred in a series of waves, first from Europe, especially the Rhineland, and then from Ireland. The fortified sites of Traprain Law (East Lothian ▲ *133*) and Tap o' Noth (Rhynie, Aberdeenshire ▲ *222*) confirm the accounts of such Roman historians as Tacitus, whose father-in-law Agricola invaded Scotland in AD 81. These state that the cultural and technical homogeneity of the Scottish tribes enabled them to offer a united resistance to the invaders.

THE FAILURE OF THE ROMAN CONQUEST

The Roman conquest of Britain (AD 43–78) helped to define Scotland by threatening and excluding it. Not a single Roman legion set foot in the Scottish Highlands and islands, while the expeditions sent north of the River Forth to conquer the 'barbarians' threatening the *Pax Romana* were met with fierce resistance. Although the Roman commander Agricola (AD 40–93) defeated the Caledonians led by Calgacus at Mons Graupius in AD 84, his troops were forced to withdraw shortly afterward, abandoning such fortified camps as Inchtuthil, near Dunkeld in Perthshire. By contrast, the Roman occupation of England lasted for almost four centuries and left two boundaries between England and Scotland. Hadrian's Wall, built in c. 120 between the Solway Firth and River Tyne, marked the northern boundary of *Britannia*, while the Antonine Wall, built in 142 between the River Clyde and Firth of Forth, only contained the 'barbarians' between 155 and 161. The Roman presence did, however, benefit the tribes of southern Scotland, some of whom embraced Christianity and learned to write.
Scotland was given a Latin name, *Caledonia*, and acquired a geographical and historical identity.

685 The Picts defeat the Angles of Northumbria at Forfar	839 The Vikings defeat the Picts and the Scots	1066 Norman conquest of England	1272–1307 Reign of Edward I of England
600 800	1000	1100 1200	1300
563 Saint Columba builds a monastery on Iona	c. 790 The first Viking raids	843 The Picts join forces with the Scots	1040–1057 Reign of Macbeth	c. 1160 Somerled becomes king of the Gaels (Scots)	1266 The Hebrides are ceded to Scotland by the Treaty of Perth

TOWARDS UNIFICATION

PICTS, SCOTS, BRITONS AND ANGLES

The Romans called the inhabitants of Caledonia the *Pictii* (Picts or 'painted men'). The Picts, of Celtic stock, are thought to have come to Scotland from the Continent. The Picts left many standing stones, decorated with strange inscriptions, which attest to the fact that the region between the Forth and Moray Firths lay at the heart of their territory.

In the 3rd and 4th centuries the Scots, or Gaels, arrived from Ireland. These Christianized Celts colonized western Scotland, including Kintyre, Argyll and the islands, and established the kingdom of Dalriada. The Celtic monk St Columba built a church and monastery on the island of Iona (563) and continued the task of converting Scotland to Christianity.

In the 4th century the Britons, Romanized Celts from Wales, founded the kingdom of Strathclyde in southwestern Caledonia, stretching from the Clyde to the Solway. The Teutonic Angles, who came from the lands between the Rhine and the Baltic, settled south of the Forth. By 650 their powerful kingdom extended as far south as Northumbria.

ROYAL AND RELIGIOUS AUTHORITY

By the late 7th century Scotland had been converted to Christianity, from two different sources. The first Christian missionary, who came to Strathclyde in the 5th century, was St Ninian, a Briton who was consecrated bishop in Rome. Missionaries also came in the 6th century from the Celtic Church in Ireland, led by St Columba, who established a church on Iona. The two branches of Christianity had differences, especially on the subject of episcopal authority, but the Celtic Church finally agreed to accept the Roman form of worship in 716. But Columba's more democratic idea that there could be no legitimate authority without the endorsement of the people also persisted: Scottish kings could not conceive of reigning without the approval of their kingdom (Church and nobility). In 1314 the relics of St Columba (*above*), taken by

Kenneth MacAlpin to Dunkeld, were carried into battle by Robert Bruce, together with the cross of St Andrew, the symbol of Roman orthodoxy.

THE UNIFICATION OF SCOTLAND AND THE VIKING ENCLAVE

From 790, after a series of devastating raids against Shetland, Orkney, Hebrides and Western Isles, the Vikings began to found settlements in this part of Scotland, including Caithness and Sutherland. Following their defeat by the Vikings in 839, the weakened Picts joined forces with the Scots (c. 843) under the leadership of Kenneth MacAlpin, king of Dalriada, who established his capital at Scone, near Perth ▲ 180. His descendant Malcolm II (1005–34) finally defeated the Angles and annexed the Lothians in 1018. When Malcolm died, his grandson Duncan I, who ruled the Britons of Strathclyde, came to the throne (1034–40), thereby unifying most of Scotland. Only Shetland, Orkney, the Hebrides and the northern coast remained under Viking control. The Hebrides and Kintyre ▲ 191 were ceded to Norway by treaty in 1098. However, in the 1150s Somerled, a descendant of the kings of Dalriada, recovered Iona and established an island domain over Argyll, Lochaber and the southern Hebrides.

| 1297 William Wallace defeats the English at Stirling Bridge | 1337 Start of the Hundred Years War | 1399 Henry IV: the first Lancastrian king of England | 1412 The first Scottish university is founded at St Andrews | 1485 Henry VII: t first Tudor king of England |

1250 — 1300 — 1350 — 1400 — 1450 — 1500

| 1266 The Hebrides are ceded to Scotland by Norway | 1314 Robert Bruce wins the Battle of Bannockburn | 1328 Treaty of Northampton | 1412 The first session of Parliament | 1470 Orkney and Shetland become part of Scotland |

FEUDAL SCOTLAND

THE ANGLO-NORMAN INFLUENCE

When Duncan I was murdered by Macbeth, chief of Moray ▲ *231*, in 1040, his son Malcolm III Canmore (1058–93) had to appeal to the English for help to regain the throne. Malcolm's Anglo-Saxon wife Margaret, who welcomed the nobles expelled from England after the Norman conquest, anglicized the court and Church. Her work, continued by her sons, became a process of feudalization when her son, David I (1124–53), allowed noblemen from England and Europe to settle throughout Scotland. In this way the Celtic and Pictish aristocracy was joined by such nobles as the De Bruses from Normandy and the Breton Fitzalains, whose hereditary title Steward became their family name *Stewart*.

THE STRUGGLE FOR INDEPENDENCE

Although fiercely attached to its independence, Scotland was nevertheless forced to recognize English sovereignty on a number of occasions. However, the royal lineages of the two countries were allied by marriage and each owned territory in the other's kingdom. But the death of Alexander III in 1286 provoked a crisis of succession which ended with an English invasion in 1296. William Wallace, who led the Scottish resistance, was defeated in 1305. In 1306 Robert Bruce (1306–29) seized the throne. He defeated the English at the Battle of Bannockburn (1314) and gradually restored Scotland's royal power. In 1357 England was finally forced to recognize Scottish independence ● *39*.

THE 'THRIE ESTAITIS' (THREE ESTATES)

In spite of these wars, the unification of Scotland continued under the centralizing influence of the feudal system. The Vikings ceded the Hebrides after they were defeated at Largs, in 1263, and the islands were gradually integrated into the kingdom while remaining under the rule of the Lords of the Isles (the MacDonalds). Orkney and Shetland became part of Scotland by treaty in 1470. The Scottish kings, whose legitimacy depended as much on the Church as on their lineage, encouraged the foundation of monasteries. They also granted legal and commercial privileges to the first *burghs* (towns), thereby encouraging the settlement of Flemish merchants along the east coast and promoting trade with Scandinavia, the Netherlands, England and France. Under William the Lion (1165–1214), representatives of the royal burghs were granted the right to sit with the churchmen and nobles in the assembly that preceded Parliament.

THE AULD ALLIANCE

Scotland early established unique ties with France, the rival and bitter enemy of England. The first treaty of alliance was signed in 1165 by William I, or William the Lion, before he launched a disastrous invasion of England. This *Auld Alliance* was renewed on the eve of the wars of independence, and consolidated by Scotland's entry into the Hundred Years War as France's ally. It was cemented by such marriages as that of James V and Madeleine of France, daughter of François I, and, later, Mary of Guise. Mary, who became Regent in 1542, rewarded her loyal courtiers with French titles. Her daughter, Mary Stuart, was brought up in France and became Dauphine in 1558 when she married the future François II. Many Scots went to study in Paris at this time. In 1560 the Reformation ● *41* severed this alliance, which was revived in the 18th century by the Jacobites. Words of French origin were introduced into the Scottish language ● *46*, and Scots continued to emigrate to France until the 1850s.

1509 Henry VIII becomes King of England	**1559–1560** Protestant Reformation in Scotland	**1611** 'Plantation' of Ulster by Scottish Presbyterians	**1642** The English Civil War	**1649** Charles I executed; Parliament acclaims Charles II
1510	1550	1600	1625	1650	1675
1513 The English defeat the Scots at the Battle of Flodden	**1558** Mary Stuart marries the French Dauphin	**1603** James VI of Scotland becomes James I of England	**1638** Signing of the *National Covenant*	**1642** Charles II crowned King of Scotland at Scone

THE ADVENT OF MODERN SCOTLAND

THE ROYAL HOUSE OF STEWART

David II (1329–71), son of Robert Bruce, was succeeded by his nephew Robert II (1371–90), the first Stewart to accede to the throne of Scotland. Robert's grandson, James I (1406–37), attempted to restore order and prosperity by strengthening the country's institutions. His successors more or less succeeded in asserting their authority over the recalcitrant nobility, and promoted the arts

and literature. The first universities were established at St Andrews (1412), Glasgow (1451) and Aberdeen (1495), while palaces and stately homes were modeled on the Loire châteaux. Gavin Douglas translated Virgil's *Aeneid* into Scots verse (1553), Hector Boethius (c.1465–1536) wrote a Latin history of Scotland, and George Buchanan (1506–82) became a renowned Latin poet.

Reconciliation with England seemed possible in 1503, with James IV's marriage to Margaret Tudor, sister of the future Henry VIII. But James' alliance with France led him to war with Henry in 1513. The campaign ended in a disastrous defeat at Flodden, with the death of James and many nobles and clan chiefs. The dynasty soon had to confront a new enemy, this time internal. From 1555

the ideas of the Reformation, preached by John Knox, won the support of many Scottish lords. These 'Lords of the Congregation' deposed the Catholic Regent, Mary of Guise, in 1559 and founded a Reformed Church. Mary Stuart then succeeded to the throne, but was forced to abdicate in 1567 and seek refuge in England. Elizabeth I, her cousin, had her executed in 1587 ● *41*.

THE ANGLO-SCOTTISH CROWN

The matrimonial alliance between the Scottish Stuarts and English Tudors became a key issue in 1603 when Elizabeth I died without an heir and her cousin and godson, James VI of Scotland

(1566–1625), was crowned James I of England. He immediately established his court in London, returning to Scotland briefly in 1617. His son Charles I (1625–49) only went to Scotland to be crowned at Holyrood in 1633. The union of the English and Scottish crowns left Scotland very much in the background.

THE NATIONAL COVENANT AND CIVIL WAR

Although it put an end to incursions on both sides of the border, the union of the English and Scottish crowns did not mean the union of the two kingdoms. Invoking the absolute power of the monarchy, James VI and I, and later his son, Charles I, attempted to impose the Anglican liturgy and the authority of the bishops in Scotland. Both were anathema

to Presbyterians, who remained loyal to the egalitarian principles of John Knox ● *41*. The Scots responded by signing a *National Covenant* in 1638, which condemned episcopacy and challenged the royal authority. In 1643 the Covenanters formed an alliance with the English Parliamentarians against Charles. However, disappointed by Oliver Cromwell and shocked by the execution of the king in 1649, they offered the throne to Charles II if he agreed to

uphold the Covenant. The English Civil War thus also became a war between England and Scotland, with Cromwell's army defeating the Scottish Royalists at the Battle of Dunbar in 1650. Charles II was crowned at Scone in 1651 but immediately had to go into exile in France. Scotland was forced to join the Commonwealth and remained occupied until Cromwell's death (1658) and the Restoration of Charles II (1660) following General Monck's march on London.

1715 The Jacobites rebel against union with England	1727 Foundation of the Royal Bank of Scotland	1769 James Watt develops his steam engine	1786 Robert Burns publishes his first poems	1843 Split within the Church of Scotland: creation of the *Free Church*
1700 1725	1750	1775	1800	1825
1707 Union of the Scottish and English Parliaments	1745–1746 Jacobite Rising and the Battle of Culloden	1758 Work begins on the New Town of Edinburgh	1790–1850 Eviction of Highland crofters	

SCOTLAND WITHIN THE BRITISH UNION

THE UNION OF THE SCOTTISH AND ENGLISH PARLIAMENTS

Once restored to the throne, Charles II broke his promise and reestablished the episcopacy in 1661. The Covenanters were persecuted, especially in the southwest of Scotland, in the early 1680s. The situation worsened after the accession of James VII (James II of England). The Protestant lords therefore appealed for help to William of Orange, James' nephew and son-in-law, who deposed him in 1688. In 1690 the Church of Scotland was recognized as independent and distinct from the Church of England. This led to the repression of the Catholics, Episcopalians and Jacobites (loyal to James VII ● 42), especially among the Highland clans who suffered such acts of persecution as the Glencoe Massacre in 1692 ▲ 198. A new crisis of succession dominated the union of the Scottish and English Parliaments. Since William and Mary (the eldest daughter of James VII/II) were childless, the death of the only surviving child of Mary's sister, Princess Anne, left them without an heir. Parliament wanted to transfer the succession to their cousin, Sophia of Hanover, and her descendants. If the Scots agreed to accept the new dynasty, they would be assured of commercial advantages provided they renounced their political independence. The failed attempt to colonize the Isthmus of Panama had left Scotland facing financial ruin and the financial argument eclipsed the desire for independence. In 1707 the Act of Union united the two Parliaments at Westminster.

ECONOMIC PROSPERITY IN THE LOWLANDS

Although this union proved to be a political catastrophe, it was a great economic success. Cattle and linen exports replaced the traditional activities of fishing and salt production. Glasgow and the Clyde ports grew rich on trade with America, and Scotsmen made their fortunes throughout the British Empire. It was the great age of exploration. James Bruce (*left*) explored Abyssinia and the Blue Nile (1768–72), Alexander MacKenzie crossed northern Canada (1789–93), Mungo Park explored West Africa (1795–97) and David Livingstone traveled in South and East Africa from the 1840s until his death in 1873. This same period saw an unprecedented intellectual, literary and artistic development taking place in Scotland from the 1740s onwards ● 44.

THE HIGHLANDS' DARKEST HOURS

The Highlands, with their Gaelic language and culture, paid the price of their support for the Jacobite cause after the last Rising was crushed in 1746 ● 43. The structure of the 'clan society' was dismantled and Highlanders were even forbidden to wear tartan ● 51. Their hereditary chiefs, deprived of their customary rights, became landowners and their clansmen became tenants, or crofters. From the 1790s onwards, these tenants were driven from the inland valleys (straths) and replaced by sheep farmers whose large flocks gave a high yield of wool (and income). In Sutherland, the region most affected by these 'Highland Clearances', displaced families were encouraged to settle on the coast and take up fishing or kelp gathering. The failure of such initiatives, exacerbated by the terrible famine of 1846, resulted in an influx of impoverished people into the cities and wholesale emigration to Canada, Australia and New Zealand. The Highlands and islands were depopulated and the dispersion of their inhabitants led to the gradual disappearance of the Celtic culture.

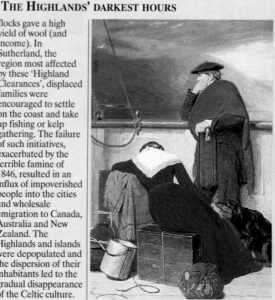

1848 Queen Victoria acquires Balmoral

1914–1918 74,000 Scots killed in World War One

1929 Alexander Fleming discovers penicillin

1967 First oil drillings in the North Sea

1979 First referendum on Devolution

1850   1900   1920   1950   1975   2000

1886 The Crofters' Act guarantees security of tenure for crofters

1900 Foundation of the Labour Party

1928 Birth of the National Party of Scotland

1947 Creation of the Edinburgh International Festival

1999 Restoration of the Scottish Parliament

THE SCOTTISH REVIVAL

A ROMANTIC VIEW OF THE HIGHLANDS

The English who ventured into the Highlands in the 18th century were dismayed by the 'dreariness' of the landscape and the poverty of the inhabitants. The 'translation' (invention) of the poems of Ossian by James Macpherson (1760) dispelled these stereotypes by offering a romantic interpretation of Celtic mythology. In the early 19th century, influenced by the works of Sir Walter Scott, scholars became ardent students of Highland folklore. Dorothy Wordsworth, sister of the poet William Wordsworth (1770–1850), was among the first to enthuse over the Scottish landscape. In 1822 an extraordinary display of tartans greeted the official visit of George IV to Edinburgh. Twenty years later Queen Victoria and Prince Albert made Balmoral Castle ▲ *214* their summer retreat. When the Queen's Scottish journal was published in 1867, the words 'Romantic' and 'Highlands' were already firmly associated. Foreigners wearing kilts came to Scotland to hunt deer and fish for salmon. Tartan became a clan emblem and was adopted as the national costume ● *50*.

THE 'RED CLYDE'

This romantic image of the Highlands was in stark contrast to the reality of southern Scotland, which was becoming rapidly industrialized. In the 18th century Glasgow grew rich on its tobacco industry, while cotton imports made the Lowland textile industry the driving force of Scotland's economy. During the second half of the 19th century this was replaced by heavy industry as new technology placed the region at the forefront of manufacturing and led to the meteoric development of iron and steel. The shipyards of the Clyde became the largest in the United Kingdom. The banks of the river bristled with cranes and the surrounding fields were covered by slums. But in the early 20th century the industry suffered a slump, and the resulting high unemployment provoked a growing sense of awareness among the working classes. In the 1920s radical socialists and communists moved the 'Red Clyde' into the political arena, where it remained until Scotland's heavy industry was dismantled in the 1970s.

ANGLO-SCOTTISH UNION UNDER THREAT?

The unemployment and hunger marches of the Great Depression in the 1930s caused great bitterness. Once again the Scots questioned the Westminster Parliament's commitment to finding solutions to their problems. During the 1970s and '80s the indifference of successive Conservative governments, none of which had a majority in Scotland, caused even more disillusionment. The Scottish National Party (SNP), founded in 1934, enjoyed increasing popularity in the early 1970s when the discovery of oil in the North Sea seemed to promise a brilliant economic future for a Scotland that was at least autonomous, if not independent. The SNP also benefited from the hopes raised by Britain's membership of the European Economic Community (EEC) in 1973. It held out the prospect of an economic revival similar to that of Ireland, and equal sovereignty with England. The Labour and Liberal parties made it part of their election manifestos to support the devolution of certain legislative powers to a Scottish Parliament. The referendum held in 1998 resulted in an overwhelming majority in favor of the restoration of the Scottish Parliament in Edinburgh, which Scottish Nationalists saw as one step further on the road to independence. Only time will tell...

37

THE WARS OF SCOTTISH INDEPENDENCE, 1296–1357

Between the 13th and 16th centuries the ambitions of the kings of England threatened the neighboring kingdoms. While Wales and Ireland were defeated, Scotland resisted by forming an alliance with France. The wars of Scottish independence, fought by the Scots against the English between 1296 and 1357, were provoked by a crisis of succession. They were the first expression of the strength of Scottish nationalism.

THE ENGLISH CONQUEST OF 1296

On the death of Alexander III in 1286 his two-year-old granddaughter Margaret 'the Maid of Norway', was proclaimed queen. Edward I of England proposed that she marry his son, but Margaret died on the voyage from Norway. Edward was then asked to choose a king from among the competitors for the Scottish throne. He decided in favor of John Balliol in 1292. Although the latter was forced to recognize Edward as his feudal lord, he signed a treaty of alliance with France in 1295 and prepared to invade England. But Edward soon defeated the Scots, and in 1296 2000 nobles and landowners were compelled to do homage to him. Edward took back to London the famous Stone of Scone ▲ 116, which had been used for the crowning of Scottish kings since Kenneth MacAlpin.

WILLIAM WALLACE (c. 1270–1305)

This son of a knight became the leader of a movement of national resistance against Edward I. In 1297 he led a force of Scottish warriors from all over Scotland against a large English army at Stirling Bridge. After his brilliant victory he was proclaimed 'guardian of the kingdom' and ruled in Balliol's name. However, he was defeated the following year by Edward at the Battle of Falkirk and never again commanded an army. Betrayed and captured in 1305, he was taken to London where he was hung, drawn and quartered. It seemed as if Scottish resistance would now be at an end, but his execution made him a national hero and the symbol of Scotland's resistance to English oppression.

THE BATTLE OF BANNOCKBURN (1314)

Edward II came north with a large army to relieve Stirling Castle. Bruce was waiting for him at the Bannock Burn below the castle. He was outnumbered three to one, but his army was drawn up on the higher ground. The clever choice of terrain prevented the enemy archers deploying effectively, while the armored English knights were soon bogged down in the heavy wet ground. By midday the English were in flight south towards the border.

ROBERT BRUCE (1274–1329)

Robert de Brus was of Norman descent, and son of one of the competitors for the throne in 1292. He owned vast estates in Scotland and England, and had paid homage to Edward. But in 1306 he killed Sir John Comyn 'the Red', leader of the Balliol family, who was also a claimant to the throne. He then raised the Royal Standard and had himself crowned King of Scots at Scone. Edward sent a strong army, but Bruce gradually rallied the support of the Scottish feudal lords. By 1309 Bruce controlled most of Scotland north of the Forth and Clyde. The Church in Scotland came out on his side, and in 1311 he invaded and sacked northern England. By 1314, the English held only Stirling Castle
▲ *169*.

THE DECLARATION OF ARBROATH (APRIL 1320)

The declaration of Scottish independence was prompted by Edward II's request to the Pope to excommunicate Bruce. The nobles, clergy and commons of Scotland gathered at Arbroath and drew up this declaration to the Pope. They swore that if Bruce ever surrendered his kingdom to the king of England they would drive him out and choose another king to defend them. They stated: 'We fight not for glory, nor riches, nor honour, but only for that liberty which no true man relinquishes but with his life.'

INDEPENDENCE REGAINED (1357)

The Treaty of Northampton, 1328, recognized Scottish independence. But Bruce died in 1329 and Edward III relaunched the offensive by trying to help Edward Balliol to gain the Scottish throne. Bruce's son David was sent to France for safety, and his grandson Robert Stewart became Regent. By 1340 Stewart had cleared Scotland of the English and David returned from France. But in 1346 the French appealed for help in the Hundred Years War, and so David invaded England. He was captured by Edward III and spent the next 12 years at the English court. Edward finally agreed to free David in return for a large ransom, and a treaty was signed at Berwick on October 3, 1357.

● MARY STUART AND THE REFORMATION

Between 1540 and 1640 Scotland was torn by civil and religious wars. These conflicts were exacerbated by two long regencies, a dynastic crisis in England and the presence on the Scottish throne of a fervent Catholic queen whose contradictions gave rise to a tragic turn of events. Although the Reformation encouraged learning and provoked social awareness, it also made Scotland the bastion of Calvinism. At the end of this period civil war loomed in England, while in Scotland the National Covenant rejected the Divine Right of Kings.

'THE ROUGH WOOING'

Mary Stuart was only six days old when her father James V died in 1542. Henry VIII, who had designs on Scotland, sought to win Mary as a bride for his son Edward. A marriage was negotiated with the Regent Arran, but Mary of Guise, her mother, and Cardinal Beaton had Mary crowned Queen at Scone, and the Estates were persuaded to repeal the treaty. Henry launched a bloody campaign of reprisals in 1544 ('rough wooing') that devastated southern Scotland. For her own safety, Mary was sent to the island of Inchmahome ▲ 173 and from there to France, in 1548. In 1558 she married the Dauphin, who later became François II. She returned to Scotland (*left*) in 1561, after the death of her husband.

JOHN KNOX (C. 1514–72) AND THE REFORMATION

Ordained in the Roman Catholic Church, John Knox soon converted to Protestantism. He lived in England for a while, but was forced into exile in 1553 when the Catholic Mary Tudor came to the throne. He visited Geneva, where he came strongly under the influence of the reformer Calvin. He returned to Scotland in 1559 at the request of the Protestant faction. In 1560 Parliament abolished papal jurisdiction and banned the Latin mass. Knox (with Mary Stuart, *below*) formulated the creed of the new Church in his *Confession of Faith* and *The First Book of Discipline*.

MARY, WIFE AND QUEEN (1561–67)

In 1561 Mary returned to Scotland from France and agreed to recognize the Reformed Church. As the most likely heir to her cousin Elizabeth I (who never forgave her for daring to challenge her succession to Mary Tudor in 1558) this young widow had several suitors. However, she made two disastrous marriages. The first was to her seventeen-year-old cousin Henry, Lord Darnley, in 1565. A year later the jealous Darnley murdered Mary's Italian secretary Rizzio in her presence. In 1567 Darnley was in turn murdered and eight weeks later Mary married James Hepburn, Earl of Bothwell, who was suspected of the murder. The ensuing scandal forced Mary to abdicate in favor of her one-year-old son James VI.

EXILE AND DEATH

Mary Stuart had lost two crowns in seven years. Imprisoned in Loch Leven Castle ▲ *178*, she escaped in 1568 and rallied troops to her cause, but was defeated at the Battle of Langside, near Glasgow, by her half-brother the Earl of Moray. Hoping to win the support of Elizabeth, she sought refuge in England. Elizabeth imprisoned Mary in Fotheringhay Castle, where she found herself at the center of French and Spanish plots against the Protestant queen. These subversive intrigues finally proved her undoing. She was convicted of attempted regicide (*above*) and executed on February 8, 1587.

DEFENDERS OF THE REFORMATION

A *National Covenant*, a declaration of the Calvinist faith similar to the *First Covenant* signed in 1557, was drawn up in 1638. It was written in angry protest at Charles I's attempt to impose the Anglican order of service and the Revised Prayer Book on Scotland. The document (*left*), whose 300,000 signatories pledged to defend their faith to the death, became the cornerstone of the Scottish Reformed Church.

THE JACOBITE RISINGS

Following the dethronement of James II in favor of William of Orange, many Scots remained faithful to the Stuarts, especially the Catholics and Episcopalians of the Highlands. The first rebellion, led by John Graham, 1st Viscount of Dundee ('Bonnie Dundee') in 1689, was soon quelled. However, the disillusionment caused by the Act of Union (1707) aroused a great deal of sympathy for the Jacobite cause (from *Jacobus*, the Latin equivalent of James). In spite of a failed invasion attempt in 1708, the Risings of 1715 and especially 1745 enjoyed a short-lived but very real success. Today, their memory is shrouded in nostalgia and romanticism.

A FAILED RISING (1715)
On the death of James VII/II in 1701, his son James Edward (1688–1766) was proclaimed King of Scotland and England by the French King Louis XIV. At the request of this Old Pretender (*left*), the Earl of Mar organized a Rising in 1715 against George I. Erskine won support throughout the north of Scotland, 12,000 armed clansmen rallying to the standard. But he led his campaign so disastrously that he was heading for certain defeat when the Prince landed at Peterhead ▲ *218* on December 22, 1715. Much of their support melted away, and both had to leave secretly for France in February 1716.

BONNIE PRINCE CHARLIE
Charles Edward Stuart, Bonnie Prince Charlie (*right*), combined dreams of courage and glory with dazzling charm. The Young Pretender contracted heavy debts to mount his campaign and, in August 1745, landed in the Outer Hebrides with a few loyal supporters. Following the lead of the MacDonalds and Camerons, there was no shortage of adherents to the Jacobite cause. On August 19 an army of supporters raised the standard of the Stuarts near Glenfinnan ▲ *236*, the signal that the Rising had begun.

GLENSHIEL (1719)
The peace treaty signed by England and France at Utrecht, in 1713, forbade the latter to support 'James VIII'. James and his court therefore went into exile in Rome where his son Charles Edward was born in 1720. The Old Pretender gained the support of Spain and preparations were made to invade England while carrying out diversionary tactics in Scotland. The invasion attempt failed, but the Scottish expedition was already under way. An army composed of Jacobite nobles and Spanish soldiers landed at Kintail and captured Eilean Donan Castle ▲ *239*. However the army was defeated at Glenshiel (*above*) on May 11, 1719.

THE FORTY-FIVE RISING

Bonnie Prince Charlie crossed the Highlands unchallenged and gathered his troops at Perth. He entered Edinburgh in triumph on September 6, and on September 18 his army defeated government troops at Prestonpans. He was now master of Scotland and decided to march on London. He reached Derby in December without setback, causing panic in London, but his advisers urged him to return to Scotland. After another victory at Falkirk on January 17, 1746 he set up his winter quarters at Inverness. He was still undefeated, but food and money were in short supply.

DEFEAT AT CULLODEN

Meanwhile the English Government was assembling a large, well-trained army at Aberdeen. Led by the Duke of Cumberland they advanced on Inverness in April. Charles gathered his Highlanders, hungry and ill-equipped, on Culloden Moor ▲ *231 (above)* on April 16 where they were cut to pieces. The prince was pursued and sought refuge first on the island of South Uist and then Skye (with the help of Flora MacDonald ▲ *250*). From there he escaped to France, to spend the rest of his life as an unhappy exile. He died in Rome in 1788.

Between 1730 and 1830 Glasgow, Aberdeen and especially Edinburgh experienced a period of intellectual activity which brought Scotland into line with the European Enlightenment and earned it the title of 'republic of letters', compensating for its political eclipse after the Union. Based on the work of 17th-century legal theoreticians, doctors, mathematicians and geographers, and favored by its excellent educational system, the Scottish Enlightenment covered the fields of philosophy, the sciences, arts and technology. Speculation was challenged in favor of experimental research and critical reasoning. With its magnificent Georgian buildings and scholarly societies, Edinburgh became the 'Athens of the North'.

THE TRIUMPH OF TECHNOLOGY
From 1750 science and technology flourished in Scotland. James Hutton (1726–97) founded the science of modern geology, Joseph Black (1728–99) discovered carbon dioxide, and John McAdam (1756–1863) invented the macadam road surface. James Watt (1736–1819), appointed manufacturer of mathematical instruments for Glasgow University, developed the steam engine that would revolutionize the transport industry.

ACADEMIES AND SCHOLARLY SOCIETIES

In Edinburgh and other Scottish cities, professors, judges, ministers, magnates and educated members of the middle-classes debated new ideas in such clubs as the Select Society, founded by David Hume, Adam Smith and the poet Allan Ramsay ● *48* in 1754. This intellectual effervescence was reported in reviews, for example the *Edinburgh Review*, and many other publications, including the *Encyclopaedia Britannica*, first published in 1768. Edinburgh became one of the main centers of British publishing, while Glasgow printed some superb editions of the Greek and Latin classics.

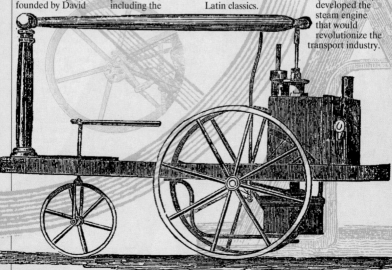

EXPERIMENTATION AND CRITICAL REASONING

In *A Treatise of Human Nature* (1739) the philosopher, historian and economist David Hume (1711–76) (*right*) proposed to adopt the precepts of Isaac Newton and reject conventional beliefs in favor of experiment, in an attempt to create a 'human science'. His experimental scepticism cost him the chair of philosophy at Edinburgh University, but earned him recognition throughout Europe. His ideas influenced Kant and Adam Smith, and made him a leading figure of the Scottish Enlightenment alongside such philosophers as Francis Hutcheson and Thomas Reid.

THE BIRTH OF LIBERALISM

In 1776 Adam Smith (1723–90) published *An Inquiry into the nature and causes of the Wealth of Nations*, a synthesis of contemporary politico-economic theory. He maintained that individual interest served the general interest via spontaneous economic mechanisms, that wealth was generated by work rather than natural resources, and that free trade should promote the international division of labor. Smith's theories (a reduction in the role of the state, the liberalization of trade) were soon applied in Great Britain, which was suffering badly from the loss of its American colonies.

THE AGE OF INVENTION

The passion for experimentation extended beyond scientific and intellectual circles. Landowners joined such societies as the Society of Agricultural Improvers and exchanged new ideas and techniques. The *Gentleman Farmer* (1776), a book by the lawyer, agriculturalist and philosopher Henry Home, Lord Kames (1696–1782), proved a huge success. The sickle was gradually replaced by the scythe and the swing-plow by the iron plow. In the industrial sector, there were many innovations in the weaving of cotton, a major activity from 1760 onwards. The introduction of steam-powered machinery heralded the industrial revolution.

THE GOLDEN AGE OF THE ARTS

While the Scottish soul was revealed by the poems of Robert Burns ● *98* ▲ *142*, artists such as Allan Ramsay (son of the poet) and Henry Raeburn ● *87* were applying the principles of 'human science' to the art of portraiture. Architecture was also experiencing a revival with Robert Adam (1728–92) (*left*), a master of neo-classicism and the creator of a sophisticated decorative style. Widespread urban development was inspired by sanitary improvements, with the spectacular Georgian New Town of Edinburgh ▲ *124* providing a fine example of the Enlightenment's desire for clarity and harmony.

Three languages are spoken in Scotland: English, Scottish Gaelic and Scots (also known as Lowland Scots or Lallans). English has been the official language since 1707. Unlike Welsh, Scots and Gaelic have no official status within the United Kingdom. They are both regarded as regional languages of the European Union.

GAELIC

Scottish Gaelic belongs to the Celtic branch of the Indo-European languages.

It is very close to Irish Gaelic and Manx, previously spoken on the Isle of Man. These northern Celtic or Goidelic languages are different from the southern Celtic or Brythonic languages, Breton, Welsh and Cornish. For example, 'four' is *ceithir* in Scottish Gaelic and *pedair* in Welsh. Until the Middle Ages Scottish Gaelic was the language of the Highlands, the Hebrides and other Scottish islands, and certain parts of Galloway, which meant it was spoken by half the population of Scotland. Today, the Gaelic-speaking area (Gaidhealtachd) is limited to the Outer Hebrides, Argyll and the Isle of Skye, and the 10 percent of Gaelic speakers living in towns and cities, mainly Glasgow and Edinburgh.

The 1991 census recorded 69,000 Gaelic speakers aged three and over (1.4 percent of the population), compared with 82,600 (1.6 percent) in 1981. There is a standard form of written Gaelic as well as several spoken dialects, used by local authorities, the local media, in teaching, religion and the oral tradition.

HISTORY

Gaelic was imported from the northeast of Ireland by the founders of the ancient kingdom of Dalriada in the 3rd and 4th centuries. During the next five hundred years Gaelic spread throughout most of Scotland, including the Outer Hebrides. It began to decline in the 12th century when French-speaking Anglo-Norman families emigrated to Scotland with their English- and Norse-speaking servants and retainers. As a result the Celtic language and culture lost their dominant position in the major power centers, from then on located in east and central Scotland. By 1500 the country was divided into two linguistic regions, with Gaelic spoken only in the Highlands and islands, and English and Scots dialects dominating the south and northeast. In an attempt to impose their authority on the semi-independent clans of the Highlands and islands, successive governments adopted measures that were openly hostile to Gaelic, a policy that continued after unification in 1707. James Macpherson (1736–96), the 'translator' of poems glorifying the ancient Celtic heroes, and Walter Scott (1771–1832), the bard of Highland romanticism, reintroduced the Gaelic language and culture with the result that it began to enjoy a more flattering image. However, the Highland Clearances of the 19th century brought Gaelic to the brink of extinction by reinforcing the tide of migration toward the industrial south and the colonies. The Gaels formed societies to promote their language and encourage the study of Gaelic literature in schools. In spite of a certain degree of success, financial backing and a more positive attitude on the part of the authorities, Gaelic continues to remain marginalized.

Tiree High School
Ard-Sgoil Thiriodh

GAELIC: A FEW FACTS

ALPHABET

Gaelic uses 18 letters of the Roman alphabet: the vowels a, e, i, o, u, and the consonants b, c, d, f, g, h, l, m, n, p, r, s, t. Vowels can be long or short, or combined in diphthongs. Long vowels are indicated by an accent: à, è, é, ì, ò, ó, ù.

GENDERS AND DECLENSIONS

There is no neuter gender. The initial consonants of adjectives agree in the feminine, as does the definite article. The genitive and dative are indicated.

SYNTAX

The verb precedes the subject. The adjective usually follows the noun it describes. The possessive form (genitive) can be expressed by the verb 'to be' + noun (object possessed) + preposition + noun or pronoun (possessor).

GAELIC IN LITERATURE

EARLY TEXTS

The earliest surviving writings in Gaelic are the 12th-century annotations in the margin of the 9th-century Latin manuscript known as the *Book of Deer*. At the time Gaelic Scotland and Ireland were very closely linked, and classical Irish and Latin were the principal languages of literature. Tales, songs and poems were also passed on in the oral tradition. A major early 16th-century work, *The Book of the Dean of Lismore*, was an anthology of poetry that brought together works from the two traditions.

PRINTING AND RELIGIOUS WORKS

The first book printed in Gaelic was a translation of John Knox's *Book of Common Order* (1567). A complete translation of the Bible was not published until 1807. However, the many religious works printed in Gaelic from the 18th century onwards greatly contributed to its survival.

SECULAR POETRY

The 18th century also witnessed the development of Gaelic as a literary language. The first secular work to be published was a book of poetry by Alasdair Mac Mhaighstir Alasdair: *The Resurrection of the Ancient Scottish Tongue* (1751). Duncan Ban MacIntyre (1724–1812) wrote one of the most beautiful odes to nature ever written in Gaelic: *Praise of Ben Doran*. This poetic tradition was perpetuated in the 20th-century Scottish Renaissance, notably by Sorley Maclean (1911–98) and Ian Crichton-Smith (1928–99), whose works were also published in English.

THE ORAL TRADITION

The oral tradition has been perpetuated through the painstaking work of folk historians, who have collected tales, songs and poems. Songs were used to create a rhythm to accompany work and *port a beul* ('mouth music'), based on onomatopoeic sounds, forms an entirely separate genre. An Comunn Gaidhealach, an association founded in 1891, organizes an annual festival of Gaelic songs and poetry (*Mod*) in which everyone, young and old, is invited to take part.

SCOTS

Scots incorporates different Lowland and coastal dialects as far north as the Moray Firth, as well as variations from Caithness, Orkney and Shetland. Its strongest forms of expression are found in the northeast, the Borders, Shetland and around the major urban centers of Glasgow, Edinburgh, Aberdeen and Dundee. Scots could be described as a series of variations on the English language, but this definition is far too vague for the purposes of making a census of Scots speakers.

HISTORY

Scots is derived from Anglian, an Old-English dialect imported into Great Britain by Germanic peoples in the 5th century. It belongs to the western Germanic group of the Indo-European languages. In the early 7th century Anglian-speaking peoples from the kingdom of Northumbria colonized what is now the southeast of Scotland ● 33. This region, with its typically Anglian place names (Haddington, Tyningham, Hawick), was absorbed by the kingdom of Scotland in the 10th century. In the 12th century the immigration of groups from northern England, who spoke a form of English combined with Scandinavian, meant that Anglian spread throughout southern Scotland and northward along the east coast. Scottish Anglian developed into a distinct group of dialects, some of them still surviving, which incorporated many words of Scandinavian, French and Flemish origin.

THE LITERARY TRADITION

The first major work written in Scots was *The Brus* (1375), an epic poem by John Barbour which told the story of Bruce's struggle for independence ● 38. During the 15th century Scots was used, alongside Latin, as the language of business and administration. It became a literary language in its own right through the works of the poets Robert Henryson (c. 1420–90), William Dunbar (c. 1460–1515) and Gavin Douglas (c. 1475–1522), who translated Virgil's *Aeneid* into Scottish verse. The first printed Scots text was published in 1508.

ANGLICIZATION
The Reformation (1560) marked the beginning of Anglicization. The Protestants opted for an English version of the Bible, and Scots lost its literary status with the union of the crowns (1603) and the transfer of the Scottish court to London. English became the language of scholarship in the 17th century, and the official language of Scotland after unification (1707). However, while the educated and ambitious spoke and wrote English, Scots remained the language of the Lowlands, with the result that a complex relationship developed between the two languages.

A LITERARY REVIVAL
Scots recovered its literary status with the poets Allan Ramsay (1686–1758), Robert Fergusson (1750–74) and Robert Burns (1759–96) ▲ 142. The works of Walter Scott (1771–1832) ● 99, ▲ 113 included dialogues in Scots, and Robert Louis Stevenson (1850–94) ● 101 also used dialect in his poems and novels.

A LIVING DIALECT
Scots was given a new lease of life by the poet Hugh MacDiarmid (1892–1978), a leading figure of the Scottish Renaissance of the 1920s and '30s ● 102. Today it continues to be a living form of expression for a number of Scottish poets (Sheena Blackhall, Tom Leonard, Edwin Morgan), writers (James Kelman, Irvine Welsh) and playwrights (Liz Lochhead, Peter MacDougal). In recent years this has led to the revival of urban dialects which had previously fallen into decline. However the media rarely use Scots due to its variety and the absence of a standardized literary form.

GAELIC: A FEW FACTS

Scots differs from English in:

● certain grammatical forms;

● pronunciation (which also has regional variations);

● vocabulary: many words are common to both languages, but Scots also has an extensive vocabulary of its own.

English.	Scots
one	*yin*
two	*twa*
more	*mare*
do	*dae*
know	*ken*
go	*gang*
child	*bairn*
eye	*ee*
head	*heid*
stone	*stane*
stream	*burn*
church	*kirk*
house	*hoos*
cup	*tassie*
plate	*ashet*
bag	*pock*
left	*carr*
dreary	*dreich*
troubled	*fasht*

Arts and traditions

Liz Arthur, Pierre Dubois, John Kenny,
George McMurdo, Martine Nouet, Judy Urquhart

50 Tartan
52 Music and dance
54 Highland Games
56 The 'Little People'
58 Golf
60 Scotch whisky
62 Food: cranachan and
    shortbread
64 Specialties

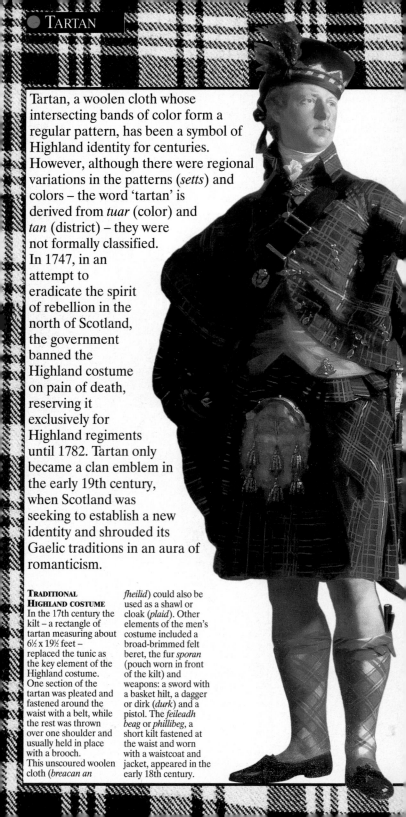

Tartan, a woolen cloth whose intersecting bands of color form a regular pattern, has been a symbol of Highland identity for centuries. However, although there were regional variations in the patterns (*setts*) and colors – the word 'tartan' is derived from *tuar* (color) and *tan* (district) – they were not formally classified. In 1747, in an attempt to eradicate the spirit of rebellion in the north of Scotland, the government banned the Highland costume on pain of death, reserving it exclusively for Highland regiments until 1782. Tartan only became a clan emblem in the early 19th century, when Scotland was seeking to establish a new identity and shrouded its Gaelic traditions in an aura of romanticism.

TRADITIONAL HIGHLAND COSTUME

In the 17th century the kilt – a rectangle of tartan measuring about 6½ x 19½ feet – replaced the tunic as the key element of the Highland costume. One section of the tartan was pleated and fastened around the waist with a belt, while the rest was thrown over one shoulder and usually held in place with a brooch. This unscoured woolen cloth (*breacan an fheilid*) could also be used as a shawl or cloak (*plaid*). Other elements of the men's costume included a broad-brimmed felt beret, the fur *sporan* (pouch worn in front of the kilt) and weapons: a sword with a basket hilt, a dagger or dirk (*durk*) and a pistol. The *feileadh beag* or *phillibeg*, a short kilt fastened at the waist and worn with a waistcoat and jacket, appeared in the early 18th century.

TARTAN AS A UNIFORM

In 1756 the government decided to create a military uniform that would encourage Highlanders to enlist in the army. The 'government' pattern, with its broad green and blue bands and black lines, became the tartan of the Black Watch which, from 1729, was responsible for maintaining order in the Highlands. As new regiments were formed, different colored bands and lines were added to this pattern to create distinctive regimental tartans. A red jacket, red and white stockings, black buckle shoes and a plumed hat completed the uniform.

CLANS AND TARTANS

After 1782 there was a movement toward the restoration of Scotland's Gaelic culture. In 1815 the Highland Society of London began to collect traditional tartan patterns by inviting clan chiefs to provide samples of their clan tartan. This enabled manufacturers to standardize the *setts* and give them historic authenticity by attributing clan names. The demand was so great that there were soon as many *setts* (often invented) as Scottish surnames.

WOMEN'S TARTAN

Until 1747 the women of the Highlands usually covered their head and shoulders with a tartan plaid, which fell in folds over their arms. The most sophisticated plaids were lined with silk and the most sought after were woven in the Hebrides. When tartan became fashionable in the 19th century, thanks to Queen Victoria, it was also used to make dresses, and factories had to expand to meet the ever-increasing demand.

BREECHES AND SOCKS

In the 17th century clan chiefs and aristocrats wore close-fitting breeches or *trews* (a kind of fitted trousers, inherited from distant Celtic ancestors) in bad weather or when on horseback.

In the 18th century hose were made from pieces of woven tartan, cut on the bias and sewn behind the calf. The resulting diamond-shaped patterns were subsequently reproduced on the first knitted socks.

THE 'TARTAN REVIVAL'

In the 19th century tartan became a romanticized symbol of Scotland. The fashion for tartan was launched in 1822 when clan chiefs welcomed George IV to Edinburgh wearing ceremonial dress, while the king himself wore the 'Royal Stuart' tartan. Then Queen Victoria became infatuated with the Highlands and tartan was very much in demand in Great Britain and Europe. Kilts were now cut with care, their pleats sewn in a regular manner, while a finely crafted silver pin held the overlapping front panel in place.

MANUFACTURE

Tartan is made from colored threads woven in a simple twill weave (the bands of color of the warp are the same as for the weft). Since the 1850s synthetic dyes have made it possible to produce much brighter and more varied colors than those produced with vegetable dyes. Today there are more than 1600 *setts*.

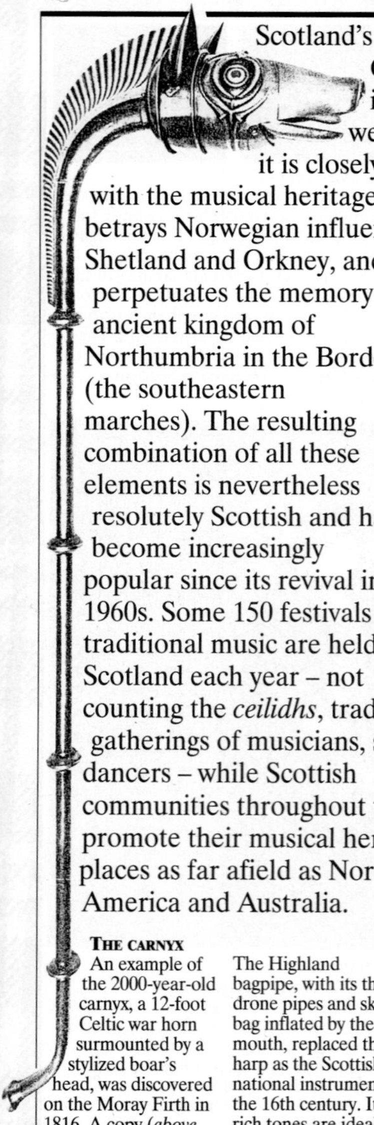

Scotland's musical heritage shows Pictish, Celtic, Anglo-Norman and Viking influences. In the Highlands and west of Scotland it is closely associated with the musical heritage of Ireland. It betrays Norwegian influences in Shetland and Orkney, and perpetuates the memory of the ancient kingdom of Northumbria in the Borders (the southeastern marches). The resulting combination of all these elements is nevertheless resolutely Scottish and has become increasingly popular since its revival in the 1960s. Some 150 festivals of traditional music are held in Scotland each year – not counting the *ceilidhs*, traditional gatherings of musicians, singers and dancers – while Scottish communities throughout the world promote their musical heritage in places as far afield as North America and Australia.

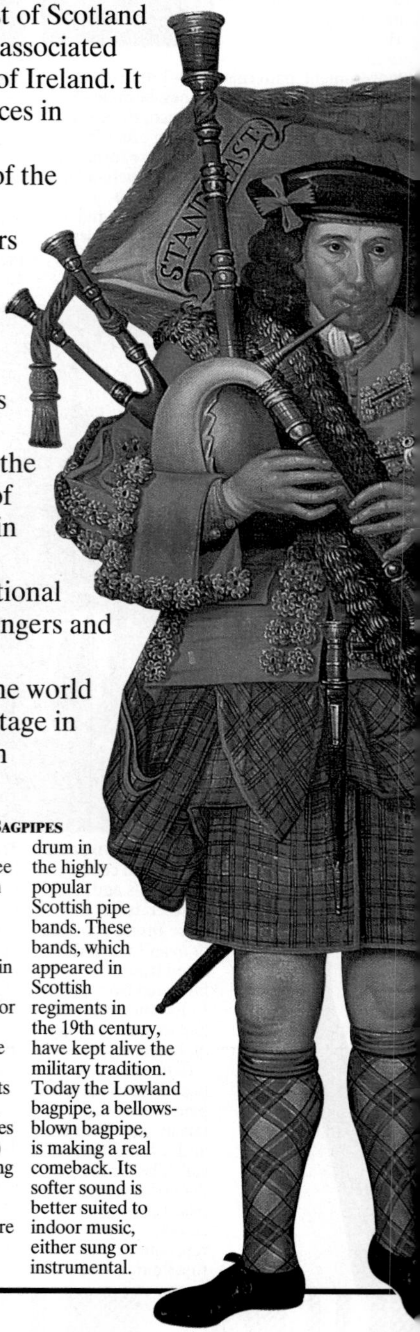

THE CARNYX

An example of the 2000-year-old carnyx, a 12-foot Celtic war horn surmounted by a stylized boar's head, was discovered on the Moray Firth in 1816. A copy (*above, left*), was made in 1994 under the direction of the composer Dr John Purser, and is used for concerts and recordings in Great Britain and other countries. The original and copy can be seen in the Museum of Scotland, in Edinburgh ▲ *123*.

BAGPIPES

The Highland bagpipe, with its three drone pipes and skin bag inflated by the mouth, replaced the harp as the Scottish national instrument in the 16th century. Its rich tones are ideal for open-air music. The repertoire of bagpipe music ranges from light accompaniments to dances and songs, to more erudite pieces (*ceol mor* or *pibroch*) with complex phrasing that requires great skill and dexterity. Highland bagpipes are also played in association with the drum in the highly popular Scottish pipe bands. These bands, which appeared in Scottish regiments in the 19th century, have kept alive the military tradition. Today the Lowland bagpipe, a bellows-blown bagpipe, is making a real comeback. Its softer sound is better suited to indoor music, either sung or instrumental.

DANCE MUSIC OF SCOTLAND.

HARPS

The triangular harp, with its characteristic sound box, was invented in Scotland and can be seen carved on Pictish stones ▲ *184* almost 2000 years old. The small Celtic harp or *clàrsach*, the instrument of medieval bards and kings, sank into obscurity for centuries before being revived in the late 19th century. Today it features in folk groups and is also used to play modern music.

DANCE

During the revival ● *37* of the 18th and 19th centuries, Scottish society became infatuated with traditional country dances (jigs, reels and strathspeys) and even invented new ones. Today, Scottish country dance societies perpetuate the tradition. Two accordions, a violin, piano, drum and double bass often accompany the dancers.

SONGS

Ballads and epic songs belong to the 'classic' genre or *oran mor*, while the popular repertoire includes lullabies, counting rhymes, love songs, dirges and songs to accompany work or dancing. Poets and writers such as Robert Burns, Allan Ramsay and Walter Scott staunchly supported this musical heritage from the 18th century onwards.

TRADITION AND MODERNITY

Great jazz musicians such as Tommy Smith compose and perform their own, very personal works within the context of regional tradition. Celtic rock groups such as Run Rig and, more recently, Avalon have also been hugely successful.

Meanwhile, artists from other countries, such as Canadian-born Ashley MacIsaac (*below*), reinterpret the repertoire bequeathed by their Scottish ancestors.

THE VIOLIN

The violin, which is an integral part of western Gaelic culture and the traditions of Shetland and Orkney, is one of the most widely played instruments in Scotland. The style known as 'Scotch snap', with its distinctive bow technique, flourished during the 16th century and was widely imitated throughout Europe. Played at dances and other public events, the violin enjoyed its golden age with brilliant player-composers such as Niel Gow (1727–1807) and James Scott Skinner (1843–1927), the 'king of the strathspey'.

Highland Games or Highland Gatherings combine traditional athletic events with folk-music and dance contests, with prizes awarded to the winners. These gatherings date from the Middle Ages, when kings and chiefs used them as a means of choosing soldiers for their private armies. Over 100 gatherings are organized throughout Scotland each year, between May and mid-September. The strains of bagpipes and the swirl of multicolored kilts contribute to the picturesque quality of these games which are often held in a spectacular setting. The most famous is the Royal Braemar Gathering (Aberdeenshire) which is regularly attended by the Royal Family.

ORIGINS

According to some, the first Highland Games were held at Ceres (Fife) in 1314, when Scottish archers returned victorious from the Battle of Bannockburn ● 39. Others believe they were founded by Malcolm Canmore ● 34, who organized a race to the top of Craig Choinnich, near Braemar ▲ 215, and made the winner his messenger after presenting him with a warrior's belt.

THROWING THE HAMMER

This contest is similar to the Olympic event, but the hammer has a wooden handle rather than a chain. The thrower, having coated his hands with resin, swings the hammer round and round above his head before throwing it as far as possible.

TOSSING THE CABER

Tossing the caber is the most spectacular of the athletic contests. Competitors have to throw a tapered fir pole some 17 feet long and weighing about 90 pounds. With the impetus gained by the run-up, the pole is thrown so that it turns end over end and lands in as straight a line as possible in front of the thrower.

FOLK MUSIC ● 52

Pipe-band and solo bagpipe contests are also held at Highland Games. Soloists compete in three categories: *pibrochs* (variations on a classical theme), military marches, and dance tunes (jigs, reels and strathspeys). The winner of the pibroch category is also the overall winner of the contest.

TOSSING THE WEIGHT

The weight (28–55 pounds) is attached to a short chain with a ring at the end. The thrower, who holds the ring in one hand, has to throw the weight as far as possible or over a bar (up to 15 feet high) located behind him.

OTHER ATHLETIC CONTESTS

Throwing the stone (15–30 pounds), running, wrestling and archery contests between two teams also feature on the games' extensive program.

COUNTRY DANCING

Girls of all ages are the main competitors in the Scottish country dancing contests. The most famous is the legendary sword dance, which dates from 1054. After killing a supporter of the Scottish king Macbeth, Malcolm Canmore is said to have executed a dance around his own and his enemy's swords crossed on the ground, taking care not to step on them, in order to ward off misfortune before going into battle.

The Highland fling, originally danced on a shield, imitates the movements of a young deer as the dancers whirl round and round, their arms raised above their heads. The *sean truibhas* or 'old trouser' dance, associated with the Battle of Culloden and the outlawing of the kilt, expresses the Highlanders' hatred of trousers.

In Scottish folklore there is a ghost in every castle, and as many fairies, elves and brownies as there are purple foxgloves and sprigs of heather. According to tradition, if travelers put an ash leaf in their right shoe, a willow leaf in their left and a sprig of hawthorn in their pocket, and greeted the first swirl of dust they encountered with a polite '*God spey ye*', a magnificent royal procession of nymphs, winged elves and horsemen clad in gold armor – so tiny they were mounted on bees, beetles and butterflies – would appear before them. But a sudden gesture or hasty word was enough to break the spell, and the dazzling, ethereal procession would be transformed into an unruly mob of demons, ready to seize the unwary and carry them off to a life of eternal wandering.

KELPIE
The kelpie (*ech-ushkya*) was a water spirit that haunted rivers, lochs, waterfalls and lonely pathways. It took the form of a winged serpent, a long-necked lizard-like creature, or a horse. It could change into a magnificent charger that drowned its unsuspecting rider, or a seductive bather who lured fishermen to their death. Perhaps the Loch Ness monster ▲ *240* is a kelpie!

BROWNIES
These impish sprites were the ideal companions of beer and whisky drinkers, for they were said to have inspired the magic alchemy of these drinks. Brownies were also poets and book-lovers. They could be enticed with pinches of snuff.

FAIRIES (*SITHS*)

Fairies were the most powerful group of 'little people' of Scotland, creating the mountains, waterfalls and lochs. Standing stones and ruined fortresses are witness to their reign. But disillusioned by human behavior and driven out by the new religion, they shrank in size until they disappeared into Fairyland. Robert Kirk, minister at Aberfoyle, described them in *The Secret Commonwealth of Elves, Fauns and Fairies* as intermediaries between men and angels, who tended to be seen at dusk. Legend says that one night in 1692 they imprisoned him in the Fairy Knowe at Aberfoyle...

'RED CAP'

Red Cap was a deformed and extremely dangerous bogeyman. He would lie in wait for lost travelers, cut their throats and use their blood to dye the bright red cap he wore so proudly. When the color began to fade, he would sharpen his ax again...

BANSHEE ('BAN SITH')

This pale, emaciated spirit, dressed in a white shroud, was a bringer of bad tidings. Her long hair flowed down over her bony shoulders, which looked like wings, and the folds of her plaid flapped in the wind as she wandered and wailed among ruins and on deserted battlefields. Banshees were attached to a clan, and would appear at night to warn of an impending disaster or death with their mournful wailing or 'keening'. They foretold the death of those who heard or saw them.

John Whyte Melville (seen here in 1874) was a member of the Royal and Ancient Golf Club for 67 years.

The rules of golf were first laid down (1744) in Scotland, where it has been played since the 15th century. It was there too that the major developments in the game took place, before 1900. Today, Scotland's 450 golf courses (the highest per capita ratio in the world) are still characterized by the sporting spirit embodied in the motto of the Troon golf club: *Tam Arte Quam Marte* ('through skill rather than effort').

GOLF IN HISTORY

Although its origins are obscure, the term probably derives from the Scots word *gowff* ('to strike'). Golf was first mentioned in 1457 when James II banned it by decree because it was distracting his archers from their training.

The game became popular at the royal court in the early 16th century. When James VI became King of England in 1603 and the court was transferred to London ● 35, the royal luggage included golf balls and clubs.

In 1744 the Honorable Company of Edinburgh Golfers established the thirteen original rules of the game. The golden age of golf was between 1880 and 1909, when almost half the present courses were opened.

BASIC PRINCIPLES

The game involves hitting a ball from one hole to the next, using a stick known as a 'club', in the least number of 'strokes'. A course has eighteen holes and covers a distance of between 6230 and 7100 yards.

BALLS

The first golf balls were made of wood, then of leather stuffed with feathers and, after 1848, gutta-percha. Today they have a polymer center and a honeycomb outer shell made of balata.

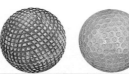

GOLF CLUBS

The first golf clubs were formed in the 18th century and provided a venue for meetings and banquets. The most famous, the Honourable Company of Edinburgh Golfers, was founded in Leith ▲ *127* in 1744, and is now based in Muirfield ▲ *131*. St Andrews golf club ▲ *177*, founded in 1754, became the Royal and Ancient Golf Club in 1834. Since 1897 it has established the rules in force throughout the world, except the United States and Mexico. Although only 15 percent of Scotland's 450 golf clubs are public, most private clubs welcome visitors, subject to certain conditions.

COURSES

Each of the eighteen holes of a golf course is located on a 'green' and marked by a flag. The green is approached via an avenue of short grass (fairway) between 100 and 160 feet wide. The green is bordered by bunkers (sand traps), areas of long grass (rough), water courses and streams, while the natural setting also features in the game. A typical Scottish course is a windswept coastal links covered with short, dry grass. St Andrews (*left*) and Muirfield (*top right*) are the most prestigious.

TOURNAMENTS

The most important, the Open, dates from 1860. Its circuit includes the Scottish links of Muirfield, St Andrews and Carnoustie on the east coast, and Turnberry and Troon on the west coast. Scotland no longer dominates these tournaments as in the past, but it still produces outstanding players.

CLUBS

Until the solid ball was invented, mainly wooden-headed clubs were used, with only one iron-headed club that ran the risk of destroying the feather-filled ball. Today players are allowed to use fourteen clubs: 'woods' (often with a metal head) for long-distance, and 'irons' for precision shots.

The Scots have elevated the distillation of malt whisky into an art form. Scotch whisky is produced by a subtle process involving the pure water of mountain springs and streams, barley, peat – and the weather. They have also developed the art of producing blended whisky, and have made their national drink a world leader in the field of alcohol sales. Scotch whisky now accounts for 25 percent of the spirits sold worldwide, which makes this industry the country's main source of export revenue.

THE HISTORY OF SCOTCH WHISKY

The monks who emigrated from Ireland in the 6th century may well have taught the Scots how to make *aqua vitae* ('water of life'), which became *usque baugh* in Celtic, *uisge beatha* in Gaelic and 'whisky' in English. Distilling soon became a domestic activity, but was forced underground in 1644 when Charles I decided to finance his armies by levying a tax on every pint of alcohol sold in Scotland. As a result, in 1777 only eight of the 408 stills operating in Edinburgh were registered. The Walsh Act put an end to this tax war in 1823 by introducing licensing and reducing government royalties. During the reign of Queen Victoria high society in London, deprived of French cognac and wines due to the ravages of vine phylloxera in the 1870s, soon adopted whisky as its favorite spirit. In 1898 there were 161 legal malt distilleries in Scotland. At the same time, with the development of blended whisky in the 1860s, production became industrialized and whisky began to be exported. In the 20th century, having usurped the place of Irish whiskey in the United States, Scotch whisky soon conquered Europe when it was introduced in 1944 by American GIs.

1. MALTING
After the impurities have been removed, the barley is soaked in water for 2 days, drained and left to germinate for 7 days (the starch is transformed into maltose). Then germination is halted by drying the malted barley in warm air and then over a peat fire.

2. BREWING
The husks are removed from the malt, which is crushed and mixed with hot water. The resulting mash is transferred to a vat (the remaining starch is converted into sugar). The solids are separated out (to be used for cattle feed) leaving a sweet liquid (must).

3. FERMENTATION
The must, cooled to 75° F, is transferred into vats. Yeast is added, which transforms the sugar into alcohol and carbon dioxide. After 60 hours this 'beer' or 'wash' forms a solution of between 7 and 8 percent alcohol.

4. DISTILLATION
The wash is distilled twice in copper pot stills.

5. MATURATION
The colorless but already perfumed distillate is matured in oak casks that have previously contained sherry, bourbon or single malt. The solution, which is now 63.4 percent alcohol, will lose some of its alcohol content but gain color and aroma. To have the right to be classified as Scotch whisky, the grain or malt spirit must have been distilled in Scotland and matured for at least three years in an oak barrel.

TYPES OF WHISKY

SINGLE MALT: malt whisky produced by a single distillery.
VATTED MALT: a blend of single malts from several distilleries.
BLENDED WHISKY (SCOTCH): a blend with a high proportion of grain spirit (corn, oats, wheat, rye), distilled in a continuous distillation system, and a fairly high percentage of single malts. It represents about 85 percent of the market of Scotch whisky.

FOUR MAJOR REGIONAL PRODUCERS

• LOWLANDS: light, smooth single malts with herby or floral aromas.
• HIGHLANDS: drier, extremely fragrant malts, with hints of smoke, honey, heather and the occasional touch of salt. The Highland region includes all the Scottish islands except the island of Islay.

Today, two-thirds of Scotland's active distilleries are concentrated in an area of only 15 square miles in the region of Speyside ▲ 220. Irrigated by the River Spey, this region produces a wide range of smooth, rounded whiskies, with an aroma that is sometimes fruity, sometimes herby.

• ISLAY: produces single malts which powerfully and vigorously assert their maritime heritage with aromas of peat, iodine and kelp.
• CAMPBELTOWN: in the only three remaining malts a touch of salt attests to the maritime influence, with hints of caramel and butter.

Barley and oats, which used to be the staple Highland diet, still occupy an important place in Scottish cooking. Oats form the basis of porridge, the savory oatmeal purée eaten for breakfast, and are used in the famous haggis recipe: a sheep's stomach filled with chopped sheep's liver, heart and lungs, mixed with beef or mutton suet and oatmeal, and flavored with herbs and spices. Pearl barley is used in Scotch broth, a thick soup made with vegetables and neck of lamb, while oats are used to make the oatcakes eaten mainly with cheese. Although succulent Aberdeen Angus beef and spring lamb are among the local specialties, Scottish culinary tradition also gives pride of place to Highland game such as venison and grouse, and smoked fish: smoked salmon, herrings (kippers) and haddock (Arbroath smokies and Finnan haddie).

CRANACHAN
INGREDIENTS (SERVES 6)
3 rounded tbsp
  porridge oats
5 fl oz double cream
½ cup cottage cheese
  (20–40 percent fat)
2 tbsp clear honey
  (preferably heather honey)
4 tbsp whisky (preferably single malt ● 60)
1¼ cups raspberries

1. Lightly toast the porridge oats over a medium heat in a non-stick frying pan. When they begin to brown, remove from the heat and leave to cool.

3. Arrange some of the raspberries in the bottom of six dessert dishes and fill with alternate layers of the mixture and raspberries.

2. Beat the cream with an electric whisk. As it begins to thicken gradually add the honey, whisky and cottage cheese. Continue to whisk the mixture for a few seconds.

4. Leave to stand for at least 2 hours. Before serving, sprinkle with toasted porridge oats. Serve with a small glass of whisky.

SHORTBREAD
INGREDIENTS (20 BISCUITS)
1 cup wheat flour
½ cup rice flour
¼ cup Demerara sugar
¼ cup each of salted
and unsalted butter

1. Preheat the oven to 355° F (180°C, Gas Mark 6). Mix the flours and Demerara sugar together in a bowl. Chop the butter into small pieces and rub lightly into the dry ingredients with your fingertips to obtain a short pastry but *do not* add water. Roll the pastry into a ball.

2. Place the pastry on a floured board and roll out gently, taking care not to press too hard, until it is about ½ inch thick. Cut out the biscuits with a pastry cutter and place them on a lightly greased baking sheet (or covered with greaseproof paper).
Prick the biscuits with a fork.

3. Cook in a moderate oven for 15–20 minutes, depending on the size of the biscuits. They should be golden, but paler than shortcrust pastry to keep their crumbly texture.

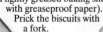

● SPECIALTIES

SMOKED FISH AND HAGGIS
Salmon, trout, kippers and smoked haddock
are among the Scottish specialties, together
with haggis, celebrated by Burns as 'chieftain
o' the puddin' race'. It is served in his honor
on January 25 ▲ *143*.

Although haggis is Scotland's ultimate culinary specialty, it is
almost impossible to find in other countries and even the Scots
eat it only on rare occasions, such as Burns' Night (January 25).
Scotland's better-known specialties are its smoked fish,
shortbread and, of course, its whiskies, which represent
Scotland throughout the world.

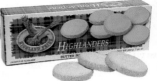

DUNDEE CAKE
This beautiful amber-colored
fruit cake is not a specialty of
Dundee. Variations have been
found throughout Scotland since
the 18th century.

SHORTBREAD ● *63*
Scottish biscuits are as varied as
they are famous. On Hogmanay
shortbread is offered to the first
person to cross the threshold.

DUNDEE MARMALADE
This was invented by
a Dundee grocer's
wife in 1797, using a
batch of oranges that
were too bitter to sell.

WHISKY AND BEER
Scotland's 100 or more single malts ● *60*
can be discovered by following the 'whisky
trail' ▲ *220*. The Scots are also great beer
drinkers and the bars of Edinburgh are
renowned for their 'real ales'. Although
these rich – pale or brown – ales vary in
strength, none is artificially carbonated
and all are additive free.

Architecture

Hilary Macartney
Ann MacSween

66 Early Scottish architecture
68 Popular architecture
70 Churches and monasteries
72 Feudal castles and tower-houses
74 Scottish Renaissance palaces
76 Country residences
78 Urban and rural planning
80 The industrial age: housing
82 The industrial age: public and
    commercial buildings
84 Mackintosh and
    the Glasgow Style

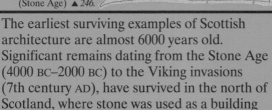

Grey Cairns of Camster
(Stone Age) ▲ 246.

1   **2**

The earliest surviving examples of Scottish architecture are almost 6000 years old. Significant remains dating from the Stone Age (4000 BC–2000 BC) to the Viking invasions (7th century AD), have survived in the north of Scotland, where stone was used as a building material. In the south, where wood was widely used, there are far fewer remains.

STONE AGE AND BRONZE AGE CHAMBERED CAIRNS
The dead were buried in a communal burial chamber with an entrance corridor, or individually in a stone tomb covered by a long tumulus or barrow (1) or a circular mound (2). These tombs often had a very specific orientation, as at Camster.

A VERY UNUSUAL CAIRN: MAES HOWE (c. 2700 BC)

This impressive mound – 115 feet in diameter and 23 feet high – stands on an artificial platform surrounded by a broad ditch. The central chamber (195 square feet) has a remarkable sandstone dressing and incorporates what are probably three funerary niches. The 30-foot entrance corridor is in line with the rising sun during the winter solstice.

A STONE AGE VILLAGE

The remarkably well-preserved site of Skara Brae (*below* ▲ 260) gives a good idea of what a Stone Age village must have looked like. The houses and workshops were built partially below ground and were linked by narrow passageways. Each dwelling had a central stone hearth, beds edged with stones and lined with moss, and a stone dresser. There were one or more underground larders and other storage spaces set into the walls. The roof, made of peat, heather or turf, was supported by slender poles.

It served both as insulation and protection, and because it was fairly porous, it allowed the smoke to escape.

1 entrance to the village
2 main passageway
3 secondary passageway
4 doorway
5 hearth
6 dresser
7 beds
8 niches
9 cell
10 larder
11 outer corridor
12 other houses

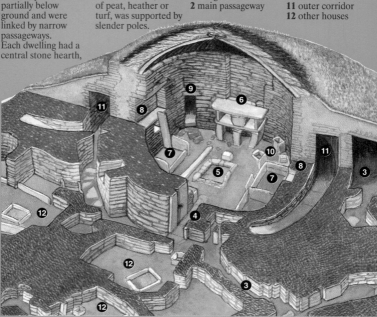

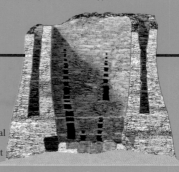

Plan and cross-section of the broch at Mousa (1st–2nd century) AD.

IRON AGE BROCHS
(700 BC–AD 400)
These round forts are found only in Scotland, especially in the north and west. The double dry-stone walls sometimes enclosed a flight of steps, while a single entrance opened onto a central courtyard. Brochs were often associated with a group of buildings, like fortified farms, the central courtyard serving as a cattle pen and a place of refuge. The best preserved example is the 42-foot broch of Mousa (Shetland) ▲ 264.

IRON AGE ROUND HOUSES

Reconstruction of a round house at Rennibister Orkney and its underground chamber ▲ 259.

These houses were found throughout Scotland, in isolation or grouped together in hamlets. Like Bronze Age houses they had a central hearth, but their structure was more elaborate: a vaulted dry-stone wall supported a conical framework reinforced by posts. Some had underground chambers in which foodstuffs and seeds were stored, and which could also have been used as a place of refuge or even as a tomb when the house was abandoned. For example the remains of 18 people were discovered in the Rennibister round house.

PICTISH STONES
The Romans referred to the inhabitants of northern and eastern Scotland as the *Pictii*. The most remarkable monuments left by these people were stones decorated with symbolic motifs ▲ 184 like those of Aberlemno (*right*). There has been much speculation about the function of these stones. They may have been used as boundary markers and their symbols may have represented the families or associated groups who occupied the marked territory.

CELTIC CROSSES
The Scots, who came from northern Ireland c. 500, introduced Irish Christianity and its decorative motifs. They erected crosses carved with a halo which combined biblical scenes and traditional Scottish images in bas-relief. One such example is the cross of St Martin (7th century) on the island of Iona ▲ 204.

VIKING HOUSES
Rectangular houses were introduced by the Vikings in the late 8th century. These long structures, built on a slight slope, housed both people and animals. The lower part with its central drain was reserved for the animals, while the dwelling was surrounded by benches, for example Jarlshof (Shetland) ▲ 264 (*above*). The double-pitched roof rested on the two vaulted walls. Its framework consisted of posts and branches covered with layers of peat and turf. Holes along the ridgepole allowed the smoke to escape and also let in light.

● POPULAR ARCHITECTURE

Tiles (Flemish tiles, *left*) were an inexpensive alternative to thatch, especially in eastern Scotland.

ROOFING MATERIALS
In the 19th century thatch was gradually replaced by more hard-wearing materials such as slate, roofing stones (especially in the north and Orkney) and tiles. Roofing felt and corrugated iron, the cheapest option, was used more or less everywhere.

Until the 18th and 19th centuries the traditional Scottish dwelling was a single-story cottage. Farmers lived on individual smallholdings (*crofts*) or in farming communities (*ferm touns*). In the many towns on the east and south coast, stone houses decorated with sculptures attested to the relative wealth of the merchants.

TOLBOOTHS (Culross ▲ *175*)
The *tolbooth*, where tolls were paid on goods to be consumed in the town, also housed the town council, the law court and the prison. *Jougs*, irons placed around the neck of thieves on market days, were set in the outer wall of these medieval tolbooths to which clocktowers were added from the 18th century onward. The quality of materials (stone and slate) and the care with which they were built makes it easy to identify these symbolic buildings.

MERCAT CROSSES
The mercat cross stood on the market place (*mercat*) along with the public weighbridge (*tron*). It symbolized one of the fiscal and judicial privileges granted to a town in the Middle Ages: the right of free trade.

MERCHANTS' HOUSES
(late 16th–17th century, *below*) Trade was carried on under the arcades or in the courtyard at the back of the house. Stepped gables were often found on the east side of the house. Decorations and inscriptions on the door and window lintels and the walls often commemorated marriages or recorded the commercial activities of the owner.

FISHING VILLAGES
Most fishing villages date from the late 19th century when fishing enjoyed its golden age. On the north and east coast houses clustered together, their gables facing the violent winds, to provide protection against storms. Houses were painted, with features such as corner-stone joints, window and door frames, and foundations picked out in contrasting colors.

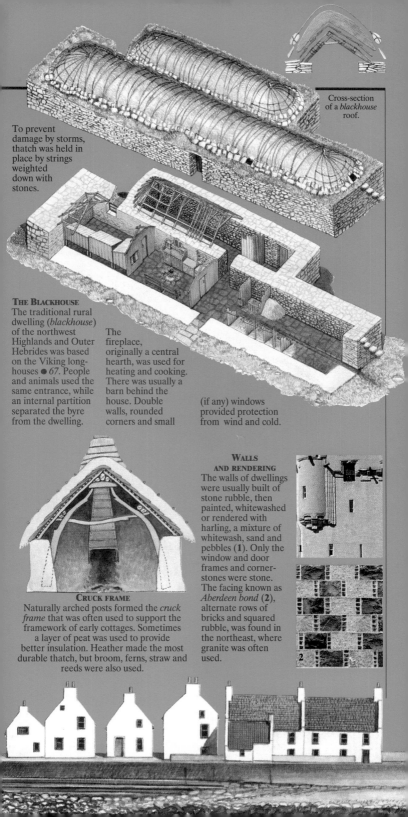

Cross-section of a *blackhouse* roof.

To prevent damage by storms, thatch was held in place by strings weighted down with stones.

THE BLACKHOUSE

The traditional rural dwelling (*blackhouse*) of the northwest Highlands and Outer Hebrides was based on the Viking long-houses ● 67. People and animals used the same entrance, while an internal partition separated the byre from the dwelling.

The fireplace, originally a central hearth, was used for heating and cooking. There was usually a barn behind the house. Double walls, rounded corners and small (if any) windows provided protection from wind and cold.

CRUCK FRAME

Naturally arched posts formed the *cruck frame* that was often used to support the framework of early cottages. Sometimes a layer of peat was used to provide better insulation. Heather made the most durable thatch, but broom, ferns, straw and reeds were also used.

WALLS AND RENDERING

The walls of dwellings were usually built of stone rubble, then painted, whitewashed or rendered with harling, a mixture of whitewash, sand and pebbles (**1**). Only the window and door frames and corner-stones were stone. The facing known as *Aberdeen bond* (**2**), alternate rows of bricks and squared rubble, was found in the northeast, where granite was often used.

PRE-NORMAN ARCHITECTURE (Brechin ▲ 186)
Like the tower at Abernethy, the Brechin Round Tower, built by the Scottish Church in the 11th century, attests to Irish influence. Its design was based on that of the bell-towers of early Irish monasteries.

When, with the support of the Scottish monarchy, the Roman form of Christianity replaced the Celtic, a new style of architecture developed. Initially Norman and then Gothic, it combined English and French influences. During the Reformation (1560s) many abbeys and cathedrals were destroyed, and new parish churches were built with a different layout and an austere decor. In the 19th century the various churches embarked upon a vast construction program that gave pride of place to the neo-Gothic style.

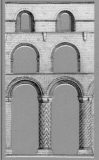

NORMAN ARCHITECTURE
Characterized by the triple elevation of the nave, the Norman style attests to the Anglo-Norman influence in 11th-century Scotland. In Dunfermline Abbey (*left*) cylindrical pillars with grooved spiral and zigzag motifs are reminiscent of those in Durham Cathedral.

NORMAN DECORATION
Dunfermline Abbey ▲ 174 was a major source of inspiration for Norman architecture in Scotland. Many Scottish churches had blind arches, corbels carved with gargoyles, and arch moldings that combine heads, animals and intertwined plants (porch of Dalmeny Kirk ▲ 128, *left*).

FROM NORMAN TO GOTHIC ARCHITECTURE (reconstruction of Jedburgh Abbey ▲ 138)

Jedburgh Abbey was one of the richest of the many churches founded in the 12th century by the Scottish monarchy. It is a fine example of the transition from the Norman to the Gothic architectural style with its characteristic pointed arches. Pillars were no longer cylindrical (**1**) but composite (**2**). The Norman choir with its apse and apsidal chapels (**3**) was replaced by a choir with a flat apse (**4**) and three horizontal levels: blind arches (**5**), triforium (**6**) and high bays (**7**). The cruciform layout was reinforced by the addition of a rectangular presbytery (**8**) to the crossing of the transept. On the original plan the side aisles were vaulted, but the nave and choir probably had an open-frame roof.

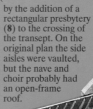

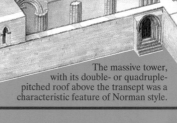

The massive tower, with its double- or quadruple-pitched roof above the transept was a characteristic feature of Norman style.

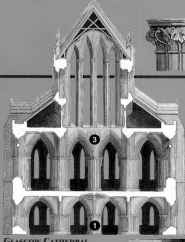

CROWNED STEEPLE
(St Giles' Cathedral,
Edinburgh ▲ *118*)
The crowned steeple
appeared in the late
15th century on some
churches associated
with the monarchy.
The traditional spire
was replaced by
pinnacled buttresses
supporting a
keystone in the form
of a crown

GLASGOW CATHEDRAL
Glasgow Cathedral, begun
c. 1240, is the only Gothic
cathedral in Scotland that is
still virtually intact ▲ *155*. It
has an unusual stone rood
screen and an impressive crypt
(**1**) whose complex ribbed
vault is echoed by the massive
pillars with their leaf-work
capitals (**2**). Above the crypt is
a flat apse with a vaulted
paneled ceiling (**3**). Two
towers once stood on the
cathedral's west façade.

COLLEGIATE CHURCHES
During the 15th century many collegiate
churches were erected. The elaborate
decoration of Rosslyn Chapel ▲ *130*, founded
in 1477, makes it the finest example of
Scottish late-Gothic: the chapel's Prentice
Pillar (*left*) with its quadruple leaf spiral.

**THE REFORMATION
(1560)**
(Cromarty ▲ *247*)
The Latin cross layout
and other symbols of
Catholicism (the internal
nave-transept-choir division)
disappeared from churches
built after 1560. The layout
was usually T-shaped, and the
altar was replaced by the pulpit, where
the minister read from the Bible.

GALLERIES AND CHAPELS

Although
Presbyterian churches
were intentionally
austere, they still had
elaborately decorated
galleries reserved for
the nobility. Noble
families often
had funerary or
commemorative

chapels built in the
side aisles. The
Skelmorlie Aisle at
Largs (1632) ▲ *149*
(*below*) has an upper
gallery above a tomb.

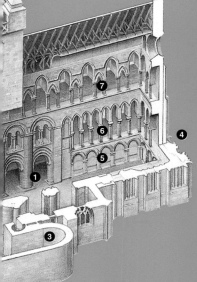

THE 19TH-CENTURY BUILDING BOOM

Many churches were built when the
Episcopalian and Catholic churches were
reestablished and there was a split within
the Church of Scotland. One of the most

spectacular is St Vincent Street Church,
Glasgow. It was built by Alexander Thomson
● *82* ▲ *155*, inspired by ancient Greek and
Egyptian elements.

71

FEUDAL CASTLES AND TOWER-HOUSES

EARLY CASTLES (Duffus ▲ 224)
Early castles were often old feudal mottes: a square wooden tower built on a mound, which dominated a courtyard, the whole structure fenced round, sometimes with a moat.

The introduction of the Anglo-Norman feudal system in the 12th century was accompanied by the construction of mottes or *motes* (a mound surmounted by a tower or castle) and baileys (the outer wall of a castle). In the late 12th and early 13th centuries the mottes were replaced by solid castles with a keep and a stone outer wall, and sometimes surrounded by moats. The tower-house appeared in the 14th century, after the Scottish wars of independence, but by the 16th century its defensive features had become purely decorative.

WALLED CASTLES
Under the Norman influence, the 13th century witnessed the construction of huge, circular stone enclosures with a central courtyard whose defenses were gradually strengthened. For example, the enclosure wall of Rothesay Castle was surmounted by a rampart walk and surrounded by moats, before being flanked by two angle towers in the 13th century. A fortified entrance was added in the 16th century.

WALLED CASTLES
(Rothesay Castle ▲ 200)

- ■ 13th century
- ■ 14th century
- ■ 16th century

NATURAL DEFENSES
The Scottish landscape provides many naturally defensive sites: Edinburgh Castle ▲ 116 is perched on a volcanic outcrop, while Dunnottar Castle ▲ 212 (*above*) stands on a rocky promontory that is unassailable on three sides.

TOWER-HOUSES
(Drum Castle ▲ 213)
In the 14th and 15th centuries a number of stone keeps were transformed into tower-houses. Even if the enclosure wall contained outbuildings, the tower was still designed as a virtually autonomous unit. The only entrance was reached by means of a ladder or movable wooden staircase. The cellars and dungeons were in the basement, the kitchens occupied an entire floor or adjoined the banqueting hall, and the private apartments were above. There was often another reception room on the top floor. An easily defended spiral staircase linked the different levels.

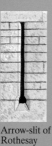

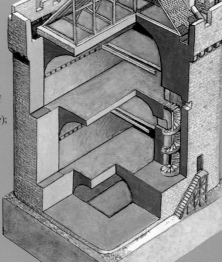

Arrow-slit of Rothesay Castle (*above*); loophole of Threave Castle (*below*).

L-shaped layout of Scalloway Castle (Shetland) ▲ *263* (*left*); Z-shaped layout of Claypotts Castle, Dundee (*right*).

Increased height and fewer, narrower apertures were two of the defensive features of tower-houses.

LAYOUT

Until the early 17th century the typical Scottish manor was a tower-house. The need for space saw the addition of one or two towers which gave rise to the L- and Z-shaped layouts.

DEVELOPMENT OF OUTLINE

(Crathes Castle ▲ *214*) In the 16th century the emphasis was very much on outline. Roof decorations became more individual, with turrets, skylights, gables and corbeled chimneys crowning former rampart walks. Machicolations, cannons and crenelations lost their defensive function and became purely symbolic. This decorative exuberance created a link between the Scottish châteaux of the period and the Renaissance of northern Europe.

TOWARD THE SCOTS BARONIAL STYLE (Thirlestane Castle ▲ *138*)

During the 17th century many tower-houses were redesigned and extended to meet the new criteria of symmetry, space and the separation of public and private spaces. In the case of Thirlestane Castle, two pavilions were added to the main building in the 1670s. The former tower-house was given a monumental staircase and its windows were enlarged. Two wings with pavilions were added in the early 19th century.

73

SCOTTISH RENAISSANCE PALACES

SYMBOLS OF ROYALTY: royal coats of arms occupy pride of place above the monumental entrance of Linlithgow Palace ▲ *130*.

In the 15th and 16th centuries the Stewart kings, and James IV and James V in particular, believed that sophistication and culture increased the prestige of the monarchy. The renovation of royal castles and palaces – one of the chief forms of expression of the ideals of the Scottish Renaissance – reflected a growing interest in the artistic and intellectual trends in countries such as France, Italy and England. Influenced by these new architectural ideas, the nobility followed suit and built magnificent castles and public buildings.

RENAISSANCE PALACE
(Reconstruction of Linlithgow Palace ▲ *130*)
Linlithgow Palace, begun by James I in 1425, was the first royal residence to meet the new requirements of the royal court. This involved providing apartments and privacy for the royal family and their entourage in a safe, modern castle built around a central courtyard.

ENDURING FEUDAL TRADITIONS
(Fortified entrance of Falkland Palace ▲ *178*)
Like Holyroodhouse ▲ *121*, Falkland Palace – a former hunting lodge redesigned in the 15th and 16th centuries by the Stewarts – had a fortified entrance. Although the palace retained some of its defensive features, the entrance became purely emblematic, evoking the medieval ideals of chivalry to symbolize the power of the Stewarts.

A HIERARCHICAL DIVISION OF SPACE
The west wing added at the end of the 15th century housed the king's apartments: the antechamber with the royal guard opened onto the throne room where ambassadors were received. Affairs of state were discussed in the bedchamber, while the study was the most private room.

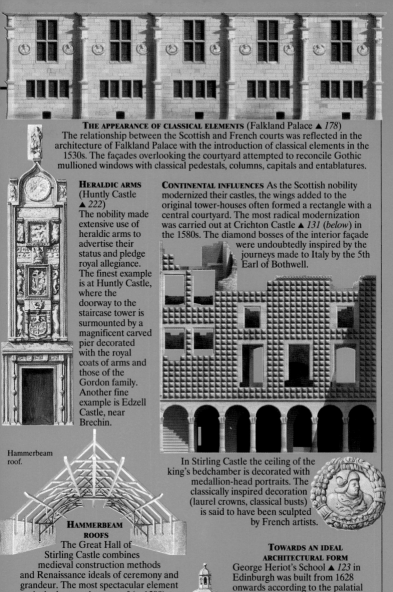

THE APPEARANCE OF CLASSICAL ELEMENTS (Falkland Palace ▲ 178)
The relationship between the Scottish and French courts was reflected in the architecture of Falkland Palace with the introduction of classical elements in the 1530s. The façades overlooking the courtyard attempted to reconcile Gothic mullioned windows with classical pedestals, columns, capitals and entablatures.

HERALDIC ARMS
(Huntly Castle
▲ 222)
The nobility made extensive use of heraldic arms to advertise their status and pledge royal allegiance. The finest example is at Huntly Castle, where the doorway to the staircase tower is surmounted by a magnificent carved pier decorated with the royal coats of arms and those of the Gordon family. Another fine example is Edzell Castle, near Brechin.

CONTINENTAL INFLUENCES As the Scottish nobility modernized their castles, the wings added to the original tower-houses often formed a rectangle with a central courtyard. The most radical modernization was carried out at Crichton Castle ▲ 131 (below) in the 1580s. The diamond bosses of the interior façade were undoubtedly inspired by the journeys made to Italy by the 5th Earl of Bothwell.

Hammerbeam roof.

In Stirling Castle the ceiling of the king's bedchamber is decorated with medallion-head portraits. The classically inspired decoration (laurel crowns, classical busts) is said to have been sculpted by French artists.

HAMMERBEAM ROOFS
The Great Hall of Stirling Castle combines medieval construction methods and Renaissance ideals of ceremony and grandeur. The most spectacular element is the hammerbeam roof (c. 1500) which attests to links with England. This complex wooden framework opens up a large amount of space, both vertically and horizontally.

TOWARDS AN IDEAL ARCHITECTURAL FORM
George Heriot's School ▲ 123 in Edinburgh was built from 1628 onwards according to the palatial model (rectangular layout punctuated by towers). The pepper-pot watch turrets and window pediments may have been inspired by the north wing of Linlithgow.

In the 18th century castles were replaced by classical-style symmetrical mansions. They offered greater privacy and comfort by attributing a specific function to each particular area. Robert Adam emphasized the relationship between architecture and the landscape by choosing spectacular settings for his Scottish houses which served to emphasize their neoclassical harmony. The 19th century reinterpreted medieval and Renaissance styles by creating the Scots Baronial style which combined past architectural styles with modern comfort.

TOWER-HOUSES: A THING OF THE PAST
William Bruce (c. 1630–1710) was one of the first Scottish architects to use a classical design: symmetrical layout and façades pierced by large windows. A skilful use of gardens integrates Kinross House ▲ *178* into its surroundings.

A FAMILY OF ARCHITECTS
William Adam (1689–1748) (*right*) and his sons John (1721–92), Robert (1728–92) – the best known – and James (1732–94) belonged to an established family of Scottish architects. Their influence extended to Europe and America.

PALLADIAN MANSIONS (Duff House ▲ *219*)
The classical style inspired by Italian villas and palaces was very much in vogue during the late 17th century. Freestone replaced rubble and harling ● *69*. Façades were characterized by the use of different materials, architectural devices and finishes. Galleries linked the central body of the building to pavilions or outbuildings according to techniques used by Italian architect Andrea Palladio (1508–80).

The dimensions and quality of William Adam's creations demanded massive financial investment. This was why Duff House (reconstruction, *below*) was never finished.

GOTHIC REVIVAL (Inverary Castle ▲ *195*)
Architects William Adam and his son John were involved in the design and construction of this huge, 1740s square castle punctuated by towers. The castle replaced a 15th-century tower-house as the residence of the Duke of Argyll, the powerful chief of the Campbell clan. The unusual combination of a symmetrical layout and neo-Gothic architecture was more in keeping with the concept of feudal power than that of clan chiefs.

Inverary Castle (1746) by Roger Morris.

BETWEEN CLASSICISM AND ROMANTICISM

Robert Adam was very much aware of the concepts of the 'picturesque' and the 'sublime'. In his architecture he made every effort to reconcile Scottish national tradition with his preference for classical design, and to integrate his creations into a Romantic vision of the surrounding landscape.

Detail of moldings (*above*) and a ceiling motif (*below*) designed by Robert Adam for the Round Drawing Room of Culzean Castle ▲ *147*.

THE ADAM STYLE

After studying classical and Renaissance architecture in Rome between 1755 and 1757, Robert Adam developed a vast repertoire of classically inspired motifs which he used in the decoration and furnishing of the many mansions he was commissioned to design. Their fineness suited the rococo and neoclassical styles currently in vogue and made the 'Adam style' famous throughout Europe.

'BARONIAL' DECOR

The novelist Walter Scott ● *99* ▲ *113* was a champion of ancient Scottish traditions and created the fashion for a Romantic image of feudal Scotland. The interior of his house at Abbotsford ▲ *138*, designed between 1817 and 1823 by the English architect William Atkinson, was a major source of inspiration for the Scots Baronial style. The entrance hall (*above*) is reminiscent of a medieval armory.

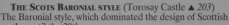

THE SCOTS BARONIAL STYLE (Torosay Castle ▲ *203*)

The Baronial style, which dominated the design of Scottish castles until the 20th century, is characterized by the marked asymmetry of the façades. Those of Torosay Castle, built in 1850 by David Bryce, appear even more asymmetrical when viewed from the gardens below: stepped gables, corbeled towers, split-level roofs and projections create an interplay of light and shadow.

During the 18th century Scotland's towns and countryside were transformed under the impetus of the Scottish Enlightenment. The rational approach of the Enlightenment was reflected in the introduction of town and country development plans which aimed to offer a more spacious and healthier living environment – at a time when Scotland was becoming increasingly urbanized and industrialized. The use of the classical style gave rise to a certain architectural uniformity which was eclipsed in the early 19th century by the development of Romanticism and the search for a style of architecture that was better able to reflect national aspirations.

PLANS

FORT GEORGE ▲ 231
When it was completed in 1769 Fort George, with its bastioned ramparts, was one of the most modern fortified towns in Europe. The project, executed by William Adam and his sons, reflects the principles of the Enlightenment. The austere classical buildings are arranged around a straight, central thoroughfare linking the entrance and the chapel.

BOWMORE ▲ 202
Bowmore (1768) was one of the many villages designed at the instigation of local *lairds* according to a rectilinear plan: the main thoroughfare links the jetty and the circular church. The houses provided by the landowner for his agricultural workers were spacious and of a high standard for the period. The space was divided into three main areas: the castle, village and agricultural buildings.

THE MONUMENTAL STYLE, EDINBURGH
When he built Edinburgh's Charlotte Square ▲ 126, in 1792, Robert Adam created architectural unity by giving the houses on each side of the square a single, monumental palace-like façade.

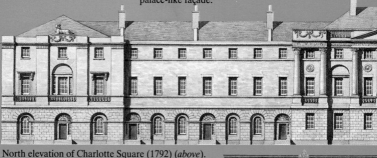

North elevation of Charlotte Square (1792) (*above*).

EDINBURGH. The New Town ▲ *124* was originally designed as a residential suburb for the aristocracy. On either side of a broad thoroughfare (1) linking two squares (A and B), two avenues (2 and 3) border a series of rectangular blocks of houses (4) each crossed by a narrow service road (5). This functional, rectilinear plan was designed by James Craig in 1767. It was extended in 1801 by Robert Reid and William Sibbald, who broke away from the regularity of the original layout. They designed larger, less regular blocks of houses which formed crescents (6) and circuses (7), and made more use of natural features.

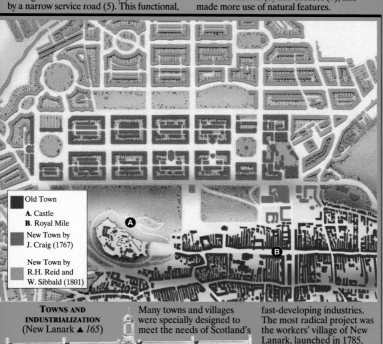

Old Town
A. Castle
B. Royal Mile
New Town by J. Craig (1767)

New Town by R.H. Reid and W. Sibbald (1801)

TOWNS AND INDUSTRIALIZATION (New Lanark ▲ *165*)

Many towns and villages were specially designed to meet the needs of Scotland's fast-developing industries. The most radical project was the workers' village of New Lanark, launched in 1785. The mills and workers' dwellings were built in 'rows'. These alignments of sober, communal buildings became widespread in Scotland.

'ROWS' (New Town, Edinburgh). The original plan for the New Town (1767) designed the blocks of houses in simple 'rows'. In 1801 each row was given a single, unified façade – based on the design of Charlotte Square – which created a monumental effect.

National Gallery of Scotland (1854) ▲ *125* (*below*).

'ATHENS OF THE NORTH'
To link the Old Town and New Town, a series of green spaces and monumental public buildings were designed and built, in the early 19th century, on the 'acropolis' of Calton Hill and at the foot of the Castle. The 'Greek temples' designed by William Playfair (1790–1857) – such as the National Gallery of Scotland (1850–58) – earned Edinburgh the epithet 'Athens of the North'.

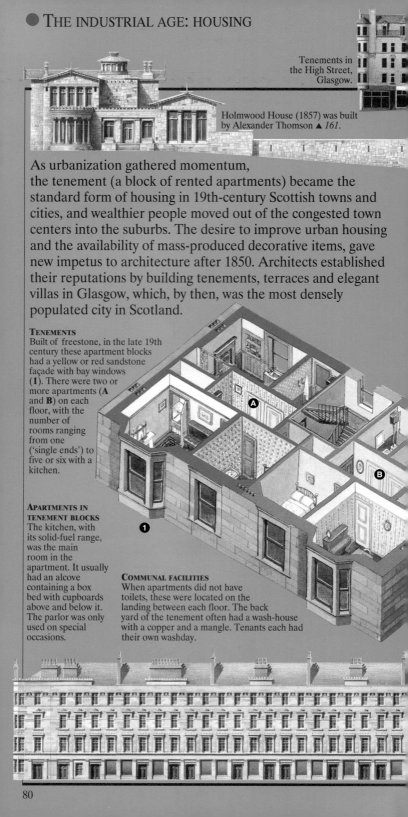

THE INDUSTRIAL AGE: HOUSING

Tenements in the High Street, Glasgow.

Holmwood House (1857) was built by Alexander Thomson ▲ *161*.

As urbanization gathered momentum, the tenement (a block of rented apartments) became the standard form of housing in 19th-century Scottish towns and cities, and wealthier people moved out of the congested town centers into the suburbs. The desire to improve urban housing and the availability of mass-produced decorative items, gave new impetus to architecture after 1850. Architects established their reputations by building tenements, terraces and elegant villas in Glasgow, which, by then, was the most densely populated city in Scotland.

TENEMENTS
Built of freestone, in the late 19th century these apartment blocks had a yellow or red sandstone façade with bay windows (**1**). There were two or more apartments (**A** and **B**) on each floor, with the number of rooms ranging from one ('single ends') to five or six with a kitchen.

APARTMENTS IN TENEMENT BLOCKS
The kitchen, with its solid-fuel range, was the main room in the apartment. It usually had an alcove containing a box bed with cupboards above and below it. The parlor was only used on special occasions.

COMMUNAL FACILITIES
When apartments did not have toilets, these were located on the landing between each floor. The back yard of the tenement often had a wash-house with a copper and a mangle. Tenants each had their own washday.

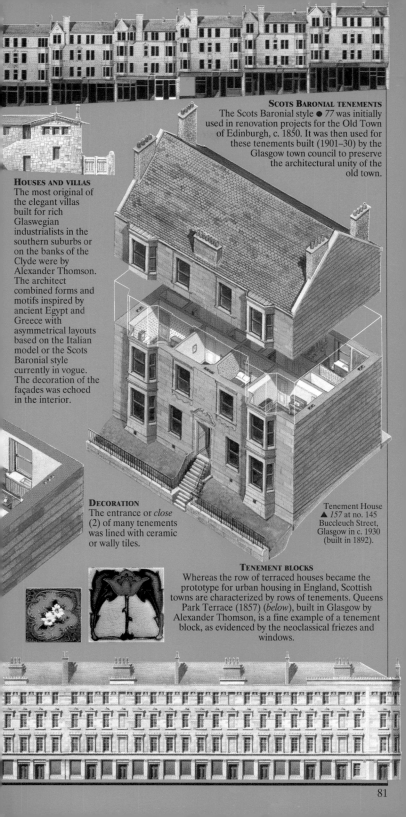

The Scots Baronial style ● 77 was initially used in renovation projects for the Old Town of Edinburgh, c. 1850. It was then used for these tenements built (1901–30) by the Glasgow town council to preserve the architectural unity of the old town.

HOUSES AND VILLAS

The most original of the elegant villas built for rich Glaswegian industrialists in the southern suburbs or on the banks of the Clyde were by Alexander Thomson. The architect combined forms and motifs inspired by ancient Egypt and Greece with asymmetrical layouts based on the Italian model or the Scots Baronial style currently in vogue. The decoration of the façades was echoed in the interior.

DECORATION

The entrance or *close* (2) of many tenements was lined with ceramic or wally tiles.

Tenement House ▲ 157 at no. 145 Buccleuch Street, Glasgow in c. 1930 (built in 1892).

TENEMENT BLOCKS

Whereas the row of terraced houses became the prototype for urban housing in England, Scottish towns are characterized by rows of tenements. Queens Park Terrace (1857) (*below*), built in Glasgow by Alexander Thomson, is a fine example of a tenement block, as evidenced by the neoclassical friezes and windows.

THE INDUSTRIAL AGE:
PUBLIC AND COMMERCIAL BUILDINGS

In the second half of the 19th century the Industrial Revolution made Glasgow the Scottish center of ironworks and heavy industry. The city's architecture reflects its rapid increase in wealth and attests to its economic activity via its public monuments. Industrialization and its products (plate glass, cast iron, wrought iron) made the city a melting pot of architectural research and forms of expression.

CHURCHES

Unlike the other Churches which favored the neo-Gothic style, the United Free Church to which Alexander Thomson belonged drew its inspiration from the Old Testament. The architect wanted St Vincent Street Church ▲ 155 (1857–59) to evoke Solomon's Temple and dramatized the sloping site by building a 'Greek temple' on a replica of a cryptoporticus. The entire structure combined elements inspired by ancient Egypt and Greece. Thomson also made use of industrial techniques to achieve certain recurrent themes in the decor: the wooden paneling and cast-iron columns were manufactured on machines in the Glasgow shipyards.

PUBLIC BUILDINGS

Glasgow's town hall (City Chambers), was built on George Square ▲ 152 by William Young. It embodies the wealth and pride of 'the second largest city in the Empire.' With its impressive dimensions, classical composition, elaborate baroque façade and opulent interior decor, it is a fine example of the eclectic style that was currently in vogue.

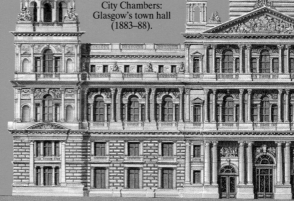

City Chambers: Glasgow's town hall (1883–88).

WAREHOUSES AND FACTORIES

(Egyptian Halls, 84–100 Union Street, Glasgow, 1871) Industrialization was accompanied by a building program in the very heart of Glasgow, with stores, workshops and factories occupying large multifunctional spaces. To open up the space in the six-story building (including a basement) known as Egyptian Halls, Alexander Thomson replaced the traditional load-bearing walls with a system of cast-iron pillars. The commercial building was lit by light wells and large bay windows. The austere interior contrasted strikingly with the exuberant decor of the façade which ensured that the building would blend into the urban landscape.

UNITY OF STYLE

Alexander Thomson combined ancient forms (pyloned doorways, left) and outlines (friezes, Greek borders, acroteria) to create an eclectic repertoire of architectural elements which he used, with great attention to detail, on all his buildings regardless of their end use.

METALLIC ARCHITECTURE

In the 1850s many architects experimented with cast and wrought iron in the structure and composition of their façades. Huge plate-glass windows emphasized the 'lightness' of Gardner's Warehouse (*above*), designed and built in 1856 by the architect Baird and the metal-founder McConnell at no. 36 Jamaica Street, Glasgow.

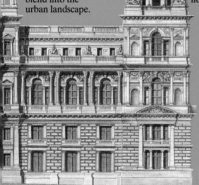

ECLECTIC ARCHITECTURE

Experiments were also made with architectural styles. Templeton's Carpet Factory ▲ 154 (*right*), built in 1889, is an extremely striking building. The combination of sandstone, colored brick and tiles on the Venetian-style façade suggests the design of the carpets woven in the building.

MACKINTOSH AND THE GLASGOW STYLE

Charles Rennie
Mackintosh (1868–1928).

The group known as the Glasgow Four, formed at the Glasgow School of Art by Charles Rennie Mackintosh, was the embodiment of the Glasgow Style. The movement revived architecture and the decorative arts in the 1890s. It combined purely Scottish stylistic elements with various other influences (including Celtic tradition and Japanese art) and had similarities with European Symbolism.

THE GLASGOW FOUR
Mackintosh and his friend Herbert MacNair first met the Macdonald sisters, Margaret and Frances, in 1891. The Glasgow Four worked together for the next ten years, with Mackintosh and Margaret remaining together for the rest of their lives.

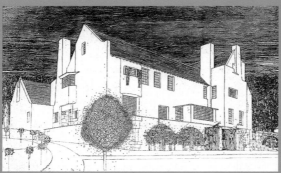

A TRADITIONAL MODERNISM

From 1891 Mackintosh ▲ 162 enthused about the architecture and functionalism of Scottish castles. Hill House ▲ 189 (above), the villa he built at Helensburgh, between 1902 and 1904, reflected the influence of the Scots Baronial style. Windows, towers, gables and chimneys were arranged in such a way as to create asymmetrical façades and the interior space organized to create an asymmetrical layout. However, the forms were simplified and cement rough-rendering replaced the traditional harling ● 69. With his design for Scotland Street School (1906) ▲ 161, in Glasgow, Mackintosh improved upon the archetypal model of the school. Various elements – the size of the stair wells, their glazed surfaces and the tiered arrangement of broad horizontal windows – heralded the Modernist movement, while the 'pepper-pot' roofs of the staircase towers reflected Mackintosh's admiration of traditional styles.

STYLIZED DECORS
This stained-glass window, decorated the Rose Boudoir, was designed by the Glasgow Four for the Turin Exhibition of Decorative Art (1902). In direct contrast to the Victorian style, Mackintosh and his collaborators favored austere interiors dominated by stylized – and highly symbolic – decorative motifs.

SHOOL BOARD & GLASGOW SCOTLAND STREET PUBLIC SCHOOL.

Scotland
as seen by painters

Hilary Macartney

86 From royal portraits to
personal portraits

88 Wild and romantic landscapes

90 Modern Scotland:
myth and reality

92 The sea, a boundless source
of inspiration

Until the early 17th century Scotland produced mostly religious paintings and royal portraits by foreign – predominantly Flemish – artists. The two themes are combined in a magnificent portrait of James III, which forms one of the panels of the *Holy Trinity Altarpiece* (**1**), attributed to the Flemish painter HUGO VAN DER GOES (d. 1482). Van der Goes, who became a master in 1467, never traveled to Scotland and never met the king. He is therefore not concerned with producing an accurate likeness, but conveys the status of the central figure by the richness of his garments, and his identity by the

genres became increasingly popular: landscapes and portraits. The portraitist Henry Raeburn (1756–1823) was the first successful Scottish painter to spend almost his entire career in his own country. Most Scots of the period would have recognized the portrait of Niel Gow, c. 1793 (**2**), the famous composer and violinist who revived local folklore ● *53*. Raeburn rejected the academic tradition and drew straight onto the canvas with his brush without making a preliminary drawing. By depicting the musician lost in thought, he produced a fascinating study of the process of artistic creation. The dramatic contrast of light and shadow heralds the intense eloquence of the Romantic generation. *William Chalmers Bethune, his wife and their daughter*, 1804 (**3**), is an early work by DAVID WILKIE (1785–1841). This remarkably frank family portrait reflects the artist's desire to produce a realistic and honest likeness. The portrait is obviously posed, but has a naturalness that prefigures the photographic portrait: the mother appears not to have had time to raise her head before the 'snapshot' was taken. The work is nevertheless more structured than it at first appears and illustrates the artist's gift for psychologically analyzing his subjects. Wilkie settled in London where he became a prominent painter.

presence of St Andrew, the patron saint of Scotland, and the lion on the coat of arms. Paradoxically Scottish painting flourished when its two main patrons, the Church and the royal court, no longer financed the arts. The Reformation condemned religious works of art and, following the Union of the Crowns in 1603, the court moved to London. Subsequently Scottish painters often began their careers as decorators of stately homes. In the late 18th century, two

In 1771 the Scottish landscapist JACOB MORE (1740–93) painted *Corra Linn* (**2**), the upper fall on the River Clyde, a view that was very popular at the time. The work reflects the sense of the 'sublime' inspired by the power of nature, as suggested by the figures in the foreground. In the early 19th century the wildness of Highland landscapes captured the imagination of the European Romantics. Painters and poets visited the isolated Loch Coruisk, on the Isle of Skye, described by Walter Scott in *The Lord of the Isles* (1815). JOSEPH MALLORD WILLIAM TURNER (1775–1851) went there in 1831 to illustrate the text and painted the loch under a stormy sky (**3**). The watercolor demonstrates the artist's ability to capture the nuances of light. In 1851 another British artist, EDWIN LANDSEER (1802–73), produced one of the most famous images of Scotland when he painted *Monarch of the Glen* (**4**). This noble stag standing proudly in a majestic setting reveals Landseer's talent as an animal portraitist, his passion for Scottish landscapes and for hunting. The landscape is represented as a vast game reserve, an image that was all too realistic since the countryside had already been cleared of its inhabitants to make way for grouse ● *25* and deer. Like Turner and the Impressionists, WILLIAM MCTAGGART (1835–1910) made bold use of his subject matter to render the effects of light in his seascapes of the west coast. The *Sailing of the Emigrant Ship*, 1895 (**1**) evokes the wholesale emigration that followed the 'Highland Clearances' and changed the face of the landscape forever. The figures gathering kelp in the foreground represent the artist's attachment to local traditions.

The Celtic Revival of the late 19th century reinstated Scottish customs and traditions, and the poetic soul attributed to the ancient Celts. This legacy was reinterpreted by writers, musicians and painters, whose strong symbolist movement is illustrated by *The Druids, Bringing in the Mistletoe* (**2**), painted in 1890 by GEORGE HENRY (1858–1943) and EDWARD A. HORNEL (1864–1933). Both artists were members of the group known as the Glasgow Boys, who benefited greatly from the city's artistic revival. Rich industrialists became patrons of the arts, under the guidance of such art dealers as Alexander Reid, who introduced them to Impressionism. Early 20th-century painting paid more attention to scenes from urban life, while the Scottish Colourists echoed the European Impressionist and Fauvist movements.

Interior: the Orange Blind (**1**), painted c. 1928 by FRANCIS C. B. CADELL (1883–1937), one of the four Colourists, shows an elegant Edinburgh apartment. The colors and composition of the work, which evoke the 1920s, attest to the influence of Matisse and of Japanese prints. The cycle known as *Shipbuilding on the Clyde*, commissioned by the War Artists'

Advisory Committee from the English painter STANLEY SPENCER (1891–1959), depicts a completely different world: that of the Lithgow shipyards of Port Glasgow. In *Furnaces*, 1946 (**3**) the shipyard workers are painted almost as caricatures, but are transfigured by collective effort and the mysterious process of industrial transformation.

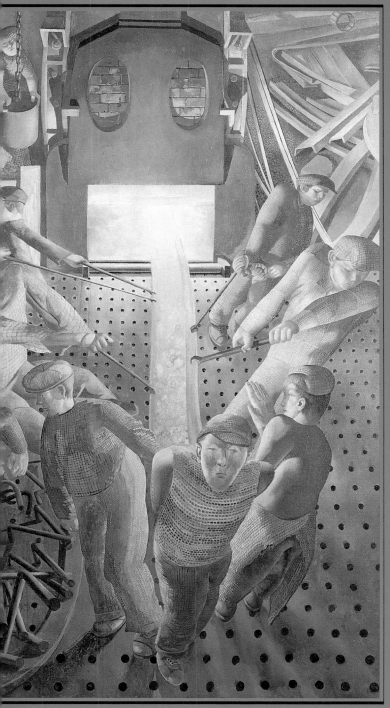

91

THE SEA,
A BOUNDLESS SOURCE OF INSPIRATION

Scottish landscapes transformed the life and career of the American abstract expressionist JON SCHEULER (1916–92). Scheuler settled in Mallaig after spending the winter of 1957 in this port on the northwest coast of Scotland. His seascapes, like those of Turner and McTaggart, evoke the struggle between the elements, but also express the artist's internal conflicts, as for example in *Storm Light and Black Shadow*, 1974 (**2**). WILL MACLEAN was born (1941) the son of a fisherman and was for a time a fisherman himself. He paints the sea and the harsh existence and traditions of those who make their living from it. His distinctive style combines painting, collage and the assemblage of painted objects. *Ex-voto South Minch*, 1993 (**1**) is based on the superstitions of the Highland fishermen.

Scotland
as seen by writers

EARLY TRAVELERS IN SCOTLAND

A HUMANIST VIEW

The great humanist Aeneas Sylvius Piccolomini, Pope Pius II, born in 1405, is one of the most interesting Popes of the early Renaissance. As a young man he was sent to negotiate with James I who defrayed his expenses and presented him with two horses and a pearl. Aeneas found the following facts relating to Scotland worthy of mention.

❝Scotland makes part of the same island as England, stretching northwards 200 miles with a breadth of 50. Its climate being cold it produces few crops and is scantily supplied with wood. A sulphurous stone dug from the earth is used by the people for fuel. The towns have no walls, and the houses are for the most part constructed without lime. The roofs of the houses in the country are made of turf, and the doors of the humbler dwellings are made of the hide of oxen. The common people are poor, and destitute of all refinement. They eat flesh and fish to repletion, and bread only as a dainty. The men are small in stature, bold and forward in temper; the women, fair in complexion, comely and pleasing, but not distinguished for their chastity, giving their kisses more readily than Italian women their hands.

There is no wine in the country unless what is imported. All the horses are amblers, and are of small size. A few are kept for breeding, the rest being gelded. They are never touched either with an iron bush or a wooden comb, and they are managed without a bit. The oysters of the country are larger than those found in England. Hides, wool, salted fish, and pearls are exported to Flanders. Nothing pleases the Scots more than the abuse of the English. There are said to be two distinct countries in Scotland – the one cultivated, the other covered with forests and possessing no tilled land. The Scots who live in the wooded region speak a language of their own, and sometimes use the bark of trees for food.❞

EARLY TRAVELLERS IN SCOTLAND,
ED. P. HUME BROWN,
JAMES THIN, 1978

AN INFORMED OPINION

Fynes Morrison (1566–?), having taken degrees in both Cambridge and Oxford, then embarked in 1589 on a ten-year journey that took him all over Europe and as far afield as Poland. He did this 'for the ornament of this profession [Civil Law]... and to gain experience by travelling into forraigne parts...' He visited Scotland in 1598, by which time he had gained some experience, so his remarks should be given due weight.

❝On the West side of Scotland are many Woodes, Mountaines, and Lakes. On the East side towards the Sea, I passed Fife, a pleasant little Territory of open fields. Without inclosures, fruitfull in Corne (as bee all the partes neare Barwick, save that

they yeeld little wheate, and much Barley and Oates), and all a plaine Country, but it had no Woodes at all, onely the Gentlemens dwellings were shaddowed with some little Groves, pleasant to the view. Scotland abounds with Fish, and hath plenty of all Cattell, yet not so bigge as ours, and their Horses are full of spirit, and patient of labour, but very little, so as the Scots then would give any price for one of our English Gueldings, which notwithstanding in Queene Elizabethe time might not upon great penalty be sold unto them...

Touching their diet: They eate much red Colewort and Cabbage, but little fresh meate, using to salt their Mutton and Geese, which made me more wonder, that they used to eate Beefe without salting. The Gentlemen reckon their revenewes, not by rents of monie, but by chauldrons of victuals, and keepe many people in their Families, yet living most on Corne and Rootes, not spending any great quantity on flesh. My selfe was at a Knights House, who had many servants to attend him, that brought in his meate with their heads covered with blew caps, the Table being more then halfe furnished with great platters of porredge, each having a little peece of sodden meate: And when the Table was served, the servants did sit downe with us, but the upper messe in steede of porredge, had a Pullet with some prunes in the broth. And I observed no Art of Cookery, or furniture of Houshold stuffe, but rather rude neglect of both, though my selfe and my companion, sent from the Governour of Barwicke about bordering affaires, were entertained after their best manner. The Scots, living then in factions, used to keepe many followers, and so consumed their revenew of victuals, living in some want of money. They vulgarly eate harth Cakes of Oates, but in Cities they have also wheaten bread, which for the most part was bought by Courtiers, Gentlemen, and the best sort of Citizens. When I lived at Barwicke, the Scots, weekely upon the market day, obtained leave in writing of the Governour, to buy Pease and Beanes, whereof, as also of Wheate, their Merchants at this day send great quantity from London into Scotland.

They drinke pure Wines, not with sugar as the English, yet at Feasts they put Comfits in the Wine, after the French manner, but they had not our Vinteners fraud to mix their Wines. I did never see nor heare that they have any publike Innes with signs hanging out, but the better sort of citizens brew ale, their usuall drinke (which will distemper a stranger's bodie), and the same Citizens will entertaine passengers upon acquaintance or entreaty. Their bedsteads were then like Cubbards in the wall, with doores to be opened and shut at pleasure, so as we climbed up to our beds. They used but one sheete, open at the sides and top, but close at the feete, and so doubled. Passengers did seeke a stable for their Horses in some other place, and did there buy hors-meat, and if perhaps the same house yeelded a stable yet the payment for the Horse did not make them have beds free as in England. 🙶

EARLY TRAVELLERS IN SCOTLAND,
ED. P. HUME BROWN,
EDINBURGH 1891

IN SEARCH OF THE WILD

In 1773 the famous lexicographer Samuel Johnson made a journey to Scotland and the Western Isles in the company of his friend James Boswell, his future biographer. Johnson was sixty-three and Boswell thirty-two. Their trip lasted three months, and was subsequently described in A Journey to the Western Islands of Scotland, *published in 1775. Johnson had hoped to encounter the wild, even the primitive. But the old ways were already changing, in the wake of Culloden and the enforced pacification, and the clan system was in decay. 'We came too late,' he wrote, to see what we had expected.' He was impressed, however, with the warmth and hospitality of the Highlanders.*

❛...As we sat at sir Alexander's (Macdonald) table, we were entertained, according to the ancient usage of the north with the melody of the bagpipe. Everything in those countries has its history. As the bagpipes were playing, an elderly gentleman informed us that in some remote time, the Macdonalds of Glengarry having been injured, or offended by the inhabitants of Culloden, and resolving to have justice or vengeance, came to Culloden Church which they set on fire; and this, said he, is the tune that the piper played while they were burning.

Narrations like this, however uncertain, deserve the notice of the traveller, because they are the only rewards of a nation that has no historians and afford the most genuine representation of the life and character of the ancient Highlanders...

A man of the Hebrides, for of the women's diet I can give no account, as soon as he appears in the morning, swallows a glass of whisky.; yet they are not a drunken race, at least I never was present at much intemperance; but no man is so abstemious as to refuse the morning dram, which they call a skalk...

Not long after the dram, may be expected the breakfast, a meal in which the Scots, whether of the Lowlands or mountains, must be confessed to excel us. The tea and coffee are accompanied not only with butter, but with honey, conserves, and marmalades. If an epicure could remove with a wish, in quest of sensual gratification, wherever he had supped he would breakfast in Scotland...

A dinner in the Western Islands differs very little from a dinner in England, except that, in the place of tarts, there are always set different preparations of milk. This part of their diet will admit some improvement. Though they have milk, and eggs, and sugar, few of them know how to compound them in a custard. Their gardens afford them no great variety, but they have always some vegetables on the table. Potatoes, at least, are never wanting, which, though they have not known them long, are now one of the principal parts of their food. They are not of the mealy, but the viscous kind.

Their more elaborate cookery, or made dishes, an Englishman, at the first taste, is not likely to approve, but the culinary compositions of every country, are often such as become grateful to other nations only by degrees; though I have read a French author, who, in the elation of his heart, says, that French cookery pleases all foreigners, but foreign cookery never satisfies a Frenchman.

Their suppers are like their dinners, various, and plentiful. The table is always covered with elegant linen. Their plates for common use are often of that kind of manufacture, which is called cream-coloured, or queen's ware. They use silver on all occasions where it is common in England, not did I ever find a spoon of horn but in one house.

The knives are not often either very bright, or very sharp. They are, indeed, instruments of which the Highlanders have not been long acquainted with the general use. They were not regularly laid on the table, before the prohibition of arms, and the change of dress. Thirty years ago the Highlander wore his knife as a companion to his dirk or dagger, and when the company sat down to meat, the men, who had knives, cut the flesh into small pieces for the women, who with their fingers conveyed it to their mouths.

There was, perhaps, never any change of national manners so quick, so great, and so general, as that which has operated in the Highlands by the last conquest, and the subsequent laws. We came thither too late to see what we expected, a people of peculiar appearance, and a system of antiquated life. The clans retain little now of their original character; their ferocity of temper is softened, their military ardour is extinguished, their dignity of independence is depressed, their contempt of government subdued, and their reverence for their chiefs abated. Of what they had before the late conquest of their country, there remain only their language and their poverty. **)**

SAMUEL JOHNSON AND JAMES BOSWELL,
*A JOURNEY TO THE WESTERN ISLANDS OF SCOTLAND
AND THE JOURNAL OF A TOUR TO THE HEBRIDES*,
PENGUIN BOOKS, LONDON, 1984

AN ECONOMY DESTROYED

Daniel Defoe (1660–1731) was at the height of his literary career when A Tour thro' the Whole Island of Great Britain *was published in 1724–6. The conditions he describes are those he discovered while acting as a secret agent for the English government – it was anxious to know the true state of affairs in Scotland, following the Act of Union. Defoe, who was an accurate and impartial observer, was at pains to correct some of the misconceptions of his contemporaries and to reveal some little known aspects of Scotland, hitherto so disparaged.*

(I take the decay of all these sea-port towns, which 'tis evident have made a much better figure in former times, to be owing to the removing of the court and nobility of Scotland to England; for it is most certain, when the court was at home, they had a confluence of strangers, residence of foreign ministers, being of armies, &c. and consequently the nobility dwelt at home, spent the income of their estates, and the product of their country among their neighbours. The return of their coal and salt, and corn and fish, brought them in goods from abroad, and, perhaps, money; they sent their linen and other goods to England, and received the returns in money; they made their own manufactures, and though not so good and cheap as from England, yet they were cheaper to the public stock, because their own poor were employed. Their wool, which they had over and above, went to France, and returned ready money. Their lead went to Holland, and their cattle and sheep to England, and brought back in that one article above 100,000 l. sterling per ann.

Then it was the sea-port towns had a trade, their Court was magnificent, their nobility built fine houses and palaces which were richly furnished, and nobly finished within and without. They had infinitely more value went out than came back in goods, and therefore the balance was evidently on their side, and yet scarcely takes it off at home; if the cattle goes to England, the money is spent there too. The troops raised there are in English service, and Scotland receives no premio for the levies, as she might have done abroad, and as the Swiss and other nations do at this time.

It is true, Scotland would have an advantageous trade with England, and not the worst for the Union, were not the Court removed, and did not their nobility dwell abroad, and spend their estates abroad. Scotland has a plentiful product for exportation, and were the issue of that product returned and consumed at home, Scotland would flourish and grow rich, but as it is, I may venture to say, it is not to be expected.'

DANIEL DEFOE,
A TOUR THRO' THE WHOLE ISLAND OF GREAT BRITAIN,
ED. PAT ROGERS, WEBB & BOWER, 1989

ROMANTIC VISIONS

CALVINISM

The poet Robert Burns (1759–1796) composed the following piece, which is 'Written with a Pencil over the Chimneypiece, in the Parlour of the Inn at Kenmore, Taymouth' in August 1787, while walking in the Highlands and being inspired by the beauty of the estate of the count of Breadalbana, on the Tay river. Robert Burns, then 28 years old, was already famous thanks to his Poems, Chiefly in the Scottish Dialect *(1786). A few intellectuals are still hostile to Burns' poetry, but it is largely met with popular enthusiasm and the admiration of the Scottish intelligentsia.*

'Admiring nature in her wildest grace,
These northern scenes with weary feet I trace
O'er many a winding dale and painful steep,
th'abodes of covey'd grouse and timid sheep,
my savage journey, curious, I pursue,
till fam'd Breadalbane opens to my view.
The mating cliffs each deep-sunk glen divides,
The wooden wild-scatter'd, clothe their ample sides;
Th'outstretched lake, imbosomed among the hills,
The eye with wonder and amazement fills;
The Tay meand'ring sweet in infant pride,
The palace rising on his verdant side;
The lawns woods fring'd in Nature's native taste;
The hills dropt in Nature's careless haste;
The arches striding o'er the new-born stream;
The village glittering in the Noontide beam –
....
poetic ardors in my bosom swell,
home wand'ring by the hermits' mossy cell
the sweeping theatre of hanging woods;
the'incessant roar of headlong tumbling floods –
....
Here Poesy might wake her heav'n-taught lyre
And look through Nature with creative fire;
Here to the wrongs of Fate half-reconcil'd,
Misfortune's lighten'd steps might wander wild;
And disappointment, in these lonely bounds
Find balm to sooth her rankling wounds:
Here heart-struck Grief might heav'n-ward stretch her seam
And injur'd Worth forget and pardon man'

ROBERT BURNS

SCOTLAND AS SEEN BY WRITERS

LOCH KATRINE

‘ *Walter Scott (1771–1832) was brought up from early childhood to the poetry of the places and past of his native land. Rocked in his cradle to Scottish ballads, he stored in his memory the legends and traditions of Scotland. His early works, before he embarked on his career as a novelist, were dramatic poems in which he conveyed his enthusiasm for the past and his admiration for the grandeurs of the Scottish landscape.* The Lady of the Lake *(1810) is a long narrative poem in which the action takes place during a stag hunt in the Trossachs. It was an instant success, and a wave of tourists soon descended on the shores of Loch Katrine to discover for themselves its wild, unspoiled splendour.*

‘ Boon nature scatter'd, free and wild,
Each plant or flower, the mountain's child.
Here eglantine embalm'd the air,
Hawthorn and hazel mingled there;
The primrose pale, and violet flower,
Found in each cliff a narrow bower;
Fox-glove and night-shade, side by side,
Emblems of punishment and pride,
Group'd their dark hues with every stain
The weather-beaten crags retain.
With boughs that quaked at every breath,
Grey birch and aspen wept beneath;
Aloft, the ash and warrior oak
Cast anchor in the rifted rock;
And, higher yet, the pine-tree hung
His shatter'd trunk, and frequent flung,
Where seem'd the cliffs to meet on high,
His boughs athwart the narrow'd sky.
Highest of all, where white peaks glanced,
Where glist'ning streamers waved and danced,
The wanderer's eye could barely view
The summer heaven's delicious blue;
So wondrous wild, the whole might seem
The scenery of a fairy dream…
One burnish'd sheet of living gold
Loch Katrine lay beneath him roll'd
In all her length far winding lay,
With promontory, creek and bay,
And islands that, empurpled bright,
Floated amid the livelier light,
And mountains , that like giants stand,
To sentinel enchanted land. ’

WALTER SCOTT,
SELECTED POEMS,
ED. JAMES REED, CARCANET, 1992

FINGAL'S CAVE, JEWEL OF THE ISLAND OF STAFFA

The French geologist Barthélemy Faujas de Saint-Fond (1741–1819) made numerous journeys in his capacity as royal commissioner for mines, notably in England and Scotland in 1784. In 1793 he was appointed Professor of Geology and Natural Science at the Jardin des Plantes in Paris. He was one of the first Frenchmen to travel to Scotland for the purposes of study and research; here he describes Fingal's Cave, on the island of Staffa, which was to become a major shrine for romantically-minded tourists in the 19th century.

❛This impressive space…its origins lost in the mists of time, conveys so striking a sense of order and regularity that it is difficult for even the most cold and insensitive observer of terrestrial phenomena not to be astonished with wonderment at the appearance of this natural palace…

I have seen many ancient volcanoes, reported on superb basalt causeways and beautiful caves; but I have found nothing to compare with this, whether it be for the amazing regularity of its columns, the height of the roof, its site and shape, the elegance giving this work of nature the appearance of an artistic masterpiece, although art had nothing to do with it; so it is not surprising that tradition has made it the dwelling-place of a hero.❜

BARTHÉLEMY FAUJAS DE SAINT-FOND,
VOYAGE EN ANGLETERRE, EN ECOSSE ET AUX ÎLES HEBRIDES AYANT POUR OBJET LES SCIENCES, LES ARTS, L'HISTOIRE NATURELLE ET LES MŒURS,
H J JANSEN, PARIS, 1797

THE CAPITAL

A VIEW OF EDINBURGH

The Scottish writer Robert Louis Stevenson was born in Edinburgh in 1850 and died in Samoa in 1894. He is famous for his adventure stories: Kidnapped, Treasure Island, Dr Jekyll and Mr Hyde, *and for his travel books, such as* Travels with a Donkey in the Cevennes. *Several of his books are set in Scotland, particularly Edinburgh, his birthplace, which he described with feeling in* Edinburgh: Picturesque Notes *(1879)*

❛The ancient and famous metropolis of the North sits overlooking a windy estuary from the slope and summit of three hills. No situation could be more commanding for the head city of a kingdom; none better chosen for noble prospects. From her tall precipice and terraced gardens she looks far and wide on the sea and broad champaigns. To the east you may catch at sunset the spark of the May lighthouse, where the Firth expands into the German Ocean; and away to the west, over all the carse of Stirling, you can see the first snows upon Ben Ledi.

But Edinburgh pays cruelly for her high seat in one of the vilest climates under heaven. She is liable to be beaten upon by all the winds that blow, to be drenched with rain, to be buried in cold sea fogs out of the east, and powdered with the snow as it comes flying southward from the Highland hills. The weather is raw and boisterous in winter, shifty and ungenial in summer, and a downright meteorological purgatory in the spring. The delicate die early, and I, as a survivor, among bleak winds and plumping rain, have been sometimes tempted to envy them

their fate. For all who love shelter and the blessings of the sun, who hate dark weather and perpetual tilting against squalls, there could scarcely be found a more unhomely and harassing place of residence. Many such aspire angrily after that Somewhere-else of the imagination, where all troubles are supposed to end. They lean over the great bridge which joins the New Town with the Old – that windiest spot, or high altar, in the northern temple of the winds – and watch the trains smoking out from under them and vanishing into the tunnel on a voyage to brighter skies. Happy the passengers who shake off the dust of Edinburgh, and have heard for the last time the cry of the east wind among her chimney-tops! And yet the place establishes an interest in people's hearts; go where they will, they find no city of the same distinction; go where they will, they take a pride in their old home.❜

ROBERT LOUIS STEVENSON,
EDINBURGH, PICTURESQUE NOTES,
LONDON, 1896

THE SCOTTISH RENAISSANCE

THE NORTH FACE OF LIATHACH

Hugh MacDiarmid (1892–1978) revived the Scots language known as Lallan, and so became the chief architect of the Scottish Renaissance, the literary movement of the Thirties which sought to reaffirm the cultural identity of Scotland. His finest work is A Drunken Man Looks at the Thistle *(1926), which made him one of the greatest Scottish literary figures of the 20th century.*

❛The north face of Liathach
Lives in the mind like a vision.
From the deeps of Coire na Caime
Sheer cliffs go up
To spurs and pinnacles and jagged teeth.
Its grandeur draws back the heart.
Scotland is full of such places.
Few (few Scots even) know them.
I think of another
Stupendous wall of rock
On the west coast of Foula
Rising eleven hundred feet from the sea.
Keep all your 'kindly brither Scots,'
Your little happinesses,
Your popular holiday resorts,
Your damned democracy.
This is no place for children
Or for holiday dawdling.
It has no friendly sand or cove.
It is almost frightening
In its lack of anything in common
With Dunoon or Portobello or Aberdeen.
It has no modern conveniences at all
Only its own stark magnificence
Overwhelming the senses.
Every Scot should make a pilgrimage here
Just once, and alone.❜

HUGH MACDIARMID,
COMPLETE POEMS,
CARCANET, 1994

FAIRYTALES AND LEGENDS

BONNY KILMENNY

James Hogg, 'the Ettrick Shepherd' (1772–1835) was the protégé of Sir Walter Scott, who first met him when collecting ballads from his mother. It was her legendary tales of brownies, kelpies, witches and fairies that appeared in Scott's Minstrelsy, and that also deeply influenced her son's poetry, so that he became known as the 'Poet of the Fairies.' He is perhaps best known today for his strange novel Confessions of a Justified Sinner, but Kilmenny is one of his most haunting poems.

❛Bonny Kilmenny gaed up the glen,
But it wasna to meet Duneira's men,
Nor the rosy monk of the isle to see,
For Kilmenny was pure as pure could be...
When many a day had come and fled,
When grief grew calm and hope was dead,
When mass for Kilmeny's soul had been sung
When the bedes-man had prayed and the dead bell rung...

Late, late in the gloamin' Kilmeny came hame!
Kilmeny looked up with a lovely grace,
But nae smile was seen on Kilmeny's face;
As still was her look, and as still was her ee,
As the stillness that lay on the emerald lea,
Or the mist that sleeps on a waveless sea.
For Kilmeny had seen what she could not declare;
Kilmeny had been where the cock never crew,
Where the rain never fell and the wind never blew;
But it seemed as the harp of the sky had rung,
And the airs of heaven played round her tongue,
When she spake of the lovely forms she had seen,
And a land where sin had never been;
A land of love, and a land of light,
Withouten sun, or moon, or night;
Where the river swa'd a living stream,
And the light a pure celestial beam:
The land of vision it would seem,
A still, an everlasting dream…
When seven lang years had come and fled;
When grief was scarce and hope was dead;
When scarce was remembered Kilmeny's name,
Late, late in a gloamin' Kilmeny came hame! **

A BOOK OF SCOTTISH VERSE,
OXFORD, THE WORLD'S CLASSICS, 1960

● SCOTLAND AS SEEN BY WRITERS

HEAVENLY VISIONS

THE EXTRAORDINARY LIGHT OF THE SCOTTISH LANDSCAPE

The Swiss writer Nicolas Bouvier (1929–1998), having completed his studies in law and literature, set out to travel the world on a voyage of discovery. The books which were the outcome of his numerous journeys brought him a certain celebrity. Hailed as a master of travel writing, this 'wandering scholar' always manages to combine knowledge with poetry and humour.

❝I had been told over and over again that the scenery of Scotland was amongst the most beautiful in the world. But I had not been told that it was the light and not the geology that did all the work. The geology is the same as it is everywhere: a worn crust, softened or still rough and jagged. The light (fast-moving skies, enormous galloping clouds, an illumination committed to constant change) is unimaginable and creates in a day more magic images than the eye can take in…Only in the East, in Iran or Java, have I seen such free and rapid play with what the planet has to offer. I now understand much better how it is that the Scots can be simultaneously so poetic and so sparing of rhetoric: they are battered by the light like a punch-drunk boxer.❞

NICOLAS BOUVIER, 'VOYAGE DANS LES LOWLANDS'
IN ÉCOSSE, PIERRE, VENT ET LUMIERE,
AUTREMENT, PARIS, 1988

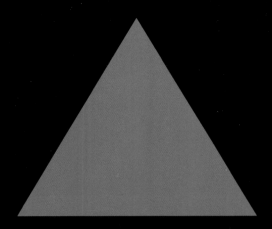

Itineraries

111 Edinburgh, Glasgow and
     the South
167 East Central
187 The West
207 The Northeast
225 The North

▲ Tantallon Castle

▲ Beach on the island of Harris

▼ Castle Stalker on Loch Linnhe

▲ Rannoch Moor

▲ East Princes Street Gardens, Edinburgh ▼ The Grampian Mountains

▲ Sheep in the snow

▲ Loch Ness

▼ Waterfalls in Glen Orchy

▲ The cantilever railway bridge across the Firth of Forth

▲ Façade in Dundas Street, Glasgow   ▼ Houses on the island of Lewis

Edinburgh, Glasgow and the South

Callum Brines, Wendy Lee, Hilary Macartney,
Ruth Noble, A. J. Paterson

114 Edinburgh

128 Lothian

134 The Borders

140 Dumfries and Galloway

142 *Robert Burns*

148 Ayrshire

150 Glasgow

162 *Charles Rennie Mackintosh in Glasgow*

164 The outskirts of Glasgow and the Clyde Valley

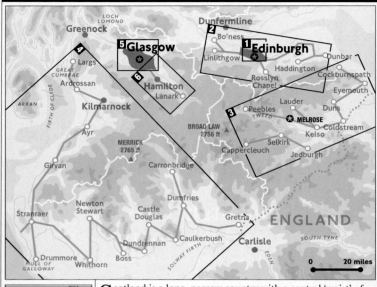

1. Edinburgh ▲ 114
2. Lothian ▲ 128
3. The Borders ▲ 134
4. The Southwest ▲ 140
5. Glasgow ▲ 150
6. The outskirts of Glasgow and the Clyde Valley ▲ 164

THE SOUTHERN UPLAND WAY
The Southern Upland Way is the longest footpath (210 miles) in Scotland. It crosses the southern part of the country, from Portpatrick ▲ 147 on the west coast to Cockburnspath ▲ 134 on the east coast. The path is well marked and presents no major difficulties, but walkers should be well prepared for the sections that cross the region's wild valleys.

Scotland is a long, narrow country with a central 'waist' of only 30 miles between the Firth of Forth in the east and the Firth of Clyde in the west. The Romans made use of this geographical feature c. 140 to try and contain the Picts by building the Antonine Wall between Bo'ness on the River Forth and Old Kilpatrick on the Clyde ● 32. The Forth/Clyde Canal, opened in 1790, followed the line of the Wall, but with the entirely different aim of enabling people and merchandise to cross this fast-developing industrial region. It also gave the ports on the west coast access to European trade and opened up the ports on the east coast to American markets. Today, while the canal is being restored to meet the demands of the leisure and tourist industries, road and rail provide the major transport links between Scotland's two major cities.
Edinburgh ▲ 114 and Glasgow ▲ 150 are in fact only 45 miles apart: 50 minutes by train or 1 hour on the motorway. Even so, they have very different identities, especially in climate, which is drier and colder in the east and milder and wetter in the west. The rivalry between the two cities, reflected in the 1980s slogan 'Glasgow's miles better', may have led some people to exaggerate these differences, whether in terms of attitude, accent, architecture or ambiance. The two Firths are also very different although, in the 19th and early 20th centuries, both provided beaches and resorts for their respective cities. The islands and long coastline of the Firth of Clyde offered a particularly wide choice to day-trippers, or the holiday-makers who sailed down the Clyde on paddle steamers such as the *Waverley* ▲ 159.
CATTLE AND SHEEP FARMING. The Southern Uplands, which lie to the south of Edinburgh and the Clyde Valley, form an undulating landscape of moorland and hills: the Pentlands, Lammermuirs and Cheviots. The Cheviots have given their name to a breed of sheep, while many of the Border towns ▲ 134 along the River Tweed, Hawick and Galashiels ▲ 138 for example, were centers for the tweed and cheviot (a twill-

weave woolen suiting fabric) industry until competition and the high rate of exchange led to its decline. The damp climate of the southwest has favored the development of dairy farming, an activity that has long relied on the merits of two breeds of cattle: the Galloway and Ayrshire. Local agricultural produce has a well-established reputation and includes such notable items as Ayrshire bacon and tomatoes from the Clyde Valley.

A BITTERLY DISPUTED BORDER. For a long time the proximity of England made the Borders an unstable region. During the Middle Ages its rich abbeys were an easy prey for invading armies and, until the 17th century, it was the stronghold of 'reivers' who lived by plundering raids, particularly stealing cattle. For this reason the architecture of many castles, for example the tower stronghold of Threave Castle, reflected the need for the region's powerful families to defend themselves against raids and vendettas. In many towns in the Borders, Dumfries and Galloway, the tradition of the 'Common Ridings' or 'Riding of the Marches' (an annual event which reestablishes a collective right to a territory by riding round the boundaries on horseback) has survived from these troubled times, which may also be the origin of the friendly rivalry between local rugby teams. The region experienced

some of its darkest hours in the 16th and 17th centuries. In 1513 James IV crossed the Tweed at Coldstream as he led his army against England. His tragic defeat at the Battle of Flodden was followed by that of James V at Solway Moss in 1542. In the 1680s ● 36, a period known as the 'Killing Time', the Covenanters of the southwest were horribly persecuted and the Wigtown martyrs ▲ 146 (two women who were tied to a stake in the estuary and drowned in the rising tide) are still remembered today.

FAMOUS SONS. Several well-known figures from the south of Scotland embody some of the region's most noble traditions. Two great medieval scholars, the mathematician, linguist and alchemist Michael Scott (c. 1175–1232 ▲ 146) and the Franciscan philosopher John Duns Scotus (c. 1266–1308), are said to have been born in the Borders. Sir Walter Scott ▲ 137, 138 and his protégé James Hogg (1770–1835), the poet known as the 'Ettrick Shepherd' ▲ 139, are also closely associated with the region, and a statue outside the inn at Clovenfords commemorates their frequent meetings there. Similarly, parts of Ayrshire and Dumfriesshire are closely linked to the life and works of Robert Burns ▲ 142 to the point that, for many, the southwest has become 'Burns country'.

WALTER SCOTT
Walter Scott was born on August 15, 1771. As the son of an Edinburgh advocate, he was destined for a legal career. He was called to the bar in 1792, and became Sheriff of Selkirk in 1799. Since childhood he had been fascinated by the historical tales and traditional folk legends of the Borders, which he learned from his maternal grandparents. In 1792 he began to compile a collection of popular ballads (*Minstrelsy of the Scottish Borders*, 1802–1803), before composing the epic poems *Lay of the Last Minstrel* (1805), *Marmion* (1808) and *The Lady of the Lake* (1810) ● 99. Fame and wealth enabled him to build Abbotsford, a baronial mansion on the banks of the Tweed near Melrose, where he spent the rest of his life. In 1814 he published *Waverley* anonymously, and the novel's huge success encouraged him to devote his time to writing historical novels. When *Ivanhoe* was published in 1820 it was read throughout Europe. But in 1826 the bankruptcy of his publishers, in which he was a partner, forced him to increase his output, in spite of his failing health, in order to pay off his debts. He died, exhausted, in 1832, leaving a legacy of more than thirty novels and the vision of a romantic and picturesque Scotland that would inspire generations of novelists, poets and painters.

▲ EDINBURGH

The city of Edinburgh from Calton Hill.

The Monuments of Edinburgh (opposite), by D. Rhind Capriccio.

THE INTERNATIONAL EDINBURGH FESTIVAL For three weeks in August the city hosts the International FESTIVAL OF MUSIC AND DRAMA which includes dance, opera, theater and classical music. A number of other cultural events are held in conjunction with the main festival: a fringe festival (THE FRINGE), whose many productions (theater, café-theater, poetry, music, art and photographic exhibitions) are held in the pubs, churches and streets, a FILM FESTIVAL, a JAZZ AND BLUES FESTIVAL and a BOOK FESTIVAL. The MILITARY TATTOO, a colorful military parade which has always been popular with the public, is held on the Castle Esplanade.

Musicians on the hills above the city (*below*).

The city of Edinburgh is renowned for its many historic monuments, which stand in a natural setting of volcanic hills and lochs. From an architectural point of view it is in fact two cities in one, with the winding alleys (vennels) of the old medieval center (Old Town) offering a striking contrast to the elegant, neoclassical façades and geometric layout of the Georgian New Town, which opens onto the countryside of Lothian and the Firth of Forth. The city, which has a population of 500,000, is proud of its status as the administrative and intellectual capital of Scotland, although this creates a certain tension with its long-standing rival Glasgow ▲ *150*, which reproaches Edinburgh for adopting a superior attitude. However, Edinburgh deserves its reputation as a city of art and culture, with its universities, museums, art galleries and theaters, not to mention the International Festival of Music and Drama which has been held here each summer since 1947.

HISTORY

ANCIENT ORIGINS. The first occupants of the site were probably Stone Age hunter-gatherers, then c. 900 BC a Bronze Age people settled on the edge of the Water of Leith ▲ *126* and built a palisade on the basalt outcrop (Castle Rock) which is today dominated by Edinburgh Castle ▲ *116*. The Romans built a fort at Cramond ▲ *128*, to the west of the site, and a port at Inveresk, to the east. The fortress of Dun Eidyn was built in the 7th century by the Angles of Northumbria to defend a border that Malcolm II pushed south of the Tweed in 1018. A town grew up at the foot of the fortress when Malcolm III took up residence there several years later, and expanded rapidly when David I founded Holyrood Abbey ▲ *120* in 1128.

MEDIEVAL PROSPERITY. By 1329, the port of Leith was under the control of Edinburgh, enabling the town to become a flourishing trading center. By the end of the 15th century James II had made it the administrative and political capital

A CITY BY ANY OTHER NAME
When the Angles captured the site in the 7th century their king, Edwin, built a fortress on the hill which was known as Edwin's Burgh or *Dun Eidyn* ('Edwin's Fortress') in Gaelic. The city's nicknames attest to its dual image: 'Athens of the North' pays tribute to the architecture of the New Town, inspired by Ancient Greece, and the intellectual flowering of the 18th century, while 'Auld Reekie' is a reference to the smoky city of the Victorian age.

of his kingdom and it had become the largest city in Scotland. It began to expand upwards with tenements in the 16th century, since the city walls built in 1513 after the Battle of Flodden ● *35* made any other form of expansion impossible.

THE AGE OF RELIGIOUS CONFLICT.
The Scottish Parliament's declaration of Presbyterianism as the official religion, in 1560, and the accession of Mary Stuart ● *40*, in 1561, made Edinburgh the scene of bitter disputes between Catholics and Protestants. The city acquired a university in 1582, but lost its cultural status in 1603 when James VI was crowned James I of England, and transferred his court to London. He returned only once to Scotland. The religious conflicts became even more acrimonious when Charles I attempted to impose the Anglican Book of Common Prayer and reestablish the authority of the bishops. When the new prayer book was used for the first time in St Giles in 1637 a riot ensued. The Presbyterians responded by signing the National Covenant in Greyfriars Kirk ▲ *123* in 1638. This pledged to maintain the 'true religion' and rejected the doctrine of the divine right of kings. The period of conflict ended with the 'Glorious Revolution' of 1688, and a protestant on the throne. The Act of Union of 1707 ● *36* guaranteed Scotland's national institutions and religious independence, and allowed Edinburgh to maintain its cultural influence and status as a capital.

THE GOLDEN AGE OF THE 'ATHENS OF THE NORTH'. In 1764, with overcrowding and insanitary conditions in the Old Town giving serious cause for concern, the municipal authorities decided to build spacious and elegant residential districts to the north. Work began on the New Town ▲ *124* in 1767 and continued until the end of the Scottish Enlightenment, when Edinburgh enjoyed a golden age of intellectual and artistic flowering ● *44*.

EDINBURGH TODAY
Today the city is still the administrative, religious and cultural capital of Scotland. In 1997 a referendum reinstated the Scottish Parliament in Edinburgh and opened up new prospects for the future. Its traditional industries (biscuit-making, brewing, printing, publishing) continue to flourish, it has a rapidly expanding service sector (banking, finance, insurance, computer technology), while its architectural and artistic heritage is attracting an increasing number of tourists, particularly during the Edinburgh International Festival.

The Crown Room contains the Honours of Scotland, discovered by Sir Walter Scott in 1818 after having lain locked in a chest since 1707. The simple gold circlet worn by Robert Bruce at his coronation in 1306 was modified and enriched with jewels by the goldsmith John Mosman ▲ *119*, in 1540, to produce the

crown (*below*) last worn by Charles II at his coronation at Scone, in 1651. James IV was presented with the royal scepter by Pope Alexander VI, in 1494, and with the sword by Pope Julius II, in 1507. The Crown Room also contains the STONE OF DESTINY (Stone of Scone), the legendary block of sandstone that Kenneth MacAlpin installed in his palace at Scone, in 838, and on which the Scottish kings were crowned until the late 13th century ● *38* ▲ *180, 185*.

AN HISTORIC CASTLE ✪
The castle, perched high on its rock (440 feet), is redolent with history, and is well worth a visit (2 hours) both for the royal treasures it contains and for its views across the city.

EDINBURGH CASTLE ◆ E B4-C4

This most visited of Scottish tourist sites has dominated the city of Edinburgh since the 11th century. Occupied alternately by the Scots and the English, it was a royal palace and then a military fortress until the 20th century.

ESPLANADE. This vast 18th-century parade ground offers some magnificent views of the city. In August it also provides the setting for the Edinburgh Military Tattoo. In the northwest corner stands the Witches' Well, erected in 1894 on the spot where 300 women accused of 'witchcraft' were burned alive between 1479 and 1722.

FORTIFICATIONS. A moat dug in 1650 by Cromwell's troops separates the esplanade from the 19th-century guard house. The Half Moon Battery (16th–17th century) runs beneath the 16th-century Portcullis Gate from where visitors can climb to Argyll's Tower (19th century) and Mills Mount Battery, with

sweeping views across the New Town. Since 1861 a cannon, which originally indicated the time to ships on the Firth of Forth, is fired from the upper battery each day at 1pm.

ST MARGARET'S CHAPEL. According to legend Saint Margaret, the pious wife of Malcolm III, is said to have had this little Romanesque chapel (30 x 15 feet) built on the top of Castle Rock just before her death, in 1093. The chapel was for a long time used as a gunpowder store, until its historical value was recognized in 1845, and it was carefully restored.

PALACE. The construction of Queen Mary's Apartments, in the southeast corner of Crown Square, was begun c. 1430. Mary Stuart gave birth to the future James VI of Scotland (James I of England) in a first-floor room in 1566. In 1617 the apartments were specially refurbished for a visit by the king, their last royal guest.

OLD PARLIAMENT HALL. This large, 15th-century banqueting hall occupies the south side of Crown Square. It was restored in the early 16th century and was used to hold the sessions of the Scottish Parliament until 1639, when it was converted into a barracks and then a hospital. Its beautiful open-timber roof was restored in the late 19th century.

SCOTTISH NATIONAL WAR MEMORIAL. This monument, opposite the Great Hall, pays tribute to the Scottish soldiers killed in the two World Wars.

CASTLE VAULTS. One of the vaulted cellars houses Mons Meg, the cannon, 13 feet long and weighing 5 tonnes, made at Mons in Belgium in 1449. It was used until 1681.

NATIONAL WAR MUSEUM OF SCOTLAND. The early 17th-century buildings house a collection of uniforms, weapons, flags and medals that traces the history of various Scottish regiments.

THE ROYAL MILE, FROM CASTLE HILL TO THE LAWNMARKET ◆ E C4

The Royal Mile consists of a series of four streets – Castle Hill, the Lawnmarket (the site of the medieval market), the High Street and Canongate – that run between the Castle Esplanade and Holyroodhouse.

SCOTCH WHISKY HERITAGE CENTRE *(354 Castle Hill)*. The center, which occupies a former schoolhouse, demonstrates the various stages in the manufacture of the Scottish national drink. Visitors are also invited to sample the end product.

CAMERA OBSCURA. Housed in a 17th-century watchtower, an ingenious optical device, installed by Patrick Geddes, projects moving images of Edinburgh. There are also telescopes on the roof terrace.

THE HUB. This neo-Gothic building, surmounted by the tallest spire in the city (275 feet), was built in 1842–44 by James Gillespie Graham and Augustus Pugin to house the General Assembly of the Church of Scotland. Between the 1930s and 1981 it was used as a Presbyterian church, under the name Highland Tolbooth St John. It was then beautifully restored and since 1999 has housed The Hub, a ticket office and information center for all the festivals held in Edinburgh.

ASSEMBLY HALL. It was in this building, built in 1859, that the Church of Scotland held its General Assembly and the Scottish Parliament met until its new premises are opened on Holyrood Road ▲ *121 (entrance to the Assembly Hall in Milne's Court)*.

ALSO OF INTEREST. The vaulted passageways (closes) that open off the Lawnmarket lead to small courtyards (courts) surrounded by fine buildings. The most interesting from an historical and architectural point of view are MILNE'S COURT (no. 517), whose buildings date from 1690, and JAMES COURT (no. 493), built 1725–27 and renovated by Patrick Geddes in 1895. RIDDLE'S CLOSE (nos. 322–328) has a beautiful late 16th-century house, while the 16th–17th-century BRODIE'S CLOSE (nos. 306–310) was the home of Deacon William

THE OLD TOWN ✪
The Royal Mile forms the backbone of the Old Town and is lined by a remarkable number of historic buildings. Strolling along this mile-long, sloping street and exploring its closes (entrances to tenements) and wynds (narrow lanes), it is easy to imagine the busy life of the district between the Middle Ages and the 18th century, with its dark booths, smoky taverns and tall tenement buildings occupied by rich and poor alike, including aristocrats, lawyers and merchants.

RAMSAY GARDENS
◆ E C4 *(alley which runs down from Castle Hill)*
The poet Allan Ramsay (1686–1758), father of the portrait painter, built Goose Pie House at the north end of the alley in 1740. The other buildings were designed in the late 19th century by Patrick Geddes, a town planner who tried to encourage well-to-do citizens to move back into the Old Town.

WRITERS' MUSEUM ◆ **E** D4 *(Lady Stair's Close)*
The museum, which occupies the town house built in 1622 by Lady Stair, presents memorabilia, portraits and manuscripts of the three great names in Scottish literature: Robert Burns ● *98* ▲ *142*, Walter Scott ● *99* and Robert Louis Stevenson ● *101*.

Brodie, a respected town councilor and cabinet-maker by day and a thief by night. He was hanged in 1788, on a gallows whose mechanism he had designed himself. He is said to have inspired Robert Louis Stevenson's famous novel *The Strange Case of Dr. Jekyll and Mr. Hyde* (1886).

THE ROYAL MILE, HIGH STREET ◆ E D4-E3

The High Street, lined with closes and inner courts, runs from Lawnmarket to Netherbow. Its beautiful houses act as a reminder that, from 1677, the use of building materials other than stone, slate and tiles made the owner liable to a fine.

ST GILES' CATHEDRAL (HIGH KIRK OF EDINBURGH). The Gothic cathedral (*below*), which stands on the site of a Norman church, has many commemorative monuments. All that remains of the cruciform Norman church (c. 1120) are the four pillars supporting the square 15th-century tower and its elegant spire, the 'Crown of St Giles'. The church acquired lateral chapels in the 14th century, was extended in the 15th, and renovated a number of times after the Reformation. John Knox ● *41* was minister there (1559–72) and his statue, which once stood in the parish enclosure, near his tomb, today stands near the west door. Although 19th-century restoration work has somewhat disfigured the exterior, it has restored the original interior space. Some of the stained-glass windows are by the pre-Raphaelite painter Edward Burne-Jones. The THISTLE CHAPEL, built in flamboyant Gothic style (1911) by Robert Lorimer, has some magnificent choir stalls bearing the

GLADSTONE'S LAND
◆ **E** D4
(477B Lawnmarket)
This five-story tenement building (land) was acquired in 1617 by the wealthy merchant Thomas Gledstanes. During restoration work the frontage of a booth was discovered beneath the first-floor arcades, and its interior was reconstructed. The apartments, with the original painted ceilings and period furniture, evoke perfectly the comfortable 17th-century interior.

THE CATHEDRAL ✪
Its 'crown' has dominated Edinburgh for 500 years. It is well worth a visit for the monuments dedicated to famous figures from Scottish history and for the decoration of its Thistle Chapel, a masterpiece of 20th-century craftsmanship.

MERCAT CROSS ◆ **E** D4
The 'market cross' that stands behind St Giles' Cathedral marks the commercial center of the medieval city. It was also the place where criminals were executed and royal proclamations read. The shaft comes from a cross demolished in 1756, while the rest dates from 1885.

arms of James VII/II, founder of the Most Ancient and Most Noble Order of the Thistle (1687), his twelve knights and subsequent knights.

HEART OF MIDLOTHIAN AND TOLBOOTH. A cobblestone heart (the Heart of Midlothian) in front of the cathedral's west door marks the site of the Old Tolbooth, the town hall and law courts in medieval times. It was converted into a prison in 1639 and demolished in 1817.

LAW COURTS. On the west side of Parliament Square are the neoclassical façades of various libraries and law courts, built between 1816 and 1818 by Robert Reid according to plans by Robert Adam. A broad flight of steps, surmounted by a dome (William Playfair, 1820), leads to the SIGNET LIBRARY whose magnificent colonnaded hall houses a vast collection of law books (not open to the public).

PARLIAMENT HOUSE *(south side of Parliament Square)*. The building was the meeting place of the Scottish Parliament from 1639 until its dissolution under the Act of Union in 1707. Today it is occupied by the Court of Session and the High Court. Built by John Mylne in 1632–40, it was extended and given an Italianate façade between 1808 and 1814. It is open to the public during the week and visitors can admire the hammerbeam roof (1637), the portraits of eminent jurists from past centuries and the huge 19th-century stained-glass window in Parliament Hall.

ADVOCATES CLOSE. The building, whose oldest parts date from 1590, was the residence of Scotland's Lord Advocate between 1692 and 1713.

CITY CHAMBERS *(249 High Street)*. The City Chambers was originally built between 1753 and 1761, according to plans by John Adam, as a Royal Exchange. But merchants preferred to do business in the street, so it was bought by the city authorities in 1811 and is today the meeting place of the town council. The west wing, added in 1904, has eleven stories.

MARY KING'S CLOSE. This old entrance, walled up after the plague of 1645 and subsequently incorporated into 18th-century buildings, is said to be haunted by former occupants.

MUSEUM OF CHILDHOOD *(42 High Street)*. The museum's collection includes toys, games and books as well as artefacts and documents relating to children's clothing and education since the Victorian era.

MOUBRAY HOUSE *(43 High Street, not open to the public)*. This four-story house, built c. 1477, is said to be one of the oldest in Edinburgh, although its present façade dates from 1630.

TRON KIRK *(Hunter Square)*. This former church, built near a public weighbeam (tron) by John Mylne in 1637–63, is now an information center for the Old Town. The south wing was lost when South Bridge was built in 1785–88. Its spire, destroyed by fire in 1824, was rebuilt in 1829, while the stained-glass windows date from the Victorian era. Excavations revealed the remains of Marlin's Wynd, an alley (vennel) that lay beneath the church and was named after the French stonemason responsible for cobbling the High Street in 1532.

JOHN KNOX HOUSE
◆ **E** E3
(45 High Street)
There is some disagreement as to whether John Knox, one of the leading figures of the Scottish Reformation, actually spent the last years of his life in this house *(below)*. It is in fact two 15th-century houses combined, with an external staircase built in 1556 by John Mosman, Mary Stuart's gold- and silversmith. The building has some beautiful paneling and oak parquet floors, a 16th-century fireplace and an interesting painted ceiling (early 17th-century). Today the museum houses a collection of bibles and rare books, and a reconstruction of a goldsmith's workbench. The house forms part of the NETHERBOW ARTS CENTRE, which includes a theater, café, art gallery and the Scottish Storytelling Centre. The complex is named after Netherbow Port, the gateway that once separated the city from its eastern suburbs.

HOLYROOD ('HOLY CROSS') ABBEY
According to legend David I, attacked by a stag while out hunting, was saved by a cross which appeared in his hands and put the animal to flight. To thank Providence the king founded an Augustinian abbey on the site of the miracle in 1128. The abbey was badly damaged by the troops of Henry VIII in 1544, sacked by supporters of the Reformation and burned by Cromwell's troops. Today, all that remains of the structure are the foundations of the chapter-house and a number of other buildings, the ruins of the royal chapel, the remains of the (mainly 12th–13th century) Gothic nave, the entrance with its beautifully sculpted details and the ruins of the north tower.

THE ROYAL MILE, CANONGATE ◆ E E3–E4–F3

When he founded Holyrood Abbey in 1128 David I granted the Augustinians the right to found an independent burgh nearby, a status that Canongate ('street of the canons') retained until 1856. In the 16th and 17th centuries the district was favored by the royal courtiers of nearby Holyroodhouse, as shown by its beautiful houses, now restored.

MOROCCO LAND *(267 Canongate, not open to the public).* The house is named after the Moorish figure which decorates the façade and which is traditionally associated with the memory of Andrew Gray. This young nobleman, condemned to death c. 1625 for having fomented a riot, who managed to escape and join the Barbary pirates. When he returned in 1645, he abandoned all desire for vengeance and married the daughter of the Lord Provost.

CHESSEL'S COURT *(240 Canongate, not open to the public).* Some of the apartments in these 1750s buildings have beautiful fireplaces and rococo-style stucco moldings.

MORAY HOUSE *(College of Education, 174 Canongate, not open to the public).* This mansion, built in 1628 and flanked by a remarkable portal with pyramidal uprights, has some finely carved timbers and remarkably well-preserved stucco ceilings. Oliver Cromwell stayed here in 1648 and the Act of Union (1707) is said to have been signed in its summerhouse.

CANONGATE TOLBOOTH *(163 Canongate).* The old town hall of Canongate (1591) also served as a tollgate, law courts and later a prison. Today it houses THE PEOPLE'S STORY, a museum devoted to the lives of the ordinary people of Edinburgh from the late 18th century to the present day.

CANONGATE KIRK. This church was built in flamboyant Gothic style in 1688, next to the Tolbooth. The economist Adam Smith (1723–90) and the poet Robert Fergusson (1750–74) are buried in its cemetery.

HUNTLY HOUSE *(142–146 Canongate).* The building was formed in 1570 by combining three houses and extended in the 17th and 18th centuries. Today it houses the City Museum, Edinburgh's principal museum of local history.

WHITEHORSE CLOSE *(31 Canongate).* The splendid 17th-century White Horse Inn *(left),* from where coaches once left for London, stands here at the foot of the Royal Mile.

PALACE OF HOLYROODHOUSE ✪
Visit the official Scottish residence of the Royal Family to see its State Apartments and experience the memories associated with its Historical Apartments (1 hour). Afterwards, the 30-minute climb to the top of Arthur's Seat (825 feet) offers a panoramic view of the city and coast.

HOLYROOD

The abbey and palace of Holyroodhouse (*right*), dominated by the steeply sloping Arthur's Seat (*above*), have long played a major role in Scotland's history. James II was born, married and buried at Holyrood, while the palace became the favorite residence of James IV. It was here that Mary Stuart married Bothwell in 1567, Charles I was crowned in 1633, and Charles Edward Stuart briefly established his court in 1745. Although the abbey and royal chapel today lie in ruins, since the reign of Queen Victoria the palace has been the official residence of the Royal Family when they visit Edinburgh.

THE PALACE OF HOLYROODHOUSE. Having decided to transform Holyrood Abbey's guest house into a royal palace, James IV built the square northwest tower (1498–1501) to which his son, James V, added the main building of the palace with a central courtyard between 1529 and 1532. Although Charles II never resided at Holyrood, in the 1670s he gave the architect William Bruce and his master stonemason Robert Mylne the task of reconstructing the palace which had been devastated by fire twenty years earlier. A southwest tower was added and linked to the northwest tower by a main Renaissance-style building. Beyond the main entrance, decorated with the arms of Scotland, a small vestibule leads to the CENTRAL COURTYARD, the buildings of which are in the purest Renaissance style (notice the superimposition of the three classical orders). Inside the palace the Grand Stair leads to the STATE APARTMENTS, occupied by the Royal Family when they visit Edinburgh. The PICTURE GALLERY presents the portraits of 89 Scottish sovereigns painted between 1684 and 1686 by the Dutch artist Jacob de Wet the Younger. The other rooms, with their magnificent stucco ceilings and carved oak timbers, are hung with Flemish and Gobelin tapestries (16th–17th century) and furnished in 18th-century style. The HISTORICAL APARTMENTS occupy two floors of the northwest tower, refurbished in 1672. They are closely associated with the memory of Mary Stuart, whose apartments include the antechamber where her secretary and favorite David Rizzio was assassinated in front of her in 1566.

HOLYROOD ROAD. The new SCOTTISH PARLIAMENT building is being constructed on Holyrood Road.

HOLYROOD PARK (QUEEN'S PARK)
This vast 655-acre estate, which lies to the south of Holyroodhouse, was enclosed by a wall during the reign of James V. Queen's Drive, dominated by the volcanic outcrop known as ARTHUR'S SEAT, leads to the vaulted 15th-century well known as ST MARGARET'S WELL, ST MARGARET'S LOCH – a lake dug beside the ruins of a 15th-century chapel in 1856 – and DUNSAPIE LOCH, an artificial lake created in 1840. To the southwest of the park and DUDDINGSTON LOCH, a sanctuary for migratory birds, lies the delightful village of DUDDINGSTON. Duddingston has a 12th-century church, renovated in the 17th and 18th centuries, and one of the oldest pubs in Scotland, the SHEEP'S HEID INN, where patrons can enjoy a traditional game of skittles.

ART GALLERIES ◆ **E** D3
The COLLECTIVE GALLERY (contemporary art) and STILLS GALLERY (photography) are only a stone's throw from the High Street, on Cockburn Street, which was built in 1856 to give carriages from the Old Town direct access to Waverley Station. The galleries on Market Street are also well worth a visit: the FRUITMARKET GALLERY (modern art) and the CITY ART CENTRE, which exhibits the work of such Scottish artists as McTaggart, Fergusson, Peploe, Eardley, Redpath, Davie, Blackadder, Paolozzi and Bellany.

OLD COLLEGE
◆ **E** E4-E5
(southwest end of South Bridge and Chambers Street)
This is the oldest part of Edinburgh University. Work was begun in 1789, according to plans by Robert Adam, and completed after the architect's death by William Playfair who modified the original design. The dome was added in 1886–88. The buildings incorporate the TALBOT RICE ART GALLERY, which houses the Torrie Collection of 16th- and 17th-century European painting and temporary exhibitions of contemporary art.

The impressive Victorian hall of the Royal Museum *(Chambers Street)*.

The building, designed by the Catalan architect, the late Enric Miralles, is due to open in the autumn of 2001. Nearby is DYNAMIC EARTH, a white structure that looks like the shell of an armadillo. Its special animations (volcanic eruptions, earthquakes, tropical storms) and projection dome trace the evolution of the Earth from the Big Bang to the present day.

SOUTH OF THE ROYAL MILE ◆ **E** D4–D5

NATIONAL LIBRARY OF SCOTLAND (GEORGE IV BRIDGE). The National Library of Scotland, founded in 1682, has one of the richest and most impressive collections in Great Britain. It has over 4.5 million works – illuminated manuscripts, ancient and modern books, maps, music scores, letters – which are often the subject of literary and historical exhibitions.
VICTORIA STREET. This curved street, built c. 1840, is bordered by terraces whose first floor is occupied by delightful shops and restaurants. Its continuation, West Bow, bordered by gabled 18th-century merchants' houses, opens onto the Grassmarket. The Bow Bar is a fine traditional pub.
GRASSMARKET. The square, at the foot of the south face of Castle Rock, is particularly pleasant in summer when its cafés, pubs and restaurants put tables out on the pavements. The Saturday market held during the Edinburgh Festival evokes the original cattle and 'grass market'. The square has a sinister history, since it was for a long time the main place of public execution: the pink cobblestone cross at the east end of the square marks the site of the gallows. It was here, in the 1820s, that Burke and Hare lured their unfortunate victims to their death in order to sell their bodies to the medical school.

The Hunterston brooch (8th century), one of the exhibits in the Museum of Scotland.

COWGATE. This unprepossessing street, linking the Grassmarket and Holyrood Road, is transformed in the evening when the pubs and restaurants open. Two monuments attest to the past splendor of the 16th–18th centuries. The MAGDALEN CHAPEL, below George IV Bridge, at no. 41, is said to have been the venue for the first meeting of the Scottish Reformed Church in 1578. ST CECILIA'S HALL, on the corner of Niddry Street, became Scotland's first concert hall in 1763. Today the building belongs to Edinburgh University and houses a remarkable collection of harpsichords and clavichords.

GREYFRIARS KIRK *(Greyfriars Place).* As its name suggests, the church was built (1612) on the site of a Franciscan friary. It was here that the National Covenant was signed in February 1638 ● *35, 41*. The kirkyard (cemetery) has a 'mort safe', an iron device designed to prevent graves from being violated, at a time when selling bodies to the medical school was one way of earning a living. Among the beautiful 17th- and 18th-century funerary monuments is the memorial, on the northeast wall of the kirkyard, dedicated to the 1200 Covenanters taken prisoner in 1679 and imprisoned here for five months before being executed.

GEORGE HERIOT'S SCHOOL *(main entrance on Lauriston Place).* On the other side of the kirkyard wall stands the school, built between 1628 and 1660 for orphans and the sons of poor families. It was endowed by George Heriot, jeweler and banker to James VI/I. In summer, the pupils give guided tours of the magnificent Scottish Renaissance-style buildings. The remains of the Flodden Wall can be seen at the end of The Vennel, to the east of the school.

CHAMBERS STREET ◆ E D5

ROYAL MUSEUM. The museum's exhibits range from natural history (fossils and minerals) to technology (machines from the Victorian era and scientific instruments) and arts throughout the world (sculpture, costumes, decorative arts). It is housed in a beautiful Victorian building (1861–88) which includes a vast hall with metal framework and glass roof (*opposite*). The façade is in Venetian Renaissance style.
MUSEUM OF SCOTLAND. The museum, designed by Benson and Forsyth (1998) as an extension of the Royal Museum, houses more than 10,000 works of art, everyday objects, costumes and machines which illustrate the history of Scotland. The basement gallery presents the formation of the country's landscapes and the various stages of its settlement from 8000 BC to AD 1100. The six upper galleries trace Scotland's political, economic, social, cultural and religious development from AD 900 to the present day, including the independent kingdom (900–1707), the industrial age and the Empire (1707–1914). The 20th century is represented by some 300 objects, chosen by the Scottish people.

CANDLEMAKER ROW
◆ **E** D4-D5
At the end of Candlemaker Row, which climbs from Cowgate and the Grassmarket towards George IV Bridge and Chambers Street, a bronze statue of GREYFRIARS BOBBY (*above*) pays tribute to the faithful little Skye terrier which spent the last fourteen years of its life watching over its master's tomb in Greyfriars Kirkyard.

AN INTRODUCTION TO SCOTTISH HISTORY ✪
The Museum of Scotland's unrivaled collection of treasures from all parts of the country is presented in a very informative way. It has a movie theater, a multimedia room and, on top of the building, an elegant café and gardens that offer a magnificent view of the city.

The Vision after the Sermon
by Paul Gauguin (1888) can be seen
in the National Gallery of Scotland.

NEW TOWN ✪
The architecture
of the New Town
is a fine example
of the Scottish
Enlightenment's
ideals of order and
harmony. Notice the
façades, especially in
CHARLOTTE SQUARE
with its GEORGIAN
HOUSE.

SCOTT MONUMENT
◆ **E** C3-D3
*(Princes Street
Gardens)* The
memorial to Walter
Scott was erected by
public subscription in
1836–40. It was
designed by George
Meikle Kemp, a self-
taught architect, who
drew his inspiration
from Melrose Abbey
▲ *137*. The monument
forms a canopy above
a marble statue of the
writer and his dog
Maida, while its niches
contain statuettes of
64 characters from
Scott's novels and 16
poems. There is a
small museum on the
second floor and a
magnificent view from
the upper gallery,
reached via 287 steps.

**GENERAL REGISTER
HOUSE ◆ E** D2-E2
*(Princes Street,
opposite North Bridge)*
The building,
designed by Robert
Adam in 1774, houses
the National Archives
of Scotland. The
entrance hall opens
onto a magnificent
domed rotunda with
stucco moldings.

NEW TOWN

As the Old Town became increasingly over-populated and
insanitary, Edinburgh's middle classes wanted to move out
of the city. In 1752 the Lord Provost, George Drummond,
published his 'proposals for public works', a visionary project
for the creation of a 'new town' to the north of the city. The
first step involved draining the Nor' Loch, prior to the
construction of North Bridge which would link the medieval
city with the new residential suburbs. Drummond also
organized a major architectural competition which was won by
James Craig in 1767. The young architect's plans incorporated
squares and gardens into a grid of elegant streets whose names
symbolized the union of the Scottish and English parliaments,
while glorifying George III and the House of Hanover.
George Street, the main thoroughfare, runs
parallel to Queen Street (to the north) and
Princes Street (to the south), and links
two squares named after the patron
saints of Scotland and England:
St Andrew Square (to the east)
and St George Square (to the
west). St George Square was soon
renamed Charlotte Square in honor
of Queen Charlotte, wife of George
III. North Bridge was completed in 1772,
while an artificial hill, the Mound, was
created from the material excavated between

ROYAL SCOTTISH ACADEMY ◆ E C3
(*corner of Princes Street and The Mound*)
The academy – a Doric-style 'Greek temple'
(*below*) built 1822–26 and extended 1831–36 by
William Playfair – houses temporary
exhibitions.

**NATIONAL GALLERY
OF SCOTLAND ◆ E** C3
The National Gallery
of Scotland was
designed in the 1850s
by the architect of the
nearby Royal Scottish
Academy. It houses
one of the finest
collections of
paintings in Great
Britain. Scottish artists
(Ramsay, Raeburn,
Wilkie, Nasmyth,
McTaggart) are well
represented, but
visitors can also
admire works by the
Italian (Raphael,
Titian, Tintoretto,
Lotto, Veronese,
Tiepolo), Dutch
(Rembrandt,
Vermeer, Hals),
Flemish (Rubens, Van
Dyck), German
(Cranach, Holbein),
Spanish (El Greco,
Velázquez, Goya),
English (Hogarth,
Reynolds,
Gainsborough,
Constable, Turner)
and French (Poussin,
Watteau, Corot,
Courbet, Degas,
Renoir, Monet,
Cézanne, Gauguin)
masters.

Princes Street and the Old Town. The New Town, with its elegant, terraced façades and crescents ● *78*, became very fashionable during the 1790s. So much so, in fact, that after 1802 it was extended towards the Firth of Forth. The area, which stretches to Fettes Row in the north, has retained its residential character and classical elegance, especially Great King Street and Royal Circus, designed by William Playfair. Between 1817 and 1860 the New Town spread eastward to Calton Hill (Playfairs's Royal, Calton and Regent Terraces) and westward around Melville Crescent. James Gillespie Graham designed the network of crescents of the Moray Estate, to the north of Charlotte Square, in the 1820s and '30s.

PRINCES STREET AND GARDENS ◆ E A3-D2 This residential street, which marked the southern boundary of the New Town, became a commercial street with the advent of the railway in the 1840s. Although its Georgian façades disappeared behind hotel signs and department-store windows, Princes Street is still one of the most attractive shopping streets in Europe, with its beautiful gardens at the foot of Castle Hill. Usher Hall (a concert hall), Saltire Court (a complex comprising restaurants, offices and the Traverse Theatre which stages modern plays) and the Exchange (a new business and conference center) can be glimpsed above the trees, to the right of the castle.

GEORGE STREET ◆ E A3-C2 This broad avenue (120 feet wide) stretches impressively between Charlotte Square and St Andrew Square. While many of its beautiful houses have been converted into shops, banks and restaurants, the magnificent Assembly Rooms (1787), at no. 54, still fulfil their original function as a place for social gatherings and continue to be used as a venue for various cultural events. The Free Church of Scotland was founded in St Andrew's and St George's Church (1784) in 1843.

ST ANDREW SQUARE ◆ E D2 The square is dominated by a statue of Henry Dundas, the British politician who controlled Scottish politics between 1780 and 1805, and contains a number of long-established banks and insurance companies. The Royal Bank of Scotland, in particular, has occupied the Palladian-style mansion at no. 26 since 1825. The mansion was built by William Chambers in 1771.

**AN EXCEPTIONAL
COLLECTION ✪**
The art treasures in
the National Gallery
of Scotland are
presented in
chronological order,
and every effort is
made to show them to
their best advantage.
For example, the 38
Turner watercolors
in the Vaughan
Collection are only
exhibited in January,
since they are best
seen in winter light.

The Royal Botanic
Gardens are best in
spring when the
azaleas and
rhododendrons are in
flower. It is an ideal
place to escape from
the hustle and bustle
of the city, or to
get a few gardening
tips from the
Demonstration
Garden.

**ALONG THE WATER
OF LEITH**
Footpaths run from
Edinburgh's two
modern art galleries
to the banks of the
Water of Leith, a
coastal river which
flows down from the
Pentland Hills ▲ *131*,
through Edinburgh
and into the Forth
estuary at Leith. The
path that follows the
river from its source
to its mouth passes
through DEAN
VILLAGE, with its
beautiful old houses,
which once had as
many as eleven mills.
It runs beneath the
impressive bridge
built in 1832 by
Thomas Telford, and
past ST BERNARD'S
WELL, a small Doric
temple (1789)
housing a pump that
draws water from a
thermal spring. ANN
STREET, on the far
side of the river, is
one of the most
prestigious in
Edinburgh with its
well-preserved
Georgian houses,
each with its own tiny
front garden (1814).
The section of the
footpath that passes
through Colinton, to
the southwest of
Edinburgh, is also
extremely pleasant.

Dean Village.

SCOTTISH NATIONAL PORTRAIT GALLERY ◆ **E** D1. From its
location at no. 1 QUEEN STREET – named after Queen
Charlotte, wife of George III – the gallery offers unrestricted
views of the Firth of Forth. A generous donation by the then
owner of the Scottish daily, the *Scotsman*, financed the
construction of this huge, Gothic-style building, built in red
sandstone in 1895. Its collections trace the history of Scotland
via portraits of its kings, queens, politicians, writers, poets,
and such stars of theater and cinema as Sean Connery.
CHARLOTTE SQUARE ◆ **E** A2. Charlotte Square, designed by
Robert Adam in 1791 and completed in 1820, is the most
beautiful square in the New Town. Its symmetrical façades
look onto a private garden dominated by an equestrian statue
of Prince Albert. The official residence of the Secretary of
State for Scotland stands on the north side of the square, at
no. 6, while no. 7 houses the GEORGIAN HOUSE museum, an
elegant Georgian residence that has been restored and
furnished in late 18th-century style. Since 1964 St George's
Church, built in 1810–14 by Robert Reid on the west side of
the square, has been occupied by WEST REGISTER HOUSE, an
annex of the Scottish Record Office.

WEST OF NEW TOWN

ROYAL BOTANIC GARDENS *(Inverleith Row, north of the city
center).* The Royal Botanic Gardens created at Holyrood in
1670 was transferred to the present site in 1820. The
collections cover an area of 70 acres and include 34,000 plant
species from all over the world. They are presented in themed
gardens (rockery garden, heather garden, Chinese garden,
arboretum) and glasshouses (alpines, winter garden, cacti and
succulents, palms). Inverleith House, at the center of the
park, houses temporary exhibitions.
SCOTTISH NATIONAL GALLERY OF MODERN ART *(Bedford
Road, northwest of Princes Street).* This modern art gallery,
which occupies an 1820s neoclassical building, gives pride of
place to 20th-century Scottish painters: Peploe, Fergusson,
Cadell. It also presents a general overview of the major
international trends, from the Nabis to Pop Art. Sculptures by
Moore, Epstein and Hepworth are exhibited in the grounds.
DEAN GALLERY. Dean Gallery was opened in 1999, in a former
orphanage opposite the National Gallery of Modern Art. The
gallery has works by Dali, Ernst, Picasso, Miró, Man Ray and
Tanguy, from the collections of Sir Roland Penrose and
Gabrielle Keiller. Visitors can also see the work of the Scottish
sculptor Eduardo Paolozzi and a reconstruction of his studio.

Views of Leith; the *Britannia*.

CALTON HILL ◆ E F1-F2

This volcanic hill at the east end of Waterloo Place (the continuation of Princes Street) offers panoramic views of the city. It is surmounted by the NATIONAL MONUMENT, the 'Scottish Parthenon' designed by William Playfair in 1816, in memory of the victims of the Napoleonic Wars. The monument was never finished due to lack of funds. To the south stands the NELSON MONUMENT (1807), a tower in the form of an inverted telescope, erected in honor of the victorious commander of the Battle of Trafalgar. To the southwest are the OLD OBSERVATORY, designed by James Craig in 1776, and the CITY OBSERVATORY, designed by Playfair in 1818. CALTON OLD BURIAL GROUND has some beautiful classical-style tombs, including that of the philosopher, historian and economist David Hume (1711–76). **ROYAL HIGH SCHOOL** *(Regent Road)*. The school's former pupils include the architect Robert Adam, the writer Walter Scott and Alexander Graham Bell, one of the inventors of the telephone. The building, designed by Thomas Hamilton in 1829, housed the Scottish Parliament for a time but was ultimately considered too small.

LEITH ◆ D C3

For a long time Leith (*above*) was Scotland's busiest commercial port. Although its deprived districts attest to the decline of its maritime trade and shipyards, its old warehouses have been gradually converted into offices and up-market apartments, not to mention the seafood restaurants and fashionable cafés along THE SHORE and other streets near the Water of Leith. ANDREW LAMB'S HOUSE in Burgess Street is named after the rich merchant who welcomed Mary Stuart on her return from France in 1561. It was on LEITH LINKS that the first written rules of golf were laid down in 1774 ● *58*.

THE *BRITANNIA*
The former royal yacht, taken out of commission in 1997, is moored at North Leith where it is open to the public. The yacht, launched from the Clyde shipyards in 1953, sailed over 1 million miles on its 968 official voyages throughout the world.

ROYAL OBSERVATORY
(3 miles south of the city center on the A7) Since 1896 the Royal Observatory has occupied this site on top of Blackford Hill, which offers a magnificent view across Edinburgh and Lothian. Visitors can find out about the history of astronomical observation and see Scotland's largest telescope (3 feet in diameter).

A round Edinburgh the rolling hills and valleys of Lothian offer some pleasant excursions. The Pentland Hills, to the south, and the Lammermuirs, to the southeast, are a hikers', horse-riders' and cyclists' paradise. To the west of the city (West Lothian) the unmistakable outline of the Rail Bridge (1890) across the Firth of Forth dominates the Georgian mansions and medieval castles built along the Forth's southern shore. The shores of East Lothian are famous for their beautiful sandy beaches, bird sanctuaries and golf courses, while the interior is full of villages and castles steeped in history.

View of the road and rail bridges across the Firth of Forth (Queensferry).

HOUSE OF THE BINNS
◆ **D** B3-C3
(*on the A904, 4 miles west of South Queensferry*)
The House of The Binns is named after the twin hills to the east. The original house, which was probably 14th century, was bought in 1612 by the merchant Thomas Dalyell, who built the present house. It was extended in 1630 and crenelated towers were added in the early 19th century. Today it houses a collection of paintings, furniture and porcelain, and has some beautiful 17th-century stucco ceilings.

THE FIRTH OF FORTH, WEST OF EDINBURGH ◆ **D** C3-D3

LAURISTON CASTLE (*Cramond Road South*). The tower-house, built c. 1590 by Sir Archibald Napier (father of the mathematician, John Napier, who invented logarithms), was the birthplace of the Scottish financier John Law (1671–1729). It was extended in the 19th century, then bought in the early 20th century by William Robert Reid, a famous cabinet-maker who put together an attractive collection of engravings, paintings, furniture, tapestry, porcelain and 'Blue John' china (named after a bluish-yellow amethyst mined in Derbyshire).
CRAMOND (*via the A902*). In the 17th and 18th centuries this delightful village on the mouth of the River Almond had a number of small ironworks. Near the church (1656) are the foundations of a fort built by the Romans in AD 142 to defend the harbor ▲ *114*.
DALMENY (*via the A90*). The small Norman church of Saint Cuthbert (12th century) is well worth a visit, in particular for the heads and silhouettes of mythical animals that decorate the Romanesque south door.
SOUTH QUEENSFERRY. This former royal burgh and port lies at the foot of the two huge bridges across the Firth of Forth.

The Napoleon room,
Dalmeny
House.

The ROAD BRIDGE, a toll bridge opened in 1964, replaced the ferry service ('the Queen's ferry') established by Queen Margaret, the pious wife of Malcolm III Canmore (1058–93), for pilgrims traveling to Dunfermline and St Andrews. The CANTILEVER RAIL BRIDGE, built in 1883–90 by Sir John Arthur Fowler, is a fine example of Victorian civil engineering and is still in use today.

In the town's well-preserved main street stands the Hawes Inn, where Robert Louis Stevenson (1850–94) set one of the scenes in his novel *Kidnapped* (1886).

HOPETOUN HOUSE (*2 miles northwest of South Queensferry*). This impressive mansion (*below*) was built for the Earl of Hopetoun, ancestor of the Marquess of Linlithgow. It stands in a vast, formally landscaped park which has two deer herds. The square, classical-style building was built by William Bruce in 1699–1704. It was extended between 1721 and 1754 by William Adam, who built the baroque east façade with its curved colonnade, and his sons, Robert and John, who completed their father's work by adding the main entrance and redecorating the state apartments, including the famous

yellow drawing room. The rooms open to the public contain period furniture, tapestries, Meissen porcelain and paintings by Ramsay, Raeburn, Gainsborough, Titian, Rubens and Canaletto. A roof terrace offers a magnificent view of the park and the Firth of Forth.

BLACKNESS CASTLE (*via the B9109 or B903*). This castle overlooking the Firth of Forth is one of the four main Scottish castles, along with Edinburgh, Stirling and Dumbarton, where the English maintained a garrison after the Act of Union in 1707. The central 15th-century tower-house served in turn as a royal castle, a Covenanters' prison and then a gunpowder store in the 1870s.

LINLITHGOW ◆ D B3

This peaceful town on the shores of a small loch, about 17 miles west of Edinburgh, was the birthplace of James V (1512) and his daughter Mary Stuart (1542). The impressive 16th- and early 17th-century façades on the High Street evoke the former prosperity of this royal burgh chartered by David I. In 1302 Edward I of England built a tower-house here, which David II and his successors incorporated into a royal palace.

DALMENY HOUSE
◆ **D** C3
Since 1662 this estate on the shores of the Firth of Forth has belonged to the Primrose (Rosebery) family. The house was the first to be built (1817) in Scottish neo-Gothic style. The drawing room houses the Mentmore Collection, a collection of 18th-century French tapestries, porcelain and furniture, bequeathed by Baron Mayer de Rothschild, from Mentmore Tower in the English county of Buckinghamshire. The dining room has paintings by Gainsborough, Raeburn, Reynolds and Lawrence, while the former billiard room has furniture and objects that once belonged to Napoleon. The medieval keep of Barnbougle, on the shores of the Firth of Forth, was converted into a library in the 20th century.

HISTORIC LINLITHGOW ★
The Church of St Michael, the ghostly ruins of Linlithgow Palace and the beautiful old houses that border the High Street are an integral part of the charm of this delightful town. In fine weather, a walk beside the loch makes a pleasant end to a visit to the royal palace.

The archeological site of Cairnpapple Hill (*above*); Linlithgow Palace and the Church of St Michael (*right*).

CAIRNPAPPLE HILL ◆ D B3
(*3¾ miles south of Linlithgow, in the Bathgate Hills*)
Five archeological periods have been identified on the site (*above*), used during ritual and funeral ceremonies between 2500 BC and the 1st century AD. Today the site has been reconstructed and the top of the hill offers magnificent views of the surrounding area. Nearby is TORPHICEN PRECEPTORY, historic seat of the Knight's Hospitaler of St John.

SCOTTISH MINING MUSEUM ◆ D C3
The museum has been built around a late 19th-century coal mine near NEWTONGRANGE, a few miles east of Roslin (Rosslyn). Visitors can see the pit head and admire Scotland's largest steam engine. Audio-tapes and interactive exhibitions give visitors an insight into the daily life and working conditions of the miners.

ROSSLYN CHAPEL, A SCULPTURAL GEM ★
Visitors will be amazed by the richness and intricacy of the stone carving in this unique Scottish chapel. Allow at least an hour to take in the atmosphere and elusive detail.

LINLITHGOW PALACE. An impressive gateway, built in c. 1535, opens onto the park that provides the setting for Linlithgow Palace and the Church of St Michael (*above*). In 1424 the palace was devastated by fire and only the walls of the original house (the square southwest tower) were left standing. The reconstruction and embellishment of the residence, begun by James I in 1425, included the construction of the west wing which housed the royal apartments. In the 16th century James IV and James V added the south (the chapel) and east (the 90-foot great hall) wings, architecturally the finest parts of the palace. The palace was abandoned after the Union of the Crowns (1603) and the transfer of the court of James VI to London ● *35*. The north wing, which collapsed in 1607, was rebuilt in 1618–30. Cromwell occupied the palace in the 1650s, and Bonnie Prince Charlie stayed there briefly in 1745, shortly before the troops of the Duke of Cumberland set fire to it and left it in ruins. In the interior courtyard (the Quadrangle) stands the beautiful stone fountain (c. 1530) said to have flowed with wine on the occasion of James V's marriage to Mary of Guise in 1538.

CHURCH OF ST MICHAEL. The church, consecrated in 1242 and rebuilt (1425–1531) in Flamboyant style, is one of the largest churches built in Scotland before the Reformation. The supporters of John Knox stripped it of its statues, while Cromwell's soldiers stabled their horses in it. The original openwork crown of the tower, demolished in 1820 for reasons of safety, was replaced in 1964 by a modern 'crown of thorns' made of aluminum and laminated wood. Of particular note is the finely carved window of the chapel where a ghost is said to have warned James IV of the fatal outcome of the Battle of Flodden ● *35*.

SOUTH OF EDINBURGH ◆ D C3-C4

CRAIGMILLAR CASTLE (*on the A68*). It was in this castle that the Preston family received Mary Queen of Scots after the murder of David Rizzio ▲ *121*, in September 1563. It was here, too, in 1566, that the queen's advisers urged her to divorce her second husband, Lord Darnley. The 14th-century castle was surrounded by an early 15th-century crenelated curtain wall, while the apartments were added in the 16th and 17th centuries. Abandoned in the 1750s, the castle gradually fell into ruins. The great banqueting hall on the second floor still has its beautiful canopied fireplace.

ROSSLYN CHAPEL (*via the A701*). This magnificent 15th-century chapel nestles in the lush valley of the River Esk, near

Rosslyn Chapel (*below*); two of the interior
façades of Crichton Castle (*center and right*).

Roslin (Rosslyn). It is a masterpiece of decorative sculpture
by craftsmen brought from all over Europe by William
Sinclair, 3rd Earl of Orkney. The chapel of St Matthew, in
late Gothic style (1446–86), is in fact the choir of a cruciform
collegiate church that was never finished. Its barrel vaults are
entirely sculpted, while the walls and pillars are decorated
with biblical scenes, and floral and animal motifs. One of the
most remarkable decorative elements is undoubtedly the
'Prentice Pillar' at the east end of the south aisle. According
to tradition an apprentice carved the pillar in his master's
absence. On his return the mason, jealous of the exquisite
handiwork, beat the young man to death with a mallet. The
exterior decoration of the chapel – damaged in 1592 and
1688, and restored in 1862 – is just as lavish and intricate.
Nearby Roslin Castle was built by the Sinclairs in the 14th
century, and rebuilt in the 16th and 17th centuries.

CRICHTON CASTLE (*via Pathhead on the A68*). These
impressive ruins stand on a small hill above the River Tyne.
The original tower-house was built in the 15th century by
William Crichton, chancellor to James II. One hundred years
later it passed to the earls of Bothwell, who transformed it
into an elegant Italianate mansion around a central courtyard.
The remarkable diamond bosses that decorate the interior
façade of the north wing were commissioned (1581–91) by
Francis Hepburn, the 5th Earl of Bothwell. James VI,
outraged by the earl's insolence in displaying such
magnificence, ordered the castle to be destroyed, but the
order was never carried out and Crichton Castle was left to
fall slowly into decline.

THE FIRTH OF FORTH, EAST OF EDINBURGH ◆ D C3-D3

MUSSELBURGH (*on the A199*). This town on the mouth of the
River Esk is renowned for its bird colonies. It also has the
oldest racecourse in Scotland.

PRESTONPANS (*via the B1398*). The town has some well-
preserved 15th–17th century houses and a magnificent
sandstone street cross surmounted by a unicorn. To the east
of the town is the site of the famous Battle of Prestonpans
(September 1745) in which the Jacobites under Bonnie Prince
Charlie defeated the Hanoverian government troops ● 43.
(*Take the A198*)

GULLANE. Gullane lies to the east of Aberlady Bay and its bird
sanctuary (200 recorded species). The town's five golf courses
include the championship course of Muirfield, one of the
venues for the Open ● 59.

PENTLAND HILLS
◆ D C3-C4
(*15½ miles southwest
of Edinburgh*)
The Pentland Hills
rise to a height of
1970 feet and offer
some magnificent
views of Edinburgh,
the surrounding
countryside and the
Firth of Forth, from
Bass Rock in the east
to South Queensferry
in the west. On a
clear day it is even
possible to see the
Trossachs in the
distance. From
FLOTTERSTONE
visitors' center there
is an easy walk to
GLENCORSE
RESERVOIR, while
footpaths from WEST
LINTON, CARLOPS and
NINE MILE BURN
cross some
spectacular
landscapes. There is
a road to the broch
(hill-fort) of
CASTLELAW, and
footpaths and a
chairlift to the top of
the dry-ski slopes of
HILLEND COUNTRY
PARK, from where
there are panoramic
views of the
surrounding
countryside. Walks in
the lower, western
hills include
THREIPMUIR
RESERVOIR, a
bird-watchers'
paradise, and the
delightful village
of SWANSTON, where
the young Robert
Louis Stevenson
● *101* spent family
holidays.

JOHN MUIR COUNTRY PARK ◆ D D3
(*Belhaven Bay, west of Dunbar*)
This nature reserve was founded in honor of Dunbar's famous son, John Muir, a pioneer of the protection of the environment and founding father of the American national parks.

A DRAMATIC CASTLE ★
The ruins of Tantallon Castle occupy a truly magnificent setting. They are best seen in the evening when the castle's impressive red-sandstone walls are set ablaze by the setting sun.

Tantallon Castle and Bass Rock by Alexander Nasmyth (1816).

DIRLETON. Old cottages and trim little gardens make this a truly picturesque village. The CASTLE, built in the early 13th century and demolished by Cromwell's troops in 1660, still has it original massive keep and great hall (15th century). Within its walls are a garden, bowling green and dovecote (17th century).

NORTH BERWICK. This small fishing port and former royal burgh is today a pleasant coastal resort. Near the harbor are the ruins of a 12th-century church, the AULD KIRK, and the newly opened SCOTTISH SEABIRD CENTRE About a mile south of the town center, the hill known as BERWICK LAW (610 feet) offers some magnificent views of the surrounding countryside. It is surmounted by a strange archway made from the jawbone of a whale.

BASS ROCK (*excursions from North Berwick*). A lighthouse and the ruins of a 16th-century chapel stand on this basalt island (350 feet) in the Firth of Forth. Bass Rock is famous for its huge colonies of seabirds, including gannets, puffins, guillemots and fulmars.

TANTALLON CASTLE (*3 miles east of North Berwick*). The ruins of this red-sandstone castle stand on a rocky promontory opposite Bass Rock. It was built in 1375 by the Earl of Douglas and reinforced in the 16th century to withstand artillery attacks. The only landward access was defended by a double moat and a 50-foot rampart wall. It was besieged many times by the English before finally being destroyed by Cromwell's troops in 1651, after 12 days of bombardment.

DUNBAR. The town has had a turbulent history, as evidenced by its ruined castle above the old harbor. This strategic fortress on the road to the South was successfully attacked by Edward I of England in 1295, but valiantly withstood a six-

Chick

Young bird

Adult (winter)

Adult (summer)

week English siege in 1339. Mary Stuart and the Earl of Bothwell sought refuge here after the murder of David Rizzio, in 1566. The castle was demolished on the orders of the Scottish Parliament following the queen's defeat in 1567, and the stones were used by Cromwell to improve the harbor in 1650. The High Street still has several interesting buildings: the 17th-century TOWN HOUSE, the HOUSE (no. 126) where the naturalist JOHN MUIR (1838–1914) was born and which is now a museum dedicated to his life and work, and LAUDERDALE HOUSE, a classical-style mansion built by Robert Adam in the 18th century.

Bass Rock.

INLAND SITES ◆ D C3-D3

EAST LINTON (*on the A1*). Beyond the town are Preston Mill, an attractive 17th-century water-mill that was in working order until 1957, and PHANTASSIE DOOCOT, a Norman dovecote built with 544 nests.

HAILES CASTLE (*2 miles southwest of East Linton*). The castle of the Hepburn family, a fine example of 13th- and 14th-century defensive architecture, was demolished by Cromwell in 1650. James Hepburn, the 4th Earl of Bothwell and third husband of Mary Stuart, stayed here with the queen in 1567.

HADDINGTON (*on the A1*). The regional capital of East Lothian was the birthplace of the Scottish Reformer John Knox (1505). The town was granted a royal charter in 1147 and built its prosperity on a flourishing cloth, wool and cereal trade. In spite of repeated sieges and plundering raids, by the 16th century Haddington was Scotland's fourth largest town and went on to enjoy its golden age in the 18th century. It is an extremely pleasant town to visit, with footpaths along the River Tyne and a great many listed buildings: the colored façades of the HIGH STREET and LODGE STREET (including the home of Jane Welsh, 1801–66, wife of the writer Thomas Carlyle), the TOWN HOUSE (town hall) built in the market place by William Adam in 1748, the 17th-century architecture of MITCHELL'S CLOSE, in Market Street, and the private mansions in COURT STREET. Near the river stands ST MARY'S CHURCH (*right*), dating from the 14th–15th centuries and restored in the 19th and 20th centuries. It has some beautiful stained-glass windows, some of which are based on sketches by the pre-Raphaelite artist Edward Burne-Jones. In the Lauderdale aisle is the tomb of the Maitland family with its beautiful alabaster recumbent statues (17th century).

TRAPRAIN LAW ◆ D C3 (*south of Hailes Castle*)
The remains of an Iron-Age fort stand on top of this volcanic hill. Excavations carried out on the site in 1919 discovered a treasure comprising 160 pieces of 4th-century silver which can today be seen in the Royal Museum of Scotland, in Edinburgh ▲ *123*.

LENNOXLOVE HOUSE ◆ D D3 (*B6369, 1 mile south of Haddington*)
This 14th-century tower-house was built by the Maitlands and is today owned by the Duke of Hamilton. It houses a collection of portraits, French furniture, porcelain and petit-point embroidery from Hamilton Palace, the sumptuous residence of the dukes of Hamilton that was auctioned in 1882 and demolished in 1927. Also on display are the death mask of Mary Stuart and a silver casket, a betrothal gift from François II of France.

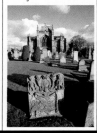

The coastal waters
(*above*) form part of
Scotland's first
marine reserve.

NORTH OF DUNS
◆ D D4
A pleasant drive
through the
countryside north of
Duns leads, via
Preston and the
B6355, to EDIN'S
HALL, one of
Scotland's rare
Lowland brochs (hill-
forts). A few miles to
the northwest are the
ruins of ST BATHANS
ABBEY, a 13th-
century monastery
dedicated to St
Columba's successor
on the island of Iona
▲ 204.

South of the plain of Lothian lie the undulating hills of the
Borders, an essentially agricultural region, irrigated by its
many rivers, that marks Scotland's border with England. Four
great medieval abbeys, a number of museums, impressive
castles and magnificent mansions attest to the turbulent history
of these Scottish marches which were the scene of many battles
from ancient times until the 18th century. Some of the region's
delightful towns have maintained the tradition of the 'Common
Ridings', which reestablishes the collective right to a territory
by riding round it on horseback. This annual event has survived
from the troubled times of the region's history when territory
had to be defended against cattle thieves and invaders. From
the 17th century wool production played a key role in the
region's economy and, in spite of its recent decline, many mills
are still open to the public and sheep continue to be farmed in
the agriculturally prosperous Tweed valley. The river, one of
the longest and most beautiful in Scotland, flows through much
of the region, to the great delight of trout and salmon
fishermen and hikers. Finally, the Borders have a claim to
literary fame as the homeland of the romantic novelist and
poet, Walter Scott (1771–1832) ● 99, and James Hogg
(1770–1835), the 'Ettrick shepherd'.

FROM COCKBURNSPATH TO COLDSTREAM ◆ D D3-D4

COCKBURNSPATH (*on the A1*). Cockburnspath has a 14th-
century church surmounted by a 16th-century round beacon-
tower and a market cross erected in 1503. About a mile to the
northwest the beautiful Dunglass COLLEGIATE CHURCH (15th
century) stands in the Dunglass House estate.
COLDINGHAM (*on the A1107*). The beach of this small resort
is extremely popular with surfers. The village also has the
remains of a 13th-century priory built on the foundations of
a late 11th-century church.
EYEMOUTH. This small resort on the mouth of the River Eye
has been a commercial fishing port since the 12th century. It
has a busy fish market and each year, in June, perpetuates the
fishing tradition by choosing a 'herring queen'. For a long time
the port was also the center of a lucrative trade in contraband
goods: tobacco, wine, alcohol and tea. The EYEMOUTH
MUSEUM, in the Auld Kirk on Market Place, is devoted to
regional traditions and history. It gives pride of place to a

> 'This is where Walter Scott stretches his bones. [...]
> His memory is rightly revered by the Scots;
> Through his works their country was revealed to the world.'
>
> Victor-Antoine Hennequin

tapestry made by local people in 1981 to commemorate the centenary of a tragedy in which 19 fishing boats and 189 men were lost in a storm just off the coast.

AYTON CASTLE (*southwest of Eyemouth, on the A6105*). Guided tours enable visitors to view the beautiful interior of this red-sandstone castle, built in 1846 by James Gillespie Graham.

DUNS. This former county town, with its central market place, is a fine example of the old freetowns of Scotland. The JIM CLARK MEMORIAL ROOM (44 Newton Street) traces the career of the motor racing champion, born in Duns in 1936 and killed in a racing accident in 1968.

MANDERSTON HOUSE (*2 miles east of Duns, on the A6105*). Scotland's most remarkable Edwardian mansion has been painstakingly restored by Lord and Lady Palmer. It was designed in the early 20th century by the architect John Kinross as the country residence of Sir James Miller, a

LADYKIRK ◆ D D4
(*Near Norham, on the B6470*)
The village is centered around the magnificent Gothic church that James IV had built in 1500 as a mark of his gratitude to the Virgin Mary for having escaped drowning as he crossed the Tweed. The upper part of the west tower was rebuilt in 1743 according to a design by William Adam.

baronet who had made his fortune from horse racing. The soberness of the classical façade contrasts with the exuberance of the interior, decorated in the style of Robert Adam and notable for the luxurious materials used – exotic woods, expensive fabrics, precious metals, marble and alabaster. The silver balustrade of the staircase leading to the second floor is a replica of the wrought-iron balustrade in the Petit Trianon at Versailles. The vast estate includes 60 acres of gardens and a number of outbuildings, including a dairy built of marble bricks and a stable block of unrivaled luxury: teak ceilings, teak stalls with copper uprights, tiled drinking troughs and a harness room in rosewood, marble and copper.

COLDSTREAM (*on the A6112*). This small town on the banks of the River Tweed, which forms a natural boundary between Scotland and England, has witnessed the passage of many armies. It was in Coldstream, in 1659, that General Monck raised the regiment – later known as the Coldstream Guards – which marched on London in 1660 and restored Charles II to the throne. The house on Market Square, where the general set up his headquarters, is now the COLDSTREAM MUSEUM. West of the town, the beautiful park of THE HIRSEL, the seat of the Douglas-Home family, is open to the public daily.

PAXTON HOUSE ◆ D D4
(*5 miles west of Berwick, on the B6461*).
This beautiful Palladian mansion was built in 1758 by John and James Adam and the interior designed by their brother Robert at the request of Patrick Home. Today it houses the largest collection of Chippendale furniture in Scotland. In the 1810s John Reid designed the art gallery – whose collection belongs to the National Galleries of Scotland – and the library (4000 volumes) furnished in Regency style by William Trotter.

ROXBURGH ◆ D D4

(*1 mile southwest of Kelso, via the A699*) This royal burgh grew up, together with its 12th-century abbey, around Marchmont Castle. The castle, perched on a small hill between the rivers Tweed and Teviot, was an important link in the defensive chain of the Borders. The town and castle fell to the English in the early 14th century. They were recaptured in 1460 but razed to the ground in reprisal for the death of James II. All that remains of the castle are a few wall sections on a massive earthwork.

SMAILHOLM TOWER ◆ D D4

(*5½ miles west of Kelso, via the B6404*) The best-preserved example of the square towers that defended the Borders in the 16th century. Inside is an exhibition centered on Walter Scott's *Minstrelsy of the Scottish Border*, based on the legends he learned as a child from his grandparents, who owned nearby Sandyknowe Farm.

THE TWEED VALLEY ◆ D D4-C4

KELSO (*on the A698*). With old cobbled streets bordered by elegant 18th-century houses and a French-style *place* dominated by the town hall (1819), Kelso is an extremely picturesque market town. Situated at the confluence of the rivers Tweed and Teviot, the town grew up around the nearby Reformed Benedictine abbey, founded in 1128 by David I near the town and royal castle of Roxburgh. It suffered a number of raids at the hands of the English, the most disastrous of which was led by Edward Seymour, Earl of Hertford in 1544–45, on the order of Henry VIII. The ruins of the Borders' most powerful abbey stand near the five-arched bridge built between 1799 and 1808 by John Rennie. The ABBEY CHURCH was built according to an original plan comprising a narthex, two transepts separated by a short nave and a choir that probably formed an apse. All that can be seen today are the narthex, the first transept and the first two bays of the nave. The tripartite structure, horizontal composition and thick walls with internal passageways attest to the Norman influence on Romanesque architecture. The projecting doorway of the north transept, with its reticulated pediment, is the only one of its kind in Scotland. The small CLOISTER (1933), to the south of the church, houses the tomb of the Ker family (the family name of the Dukes of Roxburghe).

FLOORS CASTLE (*southwest of Kelso, on the A699*). The castle, which stands in a magnificent park overlooking the Tweed, was built in 1721–25 by William Adam for the 1st Duke of Roxburghe. Between 1837 and 1845 it was transformed by William Playfair into a magnificent feudal-style mansion ● 76. It houses a collection of beautiful English, Italian and French furniture, Chinese porcelain, 17th-century Brussels and Gobelin tapestries, and paintings by Raeburn, Hogarth, Hoppner, Gainsborough, Reynolds, Matisse and Bonnard. In the park a holly tree marks the spot where James II was killed by a cannon during the siege of Roxburgh, in 1460.

DRYBURGH. The ruins of Dryburgh Abbey, founded in 1150 by the Constable of Scotland under David I for Premonstratensians from Alnwick, stand above this peaceful town in its wooded setting on the banks of the Tweed. The abbey suffered at the hands of the English on several occasions

Floors Castle (*top left*);
Melrose and Dryburgh abbeys
(*bottom left*);
the Eildon Hills from Scott's View
(*below*).

and was never rebuilt after being destroyed in 1544 by the troops of Henry VIII. The family of Walter Scott owned the abbey lands for a short time in the early 18th century and retained the right to be buried ('stretch their bones') there. Today visitors can still admire the semicircular doorway in the church's west façade (15th century) and the transept (late 12th–13th century) whose north arm contains the tombs of Walter Scott and Earl Haig, the commander of the British forces during World War One. The Romanesque monastic buildings are the best preserved in Scotland. To the east of the ruined cloister are the old vestry, the parlor, the magnificent chapter house, the warming room and the novices' day room (the dormitory occupied the entire floor above these buildings). The refectory lay to the south, above the crypt, while the kitchens, set apart to reduce the risk of fire, would have occupied the southwest corner of the building.

MELROSE ABBEY (*via the A68 and A6091*). Walter Scott's efforts to preserve the ruins of Scotland's first Cistercian abbey made the site a place of literary pilgrimage during the 19th century. The monastery, founded in 1136 by David I for monks from Rievaulx Abbey in Yorkshire, was plundered and destroyed by the troops of Edward II, in 1322, and Richard II, in 1385. It was rebuilt in the late 15th and early 16th century, but was again reduced to ruins during the campaign of terror led by the Earl of Hertford in 1544–45. Today the foundations are all that remain of the monastic buildings. However, the abbey church has some interesting Gothic ruins: the south nave aisle and its eight chapels, the east part of the nave with its stone rood screen separating the central aisle from the monks' choir (which served as a Presbyterian church between 1618 and 1810), the transept and remains of the tower, the main choir (which houses the tomb of Alexander II) and the apse, beneath whose high window the heart of Robert Bruce was said to have been buried. With its windows and finely sculpted pinnacles, niches and statues, the south façade has a remarkable decorative exuberance Today the restored Commendator's House, built in 1590, is occupied by the Abbey Museum with its collections of religious architecture and archeological remains from the Roman camp of Trimontium, built by Agricola ● *32* near Melrose. The abbey is also the departure point for St Cuthbert's Way, a footpath that runs through the Borders for a distance of 56 miles.

MELLERSTAIN HOUSE
◆ **D** D4
(*7 miles northwest of Kelso, via the A6089*)
This vast mansion, built by the Baillie family in the 18th century, has some elegant interiors designed by Robert Adam. The two wings were built by William Adam in 1725, and the central body of the building added in the 1770s by his son Robert, who also designed its magnificent ceilings, friezes and other plasterwork as well as some of the furnishings. The library is a masterpiece, with its wall decorations and delicately colored ceilings with medallions painted by Antonio Zuchi. A collection of paintings includes works by Veronese, Van Dyck, Gainsborough, Ramsay, Aikman and Nasmyth.

ROMANTIC MELROSE
✪
The delightfully exuberant Gothic decoration (15th–16th century) of Scotland's first Cistercian abbey was made famous by Walter Scott. It was ruined by Henry VIII's troops.

SCOTT'S VIEW ◆ **D** D4
(*1½ miles from Dryburgh, on the B6356*)
This viewpoint above the Tweed Valley offers a breathtaking panorama of the Eildon Hills. Walter Scott often came here to contemplate these hills steeped in legend. When his funeral cortège passed the spot, his horses stopped at Scott's View of their own accord.

137

THIRLESTANE CASTLE
◆ **D** D4 (*Lauder*)
In 1672 the Duke of
Lauderdale gave
William Bruce the
task of extending the
castle built in 1590
by his grandfather,
John Maitland,
Lord Chancellor of
Scotland. Further
extensions were
carried out by David
Bryce in 1840. The
castle ● 73 boasts
some magnificent
plasterwork ceilings
in its state apartments
(17th century) and a
collection of early
toys from the
nurseries. In one wing
of the building the
BORDER COUNTRY
LIFE MUSEUM traces
the rural history of
the Borders.

**A BEAUTIFUL
BORDERS MANSION**
★
Traquair House is the
oldest inhabited
mansion in Scotland.
Its long history is
reflected in its decor
and furnishings.

BROUGHTON ◆ **D** C4
Broughton, to the
southwest of Peebles,
has a museum
dedicated to the life
and works of John
Buchan, 1st Lord
Tweedsmuir. Before
becoming Governor
General of Canada in
1935, John Buchan
(1875–1940) wrote
more than 50 novels,
including *The Thirty-
Nine Steps*, which
Alfred Hitchcock
made into a movie in 1939.

ABBOTSFORD (*on the A7060*). Walter Scott devoted the last
twenty years of his life to converting a farm and farmhouse
into a romantic Scots Baronial mansion inspired by the great
monuments of Scotland. The house stands in a magnificent
park and its remarkably well-preserved interiors house some
9000 rare works (*left*), a collection of weapons and many
personal souvenirs. When his publishers went bankrupt in
1826, Scott worked furiously to pay off his debts and keep his
estate. He died, exhausted, on September 21, 1832, in the
dining room overlooking the River Tweed.

GALASHIELS (*on the A7*). For 700 years this town was a
flourishing textile center whose history is traced in OLD GALA
HOUSE (16th century) and the LOCHCARRON CASHMERE WOOL
CENTRE. *The other Border towns with mills open to the public
include Innerleithen, Walkerburn, Selkirk and Hawick.*

TRAQUAIR HOUSE (*south of Innerleithen, on the B709*). This
12th-century royal hunting lodge, fortified in the 13th and
extended in the 16th and 17th centuries, has welcomed a
number of English and Scottish sovereigns, including Mary
Stuart in 1566, and the Young Pretender in 1745. The chapel
in the north wing has a dozen 16th-century paintings on wood,
while the library contains more than 3500 works. The
outbuildings include an 18th-century brewhouse which still
produces excellent ales.

PEEBLES (*on the A72*). This small town nestles between green
hills on the banks of the River Tweed. It is well worth a visit
for the ruins of its 12th-century church (CROSS KIRK) and the
museum housed in the CHAMBERS INSTITUTE, a 17th-century
building given to the town in 1859 by the Lord Provost of
Edinburgh, William Chambers, a native of Peebles. West of
the town stands NEIDPATH CASTLE, built in the 14th and
extended in the 17th century.

JEDBURGH AND SELKIRK ◆ **D** D4-C4

JEDBURGH (*southwest of Kelso, on the A68*). This former royal
burgh, which stands on the River Jed about 10 miles north of
the border between England and Scotland, was attacked many
times by the English. Above the river stand the impressive
ruins of JEDBURGH ABBEY, founded in 1138 by David I for

> 'A slow, clear river winding through short grass
> or between willows and gorse.
> Sheep clustered, white pinheads against the meadow's
> green cushion. Rich, full light.'
>
> Nicolas Bouvier

Augustinian monks from Beauvais. His son Malcolm IV was crowned in the abbey in 1153. Henry VIII's campaign of 'rough wooing' ● *40* left the abbey in ruins in 1544–45, although part of the church was used for Protestant worship between 1560 and 1875. The crossing of the transept and the choir (mid-12th century) are the oldest part of the church. Its elegant west façade, supported by massive buttresses, has an elaborately decorated, projecting porchway, a high semicircular arched window framed by a blind arcade, and a pediment with a huge rose window (late 12th century). Even without a roof, the nave with its nine bays is still impressive, while its three perfectly balanced levels are a fine illustration of the transition between Romanesque and Gothic architecture. The north transept was rebuilt in the 15th century and the square tower above the crossing, in the early 16th century. The foundations are all that remain of the 14th-century monastic buildings that stood on the hillside to the south and below the church. At the top of Castlegate stands CASTLE JAIL MUSEUM, a former prison built (1823) on the site of the castle razed to the ground in 1409 to prevent it falling to the English. Also of interest is MARY QUEEN OF SCOTS' HOUSE, in Queen Street, a late 16th-century house where Mary Stuart spent several weeks, in 1566, recovering from an exhausting ride to Hermitage Castle to visit the wounded Bothwell.

SELKIRK (*via the A68 and A699*). From the 17th to the early 20th century this former royal burgh was a prosperous textile and glass-manufacturing center. In the old Town Hall an audiovisual display traces the life of Walter Scott, who was Selkirk's county sheriff for thirty-three years. Near Market Square, HALLIWELL'S HOUSE MUSEUM AND GALLERY – a former ironmonger's store – houses the museum of local history.

BOWHILL (*3 miles west of Selkirk, on the A708*). The sophisticated decor of this vast 18th-century mansion, refurbished in the 19th century by the Dukes of Buccleuch, provides the perfect setting for beautiful French furniture, exceptional Mortlake tapestries (1670) and a collection of paintings by such world-famous artists as Leonardo da Vinci, Guardi, Canaletto, Ruysdael, Reynolds, Gainsborough and Le Lorrain.

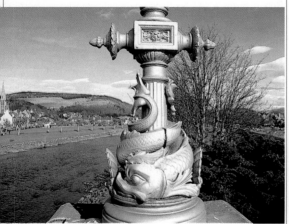

AIKWOOD TOWER ◆ D C4
(*4 miles southwest of Selkirk, on the B7009*)
The legends associated with this small tower were a source of inspiration for Walter Scott and his protégé James Hogg (1770–1835), the 'Ettrick shepherd'. Today the 17th-century tower has been restored and houses an exhibition about Hogg, who was born on a farm in the Ettrick Forest and worked as a shepherd from an early age. With the support of Scott he published his collections of popular songs and elegiac poems, often pervaded by a sense of the supernatural, as was his famous novel *The Private Memoirs and Confessions of a Justified Sinner* (1824).

Peebles and the River Tweed (*left*); Jedburgh Abbey (*above*).

ST MARY'S LOCH ◆ D C4
James Hogg was inspired by the beautiful rolling landscapes of the Yarrow Valley, between Selkirk and St Mary's Loch (on the A708). The poet often met his friends at Tibbie Shiel's Inn on the south shore of the loch, as attested by a nearby monument.

DRUMLANRIG CASTLE ◆ D B5
(18 miles northwest of Dumfries, on the A76) The impressive residence of the Duke of Buccleuch and Queensberry stands on the site of a 15th-century Douglas stronghold. The castle *(above)* was built (1679–91) from local pink sandstone for the 3rd Earl of Queensbury. It houses paintings by Holbein, Rembrandt, Murillo, Ruisdael, Ramsay, Reynolds and Gainsborough, and some beautiful 17th- and 18th-century French furniture. Charles Edward Stuart spent a night in the castle as he retreated from Derby in 1745 ● *43*.

The southwest is often neglected by tourists eager to discover the architectural and cultural heritage of the major Scottish cities, or the wild landscapes of the Highlands and islands. However the region, which lies within the triangle formed by Dumfries to the east, Stranraer to the west and the Firth of Clyde to the north, has a great deal to offer: quiet towns set in undulating landscapes given over to sheep and cattle farming, vast tracts of moorland and dense forests. It also has another major asset: almost 200 miles of indented coastline. To the south the shallow estuary of the Solway Firth, lined by marshes and tidal pools, marks Scotland's border with England while to the west, the shores of the Irish Sea stretch from Stranraer to the mouth of the Clyde, near Glasgow. The southwest has a number of early Christian and medieval remains, and it was here that Robert Bruce launched his campaign for Scottish independence in the 14th century ● *39*. Last but by no means least it is also the land of Robert Burns ▲ *142*, Scotland's national poet who was born near Ayr in 1759 and died in Dumfries in 1796. Many fervent admirers make pilgrimages to the places where Burns lived and worked.

DUMFRIES ◆ D B5

This peaceful market town with its pink-sandstone houses is the capital of Galloway. Founded on the River Nith in 1186, it suffered a number of English invasions during the 15th and 16th centuries. It was here in the Franciscan monastery that Robert Bruce murdered his rival, Sir John Comyn, in 1306, before being crowned at Scone ● *39*. The event is commemorated by a plaque on the wall of GREYFRIARS CHURCH. However, Dumfries' most famous son is Robert Burns, who spent the last five years of his life here.
GLOBE INN. Burns used to spend his evenings drinking with his friends in this dark, smoky pub located in a narrow street off the High Street.

> 'Ambition is a meteor gleam,
> Fame a restless, airy dream;
> Pleasures, insects on the wing
> Round Peace, the tenderest flower of spring [...]'

Robert Burns

BURNS' HOUSE. The poet-farmer spent the last years of his life in this ordinary house (*left*) at the south end of High Street. It has been well preserved and today houses a collection of personal items, letters and original manuscripts by Burns, as well as the famous editions of his works published in Kilmarnock and Edinburgh. The windowpane of his room, on the second floor, still bears a signature that he is said to have inscribed with his diamond ring.

BURNS MAUSOLEUM. Robert Burns was buried in the cemetery of ST MICHAEL'S CHURCH, to the south of his house. In 1815 his remains were transferred to the neoclassical mausoleum overlooking the cemetery. His wife, Jean Armour, and several of their children are also buried there.

ROBERT BURNS HERITAGE CENTRE. This small museum occupies an 18th-century mill on the bank of the River Nith. It traces the life of Burns in Dumfries and at Ellisland Farm.

DUMFRIES MUSEUM. The museum is housed in an 18th-century windmill and its annexes, which stand on a hill above the Robert Burns Heritage Centre. The exhibits in its mineralogical, archeological and historical collections range from early Christian stones to domestic, agricultural and industrial objects from the Victorian age. A CAMERA OBSCURA on the top floor of the museum presents panoramic views of the town and surrounding area.

AROUND DUMFRIES ◆ D B5-B6-E6

GLENKILN RESERVOIR SCULPTURES (*10 miles west of Dumfries, via Terregles*). On the shores of Glenkiln Reservoir a spectacular collection of monumental sculpture includes works by JACOB EPSTEIN, HENRY MOORE and AUGUSTE RODIN.

CAERLAVEROCK CASTLE (*on the B725, southeast of Dumfries*). The ruins of the castle built by the Maxwells on the northern shores of the Solway Firth are still an impressive sight (*below*). The castle, whose construction began c. 1270, was captured by Edward I in 1300 and remained in English hands until 1312. It subsequently changed hands several times before being extended in the 15th and 16th centuries, and was finally abandoned in 1640. An impressive guardhouse and two 'drum' towers mark the corners of the triangular courtyard which was surrounded by a defensive outer wall protected by a double moat. The 1st Earl of Nithsdale built the elegant Renaissance apartments overlooking the courtyard in 1621, before the castle was sacked in 1634 by the Covenanters.

ELLISLAND FARM ◆ D B5
(*6 miles northwest of Dumfries, via the A76*) Robert Burns rented this farm in June 1788 to meet the demands of his growing family. He tried to introduce new farming methods, but the land was poor and caused him great anxiety. In 1791 he gave up farming, with great relief, and moved to Dumfries where he became an Excise officer. He died there five years later. Personal items, letters and original manuscripts are exhibited in the farmhouse where the poet wrote *Tam o' Shanter*.

A CASTLE OF GREAT CHARM ★
Its hilltop setting, water-filled moats, unusual triangular layout and beautiful Renaissance carving give the ruins of Caerlaverock Castle their very individual charm.

CAERLAVEROCK WILDFOWL AND WETLANDS CENTRE ◆ D B6
Each year, some 12,000 geese from Spitzberg over-winter in this 1900-acre bird sanctuary, 3 miles from Caerlaverock Castle on the shores of the Solway Firth. Other species such as ducks (pintails and sheldrakes) and oyster-catchers also feed in the tidal reservoirs. Huts, towers and specially designed footpaths allow bird-watchers to study the birds without disturbing them.

ROBERT BURNS

AULD LANG SYNE
('old times' or 'times past')
'We'll tak a cup o' kindness yet
For auld lang syne'

Robert Burns (1759–96), the national poet of Scotland, has a cult following in his own country. The poet-farmer describes nature and the everyday life of ordinary people with loving simplicity, sometimes in English and sometimes in the Scottish dialect of his native Carrick. He was a staunch champion of Scottish folklore and also wrote a great many songs, which were sung and hummed throughout Scotland. One of the best known is *Auld Lang Syne*, sung on New Year's Eve throughout the English-speaking world.

THE POET-FARMER
As a young man, this farmer's son from Alloway ▲ *148* divided his time between working on the land and writing poetry. The meager living earned from farming placed him in financial straits from which he never really recovered and persuaded him to publish his first collection of poems – *Poems, Chiefly in the Scottish Dialect* – in 1786. The work was an immediate success and new editions were published in 1787 and 1793. Burns was acclaimed the national poet of Scotland and admitted into Edinburgh's high society. In 1788 he rented Ellisland Farm ▲ *141*, where he wrote over 160 songs and composed his last great poem, *Tam o' Shanter*, in 1790. A weak heart forced him to take a clerical post in Dumfries ▲ *140* where he died prematurely five years later after writing 115 more songs for a *Select Collection of Original Scottish Airs*.

THE SCOTTISH POET
Burns inherited the long-standing Scottish tradition revived in the 18th century by Allan Ramsay and Robert Fergusson. In his poems, written in English or the Scottish dialect ● *48*, he reintroduced old forms from France, Provence and Italy imported by the court of Mary Stuart.

THE PHILANDERER
After years of philandering Burns finally married and settled down with Jean Armour (1767–1834), who bore him nine children. However, he continued his amorous encounters with working girls while simultaneously seeking the company of society women.

BURNS

BURNS' NIGHT

If there is one night of the year when haggis is certain to be eaten, it is January 25, Robert Burns' birthday. The feasting is interspersed with poetry readings which include *To a Haggis*, an ode to Scotland's national dish. The third verse of this poem is read as the 'Great Chieftain o' the Puddin-race' is cut:
'His knife see rustic-Labour dight,
An' cut ye up wi' ready slight,
Trenching your gushing entrails bright
Like onie ditch;
And then, O what a glorious sight,
Warm-reekin, rich!'

TAM O' SHANTER (1790)

On market-night Tam of Shanter Farm went drinking with his friend, Souter Johnny. When he left the inn, night had fallen and a storm was raging. As he passed 'Alloway's auld, haunted kirk' Tam saw an incredible sight: 'Warlocks and witches in a dance' as 'Auld Nick' (the Devil) looked on. With this 'hellish legion' in hot pursuit, Tam only just managed to escape by crossing the River Doon but his mare, Meg, lost her tail. 'Remember Tam o' Shanter's meare' was a warning to any farmer who might be tempted to linger in the tavern.

THE POET OF THE ENLIGHTENMENT

Burns was a Scottish patriot, Freemason and a brilliant satirist who pilloried Puritanism. He was also an apostle of the Enlightenment, a true patriot and a champion of universal rights. His political ideals (including support for the French Revolution) made him a number of enemies.

THE PEOPLE'S POET

Born into a farming family and himself a farmer, Burns painted a detailed portrait of rural life. In his poems there was no trace of the picturesque, of the conventional arcadian image or of burning lyricism. He simply described the world he knew with moving simplicity and humanity.

RUTHWELL (*on the B725*). In 1810 Henry Duncan, minister of Ruthwell (1799–1843), founded the first Savings Bank in the village. The parish church houses the remarkable Ruthwell Cross (*left*), dating from the 8th century. The 17-foot cross, which originally stood on the shores of the Solway Firth, was demolished by the Covenanters in 1642 and restored in the 19th century. The runic motifs carved on the base are inspired by one of the first works written in Old English: *The Dream of the Rood* (c. 700). Biblical scenes illustrating Christ's life and Passion are carved on each side.

THE SHORES OF THE SOLWAY FIRTH ◆ D B6

The rocky shores of the Solway Firth are lined by saltwater marshes and tidal pools that make access to the sea difficult. Even so, a number of coastal sites and villages are well worth a visit.

NEW ABBEY (*on the A710, south of Dumfries*). To the north of the village stands SHAMBELLIE HOUSE, a 'feudal' manor built in 1850 by David Bryce. Its Victorian and Edwardian interior houses a collection of costumes dating from the late 18th to the early 20th century. Also worth a visit is NEW ABBEY CORN MILL, an 18th-century mill in perfect working order. However New Abbey is above all famous for the ruins of SWEETHEART ABBEY (*above*), a Cistercian monastery founded in 1273 by Lady Devorguilla Balliol in memory of her husband, John Balliol, who died in 1269. His inconsolable widow never went anywhere without the reliquary containing her husband's embalmed heart. When she was buried, along with the casket, in front of the high altar in the abbey church in 1290, the monks renamed the abbey *Dulce Cor* ('sweet heart').

ROCKCLIFFE AND KIPPFORD. These two picturesque holiday villages are linked by the JUBILEE PATH, which runs along the slopes of Colvend and past MOTE OF MARK, an earthwork fort built by the Celts in the 5th century. At low tide it is possible to reach ROUGH ISLAND and its bird sanctuary via the Rockcliffe tidal pools or the causeway from Kippford.

DALBEATTIE (*via the A710 or A711*). This small inland town is famous for its gray granite, which was exported throughout the world in the 19th century. It was used, among other things, to build the Bank of England in London and the port of Valletta in Malta. About 2½ miles north of Dalbeattie stands MOTE OF URR, an earthwork fort built by the Normans in the 12th century.

GRETNA GREEN ◆ D C6
In the 18th century this village on the English–Scottish border specialized in elopements, since at the time, the law was more liberal in Scotland than in England. Until 1940 many of these marriages were held in the OLD SMITHY, now a museum. Some couples still choose to take their marriage vows in this romantic Scottish village.

DUNDRENNAN ABBEY ◆ D B6
(*6 miles southwest of Kirkcudbright, on the A711*)
The mother-house of Sweetheart Abbey was founded (1142) for the Cistercian order by David I or Fergus, Lord of Galloway. The early Gothic ruins of the 12th-century church and 13th-century chapter house can still be seen today.

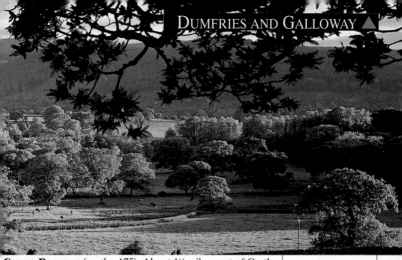

CASTLE DOUGLAS (*on the A75*). About 1¼ miles west of Castle Douglas, founded in 1791 by the merchant William Gordon, lies THREAVE GARDEN. The estate comprises just under 120 acres of woodland and a 60-acre park where 200 varieties of daffodils flower in spring. The ruins of THREAVE CASTLE, the seat of the powerful Black Douglas clan in the 14th and 15th centuries, stand on a grassy island in the River Dee. All that remains of the stronghold, dismantled in 1640, is the impressive 14th-century tower and one of the angle towers that supported the ramparts.

KIRKCUDBRIGHT (pronounced 'kirk-cou-bri'). This delightful former royal burgh on the banks of the River Dee (*bottom left*) has some beautiful old houses and a picturesque harbor. The harbor is dominated, from the end of High Street, by the ruins of MACLELLAN'S CASTLE, a turreted mansion built in 1582 by the provost Thomas Maclellan. A number of famous artists lived and worked in this street in the late 19th and early 20th centuries. For example, the landscape artist Edward Hornel ● *90* occupied BROUGHTON HOUSE (*bottom right*) between 1901 and 1933. Today the 18th-century mansion houses a collection of his works, a vast library of Scottish books and manuscripts and has a Japanese garden. The old TOLBOOTH (1629), now a museum, traces the history of this artists' colony and displays paintings by Hornel and his friends, while the first-floor studios are leased to local artists. The STEWARTRY MUSEUM, in St Mary Street, traces the natural and social history of east Galloway – the last Scottish region still administered by a steward (the Duke of Rothesay) – and the history of the Solway coast.

GATEHOUSE OF FLEET (*via the A75 and A755*). This small town, founded in 1760, is a fine example of urban planning. For a long time it lived by its shipyards and cotton mills before turning to tourism and forestry. The MILL ON THE FLEET visitor center occupies an old water mill.

GALLOWAY FOREST PARK ◆ D A5-B5
The small commercial town of NEWTON STEWART, on the banks of the River Cree, makes an ideal base for visiting this forest park (160,500 acres) in the heart of the Southern Uplands. The park has a wide range of wildlife and is ideal for open-air activities. One of the marked footpaths that leave from GLENTROOL (12½ miles north of Newton Stewart, near Bargrennan) climbs to the top of the MERRICK (2765 feet), the park's highest point. QUEEN'S WAY (A712) winds across the southern part of the park between Newton Stewart and NEW GALLOWAY. En route it passes the GLEN OF THE BAR viewpoint which overlooks a Bronze-Age archeological site and the information center (Galloway Deer Museum) of CLATTERINGSHAWS LOCH. Just beyond the dam is RAIDER'S ROAD, an old track once used by cattle thieves, which follows the River Dee for 10 miles. At this point the park is also crossed by the SOUTHERN UPLAND WAY ▲ *112*.

WIGTOWN ◆ D A6
(on the A714, 7 miles south of Newton Stewart)
This former royal burgh on Wigtown Bay is Scotland's 'National Book Town' and hosts an annual book festival. Below the town the Martyrs' Stake commemorates the Wigtown martyrs, Margaret McLachlan (aged 62) and Margaret Wilson (aged 18), two Covenanters who, in 1685, were tied to a stake in the estuary and left to drown in the rising tide.

CASTLE KENNEDY GARDENS ◆ D A6
(5 miles east of Stranraer via the A75)
The grounds of Lochinch Castle include the ruins of Castle Kennedy and its 75-acre gardens on the isthmus between the White and Black Lochs. The gardens *(below)*, designed by William Adam for the Earls of Stair in the 18th century, were restored in 1847. Rhododendrons, azaleas, magnolias and monkey-puzzle trees are very much in evidence.

THE MACHARS PENINSULA ◆ D A6

This austere, windswept peninsula to the south of Newton Stewart boasts the oldest church in Scotland.

WHITHORN *(via the A714 and A746).* It was here that St Ninian (c. 360–432), who converted the Picts and Britons to Christianity ● *33*, founded the first Christian mission in Scotland, in 397. Whithorn remained a bishopric of the Celtic and then the Northumbrian church until the Viking invasions, while the saint's tomb continued to be a place of pilgrimage until the 16th century. The PRIORY built on the ruins of the first church by Fergus, Lord of Galloway, c. 1125, was occupied by Premonstratensian monks up to the Reformation. All that remains today are the nave, two chapels and the crypt of the medieval foundations. A nearby visitor center presents artefacts discovered and models of the different phases of occupation since the 5th century. The MUSEUM, in the main street, houses a remarkable collection of early Christian crosses and stones, including the Latinus Stone (c. 450), the earliest Christian memorial in Scotland.

ISLE OF WHITHORN *(on the B7004).* This little port about 3¾ miles south of Whithorn is a popular shark-fishing center. It is also the site of the ruins of ST NINIAN'S CHAPEL (13th century) and ST NINIAN'S CAVE which was a place of pilgrimage until the 11th century.

GLENLUCE ABBEY *(about 1¾ miles north of Glenluce, 18 ½ miles northwest of Whithorn).* The foundations are all that remain of the church of the Cistercian abbey founded by Roland, Earl of Galloway, in 1192. However the magnificent 15th-century chapter house is almost intact. According to legend the alchemist Michael Scot ▲ *113* (the Wizard) imprisoned the plague in one of the abbey's vaults!

THE RHINNS OF GALLOWAY ◆ C C6 D A6

This hammer-head peninsula (rhinns in Gaelic) is warmed by the waters of the Gulf Stream and has an exceptionally mild microclimate that is particularly favorable to agriculture. STRANRAER, the region's main commercial center and ferry

TURNBERRY (*A77, north of Girvan*)
The luxury TURNBERRY HOTEL stands on the
edge of the famous golf links ● *59 (below)*. It
overlooks the lighthouse which stands amidst
the ruins of the CASTLE where Robert Bruce
is said to have been born in July 1272.

port for Northern Ireland, lies at the southern end of Loch
Ryan, on the east coast. The coast road running round the
peninsula passes through such delightful little ports as PORT
WILLIAM, GARLIESTON and DRUMMORE, Scotland's
southernmost town.

PORTPATRICK (*on the A77, on the west coast of the peninsula*).
According to legend this was where St Patrick, the patron
saint of Ireland, set foot when he crossed the Irish Sea in a
single stride. This small resort with its pastel-colored houses
(*below*) was the main ferry port for Ireland before the advent
of steam ships in the 19th century. Portpatrick lies at the
western end of the Southern Upland Way.

KIRKMADRINE CHURCH (*southwest of Sandhead, on the
B7042*). The porch of this old chapel houses the Kirkmadrine
Stones, three of the earliest Christian memorials in Britain
(5th–6th century).

LOGAN BOTANIC GARDEN (*near Port Logan, on the southwest
coast*). A magnificent collection of palms, tree ferns and other
subtropical plants flourishes in this annex of Edinburgh's
Royal Botanic Gardens ▲ *126* which enjoys the influence of
the Gulf Stream.

SOUTH AYRSHIRE ◆ **D** A4-A5

From Stranraer the A77 follows the coast into Ayrshire.
GIRVAN. In summer there are boat trips from this fishing port
and resort to AILSA CRAIG, a volcanic island (1,114 feet high)
that lies midway between Belfast and Glasgow. This granite
island, whose Gaelic name means 'Fairy Rock', is today a bird
sanctuary which provides refuge for huge colonies of seabirds.
CULZEAN CASTLE AND COUNTRY PARK (*A719*). This castle,
which dominates the Ayrshire coast, is an architectural
masterpiece by Robert Adam. David Kennedy, the 10th Earl
of Cassillis, commissioned the most famous architect of the
day to transform the ancestral tower-house into an elegant
castellated mansion. The work lasted from 1777 to 1792. Two
major features of the castle are the OVAL STAIRCASE and the
ROUND DRAWING ROOM, which was entirely furnished by
Adam and whose colors blend harmoniously with the
seascape framed by the French windows. The castle also
houses collections of 18th- and 19th-century weapons,

MULL OF GALLOWAY
◆ **D** A6
This arid cape to the
south of Drummore
is Scotland's
southernmost point.
There is something
eerie about it, with
strong tides creating
huge waves offshore
and, even on calm
and sunny summer
days, the breakers
come crashing onto
the foot of the cliffs.
An austere white
lighthouse has stood
on the 'mull' since
1830

KIRKOSWALD ◆ **D** A5
(*on the A77, northeast
of Turnberry*)
In the village where
Robert Burns went to
school is the cottage
of John Davidson, the
poet's friend and
drinking companion
who provided the
model for Souter
(cobbler) Johnny in
Tam o' Shanter.
Today SOUTER
JOHNNY'S COTTAGE is
a museum, while in
the garden, life-size
statues of Tam,
Souter Johnny, the
innkeeper and his
wife stand drinking
and talking, just as
they do in this very
realistic poem.

Culzean Castle from the walled garden; the Oval Staircase and the orangery.

CULZEAN CASTLE ★
Culzean (pronounced 'cou-lane') is the finest castle in southwest Scotland. It is well worth a visit for its exceptional site overlooking the sea, its famous Oval Staircase and its country park.

CROSSRAGUEL ABBEY ◆ D A5
(*on the A77, northeast of Kirkoswald*)
The monastery was founded in 1244 by Duncan, Earl of Carrick, for Cluniac monks who occupied it until 1592. It was largely rebuilt after the Scottish wars of independence. Today its extensive ruins include the choir of the church with its triple apse, an elegant chapter house and a fortified guard room (15th century), and a 16th-century tower house. The abbey's name is derived from the cross of Riaghail (an Irish saint sometimes associated with St Rule) which once stood on the site.

The cottage in Alloway where Robert Burns was born.

furniture, tapestries, silverware, porcelain and paintings in a suite of rooms elegantly decorated by Adam. When he gave the castle to the National Trust for Scotland in 1945, the 5th Marquess of Ailsa requested that General Eisenhower (1890–1969), supreme commander of the Allied forces in western Europe during World War II, be presented with an apartment for use during his lifetime. The American statesman paid several visits to the castle, which today houses an EISENHOWER PRESENTATION. The 560-acre park includes, in particular, a walled garden, an orangery, a small lake and a deer park. On a clear day the terrace overlooking the garden offers a magnificent view of the Isle of Arran, the Mull of Kintyre, Ailsa Craig and even the Irish coast.

ELECTRIC BRAE (*on the A719, between Culzean and Dunure*). Electric Brae or CROY BRAE is famous for an amazing optical illusion: the road seems to go down when it is in fact climbing. An information board on the parking area explains how best to observe this phenomenon.

ALLOWAY (*on the B7124*). The village where Robert Burns was born is entirely devoted to his memory. Several buildings and museums form the BURNS NATIONAL HERITAGE PARK, with BURNS COTTAGE AND MUSEUM occupying pride of place. The thatched cottage was built by William Burns in 1757 and his son Robert was born there January 25, 1759. William Burns and his wife Agnes Broun are buried in the cemetery of the AULD KIRK, where Tam o' Shanter saw the 'warlocks and witches in a dance'. The BURNS MONUMENT, a neoclassical temple dedicated to the poet's memory (1823), stands in a nearby garden. Editions of his works in various languages can be seen on the first floor, while the second offers an attractive view of the garden and, beyond, of the famous BRIG O'DOON, the 13th-century bridge over which Tam o' Shanter made his escape from the witches ▲ *143*. The LAND o' BURNS CENTER has an exhibition on the life and works of Burns, the town of Ayr in the 18th century and scenes from *Tam o' Shanter.*

AYR. Its beautiful sandy beaches have made Ayr – a former royal burgh and busy port until the 18th century – the leading resort on the Firth of Clyde. Robert Burns is also very much in evidence and the town is popular with visitors throughout the year. Burns immortalized the AULD BRIG, a 15th-century cobbled bridge across the River Ayr, and was christened in the AULD KIRK, built in 1650 and dedicated since 1957 to the memory of those killed in the two world wars. Also on the High Street, visitors can stop for a drink at the TAM O' SHANTER INN, from where Burns's hero Tam set off on his famous ride home. WALLACE TOWER, near the inn, was built in 1828 on the site of a tower from which William

Wallace (c. 1270–1305), the champion of Scottish
independence, escaped after being imprisoned by the English.
MAUCHLINE (*on the B743, northwest of Ayr*). It was in this
village that Robert Burns married Jean Armour in 1788. He
rented a room for his wife and their children in a house in
Castle Street, which is today the BURNS HOUSE MUSEUM.
The nearby pub, POOSIE NANSIE'S TAVERN, provided the
inspiration for part of *The Jolly Beggars*.

NORTH AYRSHIRE ◆ D A4

Not so long ago the inhabitants of Glasgow used to spend
their summer holidays in the small towns and villages north
of Ayr, on the coast of the Firth of Clyde. Today SALTCOATS,
ARDROSSAN and Largs are popular weekend destinations.
Ferries link these ports with the islands of Arran ▲ *200* and
Great Cumbrae in the Firth of Clyde.
LARGS (*on the A78*). Largs is undoubtedly the most attractive
family seaside resort on the Firth of Clyde. It is also the
principal ferry port for Great Cumbrae Island where, in
1263, Alexander III routed the fleet of King Hakon of
Norway ● *34*. The VIKINGAR CENTRE, on the seafront,
commemorates the battle that resulted in the Vikings of
Norway ceding the Hebrides to Scotland. In the old cemetery,
just off the High Street, SKELMORLIE AISLE, originally the
north transept of the parish church, was converted into a
mausoleum by Sir Robert Montgomerie of Skelmorlie in
1623. Beneath a richly decorated barrel-vault, his tomb ● *71*
is decorated with beautifully carved details, including his coat
of arms and various motifs symbolizing death (skull, winged
hour-glass, inverted torch). Finally the NARDINIS restaurant
and ice-cream parlor (1890) is an absolute must: a
quintessential Scottish seaside café with a superb Art
Deco setting.

IRVINE ◆ D A4
(*via the A77 and A78*)
This former royal
burgh became a 'new
town' in 1966 and is
today an industrial
center. In the
SCOTTISH MARITIME
MUSEUM several
exhibition rooms and
a collection of boats –
including the *Carrick*,
the oldest clipper in
the world – present
an attractive overview
of Scotland's
maritime history.

**GREAT CUMBRAE
ISLAND ◆ D** A4
From Largs it is only
a short boat trip to
the resort of
MILLPORT, which
stands on a delightful
bay at the south end
of Great Cumbrae
Island. Millport has
the smallest cathedral
in Britain, the
CATHEDRAL OF THE
ISLES, consecrated in
1851. A trip round
the island (11 miles)
by car or bicycle
offers spectacular
views of the islands of
Arran and Bute, and
the Ayrshire coast.

Portrait of the tobacco merchant John Glasford and his family, by Archibald McLauchlin (c. 1767).

With some 740,000 inhabitants Glasgow is Scotland's most densely populated city. For centuries it has had to compete with the city of Edinburgh, in the east, the capital of Scotland and the seat of the recently restored Scottish Parliament. The city has made the most of its cultural resources and architectural eclecticism – including an outstanding Victorian heritage – and established itself as a leading center of the arts. These valuable assets have in no way been spoilt by its recent and spectacular economic revival. Freed from its reputation of a city in crisis – despite a poor health record – Glasgow has become one of the most dynamic economic and cultural centers in Britain.

HISTORY

GREEN GLEN. Glasgow's name is derived from the Gaelic *Glas Ghu* ('Green Glen'). Its origins date from the 6th century when the abbot Kentigern (St Mungo) built a monastery on a hill blessed by St Ninian in 397, near a fishing village on the River Clyde. The town was granted a charter in 1175 and grew up around the cathedral ▲ *155* and the university founded in 1451, the second in Scotland after St Andrews ▲ *176*. Its status as a royal burgh, granted in 1459, favored the development of trade with London and Rotterdam.

THE TOBACCO LORDS. In 1707 the Act of Union enabled Scotland to develop its trade with the English colonies in America and the West Indies. Glasgow soon became the leading port that imported tobacco from the New World. It was described by Daniel Defoe (1660–1731) as 'the cleanest and beautifullest, and best built city in Britain, London excepted'. Today many of the buildings in Merchant City still

attest to the power of the the 'Tobacco Lords' who
dominated the life of the district throughout the
18th century. Although the War of American
Independence (1775–82) sounded the death knell of
the tobacco trade, these powerful merchants had
already managed to diversify by importing other
luxury products (cotton, sugar, tea) and moving into
the banking sector.

THE CRADLE OF THE INDUSTRIAL REVOLUTION. The
Industrial Revolution could be said to have begun in
Glasgow one Sunday in 1764, when an engineer named James
Watt (1736–1819) realized how to perfect the steam engine
during a walk on Glasgow Green ▲ 154. This invention ● 44,
combined with the discovery of coal deposits in the region,
enabled the city, which already had a flourishing cotton
industry, to become one of Britain's leading centers of
heavy industry (coal, iron and steel) and shipbuilding.
The city's population, increased by the influx of Highlanders
and Irish driven from their lands by poverty and famine,
increased from 77,000 in 1801 to almost 800,000 in 1900.
As the wealthy classes moved into the West End ▲ 157, the
working classes crowded alongside the river in squalid
ghettoes with the highest mortality rate in Europe.

THE SECOND LARGEST CITY IN THE BRITISH EMPIRE. In the
early 20th century Glasgow was producing sewing machines,
printing presses and luxury liners, and its steam engines
were being exported to India, Africa and South America.
The International Exhibitions held in Glasgow in 1888
and 1901 provided an international showcase for the
city's industrial power. Glasgow enjoyed the position of
'second largest city in the British Empire' until the trade
unions made it the bastion of Scottish socialism in the
1920s ● 37.

A SUCCESSFUL ECONOMIC REVIVAL. The depression of 1929
marked the beginning of a long period of decline for the
mining and shipbuilding industries. The decline continued
until comparatively recently, in spite of increased demand
during World War Two and the discovery of North Sea oil
in the late 1970s, and its economy was badly hit by the
closure of most of its shipyards and mines in the 1970s
and '80s. However, in the last decade it has managed to
diversify by turning to the latest technology, exchanging
the image of a city undermined by unemployment and
violence for that of a dynamic, up-to-date metropolis.
Nominated the European City of Culture in 1990 and
the Capital of Architecture and Design for the United
Kingdom in 1999, Glasgow is now highly recommended
on any tourist itinerary.

**FOOTBALL
AND RELIGION**
As in many other
cities football in
Glasgow is a positive
cult. The city has two
major clubs: Rangers
and Celtic. These
long-established
teams, referred to
jointly as the 'Old
Firm', are traditional
rivals and matches
sometimes give rise
to violent exchanges
both on and off
the pitch. This
antagonism is in fact
the result of the
traditional
sectarianism between
Protestants, who
support Rangers,
and Catholics, who
support Celtic.

The two faces of
Glasgow: an 18th-
century façade (*left*)
and Strathclyde
University's Blair
Hall (*right*).

THE LIGHTHOUSE
◆ F C3
(Mitchell Street, parallel to Buchanan Street)
The Scottish Centre for Architecture, Design and the City occupies the stone building designed in 1895 by Charles Rennie Mackintosh ● *84* ▲ *162* for the offices of the *Glasgow Herald*. The interior was entirely redesigned by the architects Page and Park as a showcase for the Year of Architecture and Design (1999). Temporary exhibitions highlight various aspects of modern architectural design and present the different facets of local architecture.

The main staircase of Glasgow City Chambers (*right*).

Flags on George Square.

THE CITY CENTER ◆ F D3

The city center stands on a series of small hills on the north bank of the River Clyde. Apart from the obvious difference in size, the grid layout of its streets is similar to that of New York. It has a great many Victorian monuments, museums and art galleries centered on George Square. To the east of the square lies the redeveloped commercial district of Merchant City and the East End. To the west the city's main shopping streets climb towards the terraced houses of the wealthy residential district of Blythswood Hill.

GEORGE SQUARE. The square, dedicated to George III, was built in 1781. Originally a residential square, it was surrounded by hotels with the advent of the railway before becoming the center of Merchant City c. 1850 and then the administrative center of the Victorian era. The statues of well-known celebrities that line the esplanade are dominated by an 80-foot column surmounted by a statue of Walter Scott. At the northwest corner of the square a gilded merchant vessel adorns the Italianate facade of MERCHANTS' HOUSE, built by John James Burnet in 1874 and today occupied by the Glasgow Chamber of Commerce. On the south side of the square the TOURIST INFORMATION CENTRE (no. 11) occupies the former General Post Office building (1876). The entire east side of George Square is taken up by the impressive GLASGOW CITY CHAMBERS, designed by William Young and opened in 1888 by Queen Victoria. Beyond the grandiose neoclassical façade lie magnificent interiors in Italian-Renaissance style, with majestic marble staircases and vaulted ceilings decorated with gold leaf (guided tours).

> 'Glasgow is, indeed, a very fine city; the four principal streets are the fairest for breadth, and the finest built that I have ever seen in one city together.'
>
> Daniel Defoe

MERCHANT CITY ◆ F D3-D4

After a long period of neglect this district near Central Station was the subject of an extensive redevelopment program. The warehouses and 18th-century merchants' houses were renovated to provide residential and commercial accommodation. Many of the street names, such as Jamaica Street and Virginia Street, evoke the golden age of trade with the British colonies, or pay tribute to famous merchants.

GALLERY OF MODERN ART *(Royal Exchange Square)*. Since 1996 this rich collection of modern art has been housed in a magnificent mansion built in 1780 for the tobacco lord William Cunninghame. The neoclassical building was extended in 1827 by David Hamilton, who added an impressive Corinthian portico and a dome. It subsequently became the Royal Exchange bank and then the central lending library. Four themed galleries – Fire (basement), Earth (main gallery), Water (second floor) and Air (terrace) – present works by Scottish artists such as Peter Howson, Stephen Campbell and Ken Curry, and foreign artists such as Niki de Saint Phalle, Andy Warhol and Eduard Bersudsky.

HUTCHESONS' HALL *(158 Ingram Street)*. Today a slender white tower marks the office of the National Trust for Scotland. This former business center was built (1802–1805) by David Hamilton on the site of a hospice founded in 1639–41 by the Hutcheson brothers. All that remains of the original building are the statues of the two philanthropists that decorate the façade. The elegant interior was designed by John Baird II (1876).

TRADES HOUSE *(Glassford St)*. This former charitable institution, built by Robert Adam in 1791, is worth visiting for the Venetian windows and Ionic columns of the façade.

TRON STEEPLE *(Trongate)*. This solid, square tower was added to St Mary's Church in 1631. The 15th-century church was accidentally burned down by members of the Hell Fire Club after an evening's drinking, in 1793. It was replaced by a building designed by John Adam and is today occupied by the Tron Theatre.

GLASGOW CROSS *(east end of Trongate)*. This crossroads with its market cross (1929), a replica of the original, lies to the east of Merchant City. It was the heart of the medieval city and remained the nerve center until the end of the Victorian age. Tolbooth Steeple is all that remains of the 17th-century building that served as a town hall, prison and law court. In front stood the public weighbridge *(tron)* that determined the amount of tax to be paid on merchandise entering the city.

MODERN ART AND CLASSICAL ARCHITECTURE ★
The Gallery of Modern Art is well worth visiting for its continually expanding collection of modern art and its magnificent 18th-century architecture. The top-floor café, which has a fresco by the modern Glaswegian artist Adrian Wisniewski, offers a beautiful panoramic view of the city.

HORSE SHOE BAR ◆ F C3
(17–19 Drury Sreet)
The Horse Shoe Bar is a fine example of a late-Victorian pub. Its monumental horse-shoe bar is featured in the *Guinness Book of Records* as the longest bar in the United Kingdom. It has an extremely elaborate decor – Corinthian capitals, mirrors, mosaics, stained-glass windows and two great clocks – although the focal point is obviously the 'horse shoe'.

Trongate in 1826.

NECROPOLIS
◆ F F2-F3
Although the cemetery behind Glasgow Cathedral is as old as the church, it was redesigned in the 1830s along the lines of the Père-Lachaise cemetery in Paris. It contains a profusion of abandoned tombs and neoclassical monuments erected in memory of great 19th-century industrialists and financiers.

The statue of John Knox (1825) (*above*) appears to be taking in the spectacular view of the cathedral and the city from the top of its stone column.

TEMPLETON'S CARPET FACTORY ◆ F F5
(*on the edge of Glasgow Green*)
James Templeton asked the architect of his carpet factory, William Leiper, to base his design on a world-famous architectural masterpiece. The result is an extravagant combination of colored mosaics and bricks, a pastiche of the Doge's Palace in Venice (*right*). The building was extended in the 1930s and has housed offices since 1984.

THE EAST END ◆ F E5-F6

While Merchant City has certain pretensions, this district to the east of Glasgow Cross has retained its working-class character and friendly atmosphere. Its main thoroughfare, Gallowgate, is lined with shops and pubs that evoke the old city. The Saracen's Head (209 Gallowgate) claims to be Glasgow's oldest bar and is said to have welcomed such famous literary figures as Robert Burns ▲ *142* and Charles Dickens.

THE BARRAS (*between Gallowgate and London Road*). With its old stores, open-air stalls, cafés and little restaurants, this flea market – whose name is a distortion of 'barrows' – is one of the East End's main attractions. Voluble stallholders sell all kinds of new and second-hand goods at bargain prices: furniture, bric-à-brac, clothes, household appliances, hi-fis, CDs and video games. To the north of the market, on Gallowgate, stands BARROWLAND BALLROOM which today stages modern concerts.

GLASGOW GREEN. This vast park on the banks of the River Clyde has been the center of Glasgow's public life since at least the 12th century. Glasgow's Fair Fortnight is held here in July and it is the venue for a number of processions, including the May Day procession, and public events. It also boasts Britain's first Nelson memorial, a 145-foot monument erected in 1806 to commemorate the victory of Trafalgar (1805).

Façade of a building reflecting St Vincent Street Church.

PEOPLE'S PALACE *(north side of Glasgow Green)*. This Renaissance-style palace (1898) was originally a cultural center for the workers of the East End. Today it houses an interesting museum which traces the history of Glasgow from its official foundation in 1175, placing the emphasis on the economic and social transformations of the 19th and 20th centuries. There is a pleasant tea room in the luxuriant setting of the WINTER GARDEN.

THE CATHEDRAL DISTRICT ◆ **F** E2-F3

The High Street, the main commercial street of the medieval city, climbs from Glasgow Cross to the Cathedral.

GLASGOW CATHEDRAL. This impressive Gothic cathedral enjoys the unusual distinction of having been built on two levels. It is also one of the few Gothic churches in Scotland to have been spared during the Reformation, following the intervention of the trade guilds in 1578. The first cathedral, consecrated in 1136, was destroyed by fire and work began on the present edifice in 1197. The choir was built between 1233 and 1258 in early Gothic style. The sacristy, central tower and stone spire date from the first half of the 15th century, while the nave was completed in 1480. Archbishop Blacadar (1483–1508) added the flight of steps leading to the Lower Church, the remarkable stone rood screen whose carvings represent the Seven Deadly Sins and the flamboyant Gothic side aisle named after him. The Lower Church, designed to house the tomb of St Mungo, dates from the first half of the 13th century, although its chapter house was renovated in the early 15th century. The cathedral's balanced proportions and delicate ornamentation make it a fine example of Scottish early Gothic architecture.

ST MUNGO MUSEUM OF RELIGIOUS LIFE AND ART *(2 Castle Street)*. This fascinating museum compares the world's major religions and traces the religious history of Scotland. The many religious works of art include Salvador Dali's famous *Christ of St John of the Cross* (1951). At the end of the visit there is an opportunity to relax in an authentic Zen garden.

WEST OF GEORGE SQUARE ◆ **F** A2-C3

THE HAT RACK *(144 St Vincent Street, on the corner of Hope Street)*. With its lead roof and finely carved ridgepole, the tall building designed in 1902 by James Salmon Junior does indeed look like a hat rack. Its narrow façade pierced by numerous windows and the delicate Glasgow Style details are reminiscent of the work of the Catalan architect Antonio Gaudí.

ST VINCENT STREET CHURCH *(265 St Vincent Street, on the corner of Pitt Street)*. This colonnaded church built on monumental foundations and surmounted by a slender spire is one of the few surviving churches by Alexander Thomson. It was built in 1857–59 and combines Egyptian, Greco-Roman and Indian architectural styles. Behind its austere façade lies an interior bathed in light from the spectacular windows and richly colored by the reds, greens and blues of its walls, cornices, friezes and cast-iron columns.

THE CATHEDRAL: SYMBOL OF A LONG HISTORY ★
The Gothic edifice stands on the site of the 6th-century church built by St Mungo. Its remarkable stone rood screen (c. 1500) is unique in Scotland, while the Lower Church (13th century) is a masterpiece of medieval Scottish architecture.

PROVAND'S LORDSHIP ◆ F E3
(3 Castle Street)
The oldest house in Glasgow was built probably in 1471 for the priest in charge of St Nicholas Hospice, which has since disappeared. The house was subsequently occupied by a bar and a sweet shop. Today it houses a reconstruction of an early 16th-century parlor, as well as various objects and furniture evoking the building's long history. The peaceful Garden of St Nicholas, at the back of the building, is filled with medieval medicinal plants.

WINDOW SHOPPING
Glasgow is Scotland's largest shopping center. As well as the many shops centered on Argyle Street, Buchanan Street and Sauchiehall Street, there are three shopping malls. The most elegant is the PRINCES SQUARE mall (48 Buchanan Street), built beneath the glass roof of a building erected in 1841, while the largest is ST ENOCH SHOPPING AND LEISURE COMPLEX (corner of Argyle Street and Buchanan Street). The third, the BUCHANAN GALLERIES, shares an impressive sandstone building at the top of Buchanan Street with the Royal Concert Hall. ARGYLE ARCADE (1872), near Princes Square, is a replica of the early 20th-century Parisian shopping arcades and is famous for its jewelers' stores. The ITALIAN CENTRE in John Street (Merchant City) is a favorite rendezvous for lovers of design, and at weekends bargain-hunters converge on the East-End flea market, the BARRAS ▲ 154.

BLYTHSWOOD SQUARE *(northeast of St Vincent Street Church).* The square is surrounded by elegant terraced houses built in the 19th century for well-to-do Glaswegians. Today they are mostly occupied by offices. The Glasgow Style door of no. 5 was designed by Charles Rennie Mackintosh (1868–1928).

PIPING CENTRE *(30–34 McPhater Street, behind the Royal Scottish Academy of Music and Drama).* The Piping Centre, dedicated to the teaching and history of the bagpipes, occupies a former church. It incorporates a school, concert hall, a museum tracing the history of Scotland's national instrument from the 14th century to the present day, a library and a café.

WILLOW TEA ROOMS *(217 Sauchiehall Street).* Like the three other tea rooms owned by Miss Kate Cranston, the Willow Tea Rooms were entirely designed and decorated by Charles Rennie Mackintosh ▲ 162. Kate Cranston was one of the architect's fervent admirers and a member of a temperance society. She decided to fight drunkenness by opening sophisticated establishments that would attract regulars away from the pubs. The Tea Rooms, open between 1904 and 1926, were restored in 1980. Today the first floor is occupied by a jeweler's store and art gallery.

McLELLAN GALLERIES *(270 Sauchiehall Street).* The building was constructed in 1855 by James Smith to house the private collection of Archibald McLellan (1797–1854), which mainly consisted of paintings by Italian, Dutch and Flemish masters. These works are now in the Glasgow Art Gallery and Museum ▲ 158 and the McLellan Galleries hold major temporary exhibitions.

CENTRE FOR CONTEMPORARY ARTS *(350 Sauchiehall Street).* This elegant cultural center specializes in innovative forms of expression: multimedia, modern dance, poetry, painting, sculpture, music and theater. It has a library and café-restaurant.

GLASGOW SCHOOL OF ART ▲ *162 (167 Renfrew Street, just beyond Sauchiehall Street).* Charles Rennie Mackintosh was only 28 when he won the competition to design this school of architecture. The building, which was constructed in two stages, 1896–1899 and 1907–1909, is regarded as the architect's greatest work. It is both elegant and functional and combines traditional Scottish architecture with modern techniques and materials. The Mackintosh touch is applied to the slightest decorative detail, as illustrated by the geometric

and floral motifs which appear on the fireplaces, wall lamps, carpets, enameling and furniture. The Mackintosh Room and the Furniture Gallery house collections of the architect's furniture, designs and watercolors. The oak-paneled Library is particularly impressive with its suspended ceiling, its positively vertiginous windows, its mezzanine gallery with carved and painted balusters and the metal and glass light fittings in the reading room.

THE WEST END

The university district is also one of the most pleasant districts in Glasgow, with its Victorian terraces, beautiful sandstone mansions, museums and art galleries, and green spaces. It has retained the peaceful atmosphere that, in the 19th century, attracted wealthy Glaswegians seeking to escape the hustle and bustle of Merchant City and the smoke from the factories along the banks of the Clyde.

CHARING CROSS MANSIONS ◆ F A2-B2 *(corner of Sauchiehall Street and St George's Road)*. These mansions, built by John James Burnet between 1889 and 1891, represent the most ambitious tenement project ▲ *80* ever designed for the city center. Its amazing French-Renaissance façades saved it from demolition during the construction of the M8 motorway.

MITCHELL LIBRARY ◆ F B3 *(Kent Road)*. South of Charing Cross is the green dome of the Mitchell Library (1906–11), which was designed by W. B. Whitie to house the public library founded in 1874 by Stephen Mitchell, a rich tobacco merchant. Today the library has over one million volumes and, unsurprisingly, gives pride of place to Scottish literature and the history of Glasgow.

PARK CONSERVATION AREA. Most of the elegant terraces (1855–57) of Woodlands Hill were designed by Charles Wilson, who also designed TRINITY COLLEGE (1861) with its Italianate towers. However, the architect's greatest work is undoubtedly the beautiful Georgian terraces of PARK CIRCUS (1857–63). At about the same time Sir Joseph Paxton, the designer of the Botanic Gardens ▲ *159* and Queens Park in the South Side, laid out KELVINGROVE PARK. This vast public park, crossed by the River Kelvin, hosted the International Exhibitions of 1888 and 1901.

A MAJOR WORK OF EUROPEAN ARCHITECTURE ✪
The Glasgow School of Art designed by Charles Rennie Mackintosh is a masterpiece of functionalism that has stood the test of time. Guided tours by the students.

TENEMENT HOUSE
◆ F B2
(145 Buccleuch Street, northwest of the School of Art)
The first floor of this Victorian tenement building (1892) houses an exhibition on these tall blocks of flats built in the late 19th century in response to the housing crisis. On one of the upper floors is the apartment occupied between 1911 and 1965 by a shorthand typist, Miss Agnes Toward, who was not interested in progress. The apartment (parlor, bedroom, kitchen and bathroom) was bought as it stood by the National Trust for Scotland. Today, its furniture and decoration provide a fascinating insight into everyday life in Glasgow in the 1930s.

MUSEUM OF TRANSPORT
(Kelvin Hall, 1 Bunhouse Road)
Horse-drawn vehicles, prams and pushchairs, bicycles, mopeds, locomotives, cars, trams, trolleybuses and fire engines trace the history of overland transport. Maritime transport is covered in the CLYDE ROOM which has an exhibition on some of the vessels built in the Scottish shipyards. These include the *Comet*, the world's first passenger steamer, which operated between Glasgow and Greenock from 1812 to 1820, and the three Queen-class liners on which the Clyde shipyards built their excellent reputation. Another of the museum's attractions is KELVIN STREET, a reconstruction of a Glasgow street in the late 1930s, including an underground station and a film theater which screens old films.

KELVINGROVE ART GALLERY AND MUSEUM *(Kelvingrove Park)*. The city's Art Gallery and Museum (*above*), opened in 1902, has one of the richest collections in Britain: 3000 paintings, 12,500 drawings and engravings and 300 sculptures. The first floor presents Scotland's natural history and archeology, as well as weapons and armor from Europe and the East. The second-floor balconies are devoted to the decorative arts (gold and silverware, jewelry, glass and ceramics) while its galleries present a remarkable collection of paintings. The Continental (west) Wing gives pride of place to the Italian (Bellini, Botticelli, Giorgione, Caravaggio), Dutch (Rembrandt, Ruisdael), Flemish (Brueghel the Elder, Rubens) and French (the Barbizon School, Impressionism, Fauvism, Cubism) masters. Scottish painting from the 16th century to the present day is particularly well represented in the British (east) Wing by Ramsay, Raeburn, Wilkie, McTaggart, the Glasgow Boys and the Scottish Colourists.

GLASGOW UNIVERSITY *(north of Kelvingrove Park)*. The university was founded in 1451 by Bishop William Turnbull. Lectures were initially held in the cathedral and then in various buildings in the High Street. In 1870 it was transferred to the Gilmorehill campus. The main building (GILMOREHILL BUILDING), designed by Sir George Gilbert Scott in 1866, was inspired by the cathedral. Alexander Thomson, whose more innovative plans had been rejected by the municipal authorities, lost no time in criticizing the massive 19th-century Gothic structure. Scott's son, John Oldrid, built Bute Hall in 1882 and the tower in 1887. The VISITOR CENTRE provides visitors and would-be students with information on the university's history and architecture, and the layout and organization of the campus.

HUNTERIAN MUSEUM *(Gilmorehill Building, entrance on University Avenue)*. Glasgow's oldest museum is centered on the eclectic collection bequeathed to the university by a former student, Dr William Hunter (1718–83). This famous doctor of medicine, professor of anatomy and royal physician was also a keen collector of paintings, archeology, zoology and mineralogy. The numismatics collection (30,000 coins and medals) constitutes its main attraction.

'The proximity of the mountains attracts quite a large number of Highlanders to the city: their ancient mode of dress [...] is in stark contrast to that of the women and [the city's] other inhabitants.

Faujas de Saint-Fond

HUNTERIAN ART GALLERY (*University Avenue, opposite Gilmorehill Building*). Admirers of James McNeill WHISTLER (1834–1903) will be amazed by the gallery, which houses the largest European collection of paintings and personal items belonging to the Scottish-American painter. The MACKINTOSH HOUSE is a reconstruction of the Glasgow home of this pioneering architect. The exhibition, on three floors, shows some 60 pieces of furniture and numerous drawings, sketches and watercolors by the famous architect and designer. Several galleries are devoted to 19th- and 20th-century Scottish painting. The collections also include some remarkable prints and engravings belonging to the university, paintings by Rembrandt, Rubens, Stubbs and Chardin, a number of French Impressionist paintings and a collection of modern sculpture.

Detail of a panel (*below*) in the White Bedroom of the Mackintosh House.

BOTANIC GARDENS (*730 Great Western Road*). The gardens, which occupy a 50-acre site on the banks of the River Kelvin, are renowned for their collection of ferns, begonias and orchids. They also contain the Kibble Palace (above), one of the largest Victorian glasshouses in Britain. The huge metal-and-glass structure was originally built in 1864 on the shores of Loch Long by the engineer John Kibble. It was transferred to its present site in 1874 and served as a conference venue and concert hall before being used to house plant specimens from all over the world, including a remarkable collection of tree ferns from Australia and New Zealand. Other glasshouses contain some amazing species of tropical plants. The Tropicarium, for example, reproduces the conditions of a rain forest.

QUEEN'S CROSS CHURCH (*870 Garscube Road, northwest of the Botanic Gardens*) The Charles Rennie Mackintosh Society has its headquarters in the only church built by the famous architect (1898). The interior decor and furnishings bear the hallmarks of his style.

MUSEUMS 🔾
The MUSEUM OF TRANSPORT will delight old and young alike. Art lovers will be stunned by the masterpieces in the KELVINGROVE ART GALLERY AND MUSEUM, and the Whistler collection and Mackintosh House in the HUNTERIAN ART GALLERY.

THE QUAYS OF THE CLYDE ◆ F D5-B4

The quays of the Clyde, reduced to an industrial wasteland by the closure of the shipyards, are still waiting to be redeveloped. Nevertheless, they are well worth a visit.
CLYDE WALKWAY. The path follows the quays past VICTORIA BRIDGE, a granite structure built in 1854 to replace a medieval bridge, and the pedestrian SUSPENSION BRIDGE (1851–71).

THE WAVERLEY ◆ F A4
(*Anderston Quay*) In summer, enjoy a trip down the Clyde on board the steamship *Waverley*. Known as the 'pride of the Clyde', it is the last seagoing paddle-steamer in the world still in service.

Finnieston Crane (*below, left*);
the Suspension Bridge (*below, right*);
the Clyde Auditorium, whose shiny, metal roof
looks rather like the shell of an armadillo, and
the Suspension Bridge (*bottom*).

FINNIESTON CRANE
This 170-foot crane, erected in 1932, was used to load steam locomotives aboard cargo ships when Glasgow was Europe's leading center of shipbuilding.

BROOMIELAW QUAY
Under pressure from traders the central channel of the Clyde was deepened in the 1780s to enable deep-draught vessels to sail up the river to Broomielaw, the city's leading port. In the 19th century the quay was the landing stage for the steamer services that operated between the port and suburbs that lay downstream. A dozen or so navigation companies competed for the steamer link between Broomielaw, Port Glasgow, Greenock and the resorts on the Firth of Clyde. For thousands of Glaswegian families this was the starting point of the summer migration 'doon the watter'.

SECC AND THE CLYDE AUDITORIUM *(Queen's Dock)*. The Scottish Exhibition and Conference Centre (SECC) has hosted exhibitions, conferences and concerts since 1985. The nearby Clyde Auditorium, also a conference center, was designed by Norman Foster in 1997.

CLYDE MARITIME CENTRE *(Stobcross Quay)*. The *Glenlee* (1895), a floating museum moored near the heliport, is one of five yachts still afloat that were built on the Clyde. The PUMPHOUSE, which once supplied the electricity for the hydraulic cranes and swing bridges of the docks, has been converted into a museum tracing the history of the Clyde shipyards. Its café-restaurant offers fine views of the river's south bank and the shipyards, Govan and Scotstoun, still working today.

SOUTH OF THE CLYDE

Beyond GOVAN and GORBALS, once infamous inner-city areas which have been extensively redeveloped, lie the well-to-do

> 'Yesterday [...] I greeted the banks of the Clyde with their elegant minarets and modern buildings, built on Gothic foundations. I watched the women in their dresses of multicolored plaid ...'

Adolphe Blanqui

suburbs of the SOUTH SIDE, with their golf courses and other green spaces. Two of Glasgow's leading museums stand in the lush setting of POLLOK PARK, a 420-acre park about three miles south of the city center.

POLLOK HOUSE. This beautiful Georgian house was built c. 1750 by William Adam and sons for the Maxwell family, owners of the vast Pollok Park estate since the 13th century. The elegantly furnished rooms provide the ideal setting for Britain's finest private collection of Spanish paintings (El Greco, Velázquez, Murillo, Goya) as well as paintings by Italian, Flemish and English masters. The collection was assembled by William Stirling Maxwell (1818–78) who also added the great hall and the formal French-style gardens.

BURRELL COLLECTION. In 1944 the wealthy Glasgow shipowner William Burrell (1861–1958) donated his art collection to the City of Glasgow. The collection, remarkable for its size and diversity, was the fruit of a lifetime of research and acquisition. The building designed by Barry Gasson to house the collection was opened in 1983. Some 3000 of the 8000 pieces are on permanent display, while the others are displayed in rotation. The courtyard is dominated by the Warwick Vase, an 18th-century reconstruction of a 2nd-century marble vase from Hadrian's villa at Tivoli. The HUTTON CASTLE ROOMS, a reconstruction of the hall, drawing room and dining room of Hutton Castle which Burrell owned, are filled with tapestries, oriental carpets and antique furniture. The galleries devoted to ANCIENT CIVILISATIONS present pieces from Mesopotamia, Egypt, Greece and Rome. The ORIENTAL ART collection comprises Persian, Turkish and Indian carpets, Japanese prints and Chinese objets d'art (jade, bronzes, pottery and porcelain) dating from the third millennium BC to the 19th century (*right*, Ming Dynasty earthenware figure of a Buddhist disciple, decorated with colored enamel). The collection of MEDIEVAL AND POST-MEDIEVAL EUROPEAN ART brings together more than 150 tapestries, 600 stained-glass windows and 300 stone and wood statues. Three PERIOD GALLERIES house works by 17th- and 18th-century British masters, while the paintings, drawings and bronzes on display on the mezzanine floor include works dating from the 15th century (the elder Cranach) and works by such 19th-century French artists as Géricault, Degas, Boudin, Sisley and Cézanne.

'HOUSE FOR AN ART LOVER' (*Bellahouston Park, 10 Dumbreck Road*). The 'Haus eines Kunstfreundes' is today part of the Glasgow School of Art. It was inspired by the plans designed in 1901 by Charles Rennie Mackintosh ● *84* ▲ *162* and his wife Margaret Macdonald for a competition in a German design magazine. The entrance hall, dining room, music room and oval room enable visitors to compare the design project, which greatly contributed to establishing the architect's international reputation, with the work carried out (1989–96) by William Roxburgh and a team of modern interior designers.

SCOTLAND STREET SCHOOL MUSEUM OF EDUCATION (*225 Scotland Street*). The school was designed by Mackintosh. It is now a museum which traces the development of the Scottish education system from the Victorian age to the present day.

POLLOK HOUSE ★
A remarkable collection of Spanish paintings in a magnificent Palladian mansion.

HOLMWOOD HOUSE
(*61–63 Netherlee Road*)
This villa, built in 1857–58 for the paper-mill owners James and Robert Couper, is the most beautiful of the surviving works by Alexander Thomson. The decorative elements of the façade and interior are borrowed from Ancient Greece, while the decoration of the rooms uses wood, plaster and marble and includes some extremely well-restored friezes and stencil drawings. Like Mackintosh, Thomson combined architecture and interior design, even designing the hangings and the smallest ornaments.

BURRELL COLLECTION ✪
It is worth visiting Glasgow just to see this incredibly rich and admirably presented collection.

The name of Charles Rennie Mackintosh (1868–1928) is closely associated with Glasgow, one of the few, if not the only town where his work can still be admired today. This leading figure of the Glasgow Style believed that architecture should meet people's material and spiritual needs at a particular point in time. While expressing beauty, it should also be functional. In spite of his reputation Mackintosh only completed a relatively small number of architectural projects. Even so he is acclaimed as the embodiment of Scottish Art Nouveau.

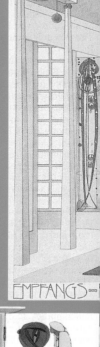

ARCHITECTURE ● 84
The Glasgow School of Art (1896–1909) is regarded as Mackintosh's architectural masterpiece ▲ 157. Its façades, like those of so many Scottish castles, are all different. In the slightly asymmetrical north façade (*above*) large bay windows allow the maximum amount of natural light into the studios.

FURNITURE
Mackintosh designed pieces of furniture as part of the redesign of the interior of a house in Glasgow, in 1902. The sideboard (*right*) reflects a desire for balance between the vertical and horizontal lines, which are softened by the curved, convex surfaces. The rose symbolizing love, the source of life, and the female figure are two of the designer's favorite motifs.

WROUGHT IRON
Mackintosh made extensive use of wrought iron and stained glass. He gave free rein to his imagination and continually redesigned forms and motifs. The wrought-iron gate of the Glasgow School of Art (*detail, below*) incorporates Japanese heraldic crests (mon) and floral motifs.

PAINTING AND FABRIC DESIGN. After the failure of his dream of a Scottish architectural revival, Mackintosh moved to London with his wife, in 1915, where he earned a living creating textile designs ('rose and tear', *left*) and painting. Between 1923 and 1927 the couple lived in Port-Vendres in the Roussillon region of France, where Mackintosh devoted himself to painting watercolors. He died in London in 1928.

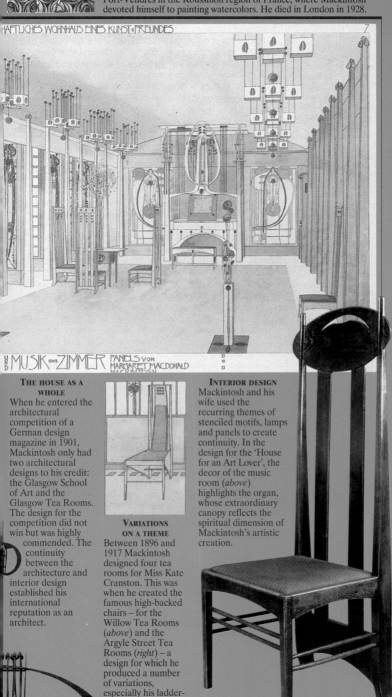

...AFTLICHES WOHNHAUS EINES KUNST·FREUNDES 7

...UND MUSIK·UND·ZIMMER PANELS VON MARGARET MACDONALD MACKINTOSH

THE HOUSE AS A WHOLE

When he entered the architectural competition of a German design magazine in 1901, Mackintosh only had two architectural designs to his credit: the Glasgow School of Art and the Glasgow Tea Rooms. The design for the competition did not win but was highly commended. The continuity between the architecture and interior design established his international reputation as an architect.

VARIATIONS ON A THEME

Between 1896 and 1917 Mackintosh designed four tea rooms for Miss Kate Cranston. This was when he created the famous high-backed chairs – for the Willow Tea Rooms (*above*) and the Argyle Street Tea Rooms (*right*) – a design for which he produced a number of variations, especially his ladder-back chair.

INTERIOR DESIGN

Mackintosh and his wife used the recurring themes of stenciled motifs, lamps and panels to create continuity. In the design for the 'House for an Art Lover', the decor of the music room (*above*) highlights the organ, whose extraordinary canopy reflects the spiritual dimension of Mackintosh's artistic creation.

▲ The outskirts of Glasgow and the Clyde Valley

David Livingstone (1813–73).

The lower reaches of the Clyde were deepened in the 18th century to accommodate deep-draught vessels, and developed in the 19th century to meet the needs of heavy industry and shipbuilding. By contrast its upper reaches, south of Glasgow, are much more peaceful and the banks become more rural as you approach its source. The most interesting feature is the industrial village of New Lanark, founded at the beginning of the Industrial Revolution near the Falls of Clyde. The small town of Paisley, to the southwest of Glasgow, is an ideal starting point for a visit to the valley.

PAISLEY ◆ D A4

The town grew up around a 12th-century priory built by Walter Fitzalan, steward of David I and an ancestor of the first Stewart king of Scotland ● 35. It enjoyed its golden age in the 17th century when it became a center for the textile industry which copied the much sought-after cashmere shawls. 'Paisley' shawls became so popular that the term was used to refer to both the garment and the design.

PAISLEY ABBEY (*High Street*). The church opposite the town hall is all that remains of the priory of Pasletum which housed the Cluniac monks of Wenlock (c. 1163) and the relics of St Mirren before becoming an abbey in 1249. Rebuilt c. 1450 and restored several times, it has a beautiful early-Gothic porch dating from the 13th century, while the nave, long used as the parish church, still has its rich 15th-century decoration. In St Mirren's Chapel (1499) a series of 12th- and 13th-century panels depict the life of the saint, who was a friend of St Columba. The choir houses the tombs of six High Stewards of Scotland, Robert III, the two wives of Robert II and possibly Marjory Bruce, the daughter of Robert Bruce and mother of Robert II.

THOMAS COATS MEMORIAL CHURCH. This Baptist Church built by Hippolyte Blanc in 1894 is an amazing Gothic Revival building with massive buttresses and an interior decor overloaded with marble and alabaster.

PAISLEY MUSEUM AND ART GALLERY. The museum, at the end of the High Street, traces the town's history and, in particular, the history of the famous Paisley shawls. Its small collection of paintings includes works by the Glasgow Boys Hornel ● 90, Guthrie and Lavery.

SMA' SHOT COTTAGES (*George Place*). The interior of these cottages evokes the everyday life of the 18th-century weavers and 19th-century mill workers.

THE CLYDE VALLEY ◆ D B4

BLANTYRE (*9 miles southeast of Glasgow*). In Blantyre, the birthplace of David Livingstone (1813–73), a MUSEUM traces the life and career of the intrepid missionary and explorer. From the age of ten Livingstone worked in a local textile mill before going on to study medicine and theology in Glasgow. He went to southern Africa as a missionary in 1841 and explored the east and south of the continent. He

> 'The most famous of the Falls of Clyde is the one known as Cora Linn, named after the castle of Cora extolled by Ossian. [...] To me, it was still one of the most impressive [falls] in the world.'

This painting by John Knox (1778–1845), a landscape artist born in Paisley, shows the first steamship on the River Clyde.

discovered the Victoria Falls and then went in search of the source of the Nile with Stanley (1841–1904). He died of exhaustion in what is now Zambia.

BOTHWELL CASTLE *(1 mile north of Blantyre)*. A few miles further on, near Uddingston, the red-sandstone ruins of Bothwell Castle, one of the most impressive 13th-century fortresses, stand above the River Clyde. The castle was built by Walter de Moravia (later Moray, then Murray), in 1242, but work was interrupted by the wars of independence in the late 13th century and the castle was never completed. In 1301 it was besieged by Edward I who demolished the ramparts using a machine made specially in Glasgow. It changed hands repeatedly over the years and was rebuilt and demolished a number of times. Although partly ruined, its circular keep is a fine example of 13th-century defensive architecture.

LANARK. This market town, which became a royal burgh in 1140, has a long history. Kenneth II convened the Scottish Parliament here in 978, and the town also witnessed the beginning of William Wallace's rebellion against the English. Outlawed for the murder of the Sheriff of Lanark, Wallace gathered a small army and returned to massacre the English garrison in May 1297. His statue (1822) on the façade of St Nicholas' Church shows him, unusually, with a beard. During the annual Lanimers festival, held in the first week of June, a 'queen' is crowned at the foot of the statue.

NEW LANARK. This 19th-century workers' village, nestling in a steep-sided valley on the Clyde, was one of the earliest social experiments to provide decent working and living conditions for a large workforce. The village was classified as a World Heritage Site in 1986 and most of the buildings have been restored. In 1783 Richard Arkwright (1732–92), who invented the water frame, was commissioned by the industrialist David Dale (1739–1806) to design a cotton mill powered by the water of the Falls of Clyde. The mill *(above and left)* soon became the largest in Scotland. It employed 1500 workers and

CRAIGNETHAN CASTLE ◆ D B4 *(near Crossford, 5 miles northwest of Lanark)*
The castle, one of the strongholds of the Hamiltons, was built in the 15th century to resist artillery attacks. The steep outcrop on which it stands made it impregnable on three sides, while the only vulnerable side was defended by a fortified outer courtyard and a dry moat with a caponier (a large vaulted chamber which was set across the floor of a broad, dry moat to deliver grazing fire), one of the first of its kind in Britain. A 17th-century manor house stands in one corner of the outer courtyard.

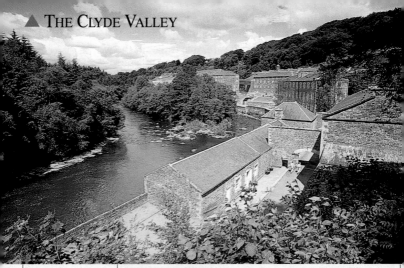

OWEN AND OWENISM
In 1820 Robert Owen published his *Report to the County of Lanark* in which he argued in favor of a society in which each member would receive a fair share of what he produced and enjoy an equal right to education. He decided to put his principles into practice in cooperative villages. In 1825 he went to the United States where he founded the colony of New Harmony in Indiana. He returned to England in 1829 and, in 1834, helped to found the Grand National Consolidated Trade Union, but the movement was crushed by the government and employers. He withdrew from public life but published the *Book of New Moral World* in 1844 and his autobiography in 1858.

by 1799 was supporting 2500 people living and working on the site. Robert Owen (1771–1858) took over his father-in-law's enterprise in 1800 and soon decided to introduce his own progressive ideas. Convinced that the well-being and education of the workforce were the key to improved production, he founded a kindergarten for the children of his employees in 1809. This was followed, in 1816, by an 'institute for the formation of character' which fulfilled the functions of a chapel, library, dance hall and public baths. Today the center is occupied by the NEW MILLENNIUM EXPERIENCE, a multimedia exhibition that highlights the historical importance of New Lanark. In 1816 Owen opened a free school, compulsory for children between the ages of 18 months and 10–12 years, which favored the use of encouragement and rewards rather than a system of corporal punishment . Some of the WORKERS' DWELLINGS and the COOPERATIVE STORE have been restored to their original state and are open to the public. Before 1813 the mill workers had to pay inflated prices for their basic necessities. Seeing that they were suffering from malnutrition and chronic debt, Owen decided to buy these necessities, such as foodstuffs, fuel, clothes and household objects, wholesale and open a shop where they could be sold at reasonable prices. The amount spent by each family was recorded in a ledger and a percentage refunded as a 'dividend', which enabled them to make additional purchases. This new type of organization provided the basis for the cooperative movement, founded in Rochdale in 1844, which became a worldwide institution.

The workers' dwellings, or NEW BUILDINGS, built in 1798 on the slopes opposite the mill, made the best possible use of the space available. Although each family had only one or two rooms, health officers tried to enforce standards of hygiene and cleanliness. ROBERT OWEN HOUSE contains personal posssessions of the mill owner and documents relating to his utopian philosophy.

THE FALLS OF CLYDE. A path leads from the mill through woods to the BONNINGTON LINN and CORA LINN falls ● *88*. These spectacular sites are today part of the FALLS OF CLYDE WILDLIFE RESERVE.

East Central

Callum Brines, Catherine Ianco,
Hilary Macartney, Ruth Noble, Nicola Taylor

169   Stirling and surroundings
174   Fife
179   Perthshire
184   *Pictish Stones*
185   Angus

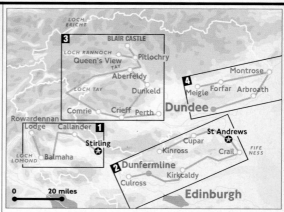

1. Stirling and
   surroundings ▲*169*
2. Fife ▲*174*
3. Perthshire ▲*179*
4. Angus ▲*185*

'There absolutely is no need for letters of introduction when visiting Scotland; the country is inhabited by such obliging people that on every road, in every tavern, in carriages and on steamers, you encounter real friends who take it upon themselves to offer you every kind of assistance which in any other country you would scarcely dare to expect from the people with whom you live.'

Astolphe de Custine

STIRLING
OLD BRIDGE ◆ D B3
(north of Stirling)
The stone bridge built across the Forth in the early 15th century was of great strategic importance. It was the river's most southerly crossing until a second bridge, Main Road Bridge, was built below it in 1831. All the Scottish sovereigns, from Robert III to Charles II, are said to have passed over Stirling Old Bridge. The wooden bridge that gave its name to the famous battle in which William Wallace defeated the English, in September 1297 ● *38*, stood nearby.

The central regions of Stirlingshire and Perthshire, and the eastern regions of Fife and Angus, are bounded by the Highlands to the north and the Southern Uplands to the south. Most of Stirlingshire lies to the north of the Highland Boundary Fault ● *16*, the large geological fault that runs northeast/southwest and passes through Perthshire and the Trossachs. To the south of the fault lie the rich agricultural lands of Strathmore and the Carse of Gowrie, whose fruit production formed the basis of the Dundee jam and marmalade industry. Major coal and slate deposits played an even more important role in the region's economy in the 19th century. To the north of the fault the land is more mountainous. Due to its geographical position the region also played a key role in Scotland's history. Angus, one of the main centers of Pictish settlement, has a remarkable legacy of symbolic carved stones ▲ *184*. One of these is thought to commemorate the decisive victory of the Picts over the Angles in 685, which prevented the expansion of the kingdom of Northumbria. In the 11th century the center of power was displaced to the southwest when Scone ▲ *180* became the capital of the kingdom of the united Scots (Picts and Scots) of Dalriada. During the wars of Scottish independence ● *38* it was Stirling's turn to become the 'key to the kingdom' and the focus of crucial battles, with Scottish independence finally proclaimed at Arbroath Abbey ▲ *185* in 1320. Fife also played a major role in the history of the kingdom. In the 11th century Malcolm III married Margaret at Dunfermline ▲ *174*, where they founded the first Benedictine abbey. They also encouraged the worship of the relics of St Andrew, the patron saint of Scotland, at St Andrews ▲ *176*. In the 15th century St Andrews, the ecclesiastical capital and first university town in Scotland, lived through some of its darkest hours during the Reformation. Perth ▲ *179*, a former royal residence, also experienced some troubled times, while Perthshire was the theater of two great battles during the Jacobite Risings: Killiecrankie in 1690, and Sheriffmuir in 1715. Finally, the Trossachs ▲ *172* owe their success as a tourist venue to the poet and novelist Walter Scott who immortalized their lochs and wild valleys in one of his poems and made Rob Roy, a famous local outlaw, the hero of one of his novels (*Rob Roy*, 1817).

The plain of central Scotland lies on either side of the River Forth, forming a natural corridor between the Southern Uplands and the North. It is dominated by Stirling Castle, which played a major role in the history of the kingdom. To the west the magnificent landscapes of the Campsie Fells, Trossachs and Loch Lomond, with their wooded hills, sparkling lochs and delightful villages, are only an hour by road from Edinburgh or Glasgow.

STIRLING ◆ D B3

This small town, with its former royal residence and historic center, is one of Scotland's leading tourist destinations. It is not unlike Edinburgh, only on a smaller scale, with its castle perched on a steep rock and an urban development that combines the old (cobbled streets and houses with stepped gables) and the new (shopping malls and streams of traffic), and University, nearby, at Airthrey.

GATEWAY TO THE HIGHLANDS. The history of Stirling is closely linked to that of its castle, which stands on a 250-foot volcanic outcrop above the best crossing on the River Forth, a strategic position which explains its turbulent past. The rock was fortified during the Iron Age and may have been occupied by the Romans. The castle was first mentioned in history in connection with the death of Alexander I in 1124. The town was elevated to the status of a royal burgh by David I and soon became one of the 'courts of the four burghs', along with Berwick, Edinburgh and Roxburgh. It occupied a strategic position on the road to the Highlands and whoever controlled it also held the 'key to the kingdom'. As a result the castle became the focus of bitter struggles. It fell into the hands of the English in 1296 but was recaptured a year later by William Wallace. In 1304 it was captured by Edward I after a long siege, but his son Edward II had to abandon it to Robert Bruce in 1314, following his defeat at the Battle of Bannockburn ● 39. Dismantled on the order of Robert Bruce, the castle was rebuilt by the English in the 14th century and subsequently became the permanent royal residence of the Stewarts. It was the birthplace of James III in 1452, James V spent the first years of his reign there, his nine-month-old daughter Mary was crowned queen there in 1543, and his grandson James VI was baptized there, in 1566. Although Stirling lost its status as a royal residence when the court moved to London in 1603, it continued to prosper. Today Stirling is an active agricultural and commercial center and has been a university town since 1967.

STIRLING ✪
This old town and former royal residence has always been an obligatory crossing point to the North. It is dominated by its castle which symbolizes the long struggle for Scottish independence.

WALLACE MONUMENT ◆ D B3
(½ mile northwest of Stirling, on the A9 and B998)
This 220-foot tower was erected on Abbey Craig hill in 1869 in memory of William Wallace (c. 1270-1305) ● 38. It houses an exhibition which includes Wallace's two-handed sword, while beneath his battle tent is an audiovisual display tracing the exploits of the Scottish hero and patriot, and a series of marble busts of famous Scotsmen. The top of the tower (246 steps) offers sweeping views of the Ochil Hills to the east, Stirling to the south and the Trossachs to the west.

Stirling in the time of the Stuarts, by Johannes Vorsterman (late 17th century).

BANNOCKBURN HERITAGE CENTRE ◆ D B3
(2 miles south of Stirling on the A9)
The site commemorates Robert Bruce's (1274–1329) decisive victory over Edward II of England on June 24, 1314 ● *39*. A bronze equestrian statue of Bruce *(below)* stands next to a rotunda enclosing the site traditionally regarded as his command post and the site of the borestone in which he planted his standard after the English defeat. Fragments of the stone can be seen in the visitor center, which also houses an exhibition on the Scottish wars of independence and an audiovisual presentation of the battle.

STIRLING CASTLE. Although some parts of the castle date from the 12th century, most of the buildings were constructed in the 15th and 16th centuries, when James IV and James V transformed the fortress into a comfortable Renaissance palace. The castle was converted into a barracks after 1745, but since it was vacated by the army, in 1964, there have been a series of restoration campaigns. On the esplanade, guarded by an equestrian statue of Robert Bruce, the ROYAL BURGH OF STIRLING VISITOR CENTRE provides an informative introduction to the town's history. Beyond the defensive outworks (1708–17), a ramp climbs to the entrance in the center of the early 16th-century Gatehouse, past Queen Anne's Garden on the left, and leads onto the Lower Square. On the left of the square is the elegant east façade of the Palace, with its alternate windows and statue niches, and, opposite, the south gable of the Great Hall. The PALACE, built in the 1540s, houses the royal apartments, which are almost bare except for the magnificent carved oak heads ('Stirling Heads') that originally decorated the ceiling of the king's apartments. Today the heads are displayed on the walls of the queen's apartments. The Great Hall, built in 1500 in late Gothic style and converted into a barracks in the 18th century, has now been entirely restored. The Lower Square also gives access to the vaults that housed the kitchens. The doorway between the Great Hall and the Palace opens onto the Upper Square. On the far side of the square stands the 12th-century CHAPEL ROYAL, refurbished in 1594 by James VI for the baptism of his son, Prince Henry. Visitors can still admire the ceiling and wall paintings executed by Valentine Jenkin in 1628. On the west side of the square the King's Old Buildings, refurbished as officers' quarters in the 18th century, today houses the Museum of the Argyll and Sutherland Highlanders (collections of silverware, memorabilia and military medals). The rampart walk on the north and east sides of the main rampart offers a magnificent view of the town and surrounding countryside.

THE OLD TOWN. In Castle Wynd, the street leading down from the castle, is ARGYLL'S LODGING, an impressive town house built in 1632 by Sir William Alexander of Menstrie, a poet, statesman and courtier under James VI. In the 1620s Menstrie founded and colonized the region of Nova Scotia in Canada. On his death the mansion passed to the Argyll family who extended it in 1674. The apartments that lie behind the beautiful Renaissance façade have

Cowane's Hospital (or Guildhall)
and Church of the Holy Rude,
Stirling (*below*)

**CAMBUSKENNETH
ABBEY ◆ D B3**
(*1 mile east of Stirling*)
All that remains of
the monastery
founded by David I in
1147 is the beautiful
14th-century bell-
tower and the
foundations of the
monastery buildings.
This rich abbey
hosted several
meetings of the
Scottish Parliament,
including the first at
which the royal

been entirely restored and furnished in 17th-century style. A
little further down the street is the once beautifully worked
façade of Mar's Wark, all that remains of the Renaissance
palace commissioned in 1569 by John Erskine, 1st Earl of
Mar and Regent of Scotland, but which was never finished. In
the CHURCH OF THE HOLY RUDE, on the corner of St John
Street, the infant James VI was crowned king in 1567. The
15th-century nave has a remarkable oak roof and vaulted
aisles dating from the same period, while the choir and apse
date from the 16th century. To the southwest of the church is
COWANE'S HOSPITAL, a charitable hospice built between 1634
and 1649 by John Cowane, a member of the Scottish
Parliament. The OLD TOWN JAIL, at the top of St John Street,
dates from 1867. The costumed guides who conduct tours of
the cells describe the various punishments meted out to the
prisoners. The roof of the prison offers views of Stirling and
the surrounding area. On Dumbarton Road, to the southwest
of the town, the SMITH ART GALLERY AND MUSEUM was
founded in 1874 with a bequest by a local artist, Thomas
Stuart Smith. As well as a collection of paintings the museum
also houses a permanent exhibition on Stirling.

burghs were
represented (1326). A
memorial erected on
the order of Queen
Victoria marks the
tomb of James II
(1452–88) and his
wife, Margaret of
Denmark.

STIRLING AND SURROUNDINGS ◆ D B3

DUNBLANE (*4 miles north of Stirling*). This delightful little town
has a cathedral (*right*) founded in 1150 on the site of a 6th-
century church. All that remains of the original cathedral are
the first two floors of the tower; the rest was built between
1233 and 1258 by Bishop Clement. Extended in the 15th
century and restored in the 19th and 20th centuries, the
cathedral has a magnificent Gothic façade and beautiful 15th-
century carved choir stalls. Dean's House (1624) is occupied
by a small cathedral museum and an exhibition of local history.
DOUNE CASTLE (*west of Dunblane, on the A820*). This
impressive castle, which stands above a bend in the River
Teith, was built in the late 14th–early 15th century by Robert
Stewart, Duke of Albany (d. 1419) and his son Murdoch, both
regents of Scotland under James I. The king had Murdoch
executed on his release from captivity, in 1424, and the castle
passed to the earls of Moray, another branch of the Stewart
family ● *35*, who still own it today. The curtain wall and the
massive 100 foot-high keep, with its huge state room and vast
kitchens, give some idea of the past power of this castle. The
keep has been extremely well restored.

**CASTLE
CAMPBELL ◆ D B3**
(*7 miles northwest of
Stirling, on the A91*)
The castle owned by
the Campbell family
stands above Dollar,
famous for its school
(Dollar Academy).
Perched high on a
rocky outcrop, it
dominates the
surrounding area as
far as the Firth of
Forth. The tower-
house was built in the
15th century by the
1st Earl of Argyll,
while the two wings
and gardens were
added in the 16th
and 17th centuries.
Unsuccessfully
besieged by the Duke
of Montrose in 1645,
it was burned by
Cromwell's troops
in 1654.

On his
father's
death, he became
clan chief and a
wealthy cattle-driver.
Wrongly accused of
stealing £1000 from
the Duke of
Montrose, he was
outlawed in 1713
and forced to take to
the hills. He was
pardoned in 1725 and
lived the rest of his
life peacefully in
Balquhidder, on the
shores of Loch Voil.
*Rob Roy and the
magistrate*, by John
Watson Nicol (1886)
(*above*).

THE TROSSACHS ★
The 'bristly country'
so dear to Walter
Scott has retained
all its wild beauty.
In summer its
unforgettable
landscapes are best
enjoyed before the
tourists flock onto
the hills and along the
wooded shores of
the lochs.

THE TROSSACHS ◆ D A3-B3

The Trossachs, which means the 'bristly
country' in Gaelic, is in fact the wild
gorge that links Loch Achray and Loch
Katrine. Its idyllic landscapes are described
by Walter Scott in *The Lady of the Lake*
(1810) ● *98*. Today, the name of this wooded
gorge is used to refer to the region that lies between
Loch Venachar, to the northwest of Stirling, and Loch
Lomond. These hills and lochs, which have attracted tourists
since the 18th century, are also associated with Rob Roy
MacGregor, the outlaw whose exploits inspired a number of
writers during his lifetime, and who was immortalized by
Walter Scott in his novel *Rob Roy* (1818).

CALLANDER. This small town on the eastern edge of the
Trossachs is the region's main summer resort. Its many tea
rooms and souvenir shops are part of a flourishing tourist
industry which dates from the 19th century and owes much
to the works of Walter Scott and William Wordsworth.
The ROB ROY AND TROSSACHS VISITOR CENTRE, housed in a
former church on Ancaster Square, presents a lively and
romanticized version of the life of the famous outlaw. The
slopes of Ben Ledi (2885 feet), to the northeast of Callander,
offer some beautiful walks.

LOCH KATRINE. From Callander the A821 follows a
picturesque route westward along the shores of Loch
Venacher and Loch Achray. One branch of a fork at the
western end of Loch Achray leads to the southern tip of Loch
Katrine. This impressive loch, which provided the inspiration
for Walter Scott's THE LADY OF THE LAKE, has been the
reservoir for the city of Glasgow since 1859. Its charm can
best be experienced by following the footpath along the north
shore or, in summer, taking a trip across the loch aboard the
Sir Walter Scott, which stops at Stronachlachar on the west
shore. Experienced climbers and hikers will enjoy climbing
Ben Venue (2360 feet) and Ben A'an (1520 feet) on the loch's

'If Loch Lomond were situated beneath an Italian sky, I would want to end my days on one of its islands.'

Adolphe Blanqui

On the shores of Loch Katrine, by the landscape artist John Knox (1778–1845).

south shore. Their efforts will be well rewarded by the magnificent views of the surrounding hills and lochs.
ABERFOYLE. To the south of Loch Katrine the A821 winds its way up to Dukes Pass and then down through the Achray Forest to Aberfoyle. This peaceful little town in the heart of the Trossachs is almost unrecognizable in summer when it is inundated with tourists. The visitor center of QUEEN ELIZABETH FOREST PARK, to the north of Aberfoyle, is an ideal starting point from which to explore the park's 74,000 acres of forests, lochs and mountains.

CAMPSIE FELLS ◆ D A3

This region to the southwest of Stirling is characterized by delightful villages, pastureland and gently rolling hills: the Fintry hills in the north and the Campsie Fells in the south. The treacherous marshes of the Carse of Forth, which lay on the route between the Southern Uplands and the North, were drained in the 18th century to create this fertile region which is today crossed by the A811 between Stirling and Loch Lomond.
LOCH LOMOND. Loch Lomond (23 miles long) is the largest freshwater area in Great Britain. It is a breathtaking sight, even on summer weekends when jet skis disturb the tranquillity of its shores. Boat trips are organized from BALLOCH at the south end of the loch. The road that runs along the east shore, more wooded and less busy than the west shore, comes to an end at Rowardennan Lodge. This is a popular destination for hikers following the West Highland Way toward Queen Elizabeth Forest Park or climbing BEN LOMOND (3195 feet). CONIC HILL (1175 feet) is an easy climb, even for young children. It starts from the Balmaha car park, to the south of Rowardennan Lodge. On a clear day there is a superb view of the loch and Ben Lomond from the top of the hill.

LAKE OF MENTEITH
◆ D B3
(4 miles east of Aberfoyle)
This is the only freshwater lake in Scotland that isn't a referred to as a loch. The lake's largest island can be reached by boat from Port of Menteith. It is the site of the romantic ruins of Inchmahome Priory, founded c. 1238 by Walter Comyn, Earl of Menteith, for Augustinian Canons. In 1547, after their defeat at Pinkie by the English, the Scots hid the five-year-old Mary Stuart on the island before sending her secretly to Dumbarton ▲ *189* and from there to France ● *40*.

MUNRO
In the United Kingdom the term munro is applied to any summit above 3000 feet. It is derived from the name of Sir Hugh T. Munro who recorded the height of all the Scottish summits in 1891. There are over 280 munros in Scotland.

Loch Lomond.

The nave of Dunfermline Abbey Church.

Andrew Carnegie emigrated to America in 1848. He rose to become head of the most powerful steel company in the United States. After retiring in 1901 he sponsored many charitable works on both sides of the Atlantic. He made a gift of Pittencrieff Park, a school and a public baths to his native town of Dunfermline, as well as the first of the many public libraries that he financed throughout the United Kingdom.

Andrew Carnegie.

INCHCOLM ◆ D C3
(ferries from Aberdour, North Queensferry and South Queensferry)
This island in the Firth of Forth, home of seabirds and seals, is also the site of ST COLM'S ABBEY. To thank the hermit who helped him when he was shipwrecked, Alexander I founded a priory in 1123, which was raised to the status of an abbey in 1235. The monastic buildings, which include a late 13th-century octagonal chapter house with a stone roof and a 14th-century cloister with a dormitory above, are some of the best preserved in Scotland.

The Fife Peninsula, bounded by the Firths of Forth and Tay, has long been one of the richest regions in Scotland. In addition to such architectural treasures as Dunfermline Abbey, Falkland Palace and the town of St Andrews, it has the delightful ports of the East Neuk ('east corner') and, further inland, an opulent patchwork of fruit and cereal crops.

DUNFERMLINE ◆ D C3

The development of this royal burgh, a favorite town of Scottish sovereigns from the late 11th to the 14th century, was closely linked to its religious influence. After marrying Malcom III (1031–93), in 1070, the pious Queen Margaret (1045–93) founded a priory which her son David I made a Benedictine abbey in 1128. Several Scottish kings and queens are buried there, the abbey having superseded Iona ▲ *204* as a royal place of burial in the 12th century. Dunfermline was one of the principal centers of the linen industry from the 16th to the early 20th century, but it is primarily known as the birthplace of Andrew Carnegie (1835–1919), the steel magnate and philanthropist to whom it owes its annual festival of music and drama.

DUNFERMLINE ABBEY. The ABBEY CHURCH stands on the site of a church founded by David I. Over the centuries it has been ruined and rebuilt many times. By contrast the interior of the nave, inspired by that of Durham Cathedral and skillfully restored by William Shaw (1550–1602), has retained all its Norman grandeur: its semicircular arches are supported by tall, cylindrical piers, four of which are carved with Norman motifs. Today the only part of the abbey used for worship is the Gothic CHOIR, rebuilt in 1817–22, where Robert Bruce is buried ● *34, 39*. Beyond the apse of the sanctuary are the foundations of the 13th-century chapel which housed the remains of Malcolm III and the relics of St Margaret and was for a long time a place of pilgrimage. To the south of the church are the ruined MONASTERY BUILDINGS (13th-century refectory) and the kitchens of the abbey guest house,

> 'On the shore of the firth, farther down, stands the town of Culross, a neat and agreeable town [...] Here is a pretty market, a plentiful country behind it, and the navigable firth before it.'
>
> Daniel Defoe

transformed in the 14th century into a royal palace where several Scottish kings were born.

PITTENCRIEFF PARK *(west of the abbey)*. In the lush setting of Pittencrieff Park stands PITTENCRIEFF HOUSE, a 17th-century manor which now houses a museum of local history and costume. There are also the ruins of Malcolm's TOWER where, in 1068, Malcolm III received his future wife and her brother, Edgar Atheling, who fought against William the Conqueror.

ABBOT HOUSE *(Maygate, north of the abbey)*. This delightful 15th-century abbot's house, with its walled garden, houses an attractively presented introduction to the town's history.

OTHER PLACES OF INTEREST. The ANDREW CARNEGIE MUSEUM (Moodie Street), housed in the weaver's cottage where Carnegie was born, traces his life and work. DUNFERMLINE MUSEUM (Viewfield, east of High Street) traces the history of the linen and damask industry.

CULROSS ◆ D B3

This old port on the Firth of Forth is one of the gems of Scottish vernacular architecture, dating from the 16th–17th century. Its cobbled streets and white houses with red-tiled roofs have been carefully restored. A flourishing coal and salt trade with the Netherlands and the Baltic countries enabled Culross to obtain a charter in 1588. However, the development of trade with the American colonies marked the beginning of its decline in the late 17th century.

TOWN HOUSE. The visitor center, housed in the stone and slate town hall or tolbooth (1626) overlooking the River Forth, has an audiovisual presentation on Culross.

CULROSS PALACE. This beautiful town house with its ocher-colored rough-rendering *(top right)*, stands on the banks of the River Forth. It was built for Sir George Bruce in 1597 and enlarged in 1611. The pine-paneled walls, decorative paintings, numerous chimneys, fire-proof strong room and period furniture reflect the lifestyle of a rich merchant of the time.

MARKET PLACE. On the market place *(center right)* stand the oldest house in Culross (1577) and THE STUDY of Bishop Leighton (1610), a corbeled out-turret with beautiful painted ceilings. Visitors can also admire the restored façades of the residence of Bishop Robert Leighton, in Mid Causeway, and a convent and a hostel (The Ark), in Wee Causeway.

CULROSS ABBEY. At the top of the town stand the remains of a Cistercian abbey founded in 1215 by Malcolm, Earl of Fife. The parish church occupies the choir of the 14th-century abbey church and houses the beautiful funeral memorial of Sir George Bruce (d. 1625) and his family. The monastic buildings were demolished and their stone used to build nearby Abbey House, begun in 1608.

KIRKCALDY ◆ D C3
Kirkcaldy, the birthplace of the economist Adam Smith (1723–90) and the architect Robert Adam (1728–92) ● *44* was also the birthplace of the linoleum industry in 1847. This fairly unprepossessing town has a dynamic recreational and cultural life. Although modest, the collection in the Art Gallery includes some remarkable works by William McTaggart (1835–1910) ● *88* and S.J. Peploe (1871–1935).

A SMALL SCOTTISH TOWN (16TH–18TH CENTURY) ★
The exceptionally well-preserved royal burgh of Culross (pronounced 'coo-ross') attests to the golden age of the east-coast ports. It is the pride and joy of the National Trust for Scotland.

LOWER LARGO ◆ D C3
This tiny port was the birthplace of Alexander Selkirk (1676–1721), the sailor who was marooned on a Pacific island for four years and four months and provided the inspiration for Daniel Defoe's novel *Robinson Crusoe* (1719).

KELLIE CASTLE ◆ D C3
(10 miles south of St Andrews)
This 16th-century castle perched on a wooded hillside was restored and given a Victorian garden ▲ *197* by the Lorimer family in the 1880s. It has a T-shaped layout, some distinctive stuccoed ceilings and painted wall panels (17th century), and furniture designed by Robert Lorimer.

ST ANDREWS: A PRESTIGIOUS TOWN ✪
The most prestigious golf course in the world, a university with a long-established reputation and a cathedral that attests to its former religious power are the crowning glories of this delightful summer resort.

EAST NEUK ◆ D D3

The southeast coast of the Fife Peninsula is dotted with delightful little fishing ports. Between the 11th and 17th centuries they also traded with the Netherlands and the Baltic countries.

ANSTRUTHER. The SCOTTISH FISHERIES MUSEUM is the main attraction of this former herring port which, in summer, runs boat trips to the ISLE OF MAY and its BIRD SANCTUARY. The museum, housed in 16th- to 19th-century buildings, traces the history of fishing in Scotland: reconstructions of interiors, scenes of fishermen at work, models, equipment, paintings and photographs.

CRAIL. This former royal burgh, with its two hundred year-old golf course, is the most delightful port on this stretch of coast. A small museum occupies one of the elegant 16th- to 19th-century houses that stand on the market place at the top of the town. Other old houses border the narrow streets leading down to the harbor and quays.

ST ANDREWS ◆ D C2

St Andrews, the former ecclesiastical capital of Scotland, a renowned university town and the birthplace of golf, is also a delightful coastal resort. Traditionally its history dates from the 4th century when St Regulus (St Rule) was shipwrecked here and buried the relics of St Andrew which he was bringing back from Patras. The relics of the patron saint of Scotland, which were more probably brought here in the 8th century just before the foundation of a Celtic monastery, soon became the focus of popular pilgrimage. The cathedral, built between 1160 and 1318, was the largest in Scotland. With the foundation of Scotland's first university, in 1412, and the elevation of the diocese to an archbishopric and metropolitan see, in 1471, St Andrews became a prestigious and influential town. However, it lost its religious status during the Reformation, and the university did not recover its prestige until the late 19th century, when the aristocracy developed a passion for golf and made the town a fashionable resort.
ST ANDREWS CATHEDRAL. The town's three main streets (South Street, Market Street and North Street) converge on

the ruins of the cathedral precinct and THE PENDS, its main entrance. In 1559 Reformers pillaged the cathedral, throwing its statues and paintings into the sea, while the stones were used for building materials. The least damaged sections are the flat apse (12th century), the façade (1273–79) and the south wall of the nave (12th–13th century). To the south of the cathedral are the foundations of the monastic buildings and, to the southeast, all that remains of the Church of St Rule (11th or 12th century): the choir and a large square tower (108 feet) which offers a splendid view of the town from the top of its 159 steps. The CATHEDRAL MUSEUM has a rich collection of sculpted crosses (8th–10th century) and a magnificent early 9th-century tomb.

ST ANDREWS CASTLE. The Scores, the promenade that borders St Andrew Bay, links the cathedral and castle, a fortified bishop's home that was founded in 1200. They include the bottle-shaped dungeon in the northwest tower (Sea Tower), where the Protestant George Wishart was imprisoned before being burnt at the stake on the order of Cardinal Beaton, in January 1546. In May 1546 Wishart's friends captured the castle and killed the cardinal. They were joined by other Reformers, including John Knox, and held the castle for a year before being ousted by a French fleet and sent to the galleys. A tunnel dug by the castle's attackers to undermine its foundations can still be seen in the courtyard.

THE UNIVERSITY. St Andrews University was founded in 1412 by Bishop Henry Wardlaw and recognized by papal bull in 1413. The first faculty, ST SALVATOR'S COLLEGE, which opened in North Street in 1450, was replaced in 1741 by United College. All that remains today is the Gothic chapel which houses the elaborately carved tomb (1460) of its founder, Bishop James Kennedy. The initials carved on the paving stones in front of the entrance are those of Patrick Hamilton, one of the first Reformers, who was burnt at the stake on this very spot in 1528. ST LEONARD'S COLLEGE (1512), where John Knox and other Reformers studied, has been replaced by a girls' school. The University Library occupies Queen Mary's House, a beautiful 16th-century house on South Street. A little further on stands ST MARY'S COLLEGE (1537) which has housed the theological faculty since 1579.

A street in Crail (*far left*); St Andrews Cathedral, with the ruined castle in the background (*center*); Crail harbor (*above*).

OTHER PLACES OF INTEREST
South Street: HOLY TRINITY CHURCH, built in 1410 and restored in 1906–09, where John Knox delivered his first public sermon in 1547; BLACKFRIARS CHAPEL (16th century), all that remains of a Dominican monastery destroyed during the Reformation; WEST PORT (1589), one of Scotland's few surviving town gates. North Street: ST ANDREWS PRESERVATION TRUST MUSEUM, a beautiful merchant's house converted into a museum of local history. On the sea front, near the British Golf Museum, children will love the SEA LIFE CENTRE with its aquariums full of fish and other sea creatures.

FROM ST ANDREWS TO FALKLAND ◆ D C2-C3

LEUCHARS (6 miles north of St Andrews). In addition to St Andrews Station and a Royal Air Force base, the village has a remarkable 12th-century Norman church dedicated to St Athanasius. The nave has been rebuilt, but the choir and apse (apart from the 17th-century tower) are original.

CUPAR. The former county town of Fife has an attractive town hall and a 17th-century market cross. About 2 miles to the south is the HILL OF TARVIT, an Edwardian-style mansion designed by Robert Lorimer to house the collections of paintings, bronzes, Chinese porcelain and Chippendale furniture owned by the rich Dundee industrialist, Frederick Bower Sharp. The Hill of Tarvit holds the keys for SCOTSTARVIT TOWER, an L-shaped tower-house dating from the 16th century.

CERES. The collections of the FIFE FOLK MUSEUM occupy several old houses in this delightful village.

FALKLAND. This medieval village, raised to the status of a royal burgh in 1458, has carefully maintained its old weavers' cottages and beautiful 17th- and 18th-century mansions with their carved lintels. FALKLAND PALACE on the High Street is a former Stewart hunting lodge which was transformed into a magnificent palace in the 15th and 16th centuries. The building, abandoned after 1650, has been the subject of several restoration programs since the late 19th century. The south wing, the best preserved, has a magnificent Renaissance façade (1537–42) and houses a collection of 17th-century Flemish tapestries and a royal chapel dating from the 16th century. James V died in 1542 in the royal apartments of the east wing, only a few days after the birth of his daughter Mary. In the gardens are the foundations of the north wing and a wallcourt, dating from 1539, for real or royal tennis.

KINROSS ◆ D C3
(12 miles north of Dunfermline)
This small town stands on the shores of Loch Leven, popular with trout fishermen. KINROSS HOUSE ● 76, built and owned by the architect William Bruce in the 1680s, and its gardens (*above*) are open to the public. On an island in the loch are the ruins of the CASTLE where Mary Stuart was imprisoned in June 1567 and from which she escaped in May 1568 ● 41 with the help of her jailer's son. VANE FARM NATURE RESERVE, south of Kinross, offers an opportunity to observe the waterfowl that nest and over-winter on the loch.

ABERNETHY ◆ D C2
The village was the seat of the Church of Scotland from the 11th to the 15th century. At the entrance to the churchyard stands the 75-foot round tower that served as the monastery watch tower. The lower section is 9th century.

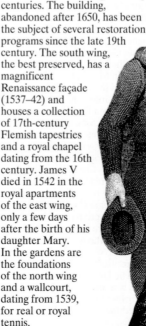

As the point of passage between the Highlands and Lowlands, the region of Perth featured early in Scottish history, as evidenced by its many castles, cathedrals and abbeys. Its vast landscapes have always fired the imagination. The first chapter of Walter Scott's *The Fair Maid of Perth* begins: 'Among all the provinces in Scotland, if an intelligent stranger were asked to describe the most varied and the most beautiful, it is probable he would name the county of Perth'.

PERTH AND SURROUNDINGS ◆ **D** C2

After 846 Perth, which may have been built on the site of a Roman camp, was overshadowed by Scone, capital of the kingdom of Dalriada ● *33*. In the 12th century the town obtained a charter, due to its port on the River Tay, which linked it to the east coast, and became the principal residence of the Scottish monarchy. After James I was assassinated in one of the town's monasteries in 1437, however, James II transferred the royal residence to Edinburgh. Perth's political eclipse did nothing to protect it: in 1559 rioters destroyed its monasteries; it was occupied by the troops of the Duke of Montrose in 1644, by Cromwell's troops in 1651, and by the Jacobites in 1689, 1715 (when the Young Pretender was proclaimed king in the town) and again in 1745. The capital of Perthshire has a rich architectural heritage from the Georgian period, a famous golf course, a well-established dramatic and musical tradition, and an emblematic figure: the Fair Maid of Perth, heroine of the novel by Scott.

ST JOHN'S KIRK *(St John Street, behind the town hall)*. Perth owes its original name of 'St John's Toun' to this church founded in 1126 by David I and renovated in the 15th century. On May 11, 1559 John Knox preached a sermon in the church which denounced papist idolatry. St John's Kirk was restored in the 1920s and today houses a war memorial by Robert Lorimer.

FAIR MAID'S HOUSE. In North Port stands the cottage on which Walter Scott modeled the house of the Fair Maid of Perth.

PERTH ART GALLERY AND MUSEUM *(78 George Street)*. This classical-style building houses a museum of natural history, archeology and local history, which gives pride of place to the whisky and glass industries. Its art gallery has works by British and foreign artists.

FERGUSSON GALLERY *(Marshall Place)*. Works by the Scottish Colourist John Duncan Fergusson (1874–1961) are on display in this elegant water tower (1832) near South Inch.

NORTH AND SOUTH INCH ◆ **D** C2
To the south and north of the town, on the west bank of the River Tay, are two vast public parks: SOUTH INCH and NORTH INCH. North Inch was the scene of a fierce chivalric tournament, described in *The Fair Maid of Perth*, between the champions of the Chattan and Quhele (Kay) clans in 1396. On the east bank of the Tay is the delightful BRANKLYN GARDEN, renowned for its collections of rhododendrons and Alpine plants (entrance on Dundee Road).

BALHOUSIE CASTLE ◆ **D** C2
(west of North Inch, north Perth)
The 15th-century castle, extended in Scots Baronial style in the 19th century, houses the BLACK WATCH REGIMENTAL MUSEUM, dedicated to the first Highland regiment, formed in 1739 by General Wade to maintain order in the Highlands ▲ *233*.

HUNTINGTOWER CASTLE ◆ **D** C2
(3 miles northwest of Perth, on the A85)
The castle comprises two square, 15th-century towers linked by a 17th-century building. The walls and ceiling of the hall on the second floor of the east tower have retained their 16th-century painted decor.

SCONE PALACE *(2 miles north of Perth, on the A93)*. In 1808 the town of Scone was relocated a few miles from its original site and renamed New Scone to make way for the palace (above and left) built by William Atkinson for the earls of Mansfield. The style of the palace was designed to evoke the long history of the town as the capital of the kingdom of Dalriada, the capital of Kenneth MacAlpin (835), the seat of the Scottish Parliament (1284–1402) and the see of a great abbey (1114–1559). Scone owed much of its prestige to the 'Stone of Destiny' associated with the crowning of Scottish kings until the 13th century ● *38* ▲ *116*. The ceremony took place on top of Moot Hill which, according to legend, was formed from the earth brought to Scone on the soles of the shoes of foreign ambassadors. The stone was transported to London by Edward I in 1275. However, this did not deter Scottish sovereigns from being crowned at Scone, and the tradition continued for almost 400 years, ending with Charles II in 1651. The stone was finally returned to Scotland at the end of the 20th century. The red-sandstone palace, a fine example of Scots Baronial style, houses some beautiful collections of ivory, porcelain and 18th-century French furniture. It stands in a vast park inhabited by peacocks, sheep, donkeys and Highland cattle.

DAVID DOUGLAS (1799–1834)
David Douglas, the son of a stonemason employed by the Earl of Mansfield, was born on the Scone estate. This 'hero of modern times' significantly altered the face of European horticulture. Between 1824 and his accidental death in 1834, he traveled in North America on behalf of the Royal Horticultural Society and sent back over 200 species of plants and trees which have since been introduced into Europe. Among them was the Douglas Fir *(below)* of which the oldest European specimen can be seen in the Scone Pinetum.

FROM PERTH TO DUNKELD ◆ D B2

CRIEFF *(20 miles west of Perth, on the A85)*. Before the advent of the railroad made it a fashionable Victorian spa town, Crieff was famous for its cattle markets. Today its principal attraction is GLENTURRET DISTILLERY, one of the oldest distilleries in Scotland (1775). South of the town, on the A822, are the formal gardens of DRUMMOND CASTLE ▲ *197* – built in the late 15th and rebuilt in the 19th century – and the remains of ARDOCH ROMAN CAMP (1st–2nd century), near Braco. TULLIBARDINE, to the southwest of Crieff, on the A823, has one of Scotland's best-preserved medieval churches. The red-sandstone church, built in 1446 and enlarged c. 1500, houses the tombs of the earls of Perth.
SMA' GLEN *(north of Crieff, on the A822)*. Ossian, the famous 3rd-century Scottish bard, is said to lie buried beneath the steep slopes of Sma' Glen, the 'narrow glen' immortalized by the poet William Wordsworth (1770–1850). A huge stone surmounts the bard's supposed tomb, at the north end of the valley, once guarded by a Roman camp. The A822 continues along the wild and deserted valley of Glen Quaich, following

> 'The further you go, the more picturesque and original the scenery becomes; mountains rear up, covered with woods which seem to merge with the dark waters of the Tay.'
>
> Pierre Trabaud

the route taken by the Young Pretender when he marched on Culloden ● *43* and then turned off to Dunfermline.

DUNKELD. The seven-arched bridge, built across the River Tay by Thomas Telford in 1809, offers a sweeping view of the town nestling on the banks of the river below wooded mountains. This Pictish stronghold became a principal place of pilgrimage when Celtic monks, driven from Iona ▲ *204* by Vikings, brought the relics of St Columba to Dunkeld in 850. The cathedral, built between 1260 and 1501, evokes the town's golden age. It was twice destroyed: in 1600 by the Reformers and, in August 1689, during a battle which ended with the defeat of the Jacobites, who only a month before had defeated the English at the battle of Killiecrankie. The roofless nave stands open to the sky, its grassy floor paved with tombs. The choir has been restored several times and is now used as the parish church. It has a carved oak screen which conceals the tomb of the 'Wolf of Badenoch' ▲ *232*, the natural son of Robert II who, amongst other evil deeds, burned the Cathedral of Elgin in 1390. The cathedral, which stands on lawns planted with trees on the banks of the River Tay, occupies a truly idyllic setting. Beyond its monumental gate, the white façades of Cathedral Street and High Street provide a striking contrast with the severity of some Scottish villages. These 'Little Houses' were built on the ruins of old Dunkeld, which was burned in 1689 along with the cathedral.

LITTLE DUNKELD AND BIRNAM. Niel Gow ● *53, 87*, fiddler by appointment to the dukes of Atholl and writer of traditional Scottish folk music, is buried in Little Dunkeld churchyard. Beatrix Potter spent childhood holidays in the region and, in 1893, wrote the first of her widely acclaimed Peter Rabbit stories in Dunkeld. Today, the creatures she created populate BEATRIX POTTER'S GARDEN in Birnam. This Victorian resort is said to possess the last oak of Birnam Wood, the same wood that heralds the death of the hero in Shakespeare's *Macbeth*.

FROM LOCH EARN TO LOCH TAY ◆ D B2
The small town of Comrie (west of Crieff, on the A85) lies on the Highland Boundary Fault and frequently experiences earth tremors. From Comrie the A85 continues along the north bank of the River Earn to Loch Earn, a popular water-sports center. Beyond Glen Ogle the A827 leads to the delightful village of Killin, near the Falls of Dochart and Loch Tay. This beautiful loch, famous for its salmon, stretches for 13 miles along the foot of Ben Lawyers (3980 feet). One of the artificial islands (crannogs) built on the loch by the ancient Celts has been reconstructed at the SCOTTISH CRANNOG CENTRE of Kenmore.

Loch Earn.

A CASTLE MUSEUM ★
The thirty-one rooms of Blair Castle are open to the public and present some magnificent 18th-century interiors. The works of art contained in the castle have earned it the name 'Victoria & Albert Museum of the Highlands'.

ABERFELDY ◆ D B2
This little town has been immortalized in a poem by Robert Burns ● *98* ▲ *142*, *The Birks* ('silver birches') *of Aberfeldy*. A walk starting on the central square (The Square) leads through woodland to the place where Burns was inspired to write his poem. The association with Burns is not the town's only claim to fame: its bridge across the Tay is one of the most photographed bridges in Scotland. Near this massive work of art, built in 1733 by General Wade, a statue of a kilted soldier commemorates the formation of the Black Watch Regiment at Aberfeldy, in 1739. CASTLE MENZIES lies to the northwest of the town, on the B846. It is a fine example of a 16th-century Z-shaped tower-house and is currently being restored. In Grandtully, to the northeast of Aberfeldy, on the A827, ST MARY'S CHURCH (16th century) has a magnificent painted ceiling dating from the 1630s.

THE HERMITAGE *(2 miles west of Dunkeld)*. In the woods of the Hermitage, hillside paths lead to Ossian's Hall, an 18th-century folly above the Braan Falls and a mecca of Romanticism. Wordsworth, Turner and Mendelssohn visited this viewpoint from where salmon can be seen leaping up the river to their spawning ground in the loch.

PITLOCHRY AND SURROUNDINGS ◆ D B1-B2

PITLOCHRY. This town in the Tummel valley enjoyed its golden age in the late 19th century, when it became a fashionable spa town. Tourists continue to flock here, attracted by its invigorating air, summer drama festival, two distilleries, salmon ladder and, above all, its magnificent surroundings.
LOCH TUMMEL. To the northwest of Pitlochry, the B8019 enters the magnificent Tay Forest. A series of hairpin bends climbs to the Queen's View viewpoint, from where Queen Victoria enjoyed the breathtaking view of Loch Tummel. The loch stretches majestically between the mountains, dominated by the conical outline of Schiehallion (3545 feet), while the summits of Glen Coe ▲ *199* can be seen in the distance. The B8019 joins the B846 which comes to an end on the borders of Perthshire, on the edge of Rannoch Moor. Only the most hardened hikers venture onto the vast, desolate wastes, bristling with rocky outcrops and scattered with small lochs.
KILLIECRANKIE PASS *(on the A9)*. This wooded pass, which forms a strategic link between the Highlands and Lowlands, was the scene of the first great encounter between the Jacobite and government forces. On July 27, 1678 John Graham of Claverhouse, popularly known as Bonnie Dundee, routed the army of William III of Orange before dying of his wounds. He is buried in the ruined church of Old Blair, behind Blair Castle. A footpath leads to SOLDIER'S LEAP, where a Redcoat is said to have jumped 20 feet to escape

> 'I have just walked through Dunkeld park [...] fifty-five gardeners are employed solely to maintain seventeen leagues of sandy paths, and twenty leagues of grass ones.'
>
> Astolphe de Custine

Blair Castle (*above*); the Braan Falls (*below*), in The Hermitage woods, near Dunkeld.

from his Jacobite pursuers. The pass is inhabited by a wide range of wildlife and has been declared a site of scientific interest. The most elusive species is the wildcat, which only comes out at night, while the most sought after is the salmon, once so abundant that peasants used to hang baskets in the River Garry and wait for the fish to get caught in them as they swam upriver.

BLAIR CASTLE. The impressive white castle, the home of the dukes of Atholl, stands in a wooded hillside setting like something out of a novel by Walter Scott. The tower-house, built in 1269 to defend the Grampians and the road to Inverness, has been attacked and rebuilt many times over the centuries. It was rebuilt in Georgian style in the late 18th century and refurbished in Scots Baronial style by the architect David Bryce c. 1870. The entrance hall is hung with ancient weapons, including muskets and shields from Culloden which evoke the castle's turbulent past. During the Jacobite Risings the Murray brothers of Atholl fought on opposite sides, with the result that one of them besieged his own castle in 1746. In addition to Jacobite memorabilia, collections of furniture, portraits, tapestries and porcelain, there are some remarkable papier-mâché objects made on the Isle of Man, which was ruled by the family in the 18th century. The dukes are renowned for their intensive reforestation program: over the last 100 years they have planted 14 million larches in the region, finding it more efficient to sow the seeds using a cannon. The trees were all grown from seed taken from five trees on the lawns of Dunkeld Cathedral.

BRUAR FALLS. The picturesque Bruar Falls (3 miles north of Blair Castle) were planted with trees and shrubs by the dukes of Atholl. The work is said to have been inspired by a poem by Robert Burns, *The Humble Petition of Bruar Water*, in which the poet takes the part of the falls to ask their 'noble master' to 'shade [their] banks wi' towering trees, And bonie spreading bushes'.

LOCH OF LOWES WILDLIFE RESERVE ♦ D B2-C2 (*2 miles northeast of Dunkeld – marked road and footpath from the town center*) Ospreys and other species of wildlife that populate this 240-acre reserve can be observed from a hide equipped with binoculars and telescopes, on the south shore of the loch.

A LITTLE-KNOWN PEOPLE

Although it is known that the Picts occupied a large part of Caledonia in the early 5th century, little is known of the identity and history of these 'painted men'. The Picts' principal legacy are the 2000 or so 'symbolic stones' found north of the Firths of Clyde and Forth, especially in Angus and the Northeast. The most likely explanation is that these monuments were used to mark a boundary or burial site, commemorate an alliance or victory, or celebrate a ritual. However, the exact significance of their motifs is not known. This extremely elaborate art form disappeared after the Picts and Scots formed the kingdom of Dalriada in the 9th century.

CLASSIFICATION OF PICTISH STONES

In the absence of an exact dating system, Pictish stones are classified into three main categories. Category I comprises simple rocks or megaliths that have been reused and are inscribed with figurative or abstract motifs bearing no relation to Christian iconography. The stones in the other two categories are carved and sculpted in relief. Those in Category II often represent figurative scenes accompanied by elaborately worked symbols on one side, and a cross and Christian motifs on the other. By contrast Pictish symbols do not appear on the stones in Category III.

1

2

3

MYSTERIOUS SYMBOLS

On the inscribed stones, straight or broken lines are always combined with an abstract symbol (crescent, double disc, rectangle), objects from everyday life, a 'flower' or an animal (*above*). One of the three standing stones (1) at Aberlemno ▲ *186* is inscribed with motifs that recur in Pictish art: a serpent (possibly an allusion to reincarnation), a double disc (which could represent this world and the hereafter or the union of two families), a broken arrow in the form of a Z (possibly symbolizing a great warrior or death) and the mirror-comb combination (undoubtedly a female symbol).

AN INCREASINGLY ELABORATE ART

The combination of symbols and figurative scenes on the standing stone in Aberlemno churchyard illustrates the development of Pictish art. On one side a battle scene (2) may commemorate the victory of the Picts (bare-headed on the left) over the Angles (wearing helmets) at Nechtansmere in 685. Another work of art is the stone at Nigg ▲ *247*. It is decorated on one side with the figures of men and animals and, on the other (3), with a huge cross and abstract motifs which suggest a knowledge of Irish and Northumbrian art and may have influenced the sculpture of Iona.

The region of Angus is bounded by the Firth of Tay to the south and the Grampian Mountains to the north. Its hinterland lies in the rich agricultural basin of Strathmore, while its coastal ports in the east have long owed their prosperity to trade, fishing and the textile industry. In addition to the legacy of this past glory the region also has some remarkable Pictish remains.

DUNDEE ◆ D C2

Scotland's fourth largest city, situated on the Firth of Tay at the foot of the Sidlaw Hills, is a port, an industrial center and a dynamic university town. It was elevated to the status of royal burgh in 1190 and soon became one of the principal towns in the kingdom, as well as one of the hardest hit by internal divisions and the wars between England and Scotland. It prospered in the 18th century and enjoyed its golden age during the Victorian era due to its flourishing textile and jam industries (including the famous orange marmalade invented by Mrs Keiller in 1797) and journalism. Today, modern industries have replaced the more traditional forms of production, but Dundee remains the seat of the Thompson newspaper group which publishes Scotland's best-known Sunday paper, the *Sunday Post*.

CITY CHURCHES *(Nethergate)*. These three churches occupy a single building dominated by ST MARY'S TOWER. The tower – all that remains of the 15th-century parish church – houses a small museum of religious history.

DUNDEE CONTEMPORARY ARTS CENTRE *(152 Nethergate)*. In 1999 Scotland's largest modern art center moved into the building designed by Richard Murphy. It offers visitors the opportunity to explore all areas of artistic creation – plastic arts, decorative arts, music, dance, cinema – through exhibitions, workshops and meetings with the artists.

MCMANUS GALLERIES *(Albert Square)*. This beautiful Victorian Gothic building, designed by George Gilbert Scott in 1867, houses a museum of local history and archeology and an interesting collection of works by 19th- and 20th-century European and Scottish artists.

VERDANT WORKS *(West Henderson's Wynd)*. This old factory, founded in 1833, traces the history of the jute industry in an innovative and interesting way.

ARBROATH ◆ D D2

Arbroath, a former royal burgh, 400-year-old fishing port and center of light industry, lies 12 miles to the northeast of Dundee. It is renowned for its smokies (haddock smoked over an oak fire) and its abbey.

ARBROATH ABBEY. The red-sandstone abbey church was consecrated in 1178 by William the Lion, but the present building dates from 1285. It was in this abbey, which once housed the relics of St Columba ● *33*, that the famous Declaration of Scottish Independence ● *39* was signed in April 1320. It was here, too, that the 'Stone of Destiny' ● *38* ▲ *116, 180*, stolen from Westminster in 1950, was found on

THE PORT OF DUNDEE Dundee is extremely proud of its maritime history. It was for a long time the Scottish center of the wine trade, and acquired important shipyards before becoming the major whaling port in Great Britain in c. 1860. Two museum ships built in the Dundee shipyards are moored at its quays: the wooden frigate HMS *Unicorn* (1824), fitted with 46 guns, and the Royal Research Ship *Discovery* (*above*), in which Captain Scott (1868–1912) led his first expedition to the Antarctic in 1901–04. The nearby visitor center, DISCOVERY POINT, retraces the ship's history. The BROUGHTY FERRY MUSEUM, in Dundee's east suburbs, has a permanent exhibition on whaling.

ST VIGEANS ◆ D D2
(1 mile north of Arbroath, on the A92) The museum, housed in one of the cottages in the village, has remarkable collection of 32 Pictish sculptured stones discovered during the rebuilding of the church.

▲ Angus

GLAMIS CASTLE ★
Glamis Castle, which
is closely associated
with the royal family,
also provided the
setting for the murder
of Duncan in
Shakespeare's
Macbeth. It is said to
be haunted by the
ghost of Lady Glamis,
who was burnt at the
stake as a witch by
James V. Guided visits
only: 2 hours.

GLAMIS
*(5 miles west of Forfar,
on the A94)*
Glamis Castle (*above,
right*), a former royal
hunting lodge and fief
(feu) of the Bowes-
Lyon family, earls of
Strathmore and
Kinghorn, was the
childhood home of
HM Queen Elizabeth
The Queen Mother,
daughter of the
14th Earl, and the
birthplace of Princess
Margaret. The tower-
house built in the
15th and 16th
centuries was
enlarged in the
17th and 19th
centuries. Some of
the richly furnished
apartments and a
chapel decorated with
panels painted by the
Dutch artist Jacob de
Wet, in 1688, are
open to the public.
The collections of the
ANGUS FOLK
MUSEUM, housed
in a number of old
cottages in the village,
are well worth a visit.

Brechin Cathedral
and its round tower.

the abbey's altar in 1951. The abbey ruins, which combine
Norman and early Gothic styles, include a decorated west
doorway and the beautiful south transept with its two rows of
blind arches surmounted by a row of open arches, high Gothic
windows and a circular window (the 'Round O of Arbroath'). A
plaque marks the tomb of William the Lion. The 15th-century
sacristy is very well preserved, as is the Abbot's House
(15th–early 16th century) which today houses a museum.
SIGNAL TOWER MUSEUM. The signal tower built in 1811 to
communicate with the construction teams working on the
Inchcape or Bell Rock lighthouse, 12 miles to the southeast,
traces the history of Arbroath and the lighthouse.

FROM ARBROATH TO MEIGLE

MONTROSE *(A92).* This ancient royal burgh is a busy
commercial center and active port. It has some beautiful old,
gabled houses and a small museum of local history. The
MONTROSE BASIN NATURE RESERVE CENTRE (a mile to the
southwest, on the A92) has a presentation on the 740-acre
nature reserve on the south shore of the tidal Montrose Basin.
HOUSE OF DUN *(A935).* This impressive Georgian mansion,
designed in 1730 by William Adam and refurbished in the
19th century, still has its magnificent plasterwork and
Victorian gardens.
BRECHIN. This town on the South Esk is centered on its 13th-
century cathedral. In the adjoining churchyard stands one of
Scotland's two Irish-style Round Towers (the other is at
Abernethy ▲ *178*), a 110-foot tower dating from the 11th
century. The PICTAVIA museum, which stands in the grounds
of Brechin Castle, traces the history of the Picts.
ABERLEMNO *(B9134).* The village has some magnificent
Pictish stones ▲ *184* (7th–9th century), one in the churchyard
and three at the roadside.
MEIGLE *(7 miles southwest of Glamis, on the A94).* Twenty-five
outstanding Pictish stones (7th–10th century) from the
surrounding area can be seen in Meigle's former schoolhouse.

The West

Julia and John Keay, Mary McGrigor, Patrick Taylor

189 The right bank of the
     Firth of Clyde
190 Argyll
196 *Scotland's gardens*
200 The Inner Hebrides

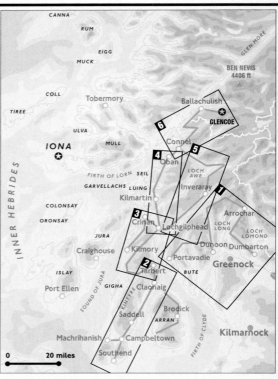

1. The right bank of the
   Firth of Clyde ▲189
2. Kintyre ▲191
3. Knapdale ▲192
4. From Lochgilphead
   to Oban ▲193
5. Inveraray
   and Loch Awe ▲194
6. North Argyll ▲198

**TRADITIONAL
AGRICULTURE**
Many of the farmers
evicted from the
Highlands in the 18th
and 19th centuries
were resettled on
smallholdings known
as 'crofts'. These
crofters kept a few
sheep, sometimes
cattle and poultry,
and grew barley, oats,
potatoes and swedes.
They dug peat to heat
their 'blackhouses'
▲ 69 and often
supplemented their
income by fishing or
collecting seaweed.
In 1886 the Crofters
Holding Act granted
these smallholders
security of tenure, the
right to bequeath
their property to their
descendants and a
rent fixed by the
'Land Court' which
sat in Edinburgh. This
traditional form of
agriculture is still
practiced from Argyll
to Sutherland, and
especially on the
islands. Crops are
farmed individually
while grazing is
shared by the crofters
who also share
certain tasks,
especially the harvest.
Many crofters are
also employed in the
fishing, tourist and
building industries.

With its mountainous relief and long peninsulas, the west coast of Scotland has an extremely jagged coastline. The West Highlands, which cover the county of Argyll and stretch for a distance of 155 miles from north to south, have no less than 2800 miles of coastline. Off the coast lies a string of islands, vast and mountainous like Mull or small and flat like Tiree. Rhododendrons and azaleas flourish at the head of lochs and bays bathed by the Gulf Stream, which accounts for the region's mild, wet climate.

HISTORY. In the early centuries AD Celtic-speaking peoples from Ireland settled along this coast and founded the kingdom of Dalriada in 498 ▲ 33, with its two capitals, Dunadd ▲ 193 and Finlaggan, on Islay ▲ 202. Christianity also came from Ireland in the 6th century, when St Columba founded a monastery on the island of Iona ▲ 204 before going on to convert the mainland. Many burial mounds (tumuli), fortifications, standing stones and carved stone crosses evoke this rich Celtic heritage. The Viking threat brought about the union of the Picts and the Scots in 843, but c. 900 the invaders still controlled the islands and most of the west coast, as evidenced by the many placenames of Norse origin. In the 12th century the decline of Viking power enabled local chiefs to establish a clan society while Somerled, a descendant of the kings of Dalriada, founded an 'island kingdom' over Argyll and Mull (c. 1150) which lasted until 1493. The Macdonalds subsequently laid claim to the kingdom, but none of the clans who bitterly disputed this territory could rival the power of

> 'The rock of Dumbarton rose from its waters [the Clyde]
> like a black pyramid; in the distance, a few motionless
> vessels awaited the incoming tide.'

Adolphe Blanqui

the Campbells of Inveraray ▲ *194*. For a long time cattle farming (and stealing) was one of the principal sources of income. This was replaced by fishing, the collection of seaweed and subsistence farming after the Highland Clearances of the 18th and 19th centuries ▲ *36*. Today, these activities are still practiced, though on a smaller scale, while the depopulated valleys are given over to forestry.

THE RIGHT BANK OF THE FIRTH OF CLYDE ◆ D A3

DUMBARTON AND ITS CASTLE *(west of Glasgow, on the A82).* This industrial town was formerly the capital of Strathclyde, the kingdom of the Britons which became part of Scotland in 1034 ▲ *33*. It is also said to be the birthplace of St Patrick (c. 387–461), kidnapped by pirates as a young man and sold into slavery in Ireland where he became a Christian and began to convert the people of Ireland in 432. Dumbarton is also the port from which Mary Stuart secretly set sail for France in 1548 ▲ *40*. Dumbarton Castle dominates the Firth of Clyde from the top of a 240-foot rock. The castle was fortified in the 13th century when it became a royal residence. In 1305 its governor used treachery to capture William Wallace and hand him over to Edward I of England. The castle, badly damaged in the wars between England and Scotland, was rebuilt after 1707, when the Act of Union stipulated that it must house a garrison. From the former Governor's House (1735–1832) steps cut out of the rock climb to the Wallace Guardhouse where two more flights of steps lead east to the magazine and west to the orientation table on the site of the White Tower. The panorama over the Clyde from this viewpoint is well worth the effort.

HELENSBURGH *(on the A814).* This elegant coastal resort stands on a hillside on the north bank of the Firth of Clyde. At the top of Colquhoun Street stands HILL HOUSE *(below)*, the beautiful house designed and decorated (1902–04) by Charles Rennie Mackintosh and Margaret Macdonald ● *84* ▲ *162* for the Glaswegian publisher Walter W. Blackie. The house combines several different styles – Arts and Crafts, Glasgow Style and Scots Baronial – and is a fine example of a design that is both functional and esthetically pleasing, both in terms of spatial organization and decoration. White and dark, wood-paneled walls punctuated by stenciled motifs, stuccoed panels and stained glass insets attest to an attention to detail that is echoed by the furniture and lighting designed by the architect. Beyond Helensburgh the A814 follows the east shores of Gare Loch and Loch Long toward Arrochar.

THE WEST HIGHLAND WAY
This 95-mile footpath runs from Milngavie, in the north of Glasgow, to Fort William ▲ *236*, at the foot of Ben Nevis. It follows old military roads and disused railway lines, running along the east shore of Loch Lomond and into the Highlands, where it passes through Glencoe ▲ *199* and crosses Rannoch Moor ▲ *182*.

REMAINS OF THE ANTONINE WALL
An earthwork at Old Kilpatrick (1 mile southeast of Dumbarton) has remains of the Antonine Wall, built by the Romans c. 143 as a defense against Pictish invasions. When it was built the wall was reinforced with a palisade and ditch, and guarded by forts. Other remains of the wall can be seen at Duntocher, 2 miles east of Old Kilpatrick.

HILL HOUSE, A MACKINTOSH TOWER-HOUSE ★
The beautiful house designed by Charles Rennie Mackintosh, in a combination of traditional Scots Baronial and Glasgow Style, is the only one to have retained its original decor.

YOUNGER BOTANIC GARDEN ◆ **D** A3
(on the A815, south of Loch Eck)
This annex of Edinburgh's Royal Botanic Gardens ▲ *126* is famous for its avenue of Californian giant redwoods, planted in 1863. The park is particularly attractive in May and June, when the azaleas and rhododendrons are in bloom. Rhododendrons 'Golden Horn', 'Sinogrande' and 'Yakushimanum' (*above*).

THE COWAL PENINSULA ◆ **C** C3-**D** A3

The southeast of Argyll is formed by the Cowal peninsula, which stretches between Loch Long and Loch Fyne like an eagle's claw closing round the Island of Bute ▲ *200*.

ARROCHAR. This little village nestling at the head of Loch Long is a favorite summer rendezvous for walkers and climbers, who come to pit themselves against the munros and other peaks of Arrochar: Ben Arthur (2890 feet), nicknamed The Cobbler because its outline resembles that of an upturned shoe, Beinn Ime (3315 feet), Beinn Narnain (3040 feet), Ben Vane (3005 feet) and Ben Donich (2780 feet).

TOWARD LOCH GOIL. The A83 winds its way up the valley of Glen Croe to the pass known as REST AND BE THANKFUL (875 feet), named by the soldiers who built the first road over the pass in 1750. From here the B828 leads to Loch Goil, via Glen Mhoil, and the B839 to Hell's Glen. At the head of Loch Goil is the little port of Lochgoilhead and, on its

west shore, the ruins of CARRICK CASTLE (14th–15th century). Mary Stuart stayed in this stronghold of the earls of Argyll on her way to Inveraray in 1563.

ARDKINGLAS WOODLAND GARDEN. This arboretum at the head of Loch Fyne (*above*) has a superb collection of conifers.

DUNOON *(on the A815 and the southeast coast).* Dunoon, the 'capital' of Cowal, stands on the bend of the Firth of Clyde. The village became a fashionable spa town in the 19th century when a ferry service was established between Dunoon and Gourock. Its pleasant Victorian villas are dominated by the ruins of a 13th-century castle, destroyed in 1685. According to tradition James III made the earls of Argyll the castle's hereditary keepers, on condition that they presented him with a red rose whenever he asked for one. A bronze statue (1896) of Highland Mary, the subject of a song by Robert Burns ● *98* ▲ *142*, stands at the foot of Castle Hill. At the end of August Dunoon welcomes the 150 or so pipe bands that take part in the COWAL HIGHLAND GATHERING. The A886 runs down the west side of the peninsula to COLINTRAIVE, the ferry port for the Island of Bute. Another ferry service links Portavadie, on the southwestern tip of the peninsula, with Tarbert, in Kintyre.

> 'In Scotland and Ireland, the roads twist and turn for no apparent reason other than to allow you to enjoy the same landscape from every possible angle.'
>
> Nicolas Bouvier

KINTYRE ◆ C C3-C5

Kintyre is the southern part of the long western peninsula of Argyll. The Kilbrannan Sound separates it from the Isle of Arran ▲ *200*, in the east, while the tiny island of Gigha ▲ *200* lies a few miles off its west coast.

TARBERT. This little fishing port and marina stands on East Loch Tarbert, at the northern end of Kintyre. Its name, derived from *an tairbeart*, meaning 'isthmus' in Gaelic, is associated with the memory of the Norse king, Magnus Barfor (or Barelegs). Legend has it that in 1098, when he was trying to persuade the king of Scotland to cede all the islands he could circumnavigate, Magnus Barfor had a galley hauled across the isthmus between East and West Loch Tarbert in order to lay claim to Kintyre. Tarbert, which has always been a herring fishing port, has five processing factories. The photographs and archeological remains on display in the AN TAIRBEART HERITAGE CENTRE trace the everyday life of this small community over the centuries. The castle, whose ruins dominate the port, was built by Alexander II or his son Alexander III, in the 13th century, and refurbished by Robert Bruce in 1325. In 1494 James IV built the keep (complete with dungeon) which faced east so that its cannons were aimed at the entrance to the port. The Earl of Argyll was appointed hereditary keeper in 1505. After serving as the headquarters of the pirate Alan-nan-Sop Maclean, the castle fell into the hands of Cromwell's troops in 1652. The inhabitants are said to have taken advantage of the absence of the garrison, which had gone to gather nuts, to regain possession of their castle. Inhabited since the 18th century, the building is at present under the guardianship of the Tarbert Castle Trust.

KENNACRAIG *(on the A83)*. This port on West Loch Tarbert is today the car-ferry port for the islands of Gigha, Islay ▲ *202*, Jura ▲ *201* and Colonsay ▲ *202*.

SKIPNESS CASTLE ◆ C C4
This impressive fortress once guarded the confluence of Loch Fyne, the Kilbrannan Sound and the Sound of Bute. The castle was built in the first half of the 13th century by a vassal of the Macdonalds of Islay and Kintyre. It was surrounded by a curtain wall c. 1300 and enlarged in the 16th century. Nearby stand the ruins of the 14th-century Gothic church of St Brendan.

East Loch Tarbert.

Crinan at the west end of the Crinan Canal.

'From the Mull of Kintyre they see Ireland very plain, it being not above fifteen or sixteen miles from the point of land, which they call the Mull to the Fair Foreland [...] on the north of Ireland. [...] Here are also the islands of Arran and Bute [which] have nothing considerable in or about them, except it be a tumultuous sea for sailors, especially when a south-west wind blows hard, which brings the sea rowling in upon them in a frightful manner.'
Daniel Defoe

CLAONAIG *(via the B8801)*. In summer this little port on the east coast of the peninsula is the car ferry for Arran.
SADDELL *(on the B824)*. The CISTERCIAN ABBEY, where its founder Somerled (d. 1164) ● *33* is said to be buried, today stands in ruins. However, the many 14th–15th century tombstones in its churchyard and those of the surrounding area attest to the talent of local medieval stonemasons.
CAMPBELTOWN. This resort at the head of Campbeltown Loch is the peninsula's main town. Formerly Kinlochkilkerran, it acquired its present name in the 17th century when Archibald Campbell, 7th Earl of Argyll, gained control of the town after a long and bitter struggle with the Macdonalds of Kintyre. It became a royal burgh in 1700 and was a herring port until the 1920s. In the late 19th century it had 34 distilleries of which two are still active today ● *60*. The fine Campbeltown Cross opposite the harbor dates from the 14th century.
TOWARD THE MULL OF KINTYRE. It was at Keil, near Southend, on the southern tip of the peninsula (B842), that St Columba is said to have first set foot on Scottish soil in 563. A minor road follows the south coast to the Mull of Kintyre, from where you can see the coast of Northern Ireland.
MACHRIHANISH *(at the end of the B843)*. This holiday resort on the west coast has long beaches and, like Southend, a beautiful golf course. From Campbeltown the A83 turns northward along the west coast of the peninsula.

KNAPDALE ◆ C C3-C4

This district of Mid-Argyll is bounded by West Loch Tarbert to the south and the Crinan Canal to the north.
SOUTH KNAPDALE. From Tarbert the B8024 offers some spectacular views as it follows the southeast and west coasts of the Knapdale peninsula. At Achahoish, at the head of

One of the two
Templewood Stone
Circles (*far left*);
footprint carved in a
stone at Dunadd Fort
(*left*).

Loch Caolisport, a poorly maintained road turns off to
ST COLUMBA'S CAVE. The cave is traditionally associated with
the missionary saint but was probably occupied much earlier.
CRINAN CANAL. Ardrishaig stands at the south end of the
Crinan Canal. This 8-mile stretch of water, which links Loch
Fyne to the Sound of Jura at the mouth of Loch Gilp, was
opened in 1810 to prevent fishing boats having to sail round
the dangerous Mull of Kintyre.
CRINAN *(via the B841)*. The attractive hamlet at the
western end of the canal is also a busy marina. The north
entrance to the bay is guarded by DUNTRUNE CASTLE, built
in the 13th century to counter Viking attacks. The castle is
closed to the public but its gardens are well worth a visit
(via the B8025).
TOWARD THE POINT OF KNAP. From Bellanoch, a minor road
runs through Knapdale Forest and along the east shore of
Loch Sween to its mouth. It passes the ruins of Castle
Suibhne (or Castle Sween), a Norman castle built in the 11th
or 12th century and dismantled in 1647. Today the castle is
surrounded by a caravan park. The road also leads to
KILMORY KNAP CHAPEL which houses some beautiful Celtic
and medieval crosses. The 15th-century MacMillan Cross,
which has a crucifixion carved on one side and a hunting
scene on the other, evokes the memory of one of the keepers
of the castle.

FROM LOCHGILPHEAD TO OBAN ◆ C C3-C2

LOCHGILPHEAD *(on the A83)*. Lochgilphead, at the head of
Loch Gilp, is the administrative center of Argyll and Bute.
The town enjoyed its golden age in the early 19th century
when the Crinan Canal was opened and it welcomed farmers
evicted by the Highland Clearances.
DUNADD *(on the A816)*. The isolated hilltop that dominates
the River Add, to the northwest of Bridgend, was fortified
during the Iron Age. Around 500 it became the site of
the capital of Fergus, the first king of Dalriada, ● *33*.
Its remains include carved stones – an inscription in the
ogham alphabet (an ancient Celtic writing system), the image
of a boar, a footprint and a shallow basin – which were
probably associated with the coronation ceremony of the
Scottish kings. The stones act as a reminder that
Dunadd was the first site of the 'Stone of Destiny'
● *38* ▲ *116, 180, 185*.

PREHISTORIC SITES
◆ C C3
There is no shortage
of late Stone Age
(c. 3000 BC) and
Bronze Age remains
in Kilmartin Glen,
between
Lochgilphead and
Kilmartin. The most
interesting are the
cup-and-ring
markings carved on
two flat rock surfaces
at ACHNABRECK
Farm, the two
TEMPLEWOOD Stone
Circles and the three
burial mounds
(tumuli) at NETHER
LARGIE.

**CARNASSARIE
CASTLE ◆ C** C3
(Carnassie, A816)
This abandoned
castle was built in the
16th century by John
Carswell, the first
Protestant Bishop of
the Isles, whose
Gaelic translation of
John Knox's ● *35, 41*
liturgy was one of the
first works published
in Gaelic (1567). The
castle still has some
beautiful fireplaces
and carved details
dating from the
Renaissance period.

OBAN AND SURROUNDINGS ◆ **C** C2

This pleasant town, which stands at the
crossroads of the Highlands and islands,
is the principal port for the Hebrides.
The fishing port founded in the 18th
century, on a bay sheltered by the island
of Kerrera, became a fashionable resort
with the advent of the railway and the
development of steam navigation in the
1850s. MCCAIG'S FOLLY, in the style of
the Colosseum in Rome, stands above
the town. It was begun in 1897 by the
banker John Stuart McCaig, who wanted
to build a family mausoleum and provide
work for the town's unemployed.
Work was suspended when this local
benefactor died in 1902. This viewpoint
on the mouth of the River Lorn is one of
the town's main attractions, along with
the distillery ▲ *221,* founded in 1794 on
Stafford Street, and the fishing port.
KERRERA. The island of Kerrera, a
walkers' paradise, protects the entrance
to Oban harbor and is linked to the town
by ferry. Alexander II was killed here, in
1249, when he fought Duncan, Lord of
the Isles, who refused to take an oath of

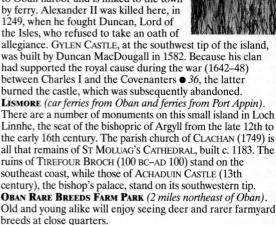

allegiance. GYLEN CASTLE, at the southwest tip of the island,
was built by Duncan MacDougall in 1582. Because his clan
had supported the royal cause during the war (1642–48)
between Charles I and the Covenanters ● *36,* the latter
burned the castle, which was subsequently abandoned.
LISMORE (*car ferries from Oban and ferries from Port Appin*).
There are a number of monuments on this small island in Loch
Linnhe, the seat of the bishopric of Argyll from the late 12th to
the early 16th century. The parish church of CLACHAN (1749) is
all that remains of ST MOLUAG'S CATHEDRAL, built c. 1183. The
ruins of TIREFOUR BROCH (100 BC–AD 100) stand on the
southeast coast, while those of ACHADUIN CASTLE (13th
century), the bishop's palace, stand on its southwestern tip.
OBAN RARE BREEDS FARM PARK (*2 miles northeast of Oban*).
Old and young alike will enjoy seeing deer and rarer farmyard
breeds at close quarters.
DUNSTAFFNAGE CASTLE (*on the A85, near the village of
Dunbeg*). In the 13th century the MacDougalls of Lorne built
a stronghold on a promontory above the entrance to Loch
Etive, said to have been the site of the court of Kenneth
MacAlpin ● *33* before he moved to Scone ▲ *180.* In the 15th
century the 1st Earl of Argyll bought the castle and appointed
the Campbells of Dunstaffnage as its hereditary captains. The
three round towers and tower-house built above the entrance
date from the 16th century.

INVERARAY AND LOCH AWE ◆ **D** A2-A3-**C** C2-C3

With its whitewashed two-story houses and classical-style
public buildings, this former royal burgh (1648) and seat of
the Campbell clan since the 15th century is a fine example of

At the north end of Loch Awe, said to be haunted by a mythical monster, stand the ruins of Kilchurn Castle (*below*). The tower-house built by Sir Colin Campbell of Glenorchy in 1440 was extended in 1693 and abandoned in the 1740s.

18th-century urban planning ● 78. When Archibald Campbell, 3rd Duke of Argyll decided to enlarge his ancestral castle in 1744, he moved the surrounding village to Gallows Foreland on the shores of Loch Fyne. The public buildings were designed by Robet Mylne and built by William Adam. One of these, the prison (1816–20), was closed in 1889 and converted into a museum: the very realistic INVERARAY JAIL has a courtroom (1820), wax figures and mechanical models. The BELL TOWER of the parish church (Front Street), erected by the 10th Duke of Argyll in memory of the Campbells killed during World War One, offers panoramic views of the town and Loch Fyne.

INVERARAY CASTLE. The castle, whose plans ● 76 were designed by Roger Morris assisted by William Adam, was built between 1746 and 1758. The interior decor was renovated (1772–82) by Robert Mylne at the request of the 5th Duke of Argyll. With their painted panels by the French artists Guinand and Girard and their coffered ceilings, the banqueting hall and drawing room – which has a magnificent collection of 18th-century Beauvais tapestry – are among the finest examples of Scottish neoclassical decor. An impressive collection of weaponry (*above, right*), family portraits (Gainsborough, Ramsay, Raeburn), furniture, gold- and silverware, and various family souvenirs complete the exhibition. The castle has been restored since it was badly damaged by fire in 1975.

LOCH AWE. To the north of Inveraray, the A819 follows Glen Aray to the shores of Loch Awe, Scotland's longest inland lake (25 miles) and a fisherman's paradise.

AUCHINDRAIN ◆ D A3
(6 miles southeast of Inveraray)
This typical West Highland village has been carefully restored. Its FOLK LIFE MUSEUM presents the everyday life of a traditional Highland croft.

INVERARAY ★
This delightful example of 18th-century Scottish urban architecture and residence of the dukes of Argyll stands against the backdrop of Loch Fyne.

195

Scotland, where horticulture has long been a national tradition, is renowned for its colorists' and collectors' gardens. The most beautiful botanical collections are undoubtedly those of Arduaine, Inverewe and Logan, on the west coast, where the mild climate (due to the influence of the warm Gulf Stream), abundant rainfall and acid soil have encouraged the development of a wide range of exotic plants. The formal French-style gardens of Pitmedden and Drummond Castle, and the exuberant borders of Crathes Castle and the House of Pitmuies are a wonderful illustration of the Scottish passion for color in the garden.

2. INVEREWE ▲ *243*
Rare and delicate plants, including many from the Southern Hemisphere, eucalyptus, myrtle and different varieties of rhododendron from the Himalayas flourish in this Scottish 'jungle'.

3. HOUSE OF PITMUIES
The planting designed by Margaret Ogilvie in the 1970s is a perfect illustration of a traditional colorist's garden. One of its multicolored borders cleverly echoes the colors of the main drawing room.

1. DRUMMOND CASTLE ▲ 180
The castle's terraced gardens were created in the 1630s, but the St Andrew's Cross design dates from the 19th century. Neatly clipped trees and shrubs, elegantly planted beds and carefully designed borders form a dazzling formal display centered on a sundial.

4. PITMEDDEN GARDEN ▲ 217
This huge garden was created by Alexander Seton in 1675 and redesigned in the 1950s. Its box hedges are shaped into elegant geometric motifs which provide a framework for a sumptuous display of annuals.

5. KELLIE CASTLE ▲ 176
This romantic composition, created in 1880 by Robert Lorimer, was inspired by 17th-century gardens with their densely planted beds, herbaceous borders, espaliered fruit trees, rose arbors and bowers.

6. CRATHES CASTLE ▲ 214
Impressive hedges of clipped yew, the remains of the classical garden laid out in the early 18th century, add a monumental dimension to the series of gardens designed in the 1930s by Sir James Burnett of Leys. His wife's planting uses sophisticated combinations of hot colors – reds, purples and yellows – to give each garden its beautiful chromatic harmony.

BLUE POPPIES
Many Scottish horticulturists brought back plants from abroad, for example the blue Himalayan poppy (*Meconopsis betonicifolia*, *above*) which flourishes in acid soil and damp conditions. David Douglas (1798–1834) sent several varieties of conifer from North America, while George Forrest (1873–1932) brought varieties of camellia and rhododendron from China and Tibet. As a result Scotland has some remarkable botanical collections.

Castle Stalker.

ST CONAN'S KIRK. The church stands on the shores of Loch Awe, to the west of Lochawe village. It was built in 1881 by Walter Douglas Campbell, a passionate architect who spent his entire life perfecting his neo-Gothic work. This unusual building houses tombs with recumbent statues of the dukes of Argyll and archeological finds from different parts of the region.

CRUACHAN POWER STATION *(on the A85).* This hydroelectric power station with its reversible pump-turbines and machine room deep within Ben Cruachan (3707 feet) is open to the public. The road leaves the Pass of Brander, where Robert Bruce defeated the MacDougalls of Lorne, the most powerful clan in Argyll, in 1308, and crosses the Awe which is famous for its salmon.

BONAWE IRON FURNACE. This coal-fueled furnace produced high-quality iron between 1753 and 1874. It has been restored as a reminder that the village of Taynuilt was once one of Scotland's major iron-smelting centers.

NORTH ARGYLL ◆ C C2-D A1-A2

ARDCHATTAN PRIORY *(via the minor road that turns off the A828, just north of Connel's cantilever bridge, and follows the south shore of Loch Etive).* The priory, founded in 1231 by Duncan MacDougall, Lord of Lorne, was bought after the Reformation by Alexander Campbell, a commendatory prior, and is still occupied by his descendants. The only parts of the priory (burned by Cromwell's troops) open to the public are the ruined cloister, which houses some monumental sculptures from the Iona school ▲ *204*, and the gardens.

BARCALDINE CASTLE *(on the southwest shore of Loch Creran, via a minor road that turns off the A828 just north of Benderloch).* This tower-house, built in 1609 by Duncan Campbell of Glenorchy, was abandoned in the late 19th century. Its restored interiors and secret passages are open to the public, and it is even possible to rent a room.

BARCALDINE SEA LIFE CENTRE *(on the A282, on the south shore of Loch Creran).* The open-air seal pool is the main attraction of this oceanographic museum which offers an insight into Scotland's marine life. As the A828 follows the shore of Loch Creran, Port Appin, the ferry port for the island of Lismore, lies off to the west.

CASTLE STALKER. This private castle, perched on a rocky outcrop at the entrance to Loch Laich, south of Portnacroish, is surrounded by an aura of romantic splendor. It was built c. 1520 by the Stewarts of Appin, abandoned c. 1800 and restored in the 1970s by Colonel Stewart Allwood.

BALLACHULISH. Near the bridge that spans Loch Leven, a granite monument marks the spot where James Stewart of Aucharn was hanged in November 1752 for the murder of Colin Campbell of Glenure, a government officer murdered during the 'Highland Clearances'. Robert Louis Stevenson based one of the characters in his novel *Kidnapped* (1886) on the main suspect, Alan Breck Stewart. Stevenson's novel illustrated the cruelty of the British government toward the supporters of the Stuart cause after Bonnie Prince Charlie had escaped to France ● *43*.

THE GLENCOE MASSACRE
After the first Jacobite Rising, in 1689, William III of Orange decided to pardon all clans who took an oath of allegiance before January 1, 1692. After a number of delays Alistair MacIan, chief of the Macdonalds of Glencoe, took the oath a week late. The Under Secretary of State, Sir John Dalrymple, and the Campbells (Presbyterians and hereditary enemies of the Macdonalds) who sat on the Privy Council decided to send troops led by Campbell of Glenlyon to punish the 'rebels'. Disregarding the rules of Gaelic hospitality, these troops spent a week with the Macdonald clan before running forty of its members through with their swords at dawn on January 13. Most of those who were not killed died of cold and exposure. The report of the massacre by two survivors led to an official inquiry, but those responsible were not brought to account. Jacobite propaganda made much of the tragedy and gained the sympathy of Catholic Europe.

GLENCOE VILLAGE *(on the south shore of Loch Leven, on the A82)*. THE GLENCOE AND NORTH LORNE FOLK MUSEUM traces the economic and social history of the region, the history of the Macdonald clan and the Jacobite Risings.

GLEN COE. This deep, narrow valley is bounded by barren mountains, including Bidean nam Bian (3743 feet), the highest point in Argyll, and its foothills, the Three Sisters of Glen Coe: Beinn Fhada, Gearr Aonach and Aonach Dubh. In addition to its harsh beauty and Highland flora and fauna, the infamous massacre that took place in the glen in 1692 has made it a site of scientific and historic interest. The GLENCOE CENTRE at Clachaig has a presentation on the geology and history of this impressive valley and organizes guided tours. Further along the valley the GLENCOE SKI CENTRE, the White Corries ski resort, has a chair-lift that climbs to 2300 feet (operational throughout the year) and offers a spectacular view of Glencoe and Rannoch Moor ▲ *182*. From the Kingshouse Hotel, at the eastern end of Glen Coe, a minor road runs southwest along the magnificent glacial valley of Glen Etive to Loch Etive.

Glen Coe in summer (*top*); Glen Coe in winter (*center*); Glen Etive (*bottom*).

EXCURSIONS IN GLEN COE ◆ D A1
Several itineraries enable seasoned walkers to discover the valley's spectacular landscapes at close quarters. From the Glencoe Centre, which provides valuable information for walkers and climbers, a marked footpath leads through woodland to Signal Rock, the former rallying point of the Macdonalds. This is a long walk over rugged terrain but the view is well worth the effort. There is also Ossian's Ladder, a steep path which climbs the slopes of Aonach Dubh to the cave where the legendary bard is said to have been born. Alternatively the Devil's Staircase follows part of an old military road from Altnafeadh to Kinlochleven (6 miles).

GLEN COE, THE EMOTIVE BEAUTY OF THE HIGHLANDS ✪
A wild valley dominated by high volcanic peaks. Grandiose landscapes that send a shiver down the spine when the wind rises and clouds gather in the sky.

GIGHA ◆ C C4
(car ferries from Tayinloan)
The island of Gigha, whose name means 'island of the gods' in Gaelic, lies 3 miles west of Kintyre. It is a tiny, fertile island bordered by beautiful beaches. The trees and shrubs of ACHAMORE GARDENS provide shelter for such delicate and exotic species as magnolias and camellias.

BUTE ◆ C C3-C4 D A3-A4

This small island in the Firth of Clyde (46 square miles) has been a popular destination for Glaswegians for over a century. There are ferry services between Rothesay and Wemyss Bay (Ayrshire), and between Rudobach, at the north end of the island, and Colintraive on the Cowal peninsula ▲ *190*.

ROTHESAY. Rothesay, the only town on the Island of Bute, is a popular coastal resort whose fountains, winter garden (1924) (including a restaurant and cinema) and extravagant public toilets (1899), now a listed building, give it a certain outdated charm. In the 13th century, after two Norse occupations, ROTHESAY CASTLE was surrounded by a circular curtain wall punctuated by four round towers. It was rebuilt in 1406 and became the summer residence of the Stewarts who added the Great Tower in the 16th century. It was burned by the Duke of Argyll in 1685 and has been partially restored since the 19th century. The Bute Museum, in the street next to the castle, presents the geology, fauna and history of the island, which was first occupied some 5500 years ago. ROTHESAY CREAMERY, the local cheese factory, presents a more up-to-date aspect of life on the island.

ARDENCRAIG GARDENS *(1 mile south of Rothesay)*. The gardens are renowned for their fuchsia collection, water garden and aviaries.

MOUNT STUART *(3 miles southeast of Rothesay)*. Robert Rowand Anderson undertook the construction of this extravagant neo-Gothic mansion at the request of the 3rd Marquess of Bute (1847–1900). The cathedral-like appearance of the vast marble

Rothesay harbor *(below)*; Mount Stuart *(right)*.

hall, with its stained-glass windows and vaulted ceiling studded with glass stars, the white marble chapel lit by purple-glass windows and the 'Horoscope' study reveal the mystical leanings of this art lover who was the patron of a dozen architects and financed some 60 building projects. With its pinetum, Victorian vegetable garden and beautiful informal gardens, the vast estate offers some pleasant walks.

ST BLANE'S CHURCH *(at the south end of the island)*. This ruined chapel, consecrated in the 12th century on the foundations of a 6th-century monastery, still has a beautiful Norman vault.

ARRAN (AYRSHIRE) ◆ C C4 -D A4

The Isle of Arran (170 square miles) lies between the mouth of the Firth of Clyde and the east coast of Kintyre ▲ *191*. The southern part of this 'miniature Scotland' is fertile and fairly flat, rather like the Lowlands, while the more austere and

MOUNT STUART, A GOTHIC MANSION ★
This monumental Victorian mansion is remarkable both for its architecture, which is a subtle blend of various Gothic influences, and its rich decoration reflecting the 3rd Marquess' espousal of Roman Catholicism.

> 'Scotland is defined by its island horizon. A distinct outline unchanging in the distance, The silhouette of a mountain with lush, green slopes, The profile of high blue peaks.'

Jacques Darras

The ruins of Lochranza Castle.

JURA ◆ **C** B3-C3
This wild island, dominated by the three summits of the Paps of Jura (the highest is 2576 feet), was named after the deer that inhabit it (*Dyr oe* in Norse). The islanders live mainly by agriculture and tourism since the only industry is the distillery at Craighouse, the island's main village. The Strait of Corryvreckan, between the northwestern tip of Jura and the uninhabited island of Scarba, is renowned for the whirlpools created by counter currents from the Atlantic and the Sound of Jura above a submerged reef. The noise can be heard for up to 10 miles away. The strait, in the past thought to be a witch's cauldron, is an extremely dangerous stretch of water.

mountainous north evokes the Highlands. This part of the island is a walkers' and climbers' paradise, and its sandy bays and delightful little ports are popular with water-sports enthusiasts, golfers and fishermen.

BRODICK. This fishing port and coastal resort is also the 'capital' of Arran. It nestles in a bay dominated by Goatfell (2867 feet), the highest point on the island (allow 3 hours to reach the summit). There is a ferry service between Brodick and Ardrossan (Ayrshire) and, in summer, Rothesay on the Island of Bute.

ISLE OF ARRAN HERITAGE MUSEUM (*Rosaburn, 1 mile west of Brodick*). The museum occupies an 18th-century farmhouse and presents the island's economic, social and natural history.

BRODICK CASTLE (*1 mile north of Brodick*). The castle's lush gardens are due to the fact that, like the rest of Scotland's west coast, Arran is subject to the influence of the warm Gulf Stream. The 13th-century castle, the home of the dukes of Hamilton between 1503 and 1958, has been enlarged several times, in particular by James Gillespie Graham in 1844. Its collections include works by Gainsborough, Turner and Watteau, and some beautiful 18th- and 19th-century furniture.

LOCHRANZA. In summer a ferry service links this little resort on the north coast of Arran with the village of Claonaig in Kintyre ▲ *191*. A whisky distillery has recently been opened in this former herring port, dominated by the ruins of its castle (14th–15th century).

MACHRIE MOOR STONE CIRCLES (*near Tormore, on the west coast*). Pottery dating from the 2nd millennium BC has been found in these stone circles, whose function remains a mystery.

LUING AND SEIL
◆ **C** C2-C3
Ferries link the small islands of Luing, renowned for its cattle, and Seil, which is also linked to the west coast of Argyll by a bridge built by Thomas Telford in 1793.

GARVELLACH ISLANDS
◆ A B4
The only way to visit
the now uninhabited
Garvellach Islands, to
the south of Mull, is
to hire a boat. The
remains of 9th-
century beehive cells
can be seen on the
southernmost island,
Eileach an Naoimh,
where St Brendan
founded a monastic
community in 542.

COLONSAY ◆ C B3
*(ferry links with Oban
and Kennacraig)*
The island has
beautiful beaches,
rich plant life, and a
number of megaliths.
To the north of
Scalasaig, the island's
only village, Kiloran
House is open to
the public. The
magnificent gardens
of this 18th-century
mansion have many
varieties of exotic
plants. They were
created by Lord
Strathcona who
bought the island
in 1904.

ORONSAY ◆ C B3
At low tide Oronsay
and Colonsay are
linked by a causeway.
On Oronsay stand
the ruins of an
Augustinian priory
built in the 14th
century on the site of
a Celtic monastery.
An Irish stonemason
from Iona, by the
name of O'Cuinn, is
said to have carved
the beautiful stone
cross (1510) to the
west of St Oran's
Chapel.

ISLAY ◆ C B3-B4

Islay, the most southerly of the Inner Hebrides, is also the
largest and most fertile. For centuries its whisky ● *60* ▲ *220*
was produced and sold illegally. Today the island has six legal
distilleries, a cheese factory and tweed mill. It is linked to
Kennacraig (Kintyre), Colonsay and Jura by ferry.
PORT ELLEN. Islay's largest town, on the southeast coast,
was rebuilt in 1821 according to plans by Walter Frederick
Campbell. The road leading to Kildalton, to the northeast of
Port Ellen, services several of the island's distilleries. It also
passes beneath Dunyvaig Castle, built in the 14th century by
the Macdonalds, Lords of the Isles.
KILDALTON. The 13th-century church houses one of Scotland's
most beautiful Celtic crosses, probably carved on Iona in the
8th or 9th century, while the churchyard has some fine
tombstones.
BOWMORE. Islay's administrative center also has its
oldest legal distillery (1779). The island was bought by
Donald Campbell of Shawfield in 1725. His grandson,
Donald the Younger, inspired by the architecture seen on a
visit to Italy, designed this model village in 1768. Its crowning
glory is Kilarow Church, whose circular plan was intended to
prevent the devil from hiding in the corners!
GRUINART FLATS NATURE RESERVE *(south of Loch Gruinart).*
The Royal Society for the Protection of Birds opened this
nature reserve to enable barnacle geese to over-winter
undisturbed on the island and return to Greenland at the first
sign of spring.
PORT CHARLOTTE. This delightful little harbor, founded in
1828 by Walter Frederick Campbell on the west bank of Loch
Indaal, has an interesting MUSEUM OF ISLAY LIFE.
LOCH FINLAGGAN. The 'Friends of Finlaggan' have opened a
small museum to the northeast of the loch. They also provide

Fulmar (*above*); the island of Staffa (*left*).

'In fine weather, when the midday sun breaks through the veil of clouds and floods the Ocean with its radiant light, the depths of the cave are resplendent with a magnificent array of glowing colors [...]. The cave is filled with the noise of the crashing waves. The Gaels called it the musical cave.'

Louis Enault

a boat to enable visitors to reach the ruined castle, a former Macdonald stronghold, that stands on an island in the loch.

PORT ASKAIG. Together with Port Ellen, Port Askraig is one of the island's two ferry ports for Kintyre and the only ferry port for Jura and Colonsay.

MULL ◆ C B2-C2

This volcanic island is wilder than the Isle of Skye but, like Skye, is renowned for the diversity of landscapes. Its highest point is Ben More (3170 feet).

CRAIGNURE. This little harbor on the northeast coast of Mull is the car-ferry port for Oban.

TOROSAY CASTLE (*miniature-train service from Craignure's old pier*). The castle was built in Scots Baronial style (1858) by the architect David Bryce for the Campbells. It stands above Duart Bay and enjoys a sweeping view of Lock Linnhe which stretches away to the Appin and Lorne mountains on the Scottish mainland. Its magnificent gardens were designed by Robert Lorimer at the request of the Guthries, who bought the estate in 1868, and decorated with marble statues by the Italian sculptor Antonio Bonazza (1698–1763).

DUART CASTLE. The castle, built c. 1250 to protect the major navigation route of the Sound of Mull, is the ancestral home of the chiefs of the MacLean clan. After a checkered history it was extensively restored in the early 19th century: the keep is all that remains of the original building. Various relics of the clan's history can be seen inside the castle.

TOBERMORY. The administrative center of Mull is also one of the most beautiful natural harbors on the west coast of Scotland. It is extremely picturesque, with its tiers of gaily colored houses built on the hillside around the harbor. Founded in 1788 by the British Society for Encouraging Fisheries, it welcomed many of the farmers evicted during the Highland Clearances. At the harbor are a small MUSEUM of regional history, an ART AND CRAFT GALLERY and a DISTILLERY founded in 1795.

DERVAIG. The principal village on the west coast of Mull, founded in 1799, has the smallest professional theater in Great Britain, the Mull Little Theatre (performances May–September). Its museum, the OLD BYRE, has presentations of the island's everyday life and natural history.

FIONNPHORT. This hamlet at the end of the A849 is the ferry port for Iona. Its visitor center provides interesting information on the island of St Columba.

INCH KENNETH, ULVA, STAFFA, AND THE TRESHNISH ISLANDS ◆ C B2
The islands that lie to the west of Mull include the fertile Inch Kenneth, the former 'granary' of Iona with its 13th-century church, Ulva (whose Gaelic name means 'island of wolves') and Staffa (*above*), an uninhabited island famous for its basalt rock formations. Staffa's huge Fingal's Cave became a place of Romantic pilgrimage in the late 18th century ● *100* and inspired Mendelssohn to write the overture known as *Fingal's Cave* (*The Hebrides*). Further west the Treshnish Islands, fortified in the Middle Ages by the Lords of the Isles ● *33*, are today a bird sanctuary. Seals bask on the rocks at the foot of the basalt cliffs that provide a nesting site for petrels and puffins ● *20*.

IONA, THE SACRED ISLAND ✪

The windswept island of Iona, the main landmark of Scottish Christianity and the burial place of Scotland's first kings, is steeped in an atmosphere conducive to a life of meditation.

ST COLUMBA (c. 521–597)

The life of St Columba was recorded by his disciple and biographer Adamnan. Born into the Tirconaill (Donegall) branch of the Irish royal family, this priest with a fiery temper was the instigator of a bloody battle in 561. His penitence was to set sail in a coracle with twelve companions. Two years later he landed on the inhospitable island of Iona – given to him by a relative, the king of Dalriada – where he founded the monastery that was to play a key role in Scottish religious history. Columba also became the intermediary between the Scots of Dalriada and the Picts who dominated the east and north of Scotland ● 33. On his way to Inverness to convert the Pictish king Brude, he saved one of his disciples from being killed by a giant serpent which is today popularly known as Nessie ▲ 240. Legend has it that, on Sunday June 9, 597, a pony, sensing the saint's imminent death, placed its head on his shoulder and cried like a child... St Columba died the same night.

IONA, THE ISLAND OF ST COLUMBA ◆ C B2

This tiny island (2 square miles), which lies off the southwest tip of the Isle of Mull, played a key role in Scotland's conversion to Christianity. The restored cathedral, the burial place of the first Scottish kings (8th–11th century) and the Lords of the Isles (14th–15th century), is a major place of pilgrimage. The island, owned by the National Trust for Scotland, is popular with bird-watchers, geologists and hikers.

HISTORY. In 563 Columba founded a monastery which was to play a decisive role in the conversion of the peoples of Scotland to Christianity. In 574 he presided, in his capacity as head of the Celtic Church, over the coronation of Aidan, king of Dalriada. After Columba's death pilgrims began to flock to his tomb and the monastery became extremely influential, devoting itself, in particular, to stone carving and the production of magnificent illuminated manuscripts. In 806 the Vikings massacred 68 monks at Port nam Mairtear and destroyed the monastery. The survivors sought refuge at Kells, in Ireland, taking with them the relics of St Columba and other treasures, which probably included part of the magnificent *Book of Kells*, today held in Trinity College, Dublin. In 1203 Reginald, son of Somerled and Lord of the Isles, founded a Benedictine monastery on the site of Columba's monastery and, some time later, an Augustinian nunnery. The Benedictine church became the seat of the see of the Isles in 1499 and was elevated to the status of cathedral in 1507. However, the entire complex was destroyed during the Reformation. The abandoned island was bought by one of the earls of Argyll, whose descendent, the 8th Duke, gave it to the Church of Scotland in 1899. The Iona Cathedral Trust restored the cathedral between 1902 and 1910. In 1938 Dr George Macleod, whose dynamism equaled that of St Columba, formed the Iona Community (now an ecumenical society) which has restored the main monastic buildings.

NUNNERY. The Augustinian nunnery was founded in the early 13th century by Reginald, whose sister, Beatrice, became the first prioress. Today its ruins stand behind the post office, to the left of the path running from the ferry to the cathedral. The church still has its choir, nave and part of its vaulted roof. To the south lie the remains of the cloister, today

A fragment of the
Book of Kells (*left*).

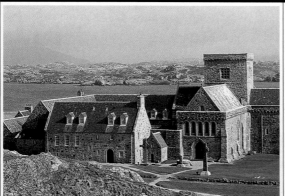

Southwest view of the
Cathedral, Iona.

INFIRMARY MUSEUM
The former infirmary,
to the northeast of
the abbey, houses a
beautiful collection of
carved stones from
the Celtic and
medieval periods,
including the original
St John's Cross (8th
century) and the most
beautiful tombstones
from St Oran's
cemetery.

ST ORAN'S CHAPEL
This tiny rectangular
chapel (*above*), built
between the 9th and
12th centuries and
restored in the 20th
century, is the oldest
building on the
island. It has a
beautiful Norman
doorway decorated
with chevrons. Two
Lords of the Isles
from the 14th–15th
century are buried
here.

occupied by a pleasant garden, and those of the chapter house
and refectory.

CHURCH OF ST RONAN. This 13th–14th century church, built
on the foundations of an 8th-century chapel to the north of
the nunnery, houses a small museum.

MACLEAN'S CROSS. The Celtic motifs decorating this 15th-
century cross that stands beside the footpath, are a fine
example of the work of the Iona school.

ST ORAN'S CEMETERY (REILIG ODHRAIN). St Oran's Chapel
stands in the center of one of Scotland's oldest Christian
cemeteries. Many clan chiefs from the Hebrides, eight Norse
kings, four Irish kings and forty-eight Scottish kings (including
Kenneth MacAlpin and Duncan I) are buried here.

STREET OF THE DEAD. A section of the Street of the Dead,
the paved road that led from the ferry and was used for
funeral processions, still links the cemetery and cathedral.

CELTIC CROSSES. In front of the cathedral's west façade
stand a beautiful St Martin's Cross (8th
century, *left*), a copy of the St John's Cross in
the Infirmary Museum, which dates from the
same period, and the broken shaft of a
St Matthew's Cross (11th century).

THE CATHEDRAL. This former 13th-century
BENEDICTINE CHURCH, built on a cruciform
plan, has been renovated a number of times.
In the 15th century the south side was
extended, a square bell tower built on the
crossing of the transept, the north aisle
transformed into a sacristy and St Columba's chapel
(said to be the saint's first burial place) incorporated
into the complex, to the west of the cloister. The beautiful
carved capitals of the south arch of the choir date from
the same period. The door in the north wall of the nave
opens onto the cloister in the center of which stands a
group by Jacques Lipchitz: *The Descent of the Spirit* (1960).
The CHAPTER HOUSE was restored in 1955 and the
REFECTORY in 1949.

INFIRMARY MUSEUM. The former infirmary, to the
northeast of the abbey, houses a beautiful collection of
carved stones from the Celtic and medieval periods,
including the original St John's Cross (8th century) and
the most beautiful tombstones from St Oran's cemetery.

ST MICHAEL'S CHAPEL
This chapel, to
the east of the
cathedral, is believed
to have been used as
a church while the
Benedictine church
was being built.

COLL AND TIRE ◆ C A2-B1-B2

These two isolated islands to the
northwest of Staffa, are linked to Oban
by ferry. Although relatively flat and
barren, these windswept islands
nevertheless hold the record for the most
hours of sunlight in Scotland.

COLL. The port of ARINAGOUR is also the
island's only village. BREACACHADH

Trawlers on Tiree.

RUM, EIGG, CANNA AND MUCK ◆ C B1
(ferry links with Mallaig throughout the year)
Scottish Natural
Heritage has made
RHUM, the largest of
this group of islands,
a National Nature
Reserve and
Biosphere Reserve.
Footpaths start from
the hotel, a castle
built by the Bulloughs
in 1901. EIGG is
inhabited by a small
farming community.
CANNA, the prettiest
of the islands, is
owned by the
National Trust and is
a favorite haunt of
seabirds. MUCK is the
smallest island in the
group. It is named
after the porpoises or
'seahogs' that
frequent its waters.

CASTLE, a 15th-century tower-house (*above*), stands at the
head of a loch on the southwest coast. The castle has been
recently restored and is now a training center for humanitarian
aid workers. It stands in the middle of a BIRD SANCTUARY
which stretches to the southern tip of the island and is
frequented by the red-throated diver and graylag goose.
The most beautiful beaches are found on the northwest coast,
once the most populated part of the island.

TIREE. In the time of St Columba the island, whose Gaelic
name means 'land lower than the waves', was the granary of
the Inner Hebrides. Today Tiree and Coll are farmed by
smallholders. SCARINISH, the main village, is situated on the
northeast coast. In summer it is inundated with surfers and
windsurfers who come to try their skill on the Atlantic rollers
that break on the island's long, sandy beaches. On the north
coast, west of Vaul Bay, are the remains of a broch, Dun Mor
Vaul, dating from the 1st century BC. Excavations have
revealed pottery shards from the 5th century BC. At the
southern tip of the island, the harbor of HYNISH was built by
Alan Stevenson in the 1830s to service the construction of the
SKERRYVORE LIGHTHOUSE on an island off the coast of Tiree.
A group of enthusiasts from the Hebridean Trust has restored
the harbor and converted its former signal station into the
Skerryvore MUSEUM which traces the history of the
lighthouse. The Trust has also reconstructed the interiors of
several cottages in SANDAIG, on the west coast of Tiree, to
reflect the everyday life of the island in days gone by.

The Northeast

Hilary Macartney
Martine Nouet

209 Aberdeen
212 Aberdeenshire
220 *The Whisky Trail*
224 Moray

1. Aberdeen ▲ 209
2. South of Aberdeen ▲ 212
3. Royal Deeside ▲ 213
4. Strath Don ▲ 215
5. Aberdeen to Turriff ▲ 217
6. The coast from Aberdeen to Buckie ▲ 218
7. From Aberdeen to Elgin ▲ 222
8. From Elgin to Forres ▲ 224

STONE CIRCLES
There are more than 90 stone circles in the Northeast, mainly near the town of Alford and along the Don Valley. They usually stand on a hill offering a clear view of the sky and are characterized by a large recumbent stone placed on two standing stones on the south side of the circle. The 'window' formed by these stones enabled the Stone Age peoples who built them to predict seasonal cycles by observing the movement of the Moon. The circles consist of 10 or 12 stones (between 3 and 10 feet high) and have a diameter of about 65 feet. The recumbent stone is often the most impressive and is usually of a different type and color to the rest. These circles date from the 3rd millennium BC and may have been used for ceremonies and fertility rituals. They were reused in the Bronze Age (c. 2000 BC) for cremations and burials.

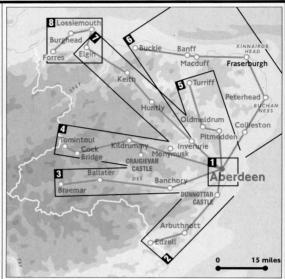

The northeast of Scotland has a drier, sunnier climate than the west coast of the Highlands and a varied landscape. The center of the region is occupied by the Grampian Mountains, whose wooded foothills, especially Strath Spey, contain some of the country's most famous whisky distilleries ▲ 220. Its rich agricultural plains (25 percent of Scotland's arable land) are mainly given over to barley and cattle and are bounded by a shoreline dotted with ports and little fishing villages. Fishing, which enjoyed its golden age in the 19th century, was partly replaced by North Sea oil in the 1970s. The industry, now in decline, greatly benefited the ports of Peterhead ▲ 218 and Aberdeen. The Northeast also has a remarkable archeological heritage. A number of Stone Age stone circles attest to the fact that the region was inhabited early in its history. The Picts also left some magnificent carved stones before they became part of the kingdom of Dalriada in the 9th century. In the 14th century Robert Bruce ● 39 gave Adam Gordon the lands he had confiscated from the Comyns, earls of Buchan. The Gordons, who later became the earls of Huntly ▲ 224, were sole masters of the region until the 16th century when the 4th Earl's rebellion against Mary Stuart led to his downfall and the confiscation of his lands. Other Catholic and Episcopalian lords suffered the same fate in the 18th century for having supported the Jacobite cause but, in spite of the persecutions, Catholic and Episcopalian beliefs remained unshaken in certain areas. Although the castles of Huntly ▲ 222, Fyvie ▲ 217 and Mar are fine examples of this period of Scottish history, the most famous of the 70 or so castles in the Northeast is undoubtedly Balmoral ▲ 214, in Strath Dee. This house was bought by Queen Victoria and Prince Albert in 1852, and since then has been the traditional summer residence of the Royal Family, making Royal Deeside the most frequently visited region in the Northeast.

With a population of almost 200,000 Aberdeen, the 'Granite City', is Scotland's third largest city. The modern conurbation was created in 1891 by the amalgamation of two medieval villages: Aulton or Old Aberdeen, on the mouth of the River Don, and the port on the Dee estuary, 2 miles to the south.

THE HISTORY OF THE PORT. In 1136 the fishing village on the Dee estuary was granted the right to levy a tithe on all vessels sailing in and out of the Dee. It received its charter as a royal burgh in 1170. In 1306 Robert Bruce sought refuge in the town and showed his gratitude by giving it the lands on which the granite quarries were situated. The town was destroyed by Edward III of England in 1337, but escaped being plundered in 1411 when the bloody Battle of Harlaw, near Inverurie ▲ 222, repelled the offensive of Donald, Lord of the Isles. In 1639, the Marquess of Montrose occupied the town with 9000 men to counter local opposition to the National Covenant ● 35, 41. He returned in 1644 at the head of a Royalist army, having changed sides, and captured the town. In the 18th century the Young Pretender stayed in Aberdeen in 1715, while the Duke of Cumberland passed through the town six weeks before the Battle of Culloden in 1746. This checkered history did not prevent the port from carrying on trade with

the Baltic countries until the 18th century, and developing its shipbuilding, whaling and herring industries until the 19th century. Aberdeen's economy was boosted in the 1970s when oil was discovered in the North Sea. The city became the capital of the European petroleum industry, acquiring a research center and developing a vast infrastructure for the off-shore rigs. Although in decline since the 1980s the industry financed the construction of many hotels, restaurants, shops and leisure facilities.

CENTRAL ABERDEEN ◆ B A6 D A1

UNION STREET. Aberdeen's main street was built in 1801 as part of a development program undertaken by the municipal authorities. It is bordered by beautiful granite buildings whose stone is ideally suited to the neoclassical austerity of their Georgian architecture. The most impressive is the Music Hall (1820) designed by Archibald Simpson, a native of Aberdeen and the architect of many of its public and private buildings. His rival, John Smith, designed the sundial (1830) which stands opposite St Nicholas' churchyard. The east end of Union Street gives way to Castle Street, named after the castle that stood behind the former church until 1337.

ABERDEEN IN BLOOM Although the Scots have a worldwide reputation for prudence, they themselves accuse the Aberdonians of 'stinginess', probably because the latter have always been particularly astute businessmen. This doesn't bother the inhabitants of the 'Granite City' who take the maintenance of their parks and gardens much more seriously. Aberdeen has in fact won the Britain in Bloom competition more than ten times, a success that owes much to the city's beautiful roses.

Gardening enthusiasts can visit the University's CRUIKSHANK BOTANIC GARDENS, the delightful JOHNSTON GARDENS, the maze in HAZELHEAD PARK, to the west of the city, and the rose and winter gardens of DUTHIE PARK on the banks of the River Dee.

ABERDEEN, A SPARKLING CITY ★ The architectural unity of this seaward-facing city is created by the gray granite that sparkles in the sun. The austerity of the stone is offset by the city's love of flowers.

Provost Skene's House.

ST NICHOLAS' KIRK *(between Union Street and Upper Kirk Gate).* The church of St Nicholas (12th–15th century) was divided in two after the Reformation. The West Church, rebuilt by James Gibbs in 1752, and the East Church, built by Archibald Simpson in 1837 and renovated in 1875, are linked by the ancient Transept. The East Church still has its 15th-century crypt, St Mary's Chapel, restored in 1898.

The tower and steeple of Aberdeen's town hall.

MERCAT CROSS *(Castlegate).* The market cross (rebuilt in 1821) was first erected on the market place of the medieval town in 1686. Its white marble unicorn (the emblem of the kingdom of Scotland), gargoyles and medallion heads of the Stewart kings make it one of the most beautiful market crosses in Scotland.

TOWN HOUSE *(on the corner of Castle Street and Broad Street).* The town hall, a Flemish-style granite building, was built between 1868 and 1874. It incorporates the tower and spire of the Tolbooth (1615), a former prison which today houses a CIVIC HISTORY MUSEUM.

PROVOST SKENE'S HOUSE *(Guest Row, a narrow street leading off Broad Street).* For a time this vast 16th-century manor belonged to the rich merchant and Provost of Aberdeen, George Skene (1619–1707). It still has its 17th-century stucco ceilings and paneling. The paintings on the ceiling of the chapel (late 16th century) illustrate scenes from the New Testament, rare in post-Reformation Scotland.

MARISCHAL COLLEGE *(Broad Street).* This Protestant university was founded in 1593 by George Keith (1553–1623), 5th Earl-Marischal of Scotland. In 1860 it merged with King's College to form Aberdeen University. The Franciscan monastery originally occupied by the college was replaced by the present buildings in 1836–1906. The neo-Gothic façade (1905) is unusually elaborate for a granite building. The MARISCHAL MUSEUM, on the far side of the courtyard, has interesting archaeological and anthropological collections.

OLD ABERDEEN

The village on the River Don expanded around its cathedral and university. This delightful district, with its cobbled streets bordered by old cottages and mansions, has been classified as a district of historic interest.

KING'S COLLEGE *(High Street).* Scotland's third largest university was founded in 1495 by Bishop Elphinstone. It was named in honor of James IV whose coat

> 'You have to like stone to understand this country. [...]
> If you can meet this initial requirement, you will feel at
> home in an hospitable landscape.'

Jacques Darras

of arms appears on the west façade, together with those of his wife, Margaret Tudor, and his natural son Alexander, Bishop of St Andrews. The Round Tower, at the southeast corner of the courtyard, is a defensive tower built in 1525, while the Square Tower (Cromwell's Tower), at the northeast corner, was built as student hall of residence in 1658. Of particular interest is the Gothic CHAPEL (1500–1505), whose tower is surmounted by a remarkable crown-shaped lantern which was restored in 1633. The chapel has a rood screen, canopied choir stalls and a beautifully carved pulpit from St Machar's Cathedral. The modern stained-glass windows are by Douglas Strachan.

OLD TOWN HOUSE. In 1891 the former Georgian town hall (1788) was converted into a public library.

ST MACHAR'S CATHEDRAL. The cathedral was founded in 1131 and dedicated to a disciple of St Columba who had built a chapel on the site in 580. The present building dates from the 14th–15th centuries. The choir was demolished during the Reformation and the transept destroyed when the central tower collapsed in 1688. The two massive defensive towers on the west façade are a feature unique to Great Britain. Their slender spires are believed to have been added by Bishop Gavin Dunbar in 1519–21, as was the nave's PANELED OAK CEILING decorated with 48 shields. The shields, arranged in three rows, bear the coats of arms of Pope Leo X, Charles V, the Holy Roman Emperor, St Margaret, and Scottish bishops and nobles during the reign of James V. They serve to confirm the role of Scotland, and Aberdeen in particular, in 16th-century Europe.

BRIG O'BALGOWNIE. A footpath leads from Seaton Park to this attractive bridge (1320s) whose Gothic arch spans the River Don.

THE PORT

Aberdeen has a modern fishing fleet whose catches are auctioned in the Albert Basin Fish Market (*above*), between 7 and 8am, Mondays through Fridays. Ferries leave Jamieson's Quay for Orkney, Shetland and, in summer, Norway, Iceland and the Faeroes. The Harbour Board occupies a strange circular building on North Pier, built by John Smeaton in 1775–81 to prevent the port silting up. Between North Pier and the beach are the delightful cottages of Footdee (pronounced 'Fittie'), a fishing village built between 1808 and 1809.

ABERDEEN ART GALLERY
(corner of Schoolhill and Blackfriar Street)
This museum gives pride of place to artists born in Aberdeen and includes works by the first great Scottish painter George Jameson (c. 1588–1644), the pre-Raphaelite William Dyce (1806–64) and John 'Spanish' Phillip (1817–67), who lived in Spain and was influenced by Murillo and Velázquez. It also presents works by Ramsay, the Glasgow Boys, the Scottish Colourists ● *90*, English artists such as Walter Sickert, Stanley Spencer ● *90* and Francis Bacon, and the French Impressionists and Nabis.

GORDON HIGHLANDERS MUSEUM
(Viewfield Road, west Aberdeen)
The museum, which traces the history of this famous 300 year-old regiment, occupies the former studio of the Victorian artist George Reid (1841–1913).

MARITIME MUSEUM
(Shiprow, between Union Street and the port)
The museum occupies a merchant's house built in 1593 and occupied in the 18th century by Provost Ross. It traces the history of the local fishing, shipbuilding and oil industries.

Stonehaven.

SOUTH OF ABERDEEN ◆ D D1

THE GLORIOUS HOURS OF DUNNOTTAR CASTLE
When Cromwell's troops invaded Scotland in 1650 the royal regalia were sent to Dunnottar Castle for safekeeping. When the castle was besieged by the English Parliamentarians in 1652, its governor Ogilvy successfully smuggled out the regalia which remained hidden beneath the floor of Kinneff Church until the Reformation. The wife of the minister of Kinneff had obtained permission to visit Ogilvy's wife and when she left, she had the royal crown hidden in her clothing, and the sword and scepter in a bundle carried by her servant. In 1685 some 167 Covenanters were held in the dungeons of Dunnottar Castle in appalling conditions. More recently, in 1990, the castle was used as the setting for Franco Zeffirelli's *Hamlet*.

FOWLSHEUGH NATURE RESERVE ◆ D D1
(near Crawton, south of Dunnottar)
This coastal reserve provides sanctuary for a large colony of seabirds (visit in April–July).

The agricultural plain of Howe of the Mearns, to the south of Aberdeen, stretches its ocher-colored expanses, interspersed with blocks of granite, to the windswept coast of the Northeast. In his famous trilogy *A Scots Quair*, the novelist Lewis Grassic Gibbon (1901–35) used the lilting Doric dialect, the local variation of Scots ● *48*, to evoke the harsh existence of the region's farmers.

STONEHAVEN *(on the A90)*. This delightful port founded by George Keith (1553–1623), 5th Earl-Marischal of Scotland, is today a suburb of Aberdeen. Near the port stands the late 16th-century TOLBOOTH where Episcopalian ministers were imprisoned in 1748–49, although this did not prevent them baptizing children through the bars of their cells. Today the building houses a MUSEUM of fishing, cooperage and local history. Stonehaven celebrates Hogmanay (New Year's Eve) with a huge firework display that lights up the port.

DUNNOTTAR CASTLE *(via the A92)*. Dunnottar Castle stands on a steep rocky outcrop separated from the mainland by a deep ravine. A Pictish fort was the first building to be built on this isolated rock. It was followed by a chapel in the 5th century, and later a castle and church which were destroyed by William Wallace in 1297. The present ruins are those of a tower-house built in 1392 by William Keith, hereditary Earl-Marischal of Scotland and, as such, guardian of the royal insignia. His descendants transformed it into what was virtually a fortified town. It was badly damaged by Cromwell's troops in 1651–52, confiscated following the 10th Earl's involvement in the Jacobite Rising of 1715, and remained abandoned until the 20th century. The oldest ruins are those of the 14th-century chapel and L-shaped tower-house.

The fortified guardroom (1575) and elegant apartments built around a square courtyard (14th–17th centuries) are attributed to the 5th Earl-Marischal and founder of Marischal College in Aberdeen ▲ *210*. A complex of domestic buildings – a kitchen, bakery, brewery, wine vault, forge and stables – is also open to the public.

ARBUTHNOTT *(via the A92 and B967).* ARBUTHNOTT HOUSE, a 15th-century mansion renowned for its plasterwork and painted paneling, is only open to the public on certain days of the year, while the gardens and 17th-century parterre are open throughout the year. ST TERNAN'S CHURCH was consecrated in 1242, but the bell tower and late-Gothic Lady Chapel (or Arbuthnott Aisle) date from 1500. James Leslie Mitchell, better know as Lewis Grassic Gibbon, is buried in the churchyard. An exhibition in the old schoolhouse is devoted to this famous novelist. (Follow the A90 south and then turn west along the B9120.)

FETTERCAIRN. This red-sandstone village has a market cross from the village of Kincardine, the home of one of Scotland's first legal distilleries but which has today disappeared. It also has a triumphal arch that commemorates a visit by Queen Victoria in 1861.

CAIRN O'MOUNTH. As it makes its way to Banchory the B974 crosses moorland and climbs the Cairn o'Mounth (1490 feet) which offers a sweeping view of Howe of the Mearns.

ROYAL DEESIDE ◆ **D** C1-D1

The A956 links Aberdeen to Braemar via the left bank of the Dee, a gracefully curving salmon river that rises in the Cairngorms. This magnificent valley, where the Royal Family has stayed regularly since the reign of Queen Victoria, is extremely popular with summer visitors.

DRUM CASTLE. The splendid square, red-granite tower that dominates the castle is the oldest in the region (1296). It is attributed to Richard Cementarius, a master mason by appointment to the king who was also the first Provost of Aberdeen. In the 14th century the castle passed into the hands of William Irvine, standard and armor bearer to Robert Bruce, and remained in the Irvine family until it was bequeathed to the National Trust for Scotland in 1976. The wing built in the early 17th century, during the reign of James IV, houses old furniture and family souvenirs.

EDZELL CASTLE ◆ **D** D1
(6 miles southwest of Fettercairn, via the B966)
The PLEASANCE, a magnificent walled garden (1604), complements the ruins of this tower-house, built in the 16th and enlarged in the 18th century.

Window of Drum Castle.

FASQUE HOUSE ◆ **D** D1
(B974, ½ mile north of Fettercairn)
The mansion (1809) was bought in 1829 by the father of the politician William Ewart Gladstone (1809–98). Its furniture and decoration reflect life in Victorian Britain and that of its Liberal prime minister who often stayed here. *Dunnottar Castle,* by Georges Reid.

Crathes Castle
and estate.

CRATHES CASTLE. The castle is an L-shaped tower-house
whose roof positively bristles with corbeled turrets, dormers
and chimneys. It was built between 1553 and 1594 by the
Burnett family, on lands granted to one of their ancestors by
Robert Bruce after the Battle of Bannockburn in 1314, and
enlarged in the 17th and 19th centuries. The interior has
some beautiful old furniture, including an impressive carved
oak bed (1594), and some magnificent 17th-century painted
ceilings (*left*). People, animals, plants, mottoes and heraldic
motifs decorate the ceilings of the Nine Nobles Room, the
Green Lady's Room (named after the resident ghost) and
the Muses' Room. The Long Gallery has a remarkable oak-
paneled ceiling, while the ivory horn inlaid with precious
stones (Horn of Leys) that hangs above the fireplace of the
main hall is said to have been a gift from Robert Bruce. Eight
magnificent walled gardens ▲ *197* designed in the 1930s set
off this castle steeped in tradition.

BANCHORY. A small museum reminds visitors that the village
was the birthplace of James Scott Skinner (1843–1927), the
'king of the strathspey' ● *53*. In spring the bridge across the
Feugh, to the south of the village, is an ideal place to watch
salmon returning upstream to their spawning grounds.

ABOYNE. This little granite village is a fine example of
19th-century urban planning. It is organized around a huge
central green which, in August, hosts a traditional Highland
Gathering ● *54*. The wooded hills of the GLEN TANAR ESTATE,
southwest of Aboyne, offer some extremely pleasant walks.

BALLATER. In 1863 this delightful early-19th-century spa town
became the terminus of a railway line from Aberdeen.
Although the line closed in 1964 the station used by the Royal
Family when visiting Balmoral is still standing. Royal Bridge,
opened in 1885, and the Victoria and Albert Memorial Halls
evoke Ballater's golden age.

BALMORAL. Queen Victoria had been looking for an estate in
the Highlands for some time when she came across Balmoral
in 1848. The Royal couple bought the estate privately, and
Prince Albert became passionately enthusiastic about the
16th-century tower-house, enlarged in 1835 by the
Aberdonian architect William Smith. The Queen helped to
promote wider interest in the region when she published her
travel journal: *Leaves from a Journal of our Life in the
Highlands*, in 1867. *More Leaves*, published in 1883 was
dedicated to John Brown, her faithful manservant and former
groom at Balmoral. The gardens and ballroom, which houses

> 'In Scotland, Sundays are strictly observed, but on
> Mondays, the people dance and sing with a joy and gay
> abandon that is unknown in London.'
>
> Stendhal

an exhibition tracing the castle's history, are open to the
public in summer, except when the family is in residence in
August. Nearby are CRATHIE CHURCH (1895), attended by the
Royal Family, and ROYAL LOCHNAGAR DISTILLERY, founded
in 1845 and suppliers by Royal Appointment since the time of
Queen Victoria. The Royal estate stretches south to
LOCHNAGAR (3786 feet) and the magnificent GLEN MUICK
(pronounced 'Mick'). It was here, on the shores of Loch
Muick, that Queen Victoria had a modest retreat built in 1868
following the death of Prince Albert. From the glen, which is
very busy at weekends and in summer, footpaths lead up the
slopes of Lochnagar, while others lead south across country
to GLEN COVA.

BRAEMAR. This tourist village is a favorite rendezvous for
hikers and climbers. It is also the venue for the famous
BRAEMAR HIGHLAND GATHERING ● *54*, held on the first
Saturday in September. The gathering has enjoyed Royal
patronage since Queen Victoria attended the event in 1848.
Robert Louis Stevenson wrote part of *Treasure Island* (1883)
in a cottage just outside Braemar, on the road to Glenshee,
where he spent the summer of 1881.

STRATH DON ◆ A F6-B A6

Like the River Dee, the Don rises in the Cairngorms. Its
valley is less touristic than Deeside, and many people find this
adds to its charm.

MEGALITHS. There is a fine example of an alignment of
recumbent stones ▲ *208* in the churchyard of MIDMAR, near
Echt (on the B9119). CULLERLIE STONE CIRCLE, south of
Garlogie, with its eight small standing stones grouped
around several cairns, reflects the development of megaliths
in the Northeast.

CASTLE FRASER (*northwest of Dunecht*). Midmar's largest
castle, built between 1575 and 1636, was the property of
the Frasers until the early 20th century. Since 1976 it
has belonged to the National Trust
for Scotland.

**BRAEMAR
CASTLE** ◆ D C1
The tower-house built
in 1628 by the Earl of
Mar was burned in
1689 by John
Farquharson.
Fortified by John
Adam, it housed a
Hanoverian garrison
after the Jacobite
Risings of 1715
and 1745. It was
subsequently bought
and restored by the
Farquharsons.

**THE HIGHEST 'A'
ROAD IN GREAT
BRITAIN**
◆ D C1-C2
With the spectacular
LINN OF DEE falls
lying off the west, the
A93 between
Braemar and
Blairgowrie follows
the route of an old
military road built by
the Hanoverian
garrison. On this
section the road
becomes the highest
'A' road in Britain
as it climbs to the
Cairnwell Pass
(2199 feet) before
continuing along the
valley of Glen Shee
to the ski resort.

The Royal Family at
Balmoral
in 1972.

Craigievar Castle.

MONYMUSK ◆ A F6
(northwest of Castle Fraser)
For a long time the priory founded on the ruins of a Celtic chapel housed the *Brec Bennoch*, the reliquary containing the relics of St Columba ● *33*, now in the Museum of Scotland in Edinburgh ▲ *123*. Near the 12th-century church, restored in the 20th century, stands a Pictish stone.

DOUNE OF INVERNOCHTY ◆ A F6
(Bellabeg)
This grassy motte surmounted by Norman ruins and surrounded by a ditch was the main fortress of the province of Mar until Kildrummy Castle was built.

THE LECHT ROAD AND TOMINTOUL ◆ A F6
The road between Cockbridge and Tomintoul crosses a desolate stretch of moorland known as the Lecht. The road's construction – by five companies of the 33rd infantry regiment during the 'pacification' of the Highlands – is commemorated by a plaque (dated 1754) at the WELL OF LECHT. It climbs to a height of 1968 feet and services the Lecht ski resort (when not blocked by snow) before descending to the weavers' village of Tomintoul, built in 1746 by the Duke of Gordon. The Museum presents various aspects of local life.

The two towers that stand diagonally opposite on either side of the main of the building were built by Thomas Leiper. Another master mason from the region, John Bell, was responsible for the castle's complex tiered corbeling, turrets, elaborately worked roofs and Renaissance-style chimneys.
ALFORD *(on the A980)*. This town in the heart of a cattle-farming region has transformed its cattle market into a museum of rural life: the ALFORD-DONSIDE HERITAGE CENTRE. The ALFORD VALLEY RAILWAY, which has the only narrow-gauge line in Scotland, has created a small railway museum in the station. The GRAMPIAN TRANSPORT MUSEUM presents an exhibition of vehicles from different periods, including the Craigievar Express, an amazing steam tricycle designed in 1895 by an imaginative postman.
CRAIGIEVAR CASTLE. This tall L-shaped castle, with its pink rough-rendered walls surmounted by turrets and gables, is like something out of a fairytale. It was built in 1626 for William Forbes, a merchant who made his fortune through trade with the Baltic, and is a fine example of 17th-century Scots Baronial style.
KILDRUMMY CASTLE *(via the A944)*. The ruins of the most powerful fortress in the Highlands are still impressive. The first castle, built during the reign of Alexander II (1214–49), was a keep protected by a curtain wall and a broad ditch. The impressive guardhouse and six round towers were probably added by Edward I, who occupied the castle between 1296 and 1303. The Scots recaptured Kildrummy shortly afterwards and, in 1306, Robert Bruce considered it a safe place for his family. However, the English obtained Bruce's surrender through the treachery of a blacksmith to whom they had promised as much gold as he could carry. The castle was besieged again in 1335, before becoming the residence of the Earls of Mar. It was confiscated following the Earl of Mar's involvement in the Jacobite Rising of 1715 and dismantled shortly afterwards.

GLENBUCHAT CASTLE. This well-preserved Z-shaped castle was built in 1590 for John Gordon and Helen Carnegie, commemorated on the marriage lintel carved with their initials.

CORGARFF CASTLE (*near Cockbridge, on the A939*). This 16th-century castle was converted into a barracks for Hanoverian troops after the Battle of Culloden (1746). Its star-shaped loopholed wall was built in 1748. In the 1830s the garrison played a key role in the suppression of smuggling, especially of whisky.

ABERDEEN TO TURRIFF ◆ B A6

PITMEDDEN GARDEN ▲ *197* (*13 miles northwest of Aberdeen, via the A90 and the B9000*). This huge garden created by Alexander Seton in 1675 reflects the influence of the French landscape designer Le Nôtre (1613–1700). The borders of the lower terrace were redesigned in the 1950s and those of the upper terrace in the 1990s.

TOLQUHON CASTLE (*north of the A920*). Although ruined the castle is a fine example of the development from the medieval castle to the Renaissance mansion. In the 1580s William Forbes had the tower-house incorporated into a much larger building with thinner walls and larger windows. The work was supervised by Thomas Leiper who also built the elaborately decorated tomb (1589) of the Forbes family in Tarves churchyard.

FYVIE CASTLE (*via the A947 to Fyvie*). When he bought the estate in 1596 Alexander Seton, the loyal manservant of Mary Stuart and future Chancellor of Scotland, decided to link the two towers (13th and 14th century) by building a large central tower. He gave the castle a magnificent south façade that bristled with turrets and dormers, and created the great 'wheel staircase', one of the most beautiful circular staircases in Scotland. The northeast tower was built in the 18th century by the Gordons. Alexander Forbes-Leith, a native of Aberdeenshire who made his fortune in the American iron industry, acquired the estate in 1889. He added the northwest tower and gave the castle its opulent Edwardian interiors which house an art collection that includes works by Gainsborough, Ramsay, some magnificent paintings by Raeburn, the portrait of Colonel William Gordon of Fyvie by Pompeo Batoni (*right*) and works by French and Dutch masters.

TURRIFF. For centuries this former Pictish capital was an important market town where farmers came to hire workers by the year, a practice recalled in a song sung by seasonal workers: *The Barnyards o'Delgaty*. The TURRIFF SHOW, held in August, is still one of the largest agricultural shows in the Northeast.

HADDO HOUSE ◆ B A6 (*4 miles north of Pitmedden*) William Adam designed this perfectly symmetrical Palladian-style mansion, built for William Gordon, 2nd Earl of Aberdeen. In the 19th century the 7th Earl and 1st Marquess of Aberdeen carried out some renovations: a hayloft was converted into an elegant library (below), and the architect G. E. Street designed the neo-Gothic chapel (1876–81) whose huge stained-glass window is signed by the pre-Raphaelite artist Edward Burne-Jones. The private apartments house a beautiful collection of portraits.

ABERDEENSHIRE FARMING MUSEUM
◆ B A6
(Mintlaw, 8½ miles west of Peterhead)
This museum has won several awards. It occupies the magnificent stables of Aden Country Park, an estate dating from the mid-18th century.

OLD DEER ◆ B A6
(1¾ miles west of Mintlaw)
Ruins are all that remain of Deer Abbey, the Cistercian abbey founded (1219) by William Comyn, Earl of Buchan, on the site of a 6th-century monastery. It was in the abbey that the famous *Book of Deer* ● *47* was written in the 9th century. The annotations in the margin are the earliest known examples of Scottish Gaelic (11th–12th century). Today the book is in Cambridge University Library.

THE COAST FROM ABERDEEN TO BUCKIE

COLLIESTON *(via the A90 and the A975)*. Migratory birds over-winter on the SANDS OF FORVIE Nature Reserve which stretches from the village of Collieston, a fishing village and former smugglers' stronghold, to the mouth of the River Ythan.

CRUDEN BAY. On a cliff to the north of the village stand the ruins of SLAINS CASTLE (16th–19th century), which quite possibly served as the model for Dracula's castle in Bram Stoker's *Dracula* (1897).

BULLERS OF BUCHAN. These 230-foot cliffs teeming with seabirds are really spectacular in rough weather. THE BUCHAN NESS LIGHTHOUSE marks Scotland's most easterly point.

PETERHEAD. The port founded in 1539 by George Keith (1553–1623), 5th Earl-Marischal of Scotland ▲ *212*, was built using the local pink granite. The Young Pretender landed here in 1715 ● *42* with the help of the 10th Earl and his brother, James Keith, who later became a field marshal in the army of Frederick II the Great of Prussia. He is commemorated by a statue presented to the town by William I of Prussia, in 1868, and which stands in front of the town hall. The vast port infrastructure, begun in 1773, enabled Peterhead to become Britain's leading whaling port, and later one of its main herring ports, in the 19th century. Today it is a supply base for the North Sea oil rigs and Europe's leading whitefish port with a busy fish market. The PETERHEAD MARITIME HERITAGE MUSEUM traces the history of the port in great detail, while the ARBUTHNOTT MUSEUM presents a collection of Inuit artefacts brought back by the whalers. Peterhead also has the oldest packing plant in Scotland (1585): the UGIE SALMON FISH HOUSE, which is still active today.

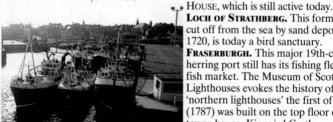

LOCH OF STRATHBERG. This former bay, cut off from the sea by sand deposits in 1720, is today a bird sanctuary.

FRASERBURGH. This major 19th-century herring port still has its fishing fleet and fish market. The Museum of Scottish Lighthouses evokes the history of the 'northern lighthouses' the first of which (1787) was built on the top floor of an old tower-house, Kinnaird Castle, on nearby

The port of Peterhead.

Kinnaird Head. The mysterious 16th-century Wine Tower is decorated with coats of arms in bas-relief. The Fraserburgh Heritage Centre has an exhibition devoted to Thomas Glover (1838–1911), who created the modern Japanese Navy and inspired Puccini's hero in *Madame Butterfly*.

MEMSIE CAIRN *(southwest of Fraserburgh, via the A981)*. This vast Bronze Age tomb was part of a complex containing two other burials.

MACDUFF *(on the A98)*. The town was built in 1783 by James Duff, 2nd Earl of Fife, on the ruins of the fishing village of Doune. The church perched on the hill was built by the 3rd Earl in 1805. The port, once one of the most active in Moray, still has its fishing fleet and docks.

BANFF. This port and former royal burgh, on the mouth of the Deveron, is one of the most attractive towns in the Northeast. It has some beautiful 18th-century houses and some older buildings and monuments, for example the market cross

The little port
of Crovie.

**BETWEEN
FRASERBURGH AND
MACDUFF ◆ B** A5
The old port of
Rosehearty is
dominated by the
ruins of Pitsligo
Castle (15th–16th
century). To the west
three villages nestle
at the foot of the
cliffs: PENNAN, part
of the setting for the
film *Local Hero*
(1983), CROVIE and
GARDENSTOWN.

DUFF HOUSE ★
This Adam house was
inspired by the Villa
Borghese in Rome. It
is the most beautiful
baroque mansion in
the Northeast.

decorated with a Virgin and Child that has stood opposite
the town hall since the 16th century.

PORTSOY. Some beautiful late-17th- and early-18th-century
buildings stand above the port built in 1692. Before the fishing
boom, Portsoy exported the serpentine marble named after
the town and used, among other things, to build the fireplaces
in Hopetoun House ▲ *129* and the Palace of Versailles.

CULLEN. This coastal resort, famous for 'Cullen Skink', a kind
of smoked-haddock soup, has an elegant Georgian upper
town. Its AULD KIRK, where the internal organs of Elizabeth
de Burgh, the wife of Robert Bruce, are said to have been
buried in 1327, was extensively renovated in the 16th century
when it became a collegiate church. It is well worth a visit to
see the sacrament house, the elaborately carved baroque
tomb of Alexander Ogilvie and the impressive Seafield Loft
(1602) in the upper gallery.

BUCKIE. The port is reached via the picturesque fishing
villages of PORTKNOCKIE and FINDOCHTY, on the A942. The
BUCKIE DRIFTER traces the history of the herring fishing
industry, which for a long time formed the basis of the port's
prosperity before its trawlers began to fish for shrimps and
clams.

TYNET *(on the A98)*. ST NINIAN'S CHAPEL, built (1755) after
the Battle of Culloden (1746) ● *43* and during the repression
of Catholicism, is a modest structure on the main road. By
contrast the CHAPEL OF ST GREGORY OF PRESHOME, built in
1788, is a baroque reaffirmation of the Catholic faith.

**DUFF HOUSE
COUNTRY HOUSE
GALLERY ● 76 ◆ B** A5
*(above, between
Macduff and Banff)*
In 1735 William
Adam laid the first
stone of this
magnificent mansion
designed for the 1st
Earl of Fife. Only the
main building was
finished since the
architect was taken to
court over the cost of
the work. Adam had
shipped top-quality
stone from his own
quarry at South
Queensferry for the
Corinthian pillars and
elaborately carved
pediment of the
façade. Today the
restored building
houses paintings by
El Greco, Ramsay,
Raeburn and
Boucher, and some
superb furniture from
Scottish national
collections.

A glass of single malt encapsulates the flavor of Scotland... The only way to fully appreciate the richness and diversity of *uisge beatha* is to follow the whisky trail. Some forty or so distilleries offer whisky lovers an opportunity to take a guided tour, sample a 'wee dram' and browse in their shop where they can buy the precious nectar and other souvenirs. Don't restrict yourself to visiting one distillery as no two are the same.

OPENING TIMES
The distillery visitor centers are usually open from Monday through Saturday, between 9.30am and 4.30pm, but it is worth phoning in advance to make sure. You may even be able to make an appointment. Visits cost between £2.50 and £4.00. Remember that many distilleries are in their 'silent season' between July 15 and August 15, when they are open to the public but not in production, which means that the visit will not be as interesting.

SPEYSIDE
The 'golden rectangle' of whisky production, bounded by the rivers Findhorn, Livet and Deveron, has some sixty or so distilleries within an area of just over 15 square miles. Seven of these distilleries and a cooperage are on the Malt Whisky Trail, a clearly signposted route of around 60 miles (brochures available from tourist offices).

Absolute musts
• DALLAS DHU (Forres ▲ 224)
Although production stopped in 1983 the distillery has been transformed into a whisky museum.
• GLENFIDDICH (Dufftown ▲ 223)
The only distillery in the Highlands offering a free visit and the opportunity to bottle your own single malt on the spot.
• SPEYSIDE COOPERAGE VISITOR CENTRE (Craigellachie ▲ 223)
A living cooperage museum.
• GLEN GRANT (Rothes)
Sample a 'wee dram' in Major Grant's 'temple', in a garden setting.
• STRATHISLA (Keith ▲ 223)
A 'dolls-house' distillery that has retained all the charm of yesteryear. Visitors are invited to take tea and shortbread before the guided tour.
Also:
• GLENFARCLAS (Ballindalloch)
• CARDHU (Knockando)
• THE GLENLIVET (Glenlivet)

Distilleries usually offer visitors a 'dram' at the end of their guided tour. Originally the dram was a measure equivalent to ⅛ fl oz, but has gradually come to mean a small glass.

EAST AND NORTH HIGHLANDS

The region doesn't have an official whisky trail, but there are possible whisky 'stops' on the road (mostly the A9) all the way from Edinburgh to the far north of Scotland and the Orkney.

• ROYAL LOCHNAGAR (Crathie ▲ 215)
This was the favorite whisky of Queen Victoria, who first sampled it on the spot. The distillery stands below Balmoral Castle, hence the name 'Royal' Lochnagar.

• DALWHINNIE (Dalwhinnie)
This isolated mountain distillery is the highest in Scotland (1070 feet). The visitor center has an exhibition covering local history,

including the flight of Bonnie Prince Charlie after the Battle of Culloden (1746).

• GLEN ORD (Muir of Ord)
A well-organized guided tour and pleasant souvenir shop in a magnificent setting.

• GLENMORANGIE (Tain ▲ 247)
A warm, spontaneous welcome, and an impressive distillation room with its shiny copper pot stills.

• HIGHLAND PARK (Kirkwall, Orkney ▲ 256)
One of the most interesting distilleries to visit when the malting areas and kiln are being used.

• OLD PULTENEY (Wick ▲ 246)
Visits to this distillery are by appointment only.

WEST HIGHLANDS AND ISLANDS

• TALISKER (Carbost ▲ 250)
The only distillery on Skye stands against the backdrop of the steep rock after which the island is named.

• BEN NEVIS (Fort William ▲ 236)
The distillery has a visitor center and a tempting shop.

• OBAN (Oban ▲ 194)
The distillery, founded in 1794, has

an interesting exhibition on the region's history.

• TOBERMORY (Tobermory, Isle of Mull ▲ 203)
Although the distillery is not in production throughout the year, visitors are always welcome.

• ARRAN (Lochranza, Isle of Arran ▲ 200)
The most recently established of the Scottish distilleries.

ISLE OF ISLAY ▲ 202

With six of its eight distilleries still active, Islay is a paradise for lovers of single malts with character.

• ARDBEG (south of Port Ellen)
A brand new visitor center and a small restaurant, The Old Kiln, with a delicious menu.

• BOWMORE (Bowmore)
A warm welcome with the added bonus of sampling a dram while admiring the sea view. A beautiful shop.

• BUNNAHABHAIN (Bunnahabhain)
Overlooking the sea, at the end of a

winding road, this is the most isolated of the distilleries. Simply superb.

• CAOL ILA (Port Askaig)
The distillation room enjoys a magnificent view of the sea and the hills of Jura.

• LAGAVULIN (Port Ellen)
Guided tours by retired distillery workers.

• LAPHROAIG (south of Port Ellen)
One of the most attractive distilleries on the island. When the tour is led by the manager Ian Henderson, there is a feeling of real enthusiasm.

The main entrance of the castle
built by the 1st Marquess of
Huntly in the early 17th century.

ABERDEEN TO ELGIN ◆ B A6-A F6-F5

INVERURIE *(on the A96)*. The county town
of Garioch is also the principal cattle
market in the Northeast. It lies at the
heart of a region that is of great
archeological interest, as evidenced by its
CARNEGIE MUSEUM. Three Pictish stones
▲ *184* stand in the churchyard at the
southeast end of the village. Nearby is
THE BASS, a feudal motte built in 1160 by
David, Lord of Garioch and brother of
Malcolm II. Another Pictish stone, the
BRANDSBUTT STONE, stands on the
northwest edge of Inverurie. It is
decorated with symbols and an Ogham
inscription (an ancient Celtic writing
system), and is thought to be a funeral
stone dating from the 6th–7th century.
LOANHEAD STONE CIRCLE *(north of
Inverurie, via the B9001 and Daviot)*.
With its central cairn, this recumbent
stone circle is a fine example of a
Neolithic monument that was reused
during the Bronze Age ▲ *208*.
MAIDEN STONE *(near the Chapel of
Garioch, 5 miles northwest of Inverurie)*.
This magnificent red-granite stone,
carved in the 11th century, combines
Pictish symbols and a Celtic cross.
BENNACHIE. The remains of a fort dating
from the early centuries AD stand at the
top of Mither Tap (1698 feet), the east
summit of Bennachie (1773 feet). The
traces of a Roman camp found at Durno, a
little to the north, suggest that Bennachie
was the site of Mons Graupius where the
troops of the Roman commander Agricola
defeated the Caledonians in AD 84 ● *32*.
OYNE *(northwest of Inverurie, on the
B9002)*. The ARCHÆOLINK PREHISTORY
PARK, created around an Iron Age fort
perched on the heights of Berryhill,
gives a detailed presentation of the
archeological history of the Northeast.
PICARDY STONE *(2 miles north of Insch)*.
This is one of the oldest known Pictish
stones. It is inscribed with a number of
symbols, including a double disc and a
serpent, both struck through with a 'Z',
and a mirror.
RHYNIE. Several Pictish stones stand in
the churchyard of this village dominated
by Tap o'Noth (1850 feet) with its Iron
Age fort.
HUNTLY *(on the A96)*. Two standing stones
mark the main square of this former royal
burgh, whose history is traced by the
BRANDER MUSEUM. The remains of

The west entrance and presbytery of Elgin Cathedral.

HUNTLY CASTLE, at the confluence of the rivers Deveron and Bogie, reflect the development of Scottish castles. The castle motte built in the 12th century by the Duncans, earls of Fife, can still be seen. So, too, can the foundations of the keep built by the Gordons in the 14th century. As fervent Catholics and key players in the Counter-Reformation, the castle of the earls of Huntly was destroyed in 1549. In 1602 George Gordon, 6th Earl of Huntly, began to restore the castle and add some magnificent features. However, the castle was abandoned shortly afterward and fell slowly into ruin. Even so the south façade is still one of the most beautiful in Britain, with its oriel windows (possibly inspired by the Château of Blois) and stone friezes bearing the names of the 1st Marquess and his wife Henrietta Stewart.

KEITH. The village was the birthplace of John Ogilvie (1580–1615), the only Scottish saint canonized after the Reformation. Near Auld Brig (1609), the STRATHISLA DISTILLERY (1786) is open to the public.

FOCHABERS. This 18th-century planned village has an interesting Folk Museum, while BAXTERS VISITOR CENTRE (west of Fochabers) traces the history of Baxters of Speyside, famous for their preserves and fine foods.

ELGIN. The attractive county town of Moray is built in the local sandstone. The medieval town and cathedral were burned in 1390 by Alexander Stewart ▲ 232, 'Wolf of Badenoch' after he had been excommunicated by the Bishop of Moray. The CATHEDRAL (1244), the 'glory of the kingdom', which had already been rebuilt after a fire in 1270, was rebuilt once again before being plundered and abandoned after the Reformation. Although the nave no longer exists, the elaborately carved entrance flanked by two 14th-century towers, and the two 13th-century transepts and choir have survived. To the north stands the octagonal chapter house with its finely carved vaults. A MUSEUM of local history, which has a large collection of fossils, stands at the end of the High Street, bordered by elegant arcaded houses (17th century). Also worthy of note are ST GILES' CHURCH (1828), built by Archibald Simpson ▲ 209, and THUNDERTON HOUSE, the 17th-century mansion where Bonnie Prince Charlie stayed on the eve of the Battle of Culloden (1746) ● 43. At the end of the street, a statue of the 5th Duke of Gordon dominates Lady Hill, the former site of the medieval castle and chapel.

DUFFTOWN ◆ A F6
(12 miles west of Huntly via the A920). This small town has eight distilleries and is the principal whisky-producing center on Speyside. MORTLACH CHURCH was built in the 11th or 12th century on the site of a church founded by St Moluag in 566, and remained the seat of the see until 1137. To the north of the town, near the GLENFIDDICH DISTILLERY ▲ 220, are the ruins of BALVENIE CASTLE, built in the 13th century and enlarged in Renaissance style in the 18th century.

CRAIGELLACHIE ◆ A F6
(on the A941 to the north of Dufftown) The town has an interesting cast-iron bridge designed by Thomas Telford in 1814. Speyside Cooperage, which produces 100,000 oak casks per year for the region's whisky distilleries, is open to the public.

Findhorn.

PLUSCARDEN ABBEY
◆ A F5-F6
(7 miles southwest of Elgin)
The priory founded in 1230 became a Benedictine abbey between 1454 and the Reformation. In 1948 it was again occupied by Benedictines whose members restored it. The Gothic church has lost its nave, but has some striking stained-glass windows.

BRODIE CASTLE ◆ A E6
(A96, 5 miles west of Forres)
The Z-shaped tower-house built in 1567 and renovated in the 17th and 19th centuries is worth a visit for its collection of European paintings, French furniture and the remarkable ceiling of the dining room. In the gardens stands the RODNEY STONE, a Pictish stone bearing an Ogham inscription.

ELGIN TO FORRES ◆ A E5-F5

SPYNIE *(on the B9103, northeast of Elgin)*. James Ramsay MacDonald (1866–1937), Britain's first Labour Party prime minister, is buried in Spynie churchyard. To the north of the village a keep with 10-foot walls stands above the ruins of the Spynie Palace (13th–15th century), which was the palace of the bishops of Moray until it was abandoned after the death of Elgin's last bishop in 1686.

LOSSIEMOUTH *(on the A941)*. The port that replaced Spynie in the 19th century was a successful herring port before it became a busy coastal resort. The LOSSIEMOUTH FISHERY AND COMMUNITY MUSEUM traces the history of the fishing industry and also has a reconstruction of the office of its famous son, Ramsay MacDonald.

DUFFUS CASTLE *(via the B9012)*. The ruins of this 14th-century stone keep stand on a 12th-century feudal motte. The castle belonged to the Moravia family (whose name later became Moray and then Murray) ▲ *165*.

BURGHEAD *(via the B9040)*. This coastal resort built on the site of a Pictish stronghold is famous for the 'Bulls of Burghead', six carved stones dating from the 7th–8th century. Two of these stones are housed in the town LIBRARY, two in Elgin Museum, one in the Museum of Scotland in Edinburgh and one in the British Museum in London. Burghead Well (King Street), whose origins are unknown, is worth a visit.

FINDHEAD *(via the B9089 and B9011)*. The village of Findhorn overlooks beautiful Findhorn Bay. It has a prestigious yacht club and an interesting HERITAGE CENTRE. Since 1962 it has been the site of an internationally renowned New Age community, the FINDHORN FOUNDATION. CULBIN FOREST, to the west of the bay, was planted to stabilize the Culbin Sands, which engulfed the first village of Findhorn in 1694.

FORRES *(on the A96)*. On the outskirts of the town stands SUENO'S STONE, a remarkable 20-foot sandstone block carved in the 9th–10th century. One side is decorated with a huge Celtic cross and the other with a series of panels depicting a battle, possibly between the Picts and the Vikings or Scots. The FALCONER MUSEUM, in Tolbooth Street, traces the history of this former royal burgh. Although no longer active, the Dallas Dhu Distillery (1 mile south of Forres on the A940) is open to the public and presents the various stages involved in the production of the national drink ▲ *220*.

The North

Richard Balharry, Syd Bangham, Greg Corbett,
Joan Dobbie, Claudine Glot, Julia and John Keay,
Ann MacSween, Olwyn Owen, Nicola Taylor

228 *The Caledonian Forest*
230 The Highlands
234 *The Cairngorms*
240 *Nessie, the Loch Ness
       Monster*
248 The Isle of Skye
252 The Outer Hebrides
256 Orkney
262 Shetland

▲ THE NORTH

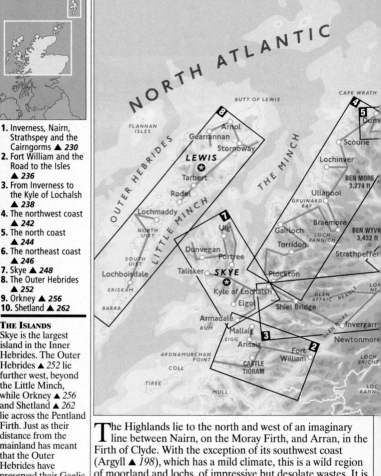

1. Inverness, Nairn, Strathspey and the Cairngorms ▲ 230
2. Fort William and the Road to the Isles ▲ 236
3. From Inverness to the Kyle of Lochalsh ▲ 238
4. The northwest coast ▲ 242
5. The north coast ▲ 244
6. The northeast coast ▲ 246
7. Skye ▲ 248
8. The Outer Hebrides ▲ 252
9. Orkney ▲ 256
10. Shetland ▲ 262

THE ISLANDS
Skye is the largest island in the Inner Hebrides. The Outer Hebrides ▲ 252 lie further west, beyond the Little Minch, while Orkney ▲ 256 and Shetland ▲ 262 lie across the Pentland Firth. Just as their distance from the mainland has meant that the Outer Hebrides have preserved their Gaelic heritage, Scandinavian culture is very much in evidence on Orkney and Shetland.

Cottage on Skye.

The Highlands lie to the north and west of an imaginary line between Nairn, on the Moray Firth, and Arran, in the Firth of Clyde. With the exception of its southwest coast (Argyll ▲ 198), which has a mild climate, this is a wild region of moorland and lochs, of impressive but desolate wastes. It is mountainous, mostly above 2950 feet, predominately infertile and sparsely populated. But although on the margins of modern Scotland, the Highlands continue to occupy a special place in the hearts of the Scottish people. In the past they were much more densely populated. Their inhabitants spoke Scots or Highland Gaelic ● 46, wore tartan and, in accordance with Celtic tradition, obeyed their clan chiefs more readily than their king. When many of these chiefs supported the Jacobite cause in the early 18th century, the government responded by installing garrisons along Glen Mor ▲ 238 (the Great Glen) and building the first roads from the Lowlands suitable for vehicles. This opening up of the Highlands, the confiscation of the lands of the clan chiefs outlawed after the Jacobite defeat

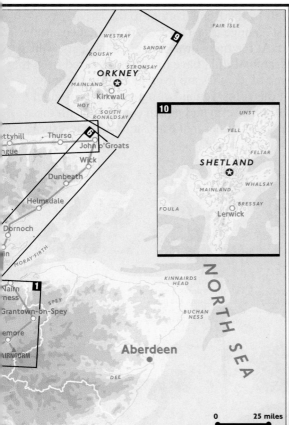

THE FLOW COUNTRY
Around Forsinard, in
the extreme north of
the Highlands, lies
Europe's largest area
of marshland, known
as the Flow Country.
Not a single tree
grows on these
floating peat bogs
interspersed with
water holes (*dhu loch*
in Gaelic). Spongy
carpets of sphagnum
moss cover a layer
of rotting vegetable
matter which first
began to form some
10,000 years ago.
At certain points it
reaches depths of
up to 20 feet. This
desolate, uniformly
flat area echoes to
the cries of the
greenshank, the
dunlin and the black-
throated diver.

EXPLOITING THE
PEAT BOGS
Peat bogs have been
exploited by man for
thousands of years,
and peat is still a
cheap source of fuel
in certain regions.
It is dug by hand
(*above*) on the islands
and elsewhere with
mechanical diggers.
The peat is extracted
in long compact strips
which are then dried.
After World War
One, many peat
bogs were planted
with conifers to
provide pit props.
Today, ecologists
are demanding
less extraction, and
the protection of
this rich natural
resource.

at Culloden in 1746 ● *43*, and the introduction of a monetary
economy undermined the basis of traditional Highland
society. The death blow was dealt by the 'Highland
Clearances' when, from 1790, entire valleys were cleared of
their inhabitants to make way for sheep farming. Today,
Gaelic is hardly spoken in the Highlands, and the traditional
Highland gatherings ● *54* held in the summer are mainly a
tourist attraction. Speyside still produces excellent whiskies
▲ *220* but North Sea oil and fish farming have enriched the
east and west coasts respectively, and green tourism has
gradually replaced subsistence agriculture ▲ *188* as the
principal source of local income. The Highlands constitute
one of the largest natural regions in Europe. They have very
specific ecosystems – for example the peat bogs of the Flow
Country (Sutherland) and the treeless expanses of the
Cairngorms ▲ *234* – and an exceptional range of wildlife. In
addition to the pleasures of walking, climbing and skiing in
the mountains, sea and river fishing and bird-watching, the
region also has a rich architectural heritage ranging from the
archeological sites of Sutherland, Caithness and Inverness to
the castles that stand guard over the cliffs of the northeast
and the now-deserted planned villages ● *78* of the northwest.

▲ THE CALEDONIAN FOREST

Written records left by the Romans refer to the 'great Caledonian Forest', a huge forest of Scots pines that covered much of Scotland. At the time it was inhabited by bears, wild boars and wolves, animals that have today disappeared from the region. While some of its pines are over 400 years old, only small stretches of this forest remain (1 percent of its original area). The smell of pine resin and pollen combined with the scent of bogbeans and heather make a visit to these forests a truly unforgettable experience.

SILVER BIRCH
This tree is easily recognized by its mottled white trunk. In winter finches and redpolls feed on its seeds.

COMMON JUNIPER
This shrub grows here and there beneath the pines alongside rowans, willows, birches and holly bushes.

CAPERCAILLIE
Its numbers are declining steadily, but the capercaillie is still one of the typical species of the Caledonian Forest.

PINE MARTEN
This nocturnal hunter feeds mainly on field mice and voles but also catches squirrels which it pursues with great agility.

WILD CAT
The wild cat is now the largest predator in Scotland. It is extremely elusive, hunting field mice and voles at dawn and dusk and sleeping in hollow branches during the day.

Male

Female

CRESTED TIT
This little bird is widely found in pine forests. It feeds on caterpillars and has a distinctive trill: *trrrri*.

SCOTTISH CROSSBILL
The crossbill's distinctively shaped beak enables it to extract seeds from pine cones.

TWINFLOWER
This northern trailing shrub is one of the many rare flowers found in Scots pine forests.

Heather

Myrtle

Juniper

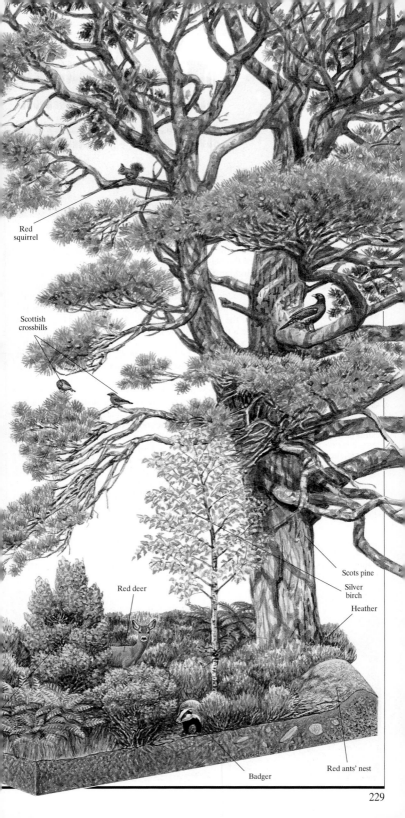

Red
squirrel

Scottish
crossbills

Scots pine

Silver
birch

Heather

Red deer

Badger

Red ants' nest

The Battle of Culloden, by David Morier (1746).

CLAVA CAIRNS
◆ **A** E6
(2 miles east of Culloden)
Clava Cairns, to the south of Nairn, are three burial mounds of a very particular type. Each of the mounds, which are at least 4000 years old, is surrounded by a circle of standing stones. Three stone pavements radiate out from the central cairn (ring-type but with no entrance) to its circle of stones. The other two are passage-type cairns. Funerary objects and human remains, some bearing evidence of cremation, were discovered on the site. The beliefs and rituals of the people who built these cairns have sunk into oblivion – for example, the significance of the cup-like depressions in some of the stones is not known – and the site remains shrouded in mystery.

Inverness from the River Ness, by Joseph Mallord William Turner (1779–1851).

INVERNESS ◆ **A** E6

Inverness is the capital of the Highlands. It stands at the mouth of the Ness, occupying a strategic site between the North Highlands and the Grampians. Early in its history St Columba ● *33* ▲ *204* came to convert the Pictish king Brude (Brudei) to Christianity. In the 11th century Macbeth built a castle here, which was later destroyed by Malcolm III to avenge the murder of his father, Duncan I ● *34*. The town was made a royal burgh by David I c. 1140 and subsequently suffered a number of sieges. It was occupied by the English during the wars of independence ● *38,* recaptured by Robert Bruce in 1307, then passed into the hands of the Highland clans, supporting Mary Stuart in 1562 and the Jacobites in 1715 and 1745. Few ancient buildings have therefore survived.
INVERNESS CASTLE. In 1746 the Jacobites destroyed the last fortress on Castle Hill. The site was cleared in 1843 to build the present castle, built in the medieval style made fashionable by Walter Scott. In front of the red-sandstone Highland Council buildings, a statue of Flora Macdonald ▲ *250*, the young woman who helped Charles Edward Stuart (Bonnie Prince Charlie) to escape after the battle of Culloden, belongs to the same Romanticized view of the Highlands.
INVERNESS MUSEUM AND ART GALLERY *(Castle Wynd)*. The well-stocked museum, which covers history, natural history, archeology, ethnography and Jacobite relics, also has an art gallery.
CHURCH STREET. The street is lined with old buildings: HIGH CHURCH (13th century, restored 1722), DUNBAR'S HOSPITAL (1688) and ABERTARFF HOUSE (1593), regional headquarters of the National Trust for Scotland.

CAWDOR ◆ **A** E6
(northeast of Kilravock, on the B9090)
The delightful village of Cawdor, with its picturesque 17th-century church, nestles at the foot of Cawdor Castle. Macbeth, chief of Moray, who

BALNAIN HOUSE *(Huntly Street)*. The Georgian mansion built by a wealthy merchant in 1762 today houses a center for research into the music of the Highlands and Islands. Instruments, videos and taped music trace the history of the region's music from the Stone Age to the present day. The center also organizes concerts and *ceilidhs* ● *52*.

INVERNESS TO NAIRN ◆ A E6

CULLODEN BATTLEFIELD *(on the B9006)*. This vast moor, five miles south of Inverness, is haunted by the bloody massacre of the Jacobites. The Battle of Culloden, on April 16, 1746, marked the end of the epic adventure of Bonnie Prince Charlie and the failure of the attempt to restore the Stuarts to the throne of Scotland. The Jacobite Risings not only divided clans and families but precipitated the disintegration of traditional Highland society ● *43*. It took less than an hour for the 9000 troops of the Duke of Cumberland, the son of George II, to crush the 5000 exhausted and demoralized Highlanders. Prisoners and wounded were not spared in the massacre, which earned Cumberland the nickname of 'Butcher'. Following the battle, the Young Pretender became a fugitive, leaving Scotland for ever five months later. The Visitor Centre has a reconstruction of the battle, while Old Leonach Cottage shows the interior of a cottage of the time. Flags mark the position of the two armies and monuments mark the spots where the clan chiefs fell. Each April a service is held in front of the Memorial Cairn in memory of those who died.

KILRAVOCK CASTLE *(pronounced 'Kilrock')*. The castle is the seat of the Roses of Kilravock. The keep of the present castle was built in the 15th century and extended in the 17th to 18th centuries. Mary Stuart was received here in 1562 and Bonnie Prince Charlie two days before the Battle of Culloden in 1746. Later guests included Robert Burns ▲ *142* and Charles Dickens.

FORT GEORGE *(at the end of the B9039)*. The fort was built by the government in 1747–69 after the Battle of Culloden, to guard the Moray Firth, but it has never been attacked in its entire history. It was designed to resist storms and Highland attacks and has barely changed since it was built. This symbol of the power of the House of Hanover occupies an area of 42 acres and remains one of the most impressive forts in Europe ● *78*. Although a garrison is still stationed here, certain buildings are open to the public and give an insight into the living conditions of soldiers in the 18th century.

murdered Duncan I and was crowned king of Scotland at Scone in 1040 ● *34*, was also Thane (baron) of Cawdor and undoubtedly owned lands nearby. Legend has it that the original tower, reached via a drawbridge, was built in the late 14th century by the Earl of Cawdor on the exact spot where, according to a dream, his donkey was in the habit of spending the night. The hawthorn bush under which the animal sheltered has been reverently preserved in the basement of the building. The vast castle gardens (above) are a blend of fantasy and formality and provide an attractive setting for the castle (enlarged in the 17th and 19th centuries).

THE FORT OF GEORGE II ★
Its defenses are as sophisticated as they are spectacular and make this Hanoverian fortress one of the most remarkable in Britain.

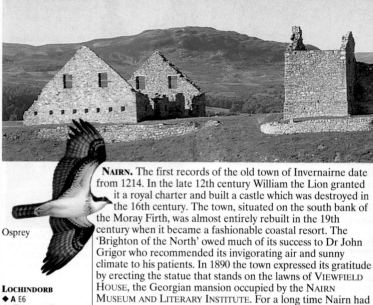

Osprey

NAIRN. The first records of the old town of Invernairne date from 1214. In the late 12th century William the Lion granted it a royal charter and built a castle which was destroyed in the 16th century. The town, situated on the south bank of the Moray Firth, was almost entirely rebuilt in the 19th century when it became a fashionable coastal resort. The 'Brighton of the North' owed much of its success to Dr John Grigor who recommended its invigorating air and sunny climate to his patients. In 1890 the town expressed its gratitude by erecting the statue that stands on the lawns of VIEWFIELD HOUSE, the Georgian mansion occupied by the NAIRN MUSEUM AND LITERARY INSTITUTE. For a long time Nairn had an active fishing community, the Nairn Fishermen's Society, founded in 1767 and believed to be the oldest cooperative in Scotland. Although the narrow streets and modest cottages of the FISHERTOWN district have changed little since the 19th century, the fishing and the herring industry declined in the 1920s and '30s. FISHERTOWN MUSEUM, in King Street, traces the history and traditions of the town's fishing industry.

STRATHSPEY AND THE CAIRNGORMS ◆ A E6-D B1

From Nairn the A939 and then the A9 lead to Strathspey ('broad valley of the Spey') and the Cairngorm Mountains ▲ *234*. Summer and winter resorts lie at the foot of this wild mountain range, much of which is now a protected site.

GRANTOWN-ON-SPEY. This elegant little town on the banks of the River Spey was built in 1776 by the then laird, Sir James Grant. It became a famous health spa whose popularity was further boosted by Queen Victoria's visit in 1860. As well as a winter-sports resort and salmon-fishing center, it is the departure point for walks along Strath Spey. It also has its own MUSEUM. On the northern edge of the town is CASTLE GRANT, the ancestral home of the Grants, built in 1563 and refurbished by Robert and John Adam in the 18th century.

ABERNETHY FOREST RSPB RESERVE. This reserve covers an area of 30,000 acres and provides sanctuary for such species as Scottish crossbills, capercaillies, whooper swans and especially the ospreys that nest on Loch Garten. The Royal Society for the Protection of Birds has built a hide from

LOCHINDORB
◆ A E6
At Dava a minor road turns right off the A939 from Nairn toward Lochindorb. On an island in the loch stand the ruins of a castle built by the Comyns in the 13th century and fortified by Edward I of England in 1303. It was demolished in 1458 on the order of James II after it was used as a stronghold by the 'Wolf of Badenoch' ▲ *232*. This was the nickname given to Alexander Stewart, Lord of Badenoch and brother of Robert III of Scotland (1390–1406), after he had plundered several villages and churches.

> 'At Nairn we may fix the verge of the Highlands; for here
> I first saw peat fires, and first heard the Erse language.'
>
> Samuel Johnson

**AVIEMORE TO THE
SUMMIT OF CAIRN
GORM ◆ A E6-D B1**
The road that climbs
from Aviemore to the
ski slopes of Cairn
Gorm (the best in
Scotland) passes
LOCH MORLICH, the
water-sports center
that lies within the
GLENMORE FOREST
PARK, and the
CAIRNGORM
REINDEER CENTRE,
which has a herd of
reindeer introduced

which, between late April and August,
visitors can observe the nests through
binoculars or on a video surveillance
screen. The small STRATHSPEY STEAM
RAILWAY operates between Boat of
Garten and Aviemore.

CARRBRIDGE *(on the A938)*. This quiet
village is named after the stone bridge
built in 1717 by John Nicolson. The
LANDMARK HERITAGE CENTRE, which has
an adventure park, enables old and young alike to discover
the region's natural heritage through its multimedia
presentations, exhibitions, arboretum and nature trails.

AVIEMORE *(on the B1952)*. Aviemore stands against the
spectacular backdrop of the peaks and pine forests of the
Cairngorms. The original village, founded in the 19th century,
was based around the whisky industry. Since the 1960s
Aviemore has been an extremely popular year-round resort
with its two water-sports centers, covered swimming pools,
ice-skating rink, theater and whisky-tasting center.

KINCRAIG. At the HIGHLAND WILDLIFE PARK, on the outskirts
of Aviemore, visitors can see (on foot or from the car) wolves,
wild cats, bison, deer, Przewalski's wild horses (the ancestors
of the domestic horse) and Highland cattle.

KINGUSSIE *(on the A86)*. The HIGHLAND FOLK MUSEUM
presents Highland traditions by means of costumes, furniture,
agricultural implements, craft demonstrations and ancient
structures such as a smokehouse for salmon, a Hebridean
cottage and barns.

RUTHVEN BARRACKS *(southeast of Kingussie, on the B970)*.
This ruined barracks is perched on an outcrop on the east
bank of the Spey, near Ruthven, the birthplace of the poet
James Macpherson (1736–96) ● *37, 46*. It was built by
Hanoverian troops (the 'Redcoats' of George II) after the
Jacobite Rising of 1715 and extended in 1734 by General
Wade. It was only defended by a dozen or so men when the
Jacobites attempted to capture it in 1745. The following year
it was attacked and captured by the Scottish artillery. The
survivors of the Battle of Culloden ● *43* ▲ *231* gathered at the
barracks and blew it up before they dispersed.

NEWTONMORE *(on the A86)*. This village makes an ideal base
for visiting the region. Many of the pieces in the collection of
the CLAN MACPHERSON MUSEUM come from Cluny Castle,
the seat of the clan chief which was destroyed by fire.

in the 1950s. The
chairlifts operate
throughout the year
to a height of 3610
feet and, in fine
weather, the summit
of Cairn Gorm
(4085 feet) offers a
sweeping view of the
Cairngorms and
beyond.

**EWEN MACPHERSON
OF CLUNY**
(c. 1700–56) After the
Battle of Culloden
(1746), Ewen
Macpherson, an
ardent supporter of
the Stuarts and chief
of the Macpherson
clan during the
Jacobite Rising
of 1745, spent nine
years in hiding before
going into exile in
France. Robert Louis
Stevenson ● *100*
described two of his
hideouts in
Kidnapped (1886):
Cluny's Cage, a hut
clinging to the slopes
of Ben Alder, and the
cave of Creag Dhu.

▲ The Cairngorms

Golden eagle
The golden eagle, symbol of wild mountain regions, hunts here. This bird of prey can have a wingspan of 8 feet or more. The adult plumage is golden on the head and dark brown on the rest of their body.

The range of granite mountains known as the Cairngorms covers an area of 100 square miles in the heart of the Grampians, between Strath Spey and Braemar. It has around 50 summits over 3000 feet high and reaches its highest point at Ben Macdui (4925 feet). Most of the Cairngorms (over 60 square miles) have been classified as a nature reserve to protect their delicate plants and wildlife, which include species only found in Scotland.

Winter

Summer

Arctic hare
This hare's ability to change color with the seasons, from reddish-brown in summer to pure white in winter, provides camouflage and protects it from predators.

Summer

Winter

Ptarmigan
Like the mountain hare, this member of the partridge family has the ability to change color with the seasons. Its winter plumage provides camouflage against the snow-covered ground.

The Cairngorms were formed by the most recent Ice Age ● 16. At high-altitude they are characterized by scree slopes and vast plateaus covered with Arctic-Alpine vegetation. The lower slopes are carpeted with heather or wooded with pines, and glacial depressions are filled with small lochs.

Lochaber and Ben Nevis (*top*); boat moored on the Caledonian canal (*above*). Glenfinnan viaduct (*right*).

BEN NEVIS ◆ D A1
Ben Nevis, the highest point in the United Kingdom (4410 feet), has an annual rainfall of around 157 inches and its summit is shrouded in mist for most of the year. Some of its north-facing ravines are covered with 'eternal snows'. According to legend, if they melted, the Camerons of Glen Nevis – the steep-sided valley whose thundering falls served as a backdrop for the films *Highlander, Rob Roy* and *Braveheart* – would lose their lands to the Crown. In fine weather it is possible to climb to the top of Ben Nevis in 4–5 hours. The less energetic can admire it from the heights of the Aonach Mor ski resort, 8 miles northeast of Fort William, or from the Commando Memorial above Spean Bridge, a few kilometers further on.

FORT WILLIAM ◆ D A1

Fort William, capital of the Lochaber district, stands on Loch Linnhe, at the foot of Ben Nevis and to the north of the famous 95 mile-long footpath known as the West Highland Way. The region has given its name to the 'Lochaber axe', an ax with a long, slender blade and a yew handle ending in a hook, designed to unseat riders. The town was named after the earthwork fort built in 1655 by General Monck and rebuilt in stone in 1690 under William III (William of Orange). The fort withstood the Jacobite attacks of 1715 and 1745, but was demolished in 1866 to make way for the railway. In spite of its lack of charm, this major road, rail and river intersection features on many tourist itineraries.
WEST HIGHLAND MUSEUM (*Cameron Square*). This small museum presents the region's natural history, popular traditions, its role in the Jacobite Risings and the wave of emigration provoked by the repression that followed.
OLD INVERLOCHY CASTLE (*Inverlochy*). Near the bridge across the River Lochy stand the impressive ruins of a tower-house that was probably built by the Comyns in the 13th century.
BEN NEVIS DISTILLERY (*Inverlochy*). Since 1825 the distillery (open to the public) has produced the whisky known as 'The Dew of Ben Nevis'.

THE ROAD TO THE ISLES ◆ C C1

The A830 between Fort William and Mallaig (46 miles) offers an opportunity to discover historical and legendary sites set in breathtaking landscapes. It is one of the most beautiful routes in Scotland and, unsurprisingly, is extremely busy in summer.
NEPTUNE'S STAIRCASE (*Banavie, 2 miles northwest of Fort William on the A830*). This series of eight locks which, over a distance of 165 feet account for a difference in height of 64 feet, is probably the most spectacular feature on the Caledonian Canal ▲ *238*. It was named by the engineer Thomas Telford (1757–1834).
GLENFINNAN. This little village is steeped in Jacobite history. It was here, at the north end of Loch Shiel, that Charles Edward Stuart rallied the Highland clans to support his cause

on August 19, 1745 ● *43* and from here that he set out, at the head of an army of 1300 men, on an epic adventure that was to end so tragically at Culloden on April 16, 1746. The event is commemorated by a column surmounted by the statue of a kilted Highlander (1815), and each year a Highland Gathering ● *54* is held in a nearby field on the Saturday nearest August 19.

LOCH NAN UAMH. Beyond Arnipol the A830 follows the shore of Loch nan Uamh (pronounced 'naan Oua'). A cairn on the water's edge marks the beach where Bonnie Prince Charlie landed in July 1745 after sailing from France via the Outer Hebrides. It was from this same spot that he went into exile a year later, with his hopes dashed and a price on his head.

ARISAIG. In 1900 it took a carriage 7 hours to travel the 34 miles from Fort William to Arisaig. Today the journey takes just an hour by car. This small harbor at the head of Loch nan Ceall has the most westerly railway station in Great Britain. Strangely enough this distant corner of the Highlands has a monumental church – St Mary's – and a good bookshop. The Sound of Arisaig offers a spectacular view of the Eigg, bought by its inhabitants in 1997, Rum, with its steep basalt cliffs, and Muck ▲ *206*. Further along the A830 the Sleat peninsula, on the Isle of Skye ▲ *248*, can be seen across the Sound of Sleat.

LOCH MORAR. Between Portnaluchaig and Morar (famous for its white silica-sand beach immortalized in the films *Rob Roy* and *Highlander*) the A830 crosses the narrow isthmus separating Loch Morar from the sea. With a depth of 1000 feet it is Scotland's deepest inland loch. It is said to be haunted by Morag, a monster which appears when a Macdonald of Clanranald is about to die.

MALLAIG. For a long time this town built on the steep slopes above a small bay owed its prosperity to herring fishing. The fishermen, whose numbers have gradually decreased, are turning increasingly to crayfish. MARINE WORLD, near the station, traces the history of these fisheries while its aquariums present the local marine life. Mallaig is linked by car ferry to Armadale (Skye) and Castlebay (Barra) and by boat to the Knoydart peninsula and the islands of Rum, Eigg, Muck and Canna.

THE WEST HIGHLAND RAILWAY ★
In summer a steam train operates between Fort William and Mallaig (2 hours). The 40-mile line, opened in 1901, offers one of the most scenic rail journeys in Europe. After crossing a spectacular viaduct 98 feet high, the train stops at Glenfinnan station, which has been converted into a railway museum.

ARDNAMURCHAN PENINSULA
◆ **C** B1-C1
South of Lochailort, the A861 crosses the Moidart to the Ardnamurchan peninsula: 200,000 acres of varied but equally rich landscapes. Against this backdrop stand the ruins of Castle Tioram (13th century), on the south shore of Loch Moidart, and those of Mingary Castle (14th century), at Kilchoan. The 60-mile journey finishes at the end of the B8007, at the Point of Ardnamurchan, the most westerly headland in the United Kingdom.

The canal was built
between 1803 and
1822 by Thomas
Telford ▲ 236
according to plans by
James Watt ▲ 44. It
was designed to link
the North Sea and the
Atlantic so that
merchant ships did
not have to make the
long, dangerous
journey round the
north coast of
Scotland. The lochs of
Glen Mor make up a
major part of this 60-
mile waterway, so that
only about 20 miles
had to be constructed.
Given the size of
modern vessels and
the small capacity of
its locks, the canal is
today only used by
pleasure craft.

GLEN URQUHART
AND GLEN AFFRIC
◆ A D6
In Glen Urquhart,
near Corrimony
(9 miles west of
Drumnadrochit
▲ 240), there is a
passage-type cairn
surrounded by eleven
standing stones. From
Cannich a minor road
leads to Glen Affric.
In spite of the
hydroelectric dam
built on its loch, the
valley's pine-covered
slopes inhabited by
deer – one of the last
remnants of the
Caledonian Forest
● 228 – make it
one of the most
beautiful valleys in
Scotland.

THE GREAT GLEN ◆ A D6-E6 D A1

The A82 between Inverness ▲ 230 and Fort William ▲ 236
follows the deep geological fault of Glen Mor ('Great Glen')
which runs diagonally across the Highlands from the
southwest to the northeast. The bottom of this rift valley,
eroded by great glaciers in the Ice Age, contains three
freshwater lochs – Loch Ness, Loch Oich and Loch Lochy –
and two fjords, the Moray Firth in the north and Loch
Linnhe in the south.
LOCH NESS. Although no more than a mile wide, Loch Ness is
one of the longest lochs in Scotland (23½ miles) and also the
most famous, due to Nessie, the mysterious monster that is
supposed to haunt its waters ▲ 240. It has an area of
almost 22 square miles, a depth of up to 820 feet in places
and an average temperature of 5°C which means it never
freezes over. The A82, which follows the west shore of the
loch and services the main tourist sites, is often jammed
with traffic in summer. The B852 and B862, which follow the
route of an old road built by General Wade along the loch's
east shore between Fort George ▲ 231 and Fort Augustus,
are much quieter and offer unspoiled views of the Great
Glen. The best way to see Loch Ness is to take a boat trip
from Inverness or Fort Augustus.

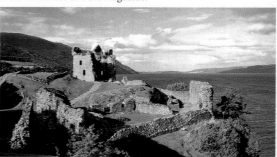

URQUHART CASTLE. The castle (*above*), built on a promontory
at the south end of Urquhart Bay to monitor ships moving up
and down the loch, stands on the remains of an Iron Age
broch. Its foundations date from the 13th century and the
tower-house, defended by a curtain wall and drawbridge, from
the 16th century. To prevent the castle falling into the hands
of the Jacobites, it was demolished by government troops in
1692.
FORT AUGUSTUS. In 1729 General Wade, governor of the
'North of Great Britain', built a fort at the south end of Loch
Ness near the mouth of the Oich. It was named after the
second son of George II, William Augustus, Duke of
Cumberland ▲ 231. Lord Lovat donated it to the Benedictine
order in 1876. The Benedictine monks from Bavaria who
occupied until recently FORT AUGUSTUS ABBEY (above left)
built the east cloister, the chapter house and St Andrews
Chapel shortly afterwards. Today the town of Fort Augustus is
crossed by the CALEDONIAN CANAL and six of its locks. The
A82 continues south, along the west shore of Loch Oich and
then the east shore of Loch Lochy before crossing Spean
Bridge into Fort William.

> 'Peaks like waves whipped up by a storm rise as far as the eye can see, following one upon the other, while the valley troughs of this petrified ocean, are occupied by lakes [...]'
>
> Astolphe de Custine

INVERGARRY TO KYLE OF LOCHALSH ◆ D A1 A C6

As the A87 climbs from Invergarry, on Loch Oich, toward Glen Garry it looks out across grandiose landscapes of trout lakes and heather-covered hillsides before following the north shore of Loch Cluanie (regulated by a dam) and dropping down into the desolate wastes of Loch Shiel. It was in this barren valley, in 1719, that the English troops of General Wightman finally routed the Highlanders of the Earl of Seaforth and their Spanish allies, after pursuing them from Eilean Donan ● 42. The Five Sisters of Kintail, the region's highest point (3504 feet), rise majestically to the north, while the view to the south is dominated by the outline of nine 'munros' (mountains above 3000 feet).

GLENELG BAY. From Shiel Bridge a small road crosses Mam Ratagan Pass (1112 feet) and passes to the west of the village of Glenelg whose name ('Glen of the Irish') may be an indication of its first inhabitants. The region has a number of brochs ● 67, including DUN TELVE (33 feet high with a diameter of 62 feet), the best preserved broch on the Scottish mainland, and DUN TRODDAN. Near Glenelg are the remains of BERNERA BARRACKS (built in 1723 and abandoned in 1790), the most westerly outpost built by the Redcoats to counter the Jacobite threat. In summer there is a ferry link between Bernera, to the northwest of Glenelg, and Kylerhea, on the Isle of Skye ▲ 248.

KYLE OF LOCHALSH. From Dornie the A87 continues to Kyle of Lochalsh, named after the narrow passage that separates it from the Isle of Skye (the Gaelic *caol* means 'strait'). It was here, in 1266, that the Norse king Hakon rallied his fleet before the Battle of Largs ● 34. Today a cantilever toll bridge, reputedly the most expensive in Europe, links the village to Skye. The bridge was privately financed and opened in 1995 amidst controversy over the abolition of the ferry service.

EILEAN DONAN CASTLE ★
Eilean Donan Castle (*above*), near Dornie, was immortalized by the film *Highlander* and is today one of the most photographed castles in Scotland. The islet located between Lochs Long, Alsh and Duich, is named after a 6th-century Celtic hermit. The castle, built c. 1220 by Alexander II to give advance warning of Viking raids, became the stronghold of the Mackenzies in the 14th century. In 1719 these fervent supporters of the Stuarts entrenched themselves in the castle with 300 Spanish soldiers who had come to support the Jacobite cause ● 42. Two months later the castle was bombarded by three English frigates. It was nothing but ruins when, in the 1920s, Farqhar Macrae and John Macrae-Gilstrap began the task of restoring it to its former glory.

STRANGE SPECTACLE ON LOCH NESS

None of the legendary creatures said to haunt the lochs and rivers of Scotland can rival the fame of Nessie, the Loch Ness monster. With dark mountains and often menacing skies reflected in its opaque waters, the loch provides the ideal setting for a legend that began in the 6th century and has captured the public imagination since the 1930s. The lack of tangible evidence has meant that Nessie's existence has never been conclusively proved, but the mystery attracts tourists in search of excitement and monster hunters from all over the world.

THE BIRTH OF A LEGEND

According to legend St Columba, who came to the region in 565, passed a funeral procession as he approached Loch Ness. The dead man had been attacked by some kind of creature while fishing. At Columba's request one of his disciples swam out to the spot where the tragedy had occurred and the monster immediately appeared from the depths. Columba forbade it to move any closer or touch his disciple and, making the sign of the cross, ordered it to return from whence it had come. The creature obeyed and those who had witnessed the miracle immediately adopted the Christian faith.

PHYSICAL CHARACTERISTICS

The monster has become affectionately known as Nessie. It is said to have a small head, a long neck, a large, brownish body with one or more dorsal humps, and four paddlelike limbs. Its size varies from 20 to 60 feet long, according to reports. Its physical characteristics suggest a plesiosaur, a marine reptile which became extinct 70 million years ago and whose fossilized remains have been found in the British Isles.

DRUMNADROCHIT ✪

The village's Official Loch Ness Monster Exhibition Centre makes it an absolute must for many tourists. The exhibition presents eye-witness accounts and details of research carried out on Nessie. The exhibition is open throughout the year (9am–8.30pm in July and August).

SCIENTIFIC EVIDENCE

A number of scientific expeditions have tried to 'flush out' the monster but the depth of the loch and the cloudiness of its waters make submarine photographs illegible and exploration dangerous.

STRANGE SIGHTINGS

Eyewitness accounts have increased significantly since a road was built along the northwest shore of the loch in 1933. When the *Daily Mail* published a photograph of the monster taken by the London surgeon Robert Kenneth Wilson in April 1934, 'monster hunters' began to flock to the loch. It was not until the 1980s that is was revealed that the photograph was a hoax! In 1960 Tim Dinsdale filmed a large and apparently live mass making its way across the loch, but the distance was too great for it to be officially identified. It also appears that Nessie has ventured onto dry land several times. In 1522 a certain Duncan Campbell saw 'a terrible creature on the shores of the loch'. More recently, in February 1999, a creature between 30 and 50 feet long was sighted on the beach near Dores.

ENCOUNTERS OF THE THIRD KIND

A number of divers claim to have seen the monster in spite of the loch's cloudy waters. In 1880 a diver encountered 'a very strange creature, like a giant frog'. In 1964 a pleasure cruiser sank after hitting an 'unidentified object'. The diver sent to locate the wreck returned to the surface distraught. He refused to say what he had seen but flatly refused to return to the water. In 1971 another diver was sent to hospital in a state of shock. He claimed to have seen 'an enormous black creature' and stated that he 'had never seen anything so hideously repugnant or terrifying' in his life.

THE APPLECROSS PENINSULA ◆ A C6
At the head of Loch Kishorn, to the north of Ardarroch, an unclassified road turns off the A896 and crosses the Applecross peninsula via BEALACH-NAM-BO (2040 feet). The pass, whose Gaelic name means 'pass of the cattle', offers spectacular views of Beinn Bhan (2940 feet), moorland scattered with small lochs, fjords to the southeast, and the Isle of Skye beyond the Island of Raasay. The road follows the edge of the peninsula, running along the shores of Lochs Torrison and Sheildag, and rejoins the A896 just south of Shieldaig.

BEINN EIGHE NATIONAL NATURE RESERVE ◆ A C5
The oldest nature reserve in Britain covers an area of 11,860 acres and provides sanctuary for red deer, roe deer, martens, golden eagles and peregrine falcons. Aultroy Visitor Centre, (1 mile north of Kinlochewe, via the A832) presents information on flora and fauna, and two nature trails on the slopes of Beinn Eighe.

THE NORTHWEST COAST ◆ A C4-C6-D4

The northwest coast of the Highlands is renowned for its mild climate, its picturesque coastal villages, its majestic lochs and its scenery: an undulating plateau punctuated by spectacular, isolated peaks. It has a number of tourist centers that attract sightseers, fishermen, hikers and experienced climbers.

PLOCKTON. Its palm trees, sheltered beaches, annual regatta (late July–early August), the fish-filled waters of Loch Carron and the nearby seal colonies make this coastal village a pleasant summer resort.

GLEN CARRON TO TORRIDON. The A890 runs along the south shore of the impressive Loch Carron and into Glen Carron. At the A890-A896 intersection turn left along the A896 which passes through the wild landscapes of the ancient county of Ross, described by Queen Victoria as totally isolated from civilization.

TORRIDON. In this small village at the head of Upper Loch Torridon, the TORRIDON COUNTRYSIDE CENTRE provides information on walks and climbs in the region as well as on its flora and fauna. Beyond Torridon the road enters the steep-sided valley of Glen Torridon dominated by Liathach (3458 feet) and the Beinn Eighe massif (3313 feet) whose red sandstone peaks (up to 800 million years old) are overlaid by white quartzite (510–550 million years old).

LOCH MAREE. From the climbing and walking center of Kinlochewe, the A832 continues to Loch Maree, the extension of Glen Docherty. This impressive stretch of water (*below*) – 12½ miles long by 3 miles wide – is named after the Irish monk, Maelrubha, who died in 722 and is said to be buried on the Isle of Maree, one of the loch's pine-covered islands.

GAIRLOCH. This former fishing port on the shores of Loch Gairloch has been a summer resort since the Victorian era. It has a golf course, fine sandy beaches, a lighthouse built by Stevenson – the engineer and grandfather of the writer, Robert Louis Stevenson – and a Heritage Museum which presents the region's maritime and agricultural traditions.

POOLEWE AND LOCH EWE. This little port nestles at the head of Loch Ewe, a fjord where a number of convoys bound for the Soviet Union were fitted out during World War Two and which is now a NATO base.

INVEREWE GARDENS ▲ *196*. In 1862 Osgood Mackenzie (1842–1922) began to create a garden on the barren, windswept and previously uncultivated Kernsary peninsula, east of Poolewe. Taking advantage of the influence of the warm Gulf Stream, he patiently put together a remarkable botanical collection. His work was continued by his daughter and today the collection comprises over 2500 species of mainly exotic plants and forms a lush garden that lies on the same latitude as St Petersburg.

GRUINARD BAY. Gruinard Island, the site of bacteriological experiments during World War Two, stands in the middle of this bay bordered by fine sandy beaches. The island was decontaminated in the 1980s. The hills overlooking the bay and the nearby slopes of An Teallach (3484 feet), whose Gaelic name means 'the forge', are inhabited by mountain goats. At the south end of Little Loch Broom, the road turns inland along the Dundonnell river and joins the A835 at Braemore Junction.

ULLAPOOL. In the 18th century, when commercial fishing was at its height, the British Fisheries Society promoted the foundation of a number of fishing villages along the northwest coast of Scotland One of these was Ullapool, founded in 1788, and then developed by Thomas Telford to exploit the rich shoals of herring in Loch Broom. Today this rich natural resource is virtually exhausted and a much-reduced fleet fishes mainly for shrimps which are sold by the pint in local bars or exported to Europe in huge refrigerated containers. Ullapool enjoyed an economic boom during World War Two, when it became a port of call for the ships avoiding the mined waters of the east coast. More recently factory ships from Eastern Europe docked here for several months at a time. This delightful village with its whitewashed houses has become a popular summer tourist resort. Ferries leave the harbor for the Isle of Lewis ▲ *252* and pleasure boats run trips to the Summer Isles. The church built by Telford (1829) houses a MUSEUM of local history.

Inverewe Gardens (*above*); on the shores of Upper Loch Torridon (*above left*).

CORRIESHALLOCH GORGE ◆ A C5
(*11 miles south of Ullapool*)
A forest path leads from the A835 to the suspension bridge built by John A. Fowler ▲ *129* across this 'terrifying gorge' carved by glaciers some 13,000 years ago. This is where the river Droma enters the Broom, plunging over the thundering Measach Falls (150 feet) and drenching the schist walls of the ravine and their lush vegetation of mosses and ferns with its fine spray. These spectacular falls can also be reached via the A832.

THE MAGIC OF THE NORTHWEST ★
While the Torridon region, Loch Maree and Inverewe Gardens are particularly worthy of note, the entire northwest coast is one of the most beautiful regions in the Highlands.

The Last of the Clan, by Thomas Faed (1865).

THE SUMMER ISLES ◆ A C4-C5
This group of islands, formerly a busy herring-smoking center, is today the preserve of seals and seabirds. In summer there are boat trips from Ullapool and Achiltibuie.

ACHILTIBUIE ◆ A C4
This coastal village stands in the magnificent setting of the Coigach peninsula (*right*). Gardening enthusiasts will love the HYDROPONICUM, a 'futuristic garden' where all kinds of exotic plants, flowers and fruit are grown under glass without soil. A traditional smokehouse for fish and meat is open to the public at Altan Dubh, 2 miles to the south.

LOCHINVER ◆ A C4
In summer this little fishing port at the head of Loch Inver and the end of the A837 is inundated with sightseers, sea and river fishermen, hikers, climbers and bird-watchers.
The coast to the north of the port is particularly beautiful, with its little inlets and villages nestling at the foot of steep cliffs.

Beyond Ullapool the A835 reaches the coast at Ardmair where it offers a magnificent view of the Isle Martin RSPB reserve before turning inland with the Coigach peninsula, dominated by Ben Mor Coigach (2437 feet), on its left.

INVERPOLLY NATIONAL NATURE RESERVE.
This 27,000-acre nature reserve incorporates the vast Loch Sionacaig and Cul Mor (2875 feet). As in the Torridon region the sandstone relief rises from a plateau of Lewisian gneiss that is 3 billion years old. The reserve has some of the last surviving remains of the Caledonian Forest and an abundant wildlife: golden eagles,

deer and wild cats. The geological trail which leaves from the KNOCKAN CLIFF Information Centre enables visitors to discover a geological anomaly: schist that is between 800 million and 1 billion years old, overlaying quartzite and other metamorphic rocks which are at most 600 million years old! Turn left at Ledmore onto the A837.

INCHNADAMPH NATURE RESERVE. The reserve at the south end of Loch Assynt lies partly on an outcrop of Cambrian limestone. Fossilized human and animal remains from the prehistoric period have been discovered in some of its caves (apply to the Lochinver Estate Office in Lochinver for permission to visit the site). Ben More Assynt (3274 feet) rises to the east.

LOCH ASSYNT. On the southeast shore of this beautiful loch stand the ruins of Ardvreck Castle (16th century), the MacLeod stronghold demolished by the Mackenzies in 1691. This was where James Graham, Marquess of Montrose, was imprisoned in 1650 before being taken to Edinburgh and executed.

SCOURIE. This small farming community on the A894 is also a trout-fishing center. Boat trips leave for HANDA ISLAND, a major nesting site for seabirds and now a Scottish Wildlife Trust reserve. North of Scourie the road leaves the coast and crosses a desolate region of scree slopes and scattered lochs.

THE NORTH COAST ◆ A D3-F3

Bathed by the North Sea, the north coast of Scotland is colder than the west and sparsely populated. Although not particularly popular with tourists, it is certainly not lacking in character with its vertiginous cliffs, wooded valleys and peat bogs interspersed with water holes (*dhu loch*).

DURNESS. This farming village, once the summer residence of the bishops of Caithness, is today a stage on the tourist route to the North. At nearby BALNAKEIL are the partially ruined Durness Old Church (1619) and the former radar station which in summer is transformed into a craft village.

SMOO CAVE. Boats can be hired at Durness and Leirinmore (2 miles to the east) to visit this spectacular marine cave. The Altt Smoo plunges over falls into its three chambers.

LOCH ERIBOLL. Loch Eriboll (394 feet deep) is the most impressive fjord on the north coast. During World War Two it was used as an allied naval base before becoming the scene of the German U-boat surrender. Leave the A838 at ACHUVOLDRACH and follow the old road to enjoy beautiful views of the Kyle of Tongue and its surroundings.

TONGUE. The village was once the stronghold of the Lords of Reay, the principal branch of the Mackay clan. The ruins of their 17th-century castle overlook the beach.

BETTYHILL. The village was founded in the 19th century by smallholders evicted from the Strathnaver valley during the Highland Clearances. The STRATHNAVER MUSEUM, housed in the former parish church of Farr, traces the history of this painful episode in Scottish history. It also has a Celtic cross and some impressive tombstones.

DOUNREAY NUCLEAR POWER STATION. Scotland's first nuclear power station (1955) was for a long time the region's principal employer – and polluter. It is currently being dismantled.

THURSO. This former Viking outpost enjoyed its golden age in the Middle Ages as the principal trading port between Scotland and Scandinavia. It reverted to fishing in the 17th and 18th centuries and owes its present activity to the ferry service between Scrabster and the Orkney ▲ 256 and Shetland ▲ 262 islands. The British surfing championships are held on Thurso beach.

DUNNET HEAD. This promontory rising 426 feet above the sea is the most northerly point in Great Britain.

JOHN O' GROATS. Today a popular tourist center, John o' Groats was named after Jan de Groot, the Dutchman who established a regular boat service between the port and the Orkney Islands at the request of James IV. Today this is still the shortest link with the islands.

CAPE WRATH ◆ A D3
(9 miles northwest of Durness – ferry from Keoldale and minibus)
The name of the northwest tip of Great Britain is derived from the Norse *hvarf* ('point of turning'). This windswept rocky promontory offers magnificent views. In fine weather the lighthouse (1828) offers views of Orkney, to the northeast, and the Isle of Lewis, to the west. Visitors can observe the colonies of seabirds that nest on the Clo-Mor Cliffs.

DUNCANSBY HEAD
◆ A F3 *(minor road from John o' Groats)*
The northeastern tip of Scotland (*below*) is worth visiting for its cliffs (213 feet) with their colonies of seabirds ● *20, 22*, and the caves, ridges, arches and bridges sculpted by thousands of years of erosion.

KEISS ◆ A F3
(4 miles north of Wick, on the A99)
The remains of two brochs can be seen beside the coastal path leading to the medieval ruins of KEISS CASTLE. Like the white castle (private property) set back from the coast, built in Scots Baronial style in the 18th century, Keiss Castle is the property of the Sinclairs, earls of Caithness.

CASTLE GIRNIGOE AND CASTLE SINCLAIR ◆ A F3
(near Noss Head, via Staxigoe)
These two adjacent castles *(above)* were built by the earls of Caithness on the wild cliffs above Sinclair's Bay in the 15th and early 17th century respectively. The ruins are potentially dangerous and are an unsuitable place for children.

Women from Cromarty (1905) *(right).*

THE NORTHEAST COAST ◆ A D5-F3

The landscape of the northeast coast of the Highlands is less pronounced than that of the west coast. Like the north coast it experienced a long period of Scandinavian occupation, as evidenced by its place names, and was as severely affected by the 'Clearances' of the 19th century ● *36*. It is also one of the poorest regions of Scotland, where sheep farming, fishing and tourism are the principal sources of income.

WICK. The name of this town on the Wick estuary, derived from the Norse *vik* meaning 'bay', attests to its history of Scandinavian occupation. Thomas Telford designed a model village and new harbor installations in 1808, when Wick became a major fishing and commercial herring port, a period of prosperity evoked in the WICK HERITAGE CENTRE (Bank Street). Today the town is well served by communication links and is renowned for its production of Caithness glass.

MEGALITHS. To the south of Wick are a number of prehistoric remains, the most remarkable and accessible of which are on the HILL O' MANY STANES, near Mid Clyth, to the northwest of Blackness. Here, some 200 standing stones, dating from c. 1800 BC, are arranged in 22 rows to form a fan shape that may have had some astrological significance. Further south, at Occumster, a minor road leads to the GREY CAIRNS OF CAMSTER, two well-preserved Neolithic burials dating from between 4000 and 1800 BC.

DUNBEATH *(on the A99).* Laidhay Croft Museum is a typical Caithness croft with outbuildings and agricultural implements dating from the early 20th century.

HELMSDALE. Like Dunbeath and many other Scottish ports, Helmsdale welcomed crofters evicted during the 19th-century 'Clearances' and who turned

Laidhay Croft Mueseum at
Dunbeath (*right*);
East Church, Cromarty,
with its 18th-century
galleries (*below*).

to herring fishing as a source of income.
The TIME SPAN HERITAGE CENTRE
presents an interesting history of the
region from prehistoric times.

DORNOCH (*on the A9*). This pleasant
family resort, renowned for its spacious
beaches and golf links, stands on the
north shore of Dornoch Firth. This
former royal burgh grew up around the
cathedral built in the 13th century by the
bishops of Caithness on the site of a 6th-
century chapel. The CATHEDRAL, destroyed by fire in 1570, was
redesigned in the 17th century, almost entirely rebuilt in
1835–37 and restored in 1924. The tower of the former
bishop's palace (16th century), opposite the cathedral, today
forms part of a luxury hotel.

TAIN. This small town on the south shore of Dornoch Firth
is Scotland's oldest royal burgh. Its patron is St Duthus
(c. 1000–1065), Bishop of Ross, who was born in the town and
whose relics were returned here in 1253. The first two chapels
built for pilgrims are now in ruins, but St Duthus Church,
built c. 1360 and now restored, has some beautiful stained-
glass windows and a pulpit that was a gift from the Earl of
Moray, Regent of Scotland, in the 16th century. TAIN
THROUGH TIME, the museum of local history, is situated near
the elegant Tolbooth (1707). Another local attraction is the
Glenmorangie Distillery ▲ *221*.

NIGG BAY. The bay, which was a Royal Naval base until 1965,
took advantage of the expansion of the North Sea oil industry
to move into the repair and reconstruction of drilling rigs.
The old church of Nigg has a beautiful Pictish stone ▲ *184*.

CROMARTY. Situated on the tip of Black Isle, the fertile
peninsula that lies between the Firths of Cromarty, Moray and
Beauly, Cromarty was once a prosperous port. It was passed
over by the development of overland communication links in
the 19th century, since when it appears to have lapsed into
inactivity. It still has its medieval market cross, beautiful
merchants' houses, East Church, with 18th-century galleries,
and the house where the self-taught geologist
Hugh Miller (1802–56) was born. The house,
along with the neighboring law court (1782),
has been converted into a museum.

ROSEMARKIE (*on the A832*). The GROAM
HOUSE MUSEUM has a vey fine Pictish
stone, which suggests that the region
was inhabited by early Christian
communities.

FORTROSE. Above the town stand the
ruins of a cathedral consecrated in 1485.
It was demolished on the order of
Cromwell and the stones used to build
the fort at Inverness ▲ *230*.

STRATHPEFFER (*just outside Tore take
the A835 and then the A834 via
Dingwall*). This delightful spa town in
the fertile Strath Peffer is no longer as
busy as it was in Victorian times.
However, visitors can still sample its
mineral water.

DUNROBIN CASTLE
◆ A E5 (*Golspie*)
This impressive
castle, the seat of the
Sutherlands since the
13th century, stands
on a natural terrace
overlooking the sea.
The foundations
(1275) and keep
(14th century) were
incorporated into
subsequent additions
to the castle. The
present building, in
Scots Baronial style,
was designed in the
early 19th century by
Sir Charles Barry,
architect of the
Houses of
Parliament. The
interior was restored
in the 1920s by
Robert Lorimer after
a fire. It houses a fine
collection of
paintings, including
family portraits by
Ramsay and
Reynolds, and two
works by Canaletto.
A small Victorian
museum, containing
hunting trophies,
family souvenirs and
some good examples
of Pictish stones,
stands on the edge of
the beautiful formal
gardens below the
castle.

CROMARTY ★
The architecture of
this peaceful little port
is typical of the old
towns and fishing
villages of the east
coast. Visitors can
take the tiny ferry,
which carries two
cars, linking Cromarty
and Nigg (April–
October, 9am–6pm).

WHERE THE SEA MEETS THE MOUNTAINS ✪
This easily accessible island is the largest in the Inner Hebrides. It is also the most spectacular. The mountains rise sheer, like the Black Cuillins, or are eroded, like the Red Cuillins. The coastline is indented by deep lochs, the interior covered with peat bogs and moorland grazed by sheep. It is a stronghold of Gaelic culture and traditions, pervaded by legends and the romantic memory of Bonnie Prince Charlie and Flora Macdonald. Although it is possible to complete a tour of Skye in a few hours, it is well worth devoting at least two days to visiting this beautiful island.

The Isle of Skye lies 1¼ miles off the northwest coast of Scotland. With an area of 60 square miles, it is the largest island in the Inner Hebrides. Its name is derived either from the Norse *ski* ('misty island') or *sgaith* ('winged island'), a reference to its shape. Its impressive landscapes – the result of intense volcanic activity during the Tertiary Period and glacial erosion during the Ice Age – attract geologists, climbers and walkers, making Skye one of Scotland's major tourist destinations. The island's economy is based on sheep and cattle, fishing and fish farming. Like the other islands of the Inner Hebrides, Skye was annexed by Norway in the 8th century and returned to Scotland in 1266. It was the theater of bloody disputes between the principal local clans – the Macdonalds, Mackinnons and MacLeods – until the 17th century and became part of the Jacobite legend when a local young woman, Flora Macdonald ▲ *250*, helped Bonnie Prince Charlie to escape after the Battle of Culloden in 1746 ● *43* ▲ *231*. Between 1882 and 1885 Lord Macdonald tried to evict the crofters who could not pay their rent. The crofters revolted, holding out against the troops called in by the sheriff and gaining widespread public sympathy. This revolt led to the Crofters' Holdings Act (1886) which gave Scottish crofters security of tenure.

SOUTHERN SKYE ◆ A B6-C6-C B1-C1

KYLEAKIN. Above this little port, linked to the Kyle of Lochalsh by a toll bridge ▲ *239*, stands the ruined keep of Castle Moil, built by the Mackinnons in the 12th–15th century. Kyleakin is named after the Norse king Hakon IV who rallied his fleet in the narrow channel between the island and mainland before the Battle of Largs ▲ *34*, in 1263.

ARMADALE (*via the A87 and the A851*). In summer car ferries operate between Mallaig ▲ *237* and this tiny port on the Sleat peninsula, the sunniest, most fertile and most densely wooded peninsula on the island. The neo-Gothic ARMADALE CASTLE (1815) stands in pleasant gardens and houses the CLAN DONALD CENTRE and a Museum of the Isles, which traces the history of the powerful Macdonald clan, Lords of the Isles during the Middle Ages ● *33, 34*. On the west coast of the peninsula, to the north of Tarskavaig, are the ruins of DUNSGAITH CASTLE, the stronghold of the Macdonalds of Sleat until the 16th century.

BROADFORD (*on the A87*). This resort nestles at the head of Broadford Bay. Its main attractions are the VIVARIUM and SKYE ENVIRONMENTAL CENTRE, which organizes walks and provides information on its natural heritage.

ELGOL (*at the end of the B8083*). In fine weather this little port on the Strathaird peninsula enjoys a spectacular view of the Cuillins. Visitors can see the cave where Bonnie Prince Charlie was invited to a farewell banquet by the Mackinnons before leaving for Mallaig. In summer you can hire a motor boat to cross Loch Scavaig and then continue on foot to Loch Coruisk, a favorite haunt of Walter Scott and Turner ● *88*.

LUIB (*on the A87*). A cottage in the village of Luib, halfway between Broadford and Sligachan, has been converted into a CROFT MUSEUM.

OTTER
Although they tend to prefer fresh water otters ● *29* are also seen along the coasts of Scotland. Visitors can see otters on the Isle of Skye and find out more about them at the SKYE ENVIRONMENTAL CENTRE in Broadford.

The Cuillins (*below*); the Old Man of
Storr in the Trotternish mountains
(*center*); Highland cattle by
the roadside, Skye (*bottom*).

Dunvegan Castle (*top*); Staffin post office (*above, left*); crofts on Skye (*above, right*).

FLORA MACDONALD (1723–1790)
This romantic heroine, distantly related to the House of Hanover, was twenty-three when she met Charles Edward Stuart on the island of Uist ▲ *254*. She helped him reach Skye disguised as a serving maid and persuaded the local clan chiefs to give him sanctuary. Before leaving the island, the Young Pretender gave her a miniature portrait of himself. Flora Macdonald was arrested and imprisoned shortly after his departure. She was pardoned in 1747 and returned to Skye where she married Captain Allan Macdonald and bore him seven children. Her funeral shroud is said to have been one of the sheets in which Bonnie Prince Charlie had slept while on the island.

THE WEST COAST ◆ A B6

THE CUILLIN MOUNTAINS. These spectacular mountains, carved out of the former magma chamber of a volcano, reach their highest point at Sgurr Alasdair (3310 feet). The BLACK CUILLINS are formed from gabbro, an extremely hard igneous rock, and their main summit describes a semicircle of sharp peaks around the glacial depression of Loch Coruisk. The other side of Glen Sligachan is dominated by the rounded crests of the RED CUILLINS, whose red sandstone has been more uniformly eroded by wind and water. Most of the excursions in the Cuillin Mountains are for experienced climbers only.
TALISKER DISTILLERY (*on the B8009, near Carbost*). The only distillery on Skye (open to the public) produces a malt whisky with a distinctive peaty flavor.
ARCHEOLOGICAL SITES. Near Struan, on the A850, stands the dry-stone Iron Age fort (2nd century BC–1st century AD) of DUN BEAG BROCH. A long walk from Glen Brittle leads to RUDH AN DUNAIN, the site of a Bronze Age broch and Neolithic tumulus ● *66*.

PORTREE AND THE TROTTERNISH PENINSULA ◆ A B5-B6

PORTREE. The island's 'capital' is situated at the head of Portree Bay with its picturesque harbor, craft shops and modern art gallery, the AN TUIREANN ARTS CENTRE. Visitors can find out more about the island's history in the AROS CENTRE and, in August, attend a traditional Highland Gathering ● *54*, the SKYE HIGHLAND GAMES, held on the Meall, a promontory above the harbor.
TROTTERNISH MOUNTAINS. The peninsula to the north of Portree is famous for its spectacular rock formations. As you head northward the STORR, an impressive escarpment (2360 feet) formed from volcanic basalt above sedimentary rocks, stretches for 10 miles to the left of the A855. Over the centuries the sedimentary rocks have subsided under the weight of the igneous rock, forming isolated pinnacles such as the OLD MANN OF STORR (165 feet), and

> 'In the house [Dunvegan] is kept an ox's horn, hollowed so as to hold perhaps two quarts, which the heir of Macleod was expected to swallow at one draught, as a test of his manhood, before he was permitted to bear arms...'
>
> Samuel Johnson

spectacular labyrinths of rocky outcrops and needles such as the QUIRAING which dominates Staffin Bay. On the side of KILT ROCK, near Elishader, the alternate layers of sedimentary rock and almost horizontal sheets of igneous rock (sills) are reminiscent of the geometric patterns of tartan.

DUNTULM CASTLE. On the northwest coast of the peninsula stand the ruins of the 15th-century castle built by the Macdonalds to guard the maritime route to the Outer Hebrides.

KILMUIR. In the local churchyard a tall Celtic cross marks the tomb of Flora Macdonald. On the edge of the village the traditional cottages (blackhouses) of the SKYE MUSEUM OF ISLAND LIFE evoke the rural life of yesteryear.

UIG. This picturesque village is the port for the Outer Hebrides ▲ 252.

NORTHWEST SKYE ◆ A A6-B6

DUNVEGAN *(via the A850)*. This west-coast resort is dominated by Dunvegan Castle, the seat of the MacLeods since the 12th century. The keep dates from the 15th century, while the 17th-century façade of the main building was rendered in the 19th century. The castle houses collections of paintings by famous artists and family souvenirs, including the Fairy Flag, a fragment of a silk flag probably woven in Rhodes in the 7th century and brought back from the Crusades by a MacLeod. According to legend a fairy, who fell in love with the 4th MacLeod chief, gave him the flag as a farewell gift, promising it would protect him and his clan.

DUIRINISH PENINSULA *(via the B884)*. The peninsula is dominated by MacLeod's Tables, two flat-topped mountains on which a clan chief is said to have invited a Scottish king to a nocturnal banquet. The peninsula's main attractions are the Croft Museum at COLBOST, and the old watermill at GLENDALE. A memorial on the slopes of the glen commemorates the crofters' revolt which began in Glendale in 1882, and which led to the signing of the Crofters' Holdings Act (1886). In fine weather, visitors can continue to NEIST POINT and climb to the top of the lighthouse.

RAASAY ◆ A B6

This island to the east of Skye can be reached by ferry from Sconser. The wooded estate of Raasay House, on the southwest coast of the island, offers some pleasant walks, and there is a breathtaking view of the Outer Hebrides and Skye from the top of Dun Caan, the extinct volcano that dominates the island (1456 feet).

GAELIC ● 46
Most of the inhabitants of Skye speak Gaelic and its use is officially encouraged, as shown by the bilingual road signs and street names. Gaelic is taught in the primary schools, and the island has its own Gaelic college, Sabhal Mor Ostaig.

Ship's chandler in Portree.

NORTH SKYE FISHERMEN Ltd.

Tel. 0478 612245

WETWEATHER GEAR — CHANDLERY — LEISURE & WORK WEAR

251

▲ THE OUTER HEBRIDES (WESTERN ISLES)

GREAT BERNERA
◆ **A** A4
(Bearnaraigh Mor)
Great Bernera, the
largest island in Loch
Roag, is linked to the
west coast of the Isle
of Lewis by a small
bridge. Near the
hamlet of Bosta
(Bostadh) is a Viking
mill and a recently
excavated, late Iron
Age village.

**CALLANISH STANDING
STONES** ◆ **A** B4
This prehistoric site
consists of 50
standing stones
erected in stages
between 3000 and
1500 BC. Thirteen of
the stones form a
circle around a huge
monolith and a small
cairn which was
probably a later
addition. Two rows
of standing stones
form a cross within
the circle, radiating
out toward the four
points of the
compass.

**MYSTERIOUS
STANDING STONES** ✪
Together with
Stonehenge, Callanish
is one of the principal
prehistoric sites in
Great Britain. The
austere beauty of the
landscape and the
mystery surrounding
the alignment – which,
along with three
smaller circles and
various nearby
monuments, once
formed a vast complex
– make this a truly
magical site.

The Outer Hebrides lie in the Atlantic off the west coast of Scotland. They stretch for a distance of 125 miles and are separated from the Scottish mainland and the Isle of Skye by the broad strait known as the Minch. Annexed by the kingdom of Norway in the 8th century, they were restored to Scotland after the Battle of Largs ● *34* ▲ *149*, in 1263. The relative isolation of these islands has enabled them to maintain their Gaelic culture and traditions. Their economy is based on fishing, sheep farming, traditional crafts and, more recently, tourism. Gaelic is the official language and enjoys equal status with English. Sundays are strictly observed on the islands: public transport is not guaranteed and most shops, bars and restaurants are closed. These unspoiled islands will fascinate those with an interest in prehistory, as well as walkers, climbers and nature lovers in search of solitude.

ISLE OF LEWIS (LEODHAIS) AND HARRIS (HEARADH)
◆ **A** A5-B3

This barren island, scattered with lochs and bordered by beautiful beaches, is the largest and most northerly of the Outer Hebrides. It is divided in two, both by the mountainous isthmus of Tarbert whose highest point, An Clisham (2620 feet) is also the highest point on the Outer Hebrides, and by an ancient schism in the MacLeod clan. It is also an island of contrasting landscapes, with the moorlands and peat bogs of Lewis to the north, and the more pronounced, rocky terrain of Harris to the south.

STORNOWAY (STEORNABHAGH). This once active fishing port was founded in the late 16th century on the east coast of Lewis. Today it is the largest town in the Outer Hebrides (population 8000) and is linked by air to Glasgow, Inverness, Benbecula and Barra, and by ferry to Ullapool ▲ *243*. The wooded park at the foot of the neo-Gothic LEWS CASTLE, built by Sir James Matheson in 1856–63, offers beautiful views of the port and, in July, hosts the Hebridean Celtic Festival. The NAN EILEAN MUSEUM, in Francis Street, traces the history of the Outer Hebrides from prehistoric times. It sometimes exhibits pieces from the collection of Viking walrus-ivory

chessmen found in 1831 by a farmer from Ardroil. The town hall houses an art gallery: the AN LANNTAIR ARTS CENTRE.

EYE PENINSULA (AN RUBHA). This peninsula, bordered by high cliffs and a number of lovely beaches, lies to the east of Stornoway and offers some magnificent views of the Minch. At Aignish (Aiginis), on the A866, stand the ruins of the 13th-century CHURCH OF ST COLUMBA, the first church built on Lewis by the MacLeods and whose churchyard contains some beautiful carved crosses.

CLACH AN TRUISEIL. This 18-foot standing stone, near the village of Balantrushal (Baile an Truiseil) on the northwest coast of the island, is reached via the A857.

ARNOL BLACKHOUSE MUSEUM *(on the outskirts of Arnol, on the west coast and the A858).* This cottage-museum was built in the 1870s and occupied until 1964. Its living room, hearth with no smoke outlet, box beds and outbuildings are typical of the island's traditional dwellings.

SHAWBOST (SIABOST). The village has a museum of local history, and a restored Norse watermill and drying kiln.

DUN CARLOWAY BROCH. The broch ● *67* was built just before the first century AD on a hill near Carloway (Carlabhagh), which offers a spectacular view of East Loch Roag and Harris.

GARENIN (GEARRANNAN). The village has been classified as a site of historic interest and its dry-stone cottages attractively restored. At the end of the A858 turn right onto the A859.

TARBERT (AN TAIRBEART). The principal port of Harris, where ferries leave for Lochmaddy (North Uist) and Uig (Skye), stands at the head of a fjord, on the narrow isthmus between North and South Harris.

LEVERBURGH (AN T-OB). Ferries leave the port for North Uist. The AN CLACHAN CENTRE has a small exhibition on the islands of St Kilda ▲ *255*.

RODEL (ROGHADAL). It is well worth a visit to St Clement's Church, built c. 1500 and restored in 1787 and 1873. It houses the tombstones of a number of Macleods from Harris and Dunvegan, including the beautiful recumbent statue commissioned by Alasdair Crotach, chief of the Macleods of Dunvegan (d. 1546), nineteen years before his death.

SCALPAY (SCALPAIGH). This boat-shaped island has an active fishing community and is linked to the east coast of Harris by a bridge.

HARRIS TWEED
This strong, warm, waterproof cloth, with its beautiful natural colors, established its reputation in the 1840s, when the Countess of Dunmore, who owned part of Harris, persuaded the British aristocracy that it was ideal for hunting and outdoor clothes. In fact Harris Tweed became so popular that it soon had to be protected against forgeries. From 1909 an Orb surmounted by a Maltese Cross identified the tweed. It is made entirely on the island's farms: from shearing the sheep, washing and scouring the wool and dyeing it with natural dyes, to carding, spinning, weaving and milling. Since then production has become industrialized. After suffering a sharp decline in the 1980s it has become popular again, particularly with the introduction of wide hand-operated looms. The weavers, usually crofters, work at home for manufacturers who provide them with the skeins of wool and produce the finished rolls of cloth. Some workshops, for example Luskentyre (South Harris), are open to the public.

BENBECULA ◆ A A6
This flat, marshy
island is linked to
Stornoway, Barra and
Glasgow by air.
Balivanich (Baile a
Mhanaich), on the
northwest coast, is the
administrative and
commercial center of
the Isles of Uist.
Liniclate (Lionacleit)
secondary school
houses a small
MUSEUM. The ruins of
Nunton Church (mid-
14th century) can be
see at Aird, and a
ruined fortress of the
Ranald clan at Borve.

**ERISKAY ◆ A A6-C A1
(EIRIOSGAIGH)**
This undulating little
island, linked by ferry
to Ludag (South
Uist), is renowned for
its patterned knitwear
and ponies. In 1941 a
cargo ship bound for
Jamaica sank off the
coast with 264,000
bottles of whisky on
board. The event gave
(Sir Edward
Montague) Compton
Mackenzie
(1883–1972) the
idea for his novel
Whisky Galore which
was made into a film
(shot on the island)
in 1948.

NORTH UIST (UIBHIST A TUATH) ◆ A A5

The Isles of Uist (North Uist, Benbecula and South Uist) are
linked by causeways (*above*). The lochs and inlets of North
Uist are a fly-fisherman's paradise, although their tendency to
overflow can make the roads impassable.
NEWTON FERRY (PORT NAN LONG). The island's most
northerly point is a port of call for ferries from Berneray and
Harris. Nearby DUN AN STICAR is a fortified Iron Age site that
was occupied until the early 17th century.
LOCHMADDY (LOCH NA MADADH). The tiny 'capital' of North
Uist is linked by ferry to Tarbert (Harris) and Uig (Skye). A
small museum and gallery, TAIGH CHEARSABHAGH, occupies
an 18th-century merchant's house. The bays and lochs here
are a paradise for otters, seals and seabirds. Take the A865.
SCOLPAIG TOWER. This folly, built in the 1830s on the site of a
broch, stands on an island in Loch Scolpaig, in the northwest
of the island.
BALRANALD NATURE RESERVE. The stretches of water in this
west-coast reserve attract almost 200 species of birds, including
the endangered corncrake (guided visits May–August).
NEOLITHIC SITES. The impressive cairn of BARPA LANGASS, a
tumulus (burial mound) on the slopes of Ben Langass, can be
seen from the A867, about 7 miles southwest of Lochmaddy.
A little further on an unclassified road turns off the A867 to
POBULL FHINN, a small circle of standing stones about 1 mile
to the southwest. Also worth a visit are the three standing
stones of NA FIR BHREIGE, 3 miles northwest of Lochmaddy.
CARINISH (CARANAIS). Ruins are all that remain of TRINITY
TEMPLE (Teampull na Trionaid), a religious foundation built
in the 13th century by the daughter of Somerled, Lord of the
Isles ● 33. The temple was a major center of learning during
the Middle Ages.

SOUTH UIST (UIBHIST A DEAS) ◆ A A6

Like North Uist this is an island of contrasting landscapes.
The east coast is mountainous and indented by deep fjords,
while the west coast – the most densely populated – has
beautiful white sandy beaches bordered by dunes and
meadows filled with flowers in summer.
OUR LADY OF THE ISLES. This remarkable statue of the
Madonna and Child (*above, left*) by Sir Hew Lorimer was
erected in 1957 by the island's Catholic population. It stands
on the slopes of Ben Rueval, to the south of Loch Bee.
LOCH DRUIDIBEG NATIONAL NATURE RESERVE. This reserve
provides sanctuary for the birds which nest on the islands of
Loch Druidibeg.

HOWMORE (TABHA MOR). This west-coast village with its attractive cottages is the burial place of the Macdonalds of Ranald. It also has two ruined medieval chapels.

MILTON (GEARRAIDH BHAILTEAS). The memorial cairn near the ruins of the house where Flora Macdonald ▲ *250* was born can be seen from the A865.

LOCHBOISDALE (LOCH BAGHASDAIL). The island's principal village is also the departure point for ferries to Mallaig ▲ *237*, Oban ▲ *194* and Castlebay (Barra).

BARRA (BARRAIGH) AND ITS ISLETS ◆ C A1

This tiny island is renowned for the beauty and diversity of its landscape. It also has 1000 different species of wildflowers. Planes from Glasgow, Benbecula and Lewis land on the Cockle Strand airfield, the sandy bay of Traigh Mhor, tide and weather permitting!

CASTLEBAY (BAGH A CHAISTEIL). The island's only village is also an active fishing port, although today, lobsters have replaced the herring catches of the past. The bay is dominated by KISIMUL CASTLE (12th and 15th century), the ancestral seat of the MacNeil clan who owned Barra between 1427 and 1838. The BARRA HERITAGE CENTRE traces its history.

OTHER PLACES TO VISIT. The cottage museum in CRAIGSTON, near Borve, on the west coast, and CILLE-BHARRA, the burial place of the MacNeil clan, near the village of Eoligarry (Eolaigearraidh), in the north of the island.

VATERSAY (BHATARSAIGH). This tiny island is linked to Barra by a causeway. A monument recalls the shipwreck in which 450 Highland emigrants bound for Quebec lost their lives when the *Annie Jane* sank in West Bay in 1826.

SANDRAY, MINGULAY, PABBAY AND BERNERAY. In summer boats link Castlebay to the most southerly islands in the Outer Hebrides. Large colonies of seabirds nest on their cliffs.

MONACH ISLES
This group of tiny islands to the west of North Uist and Benbecula are believed to have been colonized by nuns and then monks, who erected a beacon (later replaced by a lighthouse) on Shillay. Today these uninhabited islands are a sanctuary for Europe's largest colony of gray seals.

ST KILDA
This little group of islands, 25 miles west of Benbecula, is owned by the National Trust and is also a UNESCO World Heritage Site. Its spectacular cliffs are colonized by thousands of seabirds. For centuries these birds constituted the islanders' main source of food and fuel before they emigrated en masse in 1930. The abandoned cottages of Village Bay can still be seen on Hirta, the main island. (Details of guided tours from Stornoway and all tourist offices.) Boreray (*left*), one of the islands in the St Kilda archipelago.

GEORGE MACKAY
BROWN (1921–96)
The writer and poet
George Mackay
Brown was born in
Stromness. A fervent
Catholic and
champion of the
islands' history and
traditions, he evokes
the Nordic heritage of
Orkney in his novels
and poems.

A RICH
ARCHEOLOGICAL
HERITAGE ✪
The first inhabitants
of Orkney left behind
many remarkable
remains. The
Neolithic village of
Skara Brae, the best
preserved in western
Europe, the
magnificent tomb of
Maes Howe and the
remains of Pictish and
Viking settlements on
the island of Brough
of Birsay are an
absolute must for
the visitor.

THE ORKNEYINGA
SAGA
The *Orkneyinga Saga*,
written in the 12th
century in Iceland,
tells of the deeds of
Rognvald III, his
crusade to the Holy
Land, his return to
Orkney and the
foundation of the
cathedral dedicated
to his uncle,
St Magnus.

The Orkney Islands lie 12 miles off the north coast of
Scotland across the Pentland Firth, a dangerous stretch of
water scattered with reefs and swept by storms. The 67 islands
and islets in the group were worn flat by glaciers. Although
the most northerly of the islands are situated on the same
latitude as St Petersburg, the influence of the Gulf Stream
means they have a particularly mild climate throughout the
year. Today only about twenty of the islands are inhabited.
Orkney has some remarkable prehistoric remains dating from
the 4th millennium BC, including underground dwellings
(earth houses), tombs and stone circles. They were known to
the Greeks and Romans (the Greek navigator Pytheas is said
to have sailed round the islands in 325 BC) and were colonized
by the Picts in the first century AD. After two centuries of
Viking raids, the islands were annexed by the Norse king
Harald I Hárfagri in 875, and governed by the earls (jarls)
immortalized in the *Orkneyinga Saga*. The Scottish influence
began to make itself felt from the 13th century. In 1469
Christian I, king of Denmark, Norway and Sweden,
mortgaged the Orkney and Shetland islands to Scotland
against payment of his daughter Margaret's dowry on her
marriage to James III. The dowry had not been paid by 1472
and the islands were annexed by Scotland and governed by
stewards (some of whom behaved like tyrants) until they were
incorporated into the kingdom of Scotland in 1615. The
Scandinavian influence is still very much in evidence in the
islands' architecture, traditions and place names (90 percent
Norse). The economy of Orkney is based on agriculture and
livestock. Although North Sea oil refineries have been a
substantial source of income in recent years, the future of the
oil fields is uncertain. Tourism and traditional crafts are
developing but it is debatable whether this will be enough to
sustain the islands' 19,000 inhabitants, three-quarters of
whom live on the large central island, Mainland.

KIRKWALL, CAPITAL OF ORKNEY ◆ A F2

The principal town on Mainland stands at the head of
Kirkwall Bay, on the site of a former Viking trading post,
founded c. 1035 by Rognvald III. Its name is derived from the
Norse *Kirkjugavar* ('Church Place'), a reference to the church
dedicated to St Olaf, the patron saint of Norway. The port
expanded when the cathedral was built in the 12th century,
and became a royal burgh of Scotland in the 16th century.
The old town, where most of the houses date from the
16th–18th century, still lies within the area occupied by the
original Viking settlement.
ST MAGNUS CATHEDRAL. In 1137 Rognvald III decided to
build a cathedral in honor of his uncle, Magnus, who was
canonized shortly after being assassinated by his cousin and
rival Hakon, in 1116. The construction of the cathedral lasted
until the mid-13th century. The building acquired its present
form when the west extension of the nave was added in the
1550s. The height of the church, built in red and yellow
sandstone in a harmonious blend of Norman and Gothic
styles, makes up for its modest dimensions. The interior is
impressive with its imposing pillars supporting semicircular
arches, the restraint of its bays and interlacing wall-arcades,
and its beautiful ribbed vault. The cathedral houses the

St Magnus Cathedral (*left and below*).

remains of St Magnus and St Rognvald, a number of inscribed tombstones dating from the 16th and 17th centuries, and a memorial to John Rae, the Arctic explorer born in Stromness.

THE BISHOP'S PALACE. The Bishop's palace was built near the cathedral c. 1150 by Bishop William the Old and refurbished in the 16th and 17th centuries. All that remains today are the walls of the great reception hall and the angle tower, Moosie Too'r. Hakon IV of Norway, fatally wounded at the Battle of Largs ● *34*, died here in 1263.

THE EARL'S PALACE. The palace was built (1600–07) opposite the Bishop's Palace by Earl Patrick Stewart, an infamous tyrant who was executed in Edinburgh in 1615. Although badly damaged the building is still a fine example of Renaissance architecture, with its monumental staircase, corbeled windows and finely carved fireplaces.

TANKERNESS HOUSE. This beautiful 16th-century mansion houses a museum of Orkney life and a collection of objects brought back by John Rae from his Arctic expeditions.

ORKNEY WIRELESS MUSEUM. The museum is devoted to the wireless transmission systems used by the British Army from the 1930s onwards: radio, radar, air defense.

SERENITY AND GRANDEUR ★
Its remarkable proportions, the harmonious blend of styles, the sobriety of its decoration and the warm colors of the stone give St Magnus Cathedral an air of serenity and grandeur.

The Italian chapel on the island of Lamb Holm.

HMS 'ROYAL OAK'
On October 13, 1939 a German submarine broke through the defenses of Scapa Flow, where part of the Royal Naval fleet was anchored, and torpedoed HMS *Royal Oak*. The aircraft carrier and its 833-man crew lie at a depth of 90 feet, at the foot of the Gaitnip cliffs in Scapa Bay. The area has been declared a war cemetery and is out of bounds for divers.

FLOTTA ◆ A F3
Opposite St Margaret's Hope lies the small island of Flotta, a strategic military base during the two world wars. Today its oil terminal processes the crude oil piped from the Piper and Claymore oil fields in the North Sea (around 10 percent of British oil production).

EAST MAINLAND ◆ A F2

SCAPA FLOW. The A961, linking Kirkwall to the island of South Ronaldsay, follows the eastern shore of Scapa Flow, a strategic Royal Naval base during the two world wars. In June 1919 seventy-four German ships, laid up in the roadstead since the armistice of 1918, were scuttled in the bay. Sixty-three of these vessels were refloated but the wrecks that still lie on the bottom have made Scapa Flow a popular center for divers.

THE CHURCHILL BARRIERS. After the sinking of the *Royal Oak* in 1939 the Prime Minister Winston Churchill ordered four concrete dikes to be built between the islands of Mainland, Lamb Holm, Glimps Holm, Burray and South Ronaldsay. However the dikes, designed to strengthen the defenses of Scapa Flow, were not finished until the spring of 1945. These causeways still link the islands today, making communications much easier and giving motorists the impression of driving across the water. The experience is even eerier at night when the ebb tide reveals the ghostly shapes of the rusting wrecks.

ITALIAN CHAPEL *(Lamb Holm).* The Italian prisoners of war involved in the construction of the Churchill Barrier built an Italian chapel on the island using two Nissen huts and any other materials they could lay their hands on. The interior decor, by Domenico Chiochetti, even has frescos, trompe-l'oeil and false marble effects.

SOUTH RONALDSAY ◆ A F3

ST MARGARET'S HOPE. This village has some delightful 17th- and 18th-century cottages, while the OLD SMIDDY MUSEUM, which occupies the old forge, pays homage to the blacksmiths and farriers of the past.

TOMB OF THE EAGLES *(Isbister, 1 mile east of Burwick, via the B9041).* The tomb is named after the sea eagles' claws found alongside the bones of 342 people buried here in the 3rd millennium BC. The small private museum of Liddle Farm presents objects found on the site by the farmer.

WIND WICK BAY. The bay is the haunt of puffins and seals which can be seen from the top of the cliffs of Halcro Head.

ORKNEY ▲

CENTRAL MAINLAND ◆ A F2

The most outstanding of the remarkable archeological sites
in central Mainland are the tomb of Maes Howe, and the
Standing Stones of Stenness and Ring of Brodgar, 'temples'
to the Moon and Sun where the islanders still worshipped the
Norse god Odin (Woden) in the 18th century. About 2 miles
west of Kirkwall, the A965 passes the remains of the GRAIN
EARTH HOUSE, an underground chamber which was probably
used as a storehouse and place of refuge for Stone Age
farmers ● 67. Some 4 miles further on, another well-
preserved structure of the same type (reached via a trapdoor
and ladder) is situated in a farmyard at Rennibster, to the
right of the road. WIDEFORD HILL CAIRN, a burial mound to
the south of the A965 (4 miles from Kirkwall), was found to
contain animal bones, while CURWEEN HILL, to the south of
Finstown, contained human remains in addition to the
remains of a number of dogs.

MAES HOWE ● *66 (3 miles southwest of Finstown on the A965).*
This magnificent tomb built almost 5000 years ago is covered
by a mound – 24 feet high and with a diameter of 115 feet –
surrounded by a ditch. A narrow passageway leads to a burial
chamber (194 square feet) which is aligned with the rising sun
of the winter solstice. The chamber, built with huge, perfectly
cut and positioned blocks of sandstone, opens onto three
burial cells. The tomb was plundered by Norsemen in the
12th century, as shown by the runic inscriptions and images
(including the famous Maes Howe lion) carved on the walls.

STANDING STONES OF STENNESS *(½ mile from Maes Howe).*
Only three of the twelve large standing stones that formed the
original circle remain. Two smaller stones have recently been
reerected and four stones (possibly a hearth) excavated at the
center of the circle.

RING OF BRODGAR. The third point of the 'archeological
triangle' is formed by the stone circle (*below*) that stands on
the narrow strip of land between Lochs Stenness and Harray.
Only 27 of the original 60 megaliths are still standing. Like
Stenness, Brodgar is surrounded by a broad ditch, but the
earth bank that once formed the circle's outer limit has
disappeared.

UNSTAN CAIRN ◆ A F2
Some remarkable
pieces of pottery
dating from the 4th
millennium BC have
been found in this
Neolithic cairn on the
shores of Loch
Stenness.

**DEERNESS
PENINSULA ◆ A F2**
The impressive
marine caves on the
eastern shore of the
Deerness peninsula
should be approached
with caution. The
Mull Head nature
reserve provides
sanctuary for puffins,
guillemots, razorbills,
seals and otters.

The burial chamber
of Maes Howe.

259

Stone walls form the boundaries to pastures (*right*); Marwick Head (*center right*); farm on the island of Westray (*far right*).

WEST MAINLAND ◆ A F2

STROMNESS. The largest port on the island is also the ferry port for Shetland and Scotland, which the islanders refer to as 'The Sooth' (South). Before becoming a whaling and herring port in the 19th century, Stromness flourished in the 17th century as the last supply port for the ships of the Hudson Bay Company en route to Canada, and as a port of call for English ships trading with Scandinavia and Russia. THE STROMNESS MUSEUM, at the end of Main Street, presents the natural and maritime history of Orkney, while the quayside PIER ARTS CENTRE illustrates the artistic life of the islands, mainly through modern paintings and sculpture.

The port of Stromness (*top*); prehistoric earth house at Skara Brae (*above*).

HOY, THE 'HIGH ISLAND' ◆ A F2-F3 Ward Hill (1570 feet), the highest point on this island, is also the highest point on Orkney. At the foot of the cliffs on the northwest coast stands the Old Man of Hoy, a 450-foot red sandstone stack (*right*). In the north is DWARFIE STANE, a Neolithic rock tomb, where a passageway and two long cells have been carved out of a colossal, red sandstone monolith. To explain the role of Scapa Flow during the two world wars, LYNESS NAVAL BASE, on the southeast coast, has been converted into a museum.

BROCH OF GURNESS ◆ A F2 (*1 mile from Evie, on the northeast coast of Mainland*) The site, founded by Celtic peoples and occupied by the Vikings, has the best preserved broch in Orkney (c. 200 BC).

SKARA BRAE ● *66 (on the B9056).* In 1850 eyewitness accounts spoke of 'flying sheep' when a hurricane devastated west Mainland. When the storm died down the islanders discovered that the gale-force winds had uncovered the remains of a group of prehistoric dwellings at Skara Brae on the Bay of Skaill. The houses were linked by narrow passages, originally covered, and were all – except one, possibly a workshop – designed according to the same layout, with a central hearth, larder and stone seats and beds. They were built on a layer of clay and buried up to the roof in a compost of clay and household waste, which would

have provided good insulation. The site, occupied between 3100 and 2500 BC, gave a new insight into Stone Age life on the island. Near the site is SKAILL HOUSE, a 17th-century manor house which has been tastefully restored and furnished.

MARWICK HEAD. The headland, which is both a bird sanctuary and viewpoint, has a memorial to Horatio Herbert Kitchener (b. 1850), the British Field Marshal and secretary of state for war, and the crew of HMS *Hampshire*, which went down off the coast of Mainland when it hit a mine in June 1916.

BIRSAY. In this small village stand the ruins of the palace built c. 1580 by Earl Patrick Stewart. At low tide you can walk from Birsay to the neighboring island of Brough of Birsay. (Check the times of the tides.)

BROUGH OF BIRSAY. Excavations carried out on the island revealed the remains of a Pictish settlement including houses, a well and a bronze workshop, dating from the 7th–8th centuries. Between the 9th and 12th centuries there was an important Viking settlement on the island. Alongside the foundations of longhouses and a forge dating from the 10th–11th century are the remains of the earl's palace and the first bishop's palace built by Earl Thorfinn (d. 1064) in the 11th century. There are also the remains of a beautiful early 12th-century church which may well have housed the remains of St Magnus, the murdered uncle of Rognvald III. The Brough entered its period of decline when the saint's relics were transferred to Kirkwall and it was no longer a place of pilgrimage.

KIRBUSTER FARM MUSEUM. This interesting farm museum, 2 miles southeast of Birsay, traces the development of farming life on Orkney over the past 200 years. At Twatt take the A986 toward Finstown to visit the CORRIGAL FARM MUSEUM near Harray.

NORTH ISLANDS ◆ A F1-F2

With their bird and seal colonies, the northern islands of Orkney are a nature-lovers' paradise. They also have a rich archeological and architectural heritage. The islands are linked by ferry to Kirkwall.

ROUSAY. This round island has a number of prehistoric remains, including the two-story burial cairn of Taversoe Tuick and the cairns of Blackhammer and Knowe of Yarso. However the most impressive of these sites is the chambered cairn of MIDHOWE (98 feet long) hollowed out in 3500 BC. Nearby are the remains of an Iron Age broch.

WESTRAY. Apart from the ruins of two medieval churches and Noltland Castle (1560), the island is also renowned for NOUP HEAD bird sanctuary.

PAPA WESTRAY. This small, wild island – the birthplace of Christianity in Orkney – was inhabited by hermits in the early Middle Ages and was a place of pilgrimage until the 18th century. It also has two of the oldest stone houses that can still be seen in western Europe (c. 2500 BC) at KNAP OF HOWAR.

HOLM OF PAPA. The island is the site of DISS O' THE HOLM, a huge burial cairn consisting of a 65-foot central chamber, subdivided into three smaller chambers, and twelve lateral cells.

BIRD-WATCHING SITES IN ORKNEY ✪
Of the 320 species of birds recorded in Orkney, 100 nest on the islands. Noup Head, on the island of Westray, has the second largest colony of seabirds in Great Britain. They include guillemots, kittiwakes, razorbills, puffins, shags and fulmars. The cliffs of Marwick Head (Mainland) are the preserve of some 35,000 guillemots and 10,000 kittiwakes. Hen-harriers, merlins, kestrels, great skuas and Arctic skuas nest on the Birsay Moors and Cottasgarth reserve, near Finstown in the northeast of Mainland.

OTHER PLACES OF INTEREST...
For those interested in archeology: the Neolithic cairns of Vinquoy Hill on Eday, and Quoyness on Sanday. There are a number of 12th-century ruins: the Church of St Magnus, built on or near the site of the saint's assassination, on Ehilsay; Cubbie Roo's Castle, the stronghold of the Viking pirate Kolbein Hruga, on Wyre; and the Bendictine church on Eynhallow, a sacred island during the Middle Ages. Finally Balfour Castle (1847), in Scots Baronial style, stands on the island of SHAPINSAY, the most fertile of Orkney.

The Shetland Islands stretch for a distance of 68 miles, rather like giant stepping stones in the sea between Great Britain and Scandinavia. These one hundred or so islands and islets are bounded by the Atlantic to the west and the North Sea to the east. Their coastline is deeply indented by fjords (*voes*) formed by glacial erosion, which means that no point on the islands is very far from the sea. Today less than twenty of the islands are inhabited, but their many archeological sites attest to the fact that they were occupied as much as 5500 years ago. Like Orkney ▲ *256*, Shetland was colonized by the Vikings in the 7th century and annexed by the kingdom of Norway in the 9th century. Although they became part of Scotland in 1472, they did not break with their Scandinavian culture and traditions. The islands have a wide variety of landscapes: moorland and meadows dotted with wildflowers from spring until late autumn, vertiginous cliffs inhabited by huge colonies of seabirds, long white sandy beaches, and fish-filled fjords which in summer attract seals, dolphins, orcas and whales. Shetland's only towns – Lerwick, the modern capital, and Scalloway, the former capital – are both situated on the principal island of Mainland. The wild beauty and changing light of these islands, and the warm welcome extended by their inhabitants, make them a popular destination for enthusiasts of archeology, bird-watchers and walkers.

THE HISTORIC HEART OF MAINLAND ◆ B B3-C3

LERWICK. The administrative capital (7500 inhabitants) of Shetland lies on the east coast of Mainland. It expanded rapidly in the 17th century when merchants from the Hanseatic League (a commercial association of north-German towns founded in the mid-14th century) traded fishing equipment and fresh produce for herring. It soon replaced Scalloway and, in the 19th century, became a center for European fishing fleets operating in the North Atlantic and a major herring port. In recent years Lerwick has enjoyed an increase in economic activity as a port of call for the supply ships servicing the North Sea oil rigs. At the top of the town the neo-Gothic TOWN HALL (1884), whose stained-glass windows celebrate the islands' cultural links with Scandinavia, stands opposite the SHETLAND MUSEUM, which traces Shetland's natural and maritime history from prehistoric times to the present day. Below the Town Hall stands FORT CHARLOTTE, built in 1665–67 by John Mylne, the master-

mason of Charles II. It was burned in 1673 by the Dutch and finally restored in 1782. Commercial Street, the town's main street, runs the length of the port. It is bordered by beautiful 19th-century merchants' houses and craft shops selling, among other things, the famous Shetland knitwear.

CLICKHIMIN BROCH *(on the A970).* The remains of this round tower (16 feet high, *below*) stand on a vast circular platform that was once an island in Loch Clickhimin, southwest of Lerwick. The farm that occupied the site c. 700 BC was transformed, 600 years later, into a fortified camp which remained inhabited until the 5th or 6th century.

WEST BURRA ◆ B B3
Carved stones dating from the 7th century were found on this island – a center of Christianity in the early Middle Ages – to the southwest of Scalloway. The Monks Stone can be seen in the Shetland Museum in Lerwick and the Papil Stone in the Royal Museum of Scotland ▲ *123* in Edinburgh.

BRESSAY ABD NOSS ◆ B C3
A ferry links Lerwick with the inhabited island of Bressay. To the east of Bressay lies the tiny island of Noss, which is devoted to sheep farming and is also a bird sanctuary: 100,000 pairs of seabirds nest on its sandstone cliffs. An exhibition in a restored farm presents the island's bird life and recalls that, in the late 19th century, it also had a stud for breeding the Shetland ponies used to pull wagons in the coal mines.

SCALLOWAY *(via the B9073 and the A970).* This fishing port dates from the Viking period, when the court of justice and the assembly (*thing*) were held on Law Ting Holm peninsula, at the northern end of the Loch of Tingwall. Those involved set up camp at the mouth of the fertile Tingwall valley, on Huts Bay, from whose Norse name *Skalrvagr* Scalloway is derived. The resulting village remained the capital of Shetland until the early 18th century and enjoyed renewed prosperity due to fishing in the 19th century. In 1600 Earl Patrick Stewart ▲ *257* had a magnificent CASTLE built whose tower-house can still be seen today. The SCALLOWAY MUSEUM, in Main Street, traces the history of the local fishing industry and tells the story of the 'Shetland Bus', an operation mounted jointly with Norwegian fishermen and which, between 1942 and 1945, transported resistance fighters, weapons and explosives from Shetland to occupied Norway and returned with fugitives from the Gestapo.

TINGWALL. This village in the fertile Tingwall valley, to the northeast of Scalloway, has a small airport and a MUSEUM OF AGRICULTURE.

MOUSA ◆ B C4
The tiny island of
Mousa, which lies
off Leebooten
(Leebitton), on the
southeast coast of
Mainland, is famous
for its exceptionally
well-preserved broch
● *67*. The impressive
dry-stone round
tower (over 42 feet
high and with a
diameter of almost
50 feet at the base)
probably dates from
the 1st century AD. Its
hollow walls conceal a
narrow staircase
which services six
galleries and leads to
the rampart walk.
*(Ferry from Leebooten
in summer.)*

**ARCHEOLOGICAL
TREASURES ★**
The broch of Mousa,
the best-preserved in
Scotland, and the site
of Jarlshof – whose
various periods of
occupation span 3000
years of history –
make Shetland a
favorite destination
for enthusiasts of
archeology.

SOUTH MAINLAND ◆ B B4-C3

CATPUND QUARRIES. These vast soapstone (steatite) quarries
lie to the left of the A970 as it crosses the Catpund Burn, on
the outskirts of Cunningsburgh (8 miles south of Lerwick).
The quarries were exploited from the Stone Age to the
Middle Ages, and the utensils and jewelry carved out of the
soft stone by the Vikings were exported to Scandinavia and
the rest of Europe.

SHETLAND CROFT MUSEUM *(hamlet of Voe, south of Boddam).*
With its outbuilding and small water mill, this restored and
furnished farm recreates a realistic image of farm life in
Shetland in the 19th century.

JARLSHOF ● *67*. This is the most famous archeological site in
the Shetlands. It boasts the well-preserved remains of Bronze
Age oval houses (3rd millennium BC), a broch and earth
houses from the late Iron Age (2nd–1st century BC), large
circular houses with a central hearth and radiating chambers
(wheel houses) dating from the 3rd–8th century, the
foundations of Norwegian long houses (9th–14th century),
several walls from a medieval farm and the ruins of a manor
built in the 16th century by Earl Patrick Stewart. The manor
was immortalized in Walter Scott's novel *The Pirate* as
Jarlshof, a name which has now become linked with
the site *(above).*

NESS OF BURGI. At the end of this islet stand the ruins of an
Iron Age fort defended by two rock-cut moats on either side
of the massive ramparts.

OLD SCATNESS. Not far from Sumburgh Airport,
archeologists are excavating an Iron Age broch and village,
subsequently occupied by the Vikings.

SUMBURGH HEAD. The southeast tip of Mainland is an
excellent place for watching whales. Its high cliffs,
surmounted by a lighthouse (1821) designed by Robert
Stevenson, provide sanctuary for large colonies of seabirds.

QUENDALE MILL. The mill, built in the southwest of the island
in 1867, has been restored to perfect working order. Visitors can
follow the various stages involved in processing oats and rye.

LOCH OF SPIGGIE. In autumn this bird sanctuary on the west
coast welcomes large numbers of migratory birds, including
greylag geese and whooper swans.

PAPA STOUR ◆ B B2-B3 *(ferry from West Burrafirth).*
The 'Great Island of the Priests' was colonized during the Stone Age, inhabited by hermits and Christian missionaries in the early Middle Ages, and then by a 'leper' colony (in fact people suffering from skin diseases caused by malnutrition) until the 18th century. Seabirds, seals and otters frequent the island which is today inhabited by twenty or so farmers.

ST NINIAN'S ISLE. En route to Bigton the B9122 passes this delightful island linked by a sandy isthmus to the west coast of Mainland. Excavations carried out in 1958 in the isolated ruins of a medieval church revealed the remains of a chapel dating from the 7th century and a remarkable cache of Pictish silver, probably buried by the monks to save it from Viking pirates. Today these 28 objects are on display in the Museum of Scotland ▲ *123* and replicas can be seen in the Shetland Museum in Lerwick.

WEST MAINLAND ◆ B B3

The peat bogs of west Mainland have preserved a remarkable archaeological heritage: enclosed fields on hillsides dating from 3000 BC and, at their center, tombs and houses, usually primitive oval structures comprising a large main room with a central hearth and several sleeping compartments. There are a number of these sites around BRIDGE OF WALLS (Brig of Wass), in the center of the peninsula: the remains of a farm at SCORD OF BROUSTER, eight well-preserved oval houses and their cairns surrounded by enclosed fields at PINHOULLAND, and the foundations of two oval houses at GRUTING SCHOOL.

CULSWICK *(Sandsting peninsula, at the end of the B9071, via Reawick).* In a magnificent setting, between Loch Soterstad and Gruting Voe, a remarkable broch built of huge blocks of pink and white granite rises to a height of 13 feet.

STANYDALE TEMPLE. The building is almost 4500 years old and was probably used for communal or ceremonial activities. Its dimensions (130 feet by 65 feet) are twice those of the standard oval houses and its walls are up to 13 feet thick in places. Still visible in the center are two holes: the poles supporting the framework were slotted into these holes.

NESS OF GARTH. Near Melby, at the end of the A971, a prehistoric fort defended by ramparts stands on an eroded promontory. From Melby there is a clear view of the coast of Papa Stour.

FOULA ◆ B B1
'Bird Island' to the southwest of Papa Stour has the largest skua colony in Great Britain. The island can remain cut off from the outside world for long periods, so visitors should go well prepared *(ferry from Walls of Scalloway, plane from Tingwall).*

The Fair Isle Jumper, Stanley Cursiter (1887–1976).

Salmon nets on
Out Skerries.

OUT SKERRIES ◆ B C2
*(ferries from Vidlin
and Lerwick)*
These three islands –
Grunay, Bruray and
Housay – live by
fishing and salmon
farming.

SULLOM VOE ◆ B B2
Sullom Voe, the
longest fjord in the
Shetlands, was an
RAF and Norwegian
flying-boat base
during World
War Two. Europe's
main oil terminal
has stood on its
eastern shore,
7 miles northeast of
Brae, since 1978.
The terminal
processes one million
barrels of crude oil
per day.

NORTH MAINLAND ◆ B B2

At Voe (*below*) the A9071 turns off to Laxo (the ferry port for
Whalsay), Vidlin (the car ferry port for Out Skerries), and
LUNNA, the first operations base for the 'Shetland Bus'.
At Hillside the A968 turns right off the A970 to TOFT, a
hamlet linked by ferry to the island of Yell. As the A970
crosses the isthmus of Mavis Grind, at the south end of
Sullom Voe, it passes the well-preserved megalithic tombs
of ISLEBURGH and PUNDS WATER. The landscapes of the
district of Northmavine, to the north of Mavis Grind,
are undoubtedly the most beautiful in the Shetlands.
BUSTA. Beyond Brae a minor road turns left off the A970,
past a massive standing stone, to BUSTA HOUSE, a manor
built in 1714 which enjoys a magnificent view of Busta Voe.
Busta is one of the few sheltered sites in the Shetlands
and rowans, planes and elders flourish in its delightful
terraced gardens.
HILLSWICK. This fishing village is dominated by the
St Magnus Bay Hotel, a wooden building prefabricated in
Norway for the International Exhibition held in Glasgow
in 1896 and erected on its present site in 1901. Hillswick also
has Booth, the oldest inn in Shetland (1684).

ESHANESS PENINSULA. TANGWICK HAA, a beautiful late 17th-century manor, has been restored and converted into an interesting museum. To the north of the former fishing station of STENNESS, the lighthouse (1929) that stands on the northwestern tip of Mainland offers a magnificent view of the stacks known as the Drongs and the west coast of Papa Stour. The ruins of HOULLAND BROCH stand on a peninsula in Loch Eshaness.

GIANT'S GRAVE. Near Housetter (*4 miles south of Isbister, on the A970*), on the shore of the Loch of Housetter, stand two pink granite standing stones and the remains of two megalithic tombs.

RONAS HILL. At the top of this hill (1490 feet), the highest point in Shetland, is a well-preserved Stone Age or Bronze Age burial chamber.

Great skua

YELL ◆ B C1-C2

The largest of Shetland's northern islands is also the least fertile of the inhabited islands. The road linking Ulsta (ferries from Toft) with Gutcher (ferries to Unst and Fetlar) crosses peat bogs and moorland incised by deep fjords. The B9081, which follows the south and east coast of Yell, passes through a softer, less austere landscape.

BURRAVOE. OLD HAA VISITOR CENTRE, a small museum housed in a 17th-century manor, provides an introduction to local history. In the same street St Colman's Church (1900) is a delightful example of Arts and Crafts architecture.

AYWICK. A walk across the moors to the hills above the Bay of Aywick takes you past an Iron Age fort on the islet of Brough of Stoal.

MID YELL. About 1 mile to the west of Mid Yell, near the ruins of a haunted manor, Windhouse (1880), are an unexcavated broch, the remains of a Viking farm and a well-preserved megalithic tomb. The RSPB reserve of LUMBISTER, to the north of Windhouse, provides sanctuary for otters and a number of species of birds, including skuas, merlins, plovers and red-throated divers.

CULLIVOE *(on the B9082).* The northeast tip of Yell is less austere, with meadows dotted with haystacks in summer and greenhouses filled with early vegetables. To the west of Breckon beach, seasoned walkers can follow the path that skirts round Gloup Voe, at the north end of the island, crosses the moorland to the southwest and leads to the spectacular ruins of the BURGI GEOS broch.

FETLAR ◆ B C1

This island linked by car ferry to Gutcher (Yell) is the most fertile in Shetland. It was occupied in prehistoric times, as shown by the many remains including the circle of standing stones at HALTADANS, to the south of Vord Hill, and the Neolithic mound at FINNIGERT that once divided the island in two. In addition to these sites the RSPB NORTH FETLAR RESERVE protects such rare moorland species as the whimbrel and the red-necked phalarope, and is visited by the snowy owl.

HOUBIE. Fetlar's main village has a small interpretation center which presents the island's natural and social history.

WHALSAY ◆ B C2
The island has a long history of fishing and today has a modern and active fleet. The ferry from Laxo lands at Symbister, a broad roadstead used in the 16th century by merchants of the Hanseatic League who came to trade salt, tobacco and clothing for smoked fish. BREMEN BÖD, a 17th-century Hanseatic store, has been transformed into a museum. The island's archeological sites include the Standing Stones of YOXIE – two houses and a megalithic tomb c. 2000 BC on the east coast. There are also the remains of a broch on an island in the LOCH OF HUXTER, at the south end of the island.

BIRD-WATCHING SITES ✪

Shetland lies at the crossroads of the main migratory routes between Scandinavia, Iceland and Great Britain and is one of the principal nesting sites in Europe. The island of Noss has large colonies of black guillemots, common guillemots, puffins and gannets. These seabirds, along with other nesting birds such as the fulmar, also frequent the cliffs of the Hermaness National Nature Reserve, the most northerly point in the British Isles. Fair Isle, the most southerly island in Shetland, and the more inaccessible island of Foula are also major bird-watching sites for seabirds. These islands are reached by ferry, which also offers an opportunity to observe porpoises, killer whales and seals.

UNST ◆ B C1

With its green hills and attractive sandy beaches, the most northerly island in Shetland is certainly not lacking in charm. Its serpentine (ophite) deposits, the garnet that litters the beautiful bay of Woodwick, and the soapstone from the quarries of Clibberswick and Quoys will be of great interest to amateur geologists. Ferries from Gutcher (Yell) land at Belmont.

UYEASOUND. To the southeast of this former Hanseatic trading post are UYEA BRECK, a 10-foot standing stone, and MUNESS CASTLE (1598), built by Laurence Bruce, the half-brother of Robert Stewart, whose first and second floors are virtually intact. The remains of a Viking settlement dominate Sandwick beach, to the north of Muness.

LUNDA WICK. On the Westing road, near Loch Bordastubble, stands the largest megalith in Shetland. To the southwest of the bay of Lunda Wick are the ruins of St Olaf's Church (12th century) and, at UNDERHOULL, to the northwest, the remains of an Iron Age broch and a 9th-century Viking long house.

BALTASOUND. The island's main settlement enjoyed its golden age between 1880 and 1925 when its population increased from 500 to 10,000 at the beginning of the herring-fishing season.

HAROLDSWICK. The village is named after the Norse king Harald I Hárfagri (c. 860–940) whose fleet dropped anchor here in the 10th century. UNST BOAT HAVEN, on the beach, has a collection of ancient boats, while UNST HERITAGE CENTRE, to the north of the village, traces the history of the herring industry and has an attractive collection of knitwear.

HERMANESS NATIONAL NATURE RESERVE. This nature reserve, to the north of Burrafirth, provides sanctuary for hundreds of thousands of birds and is an absolute must for bird-watchers. A long walk takes you to the northern tip of the island, opposite the lighthouse (1858) on the islet of MUCKLE FLUGGA, the most northerly point of the British Isles.

Cliffs at Hermaness (*below and top right*); puffins (*bottom right*).

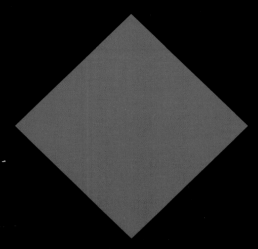

Practical information

270 Getting there

272 Getting around

274 Staying in Scotland

276 Festivals and events

277 Places to visit

300 Bibliography

302 Scottish cuisine

303 Hotels and restaurants

315 List of illustrations

318 Index

325 Map section

Key

▥	Air conditioning
🐾	Animals not allowed
✦	Children not allowed
♿	Facilities for the disabled
♠	Garden
🅿	Parking
◻	Quiet
≋	Swimming pool
▣	Television in room
◈	Tennis
⌂	Terrace
🅲	Town center
⚑	Valet parking
❦	View

◆ GETTING THERE

ADDRESSES

→ IN THE US
■ **British Embassy**
(Visa Office)
19 Observatory
Circle
NW Washington
D.C. 20008
Tel. (202) 588 7800
■ **British Consulate
General & British
Tourist Authority**
845 Third Avenue
New York
NY 10022
Tel. (212) 745 0200
(consulate)
Tel. 800 462 2748
(Tourist Authority)
www.britain-info.org

→ IN THE UK
■ **US Consulate
General**
3 Regent Terrace
Edinburgh EH7 5BW
Tel: (0131) 556 8315
*www.usembassy.org.
uk/scotland*
After-hours
emergency for
US citizens:
Tel. (0122) 485 7097

■ **London**
SCOTTISH TOURIST
BOARD
19 Cockspur Street
SW1Y 5BL
Tel. (020) 7930 2812

→ WEBSITE
*www.visitscotland.
com*
The official website
of the Scottish
tourist office.

AIR TRAVEL

→ FROM THE US
There are regular
connecting flights
from New York,
Chicago and Los
Angeles to Glasgow
and Edinburgh,
stopping over at
London or
Amsterdam.
Roundtrip flights
cost from $600 from
New York to
Glasgow.
■ **United Airlines**
Tel. 800 421 6522
*www.unitedairlines.
com*
■ **British Airways**
Tel. 800 AIRWAYS
*www.britishairways.
com*

■ **Virgin Atlantic**
Tel. 800 862 8621
*www.virginatlantic.
com*
■ **KLM**
Tel. 800 447 4747
www.klm.com

→ FROM WITHIN
THE UK
There are regular
flights from most
British airports to
destinations in
Scotland, including
daily flights from all
London airports to
Glasgow and
Edinburgh. Return
flights between
London and
Glasgow or
Edinburgh cost
on average about
£100, but you can
fly from London
Stansted to
Glasgow Prestwick
airport from as little
as £30 return.
■ **British Airways**
Tel. 0845 77 333 77
*www.british
airways.com*
■ **British Midlands**
Tel. 0870 60 70 555
*www.britishmidland.
com*
■ **Ryan Air**
Tel. 0870 333 1231
www.ryanair.com
■ **Go**
Tel. 0835 60 54321
www.go-fly.com

CAR, TRAIN AND
FERRY

→ BY CAR AND TRAIN
(LE SHUTTLE)
From Calais (France)
to Folkestone (UK)
via the Channel
Tunnel

→ TEMPERATURES(°C)		
Month	Min.	Max.
Jan.	0	6
Feb.	0	6
March	2	8
April	4	10
May	7	13
June	10	17
July	11	18
Aug.	11	18
Sept.	9	16
Oct.	6	13
Nov.	4	8
Dec.	3	7

To book in the UK:
Tel. 01227 472082
To book in France:
Tel. 0801 630 304

→ BY CAR AND FERRY
Ferry services
operate from the
European mainland.
■ **Brittany Ferries**
Tel. 0803 828 828
■ **Hoverspeed**
Tel. 0800 90 17 77

CLIMATE
Oceanic climate:
mild and wet.
The east coast is
sunnier and less
windy, while the
west coast is warmer
due to the effects of
the Gulf Stream.
Weather extremely
changeable in all
seasons with
frequent showers.
■ **Rainfall**
minimum:
March–April
maximum: July

COACH
The longest journey
time, but the
cheapest way to
travel.

■ **London–Glasgow**
8 hrs, from £22
return
■ **National Express**
National Express
Tel. (0990) 80 80 80
*www.national
express.co.uk*
Londonliner
Tel. (0990) 50 50 50
www.citylink.co.uk

COST OF LIVING
Prices more or less
the same as
mainland Europe,
except for alcohol
and cigarettes
(heavily taxed),
petrol, restaurant
meals and public
transport (slightly
more expensive) and
hotels (much more
expensive).
*NB: Accommodation
charges are per
person, not per
room.*

→ ACCOMMODATION
CHARGES
■ **Budget prices**
£20–25 per day
Youth hostels
and modest
restaurants.
■ **Average prices**
£60 per day
B&Bs, pubs and
inexpensive
restaurants.
■ **Above-average
prices**
£80 per day
Small hotels and
good B&Bs.
More expensive
restaurants.

→ Some prices
1 postcard: 40p
1 cup of coffee: £1

1 pint (¾ US pint) of beer: £1.50
1 small glass of whisky: £1.50
1 packet of cigarettes: £4

ELECTRICITY
Voltage: 240 V, 75 MHz. Adapters are necessary for foreign appliances (and are sometimes provided by hotels and B&B).

FORMALITIES
→ **DOCUMENTS**
US citizens need a valid passport; no visas are required for stays up to 6 months. EC members just need a valid passport or identity card. Authorization to leave the country of origin required for unaccompanied minors.

→ **DRIVING**
Valid driving licence, car registration papers and green card.

→ **ANIMALS**
Now admitted without quarantine, subject to innoculations and use of microchip tagging. Information from the British Consulate.

→ **CUSTOMS**
It is illegal to take perishable goods, plants and certain medication into Great Britain.

HEALTH
→ **HEALTH INSURANCE**
US visitors should check with their travel agents or insurance brokers for health coverage abroad. EU nationals and residents are entitled to free health care from NHS (National Health Service) doctors and hospitals, but you

may have a long wait. Repatriation and certain treatments are not covered, and private surgeries and clinics are often very expensive. It is advisable to take out additional insurance.

MONEY
→ **CURRENCY**
The monetary unit is the Pound Sterling and the Scottish pound (£), divided into 100 pence.
£1 = approx. $1.6

→ **CREDIT CARDS**
Visa and MasterCard are widely accepted, except in the North and the Hebrides.

→ **FOREIGN EXCHANGE**
In banks and tourist offices. Cash dispensers outside. *Warning: Cash withdrawals by card are subject to charges. Traveler's checks are recommended.*

→ **TRAVELER'S CHECKS**
Changed at banks, tourist offices and many post offices.

SPECIAL NEEDS
Public transport is poorly equipped. The 'Disabled Persons Railcard' entitles the holder to significant reductions. Specially adapted hotel rooms and hire cars are expensive. For a detailed brochure contact:
Access Travel
6 Hirrock, Astley
Manchester
M29 7BL
Tel. (01942) 888 844
Fax (01942) 891 811

TELEPHONE
→ **FROM ABROAD**
Dial the international dialing code, then 44, then the code followed

the number of the person you are calling.
Numbers beginning with **0800** are free.

TIME
→ **TIME DIFFERENCE**
In winter time (GMT) or summer time (BST), Great Britain is five hours ahead of New York and one hour behind Europe.

→ **WHAT TIME IS IT ?**
Great Britain uses the 12-hour clock system.

TRAIN
→ **EUROSTAR**
There are hourly trains from Paris and Brussels to London Waterloo.
To book in the UK:
Tel. 0990 186 186
To book in France:
Tel. 08 36 35 35 39
www.eurostar.co.uk

→ **LONDON–SCOTLAND**
From King's Cross, trains leave every hour for Edinburgh (4½ hrs) and Glasgow (5 hrs).

→ **INFORMATION**
■ National Rail Enquiries
Tel. 08457 48 49 50
■ Scot Rail
Tel. 08457 55 00 33
www.scotrail.co.uk

WHAT TO TAKE
■ **In summer:**
Light, waterproof clothing.
■ **All year round:**
Warm clothing and waterproof shoes (boots for the Highlands and Islands).
■ **High-protection insect (mosquito) repellent.**
■ **For smokers:**
Cigarettes are highly taxed in Great Britain.

WHEN TO GO
The best times:
May–June,
Sept.–Oct.

→ **May–June**
These tend to be dry, sunny months. Nature is coming back to life after a harsh winter, and there are not many tourists. An ideal time to go.

→ **July–August**
The warmest but also some of the wettest months of the year. The peak tourist season with prices to match. The main festivals and folk festivals, including the Edinburgh Festival. But be prepared for midges! The mosquito-like insects that infest the Highlands and Islands at this time of year thrive in dampness and shade and are particularly active at sunrise and sunset.

→ **September–November**
An ideal season for nature lovers. A noticeable decrease in the number of tourists from mid-September.
NB: A marked decrease in temperature at the end of October.

→ **Christmas and New Year**
Major celebrations, especially Edinburgh's Hogmanay (New Year's Eve)

→ **January–April**
Harsh climatic conditions (snow, wind, mist, rough seas). Spring heralds the beginning of the artistic season.

YOUNG PEOPLE
→ **Student card**
Some reductions (but not for the cinema) with an international student card.

AIR

→ AIRPORTS
■ **Edinburgh**
Tel. (0131) 333 1000
■ **Glasgow**
Tel. (0141) 887 1111
■ **Aberdeen**
Tel. (01224) 722 331
■ **Inverness**
Tel. (01667) 464 000

→ REGULAR FLIGHTS
Flights between
Glasgow, Edinburgh,
Aberdeen, Inverness,
Kintyre, Wick, the
Hebrides, Orkney
and Shetland. In
summer, it is
advisable to book in
advance for
Shetland.
■ **British Airways**
85 Buchanan Street
Glasgow G1 3HQ
Tel. 0845 77 333 77
*www.british-
airways.com*
■ **Loganair**
Glasgow Airport
Abbotsinch
Paisley Renfrewshire
PA3 2TG
Tel. (0141) 848 7594
Information and
reservations: contact
British Airways.

BICYCLE

Cyclists take priority
over drivers.
■ **Cycle tracks**
In Edinburgh, ask
for the map
published by:
Spokes
Tel. (0131) 313 2114
■ **Bicycles on the
train**
It is advisable to
book in advance:
ask for the 'bike it
by train' option.
*NB: You need
to be fit to cope
with Scotland's
mountainous relief
and strong winds.*

→ BIKE RENTAL
Bicycles can
be rented by the
week in most
Scottish towns and
even certain
villages.
■ **Edinburgh**
Recycling
33 Iona Street
Tel. (0131) 553 11 30
Sandy Gilchrist
Cycles
1 Cazdow Place
Tel. (0131) 652 17 60
Central Cycle Hire
13 Lochrin Place
Tel. (0131) 228 63 33
■ **Glasgow**
Billy Bilsand Cycles
176 Saltmarket
Glasgow G15LA
Tel. (0141) 552 08 41

CAR

An excellent road
network and free-
flowing traffic
throughout the year.
Freeways – indicated
by the letter M
(motorway) –
between major
cities.
*NB: Remember to
drive on the left.
You must have a
rear-view mirror on
the right.*

**→ DRIVING IN
SCOTLAND**
No priority to the
left or right: priority
is indicated by the
road signs.
Negotiate traffic
circles in a clockwise
direction and give
way to vehicles
already on the
circle. On single
track roads, carry
on if the oncoming
vehicle flashes
its headlights;
if not, allow it to
pass by stopping on
one of the passing
places (every
100 yards).
Speed limits: 70 mph
on freeways and
dual carriageways;
50 mph on two-lane
roads; 30 mph in
built-up areas. Make
a habit of topping
up with gas: outside
the major towns
and cities, most gas
stations close in the
evening and on
Sundays.

→ CAR HIRE
Expensive (at least
£40 per day).
■ **Youth Conditions**
Drivers must be
between 21 and 70
years old and have
held a driving
license for at least
one year.
■ **Car rental**
– HOLIDAY AUTOS
Tel. 0990 16 82 38
– AVIS
Tel. 0990 90 05 00
– BUDGET
Tel. 0800 18 11 81
– HERTZ
Tel. 0990 99 66 99

COACH

Slower than the
train, but much
cheaper. Tickets can
be bought from the
ticket office or on
the coach.

→ MAIN COMPANIES
■ **Scottish Citylink**
Tel. 0990 50 50 50
www.citylink.co.uk
■ **National Express**
Tel. 0990 01 01 04
*www.national
express.co.uk*

**→ ROYAL MAIL
COACHES**
In the absence of
any other means of
transport, these
coaches will take
passengers.
■ **Royal Mail Scotland**
Tel. (0131) 228 7407

→ TRAVEL CARD
With the Explorer
Pass, unlimited
travel for 3 or 8 days
on Citylink coaches,
and a 50%
reduction on
Caledonian
MacBrayne ferries.

EDINBURGH

→ BUS
A practical way to
travel, especially on
the maroon and
white buses of
Lothian Regional
Transport. Tickets
are sold singly on
the bus.
Alternatively, 1-day
or 1-week travel
cards (Touristcard)
are an ideal way to
visit the city and
surrounding areas.
■ **LRT Ticket Centre**
27 Hanover Street
Tel. (0131) 555 63 63

→ BUS TOURS
Guide Friday
Tourism Centre
provides
information on the
different tour
routes.
■ **Waverley Railway
Station**
Tel. (0131) 556 2244
*www.stratford.co.uk/
guidefriday*

→ CABS
There is no shortage
of cabs (taxis),
especially around
Waverley Bridge.
■ **Capital Castle Cabs**
Tel. (0131) 228 2555
■ **Central Radio Taxis**
Tel. (0131) 229 2468

→ PRINCIPLE DISTANCES (IN MILES)									
	ABERDEEN	AYR	DURNESS	EDIMB.	GLASGOW	INVERA.	INVERNESS	MELROSE	OBAN	ULLAP.
ABERDEEN		180	215	125	159	170	108	162	179	166
AYR	180		306	75	36	89	201	94	93	250
DURNESS	215	306		283	277	245	108	320	221	68
EDIMB.	125	75	283		46	104	177	37	124	234
GLASGOW	159	36	277	46		60	171	73	93	221
INVERARAY	170	89	245	104	60		140	170	37	190
INVERNESS	108	201	108	177	171	140		213	116	58
MELROSE	162	94	320	37	73	170	213		159	270
OBAN	179	93	221	124	93	37	116	159		165
ULLAPOOL	166	250	68	234	221	190	58	270	165	

■ **City Cabs**
Tel. (0131) 228 1211

→ CAR
Avoid driving in
Edinburgh: parking
space is at a
premium. If you
do, use the
underground
car parks – they are
well signposted.

FERRY
Scotland has a dense
ferry network; most
ferries take cars.

**→ WEST-COAST
ISLANDS**
The Hebrides
and islands of the
Firth of Clyde are
serviced by:
– CALEDONIAN
MACBRAYNE
Tel. 0990 65 00 00
Fax (0147) 563 7607
www.calmac.co.uk
■ **Firth of Clyde**
– ARRAN
Ardrossan-Brodick:
6 return trips daily
(55 mins). Very
popular in summer.
Advance booking
recommended,
especially for cars.
– BUTE
Wemyss Bay-
Rothesay (35 mins)
■ **Inner Hebrides**
– COLL
Oban–Coll
(2 hrs 40 mins)
– COLONSAY
Oban–Colonsay
(2–2½ hrs)
– EIGG, MUCK, RUM
AND CANNA
Mallaig–Eigg
(1½ hrs)
Eigg–Muck (1 hr)
Muck–Rum (1¼ hrs)
Rum–Canna (1¼ hrs)
Canna–Mallaig
(2¾ hrs)
– GIGHA
Tayinloan–Ardminish
(20 mins)
– IONA
Fionnphort–Iona
(15 mins)
– ISLAY
Kennacraig–Port
Ellen (2 hrs 10 mins)
Kennagraig-
Port Askaig (2 hrs)
– MULL
Oban–Craignure
(40 mins)

– RAASAY
Sconser–Raasay
(15 mins)
– SKYE
Mallaig–Armadale
(30 mins)
– TIREE
Oban–Coll then
Coll–Tiree (55 mins)
■ **Outer Hebrides**
– LEWIS
Ullapool–Stornoway
(2 hrs 40 mins)
Glasgow–Stornoway
(10½ hrs)
– HARRIS
Uig–Tarbert (1¾ hrs)
Otternish–
Leverburgh
(1 hr 10 mins)
– NORTH UIST
Uig–Lochmaddy
(2 hrs 50 mins)
– SOUTH UIST
Oban–Lochboisdale

(6 hrs 40 mins)
Mollaig–Lochboisdale
(3½ hrs)
– BARRA
Oban–Castlebay
(4 hrs 50 mins)
Mallaig–Castlebay
(3¾ hrs)

**→ NORTHERN
ISLES**
Orkney and
Shetland
– P&O SCOTTISH
FERRIES
Jamieson's Quay
Aberdeen
Tel. (0122) 457 2615
www.poscottish
ferries.co.uk

■ **Orkneys**
Scrabster–Stromness
(2 hrs)
John o' Groats–
Burwick (45 mins)
■ **Shetlands**
Aberdeen–
Stromness–
Lerwick (14 hrs)
Stromness–Lerwick
(8 hrs)

GLASGOW
→ BUS
A Roundabout
ticket gives
unlimited travel for
one or several days
by train or on the
underground.
■ **The Travel Centre**
Buchanan Bus
Station
Killermont Street
Tel. (0141) 332 7133

→ BUS TOURS
SCOTGUIDE TOUR
SERVICES
St George's Building
153 Queen Street
Tel. (0141) 204 0444
www.scotguide.
com

→ CAR
Parking is
difficult: use the
underground car
parks.

SCANDINAVIA
Flights and ferry
services to Denmark,
Norway and the
Faroe Islands.

→ FLIGHTS
■ **British Airways**
Tel. 08457 73 33 77
www.british-
airways.com
■ **SAS**
Tel. 08456 07 27 27
www.scandinavian.net

→ FERRIES
■ **Smyril Line**
Torshavn, Danemark
Tel. (45) 298 31 59 00
www.smyril-line.fo
■ **DFDS Scandinavian
Seaways**
Tel. 0990 33 31 11
www.scansea.com
– P&O SCOTTISH
FERRIES
Tel. (01595) 69 48 48
www.poscottishferries.
co.uk

→ TOURIST OFFICES
■ **Norwegian Tourist
Office (London)**
5 Regent Street
Tel. (020) 7839 6255
■ **Danish Tourist
Office (London)**
55 Sloane Street
Tel. (020) 7259 5959

TRAIN
Admire Scotland's
landscapes from an
observation car.

→ TRAVEL CARDS
■ **Britrail Flexipass**
On sale in all major
railway stations –
gives unlimited
travel for 8, 15, 22
days or 1 month
anywhere in the UK.
■ **Scotrail Rover**
4, 7 or 12 days.
■ **Freedom of
Scotland Travelpass**
train + ferry: 8 or
15 days.
Tourist Return
London-Edinburgh
or London-Glasgow
return.

→ INFORMATION
■ **National Rail
Inquiries**
Information on
trains throughout
the UK.
Tel. 08457 48 49 50
■ **Scotrail**
Information and
ticket sales for all
Scottish trains.
Tel. 08457 55 00 33
www.scotrail.co.uk

ACCOMMODATION

For a nominal charge, reservations can be made at tourist offices. Some of the better-known hotels require a deposit.

NB: At the height of the season, hotels are often full and it is advisable to book in advance.

→ **YOUTH HOSTELS**
These inexpensive hostels are found throughout Scotland. Comfort can be rather basic, but there is always plenty of atmosphere. SYHA Central Reservation Service Tel. 0870 155 32 55
www.syha.org.uk

→ **B&Bs AND GUEST HOUSES**
Convenient and inexpensive – found throughout Scotland. An ideal way to enjoy the warm welcome and unrivaled charm of British homes. Guest houses are a little more expensive than B&Bs (Bed & Breakfast).

→ **CAMPING**
■ **Camp sites**
Generally well maintained.
■ **Wild camping**
Possible in areas where it is not specifically forbidden. Always ask the landowner's permission.

→ **HOTELS**
■ **Prices**
Prices vary considerably depending on the hotel rating (1–5 stars). There are reductions for longer stays and 50% or more for out-of-season bookings. Breakfast is usually included and sometimes dinner.

■ **Hotel chains:**
– TRAVEL INN
Tel. (0870) 24 28 000
– TRAVELODGE
Tel. (0870) 90 56 343
■ **Annexes**
Some hotels have well-equipped, self-contained annexes for 2–8 people.
NB: Some hotels will not take children under six, ten or even twelve.

DRINK

→ **BEER**
Served by the pint (¾ US pint). A wide range of different varieties – try the traditional real ales.

→ **COFFEE**
Not particularly strong, but usually good. Decaffeinated coffee (or decaf) is also available.

→ **WINE**
In restaurants, wine is also served by the glass, usually well filled. Take advantage of this to try Chilean, South African and Australian wines.

→ **WHISKY**
Order a dram: a small glass of whisky. To help you choose from the many varieties, invest in the Collins Whisky Map of Scotland (£3.25), on sale in the shops and some Tourist Information Centers.

EATING OUT

→ **HABITS AND CUSTOMS**
■ Meals are eaten early, especially in the evening.
■ Cheese is usually served after dessert.

→ **RESTAURANTS**
■ Usually open from noon–1pm and 6.30–8.30pm. The busiest times are around 12.30pm and 5pm.
■ Prices are often quite high. Pub

meals – served in the lounge bar – are less expensive.
■ Reserve a table, especially in the evening.

→ **FAST-FOOD**
Fast-food restaurants and vendors sell hot dogs and burgers. Fish & chip shops sell take-away fish or chicken and chips (often quite greasy) at unbeatable prices. Some also sell haggis.

HEALTH

For EU nationals and residents: free health care from NHS (National Health Service) hospitals and local GPs (general practitioners). Private clinics are very expensive. Medication from the chemist (= drug store).
■ **Emergencies**
Dial 999.

MAIL

→ **POST OFFICES**
Open Mon.–Fri. 9am–5.30pm, Sat. 9am–12.30pm.

→ **INFORMATION**
■ **Royal Mail**
Postal Services
Tel. (0345) 740 740

→ **RATES**
Two rates currently in force: Second Class: cheaper but slower; First Class: more expensive but more reliable.

MONEY

→ **CURRENCY**
Pound sterling and Scottish pound (£), divided into pence (p). Coins in circulation: 50p, 20p, 10p, 5p, 2p and 1 penny. There are also Scottish coins and notes.
NB: It may be difficult to change Scottish currency

once you get home, so make sure you change (or spend) it before you leave.

→ **CREDIT CARDS**
Accepted almost everywhere, but less so in the North and the Hebrides.
NB: There is a charge for withdrawing money using a credit card.

→ **FOREIGN EXCHANGE**
In banks and tourist offices. Traveler's checks: in banks, tourist offices and many post offices (on proof of identity).

NATURE

Information from nature conservation organizations.
■ **Royal Society for the Protection of Birds**
Dunedin House
25 Ravelston Terrace
Edinburgh EH4 3TP
Tel. (0131) 311 6500
www.rspb.org.uk
■ **Scottish Natural Heritage**
12 Hope Terrace
Edinburgh EH9 2AS
Tel. (0131) 447 4784
www.snh.org.uk
■ **Scottish Wildlife Trust**
Cramond House,
16 Cramond Glebe Rd
Edinburgh EH4 6NS
Tel. (0131) 312 7765
www.swt.org.uk

NIGHTLIFE

→ **PUBS**
Pubs serve alcohol until 11pm and sometimes 1am. Drinks are ordered and paid for at the bar.

→ **NIGHTCLUBS**
There is no shortage of nightclubs in Scotland (especially Glasgow) and most are quite reasonably priced. Some pubs have 'clubs' which are much more convivial.

OPENING TIMES

→ BANKS
Open Mon.–Fri. 9.30am–4.30pm (Thur. until 6pm).

→ STORES
Open Mon.–Sat. 9am–5.30pm. Supermarkets: open Mon.–Sat. until 8 or 9pm. Many stores are open on Sundays.

SHOPPING

→ FOOD
Try the chocolate, teas, jams, marmalades (Simmers and Baxters), chutney, Indian and Chinese spices, Highland biscuits and shortbreads.

→ ANTIQUES
19th-century craft objects, firearms, copper, pewter and silverware from the various antique markets in the main towns or from antique shops.

→ BARBOUR
'Barbour' is famous for its classic waterproof (waxed cotton) jackets.

→ JEWELRY
There is some beautiful silver jewelry reproducing Celtic motifs.

→ KNITWEAR
Best-quality wool and traditionally made garments. A wide range of wool-based products, including tartan and the warm and extremely comfortable Shetland sweaters. James Pringle and Harris Tweed are two of the most prestigious wool marks.

→ POTTERY AND GLASS
The items produced by the Bridge of Allen and Wick workshops (glass), and Highland Stoneware (pottery), are renowned for their balanced composition and the clean lines of their design.

→ WHISKY
Inimitable whiskies that are only available in Scotland. Each region has its own varieties and aromas. Buy a copy of the Collins Whisky Map of Scotland (£3.25).

SMOKING
Hotels, restaurants and public places are often non-smoking areas. Cigars and pipes are frowned upon in restaurants.

SPORTS

→ HUNTING
Only on private property. Extremely expensive, especially traditional grouse hunting (Aug. 12–Dec 10.). Book well in advance with a hotel that specializes in hunting holidays (list available from tourist offices). You will need to obtain a permit in order to take your gun with you and you also need a hunting license.

→ GOLF
An extremely popular and 'democratic' sport in Scotland. There are a great many public courses (links), which are open to everyone. They are listed in the guide, Scotland Home of Golf, published by the Scottish Tourist Board.

→ FISHING
Principle rivers: the Spey, Tay and Tweed. *NB: permits for salmon fishing are exorbitant. Provisional permits are available from clubs and some hotels (list available from tourist offices). The guide* Scotland for Fishing *is published by the Scottish Tourist Board.*

TELEPHONE

→ DIRECTORY ENQUIRIES
Local: 192
International: 153

→ EMERGENCIES
Police, fire brigade, ambulance: 999

→ PHONE CARDS
Phone cards are required for most public phone boxes. Available from post offices and newsdealers displaying the BT logo.

TIPPING
■ **Hotels and restaurants**
Service is usually not included and is left to the customer's discretion (at least 7–10%). In restaurants, leave cash or make a note on your credit card slip; in hotels add to the final bill.
■ **Pubs**
No tipping required.
■ **Taxis**
Customary for a long journey (10%).

TOURIST INFORMATION

→ TOURIST OFFICES
Two sources of information: Area Tourist Boards (maps, guides, brochures) and Tourist Information Centres (TIC), usually open Apr.–Oct. Mon.–Sat. 9am–5pm. It is possible to reserve hotel rooms and travel tickets in TICs.
SCOTTISH TOURIST BOARD
Open Mon.–Thur. 9am–5.30pm,
Fri. 9am–5pm
23 Ravelston Terrace
Edinburgh EH4 3EU
Tel. (0131) 332 2433
Fax (0131) 315 4545

→ HISTORIC MONUMENTS
Many of Scotland's historic sites are managed by two organizations:
■ **Historic Scotland**
Longmore House, Salisbury Place
Edinburgh EH9 ISH
Tel. (0131) 668 8800
www.historic-scotland.gov.uk
■ **National Trust for Scotland**
28 Charlotte Sq.
Edinburgh EH2
Tel. (0131) 243 9300
www.nts.org.uk

USEFUL TIPS
The Scots have a strong sense of civic responsibility and a respect for tradition: don't drop litter in the street (a finable offense); men should wear a tie at dinner.

WALKING

→ ITINERAIRES
■ **Southern Upland Way**
Runs east-west across southern Scotland (210 miles).
■ **West Highland Way**
Glasgow–Fort William (95 miles).
■ **Speyside Way**
In the Spey valley, the home of Scotch whisky (45 miles).
NB: Footpaths are not always signposted and weather conditions can be difficult: make sure you go well prepared.

→ INFORMATION
Tourist offices and nature conservation organizations.
■ **Scottish Rights of Way Society**
24 Anandale St
Edinburgh EH7 4AN
Tel. (0131) 558 1222
Open Mon.–Fri. 9am–2pm.

◆ FESTIVALS AND EVENTS

For a complete list of Scottish festivals, contact the Edinburgh – tel: (+44) 0131 473 38 00 and Glasgow – tel: (+44) 0141 204 44 00 – tourist offices.

FESTIVALS AND HOLIDAYS

JANUARY	GLASGOW	CELTIC CONNECTIONS (CELTIC MUSIC)
	ORKNEY	THE BA' GAME (CHRISTMAS AND NEW YEAR)
	LERWICK	UP HELLY-AA (VIKING FIRE FESTIVAL)
25 JANUARY	THOUGHOUT SCOTLAND	BURNS NIGHT (ROBERT BURNS'S BIRTHDAY)
FEB	INVERNESS	MUSIC FESTIVAL (CLASSICAL AND TRADITIONAL)
MARCH	LANARK	WHUPPITY SCOORIE (CHILDREN'S RACE)
	EDINBURGH	SHOOTS & ROOTS I (FOLK LEGENDS)
MARCH–APRIL	EDINBURGH	THE PUPPET ANIMATION
APRIL	EDINBURGH	INTERNATIONAL SCIENCE FESTIVAL
	SHETLAND	FOLK FESTIVAL
APRIL–MAY	BUTE	JAZZ FESTIVAL
	SPEYSIDE	SCOTCH WHISKY FESTIVAL
MAY	ORKNEY	FOLK FESTIVAL
	GLASGOW	GLASGOW ART FAIR
	HIGHLANDS	HIGHLANDS FESTIVAL (MUSIC AND DRAMA)
	WANLOCKHEAD	GOLD PANNING CHAMPIONSHIPS
	ATOLL	GATHERING & HIGHLAND GAMES
JUNE	ARRAN	FOLK FESTIVAL
	DINGWALL	HIGHLANDS TRADITIONAL MUSIC FESTIVAL
	EDINBURGH	ROYAL HIGHLAND SHOW (AGRICULTURAL SHOW)
JULY	GLASGOW	INTERNATIONAL JAZZ FESTIVAL
	KINROSS	T IN THE PARK (ROCK FESTIVAL)
	STORNOWAY	HEBRIDEAN CELTIC MUSIC FESTIVAL
JULY–AUGUST	CALLANDER, STIRLING	WORLD HIGHLAND GAMES CHAMPIONSHIPS
AUGUST	EDINBURGH	INTERNATIONAL FESTIVAL (DRAMA, DANCE, MUSIC)
	EDINBURGH	THE FRINGE (DRAMA)
	EDINBURGH	INTERNATIONAL FILM FESTIVAL
	EDINBURGH	INTERNATIONAL JAZZ & BLUES FESTIVAL
	EDINBURGH	EDINBURGH MILITARY TATOO
	GLASGOW	WORLD PIPE CHAMPIONSHIPS (BAGPIPES)
	PORTREE	ISLE OF SKYE HIGHLAND GAMES
SEPTEMBER	LOCH LOMOND	SCOTTISH PIPE BAND CHAMPIONSHIPS (BAGPIPES)
	HAWICK	BORDERS BLUES AND JAZZ FESTIVAL
	CREETOWN	COUNTRY MUSIC FESTIVAL
	BRAEMAR	BRAEMAR GATHERING (HIGHLAND GAMES)
OCTOBER	TRAVELING	ROYAL NATIONAL MOD (GAELIC FESTIVAL)
	ABERDEEN	ABERDEEN ALTERNATIVE FESTIVAL (MUSIC AND DRAMA)
NOVEMBER	EDINBURGH	SHOOTS & ROOTS II (FOLK LEGENDS)
	THOUGHOUT SCOTLAND	ST ANDREW'S NIGHT (FESTIVAL OF THE PATRON SAINT OF SCOTLAND)
DECEMBER	EDINBURGH	EDINBURGH'S HOGMANAY (NEW YEAR)

SPORTS EVENTS

FEBRUARY–MARCH	EDINBURGH	FIVE NATION'S CUP (RUGBY)
	THOUGHOUT SCOTLAND	SCOTTISH CURLING CHAMPIONSHIPS
MAY	HEBRIDES	WESTERN ISLES CHALLENGE (TRIATHLON)
	JEDBURGH	JED-FOREST RFC ANNUAL SEVENS (SEVEN-A-SIDE RUGBY)
JULY	ABERDEEN	ABERDEEN INTERNATIONAL FOOTBALL FESTIVAL
	LOCH LOMOND	WORLD GOLF TOURNAMENT
AUGUST	LAUDER	SCOTTISH HORSE TRIAL CHAMPIONSHIPS

PUBLIC HOLIDAYS

MOST TOWNS HAVE THEIR OWN PUBLIC HOLIDAYS. ASK AT THE TOURIST OFFICE.

JANUARY	1–3	NEW YEAR
APRIL–MAY	EASTER	GOOD FRIDAY AND EASTER MONDAY
MAY	1ST MON.	MAY DAY
	LAST MON.	SPRING BANK HOLIDAY
AUGUST	1ST MON.	SUMMER BANK HOLIDAY
DECEMBER	25–26	CHRISTMAS AND BOXING DAY

Places are listed alphabetically by town, with the islands at the end.
Symbols: ▲ refers to the description given in the 'Itineraries', and ◆ to the map section.
Many sites with unrestricted access are not featured in this list; for further information contact:
Historic Scotland (0131) 668 8800 or the National Trust for Scotland (0131) 226 5922.
NB: the last visitors are usually admitted half an hour before closing time.

ABERDEEN ★		◆ D D1 B A6
ABERDEEN ART GALLERY Schoolhill Tel. (01224) 523 700	*Open all year: Mon.–Sat. 10am–5pm, Sun. 2–5pm. Admission free.*	▲ 211
CRUIKSHANK BOTANIC GARDENS Old Aberdeen Campus Tel. (01224) 272 704	*Open all year: Mon.–Fri. 9am–4.30pm (May–Sept.: Sat.–Sun. 2–5pm).*	▲ 209
GORDON HIGHLANDERS MUSEUM St Luke's, Viewfield Rd Tel. (01224) 311 200	*Open Mar.–Oct.: Tue.–Sat. 10.30am–4.30pm, Sun. 1.30–4.30pm, or by appt.*	▲ 211
KING'S COLLEGE CHAPEL College Bounds, Old Aberdeen Tel. (01224) 272 137	*Open Mon.–Fri. 9.30am–4.30pm.*	▲ 210
KING'S COLLEGE VISITOR CENTRE College Bounds, Old Aberdeen Tel. (01244) 273 702	*Open Mon.–Sat.: 10am–5pm, Sun. noon–5pm. Closed Jan. 1 and Dec. 25 Admission free.*	▲ 210
MARISCHAL MUSEUM Marischal College, Broad St Tel. (01224) 274 301	*Open Mon.–Fri. 10am–5pm, Sun. 2–5pm.*	▲ 210
MARITIME MUSEUM Shiprow Tel. (01224) 337 700	*Open Mon.–Sat. 10am–5pm, Sun. noon–3pm. Closed 1 Jan. and 25 Dec. Admission free.*	▲ 211
PROVOST SKENE'S HOUSE Guestrow Tel. (01224) 641 086	*Open all year: Mon.–Sat. 10am–5pm, Sun. 1–4pm. Admission free.*	▲ 210
ST MACHAR'S CATHEDRAL Canonry, Old Aberdeen Tel. (01224) 485 988	*Open all year: daily 9am–5pm. Admission free.*	▲ 211
ST NICHOLAS' KIRK The New Vestry, Back Wynd Tel. (01224) 643 494	*Open May–Sept.: Mon.–Fri. noon–4pm, Sat. 1–3pm, services Sun.; Oct.–Apr.: daily 10am–1pm. Admission free.*	▲ 210
TOLBOOTH (CIVIC HISTORY MUSEUM) Castle St Tel. (01224) 621 167	*Open Apr.–Sept.: Tue.–Sat. 10am–5pm, Sun. 2–5pm. Admission free.*	▲ 210
ABERFELDY		◆ D B2
CASTLE MENZIES Tel. (01887) 820 982 *Weem, north of Aberfeldy (B846)*	*Open Apr.–Oct.: Mon.–Sat. 10.30am–5pm, Sun. 2–5pm.*	▲ 182
ABERFOYLE		◆ D A3
QUEEN ELIZABETH FOREST PARK CENTRE Tel. (01877) 382 258	*Open all year: daily 10am–6pm. Closed Jan.–Feb.*	▲ 173
ACHILTIBUIE		◆ A C4
ACHILTIBUIE HYDROPONICUM Tel. (01854) 622 202	*Open Easter–Sept.: daily 10am–6pm.*	▲ 244
SMOKEHOUSE Tel. (01854) 622 353 *Altandhu, northeast of Achiltibuie*	*Open Easter–May and Sept.–Oct.: Mon.–Fri. 9.30am–5pm; June–Aug.: Mon.–Sat. 9.30am–5pm.*	▲ 244
AILSA CRAIG		◆ D A5
Tel. (01465) 713 219 *10½ miles from the port of Girvan*	*Visit by appt. with the lighthouse keeper.*	▲ 147
ALFORD		◆ A F6
ALFORD-DONSIDE HERITAGE CENTRE Mart Rd Tel. (019755) 629 06	*Open Apr.–Oct.: Mon.–Sat. 10am–5pm, Sun. 1–5pm.*	▲ 216
ALFORD VALLEY RAILWAY Dunnideer, Kingsford Rd Tel. (019755) 62 811	*Open Apr.– May and Sept.: Sat.–Sun. 1–5pm; June–Aug.: daily 1–5pm; Santa's specials: 2nd and 3rd weekend in Dec.*	▲ 216
GRAMPIAN TRANSPORT MUSEUM Tel. (019755) 622 92	*Open Apr.–Oct.: daily 10am–5pm.*	▲ 216
ALLOWAY		◆ D A4
BURNS NATIONAL HERITAGE PARK Tel. (01292) 443 700 *1¾ miles south of Ayr (B7024)*	*Open Apr.–Oct.: daily 9am–6pm; Nov.–Mar.: daily 9am–5pm.*	▲ 148

ANSTRUTHER		◆ D D3
ANSTRUTHER PLEASURE TRIPS TO THE ISLE OF MAY The Harbour Tel. (01333) 310 103	*Boats trips to the bird sanctuary May–Sept.: telephone for schedule.*	▲ 176
SCOTTISH FISHERIES MUSEUM (AND TOURIST INFORMATION CENTRE) Harbourhead Tel. (01333) 310 628	*Open Apr.–Oct.: Mon.–Sat. 10am–5.30pm, Sun. 11am–5.30pm; Nov.–Mar.: Mon.–Sat. 10am–4.30pm, Sun. noon–4.30pm. Closed Jan. 1 and Dec. 25*	▲ 176

ARBROATH		◆ D D2
ARBROATH ABBEY Tel. (01241) 878 756	*Open Apr.–Sept.: Mon.–Sat. 9.30am–6.30pm, Sun. 2–6.30pm; Oct.–Mar.: Mon.–Sat. 9.30am–4.30pm (except Thur. pm, Fri. and Sun. am).*	▲ 185
ARBROATH MUSEUM Signal Tower Tel. (01241) 875 598	*Open all year except Jan. 1–2 and Dec.: 25–26 Mon.–Sat. 10am–5pm; also Sun. July–Aug.: 2–5pm. Admission free.*	▲ 186
ST VIGEANS' SCULPTURED STONES Tel. (0131) 668 8800 *1 mile north of Arbroath*	*Open in summer. Unrestricted access.*	▲ 185

ARDKINGLAS WOODLAND GARDEN		◆ D A3
Tel. (01499) 600 263 *A83, 8 miles north of Inveraray*	*Open daily*	▲ 190

ARDUAINE GARDENS		◆ C C3
Tel. (01852) 200 366 *20 miles south of Oban (A816)*	*Open daily 9.30am–dusk.*	▲ 194

ARRAN (ISLE OF)		◆ C C4 D A4
BRODICK CASTLE Tel. (01770) 302 202 *2 miles north of Brodick*	*Open Apr.–Oct.: daily 11am–4pm; Nov.–Dec.: Fri.–Sun. 11am–3pm.*	▲ 201
HERITAGE CENTRE Tel. (01770) 302 140 *2 miles north of Brodick*	*Open 2 Apr.–Oct.: daily 10.30am–4.30pm.*	▲ 201

AUCHINDRAIN		◆ D A3
OPEN AIR MUSEUM Tel. (01499) 500 235 *6 miles southeast of Inveraray (A83)*	*Open Apr.–Sept.: daily 10am–5pm.*	▲ 195

AYR		◆ D A4
TOURIST INFORMATION CENTRE Burns House, Burns Statue Sq. Tel. (01292) 288 688		
AULD KIRK Tel. (01292) 262 580	*Open for services and ceremonies, or by appt.*	▲ 148

BALLINDALLOCH		◆ A F6
GLENFARCLAS DISTILLERY Tel. (01807) 500 245	*Open Apr.–Sept.: Mon.–Sat. 9.30am–5pm, Sun. 12.30–4.30pm; Oct.–Mar.: Mon.–Fri. 10am–4pm.*	▲ 220
GLENLIVET DISTILLERY Tel. (0154) 278 3220	*Open Mar.–Oct.: Mon.–Sat. 10am–4pm; Sun. 12.30–4pm (July–Aug.: closed daily at 6pm.)*	▲ 220

BALMORAL		◆ D C1
BALMORAL CASTLE Tel. (013397) 423 3415 *8 miles west of Ballater (A93)*	*Open Apr.–May: Mon.–Sat. 10am–5pm; June–July: daily 10am–5pm.*	▲ 214
ROYAL LOCHNAGAR DISTILLERY Crathie Ballater Tel. (013397) 42 273	*Open Easter–Oct.: Mon.–Sat. 10am–5pm, Sun. noon–4pm; Nov.–Easter: Mon.–Fri. 10am–5pm.*	▲ 215

BANCHORY		◆ D D1
BANCHORY MUSEUM Bridge St Tel. (01330) 823 367	*Open June–Sept.: Mon.–Sat. 10am–1pm and 2–5.30pm, Sun. 2–6pm; Easter, May and Oct.: Sat.–Sun. and public holidays only. Admission free.*	▲ 214

BANFF		◆ B A5
DUFF HOUSE ★ Tel. (01261) 818 181	*Open Apr.–Sept.: daily 11am–5pm; Oct.–Mar.: Thur.–Sun. 11am–4pm.*	▲ 219

BARCALDINE CASTLE	◆ C C2	
Tel. (01631) 720 598 *Ledaig, 9 miles north of Oban* *(A85)*	*Open May–Sept.: daily 11am–5.30pm.*	▲ 198

BETTYHILL	◆ A E3	
STRATHNAVER MUSEUM Clachan Tel. (01641) 521 418	*Open Apr.–Oct.: Mon.–Sat. 10am–1pm and 2–5pm.* *Shorter opening times in winter.*	▲ 245

BLACKNESS CASTLE	◆ D B3	
Tel. (01506) 834 807 *4 miles northeast of Linlithgow*	*Open summer: daily 9.30am–6pm; winter: daily* *9.30am–4pm, except Thur. pm and Fri.*	▲ 129

BLAIR CASTLE ★	◆ D B1	
Blair Atholl Tel. (01796) 481 207 *7 miles north of Pitlochry (A9)*	*Open from 1 Apr. (or Good Friday if earlier)* *to last Fri. in Oct.: daily 10am–6pm.*	▲ 183

BLANTYRE	◆ D B4	
DAVID LIVINGSTONE'S MUSEUM 165 Station Rd Tel. (01698) 823 140	*Reopened after renovation work.* *From 26 May 2000: Mon.–Sat. 9.30am–5.30pm,* *Sun. 2.30–4.30pm.*	▲ 164

BONAWE IRON FURNACE	◆ C C2	
Tel. (01866) 822 432 *12 miles east of Oban (A85)*	*Smelting furnace. Open Apr.–Sept.: Mon.–Sat.* *9.30am–6.30pm, Sun. 2–6.30pm.*	▲ 198

BOTHWELL CASTLE	◆ D B4	
Tel. (01698) 816 894 *Uddington, 7 miles southeast* *of Glasgow (B7071)*	*Open Apr.–Sept.: Mon.–Sat. 9.30am–6.30pm,* *Sun. 2–6.30pm; Oct.–Mar.: Mon.–Sat. (except Thur.* *pm and Fri.) 9.30am–6.30pm, Sun. 2–4.30pm.*	▲ 165

BOWHILL	◆ D C4	
BOWHILL HOUSE AND COUNTRY PARK Tel. (01750) 22 204	*Park open end Apr.–Aug.: daily (except Fri.)* *noon–5pm; house and park July 1–31 1–4.30pm.* *Open all year for groups, by appt.*	▲ 139

BRAEMAR	◆ D C1	
BRAEMAR CASTLE Tel. (013397) 41 219 *On the A93, northeast of Braemar*	*Open Easter–Oct.: daily (except Fri.) 10am–6pm.*	▲ 215
BRAEMAR HIGHLAND **HERITAGE CENTRE** The Mews, Mar Rd Tel. (013397) 41 944	*Open Nov.–Mar.: daily (except Fri.) 9am–5pm;* *Apr.–Oct.: daily 9am–6pm.* *Admission free.*	

BRECHIN	◆ D D1	
PICTAVIA Brechin Castle Centre, Haugh Murr Tel. (01356) 626 241	*Open Apr.–Sept.: Mon.–Sat. 9am–6pm,* *Sun. 10am–6pm.*	▲ 186

BRODIE CASTLE	◆ A E6	
Tel. (01309) 641 371 *4 miles west of Forres (A96)*	*Open Apr.–Oct.: Mon.–Sat. 11am–5.30pm,* *Sun. 1.30–5.30pm (Oct.: Sat.–Sun. only).*	▲ 224

BUCKIE	◆ A F5	
BUCKIE DRIFTER Freuchny Rd Tel. (01542) 834 646	*Open Apr.–Oct.: Mon.–Sat. 10am–6pm,* *Sun. noon–6pm.*	▲ 219

BURGHEAD	◆ A E5	
LIBRARY 16 Grand St. Tel. (01343) 830 186	*Open Tue. and Fri. 2–5pm, Thur. 5–8pm,* *Sat. 10am–noon.*	▲ 224

BUTE	◆ C C3-C4 D A3-A4	
ARDENCRAIG GARDENS Ardencraig Lane, Rothesay Tel. (01700) 504 644	*Open Easter–Sept. Mon., Wed. and Fri.–Sun.:* *castle 11am–4.30pm;* *gardens 10am–5pm.*	▲ 200

BUTE MUSEUM Stuart St, Rothesay Tel. (01700) 505 067	*Open Apr.–Sept.: Mon.–Sat. 10.30am–4.30pm,* *Sun. 2.30–4.30pm; Oct.–Mar.: Tue.–Sat.* *2.30–4.30pm.*	▲ 200
MOUNT STUART HOUSE AND GARDENS Tel. (01700) 503 877 *5 miles south of Rothesay*	*Open daily 10am–4pm.*	▲ 200
ROTHESAY CASTLE Rothesay Tel. (01700) 502 691	*Open Apr.–Oct.: daily 9.30am–6.30pm;* *Nov.–Mar.: Mon.–Thur. noon and Sat.* *9.30am–6.30pm, Sun. 2–4.30pm.*	▲ 200
ROTHESAY CREAMERY Town Head, Rothesay Tel. (01700) 503 186	*Open May–Sept.: Mon.–Fri. 8am–4.30pm,* *Sat.–Sun. 1–4.30pm.*	▲ 200

CAERLAVEROCK		◆ **D** B6
CAERLAVEROCK CASTLE ★ Tel. (01387) 770 244 *10½ miles south of Dumfries*	*Open Apr.–Sept.: daily 9.30am–6.30pm;* *Oct.–Mar.: Mon.–Sat. 9.30am–4.30pm,* *Sun. 2–4.30pm.*	▲ 141
CAERLAVEROCK WILDFOWL **AND WETLANDS CENTRE** Tel. (01387) 770 200	*Open daily 10am–5pm.*	▲ 141

CAIRNPAPPLE HILL		◆ **D** B3
Tel. (01506) 634 622 *Near Torphichen (B792)*	*Open Apr.–Sept.: daily 9.30am–6.30pm.*	▲ 130

CALLANDER		◆ **D** B3
ROB ROY AND TROSSACHS **VISITOR CENTRE** Ancaster Square Tel. (01877) 330 342	*Open Mar.–May and Oct.–Dec.: 10am–5pm;* *June–Sept.: 9.30am–6pm; July–Aug.: 9am–10pm;* *Jan.–Feb.: Sat.–Sun. 10am–5pm.*	▲ 172

CAMPBELTOWN		◆ **C** C4
HERITAGE CENTRE Big Kiln Tel. (01586) 551 400	*Open Easter–Sept.: Mon.–Sat. 10am–5pm,* *Sun 2–5pm.*	▲ 192

CARDHU DISTILLERY VISITOR CENTRE		◆ **A** F5
Knockando Tel. (01340) 872 555	*Open Mar.–Nov.: Mon.–Fri. 9.30am–4.30pm* *(July–Sept.: daily); Dec.–Feb.: Mon.–Fri. 10am–4pm.*	▲ 220

CARRBRIDGE		◆ **A** E6
LANDMARK HIGHLAND HERITAGE **CENTRE AND ADVENTURE PARK** Tel. (01479) 841 613 *On the B9153*	*Open daily July–Aug.: 10am–7pm; Apr.–June,* *Sept.–Nov.: 10am–6pm; Dec.–Mar.: 10am–5pm.*	▲ 233

CASTLE CAMPBELL		◆ **D** B3
Dollar Glen, Dollar Tel. (01259) 742 408	*Open Apr.–Sept.: Mon.–Sat. 9.30am–6.30pm,* *Sun. 2–6.30pm; Oct.–Mar.: Mon.–Sat. (except Tue.* *pm and Fri.) 9.30am–6.30pm, Sun. 2–4.30pm.*	▲ 171

CASTLE DOUGLAS		◆ **D** B6
THREAVE CASTLE Tel. (0131) 668 8800 *3 miles west of Castle Douglas* *(A75)*	*Open Apr.–Sept.: Mon.–Sat. 9.30am–6.30pm,* *Sun. 2–6.30pm.*	▲ 145

CASTLE FRASER		◆ **B** A6
Sauchen Tel. (01330) 833 463 *15½ miles west of Aberdeen (A944)*	*Open Easter, May and Sept.: daily 1.30–5.30pm;* *June–Aug.: daily 11am–5.30pm. Gardens open all* *year, daily 9.30am–dusk.*	▲ 215

CASTLE KENNEDY GARDENS		◆ **D** A6
Stair Estate Tel. (01776) 702 024 *5 miles east of Stanraer (A75*	*Open Apr.–Sept.: daily 10am–5pm (gardens only,* *castle not open to the public).*	▲ 146

CAWDOR		◆ **A** E6
CASTLE Tel. (01667) 404 615 *5 miles southwest of Nairn*	*Open May–Oct. 8: daily 10am–5pm.*	▲ 231

PLACES TO VISIT ◆

CERES ◆ D C2-C3

FIFE FOLK MUSEUM
The Weigh House, High St
Tel. (01334) 828 180

Open end Apr.–Oct.: daily 2–5pm. ▲ 178

COLDSTREAM ◆ D D4

COLDSTREAM MUSEUM
12 Market Square
Tel. (01470) 521 296

Open Apr.–Oct.: daily 10am–6pm. ▲ 135

CORGARFF CASTLE ◆ A F6 D C1

Tel. (01975) 651 460
15½ miles north of Ballater
(A939)

Open Apr.–Sept.: daily 9.30am–6.30pm; Oct.–Dec.: daily 9.30am–4.30pm (except Thur. pm, Fri. and Sun. am); Dec.–Mar.: Sat. and Sun. am. ▲ 217

CRAIGELLACHIE ◆ A F6

SPEYSIDE COOPERAGE VISITOR CENTRE
Tel. (01340) 871 108

Open all year (except 2 weeks at Christmas): Mon.–Fri. 9.30am–4.30pm; June–Sept.: Sat. 9.30am–4pm. ▲ 223

CRAIGIEVAR CASTLE ◆ A F6

Tel. (013398) 83 635
6 miles south of Alford

Open May–Sept.: daily 12.45–4.45pm. ▲ 216

CRAIGMILLAR CASTLE ◆ D C3

Craigmillar Castle Rd
Tel. (0131) 661 4445
Outskirts of Edinburgh

Open Apr.–Sept.: daily 9.30am–6.30pm; Oct.–Mar.: Mon.–Sat. 9.30am–4.30pm, Sun. 2–4.30pm (closed Tue. pm, Fri. and Sun. am in winter). ▲ 130

CRAIGNETHAN CASTLE ◆ D B4

Tel. (01555) 860 364
5 miles northwest of Lanark

Open Mar.–Oct.: Mon.–Sat. 9.30am–6.30pm, Sun. 2–6.30pm; Mar., Oct.: closed Thur. pm and Fri. ▲ 165

CRARAE WOODLAND GARDEN ◆ C C3

Tel. (01546) 886 388
10 miles south of Inveraray (A83)

Open daily in summer: 9am–6pm; winter: daylight hours. ▲ 194

CRATHES CASTLE ★ ◆ D D1

Tel. (01330) 844 525
3 miles east of Banchory (A93)

Open Apr.–Oct.: daily 11.30am–5.30pm. Gardens open all year, 9am to dusk. ▲ 214

CRICHTON ◆ D C4

CRICHTON CASTLE
Tel. (01875) 320 017

Open Apr.–Sept.: daily 9.30am–6.30pm. ▲ 131

CRIEFF ◆ D B2

DRUMMOND CASTLE
Estate Office, Muthill
Tel. (01764) 681 257

Open Easter, May–Oct.: daily 2–6pm. Grounds only. ▲ 180

GLENTURRET DISTILLERY
The Hosh
Tel. (01764) 656 565

Open Feb.–Dec.: Mon.–Sat. 9.30am–6pm, Sun. noon–6pm; Jan.: Mon.–Fri. 11.30am–4pm (last visitors admitted 1½ hours before closing). ▲ 180

TULLIBARDINE CHAPEL
Tel. (0131) 668 8800
6 miles southeast of Crieff (A823)

Open May–Sept. (ask at the nearby farm). Admission free. ▲ 180

CROMARTY ★ ◆ A E5

COURTHOUSE MUSEUM
Church St
Tel. (01381) 600 418

Open daily Apr.–Oct.: 10am–5pm; Nov.–Mar.: noon–4pm. ▲ 247

HUGH MILLER'S COTTAGE
Church St.
Tel. (01381) 600 245

Open May–Sept.: Mon.–Sat. 11am–1pm and 2–5pm, Sun. 2–5pm. ▲ 247

CRUACHAN POWER STATION ◆ D A2

Tel. (01866) 822 618
Dalmally, 18½ miles east of Oban

Hydroelectric power station. Open Easter–Nov. daily 9.30am–5pm. ▲ 198

CULLEN ◆ A F5

CULLEN AULD KIRK
Tel. (01261) 812 4189 (OT de Banff)

Open June–Sept. ▲ 219

◆ PLACES TO VISIT

CULLODEN MOOR		◆ A E6
VISITOR CENTRE Tel. (01463) 790 607	*Open daily Apr.–Oct.: 9am–6pm;* *Nov.–Mar.: 10am–4pm.*	▲ 231
CULROSS ★		◆ D B3
CULROSS ABBEY Tel. (0131) 668 8800	*Open Apr.–Sept.: daily 9.30am–6pm.* *Admission free.*	▲ 175
CULROSS PALACE West Green House Tel. (01383) 880 359	*Open Apr.–Sept.: daily 11am–5pm* *(June–Aug.: daily 10am–5pm).*	▲ 175
CULZEAN CASTLE ★		◆ D A5
Tel. (01655) 884 455 *7½ miles south of Ayr (A719)*	*Open Apr.–Oct.: daily 10.30am–5pm.* *Park open all year, daily 9am to dusk.*	▲ 147
CUPAR		◆ D C2
HILL OF TARVIT MANSION Tel. (01334) 653 127 *Via the A916*	*Open Easter–Sept.: daily 1.30–5.30pm (July–Aug.:* *11am–5pm); Oct.: Sat.–Sun. 1.30–5.30pm;* *gardens: daily 9.30am–dusk.*	▲ 178
SCOTSTARVIT TOWER Tel. (0131) 668 8800 *Via the A916*	*Open in summer.* *The key is held at Hill of Tarvit Mansion.* *Admission free.*	▲ 178
DALWHINNIE		◆ D B1
DALWHINNIE DISTILLERY Dalwhinnie Tel. (01528) 522 208	*Open Mar.–Dec.: Mon.–Fri. 9.30am–4.30pm;* *June–Oct.: Mon.–Sat. 9.30am–4.30pm;* *July–Aug.: Mon.–Sun. 9.30am–4.30pm.*	▲ 221
DIRLETON		◆ D C3
DIRLETON CASTLE AND GARDEN Tel. (01620) 850 330	*Open Apr.–Sept.: daily 9.30am–6.30pm; Oct.– Mar.:* *Mon.–Sat. 9.30am–4.30pm, Sun. 2–4.30pm.*	▲ 132
DOUNE		◆ D B3
DOUNE CASTLE Tel. (01786) 841 742 *Just outside Doune on the A84*	*Open all year: Mon.–Sat. 9.30am–6pm,* *Sun. 2–6.30pm (Oct.–Mar.: closes at 4pm,* *closed Thur. pm and Fri.).*	▲ 171
DRUM CASTLE		◆ D D1
Drumoak Tel. (01330) 811 204 *10 miles west of Aberdeen* *(A93)*	*Open Easter, May and Sept.: daily 1.30–5.30pm;* *June–Aug.: daily 11am–5.30pm; Oct.: Sat.–Sun.* *1.30–5.30pm.* *Gardens open all year 9.30am–dusk.*	▲ 213
DRUMLANRIG CASTLE		◆ D B5
Thornhill Tel. (01848) 330 248	*Open in summer: Mon.–Sat. 11am–4pm,* *Sun. noon–4pm.*	▲ 140
DRUMNADROCHIT		◆ A D6
THE OFFICIAL LOCH NESS MONSTER **EXHIBITION CENTRE** The Drumnadrochit Hotel Tel. (01456) 450 573	*Open Easter–May: 9.30am–5.30pm;* *June and Sept. 9am–6.30pm; Oct.: 9.30am–6pm;* *Nov.–Apr.: 10am–4pm.*	▲ 240
DRYBURGH		◆ D C4
DRYBURGH ABBEY Tel. (01835) 822 381 *5 miles southeast of Melrose (B6404)*	*Open Apr.–Sept.: Mon.–Sat. 9.30am–6.30pm;* *Oct.–Mar.: Mon.–Sat. 9.30am–4.30pm,* *Sun. 2–4.30pm.*	▲ 136
DUFFTOWN		◆ A F6
GLENFIDDICH DISTILLERY Tel. (01340) 820 373	*Open all year (except 2 weeks at Christmas): Mon.–* *Fri.: 9.30am–4.30pm; Easter–mid-Oct.: Sat. 9.30am–* *4.30pm, Sun. noon–4.30pm. Admission free.*	▲ 223
DUMBARTON		◆ D A3
DUMBARTON CASTLE Tel. (01389) 732 167	*Open Apr.–Sept.: daily 9.30am–6.30pm; Oct.– Mar.:* *9.30am–4.30pm, closed Thur. pm and Fri.*	▲ 189
DUMFRIES		◆ D B5
BURNS HOUSE Burns St Tel. (01387) 255 297	*Open Apr.–Sept.: Mon.–Sat. 10am–5pm, Sun.* *2–5pm; Oct.–Mar.: Tue.–Sat. 10am–1pm and* *2–5pm. Admission free.*	▲ 141

DUMFRIES MUSEUM AND CAMERA OBSCURA The Observatory Tel. (01387) 253 374	*Open Apr.–Sept.: Mon.–Sat. 10am–5pm, Sun. 2–5pm; Oct.–Mar.: Tue.–Sat. 10am–1pm and 2–5pm (Camera Obscura closed). Musem: admission free (except Camera Obscura).*	▲ 141
ELLISLAND FARM Tel. (01387) 74 426 *Holywood, northeast of Dumfries*	*Open Apr.–Sept.: Mon.–Sat. 10am–1pm and 2–5pm, Sun. 2–5pm; Oct.–Mar.: Tue.–Sat. 10am–4pm.*	▲ 141
ROBERT BURNS HERITAGE CENTRE Mill Rd Tel. (01387) 264 808	*Open Tue.–Sat. 10am–1pm and 2–5pm.*	▲ 141

DUNBAR		◆ D D3
DUNBAR TOWN HOUSE MUSEUM High St Tel. (01368) 863 734	*Open Apr.–Oct.: daily 12.30–4.30pm.*	▲ 133

DUNBEATH		◆ A F4
LAIDHAY CROFT MUSEUM Tel. (01593) 731 244 *Laidhay, north of Dunbeath (A9)*	*Open 15 Mar..-15 Nov.: daily 10am–6pm.*	▲ 246

DUNBLANE		◆ D B3
DUNBLANE CATHEDRAL MUSEUM The Cross Tel. (01786) 823 440	*Open May–end Sept.: Mon.–Sat. 10am–12.30pm and 2–4.30pm (in winter by appt.). Admission free.*	▲ 171

DUNDEE		◆ D C2
BROUGHTY FERRY MUSEUM Broughty Ferry Tel. (01382) 436 916	*Open all year: Mon.–Sat. 11am–5pm, Sun. 12.30–4pm; Oct.–Mar.: closed Mon. Closed Jan. 1 and Dec. 25.*	▲ 185
DUNDEE CONTEMPORARY ART CENTRE 152 Nethergate Tel. (01382) 432 000	*Open Tue.–Sun. 10.30am–5.30pm (Thur.–Fri. 8pm). Closed Mon.*	▲ 185
MCMANUS GALLERIES Albert Square Tel. (01382) 432 084	*Open all year: Mon.–Sat. 10.30am–5pm (Thur. 7pm), Sun. 12.30–4pm. Admission free.*	▲ 185
VERDANT WORKS West Hendersons Wynd Tel. (01382) 225 282	*Open Apr.–Oct.: Mon.–Sat. 10am–5pm, Sun. 11am–5pm; Oct.–Mar.: Mon.–Sat. 10am–4pm, Sun. 11am–4pm. Closed Jan. 1 and Dec. 25.*	▲ 185

DUNDRENNAN		◆ D B6
DUNDRENNAN ABBEY Tel. (01557) 500 262 *Southeast of Kirkcudbright (A711)*	*Open Apr.–Sept.: Mon.–Sun. 9.30am–6.30pm.*	▲ 144

DUNFERMLINE		◆ D C3
ABBOT HOUSE Tel. (01383) 624 908	*Open 10am–5pm. Closed Jan. 1 and Dec. 25*	▲ 175
ABBOT HOUSE HERITAGE CENTRE Maygate Tel. (01383) 733 266	*Open all year: daily 10am–5pm. Admission free.*	
ANDREW CARNEGIE MUSEUM Moodie St Tel. (01383) 724 302	*Open Apr.–Oct.: Mon.–Sat. 11am–5pm, Sun. 2–5pm; June–Aug.: 10am–5pm. Closed Nov.–Mar.*	▲ 175
DUNFERMLINE ABBEY AND PALACE Monastery St Tel. (01383) 739 026	*Open all year: Mon.–Sat. 9.30am–6.30pm, Sun. 2–6.30pm (Oct.–Mar. 4.30pm). Closed Tue. pm and Fri.*	▲ 174
DUNFERMLINE MUSEUM AND SMALL GALLERY Viewfield Terrace Tel. (01383) 313 838	*Open only by appt.*	▲ 175
PITTENCRIEFF HOUSE MUSEUM Pittencrieff Park Tel. (01383) 722 935	*Open all year: daily 11am–5pm. Admission free.*	▲ 175

DUNKELD		◆ D B2
DUNKELD CATHEDRAL Tel. (01350) 727 601	*Open Mon.–Sat. 9.30am–6.30pm, Sun. 2–6.30pm (Oct.–Mar.: closes daily at 4.30pm)*	▲ 181
THE HERMITAGE Tel. (01796) 473 233 *1½ miles west of Dunkeld (A9)*	*Open all year. Unrestricted access.*	▲ 182

LOCH OF LOWES **WILDLIFE RESERVE** Tel. (01350) 727 337	*Open Apr.–Sept.: 10am–5pm.*	▲ *183*
DUNROBIN CASTLE		◆ **A** E5
Golspie Tel. (01408) 633 268	*Open Apr.–Oct.: Mon.–Sat. 10.30am–4.30pm, Sun.* *noon–4.30pm; June–Sept.: daily 10.30am–5.30pm.*	▲ *247*
DUNS		◆ **D** D4
JIM CLARK MEMORIAL ROOM 44 Newtown St Tel. (01361) 883 960	*Open Easter–Sept.: Mon.–Sat. 10am–1pm and* *2–4pm, Sun. 2–4pm; Oct.: Mon.–Sat. 1–4pm.*	▲ *135*
DUNSTAFFNAGE CASTLE AND CHAPEL		◆ **C** C2
Tel. (01631) 562 465 *3 miles north of Oban (A85)*	*Open Apr.–Oct.: daily 9am–6pm;* *Nov.–Mar.: Mon.–Fri. 9am–4pm.*	▲ *194*
EAST LINTON		◆ **D** D3
HAILES CASTLE Tel. (0131) 668 8800	*Open all year.* *Admission free.*	▲ *133*
PRESTON MILL **AND PHANTASSIE DOOCOT** Tel. (01620) 860426	*Open Easter and May–Sept.: Mon.–Sat.* *11am–1pm and 2–5pm; Oct.: Sat.–Sun. 1.30–4pm.*	▲ *133*
EDINBURGH		◆ **D** C3 **E**
EDINBURGH AND SCOTLAND **INFORMATION CENTRE** 3 Princes St Tel. (0131) 473 3800		◆ **E** D2
ASSEMBLY HALL 54 George St Tel. (0131) 220 4348	*Telephone for public opening times.*	◆ **E** C4 ▲ *117*
CAMERA OBSCURA Castlehill, Royal Mile Tel. (0131) 226 37 09	*Open Apr.–Oct.: Mon.–Fri. 9.30am–6pm, Sat.–Sun.* *10am–6pm; Nov.–Mar.: daily 10am–5pm.* *Guided tours every 15 minutes.*	◆ **E** C4 ▲ *117*
CITY OBSERVATORY Calton Hill 7 Tel. (0131) 556 4365	*Open Fri. 8–10pm;* *frequent events, telephone for details.*	◆ **E** F2 ▲ *127*
DYNAMIC EARTH Holyrood Rd Tel. (0131) 550 7800	*Open Apr.–Oct.: daily 10am–6pm; Nov.–Mar.:* *Wed.–Sat.10am–5pm. Closed Dec. 24–25.*	▲ *122*
EDINBURGH CASTLE ✪ Castlehill Tel. (0131) 225 9846	*Open daily throughout the year:* *Apr.–Sept.: 9.30am–6pm; Oct.–Mar. 9.30am–5pm.* *Closed Dec. 25–26, Jan. 1 (times subject to change).*	◆ **E** B4 ▲ *116*
GENERAL REGISTER HOUSE 2 Princes St Tel. (0131) 535 1354	*Open Mon.–Fri. 9am–4.30pm.* *Admission free.*	◆ **E** D2-E2 ▲ *124*
GEORGE HERIOT'S SCHOOL Lauriston Place Tel. (0131) 229 7263	*Open during the summer, guided tours by* *students; in winter, telephone to ask about visits.* *Admission free.*	◆ **E** C5 ▲ *123*
GEORGIAN HOUSE ✪ 7 Charlotte Square Tel. (0131) 226 3318	*Open Apr. (or Good Friday if earlier)–Oct.:* *Mon.–Sat. 10am–5pm, Sun. 2–5pm.*	◆ **E** A3 ▲ *124*
GLADSTONE'S LAND 477b Lawnmarket Tel. (0131) 226 5856	*Open Apr. 1 (or Good Friday if earlier)–Oct. 31:* *Mon.–Sat. 10am–5pm, Sun. 2–5pm.*	◆ **E** D4 ▲ *118*
GREYFRIARS KIRK AND KIRKYARD Greyfriars Place Tel. (0131) 226 5429	*Open Apr.–Oct.: Mon.–Fri. 10.30am–4.30pm,* *Sat. 10.30am–2.30pm (in winter, Thur.* *1.30–3.30pm).*	◆ **E** D5 ▲ *123*
THE HUB Castlehill, Royal Mile Tel. (0131) 473 2000	*Open daily 9.30am–5.30pm.*	◆ **E** C4 ▲ *117*
HUNTLY HOUSE MUSEUM 142 Canongate, Royal Mile Tel. (0131) 529 4143	*Open Mon.–Sat. 10am–5pm, Sun. during the* *festival 2–5pm. Closed Jan. 1–2 and Dec. 25–26*	◆ **E** F3 ▲ *120*
JOHN KNOX HOUSE 43–45 High St Tel. (0131) 556 9579/2647	*Open Mon.–Sat. 10am–4.30pm.* *Closed Jan. 1 and Dec. 25*	◆ **E** E3 ▲ *119*
MAGDALEN CHAPEL 41 Cowgate Tel. (0131) 220 1450	*Open all year: Mon.–Fri. 9.30am–4pm.* *Admission free.*	◆ **E** D4 ▲ *123*

MUSEUM OF CHILDHOOD 42 High St, Royal Mile Tel. (0131) 529 4142	*Open Mon.–Sat. 10am–5pm, Sun. during the* *festival 2–5pm. Closed Jan. 1 and Dec. 25.* *Admission free.*	◆ E E4 ▲ 119
NATIONAL GALLERY OF SCOTLAND ✪ The Mound Tel. (0131) 624 6200	*Open Mon.–Sat. 10am–5pm, Sun. 2–5pm.* *Admission free.*	◆ E E3 ▲ 125
NATIONAL LIBRARY OF SCOTLAND George IV Bridge Tel. (0131) 226 4531	*Open Mon.–Fri. 9.30am–8.30pm (except Wed.* *10am–8.30pm), Sat. 9.30am–1pm. Closed Sun.* *Admission free.*	◆ E D4 ▲ 122
NELSON MONUMENT Calton Hill Tel. (0131) 556 2716	*Open Apr.–Sept.: Mon. 1–6pm, Tue.–Sat.* *10am–6pm; Oct.–Mar.: Mon.–Sat. 10am–3pm.*	◆ E F2 ▲ 127
PALACE OF HOLYROODHOUSE ✪ Holyrood Rd Tel. (0131) 556 7371	*Open daily (except Apr. 2, May 16–27, June 24–July* *8, Dec. 25–26 and when the Queen is in residence);* *Nov.–Mar. 9.30am–4.30pm; Apr.–Oct. 9.30am–6pm.*	▲ 121
PARLIAMENT HOUSE Parliament Square Tel. (0131) 225 2595	*Open Tue.–Fri. 9am–5pm.* *Admission free.*	◆ E D4 ▲ 119
PEOPLE'S STORY MUSEUM 163 Canongate Tel. (0131) 529 4057	*Open during exhibitions: Tue.–Sat. noon–5.30pm.*	◆ E F3 ▲ 120
ROYAL BOTANIC GARDEN ★ 20A Inverleith Row Tel. (0131) 552 7171	*Open daily except Jan. 1 and Dec. 25: Nov.–Feb.* *10am–4pm; Mar.–Apr. and Sept.–Oct. 10am–6pm;* *May–Aug. 10am–8pm. Admission free.*	▲ 126
ROYAL MUSEUM AND **MUSEUM OF SCOTLAND** ✪ Chambers St Tel. (0131) 247 4422	*Open Mon.–Sat. 10am–5pm (except Tue. 8pm),* *Sun. noon–5pm. Closed Dec. 25.*	◆ E D5 ▲ 123
ROYAL OBSERVATORY VISITOR CENTRE Blackford Hill Tel. (0131) 668 8405	*Open Mon.–Sat. 10am–5pm, Sun. noon–5pm.*	▲ 127
ROYAL SCOTTISH ACADEMY The Mound Tel. (0131) 225 6671	*Open during exhibitions: Mon.–Sat. 10am–5pm,* *Sun. 2–5pm.* *Admission free for children and students.*	◆ E C3 ▲ 125
ST CECILIA'S HALL Cowgate Tel. (0131) 650 2805	*Open Wed. and Sat. 2–5pm, Mon.–Sat.* *10.30am–12.30pm during the festival.* *May be closed during the school holidays.*	◆ E E4 ▲ 123
ST GILES' CATHEDRAL ✪ Royal Mile Tel. (0131) 225 9442	*Open Mon.–Sat. 9am–5pm (later in summer),* *Sun. 1–5pm.* *Admission free.*	◆ E D4 ▲ 118
SCOTCH WHISKY HERITAGE CENTRE 354 Castlehill, Royal Mile Tel. (0131) 220 0441	*Open daily 10am–5.30pm (later in summer).* *Closed Dec. 25.*	◆ E C4 ▲ 117
SCOTTISH NATIONAL GALLERY **OF MODERN ART AND DEAN GALLERY** 72 Belford Rd Tel. (0131) 624 6200	*Open Mon.–Sat. 10am–5pm, Sun. noon–5pm.* *Admission free, except during major exhibitions.*	▲ 126
SCOTTISH NATIONAL PORTRAIT GALLERY 1 Queen St Tel. (0131) 624 6332	*Open Mon.–Sat. 10am–5pm, Sun. noon–5pm.* *Admission free.*	◆ E D1 ▲ 126
SCOTT MONUMENT East Princes St Gardens Tel. (0131) 529 4068	*Open Mar.–May: Mon.–Sat. 10am–6pm;* *June–Sept.: Mon.–Sat. 9am–8pm, Sun. 10am–6pm;* *Oct.: daily 10am–6pm; Nov.–Feb.: daily 10am–4pm.*	◆ E D3 ▲ 124
TALBOT RICE ART GALLERY Old College, South Bridge Tel. (0131) 650 2210	*Open Tue.–Sat. 10am–5pm.*	◆ E E4-E5 ▲ 122
TRON KIRK 122 High St, Royal Mile Tel. (0131) 225 1637	*Open Apr.–mid-June: Thur.–Mon. 10am–5pm;* *June–Sept.: daily times to be confirmed.*	◆ E E4 ▲ 119
WRITERS' MUSEUM Lady Stair's Close, Lawnmarket Tel. (0131) 529 4901	*Open Mon.–Sat. 10am–5pm, Sun. during the* *festival 2–5pm.* *Admission free.*	◆ E D4 ▲ 118

EDZELL CASTLE AND GARDEN		◆ D D1
Tel. (01356) 648 631 *Edzell, 6 miles north of Brechin*	*Open Apr.–Sept.: daily 9.30am–6pm; Oct.–Mar.:* *Mon.–Sat. 9.30am–4pm (except Fri.), Sun. 2–4pm.*	▲ 213

EILEAN DONAN CASTLE ★		◆ A C6
Kyle, Wester Tel. (01599) 555 202	*Open Easter–Oct. 10am–5.30pm;* *Nov.–Easter: 10am–3pm.*	▲ 239

◆ PLACES TO VISIT

ELGIN		◆ A F5
ELGIN CATHEDRAL King's St	*Open Apr.–Oct.: 9.30am–6pm (Sat.–Sun. 4.30pm). Closed Thur. pm, Fri. and Sun. am.*	▲ 223
PLUSCARDEN ABBEY Tel. (01343) 890 257 *6 miles southwest of Elgin (B9010)*	*Open 4.45am–8.45pm. Admission free.*	▲ 224
ST GILES' CHURCH High St Tel. (01646) 547 208	*Open all year during services (Sat.–Sun.); July–Aug.: daily 10am–4pm.*	▲ 223

EYEMOUTH		◆ D D3
AYTON CASTLE Tel. (018907) 81212	*Open May–Sept.: Sun. 2–5pm, other days by appt.*	▲ 135
EYEMOUTH MUSEUM Old Kirk, Manse Rd Tel. (018907) 50678	*Open Apr.–June and Sept.: Mon.–Sat. 10am–5pm, Sun. 2–4pm; July–Aug.: Mon.–Sat. 10am–6pm, Sun. 11am–4pm; Oct.: Mon.–Sat. 10am–4.30pm.*	▲ 134

FALKLAND		◆ D C3
PALACE, GARDEN AND OLD BURGH Tel. (01337) 857 397	*Open Apr.–Oct.: Mon.–Sat. 11am–5.30pm, Sun. 1.30–5.30pm. Groups by appt. throughout the year.*	▲ 178

FETTERCAIRN		◆ D D1
FASQUE Tel. (01561) 340 569 *½ mile north of Fettercairn*	*Open May–Sept.: daily 11am–5.30pm.*	▲ 213
FETTERCAIRN DISTILLERY Distillery Rd Tel. (01561) 340 205	*Open May–Sept.: Mon.–Sat. 10am–4.30pm. Admission free.*	▲ 213

FINDHORN		◆ A E5
FINDHORN FOUNDATION Tel. (01309) 690 310	*Open Mon.–Sat. 9am–noon and 2–5pm, Sun. 2–5pm. Admission free.*	▲ 224
HERITAGE CENTRE Tel. (01309) 691 659	*Open May and Sept.: Sat.–Sun. 4.30–5.30pm; June–Aug.: Wed.–Mon. 4.30–5.30pm.*	▲ 224

FORRES		◆ A E5
DALLAS DHU HISTORIC DISTILLERY Manachie Rd Tel. (01309) 676 548	*Open Apr.–Sept.: Mon.–Sun. 9.30am–6.30pm; Oct.–Mar.: Mon.–Wed. and Sat.: 9.30am–4.30pm, Thur. 9.30am–12.30pm, Sun. 2–4.30pm.*	▲ 224
FALCONER MUSEUM Tolbooth St Tel. (01309) 673 701	*Open Apr.–Oct.: Mon.–Sat. 10am–5pm; Nov.–Mar.: Mon.–Thur. 11am–12.30pm and 1–3pm. Admission free.*	▲ 224

FORT GEORGE ★		◆ A E6
Tel. (01667) 462 777 *10½ miles east of Inverness*	*Open Apr.–Sept.: daily 9.30am–6.30pm; Oct.–Mar.: Mon.–Sat. 9.30am–4.30pm, Sun. 2–4.30pm.*	▲ 231

FORT WILLIAM ★		◆ D A1
BEN NEVIS DISTILLERY Lochy Bridge Tel. (01397) 702 476	*Open Sept.–June: Mon.–Fri. 9am–5pm, Sat. 10am–4pm; Easter: Sat. 10am–4pm; July–Aug.: Mon.–Fri. 9am–5.30pm, Sat. 10am–4pm.*	▲ 236
OLD INVERLOCHY CASTLE Tel. (0131) 668 8800	*Currently being restored.*	▲ 236
WEST HIGHLAND MUSEUM Cameron Square Tel. (01397) 702 169	*Open June and Sept.: Mon.–Sat. 10am–5pm; July–Aug.: Mon.–Sat. 10am–5pm, Sun. 2–5pm; Oct.–May: Mon.–Sat. 10am–4pm.*	▲ 236

FRASERBURGH		◆ B A5
FRASERBURGH HERITAGE CENTRE Quarry Rd Tel. (01346) 512 888	*Open Easter–Oct.: Mon.–Sat. 10am–5pm, Sun. 12.30–5pm.*	▲ 218
MUSEUM OF SCOTTISH LIGHTHOUSES Stevenson Rd Tel. (01346) 511 022	*Open Mon.–Sat. 10am–6pm, Sun. noon–6pm (Nov.–Mar.: 4pm).*	▲ 218

FYVIE		◆ B A6
FYVIE CASTLE Tel. (01651) 891 266 *8 miles south of Turriff (A947)*	*Open Apr. and Sept.: daily 1.30–5.30pm; June–Aug.: daily 11am–5.30pm; Oct.: Sat.–Sun. 1.30–5.30pm.*	▲ 217

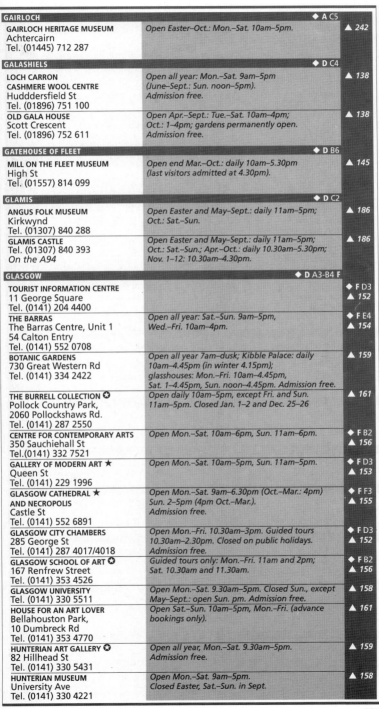

GAIRLOCH		◆ A C5
GAIRLOCH HERITAGE MUSEUM Achtercairn Tel. (01445) 712 287	*Open Easter–Oct.: Mon.–Sat. 10am–5pm.*	▲ 242
GALASHIELS		◆ D C4
LOCH CARRON **CASHMERE WOOL CENTRE** Hudddersfield St Tel. (01896) 751 100	*Open all year: Mon.–Sat. 9am–5pm (June–Sept.: Sun. noon–5pm). Admission free.*	▲ 138
OLD GALA HOUSE Scott Crescent Tel. (01896) 752 611	*Open Apr.–Sept.: Tue.–Sat. 10am–4pm; Oct.: 1–4pm; gardens permanently open. Admission free.*	▲ 138
GATEHOUSE OF FLEET		◆ D B6
MILL ON THE FLEET MUSEUM High St Tel. (01557) 814 099	*Open end Mar.–Oct.: daily 10am–5.30pm (last visitors admitted at 4.30pm).*	▲ 145
GLAMIS		◆ D C2
ANGUS FOLK MUSEUM Kirkwynd Tel. (01307) 840 288	*Open Easter and May–Sept.: daily 11am–5pm; Oct.: Sat.–Sun.*	▲ 186
GLAMIS CASTLE Tel. (01307) 840 393 *On the A94*	*Open Easter and May–Sept.: daily 11am–5pm; Oct.: Sat.–Sun.; Apr.–Oct.: daily 10.30am–5.30pm; Nov. 1–12: 10.30am–4.30pm.*	▲ 186
GLASGOW		◆ D A3-B4 F
TOURIST INFORMATION CENTRE 11 George Square Tel. (0141) 204 4400		◆ F D3 ▲ 152
THE BARRAS The Barras Centre, Unit 1 54 Calton Entry Tel. (0141) 552 0708	*Open all year: Sat.–Sun. 9am–5pm, Wed.–Fri. 10am–4pm.*	◆ F E4 ▲ 154
BOTANIC GARDENS 730 Great Western Rd Tel. (0141) 334 2422	*Open all year 7am–dusk; Kibble Palace: daily 10am–4.45pm (in winter 4.15pm); glasshouses: Mon.–Fri. 10am–4.45pm, Sat. 1–4.45pm, Sun. noon–4.45pm. Admission free.*	▲ 159
THE BURRELL COLLECTION ✪ Pollock Country Park, 2060 Pollockshaws Rd. Tel. (0141) 287 2550	*Open daily 10am–5pm, except Fri. and Sun. 11am–5pm. Closed Jan. 1–2 and Dec. 25–26*	▲ 161
CENTRE FOR CONTEMPORARY ARTS 350 Sauchiehall St Tel.(0141) 332 7521	*Open Mon.–Sat. 10am–6pm, Sun. 11am–6pm.*	◆ F B2 ▲ 156
GALLERY OF MODERN ART ★ Queen St Tel. (0141) 229 1996	*Open Mon.–Sat. 10am–5pm, Sun. 11am–5pm.*	◆ F D3 ▲ 153
GLASGOW CATHEDRAL ★ **AND NECROPOLIS** Castle St Tel. (0141) 552 6891	*Open Mon.–Sat. 9am–6.30pm (Oct.–Mar.: 4pm) Sun. 2–5pm (4pm Oct.–Mar.). Admission free.*	◆ F F3 ▲ 155
GLASGOW CITY CHAMBERS 285 George St Tel. (0141) 287 4017/4018	*Open Mon.–Fri. 10.30am–3pm. Guided tours 10.30am–2.30pm. Closed on public holidays. Admission free.*	◆ F D3 ▲ 152
GLASGOW SCHOOL OF ART ✪ 167 Renfrew Street Tel. (0141) 353 4526	*Guided tours only: Mon.–Fri. 11am and 2pm; Sat. 10.30am and 11.30am.*	◆ F B2 ▲ 156
GLASGOW UNIVERSITY Tel. (0141) 330 5511	*Open Mon.–Sat. 9.30am–5pm. Closed Sun., except May–Sept.: open Sun. pm. Admission free.*	▲ 158
HOUSE FOR AN ART LOVER Bellahouston Park, 10 Dumbreck Rd Tel. (0141) 353 4770	*Open Sat.–Sun. 10am–5pm, Mon.–Fri. (advance bookings only).*	▲ 161
HUNTERIAN ART GALLERY ✪ 82 Hillhead St Tel. (0141) 330 5431	*Open all year, Mon.–Sat. 9.30am–5pm. Admission free.*	▲ 159
HUNTERIAN MUSEUM University Ave Tel. (0141) 330 4221	*Open Mon.–Sat. 9am–5pm. Closed Easter, Sat.–Sun. in Sept.*	▲ 158

◆ PLACES TO VISIT

HUTCHESON'S HALL 158 Ingram St Tel. (0141) 552 8391	*Open Mon.–Sat.10am–5pm.* *Closed during school holidays and Dec. 24–Jan. 6.* *Admission free.*	◆ F D3 ▲ 153
KELVINGROVE MUSEUM AND ART GALLERY ✪ Argyle St Tel. (0141) 330 4221	*Open Mon.–Wed. and Sat. 10am–5pm, Fri. and* *Sun. 11am–5pm.*	▲ 158
THE LIGHTHOUSE 11 Mitchell St Tel. (0141) 221 6362	*Open Mon., Wed., Fri.–Sat., 10.30am–6pm, Tue.* *11am–6pm, Thur. 10.30am–8pm, Sun. noon–5pm.* *Admission free on Tue.*	◆ F C3 ▲ 152
MUSEUM OF TRANSPORT ✪ Kelvin Hall 1 Bunhouse Rd Tel. (0141) 1287 2000	*Open all year: Mon.–Sat. (except Tue.) 10am–5pm,* *Sun. 11am–5pm. Closed Jan. 1 and Dec. 25.* *Admission free.*	▲ 158
PEOPLE'S PALACE Glasgow Green Tel. (0141) 554 0223	*Open all year, Mon.–Sat. (except Tue.) 10am–5pm,* *Sun. 11am–5pm. Closed Jan. 1 and Dec. 25.* *Admission free.*	◆ F E5 ▲ 155
POLLOK HOUSE ★ Pollok Country Park 2060 Pollockshaws Rd Tel. (0141) 616 6410	*House open Apr.–Oct.: daily 10am–5pm;* *Nov.–Mar.: daily 11am–4pm.* *Closed Jan. 1–2 and Dec. 25–26.*	▲ 161
ST MUNGO MUSEUM OF RELIGIOUS LIFE AND ART 2 Castle St Tel. (0141) 553 2557	*Open Mon.–Sat. 10am–5pm, Sun. 11am–5pm.* *Closed Jan. 1 and Dec. 25.* *Admission free.*	◆ F E3 ▲ 155
ST VINCENT STREET CHURCH 265 St Vincent St Tel. (0141) 221 1937	*Open all year. Services Sun. 11am and 4pm.*	◆ F B3 ▲ 155
SCOTLAND STREET SCHOOL MUSEUM OF EDUCATION 225 Scotland St Tel. (0141) 287 0500	*Reopened Aug. 2000; open Mon.–Thur. and Sat.* *10am–5pm, Fri. and Sun. 11am–5pm.*	◆ F A5 ▲ 161

GLENCOE ✪		◆ D A1
GLENCOE AND NORTH LORNE FOLK MUSEUM Tel. (01855) 811 314	*Open Easter and June–Sept.: Mon.–Sat.* *10am–5.30pm.*	▲ 199
VISITOR CENTRE Tel. (01855) 811 307	*Open Mar.–Oct.: daily 10am–4pm.*	▲ 199

GLENFINNAN		◆ C C1
RAILWAY STATION AND MUSEUM Tel. (01397) 722 295	*Open June–Sept. and holidays:* *daily 9.30am–4.30pm.*	▲ 237

GLEN GRANT DISTILLERY AND GARDEN		◆ A F5
Rothes Tel. (01542) 783 318	*Open Mar.–Oct.: Mon.–Sat. 10am–4pm, Sun.* *11.30am–4pm (June–Sept.: closes daily at 5pm.)*	▲ 220

GLENLUCE		◆ D A6
GLENLUCE ABBEY Tel. (01581) 300 541 *2 miles north of Glenluce*	*Open Apr.–Nov.: Mon.–Sat. 9.30am–6.30pm* *(Oct.–Nov. 4.30pm); Dec.–Mar.:* *Sat. 9.30am–4.30pm, Sun. 2–4.30pm.*	▲ 146

GLEN ORD DISTILLERY		◆ A D6
Muir of Ord Tel. (01463) 872 004 *15 miles west of Inverness (A862)*	*Open Mar.–Oct.: Mon.–Fri.: 9.30am–5pm;* *July–Sept.: Sat. 9.30am–5pm, Sun. 12.30–5pm;* *Nov.–Feb.: by appt. Closed 1 Jan. and 25 Dec.*	▲ 221

GRANTOWN-ON-SPEY		◆ A E6
GRANTOWN MUSEUM Burnfield House, Burnfield Ave Tel. (01479) 872 478	*Open Tue.–Sat. 10am–4pm.*	▲ 232

GREAT CUMBRAE		◆ D A4
CATHEDRAL OF THE ISLES	*Open daily 11am–4pm.*	▲ 149

HADDINGTON		◆ D C3
LENNOXLOVE HOUSE Lennoxlove Estate Tel. (01620) 823 720	*Open Easter–Oct.: daily 2–4.30pm.* *Guided tours every half hour.*	▲ 133

ST MARY'S COLLEGIATE CHURCH Sidegate Tel. (01620) 825 111	*Open Apr.–Oct.: Mon.–Sat. 10am–4pm, Sun. 1–4pm.*	▲ 133
HADDO HOUSE ◆ B A6		
Tel. (01651) 851 440 *4 miles north of Pitmedden (B999)*	*Open Easter and May–Sept.: daily 1.30–3.30pm; Oct.: Sat.–Sun. 1.30–4.30pm.*	▲ 217
HELENSBURGH ✳ D A3		
HILL HOUSE ★ Upper Colquhoun St Tel. (01436) 673 900	*Open daily 1.30–5.30pm.*	▲ 189
HELMSDALE ▲ A E4		
TIME SPAN HERITAGE CENTRE Dunrobin St Tel. (01431) 821 327	*Open Apr.–Oct.: Mon.–Sat. 9.30am–5pm, Sun. 2–5pm.*	▲ 247
HOUSE OF THE BINNS ◆ D B3-C3		
Tel. (01506) 834 255 *3 miles east of Linlithgow (A904)*	*Open May–Sept.: daily except Fri.: 1.30–5.30pm; park open daily 10am–7pm (Nov.–Mar. 4pm).*	▲ 128
HUNTLY ◆ A F6		
BRANDER MUSEUM Tel. (01771) 622 906	*Open all year: Tue.–Sat. 10am–noon and 2–4pm. Admission free.*	▲ 222
HUNTLY CASTLE Tel. (01466) 793 191	*Open daily 9.30am–6.30pm (Oct.–Mar. 4.30pm).*	▲ 223
INCHCOLM ◆ D C3		
INCHCOLM ABBEY Tel. (0131) 331 4857	*Open Apr.–Sept.: Mon.–Sat. 9.30am–6.30pm, Sun. 2–6.30pm.*	▲ 174
INVERARAY ◆ D A3		
INVERARAY BELL TOWER The Avenue Tel. (01499) 302 259	*Open May–Sept.: daily 10am–1pm and 2–5pm.*	▲ 195
INVERARAY CASTLE Tel. (01499) 302 203	*Open Apr.–15 Oct.: Mon.–Sat. 10am–1pm and 2–5pm, Sun. 1–5pm.*	▲ 195
INVERARAY JAIL Church Square Tel. (01499) 302 381	*Open daily Apr.–Oct.: 9.30am–5pm; Nov.–Mar.: 10am–4pm.*	▲ 195
INVEREWE GARDEN ◆ A C5		
Tel. (01445) 781 200 *Poolewe, northeast of Gairloch*	*Open daily 9.30am–dusk.*	▲ 243
INVERNESS ◆ A E6		
BALNAIN HOUSE 40 Huntly St Tel. (01463) 715 757	*Open 10am–5pm July–Aug.: Mon.–Sat.; Sept.–June: Tue.–Sat.*	▲ 231
INVERNESS MUSEUM AND ART GALLERY Castle Wynd Tel. (01463) 237 114	*Open Mon.–Sat. 9am–5pm. Closed Sun. and public holidays. Admission free.*	▲ 230
INVERURIE ◆ B A6		
CARNEGIE MUSEUM The Square Tel. (01771) 622 906	*Open May–Sept.: Sat.–Sun. 2–4.30pm. Admission free.*	▲ 222
IRVINE ◆ D A4		
SCOTTISH MARITIME MUSEUM Laid Forge, Gottries Rd Tel. (01294) 278 283	*Open Apr.–Oct.: daily 10am–5pm.*	▲ 149
JEDBURGH ◆ D D4		
JEDBURGH ABBEY High St Tel. (01835) 863 925	*Open Apr.–Sept.: daily 9.30am–6.30pm; Oct.–Mar.: Mon.–Sat. 9.30am–4.30pm, Sun. 2–4.30pm.*	▲ 138
JEDBURGH CASTLE JAIL MUSEUM Castle Gate Tel. (01835) 863 254	*Open Apr.–Oct.: Mon.–Sat. 10am–4.30pm, Sun. 1–4pm.*	▲ 139

MARY QUEEN OF SCOTS' HOUSE Queen St Tel. (01835) 863 331	*Open Mar. and Nov.: Mon.–Sat.: 10am–3.30pm, Sun. 1–4pm; Apr.–Oct.: Mon.–Sat.10am–4.30pm, Sun. noon–4.30pm (June–Aug.: Sun. 10am–4.30pm).*	▲ 139
KEITH		
STRATHISLA DISTILLERY Tel. (01542) 783 044	*Open Feb.-Mar.: Mon.–Fri. 9.30am–4pm; Mar.–Nov.: Mon.-Sat. 9.30am–4pm, Sun. 12.30–4pm.*	▲ 220
KELLIE CASTLE	◆ D C3	
Tel. (01333) 720 271 *10 miles south of St Andrews*	*Open Apr.–Oct.: daily 1.30–5.30pm (Oct.: Sat.–Sun. only). Gardens open all year.*	▲ 176
KELSO	◆ D D4	
FLOORS CASTLE Tel. (01573) 223 333	*Open Easter–Oct.: 10am–4pm.*	▲ 136
SMAILHOLM TOWER Tel. (01573) 460 365 *5½ miles west of Kelso (B6937)*	*Open Apr.–Sept.: Mon.–Sun. 9.30am–6.30pm; Oct.–Mar.: Sat.–Sun. only.*	▲ 136
KILDRUMMY CASTLE GARDEN	◆ A F6	
Tel. (019755) 71 203/277 *10 miles west of Alford (A97)*	*Open Apr.–Oct.: daily 10am–6.30pm.*	▲ 216
KILRAVOCK CASTLE	◆ A E6	
Croy Tel. (01667) 493 258	*Guided tours Apr.–Oct.: Wed. 11am–4pm.*	▲ 231
KINCRAIG	◆ D B1	
HIGHLAND WILDLIFE PARK Tel. (01540) 651 270	*Open June–Aug.: 10am–7pm; Apr.–May and Sept.–Oct.: 10am–6pm; Nov.–Mar.: 10am–4pm, last visitors admitted 2 hours before closing.*	▲ 233
KINGUSSIE	◆ D B1	
HIGHLAND FOLK MUSEUM Am Fasgadh, Duke St Tel. (01540) 661 307	*Open Apr.–Oct.: Mon.–Sat. 10.30am–5.30pm, Sun. 1–5pm. Guided tours during the rest of the year.*	▲ 233
KINROSS	◆ D C3	
KINROSS HOUSE Tel. (01577) 862 900	*Open Apr.–Oct.: daily 10am–7pm. Grounds only.*	▲ 178
KIRKCALDY	◆ D C3	
KIRKCALDY MUSEUM AND ART GALLERY War Memorial Gardens Tel. (01592) 412 860	*Open all year: Mon.–Sat. 10.30am–5pm, Sun. 2–5pm. Admission free. Closed on public holidays*	▲ 175
KIRKCUDBRIGHT	◆ D B6	
BROUGHTON HOUSE AND GARDEN 12 High St Tel. (01557) 330 437	*Open Apr.–Oct.: daily 1–5.30pm (July–Aug.: 11am–5.30pm).*	▲ 145
MACLELLAN'S CASTLE High St Tel. (0131) 668 8800	*Open Apr.–Sept.: Mon.–Sun. 9.30am–6.30pm.*	▲ 145
STEWARTRY MUSEUM St Mary St Tel. (01557) 331 643	*Open May–Sept.: Mon.–Sat. 11am–5pm, Sun. 2–5pm (except May); July–Aug.: Mon.–Sat. from 10am; Oct.–Apr.: Mon.–Sat. 11am–4pm.*	▲ 145
TOLBOOTH ART CENTER High St Tel. (01557) 331 556	*Open all year: Mon.–Sat. 1–4pm (June–Sept.: 1–5.30pm); July–Aug.: Mon.–Sat. 11am–5pm.*	▲ 145
KIRKOSWALD	◆ D A5	
SOUTER JOHNNIE'S COTTAGE Main Rd Tel. (01655) 760 603	*Open Easter–30 Sept.: daily 11.30am–5pm; Oct.: Sat.–Sun. 11.30am–5pm.*	▲ 147
LANARK	◆ D B4	
ST NICHOLAS CHURCH The Cross Tel. (01555) 666 549 (Mr Moffat) or (01555) 662 600 (Mr Thomson)	*Open Wed. and Sun. (services at 11.00 am and sometimes in the evening). Can be opened at any time; contact Mr Thomson or Mr Moffat.*	▲ 165

LARGS		◆ D A4	
VIKINGAR Greenock Rd Tel. (01475) 689 777	*Open daily 10.30am–3.30pm (extended summer opening, flexible hours). Closed Jan. 1 and Dec. 25.*		▲ 149
LAURISTON CASTLE		◆ D C3	
Cramond Rd South Tel. (0131) 336 2060 *Outskirts of Edinburgh*	*Open Apr.–Oct.: Sat.–Thur. 11am–1pm and 2–5pm (closed Fri.); Nov.–Mar.: Sat.–Sun. 2–4pm. Guided tours only.*		▲ 128
LEITH		◆ D C3	
ROYAL YACHT BRITANNIA 100 Ocean Drive Tel. (0131) 555 5566 or (0131) 555 8800	*Open daily 10.30am–4.30pm (in summer: Sat.–Sun. 7.30pm). Visitors must book in advance, by telephone or at the Tattoo Office (32 Market Street); shuttle service.*		▲ 127
LEUCHARS		◆ D C2	
ST ATHANASIUS Tel. (01334) 839 226	*Open Mar.–Oct.: 9am–6pm.*		▲ 178
LINLITHGOW ★		◆ D B3	
LINLITHGOW PALACE Kirkgate Tel. (01506) 842 896	*Open Apr.–Sept.: daily 9.30am–6.30pm; Oct.–Mar.: Mon.–Sat. 9.30am–4.30pm, Sun. 2–4.30pm. Closed Jan. 1 and Dec. 25–26*		▲ 130
ST MICHAEL'S CHURCH Kirkgate Tel. (01506) 842 188	*Open Easter–Oct.: daily 10am–4pm; selective opening in winter. Admission free.*		▲ 130
LOCH KATRINE		◆ D A2-A3	
CRUISE Tel. (01877) 376 317	*Boats leave from Trossachs Pier Apr.–Oct.: 11am (except Sat.), 1.45pm and 3.15pm.*		▲ 172
LOGAN BOTANIC GARDEN		◆ D A6	
Tel. (01776) 860 231 *Port Logan, 14 miles south of Stanraer (B7065)*	*Open Mar.–Oct.: daily 9.30am–6pm.*		▲ 147
LOSSIEMOUTH		◆ A F5	
FISHERY AND COMMUNITY MUSEUM Flitgaveny St Tel. (01343) 813 772	*Open Easter–Sept.: Mon.–Sat. 10am–5pm.*		▲ 224
MACDUFF		◆ B A5	
MACDUFF MARINE AQUARIUM 11 High Store Tel. (01261) 833 369	*Open Oct.–Mar.: daily 10am–5pm; Apr.–Sept.: Mon.–Fri. 10am–5pm, Sat.–Sun. 10am–8pm.*		
MALLAIG		◆ C C1	
MALLAIG MARINE WORLD The Harbour Tel. (01687) 462 292	*Open June–Sept.: Mon.–Sat. 9am–7pm; Oct.–May: Mon.–Sat. 9am–5pm, Sun. 11am–5pm.*		▲ 237
MANDERSTON HOUSE		◆ D D4	
Tel. (01361) 883 450 *2 miles east of Duns (A6105)*	*Open May–Sept.: Thur. and Sun. 2–5.30pm.*		▲ 135
MAUCHLINE		◆ D A4	
BURNS HOUSE MUSEUM Tel. (01290) 550 045	*Open Easter and May–Sept.: Tue.–Sat. noon–5pm, Sun. 2–5pm.*		▲ 149
MAYBOLE		◆ D A5	
CROSSRAGUEL ABBEY Tel. (01655) 883 113	*Open Apr.–Sept.: Mon.–Sun. 9.30am–6.30pm.*		▲ 148
MEIGLE		◆ D C2	
MEIGLE SCULPTURED STONE MUSEUM Tel. (01828) 640 612	*Open Apr.–Sept.: Mon.–Sun. 9.30am–12.30pm and 1.30–6pm.*		▲ 186
MELLERSTAIN HOUSE		◆ D D4	
Tel. (01573) 410 225 *Gordon, northwest of Kelso (A6089)*	*Open Easter and May–Sept.: Sun.-Mon. 12.30–5pm (restaurant 11.30am–5.30pm).*		▲ 137

◆ PLACES TO VISIT

MELROSE ◆ D A4

ABBOTSFORD HOUSE
Tel. (01896) 752 043
*Open Mar.–Oct.: daily 10am–5pm
(Mar.–May and Oct.: Sun. 2–5pm).*
▲ 138

MELROSE ABBEY ✪
Main Square
Tel. (01896) 822 562
*Open Apr.–Sept.: Mon.–Sat. 9.30am–6.30pm, Sun.
2–6.30pm; Oct.–Mar.: Mon.–Sat. 9.30am–6.30pm,
Sun. 2–4.30pm.*
▲ 137

MINTLAW ◆ B A6

ABERDEENSHIRE FARMING MUSEUM
Aden Country Park
Tel. (01771) 622 906
*Open Easter–Sept.: daily 11am–4.30pm, and at
other times (telephone for information).*
▲ 218

MONTROSE ◆ D D1-D2

HOUSE OF DUN
Tel. (0131) 331 2451
3 miles west of Montrose (A935)
*Open Easter–Sept.: daily 10am–5.30pm
(last entrance 4.30pm).*
▲ 186

**MONTROSE BASIN
NATURE RESERVE CENTRE**
Tel. (01674) 676 336
*Open Apr.–Sept.: daily 10.30am–5pm; Oct.–Mar.:
daily 10.30am–4pm. Closed Jan. 1 and Dec. 25–26*
▲ 186

NAIRN ◆ A E6

NAIRN MUSEUM
Viewfield Drive
Tel. (01667) 455 399
Open May–Sept.: Mon.–Sat. 10am–4.30pm.
▲ 232

NEW ABBEY ◆ D B6

NEW ABBEY CORN MILL
Tel. (01387) 850 260
8 miles south of Dumfries (A710)
*Open Apr.–Sept.: daily 9.30am–1pm and 2–6.30pm;
Oct.–Mar.: Mon.–Sat. (except Thur.) 9.30am–1pm
and 2–4.30pm, Sun. 2–4.30pm.*
▲ 144

**SHAMBELLIE HOUSE MUSEUM
OF COSTUMES**
Tel. (01387) 850 375
*Open Easter–Oct.: daily 11am–5pm
(garden open from 10.30 am).*
▲ 144

SWEETHEART ABBEY
Tel. (01387) 850 397
*Open Apr.–Sept.: daily 9.30am–6.30pm; Oct.–Mar.:
Mon.–Fri. (except Tue. pm) 9.30am–4.30pm,
Sat. 9.30am–12.30pm, Sun. 2–4.30pm.*
▲ 144

NEW LANARK ◆ D B4

**FALLS OF CLYDE WILDLIFE RESERVE
AND VISITOR CENTRE**
The Dyeworks
Tel. (01555) 665 262
*Open Easter–Oct.: Mon.–Fri. 11am–5pm, Sat.–Sun.
1–5pm; Nov.–Easter: Sat.–Sun. only 1–5pm.
Closed Jan. Unrestricted access to reserve.*
▲ 166

NEW LANARK VISITOR CENTER
New Lanark Mills
Tel. (01555) 661 345
*Visitor Centre, Millworkers House Exhibitions,
Village Store Exhibition, Robert Owen's House.
Open daily 11am–5pm. Closed Jan. 1 and Dec. 25*
▲ 166

NEWTONGRANGE ◆ D C3

SCOTTISH MINING MUSEUM
Lady Victoria Colliery
Tel. (0131) 663 7519
*Open daily 10am–5pm. Closed Jan. 1–2
and Dec. 25–26.*
▲ 130

NEWTONMORE ◆ D B1

CLAN MACPHERSON MUSEUM
Clan House, Main St
Tel. (01540) 673 332
*Open Apr.–Oct.: Mon.–Sat. 10am–5pm,
Sun. 2.30–5pm.
Admission free.*
▲ 233

OBAN ◆ C C2

OBAN DISTILLERY VISITOR CENTRE
Stafford St
Tel. (01631) 572 004
*Open Easter–June and Sept.–Oct.: Mon.–Sat.
9.30am–4pm; July–Aug.: Mon.–Sat. 9.30am–8pm;
Nov.–Easter: Mon.–Fri. 9.30am–4pm.*
▲ 194

OBAN RARE BREEDS FARM PARK
New Barran
Tel. (01631) 770 608
Open Apr.–Oct. daily 9.30am–5pm.
▲ 194

OYNE ◆ B A6

ARCHÆOLINK PREHISTORY PARK
Tel. (01464) 851 500
Open Easter–Oct.: daily 10am–5pm.
▲ 222

PAISLEY ◆ D A4

COATS OBSERVATORY
49 Oakshaw St West
Tel. (0141) 889 2013
*Open all year: Tue.–Sat. 10am–1pm and 2–5pm,
Sun. 2–5pm (Nov.–Mar.: Thur. 2–9.45pm).*
▲ 164

PAISLEY ABBEY Abbey Close Tel. (0141) 889 7654	*Open all year: Mon.–Sat. 10am–3.30pm, Sun. for services only (11.00 am, 12.15pm, 6.30pm). Admission free.*	▲ 164
PAISLEY MUSEUM AND ART GALLERIES High St Tel. (0141) 889 3151	*Open all year: Tue.–Sat. 10am–5pm, Sun. 2–5pm. Admission free.*	▲ 164
SMA' SHOT COTTAGES 11–17 George Place Tel. (0141) 889 1708	*Open Apr.–Sept.: Wed. and Sat. 1–5pm. Admission free.*	▲ 164
THOMAS COATS MEMORIAL CHURCH High St Tel. (0141) 889 9980	*Open Apr.–Oct.: Mon., Wed. and Fri. 2–4pm, Sunday services: 11am and 6pm.*	▲ 164

PAXTON ◆ D D4

PAXTON HOUSE Tel. (01289) 386 291 *5 miles west of Berwick-upon-Tweed (B6461)*	*Open Easter–Oct.: daily 11am–5.30pm; gardens, tearoom and shop: 10am–dusk. Groups in winter: book in advance.*	▲ 135

PEEBLES ◆ D C4

NEIDPATH CASTLE Tweedale Tel. (01721) 720 333	*Open Apr.–May: Mon.–Sat. 11am–5pm, Sun. 1–5pm; July–Sept.: Mon.–Sat. 11am–6pm, Sun. 1–5pm.*	▲ 138

PERTH ◆ D C2

BALHOUSIE CASTLE (BLACK WATCH REGIMENTAL MUSEUM) North Inch Tel. (01738) 621 281	*Open May–Sept.: Mon.–Sat.10am–4.30pm; Oct.–Apr.: Mon.–Fri. 10am–3.30pm. Closed Dec. 23–Jan. 1.*	▲ 179
BRANKLYN GARDEN 116 Dundee Rd Tel. (01738) 625 535	*Open Mar.–Oct.: daily 9.30am–dusk.*	▲ 179
FERGUSSON GALLERY Marshall Place Tel. (01738) 441 944	*Open all year: Mon.–Sat. 10am–5pm. Admission free.*	▲ 179
HUNTINGTOWER CASTLE Tel. (01738) 627 231 *3 miles northwest of Perth (A85)*	*Open Mon.–Sat. 9.30am–6.30pm, Sun. 2–6.30pm (Oct.–Mar.: Sun. 2–4.30pm, closed Thur. pm and Fri.).*	▲ 179
PERTH ART AND MUSEUM GALLERY 78 George St Tel. (01738) 632 488	*Open Mon.–Sat. 10am–5pm. Closed Jan. 1 and Dec. 25. Admission free.*	▲ 179
ST JOHN'S KIRK St John St Tel. (01738) 621 755	*Open Easter–Sept.: Mon.–Sat. 10am–noon and 2–4pm, Sun. noon–2pm. In winter, by appt. Admission free.*	▲ 179
SCONE PALACE Tel. (01738) 552 300 *2 miles north of Perth (A93)*	*Open Easter–Oct.: daily 9.30am–5.15pm, and by appt. during the rest of the year.*	▲ 180

PETERHEAD ◆ B B6

ARBUTHNOTT MUSEUM St Peter St Tel. (01771) 822 906	*Open Mon.–Sat. 10.30am–1.30pm and 2.30–5pm, except Wed.: 10.30am–1pm. Admission free.*	▲ 218
PETERHEAD MARITIME HERITAGE South Rd Tel. (01779) 473 000	*Open daily 10.30am–5pm.*	▲ 218
UGIE SALMON FISH HOUSE Golf Rd Tel. (01779) 476 209	*Open all year: Mon.–Fri. 9am–5pm, Sat. 9am–noon. Admission free.*	▲ 218

PITMEDDEN GARDENS ◆ B A6

Tel. (01651) 842 352 *Near Ellon (A920)*	*Open May–Sept.: daily 10am–5.30pm.*	▲ 217

PITMUIES GARDEN ◆ D D2

Tel. (01241) 828 245 *Between Forfar and Arbroath (A932)*	*Open Apr.–Oct.: daily 10am–5pm.*	▲ 196

ROSEMARKIE ◆ A E5

GROAM HOUSE MUSEUM High St Tel. (01381) 620 961	*Open Easter and May–Sept.: Mon.–Sat. 10am–5pm, Sun. 2–4.30pm; Oct.–Apr.: Sat.–Sun. 2–4pm.*	▲ 247

ROSLIN		◆ D C4
ROSSLYN CHAPEL TRUST ★ Tel. (0131) 440 2159 *5½ miles south of Edinburgh (A701)*	*Open daily: Mon.–Sat. 10am–5pm,* *Sun. noon–4.45pm.*	▲ 130

ST ABB'S		◆ D D3
SAINT ABB'S HEAD Tel. (018907) 71 443 *2 miles north of Coldingham (A1107)*	*Open daily.* *Admission free, except for the nature reserve.*	▲ 134

ST ANDREWS ✪		◆ D C2
HOLY TRINITY CHURCH South St Tel. (01334) 474 494	*Open June–Sept.: 10am–noon and 2–4pm;* *Oct.–May: Sat. 10am–noon.*	▲ 177
ST ANDREWS CASTLE Tel. (01334) 477 196	*Open all year: Mon.–Sat. 9.30am–6.30pm, Sun.* *2–6.30pm (4.30pm Oct.–Mar.).*	▲ 177
ST ANDREWS CATHEDRAL **AND ST RULES TOWER** Tel. (01463) 233 535	*Open daily 10.30am–5.30pm.* *Admission free.*	▲ 176
ST ANDREWS PRESERVATION **TRUST MUSEUM** 12 North St Tel. (01334) 477 629	*Open Easter and 25 May–Sept.: daily 2–5pm.* *Admission free.*	▲ 177
SEA LIFE CENTRE The Scores Tel. (01334) 474 786	*Open all year: daily 10am–6pm (5pm Nov.–Jan.);* *July–Aug.: 9am–7pm (to be confirmed).*	▲ 177
UNIVERSITY 66 North St Tel. (01334) 462 102	*Guided tours end June–Sept.: Mon.–Sat. 11am and* *2.30pm; Sept.–May: by appt.*	▲ 177

ST CONAN'S KIRK		◆ D A2
Lochawe Tel. (01838) 200 401	*Unrestricted access.*	▲ 198

SCOTTISH CRANNOG CENTRE		◆ D B2
Tel. (01887) 830 583 *Kenmore, west of Aberfeldy (A827)*	*Open Apr.–June and Oct.: daily 10am–5pm;* *July–Sept.: daily 10am–6pm.*	▲ 181

SEA LIFE CENTRE		◆ C C2
Tel. (01631) 720 386 *Barcaldine, north of Oban (A828)*	*Oceanographic museum: open 9.30am–5pm* *Apr.–Oct.: daily; Nov.–Mar.: Sat.–Sun.*	▲ 198

SELKIRK		◆ D C4
HALLIWELL'S HOUSE MUSEUM Market Place Tel. (01750) 20 096	*Open Apr.–Oct.: Mon.–Sat. 10am–5pm,* *Sun. 2–4pm; July–Aug.: 9.30am–5.30pm (Sun. 5pm).* *Admission free.*	▲ 139

SOUTH QUEENSFERRY		◆ D C3
DALMENY HOUSE Tel. (0131) 331 1888	*Open Apr.–Sept.: Sun.–Tue. noon–5.30pm.*	▲ 129
HOPETOUN HOUSE Tel. (0131) 331 2451	*Open Mar.–Oct.: daily 10am–5.30pm.* *Groups in winter: book in advance.*	▲ 129

SPYNIE		◆ A F5
PALACE Tel. (01343) 546 358 *2 miles north of Elgin (A941)*	*Open Apr.–Oct.: daily 9.30am–6.30pm;* *Oct.–Mar.: Sat. 9.30am–4.30pm, Sun. 2–4.30pm.*	▲ 224

STIRLING ✪		◆ D B3
ARGYLL'S LODGING Castle Wynd Tel. (01786) 450 000	*Open Apr.–Sept.: daily 9.30am–5.15pm;* *Oct.–Mar.: daily 9.30am–4.15pm.*	▲ 170
BANNOCKBURN HERITAGE CENTRE Glasgow Rd Tel. (01786) 812 664	*Open Mar., 1 Nov.– 23 Dec.: daily 11am–3pm;* *Apr.–Oct.: daily 10am–5pm.*	▲ 170
CHURCH OF THE HOLY RUDE St John St Tel. (01786) 475 275	*Open May–Sept.: Mon.–Sat. 10am–5pm,* *Sunday services.* *Admission free.*	▲ 171
COWANE'S HOSPITAL St John St Tel. (01786) 473 544	*Grounds open throughout the year.* *Guided tours Apr.–Sept., during the tartans* *exhibition.*	▲ 171

OLD TOWN JAIL St John St Tel. (01786) 450 050	*Open Apr.–Sept.: daily 9.30am–6pm; Oct.–Mar.:* *daily 9.30am–4pm.*	▲ 171
SMITH ART GALLERY AND MUSEUM Dumbarton Rd Tel. (01786) 471 917	*Open all year: Tue.–Sat. 10.30am–5pm, Sun. 2–5pm.* *Admission free.*	▲ 171
STIRLING CASTLE Castle Wynd Tel. (01786) 450 000	*Open Apr.–Sept.: daily 9.30am–5.15pm;* *Oct.–Mar.: daily 9.30am–4.15pm.*	▲ 170
WALLACE MONUMENT Alloa Rd Tel. (01786) 472 140	*Open daily Mar.–Oct.: 10am–5pm/5.30pm in June* *and Sept. (July–Aug.: 9.30am–6.30pm).* *Closed Jan. 1 and Dec. 25.*	▲ 169

STONEHAVEN ◆ D D1

DUNNOTTAR CASTLE Tel. (01569) 762 173	*Open Mar.–Oct.: Mon.–Sat. 9am–6pm, Sun. 2–5pm;* *in winter: Mon.–Fri. 9am–dusk.*	▲ 212
TOLBOOTH The Harbour Tel. (01569) 766 073	*Open June–Oct.: daily except Tue. 1.30–4.30pm.* *Admission free.*	▲ 212

TAIN ◆ A E5

GLENMORRANGIE DISTILLERY Tel. (01862) 892 477 ½ mile north of Tain (A9)	*Open 10am–3.30pm June–Oct.: Mon.–Sat.;* *Nov.–May: Mon.–Fri.*	▲ 247
TAIN THROUGH TIME Tower St Tel. (01862) 894 089	*Open Easter–Oct.: daily 10am–6pm;* *Nov.–Dec. and Mar.: Sat. noon–4pm.*	▲ 247

TANTALLON CASTLE ★ ◆ D D3

Tel. (01620) 892727 3 miles east of North Berwick	*Open Apr.–Sept.: daily 9.30am–6pm; Oct.–Mar.:* *Mon.–Wed., Sat.: 9.30am–4pm, Thur.:* *9.30am–noon, Sun.: 2–4pm. Closed Fri.*	▲ 132

TARBERT ◆ C C3

AN TAIRBEART HERITAGE CENTRE Tel. (01880) 820 190 ½ mile south of Tarbert (A83)	*Open daily 10am–7pm.*	▲ 191

THIRLESTANE CASTLE ◆ D D4

BORDER COUNTRY LIFE MUSEUM Tel. (01578) 722 430 On the A68	*Open Easter–Oct. daily except Tue.: 11am–5pm (last* *visitors admitted at 4.15pm).*	▲ 138

TOLQUHON CASTLE ◆ B A6

TOLQUHON CASTLE Tel. (01651) 851 286 7 miles west of Ellon (A920)	*Open Apr.–Sept.: daily 9.30am–6.30pm;* *Oct.–Mar.: Sat. 9.30am–4.30pm.*	▲ 217

TORRIDON ◆ A C6

TORRIDON COUNTRYSIDE CENTRE Tel. (01445) 791 221 Southwest of Kinlochewe (A896)	*Open May–Sept.: Mon.–Fri. 10am–5pm,* *Sun. 2–5pm.*	▲ 242

TRAQUAIR HOUSE ★ ◆ D C4

Innerleithen Tel. (01896) 830 323	*Open Apr.–Oct.: daily 12.30–5.30pm* *(June–Aug. from 10.30 am).*	▲ 138

ULLAPOOL ◆ A C5

ULLAPOOL MUSEUM West Argyll St Tel. (01854) 612 987	*Open Apr.–Oct.: Mon.–Sat. 9.30am–5.30pm;* *July–Aug.: late-night opening 7.30–9.30pm;* *Nov.–Mar.: Mon.–Sat. noon–3pm.*	▲ 243

URQUHART CASTLE ◆ A D6

Tel. (0145) 64 50 551 On the shores of Loch Ness (A82)	*Open daily Apr.–Sept.: 9.30am–5.30pm;* *Oct.–Mar.: 9.30am–4.30pm.*	▲ 238

WHITHORN ◆ D A6

THE WHITHORN TRUST **DISCOVERY CENTRE** 45–47 George St Tel. (01988) 500 508	*Open Apr.–Oct.: daily 10.30am–5pm.*	

WHITHORN PRIORY AND MUSEUM Tel. (01988) 500 700	*Open Apr.–Oct.: daily 10.30am–5pm.*	▲ 146
WICK		◆ A F3-F4
KEISS CASTLE Tel. (01955) 602 596 (OT) *4 miles north of Wick*	*Unrestricted access. Check times of the tides.*	▲ 246
WICK HERITAGE CENTRE Bank Row Tel. (01955) 605 393	*Open June–Sept.: Mon.–Sat. 10am–5pm.*	▲ 246
YOUNGER BOTANICAL GARDEN		◆ D A3
Dunoon Tel. (01369) 706 261	*Open Mar.–Oct.: daily 9.30am–6pm.*	▲ 190

OUTER HEBRIDES

BARRA ISLAND		◆ C A1
BARRA HERITAGE CENTRE Castlebay Tel. (01871) 810 413	*Open June–Aug.: Mon.–Fri. 11am–5pm; Sept.:* *Mon., Wed. and Fri. 10am–4pm.*	▲ 255
KISIMUL CASTLE Castlebay Tel. (01871) 810 336	*Boat trips Apr.–Sept.: Mon., Wed. and Sat. 2–5pm.* *Contact Mr MacNeil* *(Tel. [01871] 810 449).*	▲ 255
LEWIS AND HARRIS		◆ A A5-B3
AN CLACHAN CENTRE Leverbugh Tel. (01859) 520370	*Open Mon.–Sat. 9am–6pm.*	◆ A A5 ▲ 253
AN LANNTAIR ARTS CENTRE Town Hall, Stornoway Tel. (01851) 703 307	*Open Mon.–Sat. 10am–5.30pm.*	◆ A B4 ▲ 253
BLACKHOUSE MUSEUM Tel. (01851) 710 395 *Arnol, north of Stornoway* *(A858)*	*Open Apr.–Sept.: Mon.–Sat. 9.30am–6.30pm;* *Oct.–Mar.: Mon.–Sat. 9.30am–4.30pm.*	◆ A B4 ▲ 253
CALANAIS STANDING STONES Tel. (01851) 621 422 *2 miles west of Stornoway*	*Megaliths. Open daily Apr.–Sept.: 10am–6pm;* *Oct.–Mar.: 10am–4pm.* *Admission free.*	◆ A B4 ▲ 252
HARRIS TWEED MILL Shawbost Tel. (01851) 710 212	*Open all year: Mon.–Thur. 8am–5pm,* *Fri. 8am–noon.* *Admission free.*	◆ A B4 ▲ 253
HARRIS TWEED WEAVING AND KNITTING 4 Plockropool, Luskentyre Tel. (01859) 511 217	*Open Mon.–Sat. 9am–7pm.* *Admission free.*	◆ A A5 ▲ 253
NAN EILEAN MUSEUM Francis St, Stornoway Tel. (01851) 703 773 / 226	*Open 10am–5pm. Easter–Sept.: Mon.–Sat.;* *rest of the year: Tue.–Sat.*	◆ A B4 ▲ 252
SHAWBOST SCHOOL MUSEUM Tel. (01851) 710 212	*Open Apr.–Nov.: Mon.–Sat. 9am–5pm.*	◆ AB4 ▲ 253
UIST ISLE		◆ A A5-A6
LOCHMADDY TOURIST OFFICE Tel. (01876) 500 321		
LINICLATE SCHOOL MUSEUM Benbecula Tel. (01870) 602 864	*Open all year: Mon., Wed.–Thur. 9am–4pm, Tue.* *and Fri. 9am–8pm (except public holidays: closes at* *7pm.), Sat. 11am–1pm and 2–4pm.*	▲ 254
TAIGH CHEARSABHAGH Lochmaddy Tel. (01876) 500 293	*Open Mon.–Sat. 10am–5pm.*	▲ 254

INNER HEBRIDES

COLONSAY		◆ C B3
COLONSAY HOUSE GARDENS Kiloran House Tel. (01951) 200 211	*Open Easter–Oct.*	▲ 202
IONA ✿		◆ C B2
ABBEY Tel. (01681) 700 404	*Unrestricted access, donations optional.*	▲ 204

HERITAGE CENTRE Tel. (01681) 700 576	Open Easter–Oct.: Mon.–Sat. 10.30am–4.30pm.	
ISLAY		◆ **C** B3-B4
BOWMORE DISTILLERY School St, Bowmore Tel. (01496) 810 441	Guided tours July–Sept.: Mon.–Fri. 10.30am–3pm, Sat. 10.30 am; Oct.–Easter.: Mon.–Fri. 10.30am and 2pm.	▲ 202
BUNNAHABHAIN Port Askaig Tel. (01496) 840 646	Open all year: Mon.–Fri. 10am–4pm. Closed 1 Jan. and 25 Dec. Admission free.	▲ 221
CAOL ILA DISTILLERY Port Askaig Tel. (01496) 840 207	Open all year: Mon.–Fri. by appt.	▲ 221
LAGAVULIN DISTILLERY Port Ellen Tel. (01496) 302 400	Open Apr.–Oct.: Mon.–Fri. 10.30am and 2.30pm.	▲ 221
LAPHROAIG DISTILLERY Port Ellen Tel. (01496) 302 418	Open all year (except July and first 2 weeks of Aug.): Mon.–Thur., visits by appt. only. Admission free.	▲ 221
LOCH FINLAGGAN VISITOR CENTRE Ballwgrant Tel. (01496) 840 644	Open Apr.: Sun., Tue. and Thur. 2.30–5pm; May–Sept.: Sun.-Fri. 2.30–5pm; Oct.: Sun., Tue. and Thur. 2–4pm.	▲ 203
MUSEUM OF ISLAY LIFE Port Charlotte Tel. (01496) 850 358	Open Easter–Oct.: Mon.–Sat. 10am–5pm, Sun. 2–5pm.	▲ 202
MULL		◆ **C** B2-C2
AN TOBAR ARTS CENTRE Argyll Terrace, Tobermory Tel. (01688) 302 211	Open Easter–Oct.: Mon.–Sat. 10am–4pm, Sun. 1–4pm; Nov.–Easter: Tue.–Sat. 10am–4pm.	▲ 203
DERVAIG OLD BYRE HERITAGE CENTRE Tel. (01688) 400 229 1½ miles southwest of Dervaig	Open Easter–Oct.: daily 10.30am–6.30pm.	▲ 203
DUART CASTLE Tel. (01680) 812 309 East coast of Mull (A849)	Open May–Oct.: daily 10.30am–6pm.	▲ 203
FIONNPHORT COLUMBA CENTRE Tel. (01786) 431 325	Open at Easter and in summer: daily 10am–5pm.	▲ 203
MULL MUSEUM Main St, Tobermory	Open Mon.–Fri. 10.30am–4.30pm, Sat. 10.30am–1.30pm.	▲ 203
TOBERMORY DISTILLERY Ledaig Car Park, Tobermory Tel. (01688) 302 645	Open Easter–Oct.: Mon.–Fri. 10am–5pm; Nov.–Easter: Tue. and Thur. 11am–4pm.	▲ 203
TOROSAY CASTLE AND GARDENS Train, de Craignure Tel. (01680) 812 421	Open Easter–Oct.: daily 10.30am–5pm; Nov.–Easter: gardens only, 10.30am–dusk.	▲ 203
SKYE ✪		◆ **A** B5-A6-C6 **C** B1-C1
PORTREE TOURIST OFFICE Tel. (01478) 612 137		
AN TUIREANN ARTS CENTRE Struan Rd, Portree Tel. (01478) 613 306	Open Mon.–Sat. 10am–5pm; in summer: Mon.–Sat. 10am–5pm, Sun. noon–4pm.	▲ 250
AROS CENTRE Viewfield Rd, Portree Tel. (01478) 613 649	Open daily Easter–Sept.: 9am–9pm; Oct.–Mar.: 10am–6pm.	▲ 250
CLAN DONALD VISITOR CENTRE Armadale Castle, Armadale Tel. (01471) 844 305	Open Apr.–Oct.: daily 9.30am–5.30pm.	▲ 248
COLBOST CROFT MUSEUM Colbost Tel. (01470) 521 296	Open Apr.–Oct.: daily 10am–6.30pm.	▲ 251
CROFT MUSEUM Luib Tel. (01471) 822 427	Open Easter–Oct.: daily 9am–4pm.	▲ 248
DUNVEGAN CASTLE Dunvegan Tel. (01470) 521 206	Open daily Mar. 23–Oct. 31: 10am–5.30pm; Nov.–Mar. 22: 11am–4pm.	▲ 251
SKYE MUSEUM OF ISLAND LIFE Kilmuir Tel. (01470) 552 206	Open Apr. 10–Oct.: Mon.–Sat. 9.30am–5.30pm.	▲ 251

SKYE VIVARIUM The Old Mill, Harrapool, Broadford Tel. (01471) 822 209	Open 10am–5pm Apr. 10–June and Sept.–Oct.: Mon.–Sat.; July–Aug. and public holidays: daily.	▲ 248
TALISKER DISTILLERY Carbost Tel. (01478) 640 314	Open Apr.–June and Oct.: Mon.–Fri. 9am–4.30pm; July–Sept.: Mon.–Sat. 9am–4.30pm; Nov.–Mar.: Mon.–Fri. 2–4pm.	

TIREE		◆ C A2
SKERRYVORE LIGHTHOUSE MUSEUM Hynish Tel. (01865) 311 468	Open daily 10am–4pm. If not open, key available from Mr Plant, Flat Five, Hynish.	▲ 206

ORKNEY ISLANDS

KIRKWALL		◆ A F2
TOURIST OFFICE Broad St Tel. (01856) 872 856		
HIGHLAND PARK DISTILLERS Holm Road Tel. (01856) 874 619	Open Mar.–Oct.: Mon.–Fri. 10am–4pm (July–Aug.: Sat.–Sun.: noon–4.00pm); Nov.–Dec.: Mon.–Fri. 2–3.30pm; Jan.–Feb.: by appt.	▲ 221
ORKNEY WIRELESS MUSEUM Kiln Corner, Junction Rd Tel. (01856) 874 272	Open Apr.–Sept.: Mon.–Sat. 10am–4.30pm, Sun. 2.30–4.30pm.	▲ 256
ST MAGNUS CATHEDRAL ★ Broad St Tel. (01856) 874 894	Open Apr.–Sept.: Mon.–Sat. 10am–6pm, Sun. 2–6pm; Oct.–Mar.: Mon.–Sat. 9am–1pm and 2–5pm.	▲ 256
TANKERNESS HOUSE MUSEUM Broad St Tel. (01856) 873 191	Open Oct.–Mar.: Mon.–Sat. 10.30am–12.30pm and 1.30–5pm; Apr.: Mon.–Sat. 10.30am–5pm; May–Sept.: Mon.–Sat. 10.30am–5pm, Sun. 2–5pm.	▲ 257

STROMNESS		◆ A F2
PIER ARTS CENTRE Victoria St Tel. (01856) 850 209	Open Oct.–May: Tue.–Sat. 10.30am–12.30pm and 1.30–5pm; June–Sept.: 10.30am–5pm. Admission free.	▲ 260
STROMNESS MUSEUM 52 Alfred St Tel. (01856) 850 025	Open May–Sept.: daily 10am–5pm; Oct.–Apr.: Mon.–Sat. 10.30am–12.30pm and 1.30–5pm.	▲ 260

OTHER PLACES ON MAINLAND		◆ A F2
BROCH OF GURNESS Tel. (01856) 751 414 Near Evie (A966)	Open daily: Apr.–Sept. 9.30am–6.30pm; Nov.–Dec. 9.30am–4.30pm.	▲ 260
BROUGH OF BIRSAY Tel. (0131) 668 8800 Near Birsay	Unrestricted access at low tide.	▲ 261
CORRIGAL FARM MUSEUM Harray Tel. (01856) 771 411	Open Mar.–Oct.: Mon.–Sat. 10.30am–1pm and 2–5pm, Sun. 2–7pm.	▲ 261
CURWEEN HILL Tel. (0131) 668 8800 Southwest of Finstown (A965)	Unrestricted access: key held at the nearest farm.	▲ 259
GRAIN EARTH HOUSE Tel. (0131) 668 8800 Hatson, 2 miles northwest of Kirkwall	Unrestricted access: key held at the Ortak Visitor Centre in Kirkwall.	▲ 259
ITALIAN CHAPEL Lambholm, St Mary's, Holm Tel. (01856) 781 268	Unrestricted access during the day.	▲ 258
KIRBUSTER FARM MUSEUM Birsay Tel. (01856) 771 268	Open Mar.–Oct.: Mon.–Sat. 10.30am–1pm and 2–5pm, Sun. 2–7pm; out of season by appt.	▲ 261
MAES HOWE Tel. (01856) 761 606 9 miles west of Kirkwall	Open Apr.–Sept.: daily 9.30am–6.30pm; Oct.–Mar.: Mon.–Sat. 9.30am–6.30pm, Sun. 2–4.30pm.	▲ 259
SKAILL HOUSE Skara Brae Tel. (01856) 841 501	Open Apr.–Sept.: Mon.–Sat. 9.30am–6.30pm, Sun. 11am–6.30pm.	▲ 261

SKARA BRAE ✪ Tel. (01856) 841 815 *18½ miles northwest of Kirkwall (B9056)*	*Open Apr.–Sept.: Mon.–Sat. 9am–4.30pm, Sun. 9am–6.15pm; Oct.–Mar.: Mon.–Sat. 9am–4.30pm.*	▲ 260

HOY		◆ A F2-F3
SCAPA FLOW MUSEUM Lyness Tel. (01856) 791 300	*Open 9am–4.30pm; May 15–Oct. 14: daily; Oct. 15–May 14: Mon.–Fri.*	▲ 260

SHAPINSAY		◆ A F2 B A2
BALFOUR CASTLE Tel. (01856) 711 282	*Visitors are taken to the castle by ferry: May 15–Sept. Wed. 2.15–5.30pm.*	▲ 261

SOUTH RONALDSAY		◆ A F3
OLD SMIDDY MUSEUM St Margaret's Hope Tel. (01856) 831 584	*Open Apr.: Sun. 2–4pm; May: daily 2–4pm; June–Aug.: daily noon–4pm; Sept.: daily 2–4pm.*	▲ 258
TOMB OF THE EAGLES Ibister, Burwick Tel. (01856) 831 339	*Unrestricted access.*	▲ 258

SHETLAND

FAIR ISLE		
GEORGE WATERSTON MUSEUM Busta Tel. (01595) 760 244	*Open May–Sept.: Mon. and Fri. 2–4pm, Wed. 10am–12.30pm. Admission free.*	▲ 265

LERWICK (MAINLAND)		◆ B B3
TOURISM OFFICE Market Cross Tel. (01595) 693 434		
FORT CHARLOTTE Town center Tel. (0131) 668 8800	*Open Apr.–Sept.: Mon.–Sat. 9am–6.30pm, Sun. 2–6.30pm. Admission free.*	▲ 262
SHETLAND MUSEUM Lower Hillhead Tel. (01595) 695 057	*Open Mon., Wed. and Fri. 10am–7pm, Tue., Thur. and Sat. 10am–5pm. Admission free.*	▲ 262

MAINLAND		◆ B B3-C3-B4
JARLSHOF PREHISTORIC SETTLEMENT ★ Tel. (01950) 460 112 *Sumburgh Head (A970)*	*Open Apr.–Sept.: Mon.–Sun. 9.30am–6.30pm.*	▲ 264
QUENDALE MILL *Quendale, 4 miles from Sumburgh*	*Open May–Sept.: daily 10am–5pm.*	▲ 264
SHETLAND CROFT HOUSE MUSEUM South Voe, Boddam	*Open May–Sept.: daily 10am–1pm and 2–5pm.*	▲ 264
TANGWICK HAA MUSEUM Eshaness Tel. (01806) 503 389	*Open May–Sept.: Mon.–Fri. 1–5pm, Sat.–Sun. 11am–7pm. Admission free.*	▲ 267
TINGWALL AGRICULTURAL MUSEUM Veensgarth, Gott	*Open June–Aug.: Mon.–Sat. 9am–1pm and 2–5pm.*	▲ 263

MOUSA		◆ B C4
MOUSA BROCH Tel. (0131) 668 8800 *Boat from Sandwick*	*Unrestricted access. Boats to the island May–Sept.: Mon.–Fri. pm, Sat. and Sun. am.*	▲ 264

UNST		◆ B C1
UNST BOAT HAVEN AND UNST HERITAGE CENTRE Haroldswick Tel. (01957) 711 528	*Open May–Sept.: daily 2–5pm. Admission free.*	▲ 268

YELL		◆ B C1-C2
OLD HAA VISITOR CENTRE Burravoe Tel. (01957) 722 339	*Open Easter–Sept.: Tue.–Thur. and Sat. 10am–4pm, Sun. 2–5pm. Admission free.*	▲ 267

◆ BIBLIOGRAPHY

ESSENTIAL READING

◆ BOSWELL AND JOHNSON: *A Journey to the Western Islands of Scotland and a Journal of a Tour to the Hebrides*, 1774, Penguin 1984
◆ FRASER, ANTONIA: *Mary Queen of Scots*, Weidenfeld & Nicolson, 1969
◆ MACLEAN, FITZROY: *Bonnie Prince Charlie*, Canongate
◆ SMOUT, T.C.: *A History of the Scottish People 1560–1830*, William Collins, 1969

GENERAL

◆ MURRAY, W.H.: *The Companion Guide to the West Highlands of Scotland*, Collins 1968
◆ WALKER, C.K.: *Walking North with Keats*, Yale University Press, 1992

ART & ARCHITECTURE

◆ BILLCLIFFE, R.: *The Glasgow Boys*, John Murray, London, 1985
◆ BILLCLIFFE, R.: *The Scottish Colourists*, John Murray, London, 1989
◆ BUCHANAN, W. (ED), JAMES, J. (ED): *The Art of Charles Rennie Macintosh*, Wigwam Digital
◆ GIFFORD, J.: *Highlands and Islands*, Perseus, 1992
◆ GOW, IAN: *The Scottish Interior*, Edinburgh University Press
◆ HOLBERTON, P., CLIFFORD, T.: *The National Galleries of Scotland*, Scala
◆ HOWARD, Deborah: *The Architectural History of Scotland from the Restoration to the Reformation 1560–1600*, Edinburgh University Press 1995
◆ LINDSAY, IAN & COSH, MARY: *Inveraray and the Dukes of Argyll*, Edinburgh University Press
◆ MACMILLAN, DUNCAN: *Scottish Art 1460–1990*, Mainstream 1990
◆ MONTGOMERY MASSINGBERD, HUGH: *Great Houses of Scotland*, Laurence King Publishing, 1997
◆ NAIDSMITH, ROBERT: *Buildings of the Scottish Countryside*, Victor Gollancz, 1989

HISTORY

◆ BATHURST, BELLA: *The Lighthouse Stevensons*, HarperCollins 1999
◆ BRANDER, M.: *The Making of the Highlands*, Constable, 1980
◆ BREEZE, D.J.: *The Stone of Destiny*, Historic Scotland, 1997
◆ BUCHAN, JOHN: *The Marquis of Montrose*, Nelson, 1913; Prion,
◆ CAMPBELL, J.L.: *Canna, the story of a Hebridean Island*, O.U.P 1984, Canongate
◆ CRAIG, DAVID: *On the Crofters Trail, in search of the Clearances Highlanders*, Cape 90, Pimlico
◆ DEVINE, TOM: *The Scottish Nation*, Penguin 1999
◆ DODGSHON, R.A.: *From Chiefs to Landlords, social and economic change in the Western Highlands and Islands, 1493–1820*, Edinburgh University Press, 1998
◆ DONALDSON, W.: *The Jacobite song: political myth and national identity*, Aberdeen University Press, 1988
◆ GRAHAM, HENRY: *The Social Life of Scotland in the Eighteenth Century*, A & C Black, 1899
◆ GRANT, F., HEDGE, RON: *Highland Folk Ways*, Kegan & Paul 1961, Birlinn
◆ GRANT, I.F. AND CHEAPE, HUGH: *Periods in Highland History*, Shepheard Walwyn 1987
◆ KEAY, JOHN: *Highland Drove*, John Murray 1984
◆ LYNCH, MICHAEL: *Scotland: A New History*, Century 1991
◆ MACKENZIE, OSGOOD: *One Hundred Years in the Highlands*, Canongate
◆ MACLEAN, CHARLES: *St Kilda: Island on the Edge of the World*, Canongate
◆ MACLEAN, FITZROY: *A Concise History of Scotland*, Thames & Hudson, 1970
◆ MACLEAN, FITZROY: *Highlanders, A History of the Highland Clans*, Adelphi & Viking 1995
◆ MACDONALD FRASER, GEORGE: *The Steel Barrets, The Story of the Anglo-Scottish Border Reivers*, HarperCollins 1995

◆ MARTIN, M.: *A Description of the Western Islands of Scotland, 1699*, Canongate
◆ PENNANT, THOMAS: *A Tour in Scotland and Voyage to the Hebrides*, 1772
◆ PREBBLE, JOHN: *Glencoe*, Secker & Warburg, 1966, Penguin
◆ PREBBLE, JOHN: *The Highland Clearances*, Secker & Warburg 1963, Penguin
◆ RICHIE, J.N.G: *Brochs of Scotland*, Shire Publications Ltd, 1998
◆ SADLER, J.: *Scottish Battles*, Canongate, Edinburgh, 1996
◆ SMOUT, T.C.: *Scottish Voices 1745–1960*
◆ SMOUT, T.C.: *A Century of the Scottish People 1830–1950*, Fontana, 1985
◆ THOMSON, D.E. (ED) *The Companion to Gaelic Scotland*, Blackwell, 1983
◆ TOBERT, M.: *Pilgrims in the Rough: St Andrews beyond the 19th hole*, Luath Press, Edinburgh, 2000

NATURAL HISTORY

◆ BERRY, R.J.: *The Natural History of Orkney*, Collins, 1985
◆ BOYD, J.M.: *The Hebrides: a Natural History*, Collins, 1990
◆ BROWN, G.M.: *Portrait of Orkney*, John Murray, London, 1988
◆ FRASER DARLING, F.: *Natural History in the Highland Islands*, Collins 1947
◆ MURRAY, W.H.: *The Companion Guide to the Western Highlands*, Collins, 1968
◆ WIGAN, MICHAEL: *The Scottish Highland Estate, preserving an environment*, Swan Hill, 1991

LITERATURE

◆ BANKS, I.: *The Crow Road*, Scribners, 1992
◆ BROWN, I.: *Summer in Scotland*, Collins, 1954
◆ BURNS, R.: *Complete Poems and Songs*, Oxford University Press
◆ DEFOE, D.: *A Tour Through the Whole Island of Great Britain*, Yale University Press
◆ HOGG, J., *Private Memoirs and Confessions of a Justified Sinner*, Everyman's Library

◆ GRANT OF ROTHIEMURENS, *Elizabeth: Memoirs of a Highland Lady*, vols 1 & 2, Canongate
◆ GRASSIC GIBBON, *Lewis: A Scots Quair*, Canongate
◆ GRAY, A.: *Lanark*, Canongate
◆ KELMAN, J.: *A Chancer*, Picador; *How Late It Was, How Late*, Vintage Books, 1995
◆ KELMAN, J. AND OWENS, A.: *Lean Tales*, Cape, 1985
◆ MCILLVANNEY, W.: *Laidlaw, Allen and Unwin*, 1975; *Docherty*, Sceptre, 1992
◆ MACDIARMID, H.: *Complete Poems* (2 vols) Carcanet
◆ MACNAB, JOHN: *John Buchan*, Nelson, 1925, Penguin
◆ SCOTT, SIR W.: *Selected Poems*, Carcanet; *The Heart of Midlothian*, Penguin; *The Bride of Lammermoor*, Oxford Paperbacks; *Rob Roy*, Everyman's Library; *Waverley*, Penguin
◆ SPARK, M.: *The Prime of Miss Jean Brodie*, Penguin
◆ STEVENSON, R.L.: *The Master of Ballantrae and weir of Hermiston*, Everyman's Library
◆ WELSH, I.: *Trainspotting*, Minerva, 1994
◆ WORDSWORTH, D: *Recollections of a Tour Made in Scotland*, Yale University Press,
◆ VICTORIA, QUEEN: *Leaves from the journal of our life in the Highlands from 1848 to 1861*, ed. Arthur Helps, Folio Society
◆ WORLD'S CLASSICS: *A Book of Scottish Verse*, Oxford University Press, 1960

CHILDREN

◆ BRASSEY, R.: *Nessie the Loch Ness Monster*, Orion Children's Books, 1996
◆ DARGIE, R., HOOK, R.: *BBC Education Scotland: Scottish Castles Through History*, Hodder Wayland, 1998
◆ STEVENSON, K.L., *illus.* HILDER, ROWLAND: *Kidnapped*, Everyman's Library
◆ VANDERSTEEN, W.: *Spike and Suzy: the Loch Ness Mystery*, Intes International (UK), 1999

300

Hotels and restaurants

Scottish specialties
Traditional specialties include the excellent Scotch broth (a thick soup made from neck of lamb, pearl barley and winter vegetables), cock-a-leekie (a sort of chicken and leek soup thickened with barley and served with stewed prunes), cullen skink (haddock soup made with milk), partan bree (crab soup), skirlie (onions sautéed in oatmeal and wild thyme), Hebridean leek tart, pork pâté flavored with green beans, slokes (purée of potatoes and seaweed), bridies (meat and vegetable pasties) and Atholl brose (oatmeal flavored with honey and whisky). Unfortunately many of these classic dishes are disappearing from Scottish menus, to make way for the wave of 'Nouvelle Cuisine' that is currently sweeping the English-speaking countries.

Haggis...
An intrinsically Scottish dish which is disgusting to describe but delicious to eat: sheep's intestines, liver, spleen, heart and lungs are chopped and mixed with beef or mutton suet, onions and oatmeal, and flavored with herbs and spices. The mixture is encased in a sheep's stomach which is poached in stock and then dried in the oven. The cutting of this blackened casing is usually accompanied

by a noise and aroma that are best left to the imagination. Even so, it tastes good – it is full of subtle flavors – and, although rather dry, goes down well with a glass of pure malt whisky. Haggis is traditionally eaten on Burns' night, when the cutting of the casing is accompanied by the recitation of a poem by the bard.

Absolute 'musts'
Scottish cuisine has not abandoned all its traditional recipes: the best of these include excellent wild salmon served poached or smoked; kippers – herrings split open, salted and smoked; porridge, traditionally eaten with salt; grouse, roasted and served with Ayrshire bacon

fried in batter; oatcakes, eaten with cheese: the creamy Highland Crowdie, Dunsyre Blue, uncooked cheese from the Mull of Kintyre, Bishop Kennedy, steeped in whisky, and the rather rubbery Dunlop.

Regional cuisine
Scottish chefs should be congratulated on their preference for a truly remarkable range of fresh produce. As well as the world-famous Aberdeen Angus beef and salmon, there is mutton and lamb from the Borders, wild hare and pheasant, guinea fowl, pigeon, duck and free-range chicken, and a wide variety of seafood and fish: turbot, bass, plaice, monkfish, halibut, sea bream, crab, lobster, prawns, kings scallops. There are also some fine vegetables – usually served boiled – and fruits, especially berries.

And not forgetting...
Oysters have become fashionable again after a period of relative neglect: in 1800 it appears that 100,000 oysters were eaten in every day Edinburgh alone! The best oysters come mainly from Loch Fyne, in Argyll. These fine-quality concave oysters are fairly fat, with a greenish tinge, and are truly exquisite when served in their own liquid (around £1 each in restaurants).

GASTRONOMIC GLOSSARY

Regional specialities
black pudding (blood sausage): pig's blood and fat in an intestine casing
bread sauce: made with breadcrumbs and seasoned milk, served with game and poultry
bridies: meat pasties
cullen skink: smoked-haddock soup
finnan haddie: smoked haddock
fishballs: balls of smoked fish cooked in batter
grouse: a game bird usually served roasted, braised or in pâtés
kippers: fresh herrings split open, salted and smoked
neeps 'n' tatties: mashed potatoes and turnips

oatcakes: oatmeal biscuits (cookies)
porridge: oatmeal or rolled oats cooked in boiling water or milk and eaten with sugar or salt (especially in Scotland)
shortbread: butter-rich biscuits (cookies) traditionally made with oatmeal (which has been widely replaced by wheat flour)
slokes: purée of potatoes and seaweed

Fish and seafood
European crab, halibut, king scallops, lobster, monkfish, mussels, oysters, plaice, prawns, queen scallops, sea bass, sea bream, velvet crabs.

Scottish cooks often have their own variation of haggis, the recipe of which is jealously guarded. Variations made with venison, milk-fed lamb, beef, lentils, or foie gras, can be light, rich and always removed from its casing. Haggis is usually served with neeps 'n' tatties (turnips and potatoes).

and bread sauce; venison in a marinade; black pudding served with vegetables; delicious, tender steaks (Scotland produces the best beef steaks in the world); finnan haddie (finnan haddock) salted, dried naturally and smoked over a peat fire; fishballs – balls of smoked fish

HOTELS AND RESTAURANTS ◆

EDINBURGH

→ HOTELS

☐ The Balmoral
◆ E D2
1 Princes St
Tel. (0131) 556 2414
166 rms. and
20 suites
Elaborately
constructed and
decorated building
in a central location.
Very pricey.
Fitness center.
Restaurants: see
Number One and
Hadrian's.
☐ ☐ ☐ ☐ P ☐ ☐

☐ The Bonham
35 Drumsheugh
Gardens
West End
Tel. (0131) 226 6050
46 rms. and 2 suites
First open in 1988,
this modern hotel
consists of three
small buildings
overlooking a
peaceful, green
square. Bright,
comfortable and
attractive.
Bathrooms
rather small.
Restaurant.
☐ ☐ ☐ ☐

☐ The Caledonian Hilton
◆ E A3
Princes St
Tel. (0131) 459 9988
233 rms. and
13 suites
This huge Edwardian
block of red
sandstone (1903),
affectionately
known as the
'Caley', has just
been taken over
by the Hilton chain.
The 6th-floor
'executive rooms',
which enjoy a
superb view of the
Castle, are of the
highest standard,
the foyer and lower
floors less so. Warm
welcome and
efficient, friendly
service.
Hydrotherapy and
fitness center.
Restaurants:
Pompadour and
Brasserie.
☐ ☐ ☐ ☐ P ☐ ☐ ☐

☐ Channings
12–16 South
Learmonth Gardens
Comely Bank
Tel. (0131) 315 2226
48 rms. and 2 suites
Five, four-story
terraced houses
(1900) form this
charming club-hotel.
Cosy and
comfortably
furnished, with
several beautifully
modern rooms.
Three gardens and a
patio.
☐ ☐ ☐ ☐

☐ The Howard
◆ E B1
32–36 Great King St
Tel. (0131) 557 3500

CHANNINGS, EDINBURGH

THE HOWARD, EDINBURGH

13 rms. and 2 suites
Closed 24–28 Dec.
An elegant and
discreet hotel
occupying three
18th-century houses
in a splendid
location. Spacious,
comfortable rooms.
Attentive service and
an interesting
basement restaurant
(see '36').

☐ Malmaison
1 Tower Pl., Leith
Tel. (0131) 468 5000
60 rms.
A Scots Baronial
(1883–5) hotel near
the docks that
describes itself –

optimistically – as
'the best hotel in the
world for under
£100'. However its
fairly successful
'designer' decor,
excellent comfort,
relaxed service and
French-style
brasserie serving
good, simply
prepared food make
it one of the most
original hotels in
Scotland.
☐ ☐ P ☐ ☐

☐ The Roxburghe
◆ E A3
38 Charlotte Square
Tel. (0131) 240 5500
Even a hotel
standing on the

most beautiful
square in Scotland
with a façade
designed by Robert
Adam has a right to
take advantage of
the conveniences
and ultramodern
comfort provided by
the MacDonald
chain (no connection
with the fast-food
business). 'Leisure
club', fitness center.
Two restaurants.
☐ ☐ ☐ ☐ ☐ ☐

✪ ☐ Sibbet House
◆ E B1
26 Northumberland
St
Tel. (0131) 556 1078

9 rms. and suites
The entrance to one
of Edinburgh's most
delightful Bed &
Breakfasts, which
occupies two
Georgian town
houses, is marked by
a simple brass
plaque. This
excellent hotel, run
by a Scottish-French
couple, is fast
establishing a
reputation by word
of mouth, often
American. The decor
– family mahogany
furniture, prints and
old nicknacks – is
tasteful, elegant and
cheerful. Friendly
welcome and service.
No restaurant but a
superb breakfast.
Expensive for a B&B,
but worth the
money.
☐ ☐ P ☐

→ RESTAURANTS
✪ The Atrium
◆ E A4
10 Cambridge St
Tel. (0131) 228 8882
Closed Sat.
lunchtime
A strong sense of
incongruity, from the
location (at the foot
of the Castle, in the
covered walkway of
the Traverse Theatre,
with a view into
neighboring offices)
to the decor – canvas
wall coverings
beneath exposed
pipework, copper-
rod light fittings,
jute-covered chairs,
varnished rough-
plank tables, rough-
plastered walls. Add
to this a service that
smilingly forgets you
and a cuisine that is
a confused mixture
of the latest culinary
trends. And yet you
are not dissatisfied
when you leave the
Atrium. The staff are
charming and chef
Andrew Radford is
really talented. Best
are the delightful
conserve of duck,
delicious cabbage
and Chinese-style
caramelized sauce,

the wonderful tagliatelle with pine nuts and Japanese mushrooms in white-truffle sauce, and the hot, sticky toffee pudding, double cream and banana fritters. Interesting wines by the glass.
☒

Blue Bar Café
◆ **E** A4
10 Cambridge St
Tel. (0131) 221 1222
Open daily
Next to the Traverse Theatre, above the Atrium, to which it belongs. A snack-type cuisine with an enthusiastically international flavor served in large, cold but attractively decorated rooms. Original and delightful. Very friendly service and reasonable prices.
☒

Creelers
◆ **E** E4
3 Hunter Sq.,
Royal Mile
Tel. (0131) 220 4447
Closed Sun.
lunchtime
The owner knows his produce and proves it by using such unusual ingredients as the strange shellfish with an elephant-like trunk – a sea gaper, a sort of clam which is served well cooked and is quite tasty. His seafood platter favors smoked fish, produced in his smokehouse on the Isle of Arran. The freshness of the produce is guaranteed, is cooked to order and is allowed to retain its own individual flavor: prawns, queen scallops and cod roasted on its skin, mussels in cider, sole and monkfish in filo pastry 'baskets'. Choose the room at the back of the restaurant rather

than the bistro at the front; it is no more attractively decorated (some disturbing paintings) and is more expensive, but you'll feel more comfortable and the waitress is charming.
☒

Café Royal
◆ **E** D2
17a West Register St
Tel. (0131) 556 4124
Open daily
The Oyster Bar, beyond the revolving door, has an atmosphere of cosy, old-fashioned elegance, with its stylish stained-glass windows, marble bar and pale green plaster moldings. White tablecloths provide the setting for an elaborate and expensive cuisine: game with juniper, lobster Newburg, sole meunière, and delicious oysters served fresh or, Rockefeller, in Pernod. Alternatively, head for the polished wood fireplace and the adjoining Circle Bar, where you can enjoy a clam chowder and one of the hundred or so whiskies at the huge oval bar (a favorite haunt of rugby fans). Magnificent Victorian decor of carved wood, green leather and ceramic pictures.
☒

✪ Dubh Prais
◆ **E** E4
123b High St
Tel. (0131) 557 5732
Closed Sat., Mon.,
2 weeks at Christmas
and 2 weeks at
Easter
Pronounced Du Prash (but ask the cab driver for 'du pray') which means 'black cooking pot' in Gaelic. However this tiny – and

fiercely Scottish – basement bistro, with its distressing decor and pink walls, doesn't serve dishes cooked in pots, but 'well done' Aberdeen Angus steaks served with braised cabbage. It also serves two of the best-known Scottish specialties, which are not widely featured on the city's menus: kedgeree, a mixture of cooked smoked haddock and rice (or pearl barley) flavored with a curry sauce, and a near-authentic haggis (not served in a sheep's stomach). James McWilliams, the bistro's friendly owner, refuses to divulge his version of the haggis recipe, but it is rich, light and full of flavor. Finish the meal with the very British sticky toffee pudding, and a drop of a vintage whisky, for example the admirable 35-year-old Springbank from Campbeltown. Service more amenable than the prices.
☒

✪ Fishers Bistro
1 The Shore, Leith
Tel. (0131) 554 5666
Open daily
Behind the restaurant's white façade one of Scotland's most original cuisines is being prepared: imaginative with a strong marine flavor. Judge for yourself: seafood poached in noodle and mushroom broth; shrimps grilled with garlic and ginger; oysters and haddock in truffle juices served in an earthenware tureen; king-scallop platter with banana and chilli; filets of mullet with saffron and coarse-grain

mustard; grilled tuna with roast beetroot and ailloli sauce flavored with coriander; fillet of turbot and Hollandaise sauce flavored with orange and spices; bass cooked in shellfish liquid; baby haddock with tapenade, oyster tart... not to mention Fishers' fish soup. It is all bursting with health, flavor and imagination. If there's no room on the terrace, find a table in the bar or perch on one of the high stools at the round tables in the bistro, at the front of the restaurant, where the food is simple but good: beautifully fresh oysters, fishballs (balls of smoked fish fried in batter) served with rocket salad, moules marinière, seafood platter. Friendly service by girls in the flush of youth, while the owner, a handsome old salt with a clear, frank expression, treats his customers like fellow seamen.
☒

FitzHenry
19 Shore Pl., Leith
Tel. (0131) 555 6625
Closed Sun.
The FitzHenry is located beneath one of the stepped gables of the impressive and austere buildings of a 17th-century warehouse near the docks. Its decor is in a very individual modernist style, while the cuisine is complicated, adventurous and subject to the variations of a constantly changing succession of chefs. At the time of writing, it has a distinctive Spanish-

HOTELS AND RESTAURANTS◆

RESTAURANTS

- ▣ < £15
- ▣ £15–£25
- ▣ £25–£45
- ▦ > £45

Italian flavor. The waiters may have pierced ears but certainly keep their eye on the ball.
▣

Hadrian's
◆ **E** E3
2 North Bridge
Tel. (0131) 557 5000
Open daily
The 'younger brother' of the Number One (see below) is less starchy, less snobbish and more accessible. The rather kitsch, pale green decor is restful, the atmosphere cheerful and the 'Scottish' cuisine deceptively simple.
▣

Haldanes
◆ **E** D1
39a Albany St
Tel. (0131) 556 8407
Closed Sat.
lunchtime and Sun.
In the basement of the Albany hotel, between a row of lemon trees (!) and a sloping garden, this quiet restaurant prides itself on serving a cuisine of plain, almost ungarnished produce: king scallops, salmon, lamb, beef, green vegetables. Gentleman-farmer atmosphere and decor, striped sofas and a peat fire.
▣

Number One
◆ **E** D2
Balmoral Hotel,
1 Princes St
Tel. (0131) 557 6727
Closed Sat. and Sun.
lunchtime
Just as other restaurants want to reach for the stars, the Number One strives for the famous Michelin star – with the result that everything in this luxury restaurant is done with this in mind. Exclusive,

almost private, with its decor of delicate Chinese ornaments beyond an intimidating foyer, and its polite but distant service, the Number One not only aspires but believes itself to be the city's leading restaurant. It is certainly not the best in terms of value for money, since customers are encouraged to eat caviar, foie gras, truffles and Bresse pigeon and drink Château Margaux.
▦

Skippers Bistro
1a Dock Pl., Leith
Tel. (0131) 554 1018
Closed Sun.
A small, painted brick house, a terrace and wooden benches above a cut-off of the Water of Leith. Although secluded, this unusual old pub-restaurant is very well known. Its decor is crammed with every kind of souvenirs from all over the world and the atmosphere is friendly and welcoming. However it lacks the innovative cuisine of its rival, Fishers, and the warm conviviality of its neighbor, the Waterfront. It serves well-prepared seafood. There are some deliciously simple dishes: fresh oysters, king prawns, grilled kippers, sautéed monkfish tails, baked bass, rhubarb cheese cake.
▣

Stac Polly
8–10 Grindlay St
◆ **E** A5
Tel. (0131) 229 5405
29–33 Dublin St
◆ **E** D1
Tel. (0131) 556 2231
Closed Sat. and Sun.

lunchtime
There are two branches of this restaurant. One, at the foot of the Castle, is 'younger' in style and renowned for its imaginative cuisine; the other, in a smart district of New Town, is more conventional, even a little sleepy, in spite of a voluble and enthusiastic French maître d'hôtel (and a French sous-chef). Stac Polly's culinary specialty is haggis 'revisited': encased in filo pastry parcels, it is fine, delicately flavored if rather soft, and served with a sweet plum sauce. Sauces are very much in evidence throughout the menu and accompany the tasty fried crab, the calf's liver, the tender if rather bland lamb. The decor of this basement restaurant consists of gray stone, red hexagonal floor tiles and black parquet, while the entrance is hung with tartan. French wines and Scottish prices with a vengeance.

✪ 36
◆ **E** B1
36 Great King St
Tel. (0131) 556 3636
Closed Sat.
lunchtime
Like the Howard hotel above it, this extremely elegant restaurant is not always full in the evening. And yet the chef Malcolm Warham did part of his training in Paris, and he has a deftness, skill and sense of presentation that is reminiscent of the great French chefs. His cuisine is perfectly in keeping with the decor of this long, stylish basement

restaurant. The innovative cuisine is in the same aloof, smooth – almost virtual – style as the decor. Warham excels in the creation of desserts and his Earl Grey ice-cream and oven-dried apple slices are absolute musts. Taken overall the restaurant can be said to be the best elegant restaurant in Edinburgh. A fine and well-constructed wine list. Prices less expensive than you might expect.
▣

✪ The Waterfront
1c Dock Pl.
Leith
Tel. (0131) 554 7427
Open daily
Sleepy during the day but positively buzzing with life in the evening, this tiny, green shuttered brick house on the canal is one of the most attractive and intriguing pub-bistros in Edinburgh. With its patinated wood fittings, low ceilings, unusual ornaments, partitions that create cosy corners, the mahogany bar with its beer pumps, the landlord with his reminiscences, the covered terrace above the black waters of the canal and the bluish-green lights, this is a pub where Sherlock Holmes or Mr Hyde would not look out of place. Good fish dishes that rival those of the nearby Skipper and Fishers: mussels in garlic, fried squid, swordfish in olive oil, crab in basil, mackerel in a thick, cold marinade sauce and some really fine oysters.
▣

◆ HOTELS AND RESTAURANTS

HOTELS

- ▫ < £75
- ▪ £75–£140
- ▦ £140–£210
- ▦ > £210

- ⊞ Luxury
- ▉ Classic
- ▊ Charming
- ■ Comfortable

The Witchery by the Castle
◆ **E** C4
Castle Hill
Tel. (0131) 225 5613
Open daily
Wedged, with its terraced courtyards and gardens, between the buttresses of Castle Rock and a church tower, this inn is particularly popular with American visitors. The decor is picturesque with some delightful touches, such as the secret garden. The cuisine – stylish but unspectacular – is reasonable but quite expensive.
▣

→**PUBS & BARS**
Many Scottish rugby fans practice their sport best during the third half, over pints of ale. They can be seen propping up the bar in some of the pubs renowned for their wide range of beers and single malt whiskies. Some of the best include:

Bow Bar
◆ **E** D4
80 West Bow
Victoria Street
Tel. (0131) 226 7667

Café Royal Circle Bar
◆ **E** D2
19 West Register St
Tel. (0131) 556 1884
(See Restaurants.)

Thompson's Bar
◆ **E** A5
182–184 Morrison St
West End
Tel. (0131) 228 5700

Wigham's Wine Cellar
◆ **E** A3
13 Hope St
Tel. (0131) 225 8674
Closed Sun.

GLASGOW

→**HOTELS**
■ **Babity Bowster**
◆ **F** E4
Blackfriars St
Tel. (0141) 552 5055
6 rms.
You are not entirely sure whether you have walked into a
private house, an inn, or onto a stage set. It is in fact a hotel that occupies a late-18th-century monastery. Welcoming, convivial and friendly with a decor of well-ordered bric-a-brac. A few cosy and comfortably old-fashioned rooms. Excellent beers and a range of bar snacks in the downstairs bar, near an imitation peat fire. The attractive and interesting second-floor bistro, the Scottische, is renowned for its haggis and sticky-toffee pudding.*
▫

⊞ **Glasgow Hilton**
◆ **F** B3
1 William St
Tel. (0141) 204 5555
315 rms. and 4 suites
Admittedly it does overlook a freeway intersection, but there is also a magnificent view across Glasgow from the top of this twenty-story building. Although not right in the center, it is located in a quiet, elegant district and is extremely modern and comfortable with an elegantly functional decor. It is expensive, but what luxury, what a welcome, what professional, friendly service! All this and the promise of the best classic dinner in the city (see Cameron's). There is also a bar, Kinsky's, with a generous buffet. Sauna, fitness center.
▦ ▣ ▦ ❄ P ▦

▦ **Hilton Grosvenor**
◆ **G** B1
Grosvenor Terrace
Great Western Rd
Tel. (0141) 339 8811
96 rms.
This smaller and
older version of the Hilton is located near the Botanical Gardens, in a beautiful Victorian building. Extremely comfortable with a pleasant and slightly faded atmosphere.*
▣ ❄ P ▦

▦ **Malmaison**
◆ **F** C3
278 West George St
Tel. (0141) 572 1000
68 rms. and 4 suites
This excellent 'chain' hotel occupies a former Greek church. It has been tastefully fitted out and its beautiful rooms have the latest mod coms. Basement bar.
▣ ▦ ❄ ▣

✪ ⊞ **One Devonshire Gardens**
◆ **G** B1
1 Devonshire Gardens
Tel. (0141) 204 5004
25 rms. and 2 suites
Three Victorian town houses – with separate entrances – form the most delightful, most elegant, and arguably one of the best hotel in Scotland, with fine antique furniture, carpets and paintings; comfort; silent and discreetly attentive butler service; and a sense of well-being that pervades you as soon as you step over the threshold – especially if you have reserved one of the extremely expensive and delightfully luxurious suites at the very top of the building. A pity that the cuisine (see Restaurants), attractive but lacking in technical expertise, strikes a discordant note in all this harmony.
▣ ▣ ▦ ▦

▦ **The Devonshire Hotel**
◆ **G** B1
5 Devonshire Gardens
Tel. (0141) 339 7878
12 rms. and 2 suites
Although less famous than its neighbor at One Devonshire Gardens, this hotel – which occupies two adjoining town houses – is by no means less elegant, even though the public rooms (foyer, hotel dining room) have less in the way of objets d'art and antiques. The rooms (some are a little less expensive) are just as delightful.
▣ ▦ ▦

→**RESTAURANTS**
The Buttery
◆ **F** B3
652 Argyle St
Tel. (0141) 221 8188
Closed Sat. lunchtime and Mon.
For chef Ian Fleming, modern Scottish cuisine means adorning traditionally Scottish produce with basil, parmesan, pancetta, tortellini and champagne. Strangely enough, it works reasonably well and is extremely popular. A delightfully old-fashioned club-style decor with mahogany furniture, crimson upholstery and waitresses dressed as Queen Victoria. The Belfry, on the first floor, is an attractive French-style bistro serving seafood.
▣

✪ **Cameron's**
◆ **F** B3
Glasgow Hilton
1 William St
Tel. (0141) 204 5555
Closed Sun.
In a somber decor that combines the woodwork of a Georgian library,

RESTAURANTS

▪ < £15
▪ £15–£25
▪ £25–£45
▪ > £45

green hangings and an Henri II sideboard, the delightful if slightly disorganized service proposes Scottish food with an international flavor. A tendency to overcook and an evident fondness for veal-based dishes does not detract from the wonderful memory of the richly flavored haggis, the light vegetable soup with haddock and seafood, the thick, tender undercut of beef topped with black pudding, and the delicately flavored rare duck with foie gras and lentils. Classic desserts and a limited choice of expensive wines (the Chilean red is to be recommended).
▪

City Merchant
◆ F D4
97–99 Candleriggs
Tel. (0141) 553 1577
Closed Sun.
lunchtime
Enjoy a warm Scottish atmosphere, with crowded tables buzzing with conversation; a decor of colored stained glass, mahogany and pitch pine; a mezzanine overlooking the animated bar and the huge old-fashioned seascape along the staircase; the accent of the politely spoken waiters; seafood cuisine and fine, well-prepared produce: prawns, seafood platter, fresh oysters, exquisite monkfish, 'rustic' haggis and hot gingerbread with orange butter. Unfortunately all this is marred by the prices which are excessive for a large but simple bistro.
▪

Gamba
◆ D B3
225a West George St, Milngavie
Tel. (0141) 572 0899
Closed Sun.
An elegant little restaurant with a contemporary terracotta decor behind a black and gold façade. It has two deliveries of fresh fish a day, so you can enjoy fish – raw (Japanese style), with garlic in a stew (French style) or in balsamic vinegar with white truffles (Italian style) – with complete confidence. However the freshness of the produce and these delicious recipes have their price.
▪

Nairns
◆ F A2
13 Woodside Crescent
Tel. (0141) 353 0707
Closed Christmas and New Year's Day
Nick Nairn is a TV personality and a first-rate chef, and it is in the latter role that he really excels. He uses only the best produce (salmon, cod, monkfish, pig's cheeks, pigeon, vegetables, butter) and has creative ideas (not to be confused with the decoration on the plates), but his timing could be slightly better. The deliciously elegant decor of the dining room – an attractive gray with beautiful white table linen and chairs covered in black – is repeated in the little rooms at garden level. The service is relaxed but professional. Prices are extremely reasonable for such an elegant restaurant. Try the South African Cabernet Sauvignon.
▪

One Devonshire Gardens
◆ G B1
1 Devonshire Gardens
Tel. (0141) 339 2001
Closed Sat. lunchtime
High-ranking Glaswegians join tourists and businessmen in the dining room of the most discreet and most elegant restaurant in Glasgow. A perfect atmosphere of muted and serene elegance, walls hung with stylish curtains, delightful chairs, numerous exquisitely tasteful wood, silver and porcelain ornaments, and an extremely elegant service. Unfortunately the cuisine does not enjoy quite the same distinction. The very original and delicately flavored little lobster, exquisitely fresh and slightly smoked, is to be recommended, but the other dishes on the short menu are not in the same league. Good wines but somewhat expensive.
▦

Rogano
◆ F D3
11 Exchange Pl.
Tel. (0141) 248 4055
Closed Christmas and Jan. 1.
This old building was given a new lease of life in 1935 with a decor inspired by the Queen Mary, then being built in the Clyde shipyards. The fish-based cuisine dates from the same period and is truly 'upper crust', both figuratively and literally (gratin). Try the lobster Thermidor or the generous seafood platter. Ceremonious welcome when you ring at the

monumental door. Many people's favorite Glasgow restaurant.
▪

Two Fat Ladies
88 Dumbarton Rd
Tel. (0141) 339 1944
Closed Sun.–Mon. and Tue.–Fri lunchtime.
The 'two fat ladies' on their large, reddish canvas are reminiscent of Botero with touches of Greuze and Picasso. They are appetizing, like the comely waitress and the seafood cuisine of chef Calum Mathieson. Nine tables in an attractively Spartan decor of shiny eggshell and paper napkins. Extremely fresh produce, generally well cooked, and imaginative recipes. Superb sole but rather softened by steaming, stir-fried vegetables and amazing oysters that even a cream sauce and the heat of a slow oven cannot spoil. The sticky toffee pudding is pleasantly overwhelming. Several good white wines from France and Australia.
▪

78 St Vincent
◆ F C3
78 St Vincent St
Tel. (0141) 248 7878
Closed Sun. lunchtime.
A French-style restaurant. Behind an austere colonnaded façade, beneath high ceilings, white-globe light fittings and Scottish clan frescos, this restaurant is the epitome of tradition, good manners and dependable value: terrine of pheasant, tenderloin of lamb with mint, cassoulet

◆HOTELS AND RESTAURANTS

(bean stew with mutton, pork or lamb), guinea fowl in whisky, creme brûlée with ginger. A wide selection of wines by the – very generous – glass. ⊡

❂ Ubiquitous Chip
◆ G B1
12 Ashton Lane
Tel. (0141) 334 5007
Closed Christmas and Jan. 1
Behind the university, Ashton Lane, a delightful little cobbled street bordered by whitewashed brick houses with black door and window frames, is like the setting for a comic strip. And what a choice of restaurants! But the Ubiquitous Chip is undoubtedly the best – and the most attractive – in the street and probably the whole of Glasgow. Imagine a glass-roofed conservatory, full of green plants, a fairly elegant adjoining room, and others upstairs (simpler dishes, soups, salads, fried fish), with seating for 120 or even 200 people. Pale girls and 'Clockwork Orange' boys, only more appealing, serve a very restrained and unpretentious modern cuisine. Who could resist the beef marinated à la juive served with acidulated mixed vegetables, the vegetarian haggis (lentils, soya, spices, a light turnip purée), the extremely ripe hare served in its juice with a wine sauce, the exceptional breast of pigeon, barley 'risotto' and two deliciously sophisticated sauces? This is cuisine at its

best, intelligent and delicate. Good cheddar but rather disappointing desserts, a richly cosmopolitan wine list and an extensive choice of pure malts. And, surprisingly, prices that leave a pleasant taste in your mouth. ⊡

Yes
◆ F C3
22 West Nile St
Tel. (0141) 221 8044
Closed Sun.
With its black shutters, blue lacquered façade, 'tulip' chairs, round

glass tables, abstract paintings, zen garden and split levels, Yes has all the modern elegance of a Milanese restaurant. The cuisine also has an Italian (antipasti) and international flavor, adventurous and not at all bad ⊡

→CAFÉS, SNACKS
Art Lover's Café
◆ G A2
House for an Art Lover,
Bellahouston Park
Tel. (0141) 353 4779
Closed Sun.

Begin your Mackintosh tour in this large white villa, designed by the architect for an 'art lover' in 1901. In summer you can enjoy a lunchtime snack or salad outside. Good jazz on Saturday evenings.

❂ The Willow Tea Rooms
217 Sauchiehall St
◆ F C2
Tel. (0141) 332 0521
97 Buchanan St
◆ F C3
Tel. (0141) 204 5242
Open daily
If you are in any

doubt as to whether Mackintosh was as great an artist as Gallé, Tiffany, Klimt or Horta (and if you are also hungry or thirsty) call in at the Willow Tea Rooms. There are two branches, but the original is in Sauchiehall Street. Mackintosh designed the clean lines of its façade just before 1900. Today the ground floor is occupied by a store selling attractive but expensive Mackintosh-style objects. It is

overlooked by a mezzanine with amazing cube-shaped colored light fittings, stained-glass windows and exquisite frescos – the famous high-backed chairs are in the 'de-luxe' room. The other tea room, in Buchanan Street, is a reconstruction of the first and is just as attractive and remarkable, with more lamps, furniture and windows. Delightfully prepared food and fresh pastries.

→PUBS
The Horse Shoe Bar
◆ F C3
17 Drury St
Tel. (0141) 229 5711
Open daily
One of the many 'longest bars in the world', but this horseshoe-shaped, polished-wood bar is truly superb. It was highly fashionable at the turn of the 19th–20th centuries, but is today reduced to holding nightly karaoke sessions (7.30pm). During the day, however, it is still possible to enjoy its legendary atmosphere, its beers at less than £1 per pint and its stimulating menus.

Uisge Beatha
◆ F A1
232 Woodlands Rd
Tel. (0141) 564 1596
Open daily
Literally 'water of life', pronounced wiskay-bê. Whisky is the order of the day in this Highland hunting cabin decor, with its old furniture, stags' heads and trophies, including the head of Margaret Thatcher, the former Prime Minister. Enjoy traditional haggis with turnip (neeps)

HOTELS AND RESTAURANTS ◆

RESTAURANTS

- 🔲 < £15
- 🔲 £15–£25
- 🔲 £25–£45
- 🔲 > £45

---

purée, mussels and roast lamb in a lively atmosphere.

SOUTH
BALLOCH

◆ **D** A3
→**HOTEL-RESTAURANT**
Cameron House
11 miles due northwest on the A82
Tel. (01389) 755 565
89 rms. and 7 suites
Luxurious and extremely comfortable, but the natural setting of Loch Lomond and the surrounding mountains is more successful than the decor of this rather pretentious mock castle. By contrast the cuisine of the Georgian House is attractive and imaginative. Fine, perfectly cooked produce.
🔲🔲🔲🔲🔲🔲 🔲🔲
🔲

DUMFRIES

◆ **D** B5
→**RESTAURANT**
Wisharts
Robert Burns Centre, Mill Rd
Tel. (01387) 259 679
Closed Sun. evening, Tue.–Sat. lunchtime, Christmas, Jan. 1, first two weeks of Jan. and July
A rather banal decor, but the cuisine uses wonderful produce that has not been martyrized by the cosmopolitan imagination of an adventurous but extremely skilful chef: for example, fillet of salmon in a crisp coating of cured Parma ham, lettuce hearts and roast peppers.
🔲

GULLANE

◆ **D** C3
→**HOTEL-RESTAURANT**
Greywalls
Duncur Rd, Muirfield
Tel. (01620) 842 144
Open. mid-April to mid-Oct.

23 rms.
Above the 18th hole of Muirfield and the Firth of Forth, a house of honey-colored stone – one of the most elegant in Scotland – stands in a large walled garden filled with roses and lavender. The decor, like the welcome, is well mannered and warm. The cuisine of chef Simon Burns does not have the reputation of the nearby La Potinière restaurant. It takes itself less seriously, but is still resolutely modernist in style. Some fine wines and whiskies.
🔲🔲🔲🔲 🔲🔲

→**RESTAURANT**
La Potinière
Main St
Tel. (01620) 843 214
Open Thur. and Sun. lunchtime, Fri.–Sat. evening. Closed first week in June and Oct.
British food critics rave about the 'masterpieces' of Hillary Brown, but the food tends to be overrated. Specialties include vanilla salmon, carrot and apricot soup, pigeon with honey and lentils, asparagus and pear salad. David Brown only abandons his air of lofty concern to offer advice and serve wine. Very little in the way of decor in this barn-like setting.
🔲

LINLITHGOW

◆ **D** B3
→**HOTEL-RESTAURANT**
Champany Inn
3 miles due northeast, Champany
Tel. (01506) 834 532
16 rms.
The only restaurant in Scotland whose main specialty is the wonderful Aberdeen

Angus beef. No trace of the 'modern Scottish' trend, but generous portions of superb, mature steak (and even burgers) grilled over a wood fire (also lobsters, king prawns and grilled salmon). The inn, with its profusion of silverware, candlesticks, paintings and tartans, is popular with tourists. Sixteen expensive rooms furnished in comfortable Edwardian style.*
🔲🔲🔲🔲

PORTPATRICK

◆ **C** C6
→**HOTEL-RESTAURANT**
Knockinaam Lodge
4 miles via the A77
Tel. (01776) 810 471
10 rms.
A neat lawn leads down to the private beach of this former whitewashed hunting lodge. Try to reserve the largest of the relatively small rooms, which are all beautifully decorated. The cuisine of chef Tony Pierce has a great reputation despite, or possibly because of, having a fixed menu that changes each day. The very fine and carefully prepared produce would probably taste just as good even without the whipped butter (grilled cod), cardamom mousse (bass with seaweed), port (milk-fed lamb) and squid ink (lobster risotto). An excellent wine list.
🔲🔲🔲 🔲🔲

TROON

◆ **D** A4
→**HOTEL**
Lochgreen House
2 miles due southeast on the B749, Monktonhill Rd, Southwood
Tel. (01292) 313 343

14 rooms, 1 suite
Thirty acres of woodland and the famous Royal Troon Golf Course are the main attractions of this pleasant little hotel with its light wood paneling, attractive paintings and peat fire. Skilfully prepared French cuisine.
🔲🔲🔲🔲🔲🔲🔲

TURNBERRY

◆ **D** A5
→**HOTEL**
Turnberry Hotel
Tel. (01655) 331 000
111 rms. and 21 suites
Very much a golfer's hotel, which offers hydrotherapy to repair strained muscles and age-related damage. A dramatic view across the vast park to the Isle of Arran. The restaurant serves fine seafood and classic cuisine. Classic rooms with a sea view, in this large Edwardian building.
🔲🔲🔲🔲🔲🔲 🔲🔲

EAST CENTRAL
ANSTRUTHER

◆ **D** D3
→**RESTAURANT**
Cellar
24 East Green
Tel. (01333) 310 378
Closed Sun.–Tue. lunchtime and Christmas
Delicious fresh seafood, meat and vegetables served in a plethora of sauces, pies, risottos, bacon, garlic and mayonnaise. Chef Mr Jukes certainly knows his job.
🔲

AUCHTERARDER

◆ **D** B2
→**HOTEL**
Gleneagles
2 miles due southwest on the A823
Tel. (01764) 662 231
215 rms. and 14 suites
The epitome of old

◆HOTELS AND RESTAURANTS

American-style elegance. Golf, shopping, horse-riding, clay-pigeon shooting, archery, a crèche, massage, a chauffeur service, golf school, falconry, swimming, fishing (salmon and trout), cross-country driving and plenty of romantic walks. The rooms have wing chairs, duchesse beds and chintz curtains. The hotel also has several restaurants.
⬚⬚⬚⬚⬚⬚⬚

CALLANDER

◆ D B3
→HOTEL-RESTAURANT
The Roman Camp
Main St
Tel. (01877) 330 003
10 rms. and 4 suites
This former hunting lodge of the earls of Perth, near the ruins of a Roman camp, is today an hotel with a luxurious decor, in modern and old-fashioned British style. Flowers everywhere and a truly remarkable garden. Private fishing. Expensive but good cuisine, with fish and poultry given an international flavor against a backdrop of tapestries.
⬚⬚⬚⬚⬚⬚⬚

CUPAR

◆ D C2
→HOTEL-RESTAURANT
The Peat Inn Hotel
Peat Inn
Cupar
Tel. (01334) 840 206
8 suites
A hamlet that has long been renowned for the cuisine of its former coaching inn. Today the Peat Inn has an annex with eight beautiful suites, where you can relax in style after eating lobster with wild mushrooms and pheasant with truffles.
⬚⬚⬚⬚⬚⬚

→RESTAURANT
Ostlers Close Restaurant
Bonnygate
Tel. (01334) 655 574
Closed Sun.–Mon.; Wed.–Thur. lunchtime and 2nd week of May
Like many Scottish restauranteurs, the Grahams, who own this tiny, old and extremely attractive inn, pride themselves on their modern Scottish cuisine. In fact they are unwittingly writing culinary prose, with fresh produce from the farm, fields, moors (grouse), woodland (wild mushrooms), river and sea allowed to express its original flavors via a subtle use of wine, saffron and Hollandaise sauce. A good restaurant, which guide books tend to ignore. Very attentive service.
⬚

DALRY

◆ A A1
→RESTAURANT
Braidwoods
1 mile due southwest via the A737, Drummastle Mill Cottage
Tel. (01294) 833 544
Closed Sun. evening, Mon.–Tue. lunchtime and first 3 weeks in Jan.
In the heart of the countryside, two fresh, rustic rooms in an old cottage. You would expect a fairly simple cuisine, but the dishes – created by true professionals using mostly local produce – are superb and perfectly cooked.
⬚

DUNBLANE

◆ D B3
→HOTEL
Hilton Dunblane Hydro
2 miles due north on the B8033
Tel. (01786) 822 551
178 rms. and 33 suites
A huge Victorian building, well situated just north of Stirling. It was completely renovated in spring 2000 and is now one of the best business hotels in Scotland. Well-equipped fitness center. Extremely comfortable.
⬚⬚⬚⬚⬚⬚⬚

→HOTEL-RESTAURANT
Cromlix House
Kinbuck
Tel. (01786) 822 125
6 rms. and 8 suites
This impressive Victorian mansion is surrounded by 2000 acres of moorland, woodland, meadows and lochs. Old-fashioned service and decor, and a comfort that is cosy, warm and deliciously outdated (huge Victorian baths). Small private chapel for weddings and christenings. Conventional cuisine – traditional and expensive – served in an elegant, rural decor.
⬚⬚⬚⬚⬚

DUNDEE

◆ D C2
→HOTEL
Hilton Dundee
Earl Grey Pl.
Tel. (01382) 229 271
126 rms. and 3 suites
An impressive modern parallelepiped-shaped building on the banks of the Firth of Tay. All the facilities, amenities and comfort of the Hilton chain. Sauna, fitness center. Good cuisine served in a restaurant with a panoramic view.
⬚⬚⬚⬚⬚⬚⬚

→RESTAURANTS
Fisherman's Tavern
12 Fort St
Broughty Ferry

Pleasant harbor-side bistro atmosphere and a wide choice of beers.
⬚

Deep Sea
81 Nethergate
Closed in the evening
This restaurant has been serving tasty fish'n'chips for sixty years.
⬚

DUNKELD

◆ D B2
→HOTELS
Hilton Dunkeld House
Tel. (01350) 727 771
93 rms. and 3 suites
This Hilton hotel, which occupies the castle of the 7th Duke of Atholl, is a complete surprise. Over 245 acres of moorland and forest; fishing, pigeon shooting, conferences and dinner-dances.
⬚⬚⬚⬚⬚⬚⬚⬚

Kinnaird
7 miles due northwest via the B898, Dalguise
Tel. (01796) 482 440
Closed Jan.–Feb.: Mon.–Wed.
9 rms. and 8 cottages (2–4 people)
A large, late-18th-century mansion nestling in the woods above the Tay valley. Elegant rooms and attentive service. After fishing for trout and salmon in the river or one of the three lochs on the estate, a game of tennis or croquet, a country walk, clay-pigeon shooting or a hack, guests can enjoy the comfortable sofas and peat fires in the Cedar Room, and the international cuisine served in an attractive decor of Italian-style frescos.
⬚⬚⬚⬚⬚⬚

HOTELS AND RESTAURANTS◆

GLENROTHES
◆ D D3
→HOTEL
Balbirnie House
2 miles due
northeast on the
B9130, Markinch
Tel. (01592) 610 066
28 rms. and 2 suites
*This magnificent,
colonnaded
Georgian castle built
in Greek classical
style offers a
plentiful supply
of fresh air,
domesticated nature
and civilized
comfort. You can
have dinner in the
orangery or lunch in
the adjoining bistro.*
⊞

PERTH
◆ D C2
→HOTELS
Within the town:
**Isle of Skye
Toby Hotel**
Dundee Rd
Tel. (01738) 624 471
*A huge, well-
appointed and
rather expensive
business hotel.
Charming view of
the Tay from some
of the rooms.*

Sunbank House
50 Dundee Rd
Tel. (01738) 442 515
*Fairly near the town
center, a Victorian
house and garden,
with a view of the
Tay and good, simple
cuisine.*

Salutation Hotel
34 South St
Tel. (01738) 630 066
*One of Scotland's
oldest hotels (1699).
It has been
extensively
modernized and,
although more
comfortable, there
are very few traces
of the past.*

On the outskirts:
Kinfauns Castle
3 miles due east via
the A90, Kinfauns
Tel. (01738) 620 777
14 rms., 2 suites
*This magnificent
hotel, with its square*

towers, has been
renovated in
Edwardian style with
painted ceilings,
marble fireplaces,
collections of objets
d'art from the Far
East, 19th-century
or teak furniture.
Large, luxurious
rooms with every
modern comfort
and service worthy
of a stately home.
The oak-paneled
dining room offers
a limited choice of
sophisticated,
attractive and
complicated cuisine
in the new British
style.*
◻◻◻⊞

The Murrayshall
1 mile via the A94,
New Scone
Tel. (01738) 551 171
28 rms.
*If golf – the main
attraction of this
mansion – is not
your cup of tea, you
can play croquet,
tennis or bowls,
work out in the gym,
go horse-riding,
pigeon shooting or
salmon fishing, walk
in the 300 acres of
parkland, meadows
and forests, enjoy a
nap in one of the
hotel's – large or
small – attractive
rooms, or the terrine
of lobster and
tenderloin of beef in
the delightfully
outdated 'Old
Master' decor of the
dining room.*
◻◻◻ ▪

→RESTAURANTS
**Kerachers Restaurant
& Oyster Bar**
168 South St
Tel. (01738) 449 777
Closed Mon. eve.
and Sun.
*An oyster bed and
adjoining bar where
they are served. On
the second floor,
lobster bisque,
mussels in garlic
cream, mullet fried
in breadcrumbs, cod
in sesame oil and
Angus steaks are*

prepared to order
and served in a
minimalist decor.*
▪

Let's Eat
77–79 Kinnoull St
Tel. (01738) 643 377
Closed Sun.–Mon.,
2 weeks in Jan. and
July.
*The only restaurant
in Perth with a real
reputation. Formerly
a theater and then
an antique store, it is
now a fashionable
bistro, informal and
not too expensive.
Unfortunately chef
Tony Heath does not
allow his excellent
produce to express
its original taste.
Parmesan, truffle oil,
garlic, olives,
peppers, basil and
Thai spices impose
the new culinary
world order.*
▪

Let's Eat Again
33 George St
Tel. (01738) 633 771
*An annex of 'Let's
Eat', this restaurant
has a more
aggressive decor
and a younger
atmosphere. The fish
mold (lunch) and
souris of lamb
(dinner) are
extremely popular.*
▪

N° 33
George St
Tel. (01738) 633 771
*Justly renowned for
its fish, crustaceans
and shellfish – and
quite a respectable
bouillabaisse –
served at the bar.*
▪

ST ANDREWS
◆ D C2
→HOTEL
The Old Course
Old Station Rd
Tel. (01334) 474 371
Closed 1 week at
Christmas
114 rms. and 32
suites
*Not recommended
for non-golfers. If
you are already*

afflicted, the
atmosphere of this
'holy of holies' will
exacerbate your
condition to the
point that you are
oblivious to the
charms of this huge
and extremely
comfortable
mansion.
Conventional French
cuisine. Well-
equipped fitness
center. Private
driving range and
putting green.*
▨▥◻▧⊞▨▨⊞

WEST
ARDUAIN
◆ C C3
→HOTEL
Loch Melfort Hotel
Arduaine
16 miles south of
Oban
Tel. (01852) 200 233
27 rms.
*Overlooking the
Askinish Bay, and
beside the famous
Arduaine Gardens,
this is a delightful,
welcoming hotel.
There are two large
superior bedrooms
in the main house
with kingsize beds
and lavish decor.
The remaining
bedrooms, in the
adjoining Cedar
wings have either a
terrace or balcony
from which you can
enjoy splendid sea
views. The elegant
restaurant offers
five-course dinners,
with the emphasis
very much on fresh
seafood. The hotel
also has a bistro,
a cocktail bar and a
comfortable library
lounge.*
◻▨▥◻▨▨

BRODICK
◆ C C4
→HOTEL-RESTAURANT
**Kilmichael
Country House**
1 mile due west,
Glen Cloy
Tel. (01770) 302 219
Closed Christmas
and Jan. 1
5 rms. and 3 suites
Everything is rather

311

◆HOTELS AND RESTAURANTS

HOTELS

⬛	< £75	⊞	Luxury
⬛	£75–£140	⊟	Classic
⬛	£140–£210	⬛	Charming
⬛	> £210	⬛	Comfortable

good in this bright, little old house in the heart of the unspoiled Isle of Arran. Its quaint and simple dining room, overlooks a park filled with rhododendrons. Sophisticated rural cuisine and a few delicately and tastefully decorated – and reasonably priced – rooms.
⬛⬛⬛⬛⬛⬛⬛

KILFINAN

◆ C C3
→HOTEL
Kilfinan Hotel
Tel. (01700) 821 201
Closed Feb.
11 rms.
A green Highland landscape, a gray loch, a delightful old whitewashed house and eleven charming rooms. The magnificently bearded owner-chef, Rolf Muelin, gives his fine regional produce what he describes as a 'sophisticated taste of Scotland'.
⬛⬛⬛⬛⬛

KINTYRE

◆ C C3
→HOTEL
The Anchor Hotel
Harbour St
Tarbert
Loch Fyne
Tel. (01880) 820 577
12 rms.
Set in the beautiful Kintyre peninsula, this is a good base for touring the surrounding lochs and mountains. Proprietress Carolyn MacDonald has spent the past few years transforming the hotel to provide modern comforts as well as a traditional welcoming atmosphere.
⬛⬛⬛⬛

MULL

◆ C B2
→HOTEL-RESTAURANT
Druimard Country House Hotel

Dervaig
Isle of Mull
Tel. (01688) 400 345
Closed Nov.–Mar.
5 rms.
Beautifully restored Victorian country house on the edge of the village of Devaig. A family hotel that prides itself on its warm welcome and relaxing, comfortable atmosphere. The hotel can arrange boat trips to the isles of Coll, Eigg, Muck and Rum, wildlife expeditions, whale watching trips or visits to the legendary Fingal's Cave. The restaurant serves tempting five-course dinners.
⬛⬛⬛⬛

PORT APPIN

◆ C C2
→HOTEL-RESTAURANT
✪ **The Airds Hotel**
Tel. (01631) 730 236
Closed Dec. 23–27
12 rms.
One of the best country hotels with a magnificent view of Loch Linnhe and the surrounding mountains. The rooms are cosy and luxuriously old fashioned, the welcome simple and courteous, and the cuisine complex but very good. The Lismore oysters in aspic, the improbable 'bouillabaisse' made with fried squid and the date pudding leave a lasting impression. Fine wine list served by a red-bearded wine-waiter in a kilt. Not cheap.
⬛⬛⬛⬛⬛⬛⬛

NORTHEAST
ABERDEEN

◆ D D1 – B A6
→HOTELS
⬛**Ardoe House**
4 miles due west,
Blairs
Tel. (01224) 867 355

70 rms. and suites
The small turreted and crenelated castle, built near the River Dee by a Victorian soap merchant, is today a fairytale hotel. In spite of a rather 'nouveau riche' luxury, its rooms are pleasantly rustic. A complicated cuisine which prides itself on being French.
⬛⬛⬛⬛

⬛**Hilton Tree Tops**
161 Springfiel St
Tel. (01224) 313 377
96 rms., 24 'club-rooms'
A slightly out-of-the-way hotel on a human scale, like cottages in the 'Granite City'. Although slightly Spartan, the rooms are extremely comfortable. Sauna, fitness center. Exotic cuisine in the Bacoa Grill.
⬛⬛⬛⬛⬛⬛⬛⬛

⬛**Simpson's**
59 Queen's Rd
Tel. (01224) 327 777
35 rms. and suites
A Mediterranean decor behind the gray façades of two granite houses. Pleasant, classically comfortable rooms. Well-prepared cuisine served on the unusual 'Andalusian' patio with its colonnades and palm trees.
⬛⬛⬛

✪⬛ **Skene House Holburn**
6 Union Grove
Tel. (01224) 580 000
39 suites
A good choice of comfortable, modern suites (one has three bedrooms, sitting room, kitchen) in traditional granite houses. Self-service bar, reading rooms, attentive

service, generous breakfasts, no restaurant. And, surprisingly, prices are the same as for a standard room in a classic hotel.

The same facilities at two other addresses:
Rosemount
96 Rosemount Viaduct
Tel. (01224) 645 971
Whitehall
2 Whitehall Pl.
Tel. (01224) 646 600
⬛⬛⬛

→RESTAURANTS
Atlantis Seafood
Mariner Hotel
349 Great Western Rd
Tel. (01224) 591 403
Closed Sat. lunchtime
The restaurant, which occupies a conservatory adjoining the hotel, serves freshly caught and simply prepared fish and good, grilled meat dishes. Wine sold by the glass. The hotel has 22 modern rooms (£65–75).
⬛

Gérard Brasserie
50 Chapel St
Tel. (01224) 639 500
Open daily
A well-established, traditional French restaurant where you can eat rare meat and lightly cooked fish. Shellfish are 'Thermidor'. Delightful winter and summer dining room.
⬛

Lairhillock Inn
Netherley, 11 miles due south
Tel. (01569) 730 001
Closed Christmas and Jan. 1
This extremely old farm has long been famous for its cheeses, whiskies and its real peat fire. It has been extensively restored

HOTELS AND RESTAURANTS ◆

RESTAURANTS

■ < £15
■ £15–£25
■ £25–£45
⊞ > £45

and is today one of the best inns in the north of Scotland. The Angus beef comes from the neighboring farm, the salmon from the River Dee and the boar from the moors. They are all prepared with respect.
■

Silver Darling
Pocra Quay, North Pier
Tel. (01224) 576 229
Closed Sat. lunchtime, Sun., Dec. 24–27 and Dec. 30–Jan. 6
The glass-roofed dining room offers a truly spectacular view, and the menu an attractive choice of fresh fish and shellfish, prepared – as you might expect with a chef called Didier Dejean – in traditional 'French' style: with mixed herbs and olives, ailloli with sorrel and chorizo, seaweed and coconut milk, and tapenade. A few interesting desserts: chocolate terrine, Drambuie soufflé.
■

BALLATER

◆ D C1
→HOTEL
Hilton Craigendarroch
Braemar Rd
Tel. (013397) 55858
39 rms. and 6 suites
This vast brick and slate building is only 6 miles from Balmoral Castle. Guests can swim, ski (artificial snow), play squash, tennis, snooker, do aerobics and sample a good pure malt from the nearby Glenlivet distillery. Luxurious Oaks Restaurant and Caribbean bar. Excellent, friendly service.
🖥️🕂🎿🐾🏊

→HOTEL-RESTAURANT
Green Inn
9 Victoria Rd
Tel. (013397) 55701
King scallops in rhubarb butter, pesto soup with prawns, home-made bread... this is the home of 'new Scottish' cuisine. But Jeff Purves is a talented chef and these unusual combinations are surprisingly good. Not many tables in the pastel dining room. Three rooms where guests can take an after-dinner nap.
■

SIMPSON'S, ABERDEEN

CULLODEN HOUSE, INVERNESS

NORTH ACHILTIBUIE

◆ A C4
→HOTEL
Summer Isles
Tel. (01854) 622 282
11 rms., cottages (2–4 people)
If you read the alluring description of the Altnaharrie Inn ◆ 314, but didn't get round to booking, you can still dine and stay in this isolated hotel some 20 or so miles to the north. It is worth it if only for the spectacle of the dazzling and shimmering sea (icy

cold or warmed by the Gulf Stream), the seabirds and seals, as well as the crab, lobster and turbot, simply prepared and served with home-made bread. Pleasant rooms in the cottages.
🏠🕂🏊🐾🎣🏕️

ARISAIG

◆ C C1
→HOTEL
Arisaig House
30 miles due southwest on the A830, Beasdale
Tel. (01687) 450 622
10 rms. and 2 suites
Rebuilt in 1937 before becoming a

training center for the British Intelligence Service, this huge, slate-gray manor has some interesting 1900s and Art Deco features, as well as others in the purest British 'cosy' tradition. Cuisine heaped with praise by the press and sauce by the chef, Mr Gibson. A magnificent view of the loch and mountains. Terraces, rock gardens, vegetable gardens, rhododendrons and rare flowers.
🏠🕂🏡🖥️🚗🎣🏊⊞

AVIEMORE

◆ A E6
→HOTEL
Hilton Aviemore
Tel. (01479) 810 681
90 rms.
If you ever go skiing in Scotland, reserve a 'club room' in this large, modern and extremely comfortable hotel at the foot of the Cairngorms. There is also another Hilton, the Coylumbridge (Tel. [01479] 810661), which stands in a wooded park and is ideal for summer sports.
🖥️🅿️🎿🏊

DUNVEGAN (SKYE)

◆ A B6
→HOTEL-RESTAURANT
The House Over-By
6 miles due northwest on the B884, Colbost
Tel. (01470) 511 258
Closed mid-Jan.– mid-Feb.
6 suites
On the glorious Isle of Skye: imagination, intelligence and taste in a relaxed, contemporary style. A few small white houses clustered around a cobbled courtyard on the shores of a sleepy loch. Furniture, fittings and finishing touches are extremely modern and sophisticated. Add to this a cuisine possibly unique in Scotland. Lobster with the merest hint of vanilla, king scallops that blend admirably with Aberdeen Angus beef, corn salad and pine nuts, while the mussels, oysters, prawns and velvet crabs are left to their own devices... One of the few Scottish restaurants to serve them without accompaniment.
🕂🏡■

313

◆ HOTELS AND RESTAURANTS

HOTELS

- ▫ < £75
- ▣ £75–£140
- ▦ £140–£210
- ▥ > £210

RESTAURANTS

- ▪ < £15
- ▪ £15–£25
- ▪ £25–£45
- ▥ > £45

ISLE OF ERISKAY

◆ A A6
→HOTEL-RESTAURANT
Isle of Eriska
Ledaig
Tel. (01631) 72037
17 rms.
Closed Jan.
Polished wood tables in an impressive gray and ocher house, across an iron bridge, on the edge of moorland, beaches and forests. Excellent produce, which hasn't been distorted by the creative talents of a 'new Scottish' chef, served with a smile: fish and crustaceans in sauce, vegetable dishes, perfectly roasted Aberdeen Angus beef, fruit soufflés, mountain cheeses. Classically comfortable rooms. Sophisticated but friendly service.
▦ ▪

FORT WILLIAM

◆ D A1
→HOTEL
Inverlochy Castle
3 miles due northwest on the A82, Torlundy
Tel. (01397) 702 177
Open March–Nov.
16 rms. and 1 suite
At the foot of Ben Nevis, everything in this hotel is on a mountainous scale: the size of the park, the Victorian-Gothic decor, the rather plain cuisine, the length of the wine list, the price of the rooms. Croquet pitch and (separate) helipad.
▥ ▣ ▦   ▥

INVERNESS

◆ A D6-E6
→HOTEL
✪ **Culloden House**
3 miles due east via the A96
Tel. (01463) 790 461
22 rms. and 6 suites
Not far from Loch Ness and near the scene of the infamous Jacobite massacre, this

historic house is certainly one of the most sophisticated and attractive hotels in the Highlands. Built by the Adam brothers in pure neo-classical style (c. 1780). Courteous hospitality, good modern and – better still – 'pure Scottish' cuisine.*
▥ ▣ ▦   ▥ ▥

KINGUSSIE

◆ D B1
→HOTEL-RESTAURANT
The Cross
Tweed Mill Brae, Ardbroilach Rd
Tel. (01540) 661 166
Open March–Nov.
9 rms.
Certainly the best cuisine on the Scottish ski slopes, served in an old tweed mill. Specialties include Puy lentils with mountain hare, Ayrshire guinea fowl and Shetland salmon, which is almost smoked to order. The prices for half-board (the rooms are very comfortable) also include dinner. No children or smokers.
▦ ▪

LOCHINVER

◆ A C4
→HOTEL-RESTAURANT
The Albannach
Baddidarrch
Tel. (01571) 844 407
Closed Jan.–Feb.
5 rms.
A spectacular view, southward over the mountains, the rustic comfort of a small 18th-century house, the peace afforded by the rather difficult and hilly access to this 'last unspoiled corner of Europe', the warm but not very liberal welcome (no children, smokers or animals), and the proximity of Scotland's 'leading fishing port for white fish' which

guarantees a regular supply of fresh fish. The cuisine, served by candlelight, in a tiny (17 places) and rather original dining room, is based on local produce and sauces, some more successful than others.*
▥ ▦ ▣ ▥   ▪ ▪

ST MARGARET'S HOPE (ORKNEY)

◆ A F3
→HOTEL
The Creel
Front Rd
Tel. (01856) 831 311
Closed Christmas and Jan.–Feb.
3 rms.
If you are attracted by Orkney, their seals, their British and German wrecks, their king scallops and their whisky, then you really must visit this good harbor bistro where you can eat the local fish stew, seafood and smoked beef served in sauce. Small, pleasant rooms.
▫

ULLAPOOL

◆ A C5
→HOTEL-RESTAURANT
✪ **Altnaharrie Inn**
½ mile by private ferry
Tel. (01854) 633 230
Open Easter–early Nov.
8 rms.
The only Scottish hotel-restaurant with two Michelin stars, widely and rightly described in glowing terms. It is in fact a fairly ordinary little Highland inn, sparsely but elegantly decorated, lost in the northwestern Highlands with extraordinary food. A private boat from the port of Ullapool takes guests to the whitewashed, slate-roofed farm on the

far side of Loch Broom. A place with no neighbors, where the waves lap at the edge of the garden, and where you can walk across heather-clad hills to see golden eagles, otters and seals. The hotel has eight rooms and you have to sleep here to dine at one of the restaurant's eight dark wood tables. The rather capricious electricity is provided by a generator which is shut down at midnight (torches on the bedside tables and lots of candles in the dining room). If you are lucky enough to obtain a reservation (book at least a year in advance if you want to stay there in the summer), you will be asked for a non-refundable deposit of £250 per room. The superb – and not excessively expensive – wines are ordered as early as 6pm, after the five-course menu (no choice but it changes each day) has been described with studied enthusiasm by manager Fred Brown. For example: prawns in filo pastry with spicy sour cream, as an appetizer, followed by lobster salad served in its cooking juices with its roe, truffles and caviar; warm cream of king scallops with walnuts; crispy wood pigeon with foie gras, wild mushrooms, wine sauce and sorb apples; a wide choice of Scottish cheeses; prune tart and peach liqueur. This is wonderful food in an extraordinarily romatic, wild setting. The price is worth paying.*
▥ ▥

Abbreviations:
B.A.L.: The Bridgeman Art Library.
D.C.: Douglas Corrance.
N.G.S.: National Gallery of Scotland.
N.T.S.: National Trust for Scotland.
S.M.P.C.: Still Moving Picture Company.
S.N.P.G: Scottish National Portrait Gallery.

10/11 Rural scene c.1920, photo © Roger Viollet.
12/13 The Victorian bridge across the Firth of Forth © Roger Viollet.
14 Highland Games: hammer thrower © Keystone.
16 Volcanos, Ardnamurchan peninsula © P. and A. Macdonald/Scottish Natural Heritage. Loch Ness © D.C. Braeriach © D. A. Gowans/Scottish Natural Heritage.
17 Peat bog © Scottish Natural Heritage. Map work © P. Mérienne/Gallimard.
18/19 illus. F. Desbordes, A. Larousse/ Gallimard.
20/21 Illus. Cl. Felloni, F. Desbordes, J. Chevallier/Gallimard.
22/23 Illus. F. Desbordes, J. Chevallier/Gallimard.
24/25 Moorland, illus. F. Desbordes/ Gallimard. Botanical diagram, Cl. Felloni. Illus. F. Desbordes, Cl. Felloni, J. Chevallier/ Gallimard.
26/27 Peat bog, illus. F. Desbordes/ Gallimard. Botanical diagram, Cl. Felloni. Illus. F. Desbordes, Cl. Felloni, J. Chevallier/ Gallimard.
28/29 Loch, illus. F. Desbordes/Gallimard. Illus. F. Desbordes, J. Chevallier, P. Robin/Gallimard. Photos © D.C. and F. Bony/Gallimard.
30 Illus. F. Desbordes, J. Chevallier, P. Robin/ Gallimard.
31 Sir Joseph Noel Paton: *At Bay*, oil/canvas, late 19th c., coll. City of Edinburgh Museums and Art Galleries © B.A.L.
32 Callinish © D.C. Antonine Wall: carved stone, coll. National Museum of Antiquities, Edinburgh © B.A.L.
33 Pictish Stone © Museum of Scotland, Edinburgh. The Monymusk reliquary © *idem*.

34/35 *Mary Stuart*, coll. His Grace the Duke of Atholl, Blair Castle, Perthshire.
35 John de Critz: *James VI of Scotland*, early 17th c., priv. coll. © B.A.L.
36 Pompeo Batoni: *James Bruce*, oil/canvas, 1762, coll. S.N.P.G., Edinburgh © B.A.L. John Waston Nichol: *Lochaber no more*, oil/canvas, 1883, coll. Robert Fleming Holding Ltd, London © *idem*.
37 Victor Dartiquenave: *Scottish fisherman*, drawing © Sotheby's Picture Library. North Sea oil © D. Laird/S.M.P.C. Demonstration © D.C.
38 John McKidy Duncan: *Robert the Bruce*, oil/canvas, 1913–1914, coll. Smith Art Gallery and Museums, Stirling © B.A.L. The Stone of Destiny © Crown copyright reserved/Historic Scotland. *The Trial of Sir William Wallace*, detail, attrib. to William Bell Scott, coll. Guildhall Art Gallery, Corporation of London © *idem*.
39 *The Battle of Bannockburn*, illum. in the Holkham Bible, coll. British Library © theartarchive. *Robert the Bruce and his wife*, Seton armorial, coll. National Library of Scotland © B.A.L.
40 H.N. O'Neil: *Mary Stuart's Farewell to France*, late 19th c. © Sotheby's Picture Library. S. Sidley: *Mary Stuart and John Knox*, coll. Townely Hall Art Gallery and Museum, Burnley, Lancashire © B.A.L.
41 A. Vanson: *Henry Darnley*, Phillips, The International Fine Art Auctioneers © B.A.L. *James Hepburn, Earl of Bothwell* © S.N.P.G. Herdmann: *Execution of Mary Stuart*, © Glasgow Museums. National Covenant © Huntu Museum.
42 François De Troy: *James-Edward Stuart*, early 18th c. © Sotheby's Transparency Library, London. Peter Tillemans: *The Battle of Glenshiel*, 1719, coll. S.N.P.G. © B.A.L.
42/43 Antoine David: *Prince Charles-Edward Stuart*, 1732, oil/canvas, S.N.P.G., Edinburgh © B.A.L.

43 W. B. Hole: *Prince Charles-Edward Stuart in Edinburgh*, © City Art Centre, Edinburgh. Culloden memorial © D.C.
44 William Stewart Watson: *Admission of the poet Robert Burns to the Lodge of Canongate*, 1787, coll. S.N.P.G. © B.A.L. James Watt: *Locomotive*, drawing in *The Illustrated London News*, 5 July 1851 © *idem*.
45 David Martin: *James Russel, professor of philosophy at the University of Edinburgh and his son James*, 1769, coll. S.N.P.G. © B.A.L. Allan Ramsay: *David Hume*, 1766, ibidem © *idem. Ib., Robert Adam, idem*.
46 Barra © D.C. Scotsman from Tree © *idem*.
47 *The Book of Deer*, detail, coll. Cambridge University Library. Fishermen on the Isle of Islay © E. Quéméré/Diaf. Signposts in Gaelic on the Shetland Islands © D.C.
48 Sydney Coodsir, Hugh MacDiarmid and Norman MacCaig at the Peacock Hotel in New Haven © George Outram & Co. Ltd.
49 Kilts © G.-B. La Guillaume.
50/51 Tartan © P. Léger/Gallimard.
50 Sir Henry Raeburn: *Colonel Alistair MacDonnel of Glengarry*, 1812, coll. N.G.S., Edinburgh © B.A.L.
51 Tartans © P. Léger/ Gallimard.Sir John Everett Millais: *Two Bairns*, coll. Roy Miles © B.A.L.
52 Carnyx © Museum of Scotland.
52/53 Richard Waitt: *William Cumming, piper to the Laird of Grant*, oil/canvas, 1714 © Museum of Scotland.
53 The Lamont harp, early 16th c. © Museum of Scotland. Walter Muirland: *The Ceilidh*, drawing © N.G.S. Ashley MacIsaac © P. Franck/ Interceltic Festival, Lorient, 1996.
54 Hammer thrower © D.C.
55 Pipe bands © D.C. The public at Ballater © *idem*. Judging a bagpipe contest © G.-B. La Guillaume. Tossing the weight © D.C. Folk dancing contest © G. B. La Guillaume.
56/57 Ambroise Paré: *Seahorse*, engraving in Oeuvres, (Book XXV), 1585, coll. BNF, est., Paris.
56 John George Naish:

The Midsummer Fairies, detail, late 19 c., coll. Christopher Wood Gallery, London © B.A.L.
57 John Anster Fitzgerald: *A Halt in the Fairy Procession*, gouache on paper, priv. coll. © B.A.L. *Red Cap*, illustration by Alan Lee in *Fearies*, London, 1978. DR.
58 Sir Francis Grant: *John Whyte Melville of Bennochy*, coll. Royal and Ancient Golf Club, St Andrews © B.A.L. Golf clubs © D.C.
59 Early golf balls © D.C. Muirfield © *idem*. Making a golf club © *idem*. Early golf clubs © *idem*.
60/61 © D.C., except the Lochnaggar Distillery © D. Faure/ Diaf.
62/63 Recipes © É. Guillemot/Gallimard. Cookery lesson in a Scottish school, photo © Keystone.
64 Smoking salmon © D.C. Dish of haggis © *idem*. Specialties © P. Léger/Gallimard.
66/67–68/69 illus. M. Pommier/ Gallimard.
70/71 illus. M. Pommier, J.-F. Penneau/ Gallimard.
72/73 illus. M. Pommier, Cl. Quiec, A. Soro, B. Lenormand/Gallimard.
74/75 illus. M. Pommier, A.-Soro/Gallimard. ph. B. Lenormand/Gallimard.
76/77 illus. A. Soro, B. Lenormand/Gallimard. Entrance hall at Abbotsford © J. Arthur Dixon. William Adam, bust © J. Mackenzie/ National Galleries of Scotland. Culzean: ceiling, Robert Adam, watercolor drawing © The Soune Museum, London.
78/79 illus. B. Lenormand, A. Soro, Cl. Quiec/Gallimard.
80/81 illus. M. Pommier, J.-F. Penneau/ Gallimard.
82/83 illus. J.-F. Penneau, B. Lenormand/Gallimard.
84 Charles Rennie Mackintosh © T & R. Annan & Sons, Glasgow. Hill House © Deutsche Kunst und Dekoration. Stained-glass window © Hunterian Art Gallery, University of Glasgow. Scotland Street School © *idem*.
85 Allan Ramsay: *Self-portrait*, c. 1739 © Picture Library, National Portrait Gallery, London.
86 Hugo Van der Goes: *Altarpiece of Holy Trinity Church*, late 15th c. © N.G.S. Sir Henry Raeburn: *Niel Gow*, 1787, coll. S.N.P.G. © B.A.L.

◆ LIST OF ILLUSTRATIONS

86/87 David Wilkie: *William Chalmers Bethune, his wife and their daughter*, 1804 © N.G.S.
88 William McTaggart: *The Sailing of the Emigrant Ship* © N.G.S. Jacob More: *Cora Linn, the Falls of Clyde*, 1771, coll. N.G.S. © B.A.L.
88/89 J. M. W. Turner: *Loch Coruisk, Skye*, c. 1815 © N.G.S. Sir Edwin Landseer: *Monarch of the Glen*, 1851, coll. United Distillers and Vintner © B.A.L.
90 Francis C. B. Cadell: *Interior: the Orange Blind* 1928 © Glasgow Museums. George Henry & Edward. A Hornel: *The Druids Bringing in the Mistletoe*, 1890 © *idem.*
90/91 Sir Stanley Spencer: *Furnaces*, 1946 © Imperial War Museum, London.
92 Will Maclean: *Ex-Voto, South Minch*, 1993 © Duncan of Jordanstone College of Art and Design, Faculty of the University of Dundee. John Schueler: *Storm Light and Black Shadow* (Skye), 1974, priv. coll., United States.
93 Shipyard workers in Glasgow © L. Freed/ Magnum.
94/95 *Dunvegan Castle*, engrav. in *Thomas Pennant's Tour*, 1772, priv. coll.
96/97 *Weaver's cottage on the Isle of Islay*, engrav. in *Thomas Pennant's Tour*, 1772, priv. coll.
98/99 *Walter Scott*, engraving, priv. coll.
100/101 Glasgow, lunch-break in the shipyards © L. Freed/Magnum.
102/103 Sheep © M. Duquet/ Gallimard.
104 St Mary's Church, Orkney Islands © P. Marlow/Magnum.
106/107 Tantallon Castle © D.C. Harris © *idem.* Loch Linnhe, Castle Stalker © G. Simeone/Diaf.
108 Glen Coe, Rannoch Moor © G. Simeone/Diaf. Edinburgh, East Princes Street Gardens © Pratt-Pries/Diaf. Grampian Mountains © *idem.*
109 The Borders © D.C. Loch Ness © G.-B. La Guillaume. Glen Orchy © G. Simeone/Diaf.
110 Rail bridge across the Firth of Forth © Pratt-Pries/Diaf. Glasgow, Dundas Street © Collections/G. Wright. Lewis © D.C.
111 Abbotsford © Y. Travert/Diaf.
113 Sweetheart Abbey © Yvan Travert/Diaf.

114 Edinburgh Festival © D.C. General view of Edinburgh © A. Lorgnier/Côtés Vues.
115 *The Monuments of Edinburgh*, capriccio by D. Rhind © City Art Centre, Edinburgh.
116 The crown of Scotland © D.C. Edinburgh Castle © A. Pinsard/Côtés Vues
117 Street names © S. Bosman/Gallimard. The Royal Mile, Lawn Market © Y. Travert/Diaf.
118 Sign for the Writers' Museum © S. Bosman/ Gallimard. St Giles' Cathedral © D.C.
119 John Knox House © W. Buss/Hoa-Qui.
120/121 Queen's Park © D.C. Hospete, *White Horse Inn*, watercolor, 1833 © City Art Centre, Edinburgh. Holyrood © Y. Travert/ Diaf.
122 Hall of the Royal Museum © D. Corrance/ S.M.P.C.
123 Hunterston fibula, 8th c. © Royal Museum of Scotland. Greyfriars Bobby © B. Lenormand/ Gallimard.
124 Paul Gauguin: *The Vision after the Sermon*, oil/canvas, 1892 © N.G.S. © B.A.L. Aerial view of the West End © D.C.
125 Façade of the National Gallery of Scotland © B. Lenormand/ Gallimard.
126 Dean Village © D.C.
127 Leith © D.C. The Britannia © Collections/ M. Fife.
128 The road and rail bridges across the River Forth © D.C.
129 Dalmeny House © D.C. Hopetoun House © *idem.*
130 Cairnpapple Hill © D.C. Linlithgow Palace © *idem.*
131 Rosslyn Chapel © B. Lenormand/Gallimard. Linlithgow Castle © D.C. Crichton Castle © B. Lenormand/Gallimard.
132 Alexander Nasmyth: *Tantallon Castle and Bass Rock*, oil/canvas, 1816 © B.A.L.
133 Puffins, illus. F. Desbordes/Gallimard. Bass Rock © J. Brun/ Explorer. Haddington, St Mary's Church © D.C.
134 *David I and Malcom IV*, illumination in the *Charter (1159) of Kelso Abbey* © National Library of Scotland. St Abb's Head, © H. Wood/National Trust.
135 Manderston © B. Lenormand/Gallimard.

136 Floors Castle © D.C. Melrose Abbey © B. Lenormand/Gallimard. Dryburgh Abbey © D.C.
137 Scott's View © D.C.
138 Abbotsford House: the library © D.C.
138/139 Peebles © D.C. Jedburgh Abbey © *idem.*
140 Burns House: interior © STB/S.M.P.C. Drumlanrig Castle © Ch. Simon Sykes/The Interior Archive.
141 Caerlaverock Castle © Y. Travert/Diaf.
142/143 Riccardo Linter: *Reminiscences of Burns*, anthology of songs © Museum of Scotland.
142 Figurines on the façade of the Tam o' Shanter Inn, Ayr © B. Lenormand/Gallimard. Charles Lucy: *The Parting of Robert and Mary*, 1844, coll. Malcolm Innes, London © B.A.L.
143 The cottage where Robert Burns was born © Sotheby's Transparency Library.
144/145 Sweetheart Abbey © STB/S.M.P.C. 144 Ruthwell Cross © STB/S.M.P.C.
145 Kirkcudbright © H. Wodd/S.M.P.C. Broughton House © *idem.*
146 Castle Kennedy Gardens © A. Johnston/ S.M.P.C.
147 Turnberry golf links © D. Ball/Diaf. Portpatrick © A. Jonston/S.M.P.C.
148 *Burns' Cottage*, postcard, priv. coll.
149 Culzean Castle: façade © D.C. Culzean Castle: Oval Staircase © Ch. Simon Sykes/The Interior Archive. Culzean Castle: orangery © N. T. S.
150 Archibald McLauchlin: *John Glassford and his family*, 1767 © Glasgow Museums.
151 Rangers supporter © A. Lorgnier/Côtés Vues.Façade © D.C. Blair Hall, Strathclyde University © Collections/G. Wright.
152 Glasgow City Chambers © D.C. Glasgow: George Square © Collections/D. Dobbie.
153 *The Trongate of Glasgow*, oil/canvas, 1826 © Glasgow Museums.
154 Glasgow Cathedral: the necropolis © S. Bosmann/Gallimard. Templeton's Carpet Factory © P. Tomkins/ S.M.P.C.
155 St Vincent Street Church © K. Paterson/ S.M.P.C.
156 Italian Centre © D.C. Princes Square © Collections/C.J. Smith.

157 Tenement House, Willow Tea Rooms, Glasgow School of Art © D.C.
158 Kelvingrove Museum © D.C.
159 Panel from the White Bedroom, coll. Hunterian Art Gallery © Collections/ G. Wright.Botanic Garden © D.C.
160 Finnieston Crane © Collections/G. Wright. Bells Bridge © Collections/ S. Walsh. The SECC and the Suspension Bridge © Collections/M. Fife.
161 Lohan, Burrell Collection © Glasgow Museums.
162/163 The Glasgow School of Art © Glasgow School of Art, Mackintosh Collection. Sideboard, courtesy of the Fine Art Society, London. Drawing of fabrics © Hunterian Art Gallery, University of Glasgow. Design for the music room of the House for an Art Lover © *idem.* Design for furniture © *idem.* High-backed chair, courtesy of Sotheby's, London.
164 Charles Need: *David Livingstone*, 19th c., coll. Royal Geographical Society, London © B.A.L.
165 John Knox: *The First Steamship on the River Clyde* © Glasgow Museums.
166 Lanark: general view © D.C. Lanark: details of a façade © G.-B. La Guillaume.
167 McCulloch: *Loch Lomond* © Glasgow Museums.
169 Johannes Vorsterman: *Stirling in the time of the Stuarts*, late 17th c., coll. Smith Art Gallery and Museum, Stirling © B.A.L.
170 Equestrian statue of Robert the Bruce © B. Lenormand/Gallimard.
171 Cowane's Hospital and the Church of the Holy Rood © B. Lenormand/ Gallimard. Dunblane Cathedral © *idem.*
172/173 John Knox: *On the shores of Loch Katrine*, early 19th c. © Sotheby's Transparency Library.
172 John Watson Nicol: *Rob Roy and the magistrate*, 1886 © B.A.L.
173 Loch Lomond © D.C.
174 Dunfermline Abbey © Bobwest/S.M.P.C. Andrew Carnegie in 1913, © Roger Viollet.
175 Culross © B. Lenormand/Gallimard. Culross © D.C. Culross Palace © K. Paterson/ S.M.P.C.

176 Crail © P. Somelet/ Diaf. St Andrews: cathedral © D. Robertson/S.M.P.C.
177 St Andrews:golf course © D.C. Crail © R. Lees/S.M.P.C.
178 Kinross House © P. Taylor.
178/179 *The Fair Maid of Perth* © Roger Viollet.
180 Scone Castle: façade © D.J. Whyte/ S.M.P.C. Scone Palace: interior © STB/S.M.P.C.
181 Loch Earn © H. Wood/S.M.P.C.
182/183 Blair Castle © A. Williams/Explorer. The Hermitage © N.T.S.
184 Standing stone, Aberlemno © D. Laird/ S.M.P.C.Standing stone, Aberlemno © Crown copyright reserved/ Historic Scotland. Standing stone, Nigg © *idem.*
185 The *Discovery* in the port of Dundee © D.C.
186 Glamis Castle Ch. Simon Sykes/ The Interior Archive. Brechin: round tower © K. Patreson/S.M.P.C.
187 Mull: Tobermory © G.-B. La Guillaume.
189 Hill House: façade © J. Eoak/N.T.S. Hill House: interior © D.C. Hill House: shower © N.T.S.
190 Ardkinglas © P. Tomkins/S.M.P.C.
191 East Loch Tarbert © D. Corrance/S.M.P.C.
192 Crinan Canal © D. Robertson/S.M.P.C.
193 Kilmartin Glen, Templewood Stone Circle and footprint at Dunadd Hill Fort © D. Robertson/ S.M.P.C.
194 Kilmartin: tombstone © D.C.
195 Loch Awe, Kilchurn Castle © G. Simeone/ Diaf. Inveraray Castle: armory © Ch. Simon Sykes/The Interior Archive.
196/197 © P. Taylor.
198 Castle Stalker © F. Bony/Gallimard.
199 Glen Coe © D.C. Glen Etive © Jouan Ruis/ Hoa-Qui.
200 Rothesay harbor © M. Brooke/S.M.P.C. Mount Stuart © *idem.*
201 Lochranza Castle © D.C.
202 Tobermory © D.C. Duart Castle © *idem.*
202/203 Staffa, Tobermory, Duart Castle © D.C.
204 *The Book of Kells* © Trinity College Library, Dublin. St Martin's Cross © G. Burns/S.M.P.C.
205 Iona Cathedral © A. Cringean/S.M.P.C.

Michael Chapel © S.M.P.C./Distant Images.
206 Coll, the port of Arinagour © D.C. Tiree © *idem.*
207 Gardenstown © D.C.
209 Views of the port of Aberdeen © D.C.
210 Provost Skene's House © Collections/ C. Inch. Town Hall © *idem.*
211 Aberdeen, Fish Market © Collections/ R. Scruton.
212 Stonehaven © Y. Travert/Diaf.
212/213 Dunnotar Castle, G. Reid © City Art Centre, Edinburgh.
213 Drum Castle: window © B. Lenormand/ Gallimard.
214 Aerial view of Crathes Castle © N.T.S. Crathes Castle: painted ceiling © D.C.
215 Balmoral: the royal family, 1972 © Keystone/ Sygma.
216/217 Lecht Road © A. Johnston/S.M.P.C.
216 Craigievar Castle © N.T.S.
217 Haddo House © N.T.S. Fyvie Castle © D.C.
218 Peterhead: the port © STB/S.M.P.C.
219 Crovie © D. Corrance/S.M.P.C. Duff House © D.C.
220 Distilleries © B. Lenormand/Gallimard.
221 Mountain stream © D.C. Dew of Ben Nevis, Fort William © K. Fergubon/S.M.P.C. Distillery: interior © D. Ball/Diaf.
222 Huntly Castle © D.C.
223 Elgin Cathedral: west entrance and presbytery © D. Robertson/S.M.P.C.
224 Findhorn © STB/ S.M.P.C. Brodie Castle, Pictish Stone © *idem.*
225 Highland cattle © F. Bony/Gallimard.
226 Skye © D.C.
227 Peat © G.-B. La Guillaume.
228/229 illus. The Caledonian Forest F. Desbordes/Gallimard. Other illustrations by Cl. Felloni, J. Chevallier, F. Desbordes, L. Lachaud/Gallimard.
230 David Morier: *The Battle of Culloden*, 1745, ph. Antonia Reeve © The Royal Collection/HM Queen Elizabeth II. J.M.W. Turner: *Inverness from the River Ness* © Sotheby's Transparency Library.
231 Cawdor Castle © B. Lenormand/Gallimard.
232 Ruthven Barracks © M. Duquet/Gallimard. Ski resort in the Cairngorms © STB/S.M.P.C.

233 Kingussie, Highland Folk Museum © D.C.
234 Illus. J. Chevallier, F. Desbordes/Gallimard.
234/235 Aerial view of the Cairngorms © A. Wright/S.M.P.C.
235 Glen More © D. Laird/S.M.P.C.Cairn Gorm © *idem.*
236 Lochaber © A. Johnston/S.M.P.C. The Caledonian Canal © Pinhole Productions/ S.M.P.C.
237 Glenfinnan viaduct © R. Beattie/S.M.P.C.
238 Fort Augustus © D.C. Urquhart Castle © G. Simeone/Diaf.
239 Eilean Donan Castle © D.C.
240/241 G. d'Achille: *The Loch Ness Monster*, litho, 1935, priv. coll. © B.A.L.
241 Badges © D.C. Nessie, photo, 19 April **1934**, postcard. DR. Drumnadrochit © STB/ S.M.P.C.Panoramic view of Loch Ness © D.C.
242/243 Loch Maree © D.C.
243 Loch Torridon © G. Simeone/Diaf. Inverewe Gardens © D.C.
244 Achiltibue © A. Johnston/S.M.P.C.
245 Thomas Faed: *The Last of the Clan*, 1865 © Glasgow Museums. Duncansby Head © Mika/S.M.P.C.
246 Castle Girnigoe and Castle Sinclair © S. Cordier/Explorer. *Women from Cromarty*, photo, 1905, coll. Grant © Edinburgh Public Library.
247 Dunbeath, Laidhay Croft Museum © B. Lenormand/Gallimard. Cromarty: interior of East Church © *idem.*
248 Otters, illus. J. Chevallier/Gallimard.
249 Skye: The Cuillins © K. Patterson/S.M.P.C. Skye: The Old Man of Storr © D. Roberstson/ S.M.P.C. Highland cattle © D.C.
250 Dunvegan Castle © D.C. Staffin post office © P. Smellet/Diaf. Crofts on the Isle of Skye © F. Bony/Gallimard.
251 Portree, Roddie Danabie © Pratt-Pries/ Diaf.
252 Lewis © D.C. Callanish © *idem.*
253 Harris Tweed © P. Léger/Gallimard. Ivory chessmen © Museum of Scotland.
254/255 Berneray © D. Robertson/S.M.P.C. Statue of the Madonna and Child © Eolas/ S.M.P.C.

255 Saint Kilda, Boreray © N.T.S.
257 Cathedral of St Magnus © B. Lenormand/Gallimard.
258 Sheep © F. Bony/ Gallimard. The Italian Chapel © D. Laidlaw/ S.M.P.C.
259 The burial chamber of Maes Howe© B. Lenormand/Gallimard.The Ring of Brodgar © D.C.
260 The port of Stromness © D.C. Prehistoric earth house at Skara Brae © *idem.* Old Man of Hoy © R. Welsby/S.M.P.C.
261 Stone walls and Marwick Head © F. Bony/Gallimard. Farm on the island of Westray © M. Duquet/Gallimard.
262 Fire Festival © D.C.
263 Clickhimin Broch © Crown copyright reserved/Historic Scotland. Stained-glass window from Lerwick Town Hall © B. Lenormand/Gallimard.
264 Jarlshof © Crown copyright reserved/ Historic Scotland.
265 Pattern for a Fair Isle jumper © N.T.S. Stanley Curister: *The Fair Isle Jumper*, 1st half of the 20th c. © City of Edinburgh Art Centre.
266 Out Skerries, salmon nets © Jouan Ries/Hoa-Qui. Voe © D. Robertson/S.M.P.C.
267 Skua © M. Duquet/Gallimard.
268 Hermaness cliffs, puffins © F. Bony/ Gallimard.

271 Eurostar © British Tourist Office, Paris
273 Cyclists at Callanish © Paul Tomkins/S.T.B./ S.M.P.C./ British Tourist Office, Paris. Glasgow, Central Station © F. Bony/Gallimard.

We have been unable to locate the copyright holders and authors of certain documents before going to print. We will, however, acknowledge these sources in the next editions if and when we are made aware of their identity. We do apologise for this.

A

Abbotsford House 77, 138
Aberdeen 35, 44, 208, **209**
– Aberdeen Art Gallery 211
– Cruikshank Botanic Gardens 209
– Duthie Park
– Gordon Highlanders Museum 211
– Hazelhead Park 209
– Johnston Gardens 209
– King's College Chapel 211
– King's College 210
– Marischal Museum 210
– Maritime Museum 211
– Mercat Cross 210
– Music Hall 209
– Old Town House 211
– Provost Skene's House 210
– St Machar's Cathedral 211
– St Nicholas' Kirk 210
– Tolbooth (Museum of Civic History) 210
Aberdeen Angus beef 62
Aberdeenshire 213
Aberfeldy 182
Aberfoyle 173
Aberlemno 184, 186
Abernethy 178
Abernethy Forest RSPB Reserve 232
Aboyne 214
Achaduin Castle 194
Achahoish 192
Achamore Gardens 200
Achiltibuie 244
Achnabreck 193
Act of Union 36, 115, 120, 189
Adam, James 76, 135
Adam, John 76, 119, 135, 215, 232,
Adam, Robert 45, 76, 77, 119, 122, 124, 133, 135, 147, 175, 232
Adam, William 76, 129, 135, 136, 146, 158, 186, 195, 217, 219
Add, River 193
Adder 24
Addresses 270
Agricola 32, 222
Agriculture (traditional) 188
Aidan 204
Aignish 253
Aikwood Tower 139
Ailsa Craig 147
Air travel 270, 272
Albert, Prince 37, 214
Alexander I 169
Alexander II 137, 194
Alexander III 34, 38
Alford 216
Alloway 142, **148**
Angles 33
Anglo-Norman 52
Angus 168, **185**
Angus Folk Museum 186
Anne, Princess 36
Anstruther 176

An Rubha 253
An Tairbeart 253
An Teallach 243
An T-ob 253
Antonine Wall 32, 189
Aonach Dubh 199
Applecross peninsula 242
Arbroath 185
Arbroath, Declaration of 39
Arbroath smokies 62, 185
Arbuthnott 213
Archives, National 124
Arctic skua 22
Ardchattan Priory 198
Ardcraig Gardens 200
Ardkinglas Woodland Gardens 190
Ardmair 244
Ardnamurchan peninsula 237
Ardrishaig 193
Arduaine Gardens 194, 196
Argyll 33, 46, 190
Argyll Forest Park 190
Arisaig 237
Arkwright, Richard 165
Armadale 248
Armour, Jean 142
Arnol 253
Arran 200
Arrochar 190
Arthur's Seat 121
Athens of the North 44, 115
Atholl, dukes of 183
Auchindrain 195
Auld Alliance 34
Auld Lang Syne 142, 148
Aulton 209
Avalon 53
Aviemore 233
Awe 198
Ayr 148
Ayton Castle 135
Aywick 267

B

Badger 229
Ba' Game 257
Bagh a Chaisteil 255
Bagpipes 52, 54, 55
Balfour Castle 261
Ballachulish 198
Ballater 214
Balliol, Edward 39
Balliol, John 38
Ballindalloch 220
Balloch 173
Balmaha 173
Balmoral 208, 214
Balnakeil 245
Balquhidder 172
Balranald Nature Reserve 254
Baltasound 268
Balvenie Castle 223
Banchory 214
Banff 218
Bank vole 24
Bannockburn, Battle of 34, 39, 54
Banshee 57
Barbour, John 48
Barcaldine Castle 198
Barfor, Magnus 191
Barpa Langass 254
Barra 255

Barraigh 255
Bass, the 222
Bass Rock 132
Bealach Nam Bo 242
Bearnaraigh Mor 252
Beer 64
Beinn Bhan 242
Beinn Eighe 242
Beinn Ime 190
Beinn Narnaim 190
Bell, Alexander Graham 127
Bellanoch 193
Bell heather 24, 25
Ben A'an 172
Ben Arthur 190
Benbecula 254
Ben Cruachan 198
Ben Donich 190
Ben Langass 254
Ben Ledi 172
Ben Lomond 173
Ben Macdui 234
Ben Mor Coigach 244
Ben More 203
Ben More Assynt 244
Bennachie 222
Ben Nevis 236
Ben Nevis Distillery 236
Ben Vane 190
Ben Venue 172
Bernera Barracks 239
Berneray 255
Berwick, Treaty of 39
Bettyhill 245
Bhatarsaigh 255
Bicycle 272
Bidean nam Bian 199
Binns, House of the 128
Birch
– dwarf 26
– silver 228, 229
Bird-watching sites 261, 268
Birnam 181
Birsay 261
Bishop's Palace 257
Black, Joseph 44
Blackford Hill 127
Blackhall, Sheena 48
Blackhouse 69
Black Isle peninsula 247
Blackness Castle 129
Black Watch 51
Blair Castle 183
Blantyre 164
Blended whisky 61
Boat of Garten 233
Boddam 264
Boethius, Hector 35
Bog asphodel 27
Bogie, the 223
Bog pimpernel 27
Bonawe Iron Furnace 198
Bo'ness 112
Bonnie Dundee (John Graham of Claverhouse) 42, 182
Bonnie Prince Charlie (see Stuart, Charles Edward)
Book of Common Order 47
Book of Deer 47, 218
Book of the Dean of Lismore, The 47
Borders 47, 52, **134**
Boreray 255
Boswell, James 96
Bothwell (see Hepburn)
Bothwell Castle 165

Bouvier, Nicolas 104
Bowhill 139
Bowmore 78, 202
Braemar 54, 215
Brandsbutt Stone 222
Brechin 70, 186
Bressay 263
Bridei (see Brude)
Bridge of Walls 265
Britannia 127
Britons 33
Broadford 248
Broch of Gurness 260
Brochs 67
Brodick 201
Brodie Castle 224
Brodie, William 117–118
Brough of Birsay 261
Broughton 138
Broughty Ferry 185
Brownie 56
Bruar Falls 183
Brus, The 48
Bruce, George 175
Bruce, James 36
Bruce, Robert 33, 34, **39**, 137, 140, 170, 174
Bruce, William 76, 121
Brude 204, 230
Brudei (see Brude)
Buchan, John 138
Buchanan, George 35
Buckie 219
Bullers of Buchan 218
Burghead 224
Burghs, royal 34
Burnett of Leys, James 197
Burns, Robert 45, 48, 53, 64, **98**, 140, 141 **142**, 148, 149, 182
Burra 263
Burravoe 267
Busta 266
Bute 190, 200

C

Cadell, Francis C. B. 90
Caerlaverock 141
Cairn Gorm 233
Cairngorms, the 232, **234**
Cairn o'Mount 213
Cairnpapple Hill 130
Cairnwell Pass 215
Caithness 47
Caledonia 32
Caledonian Canal 236, 238
Caledonian Forest 228, 238
Calgacus 32
Callander 172
Callanish (see Calanais)
Calton Hill 127
Cambuskenneth Abbey 171
Camerons, the 42
Campbell (clan) 194
Campbeltown 61, 192
Campbeltown Loch 192
Campsie Fells 173
Camster, Grey Cairns of 66, 246
Canna 206
Capercaillie 228
Cape Wrath 245
Car 270, 272
Cardhu Distillery 220
Carinish (Caranais) 254
Carlops 131

Carnassarie Castle 193
Carnegie, Andrew 174
Carnoustie 59
Carnyx 52
Carrbridge 233
Carrick Castle 190
Carse of Gowrie 168
Carswell, John 193
Castlebay 255
Castle Campbell 171
Castle Douglas 145
Castle Fraser 215
Castle Girnigoe 246
Castle Grant 232
Castle Kennedy 146
Castlelaw Broch 131
Castle Menzies 182
Castle Sinclair 246
Castle Stalker 198
Castle Suibhne 193
Castle Tioram 237
Catpund Burn 264
Catpund Quarries 264
Cawdor 231
Ceilidh 52, 231
Celtic settlement 32
Celts 52
Ceres 54, 178
Char 29
Charles I 35, 41, 60, 115, 121
Charles II 35, 36
Cheviots, the 112
Churchill Barriers 258
Clachan 194
Clach An Truiseil 253
Claonaig 192
Clark, Jim 135
Clava Cairns 230
Claypotts Castle 73
Clickhimin Broch 263
Cliffs 20
Climate 270
Clo-Mor Cliffs 245
Clyde
– Falls of 88, 166
– quays 159
– river 88, 159
– Valley 164
Coach 270, 272
Cockburnspath 134
Coigach peninsula 244
Colbost 251
Coldingham 134
Coldstream 135
Colintraive 190, 200
Coll 206
Collieston 218
Colonsay 202
Common Ridings 134
Comrie 181
Comyn, Sir John ('the Red') 39, 140
Conic Hill 173
Connel 198
Connery, Sean 126
Corgarff Castle 217
Corrieshalloch Gorge 243
Corrievreckan 201
Cost of living 270
Costume (traditional) 50
Cotton grass, common 26, 27
Counter-Reformation 223
Country Dancing 53
Cowal Highland Gathering 190
Cowal peninsula 190
Cowane, John 171
Craig Choinnich 54

Craigellachie 223
Craigievar Castle 216
Craigmillar Castle 130
Craignethan Castle 165
Craignure 203
Crail 176
Cramond 114, **128**
Cranachan 62
Cranberry 26
Crarae Woodland Garden 194
Crathes 214
Crathes Castle 73, 197, 214
Crawfish, freshwater 30
Crichton 131
Crichton Castle 75, 131
Crichton-Smith, Ian 47
Crieff 180
Crinan 193
Crinan Canal 193
Crofters Holding Act 248, 251
Cromarty 71, 247
Cromwell, Olivier 35, 120
Cross-leaved heath 27
Crossraguel Abbey 148
Crotach, Alasdair 253
Crovie 219
Cruachan Power Station 198
Cruden Bay 218
Cuillins, The 248, 249
Culbin Sands 224
Cullen 219
Cullen Skink 219
Cullerlie Stone Circle 215
Cullivoe 267
Culloden, Battle of 43, 219, 230, 231
Cul Mor 244
Culross 68, 175
Culswick 265
Culzean Castle 147, 148
Cumberland, Augustus, Duke of 43, 231, 238
Cupar 178
Curwen Hill Cairn 259

D

Dalbeattie 144
Dale, David 165
Dallas Dhu Distillery 224
Dalmeny Kirk 70, 128
Dalriada 33, 46, 188, 193, 204
Dalwhinnie 221
Dance (traditional) 52, 55
Darnley, Henry 41
David I 34, 120
David II 35
Dean Village 126
Declaration of Scottish Independence 185
Deerness peninsula 259
Defoe, Daniel 96, 150, 176
Dervaig 203
Deveron, the 218, 223
Devil's Staircase 199
Dinsdale, Tim 241
Dirleton 132
Discovery, the 185
Distillation 60
Diver
– black-throated 29
– red-throated 29

Dollar 171
Dolphin
– Atlantic white-sided 18
– bottle-nosed 18
– common 18
– Risso's 18
– striped 18
– white-beaked 18
Don
– river 209,
– Strath 215
Dores 241
Dornoch 247
Douglas, David 180, 197
Douglas, Gavin 35, 48
Doune 171
Doune of Invernochty 216
Dounreay Nuclear Power Station 245
Dr. Jekyll and Mr. Hyde 118
Drink 274
Drum Castle 72, 213
Drumlanrig Castle 140
Drummond 180, 197
Drummond, George 124
Drummore 147
Drumnadrochit 240
Dryburgh 136
Duart Castle 203
Duff House 76, 219
Dufftown 223
Duffus Castle 72, 224
Duirinish peninsula 251
Dumbarton 189
Dumfries 140
Dunadd 188, 193
Dunbar 132
Dunbar, Battle of 35
Dunbar, William 48
Dun Beag Broch 250
Dunbeath 246
Dunblane 171
Dun Caan 251
Duncan I 33, 34, 186, 205, 231
Duncan, Henry 144
Duncansby Head 245
Dun Carloway Broch 253
Dundas, Henry 125
Dundee 185
Dundee cake 64
Dundee marmalade 64
Dundonnell 243
Dundrennan 144
Dun Eadain 114
Dunfermline 174
Dunfermline Abbey 70, 174
Dunkeld 181
Dunnet Head 245
Dunnottar Castle 72, 212
Dunoon 190
Dunrobin Castle 247
Duns 135
Dunsgaith Castle 248
Dunstaffnage Castle 194
Dun Telve Broch 239
Duntocher 189
Dun Troddan Broch 239
Duntrune Castle 193
Duntulm Castle 251
Dunvegan 251
Durness 245
Durno 222
Dyce, William 211

E

Earl's Palace 257
East Linton 133
East Loch Tarbert 191
East Neuk 176
Eating out 274
Echt 215
Eday 261
Edinburgh 44, **114**, 272
– Advocates' Close 119
– Ann Street 126
– Art galleries 122
– Arthur's Seat 121
– Assembly Hall 117
– Brodie's Close 117
– Calton Hill 127
– Calton Old Burial Ground 127
– Camera Obscura 117
– Candlemaker Row 123
– Canongate 120
– Canongate Kirk 120
– Canongate Tolbooth 120
– Castle Hill 117
– Charlotte Square 78, 79, 126
– Chessel's Court 120
– City Chambers 119
– City Observatory 127
– Cowgate 123
– Dean Gallery 126
– Dean Village 126
– Duddingston 121
– Dynamic Earth 122
– Edinburgh Castle 72, 116
– Festival 114
– General Register House 124
– George Heriot's School 75, 123
– George Street 125
– Georgian House 126
– Gladstone's Land 118
– Grassmarket 122
– Greyfriars Bobby 123
– Greyfriars Kirk 115, 123
– Heart of Midlothian 119
– High Street 118
– Holyroodhouse 121
– Hub, The 117
– Huntly House 120
– James Court 117
– John Knox House 119
– Lady Stair's House 118
– Lawnmarket 117
– Magdalen Chapel 123
– Mary King's Close 119
– Mercat Cross 118
– Milne's Court 117
– Moray House 120
– Morocco Land 120
– Moubray House 119
– Museum of Childhood 119
– Museum of Scotland 52, 123
– National Gallery of Scotland 79, 125
– National Library of Scotland 122
– National Monument 127
– Nelson Monument 127
– Netherbow Arts Centre 119

– New Town 45, **79**, 115, **124**
– Old College 122
– Old Observatory 127
– Parliament House 119
– People's Story Museum (Canongate Tolbooth) 120
– Princes Street Gardens 125
– Riddle's Close 117
– Royal Botanic Garden 126
– Royal High School 127
– Royal Mile 117
– Royal Museum 123
– Royal Observatory 127
– Royal Scottish Academy 125
– St Andrew Square 125
– St Bernard's Well 126
– St Cecilia's Hall 123
– St Giles Cathedral 71, 118
– St Margaret's Chapel 116
– St Margaret's Well 121
– Scotch Whisky Heritage Centre 117
– Scott Monument 124
– Scottish National Gallery of Modern Art 126
– Scottish National Portrait Gallery 126
– Signet Library 119
– Talbot Rice Art Gallery 122
– Tolbooth 119
– Tolbooth St John's Church 117
– Tron Kirk 119
– Victoria Street 122
– Water of Leith 126
– West Register House 126
– Whitehorse Close 120
– Writers' Museum 118
Edinburgh Review 45
Edward I of England 38
Edward II 39
Edward III 39
Edzell Castle and Garden 213
Egilsay 261
Eider, common 22
Eigg 206, 237
Eildon Hills 137
Eileach an Naoimh 202
Eilean Donan Castle 42, 239
Eiriosgaigh 254
Electric Brae 148
Electricity 271
Elgin 223
Elgol 248
Elizabeth I 35, 41
Elizabeth de Burgh 219
Ellisland Farm 140, 142
Elphinstone, Bishop 210
Elves 56
Emperor moth 24, 27
English 46
Eriskay 254
Ermine 25
Eshaness peninsula 266
Eyemouth 135
Eye Peninsula 253

F

Fair Fortnight (Glasgow) 154
Fairies 56, 57
Fair Isle 265
Fair Maid of Perth, The 179
Falkirk, Battle of 38, 43
Falkland 178
Falkland Palace 74, 75, 178
Fasque House 213
Faujas de Saint-Fond, Barthélemy 100
Fergus 193
Fergusson, John Duncan 179
Fergusson, Robert 48, 120, 142
Ferry 270, 273
Festivals 52, 114, 276
Fetlar 267
Fettercairn 213
Fife 168, 174
Findhorn 224
Finlaggan 188
Finnan haddie 62
Fionnphort 203
Firth of Clyde 189
Firth of Forth 131
Firth of Tay 185
Fitzalain (family) 34
Five Sisters of Kintail 239
Flodden, Battle of 35, 115, 130
Floors Castle 136
Flotta 258
Flotterstone 131
Flow Country, 17, 26, 227
Fochabers 223
Folklore 56, 87
Football 151
Footdee 211
Forbes (family) 217
Formalities 271
Forres 224
Forrest, George 197
Fort Augustus 238
Fort George 78, 231
Fortrose 247
Fort William 236
Foula 265
Fowler, John Arthur 129, 243
Fowlsheugh Nature Reserve 212
François I 34
François II 34, 40, 133
Fraserburgh 218
Free Church of Scotland (see Scottish Reformed Church)
Fulmar, northern 20
Fyvie Castle 208, 217

G

Gaelic 46, 47, 251
Gaels 33
Gaidhealtachd 46
Gairloch 242
Galashiels 138
Galloway 46, 140
Galloway Forest Park 145
Gannet 22
Gardens 196
Gardenstown 219
Garenin 253

Garlieston 147
Garvellach Islands 202
Gatehouse of Fleet 145
Gearraidh Bhailteas 255
Gearrannan 253
Geddes, Patrick 117
George I 42
George IV 37, 51
Giant's Grave 267
Gibbon, Lewis Grassic 212, 213
Gigha 191, 200
Girvan 147
Glamis 186
Glasgow 36, 37, 44, **150**, 273
– Barras, the 154
– Blythswood Square 156
– Botanic Gardens 159
– Broomielaw Quay 160
– Burrell Collection 161
– Cathedral 71, 155
– Centre for Contemporary Arts 156
– Charing Cross Mansions 157
– City Chambers 82, 152
– Clyde Auditorium 160
– Egyptian Halls 83
– Gallery of Modern Art 153
– Gardner's Warehouse 83
– Finnieston Crane 160
– Glasgow University 158
– Glasgow Green 154
– Glasgow School of Art 156, 162
– Hat Rack 155
– Holmwood House 80, 161
– House for an Art Lover 161, 163
– Hunterian Art Gallery 159
– Hunterian Museum 158
– Hutcheson's Hall 153
– Kelvingrove Museum and Art Gallery 158
– Kelvingrove Park 157
– Lighthouse, the 152
– McLellan Galleries 156
– Mitchell Library 157
– Museum of Transport 158
– Necropolis 154
– Park Circus 157
– People's Palace 155
– Piping Centre 156
– Provand's Lordship 155
– Queen's Cross Church 159
– Queen's Park 157
– Queen's Park Terrace 81
– St Mungo Museum of Religious Life and Art 155
– St Vincent Street Church 71, 82, 155
– Scotland Street School (Museum of Education) 84, 161
– Scottish Exhibition and Conference Centre 160

– Shopping malls 156
– Suspension Bridge 159
– Templeton's Carpet Factory 83, 154
– Tenement House 80, 157
– Trinity College 157
– Trongate 153
– Victoria Bridge 159
– *Waverley*, the 159
– Willow Tea Rooms 156, 163, 308
Glasgow Boys 90, 211
Glasgow Style 84, 162
Glen Affric 238
Glen Aray 195
Glen of the Barr 145
Glenbuchat Castle 217
Glen Carron 242
Glen Coe 182, 199
Glencoe 199
– massacre 36, 198
Glendale 251
Glen Docherty 242
Glenelg 239
Glen Etive 199
Glenfiddich Distillery 220, 223
Glenfinnan 42, 236
Glen Garry 239
Glen Grant Distillery 220
Glenluce 146
Glen Mhoil 190
Glen Mor 203
Glenmorangie Distillery 247
Glen Muick 215
Glen Ogle 181
Glen Ord Distillery 221
Glen Shee 215
Glenshiel 42
Glen Sligachan 250
Glen Tanar Estate 214
Glen Torridon 242
Glentrool 145
Glen Urquhart 238
Glover, Thomas 218
Goatfell 201
Golden eagle 234
Goldeneye 28
Golf **58**, 177
Golspie 247
Gordon (earls of Huntly) 208, 223
Gourock 190
Gow, Niel 53, 87, 181
Graham of Claverhouse, John (see Bonnie Dundee)
Grampians, the 185, 208, 234
Grandtully 182
Grantown-on-Spey 232
Graupius, Mons 32, 222
Gray wagtail 30
Great Bernera 252
Great Cumbrae 149
Great Glen (see Glen Mor)
Greeen hairstreak butterfly 24, 27
Gretna Green 144
Grouse, red 25
Gruinard Bay 243
Gruinart Flats Nature Reserve 202
Guillemot
– black 20
– common 20
Guise, Mary of 34, 35, 40, 130

Guizer jarl 262
Gullane 131
Gurness 260
Gylen Castle 194

H

Haddington 133
Haddo House 217
Hadrian's Wall 32
Haggis 64, 143
Hailes Castle 133
Hakon of Norway 239, 248, 256
Hamilton, Patrick 177
Handa 244
Harald I Hárfagri 256, 268
Hare, arctic 234
Harlaw, Battle of 209
Haroldswick 268
Harp 53
Harris 252
Harris Tweed 253
Hawick 138
Health 270, 274
Hearadh 252
Heath bedstraw 24, 25
Heather 25, 228, 229
Hebridean Celtic Festival 252
Hebrides 33, 34, 46
Hebrides, Inner 248
Hebrides, Outer 252
Helensburgh 189
Hell Fire Club 153
Hell's Glen 190
Helmsdale 246
Henry VIII 35, 40
Henry, George 90
Henryson, Robert 48
Hepburn, James Francis, Earl of Bothwell 41, 121
Hermaness National Nature Reserve 268
Heron, grey 28
Highland Boundary Fault 16, 168
Highland Clearances 36
Highland fling 55
Highland Games **54**, 237, 250
Highland bagpipes 52
Highlands 46, 50, 52, 61, 88, 230
Highlands, West 188
Hillend Country Park 131
Hill House 84, 189
Hill o' Many Stanes 246
Hillswick 266
Hirsel, the 135
Hirta 255
Hogg, James 139
Hogmanay 212
Holm of Papa 261
Holmwood House 80, 161
Honourable Company of Edinburgh Golfers 58, 59
Hopetoun House 129, 219
Hornel, Edward A. 90, 145
Houbie 267
House of Dun 186
Howe of the Mearns 212, 213
Howmore 255
Hoy 260

Hudson Bay Company 260
Hume, David 44, 45, 127
Hunter, William 158
Huntly 222
Huntly Castle 75, 208, 222
Hutton, James 44

I

Inchcolm 174
Inch Kenneth 203
Inchmahome Priory 40, 173
Inchnadamph Nature Reserve 244
Industries 37
Innerleithen 138
International Festival of Music and Drama (Edinburgh) 114
Inveraray 194, 195
Inveraray Castle 76, 195
Inverewe 196, 243
Invergarry 239
Inverness 230
Inverpolly National Nature Reserve 244
Inverurie 222
Iona 33, 204
Irvine 149
Islay 61, 202
Isle of Whithorn 146
Italian Chapel 258

J

Jacobite Risings 36, **42**, 168, 198
Jacobites 34
James I 35, 179
James I of England (see James VI)
James II 121
James II of England (see James VII)
James III 86, 169
James IV 35
James V 34, 40, 178
James VI 35, 41, 58, 115, 171
James VII 36, 42
James-Edward Stuart 42
Jameson, George 211
Jarlshof 67, 264
Jedburgh 138
Jedburgh Abbey 70, 138
John Muir Country Park 132
John o' Groats 245
Johnson, Samuel 96
Jolly Beggars, The 149
Jubilee Path 144
Juniper 228
Jura 201

K

Kant, Immanuel 45
Keil 192
Keiller, Mrs 185
Keiss 245
Keith 220, 223
Keith, George 210, 212
Kellie Castle 176, 197
Kells 204
Kelman, James 48
Kelpie 56
Kelso 136

Kennacraig 191
Kentigern, Bishop (see Saint Mungo)
Kerrera 194
Kidnapped 129, 198, 233
Kilbrannan Sound 191
Kilchurn Castle 195
Kildalton 202
Kildrummy Castle 216
Killiecrankie 168
Killiecrankie Pass 182
Kilmartin 194
Kilmartin Glen 193
Kilmory Knap Chapel 193
Kilmuir 251
Kilravock Castle 231
Kilt 50
Kincardine o' Neil 214
Kincraig 233
Kingfisher 30
Kingussie 233
Kinlochewe 242
Kinlochleven 199
Kinneff 212
Kinross 178
Kinross House 76, 178
Kintail peninsula 42
Kintyre 33, 190, 191
Kippford 144
Kirk, Robert 57
Kirkaldy 175
Kirkcudbright 145
Kirkmadrine Church 147
Kirkoswald 147
Kirkwall 256
Kittiwake 20
Knapdale 192, 193
Knorr 262
Knox, John 35, **41**, 47, 118, 119, 133, 154, 165, 177, 193
Kyleakin 248
Kyle of Lochalsh 239, 248
Kyle of Tongue 245

L

Ladykirk 135
Lady of the Lake, The 172
Lammermuirs, the 128
Lanark 165
Landseer, Edwin 88
Langside, Battle of 41
Language 46
Largs 71, 149
Largs, Battle of 34, 239, 248
Lauriston Castle 128
Law, John 128
Law Ting Holm 263
Leaves from a Journal of Our Life in the Highlands 214
Lecht, the 216
Leith 59, 114, **127**
Lennoxlove House 134
Leodhais 252
Leonard, Tom 48
Lerwick 262
Lesser twayblade 26
Leuchars 178
Leverburgh 253
Lewis 252
Liathach 242
Linlithgow 129
Linlithgow Palace 74, 130
Linn of Dee falls 215

Lismore 194, 198
Lithgow 90
Little Dunkeld 181
Livingstone, David 36
Loanhead Stone Circle 222
Lochs 28–29
Lochaber 236
Loch Assynt 244
Loch Awe 195
Loch Baghasdail 255
Lochboisdale 255
Loch Bordastubble 268
Loch Caolisport 193
Loch Carron 242
Loch Cluanie 239
Loch Coruisk 88, 248, 250
Loch Druidibeg National Natural Reserve 254
Loch Earn 181
Loch Eriboll 245
Loch Etive 194
Loch Ewe 242
Loch Finlaggan 202
Loch Fyne 193
Loch Gilp 193
Lochgilphead 193
Loch Goil 190
Loch Gruinart 202
Lochhead, Liz 48
Loch Indaal 202
Lochindorb Castle 232
Lochinver 244
Loch Katrine 172
Loch Kishorn 242
Loch Laich 198
Loch Leven 178
Loch Leven Castle 41, 178
Loch Linnhe 194, 203, 236
Loch Lochy 238
Loch Lomond 173
Loch of Lowes Wildlife Reserve 183
Lochmaddy 254
Loch Maree 242
Loch Morar 237
Lochnagar 215
Loch Na Maddadh 255
Loch nan Uamh 237
Loch Ness 238, 240
Loch Ness Monster 56, 204, 238, **240**
Loch of Lowes Wildlife Reserve 183
Loch Oich 238
Lochranza 201
Loch Roag 252
Loch Shieldaig 242
Loch Sionascaig 244
Loch of Spiggie 264
Loch of Strathberg 218
Loch Sween 193
Loch Tay 181
Loch Tingwall 263
Loch Torridon 242
Loch Tummel 182
Logan Botanic Garden 147, 196
Lord of the Isles, The 88
Lorimer, Robert 197, 203
Lossiemouth 224
Lothian 128
Lower Largo 176
Lowland bagpipes 52
Lowlands 61
Luib 248
Luing 201
Lumbister 267

Lumphanan 214
Lunda Wick 268
Luskentyre 253

M

McAdam, John 44
MacAlpin, Kenneth 33, 38, 116, 180, 194, 205
Macbeth 34, 55, 186, 231
MacDiarmid, Hugh 48, 102
Macdonald of Clanranald 255
Macdonald, Flora 43, 230, 248, 250, 255
Macdonald, Margaret 189
MacDonalds, the 34, 42
MacDougal, Peter 48
Macduff 218
MacGregor, Robert (see Rob Roy)
Machars Peninsula, the 146
Machrie Moor Stone Circles 201
Machrihanish 192
MacIan (clan) 198
MacIntyre, Duncan Ban 47
MacIsaac, Ashley 53
MacKenzie, Alexander 36
Mackenzie, Compton 254
Mackenzie, Osgood 243
Mackintosh, Charles Rennie 84, 152, **162–163**, 159, 189
Maclean, Alan-nan-Sop 191
Maclean, Sorley 47
Maclean, Will 92
Maclellan's Castle 145
MacLeod's Tables 251
McManus Galleries 185
Mac Mhaighstir, Alasdair 47
Macpherson, James 37, 46, 233
Macpherson of Cluny, Ewen 233
McTaggart, William 88
Madeleine of France 34
Maes Howe 66, 259
Magnus, Saint 256, 257, 261
Maiden Stone 222
Mail 274
Mainland (Orkney Is.) 256
Mainland (Shetland Is.) 262
Maitland (family) 133
Malcolm III Canmore 33, 34, 54, 55, 174
Mallaig 92, 237
Manderston House 135
Mar, Earl of 42
Margaret ('the Maid of Norway') 38
Margaret, Saint 174
Marmalade 64
Marwick Head 261
Mauchline 149
Maxwell, William Stirling 161
Meadow pipit 26
Measach Falls 243
Meigle 186

Mellerstain House 137
Melrose 137
Memsie Cairn 218
Mendelssohn, Felix 203
Menteith, Lake of 173
Mercat cross 68
Merlin 25
Midge 27
Midmar 215
Mid Yell 267
Military Tattoo 116
Miller, Hugh 247
Millport 149
Milton 255
Minch, The (strait) 252
Mingary Castle 237
Mingulay 255
Mintlaw 218`
Mod 47
Monach Isles 255
Monck, George, General 35, 135, 236
Montrose 186
Monymusk 216
Moorland 24–25
Morag 237
Moravia, Walter de 165, 224
Moray, the 224
Moray Firth, the 47, 231
More, Jacob 88
Morgan, Edwin 48
Mosman, James 116, 119
Mote of Mark 144
Mote of Urr 144
Mound, The 124
Mount Stuart 200
Mousa Broch 67, 264
Muck 206, 237
Muckle Flugga 268
Muir, John 132
Muirfield (golf course) 59, 131
Mull 203
Mull Head 259
Mull of Galloway 147
Mull of Kintyre 192
Muness Castle 268
Music 52, 55
Musselburgh 131
Mylne, Robert 199, 121

N

Nairn 232
National Covenant 35, 41, 115, 123, 209
National Trust for Scotland 230
NATO 242
Nature 274
Nechtansmere 184
Neidpath Castle 138
Neptune's Staircase 236
Ness, the 230
Ness of Burgi 264
Ness of Garth 265
Nether Largie 193
New Abbey 144
New Lanark 79, 165
Newtongrange 130
Newtonmore 233
Newton Stewart 145
Nigg 184, 247
Nightlife 274
Nine Mile Burn 131
North Berwick 132
North Uist 254
Northern emerald 27

Northumbria, kingdom of 33, 48, 52
Norway, kingdom of 262
Noss 263

O

Oban 194
Odin (Woden) 259
Ogilvie, Alexander 219
Ogilvie, John 223
Ogilvie, Margaret 196
Oich, the 238
Old Deer 218
Old Firm 151
Old Kilpatrick 189
Old Man of Hoy, the 260
Old Man of Storr, the 249, 250
Old Scatness 264
Open, The 59, 131
Opening times 275
Orca 19
Orkney 33, 34, 47, 52, **256**
Orkneyinga Saga, The 256
Oronsay 202
Ossian's Ladder 199
Otter 29, 248
Out Skerries 266
Owen, Robert 166
Owl, short-eared 26
Oyne 222

P

Pabbay 255
Paisley 164
Papa Stour 265
Papa Westray 261
Paps of Jura 201
Park, Mungo 36
Parliament, Scottish 37, 115, 171, 180
Paxton House 135
Peat 26, 227
Peat bogs 26–27
Peebles 138
Peel Ring 214
Peffer, valley of the 247
Pennan 219
Pentland Firth 256
Pentland Hills 128, **131**
Perth 168, **179**
Perthshire 168, 179
Peterhead 42, 208, **218**
Phantassie Doocot 133
Phillip, John 'Spanish' 211
Pibroch 55
Picardy Stone 222
Pictavia 186
Pictish stones 53, **184**, 222
Picts 33, 52, 168, 184, 208, 256
Pine marten 28
Pink-footed goose 28
Pipe bands 52, 55
Pitlochry 182
Pitmedden Gardens 197, 217
Pitmuies, House of 196
Pitsligo Castle 219
Plaid 51
Plockton 193
Plover, golden 25
Pluscarden Abbey 224
Point of Knap 193
Pomona 256
Poolewe 242

Porpoise, common 18
Port Appin 198
Port Askaig 203
Portavadie 190
Port Charlotte 202
Port Ellen 202
Portnacroish 198
Portpatrick 147
Portree 250
Portsoy 219
Port William 147
Praise of Ben Doran 47
Prehistory 32
Preshome 219
Preston Mill 133
Prestonpans 43, 131
Pretender (see James-Edward Stuart)
Ptarmigan 234
Public holidays 276
Puffin 20

Q

Queen Elizabeth Forest Park 173
Queen's View 182
Quendale Mill 264
Quiraing 251

R

Raasay 251
Rae, John 257
Raeburn, Henry 45, 87
Ramsay, Allan (painter) 45
Ramsay, Allan (poet) 48, 53, 117
Ramsay MacDonald, James 224
Rannoch Moor 182, 199
Razorbill 20
Recumbent stones 208, 215
Red ants' nest 229
Red Cap 57
Red-necked phalarope 28
Red squirrel 229
Reformation 34, 40, 87
Reginald 204
Reid, Alexander 90
Reid, William Robert 128
Rennibister 67, 259
Rest and Be Thankful 190
Rhinns of Galloway 146
Rhynie 222
Rievaulx, monks of 137
Ring of Brogdar 259
River lamprey 30
Rivers 30
Rizzio, David 121
Robert II 35
Rob Roy (Robert MacGregor) 168, 172
Rockcliffe 144
Rodel 253
Roe deer 229
Roghadal 253
Roman Conquest 32
Ronas Hill 267
Rosehearty 219
Rosemarkie 247
Roslin (Rosslyn) 130
Ross, Earl of 242
Rosslyn Chapel 71, 130
Rothesay 200
Rothesay Castle 72, 200

Rough wooing 40
Rousay 261
Rowardennan 173
Roxburgh 136
Royal Deeside 208, 213
Royal Mile 117
Royal Navy 247
Royal Oak 258
Rudh an Dunain 250
Rudobach 200
Rum 206, 237
'Run Rig' 53
Ruthven Barracks 233
Ruthwell 144

S

Saddel 192
St Abb's 134
St Abb's Head Nature
Reserve 134
St Andrews 35, 59, **176**
St Blane's Church 200
St Brendan 202
St Colm 174
St Columba 33, 185,
188, 192, **204**, 216, 230,
240
St Columba's Cave 193
St Conan's Kirk 198
St Cuthbert's Way 137
Saint Duthac 247
Saint Kilda 255
Saint Maelrubha 242
Saint Magnus 256
Saint Margaret's Hope
258
St Mary's Loch 139
Saint Mirrin 164
Saint Mungo 150, 155
Saint Ninian 33, 146
St Ninian's Isle 265
Saint Olaf 256
Saint Patrick 147
St Vigeans 185
Salmon, Atlantic 30
Sanday 261
Sandpiper
– common 28
Sandray 255
Sands of Forvie 218
Scalasaig 202
Scalloway 263
Scalloway Castle 73,
263
Scalpaiagh 253
Scalpay 253
Scandinavia 273
Scapa Flow 258
Schiehallion 182
Schueler, Jon 92
Scone 33, 35, 39, 179,
231
Scone Palace 180
Scotch snap 53
Scotch whisky 60
Scots 33, 34, 46, 47,
48
Scots pine 228, 229
Scott, Captain 185
Scott, Michael **113**, 146
Scott, Walter 37, 46, 48,
53, 88, **99**, **113**, 127,
134, 137, 138, 168, 172,
264
Scottish Colourists 90
Scottish Crannog
Centre 181
Scottish crossbill 228,
229
Scottish Enlightenment
44

Scottish National Party
(SNP) 37
Scottish primrose 20
Scottish Reformed
Church 123
Scottish Renaissance
48
Scottish Wildlife Trust
244
Scott's View 137
Scourie 244
Scrabster 245
Seal
– common or harbor 19
– gray 19, 22, 23
Sea Life Centre 198
Sea pink 20
Sean truibhas ('old
trouser' dance) 55
Seil 201
Selkirk 139
Seton, Alexander 197,
217
Sgurr Alasdair 250
Shag 22
Shambellie House 144
Shapinsay 261
Shawbost 253
Sheriffmuir 168
Shetland 33, 34, 47, 52,
262
Shetland Bus 266
Shopping 275
Shortbread 63, 64
Siabost 253
Sidlaw Hills 185
Signal Rock 199
Sinclair, William 131
Single malt 61
Siths 57
Skara Brae 66, 260
Skinner, James Scott
53, 214
Skipness Castle 191
Skua, Arctic 22
Skye 43, 46, 248
Slains Castle 218
Sleat peninsula 248
Sligachan 248
Slug, great black 24
Sma' Glen 180
Smailholm Tower 136
Smith, Adam 44, 45,
120, 175
Smith, Thomas Stuart
171
Smith, Tommy 53
Smoking 275
Smoo Cave 245
Snipe 26
Society of Agricultural
Improvers 45
Solway Firth 144
Somerled 33, 192
Songs 53
Sophia of Hanover 36
Sound of Jura 193
Sound of Mull 203
Southern Upland Way
112, 145
South Queensferry 128
South Ronaldsay 258
South Uist 43, 254
Special needs 271
Specialties 64
Spencer, Stanley 90
Sperm whale 19
Speyside 61, 220, 223
Sphagnum moss 27
Sports 275, 276
Spynie 224
Staffa 203

Standing stones 246,
253, 254, 258, 267, 268
Standing stones of
Stenness 261
Stanydale Temple 265
Stenness 259
Steornabhagh 252
Stevenson, Robert
Louis 48, 101, 118, 215,
233
Stewarts, the 34, 35
Stewart, Alan Breck 198
Stewart, Alexander 'Wolf
of Badenoch' 181, 223,
232
Stewart, Patrick 257
Stirling 169
Stirling Castle 39, 75,
170
Stirlingshire 168
Stoat 25
Stoker, Bram 218
Stonehaven 212
Stone of Destiny 38,
116, 180, 185, 193
Stone of Scone (see
Stone of Destiny)
Stornoway 252
Stranraer 146
Strathaird peninsula 248
Strathclyde, kingdom of
33
Strath Dee 208
Strath Don 215
Strathisla Distillery 223
Strathmore 168, 185
Strathpeffer 247
Strath Spey 208, 234
Strathspey (dance) 53,
55
Stromness 260
Stuart, Charles Edward
42, 231, 237, 248, 250
Stuart, Mary 34, 35,
40–41, 115, 121, 169
Stuarts, the 34, 35
Sueno's Stone 224
Sullom Voe 266
Sumburgh Head 264
Summer Isles 244
Sundew, common 27
Sutherland 36
Swanston 131
Sweetheart Abbey 144

T

Tabha Mor 255
Tain 247
Talisker Distillery 250
Tam o' Shanter 141,
142–143, 147, 148
Tankerness House 257
Tantallon Castle 132
Tap o' Noth 32, 222
Tarbert (Argyll) 190, 191
Tarbert (Harris) 253
Tartan 36, **50**
Tay 179
Tay Forest 182
Telephone 271, 275
Telford, Thomas 236,
238, 243, 246
Templeton, James 154
Templewood 193
Tenement 80
Teviot, the 136
Thirlestane Castle 73,
138
Thomson, Alexander
'Greek' 82, 83, 155, 161
Threave Castle 145

Thrift 20
Thurso 245
Time 271
Tingwall 263
Tipping 275
Tiree 206
Tirefour Broch 194
Tit, crested 228
Tobacco Lords 150
Tobermory 203
Tolbooth 68
Tolquhon Castle 217
Tomb of the Eagles 258
Tomintoul 216
Tongue 245
Torosay Castle 77, 203
Torridon 242
**Tourist information
275**
Train 271, 273
Traprain Law 32, 133
Traquair House 138
Treasure Island 215
Treshnish Islands 203
Troon (golf course) 59
Trossachs 168, 172
Trotternish 249, 250
Trotternish peninsula
250
Trout, brown/sea 30
Tudor, Margaret 35
Tudor, Mary 41
Turnberry 59, 147
Turner, Joseph Mallord
William 88, 248
Turriff 217
Tweed 253
Tweed Valley 136
Twinflower 228
Tynet 219

U

Uig (Skye) 251
Uist 254
Ullapool 243
Ulva 203
Union of the English and
Scottish crowns 35, 48,
87
Union of the English and
Scottish Parliaments 36
Unst 268
Unstan Cairn 259
Up Helly-Aa 262
Urquhart Castle 238
Useful tips 275
Uyeasound 268

V

Van der Goes, Hugo 86
Vatersay 255
Verdant Works 185
Victoria 37, 51, 60, 214
Vikings 33, 34, 52, 256,
262
Violin 53

W

Wade, George General
179, 233
Walkerburn 138
Walking 275
Wallace, William
34, 38, 165, 168, 169
Wallace Monument 169
Ward Hill 260
Wars of Scottish
independence 38
Walsh Act 60

◆ INDEX

Water of Leith 114, **126**
Waterson, George 265
Watt, James 44, 151, 238
Well of Lecht 216
Welsh, Irvin 48
Wemyss Bay 200
West Linton 131
West Loch Tarbert 191
Westray 261
Wet, Jacob de 186
Whale
– blue 19
– fin 18
– killer 19
– minke 18
– northern bottlenosed 19
– Cuvier's beaked 19
– humpback 19
– pilot 18
– Sowerby's beaked 19
– sperm 19
Whalsay 267
What to take 271
Wheatear 26
When to go 271
Whisky 60, 64, 220
Whisky Galore 254
Whistler, James McNeil 159
White Corries 199
Whithorn 146
Whooper swan 28
Wick 246
Wideford Hill Cairn 259
Wigtown 146
Wild cat 228
Wilkie, David 87
William of Orange 36, 42, 198
William the Lion 34, 185, 186
Wilson, Robert Kenneth 241
Wishart, George 177
Woden (see Odin)
Wolf of Badenoch, the (see Alexander Stewart)
Wordsworth, Dorothy 37
Wordsworth, William 172, 180
Wyre 261

Y

Yell 267
Younger Botanical Garden 190
Young people 271
Yoxie 267
Ythan, River 218

HOTELS

Accommodation 274
Anchor Hotel (Kintyre) 312
Ardoe House (Aberdeen) 312
Arisaig House (Arisaig) 313
Babity Bowster (Glasgow) 306
Balbirnie House (Glenrothes) 311
Balmoral (Edinburgh) 303
Bonham (Edinburgh) 303
Caledonian Hilton (Edinburgh) 303
Channings (Edinburgh) 303
Creel (Saint Margaret's Hope) 314
Culloden House (Inverness) 314
Devonshire Hotel (Glasgow) 306
Glasgow Hilton (Glasgow) 306
Gleneagles (Auchterarder) 310
Hilton Aviemore (Aviemore) 313
Hilton Craighendarroch (Ballater) 313
Hilton Dunblane Hydro (Dunblane) 310
Hilton Dundee (Dundee) 310
Hilton Dunkeld House (Dunkeld) 310
Hilton Grosvenor (Glasgow) 306
Hilton Tree Tops (Aberdeen) 312
Howard (Edinburgh) 303
Inverlochy Castle (Fort William) 314
Isle of Skye Toby Hotel (Perth) 311
Kilfinan Hotel (Kilfinan) 312
Kinfauns Castle (Perth) 311
Kinnaird (Dunkeld) 310
Lochgreen House (Troon) 309
Loch Melfort Hotel (Arduain) 311
Malmaison (Edinburgh) 303
Malmaison (Glasgow) 306
The Murrayshall (Perth) 311
The Old Course (Saint Andrews) 311
One Devonshire Gardens (Glasgow) 306
Rosemount (Aberdeen) 312
Roxburghe (Edinburgh) 303
Salutation Hotel (Perth) 311
Sibbet House (Edinburgh) 303
Simpson's (Aberdeen) 312
Skene House Holburn (Aberdeen) 312
Summer Isles (Achiltibuie) 313
Sunbank House (Perth) 311
Turnberry Hotel (Turnberry) 309
Whitehall (Aberdeen) 312

HOTEL-RESTAURANTS

Airds Hotel (Port Appin) 312
Albannach (Lochinver) 314
Altnaharrie Inn (Ullapool) 314
Cameron House (Balloch) 309
Champany Inn (Linlithgow) 309
Cromlix House (Dunblane) 310
The Cross (Kingussie) 314
Druimard Country House Hotel (Mull) 312
Green Inn (Ballater) 313
Greywalls (Gullane) 309
The House Over-By (Dunvegan, Skye) 313
Isle of Eriska (Isle of Eriskay) 314
Kilmichael Country House (Brodick) 311
Knockinaam Lodge (Portpatrick) 309
Peat Inn Hotel (Cupar) 310
The Roman Camp (Callander) 310

RESTAURANTS

36 (Edinburgh) 305
78 St. Vincent (Glasgow) 307
Atlantis Seafood (Aberdeen) 312
The Atrium (Edinburgh) 303
Blue Bar Café (Edinburgh) 304
Braidwoods (Dalry) 310
The Buttery (Glasgow) 306
Café Royal (Edinburgh) 304
Cameron's (Glasgow) 306
Cellar (Anstruther) 309
City Merchant (Glasgow) 307
Creelers (Edinburgh) 304
Deep Sea (Dundee) 310
Dubh Prais (Edinburgh) 304
Fisherman Tavern (Dundee) 310
Fischers Bistro (Edinburgh) 304
FitzHenry (Edinburgh) 304
Gamba (Glasgow) 307
Gérard Brasserie (Aberdeen) 312
Hadrian's (Edinburgh) 305
Haldanes (Edinburgh) 305
Kerachers Restaurant & Oyster Bar (Perth) 311
Lairhillock Inn (Aberdeen) 312
Let's Eat (Perth) 311
Let's Eat Again (Perth) 311
N° 33 (Perth) 311
Nairns (Glasgow) 307
Number One Edinburgh) 304
One Devonshire Gardens (Glasgow) 307
Ostlers Close Restaurant (Cupar) 310
La Potinière (Gullane) 309
Rogano (Glasgow) 307
Silver Darling (Aberdeen) 313
Skippers Bistro (Edinburgh) 305
Stac Polly (Edinburgh) 305
Two Fat Ladies (Glasgow) 307
Ubiquitous Chip (Glasgow) 308
The Waterfront (Edinburgh) 305
The Willow Tea Rooms (Glasgow) 308
The Witchery by the Castle (Edinburgh) 306
Wisharts (Dumfries) 309
Yes (Glasgow) 308

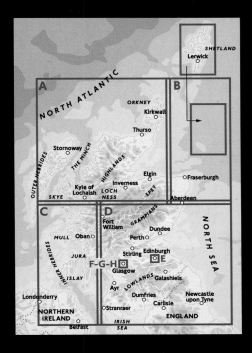

Map section

A The north
B The northeast
C The west
D The center and south
E Edinburgh city center
F Glasgow city center
G Southwest Glasgow
H Glasgow Underground

Key

▬	Motorway	▦	Urban area
▬	Primary road	●	Main town or city
▬	Secondary road	○	Secondary town
▭	Other routes	■	Place of interest
--	Ferry route	✚	Cemetery
▬	Railroad	✚	Hospital
•••	Country border		

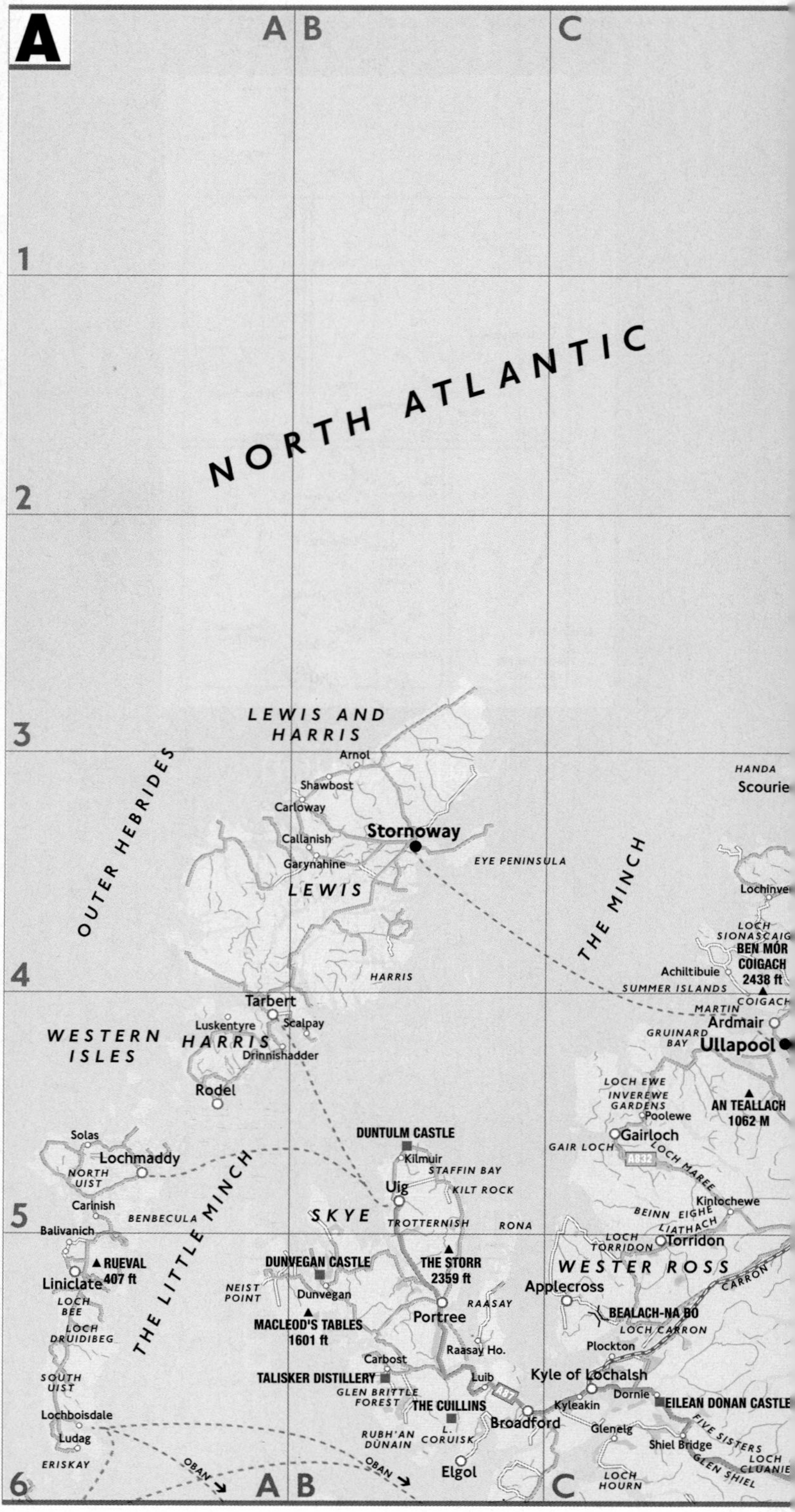

A

A B C

1

2

NORTH ATLANTIC

3

LEWIS AND HARRIS

HANDA

Scourie

Arnol

Shawbost

Carloway

OUTER HEBRIDES

Callanish

Stornoway

Garynahine

EYE PENINSULA

LEWIS

THE MINCH

Lochinver

LOCH SIONASCAIG

BEN MÓR COIGACH 2438 ft

Achiltibuie

MARTIN

COIGACH

SUMMER ISLANDS

4

HARRIS

Ardmair

GRUINARD BAY

Ullapool

Tarbert

Luskentyre

Scalpay

WESTERN ISLES

HARRIS

Drinnishadder

LOCH EWE INVEREWE GARDENS

Poolewe

AN TEALLACH 1062 M

Rodel

Gairloch

GAIR LOCH

LOCH MAREE

DUNTULM CASTLE

Solas

Kilmuir

Lochmaddy

NORTH UIST

STAFFIN BAY

Uig

KILT ROCK

Kinlochewe

Carinish

SKYE

BEINN EIGHE

LIATHACH

Torridon

Balivanich

TROTTERNISH

RONA

LOCH TORRIDON

5

BENBECULA

THE LITTLE MINCH

RUEVAL 407 ft

DUNVEGAN CASTLE

THE STORR 2359 ft

WESTER ROSS

Liniclate

NEIST POINT

Dunvegan

RAASAY

Applecross

CARRON

LOCH BEE

MACLEOD'S TABLES 1601 ft

Portree

BEALACH-NA BÒ

LOCH CARRON

LOCH DRUIDIBEG

Raasay Ho.

Plockton

Carbost

TALISKER DISTILLERY

Luib

Kyle of Lochalsh

SOUTH UIST

GLEN BRITTLE FOREST

THE CUILLINS

Kyleakin

Dornie

EILEAN DONAN CASTLE

Lochboisdale

RUBH'AN DUNAIN

CORUISK

Broadford

Glenelg

FIVE SISTERS

Ludag

OBAN

Elgol

Shiel Bridge

LOCH CLUANIE

ERISKAY

OBAN

LOCH HOURN

GLEN SHIEL

6

A B C

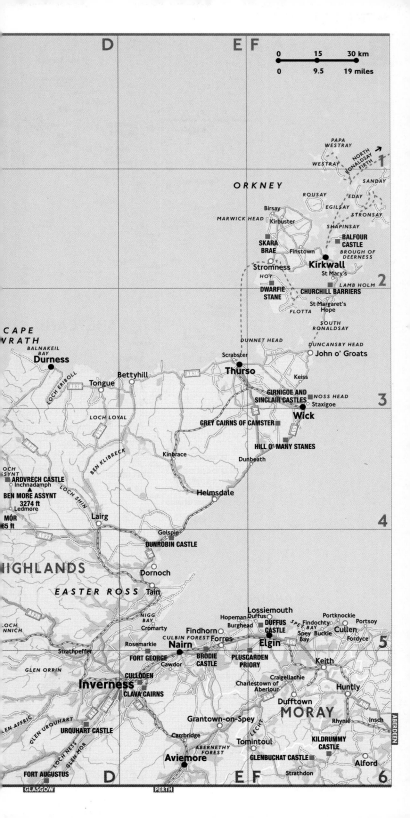

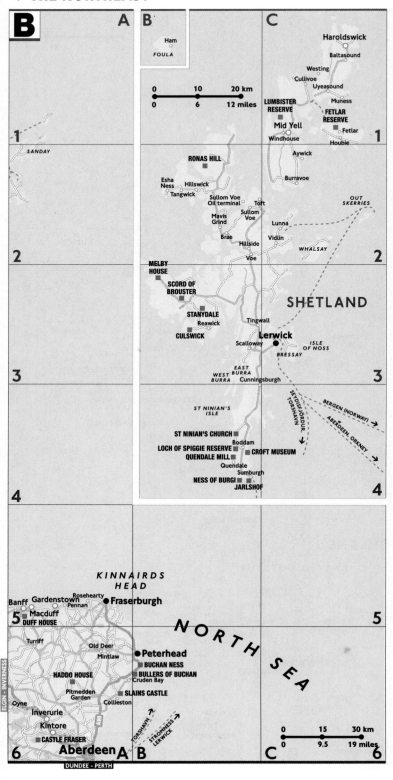

B

A

B

C

Ham
FOULA

0   10   20 km
0   6   12 miles

Haroldswick
Baltasound
Westing
Cullivoe
Uyeasound
Muness
LUMBISTER
RESERVE
FETLAR
RESERVE
Mid Yell
Fetlar
Windhouse
Houbie

1

RONAS HILL

Aywick
Burravoe

Esha
Ness
Hillswick
Tangwick
Sullom Voe
Oil terminal
Toft
Sullom
Voe
Mavis
Grind
Brae
Hillside
Lunna
Vidlin
OUT
SKERRIES
WHALSAY
Voe

2

MELBY
HOUSE
SCORD OF
BROUSTER
SHETLAND
STANYDALE
Reawick
CULSWICK
Tingwall
Lerwick
ISLE
OF NOSS
Scalloway
BRESSAY

3

WEST
BURRA
EAST
BURRA
Cunningsburgh

ST NINIAN'S
ISLE

ST NINIAN'S CHURCH
Boddam
LOCH OF SPIGGIE RESERVE
QUENDALE MILL
CROFT MUSEUM
Quendale
Sumburgh
NESS OF BURGI
JARLSHOF

SEYDISFJÖRDUR,
TÓRSHAVN
BERGEN (NORWAY) →
ABERDEEN, ORKNEY →

4

KINNAIRDS
HEAD
Banff
Gardenstown
Rosehearty
Pennan
Fraserburgh
Macduff
DUFF HOUSE

NORTH

5

Turriff
Old Deer
Mintlaw
Peterhead
BUCHAN NESS
BULLERS OF BUCHAN
Cruden Bay
HADDO HOUSE
SLAINS CASTLE
Pitmedden
Garden
Collieston
Oyne
Inverurie
Kintore
CASTLE FRASER
Aberdeen

SEA

0   15   30 km
0   9.5   19 miles

6

TORSHAVN
STROMNESS
LERWICK

A   B   C

ELGIN – INVERNESS

DUNDEE – PERTH

SANDAY

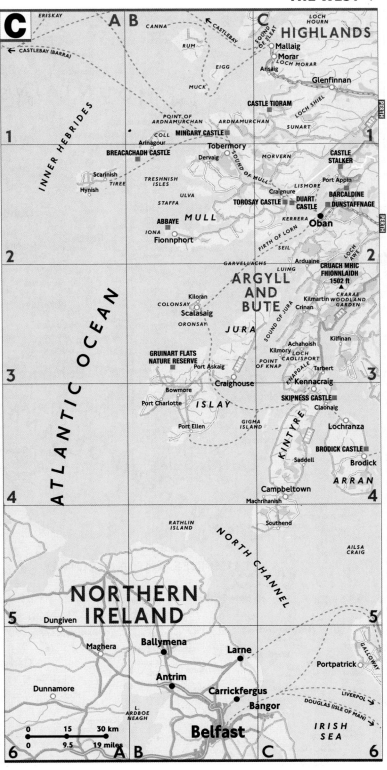

C

ERISKAY

← CASTLEBAY

← Castlebay (BARRA)

CANNA

RUM

EIGG

MUCK

A **B**

HIGHLANDS

LOCH HOURN

SOUND OF SLEAT

Mallaig

Morar

LOCH MORAR

Arisaig

Glenfinnan

LOCH SHIEL

SUNART

CASTLE TIORAM

POINT OF ARDNAMURCHAN

ARDNAMURCHAN

COLL

Arinagour

MINGARY CASTLE

1

C

PERTH

MORVERN

CASTLE STALKER

Port Appin

INNER HEBRIDES

BREACACHADH CASTLE

Scarinish

TIREE

Hynish

Dervaig

Tobermory

SOUND OF MULL

TRESHNISH ISLES

STAFFA

ULVA

MULL

LISMORE

Craignure

TOROSAY CASTLE

DUART CASTLE

BARCALDINE

DUNSTAFFNAGE

KERRERA

Oban

PERTH

ABBAYE

IONA

Fionnphort

FIRTH OF LORN

SEIL

2

GARVELLACHS

Arduaine

LUING

CRUACH MHIC FHIONNLAIDH 1502 ft ▲

CRARAE WOODLAND GARDEN

LOCH AWE

ARGYLL AND BUTE

Kiloran

COLONSAY

Scalasaig

ORONSAY

JURA

SOUND OF JURA

Kilmartin

Crinan

Achahoish

Kilmory

LOCH CAOLISPORT

POINT OF KNAP

Kilfinan

ATLANTIC OCEAN

GRUINART FLATS NATURE RESERVE

Port Askaig

Craighouse

Tarbert

Kennacraig

3

Bowmore

Port Charlotte

ISLAY

Port Ellen

GIGHA ISLAND

SKIPNESS CASTLE

Claonaig

Lochranza

KINTYRE

BRODICK CASTLE

Saddell

Brodick

ARRAN

Campbeltown

Machrihanish

4

RATHLIN ISLAND

NORTH CHANNEL

Southend

AILSA CRAIG

NORTHERN IRELAND

Dungiven

Maghera

Ballymena

Larne

GALLOWAY

Portpatrick

5

Dunnamore

Antrim

Carrickfergus

Bangor

LIVERPOL →

DOUGLAS (ISLE OF MAN) →

L. ARDBOE NEAGH

Belfast

IRISH SEA

0   15   30 km

0   9.5   19 miles

6

A **B** **C**

INVERNESS

ELGIN - FRASERBURGH

D

A B C

MALAIG

OBAN

FORT AUGUSTUS
Invergarry
GLEN ALBYN
LOCH OICH
LOCH LOCHY

HIGHLAND WILDLIFE PARK
Kingussie
Newtonmore
Kincraig
RUTHVEN BARRACKS

GLENMORE FOREST PARK
CAIRN GORM
CAIRNGORM MOUNTAINS

CORGARFF CASTLE

BALMORAL CASTLE
Braemar
Ballater Ab

LOCHNAGAR 3789 ft
GLEN MUICK
LOCH MUICK
ABER

Banavie
Neptune's Staircase
Fort William
BEN NEVIS 4409 ft

GRAMPIAN MOUNTAINS

BRUAR FALLS
BLAIR CASTLE
PASS OF KILLIECRANKIE
Pitlochry

ANGU

Glencoe
BIDEAN NAM BIAN
COE
GLEN ETIVE
RANNOCH MOOR

LOCH TUMMEL
L OF LOWES
Dunkeld
Birnam
Blairgowrie
Meigle

Forf
GLAMIS

LOCH TAY
SMA' GLEN

PERTHSHIRE AND KINROSS
Crieff

SCONE PALACE
Perth
Abernethy

Dundee

ARGYLL AND BUTE
LOCH EARN
DRUMMOND CASTLE
Muthill

Cupar
St. Andre

LOCH KATRINE
BEN LOMOND 3196 ft
THE TROSSACHS
Callander
Doune
Dunblane
Auchterarder

Falkland
Kinross
Glenrothes
L. LEVEN
Largo
Ceres
KEL CAS

Inveraray
Auchindrain
Arrochar
Rowardennan
Aberfoyle
ARGYLL FOREST PARK
Lochgoilhead
QUEEN ELIZABETH FOREST
OF MENTEITH
Kippen
Gargunnock
Stirling
Bannockburn

Kirkcaldy
Culross
Dunfermline

CARRICK CASTLE
LOCH LOMOND
Balmaha
Balloch
Fintry
CAMPSIE FELLS

THE BINNS
N. Queensferry
South Queensferry
INCHCOLM
Dalmeny
Cramond
Musselburgh

Dirle
Gullane
Hadding

Helensburgh
Greenock
Dunoon
Port Glasgow
Largs

Dumbarton

Linlithgow
CAIRNPAPPLE HILL
WEST LOTHIAN

Edinburgh
MIDLOTHIAN S
Newtongran
Crichton
Lau

GREAT CUMBRAE
Millport

Glasgow
Paisley
Blantyre
East Kilbride
Hamilton
Motherwell
Lanark

PENTLAND HILLS

SOUTHERN UPLANDS
Peebles
Broughton
Innerleithen
Galashi
Sel

Kilmarnock
Irvine
Troon
Ayr
Alloway

SOUTH LANARKSHIRE

Yarrow
ST. MARY'S LOCH
BOWHILL

Dunure
CULZEAN CASTLE
Kirkoswald
Turnberry
Girvan
CROSSRAGUEL ABBEY

DRUMLANRIG CASTLE

DUMFRIES AND GALLOWAY

GALLOWAY FOREST PARK
New Galloway

Dumfries
SWEETHEART ABBEY
New Abbey
CAERLAVEROCK CASTLE

GRETNA GREEN

CASTLE KENNEDY
Newton Stewart
Wigtown
GLENLUCE ABBEY
THE MACHARS
LOGAN BOTANIC GARDENS
Port William
Garlieston
Whithorn

Gatehouse of Fleet
THREAVE GARDEN
Kirkcudbright
Dundrennan
Dalbeattie
Kippford
Rockcliffe

Carlisl

Drummore
Mull of Galloway

Cockermouth

A B C

1 2 3 4 5 6

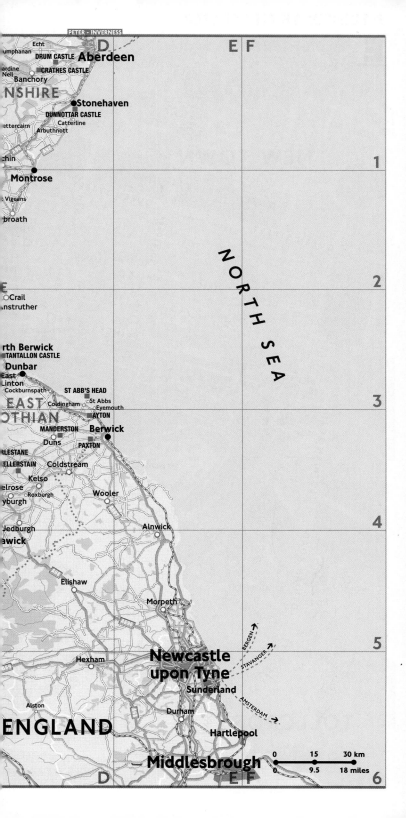

D   E   F

Echt
umphanan   DRUM CASTLE   Aberdeen
ardine   CRATHES CASTLE
Neil   Banchory
NSHIRE
                ●Stonehaven
            DUNNOTTAR CASTLE
            Catterline
ettercairn   Arbuthnott
chin
    ●Montrose

1

Vigeans

broath

N O R T H   S E A

2

E
○Crail
nstruther

rth Berwick
TANTALLON CASTLE
    Dunbar
East
Linton
Cockburnspath   ST ABB'S HEAD
        Coldingham   St Abbs
EAST   Eyemouth
OTHIAN   AYTON
    MANDERSTON   Berwick
    Duns   PAXTON
RLESTANE
ELLERSTAIN   Coldstream
elrose   Kelso
yburgh   Roxburgh
        Wooler
Jedburgh   Alnwick
awick

3

4

Elishaw
        Morpeth
                    BERGEN
Hexham   Newcastle   STAVANGER
        upon Tyne
            Sunderland   AMSTERDAM →
Alston   Durham
ENGLAND   Hartlepool

5

        Middlesbrough

0   15   30 km
0   9.5   18 miles

D   E   F

6

E

A B C

N.W. CIRCUS PLACE S.E.

ROYAL

GREAT KING ST.

HOWE STREET

CIRCUS

NORTHUMBERLAND

DUNDAS STREET

STREET

ABERCROMBY PLACE

1 MORAY

HERIOT   ROW

NEW TOWN

HERIOT   ROW

PLACE

QUEEN STREET GARDENS

QUEEN STREET

QUEEN STREET

THISTLE STREET

HANOVER

THISTLE STREET

ST ANDREW-
ST GEORGE

FREDERICK

YOUNG STREET

HILL STREET

N. CASTLE ST.

STREET

GEORGE   STREET

CHARLOTTE

2

GEORGE   STREET

CASTLE ST.

ROSE STREET

ROSE STREET

STREET

ROSE STRE

SQUARE

ROSE STREET

CASTLE ST.

ROSE STREET

PRINCES   STREET

ROYEL SCOTTISH
ACADEMY

NATIONAL GALLERY
OF SCOTLAND

PRINCES   STREET

*WEST PRINCES
STREET GARDENS*

THE MOUND

3

LOTHIAN ROAD

KING'S STABLES ROAD

RAMSAY
LODGE

ASSEM
H

OUTLOOK TOWER
AND CAMERA OBSCU

CASTLE   TERRACE

THE CASTLE

ESPLANADE

SCOTCH WHISKY
HERITAGE CENTRE

JOHNSTON TERR.

JOHNSTON TERRACE

4

LOTHIAN ROAD

GRINDLAY STREET

SPITTAL STREET

LADY

KING'S STABLES ROAD

PORT

GRASSMARKET

MORRISON ST.

BREAD STREET

WEST

LAWSON STREET

FOUNTAINBRIDGE

LAURISTON ST.

STREET

KEIR

GEOR
HERIO
SCHO

5

FOUNTAINBRIDGE

EARL GREY ST.

LAURISTON   PLACE

LAURISTON GARDENS

CHALMERS STREET

LAURISTON   PLAC

TOLLCROSS

BROUGHAM STREET

6

A B

C *THE MEADOWS*

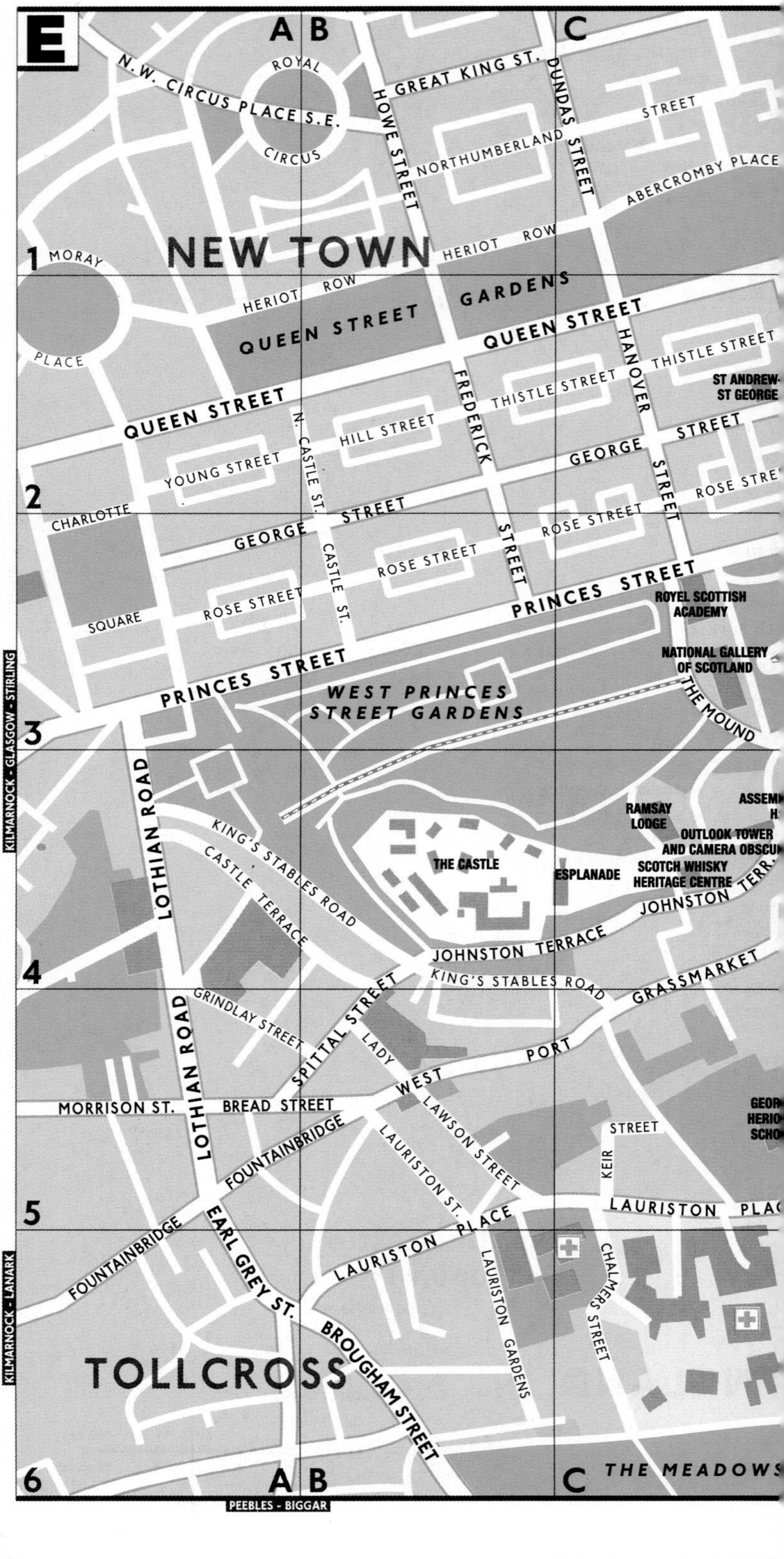

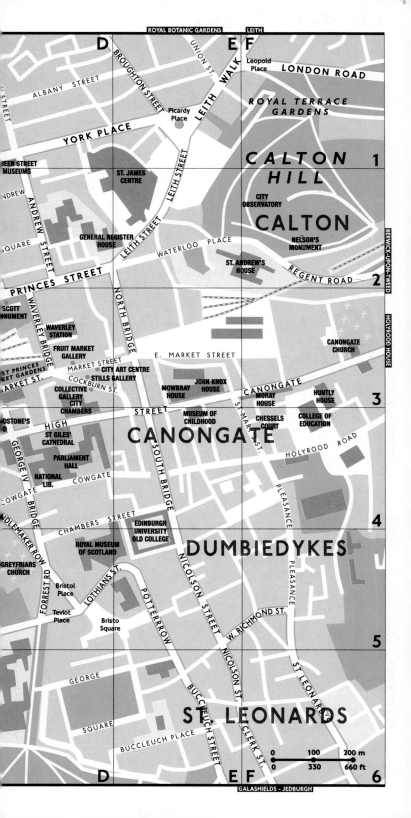

◆ GLASGOW CITY CENTER

F

GLASGOW
CALEDONIAN
UNIVERSITY

WOODLANDS ROAD

WEST PRINCES STREET

ST GEORGES ROAD

WESTERN ROAD

GARSCUBE ROAD

CRAIGHALL RD

PARK
CIRCUS

WOODLANDS ROAD

ST GEORGES RD

DOBBIE

COWCADDENS

1

KELVINGROVE
PARK

WEST GRAHAM ST.

COWCADDENS ROAD

MCPHATER

WOODSIDE PL.

RENFREW STREET

BUCCLEUCH STREET

GARNETHILL

TENEMENT
HOUSE

SAUCHIEHALL STREET

SAUCHIEHALL ST

GLASGOW
SCHOOL
OF ART

MCLELLAN
GALLERIES

ROYAL SCOTTISH
ACADEMY OF MUSIC
AND DRAMA

THEAT
ROYA

BERKELEY   STREET

ELDERSLIE STREET

MITCHELL LIBRARY
& THEATRE

SAUCHIEHALL ST

RENFREW STREE

BATH STREET

KINGS
THEATRE

PITT STREET

BATH STREET

SHOPPING
CENTRE

HOPE STREET

RENFIELD STREET

2

CHARING
CROSS

ST VINCENT STREET

REGENT STREET

BLYTHSWOOD
SQUARE

WEST   GEORGE   STREET

HOULDSWORTH ST

ARGYLE ST

WILLIAM
STREET

SAINT VINCENT STREET

ST VINCENT ST

HOPE STREET

DRURY
ST

MITCHELL STREET

ANDERSTON

ANDERSTON
CROSS CENTRE

BOTHWELL STREET

STOBCROSS

WATERLOO STREET

WEST CAMPBELL STREET

ANDERSTON
CROSS CENTRE

CADOGAN STREET

CENTRAL
STATION

3

LANCEFIELD QUAY

HYDE PARK STREET

ANDERSTON QUAY

ARGYLE STREET

ARGYLE STREE

JAMES WATT ST.

CENTRAL

BROOMIELAW

BROOMIELAW QUAY GARDENS

KINGSTON
BRIDGE

RIVER CLYDE

GEORGE V
BRIDGE

GLASGOW
BRIDGE

ST ANDREW
CATHEDRA

CLYD

SUSPENSIO
BRIDGE

4

PAISLEY

PAISLEY   ROAD

PAISLEY   ROAD

KINGSTON

ST WEST STREET

BRIDGE ST

CARLTON   STR

MORRISON NELSON STREET

NORFOLK ST

WALLACE   ST   STREET

KINGSTON

GLOUCESTER ST

COOK STREET

EGLINTON STREET

BEDFORD STREET

POLLOKSHIELDS

GREENOCK

SCOTLAND STREET

SCOTLAND ST

ST WEST STREET

CUMBERLAND STREET

5

SHIELDS ROAD

GOVANHILL

CATHCART ROAD

GORBA

ST ANDREWS DRIVE

ST ANDREWS ROAD

SHIELDS ROAD

EGLINTON STREET

POLLOKSHAWS ROAD

6

A   B

C

PAISLEY